Immigrant and Passenger Arrivals

A Select Catalog

of

National Archives

Microfilm Publications

National Archives Trust Fund Board
Washington, DC
1983

Library of Congress Cataloging in Publication Data

United States. National Archives and Records
   Service. Immigrant and passenger arrivals.

   Includes index.
   1. United States—Genealogy—Bibliography—
Microform catalogs. 2. Ships—Passenger lists—
Bibliography—Microform catalogs. 3. United
States. National Archives—Microform catalogs.
4. Documents on microfilm—Catalogs. I. Title.
Z5305.U5U54 1983 [CS47] 016.929′373 83-13403

ISBN 0-911333-05-3

Revised 1991

Foreword

The National Archives and Records Administration is responsible for administering the permanently valuable noncurrent records of the Federal Government. The holdings of the National Archives now amount to more than 1.3 million cubic feet. They date from the First Continental Congress and consist of the basic records of the legislative, judicial, and executive branches of Government. The Presidential libraries of Herbert Hoover, Franklin D. Roosevelt, Harry S. Truman, Dwight D. Eisenhower, John F. Kennedy, Lyndon B. Johnson, Gerald R. Ford, and Jimmy Carter contain the papers of those Presidents and many of their associates in office. These research resources document significant events in our Nation's history, but most of them are preserved for continuing practical use in the ordinary processes of Government; for the protection of individual rights; and for the research use of scholars, students, and other individual researchers.

The National Archives Microfilm Publication Program

Since 1941, the National Archives has been microfilming selected groups of Federal records that have high research value. Under this program, negative microfilm is retained by the National Archives, and positive prints are made from these master negatives and sold at moderate prices. The chief purposes of the program are to make archival sources more easily accessible to libraries, research centers, and individuals and to ensure against loss of valuable information should the original records be destroyed. In this way, microfilm publications are a partial answer to the researcher's need for more extensive publication of archival materials because they provide a relatively inexpensive method by which he or she can obtain facsimile reproductions of entire series of documents.

Although the microfilm publication program is one of the oldest continuing programs of the National Archives, it was not firmly established financially until 1948, when a grant of $20,000 from the Rockefeller Foundation provided for accelerated production of microfilm and ensured the continuation of the program through the establishment of a revolving fund. By 1991, nearly 200,000 rolls of master negative microfilm had been produced.

National Archives microfilm publications now provide basic documentation for research in the fields of American, European, Far Eastern, African, and Latin American history as well as in local history and genealogy. They are also valuable for work in other fields, such as economics, public administration, political science, law, and ethnology. As the program has developed, more emphasis has been placed on microfilming groups of records that are directly related to one another, as in the case of records relating to the same general subject or to a specific geographic area. In this way, researchers can obtain reasonably complete documentation in many fields of interest. For example, a number of microfilm publications document diplomatic, consular, and naval relations between the United States and the Far Eastern countries of China, Japan, and Korea from the late 18th century. Similarly, almost complete coverage of relations between the United States and other countries throughout the world is provided. Microfilm publications have also been produced concerning the administration of affairs in individual territories of the United States.

Types of Microfilm Publications

National Archives microfilm publications are divided into two series, identified by "M" numbers and "T" numbers. In general, records selected for filming as "M" publications have high research value for a variety of studies, and the ratio of research value to volume is high. Usually each publication reproduces an entire series of records. Most "M" publications include explanatory material prepared by archivists to help researchers glean information from the filmed records more easily. "M" publications usually have an introduction that describes the origin, content, and arrangement of the filmed records and lists related records. Some introductions also include special aids, such as indexes and registers.

Descriptive pamphlets (DPs) are available for many "M" publications. Each pamphlet contains the publication's introduction (including special lists or indexes prepared to simplify the use of the microfilm publication) and a table of contents that identifies the material contained on each roll. "M" publications that have descriptive pamphlets are indicated in this catalog by the symbol DP at the end of a publication title. The pamphlets are made available on request to prospective purchasers so they can evaluate more thoroughly the value of the publication's contents for their research.

"T" publications, unlike "M" publications, do not usually reproduce a complete series of records; that is, they may contain only segments, by date or subject, of a larger series. In many cases, "T" publications were produced in response to specific reference requests. Also, over the years the National Archives has accessioned as record material microfilm produced by other Federal agencies. Some of this film, when it is not defense classified and is deemed of sufficient research value, is reproduced and made available for sale as "T" publications. These publications are reproduced and sold exactly as they were filmed; they contain no introductions, nor are descriptive pamphlets available for them. All of the Immigration and Naturalization Service (INS) records described in this catalog are "T" publications that were filmed by and accessioned from the INS.

Catalogs of Microfilm Publications

This catalog is one in a series describing National Archives microfilm publications related to subjects of high research interest. Each catalog is compiled through an extensive review of all microfilmed records to locate publications relevant to each topic. The catalogs contain both detailed descriptions of the records and roll-by-roll listings for each publication.

The other six catalogs in this series cover the following topics:

American Indians
Black Studies
Diplomatic Records
Genealogical and Biographical Research
Military Service Records
Federal Court Records

These catalogs are part of a larger effort undertaken by the National Archives Trust Fund to increase public awareness of the availability of the records in the National Archives and to improve access to them. If you have suggestions for new catalog topics, new types of products based on the holdings, or new ways in which the Trust Fund can help you with your research, please contact the National Archives Trust Fund Board (NAJ), National Archives, Washington, DC 20408.

Microfilm Pricing Policy

The price of each roll of microfilm in this catalog is $23. Prices are subject to change without advance public notice. Film can be bought as either individual rolls or a complete publication. The microfilm price includes the cost of film stock, chemicals, boxes and reels, postage, and salaries. A fixed price per roll has been established because most of the costs of reproducing and selling microfilm are the same for all rolls of film, regardless of length. The establishment of such a price permits a substantial savings in order processing costs.

The National Archives microfilm publications program is financed from a trust fund established by the National Archives Trust Fund Board Act (44 U.S.C. 2307). Revenue received through the sale of microfilm publications is returned to the Trust Fund for use in financing additional publications and other products designed both to facilitate access to Federal records held by the National Archives and to make them more widely available to a larger portion of the public.

Microfilm Specifications

All microfilm sold through the National Archives Microfilm Publications program is silver-halide positive microfilm. Unless otherwise specified, it is 35mm reel microfilm, with plastic reels. Reduction ratios used range from 12:1 to 20:1. The number of frames on each reel varies.

In some instances, it is possible to obtain either microfilm in a different form (e.g., duplicate negative rather than positive) or paper copies. If you desire such services, please contact Publications Services (NEPS), National Archives, Washington, DC 20408 (phone: 202-501-5240), for a price quotation.

Contents

Foreword iii

The National Archives Microfilm Publication Program v

Catalogs of Microfilm Publications vii

Microfilm Pricing Policy ix

Microfilm Specifications ix

Introduction 1

Records of the U.S. Customs Service, 1820–ca. 1891 3
    Atlantic, Gulf, and Great Lakes Ports 3
    Baltimore, Maryland 5
    Boston, Massachusetts 7
    New Orleans, Louisiana 10
    New York, New York 12
    Philadelphia, Pennsylvania 20

Records of the Immigration and Naturalization Service, 1891–1957 23
    Alabama, Florida, Georgia, and South Carolina 23
    Baltimore, Maryland 23
    Boston, Massachusetts 25
    Detroit, Michigan 32
    Galveston, Texas 33
    Gloucester, Massachusetts 34
    Gulfport and Pascagoula, Mississippi 34
    Key West, Florida 34
    New Bedford, Massachusetts 35
    New Orleans, Louisiana 35
    New York, New York 39
    Philadelphia, Pennsylvania 126
    Portland, Maine 129
    Providence, Rhode Island 129
    St. Albans, Vermont, District 130
    San Francisco, California 144
    Savannah, Georgia 155
    Seattle, Washington, and Other Washington Ports 155

Guide to the Soundex System 163

Index to Publication Numbers 164

Index to Publications by Port 165

Index to Publication Numbers by Port 167

Index to Microfilm Holdings in the Regional Archives 169

Instructions for Ordering Microfilm Publications 171

Introduction

This catalog lists National Archives microfilm publications of records relating to the arrival of passengers, crew members, and vessels in U.S. ports. Most of the records before 1891 are from the Records of the U.S. Customs Service, Record Group 36. Later records are part of the Records of the Immigration and Naturalization Service (INS), Record Group 85. The publications are arranged by record group and thereunder alphabetically by the name of the port.

The second edition features five new ports of entry: Detroit, Michigan; Galveston, Texas; the St. Albans, Vermont, District, encompassing territory along the Canadian border from Maine to Washington; San Francisco, California; and Seattle, Washington. The catalog now includes complete roll listings for every microfilm publication, providing the researcher with a more thorough understanding of the records each publication contains. In addition, there are three new indexes at the back of the catalog: publications are arranged by port, by title, and by their inclusion in the microfilm holdings of each regional archives.

Records of the United States Customs Service, Record Group 36

Early records relating to immigration originated in regional customhouses. An act of March 2, 1819 (3 Stat. 489) required the captain or master of a vessel arriving at a port in the United States or any of its territories from a foreign country to submit a list of passengers to the collector of customs. The act also required that the collector submit a quarterly report or abstract, consisting of copies of passenger lists, to the Secretary of State, who was required to submit such information at each session of Congress. After 1874, collectors forwarded only statistical reports to the Treasury Department. The lists themselves were retained by the Collector of Customs. Customs records were maintained primarily for statistical purposes.

Records of the Immigration and Naturalization Service, Record Group 85

In 1882, Congress passed the first Federal law regulating immigration; between 1882 and 1891 the Secretary of the Treasury had general supervision over immigration. The Office of Superintendent of Immigration of the Department of the Treasury was established under an act of March 3, 1891, and was designated a bureau in 1895 with responsibility for administering the alien contract-labor laws. In 1900, administration of the Chinese-exclusion laws was added. In 1903, the Bureau became part of the Department of Commerce and Labor. Functions relating to naturalization were assigned to the Bureau in 1906, and its name was changed to the Bureau of Immigration and Naturalization. It was transferred in 1940 to the Department of Justice.

The records of the Immigration and Naturalization Service listed in this catalog were transferred to the National Archives on microfilm. The original records were destroyed by the INS. In some instances, there are indexes for which the National Archives has no list. Some of the records were microfilmed as they appeared in volumes and the date spans may overlap. Errors in arrangement or omission cannot be corrected. Not all passenger lists are indexed. Many of the indexes are difficult to read. This catalog describes contents of individual rolls of microfilm.

The Records

In this catalog, passenger arrival records are preceeded by their indexes. The date spans for the indexes and the records do not always exactly correspond.

Card Indexes

The quantity of information in each of the indexes varies. They may be simple alphabetical listings or arranged in the Soundex coding system (for a full explanation of how to use the Soundex system, see p. 43). The indexes may contain the name, age, occupation, nationality, and last permanent residence of the passenger; the port of entry; the name of the vessel; and the date of arrival. The Soundex index cards may contain only the passenger's name, age, and sex, and the volume number, page, and line where the name may be found.

Book Indexes

These records consist of alphabetical listings of passengers provided to the Immigration and Naturalization Service by the shipping lines. The lists are usually arranged chronologically by date of arrival. The lists include the passenger's name, age and destination.

Passenger and Crew Lists

Customs Passenger Lists and Abstracts

Customs passenger lists contain each passenger's name, age, sex, occupation, nationality, and the name of the country in which each intended to reside. Entries are arranged by date of arrival and sometimes by the passenger or crew member's occupation and the port from which he or she sailed. Lists may also include notations as to the number and causes of deaths on board. The abstracts, which are consolidated lists of all the passengers who arrived at a port during the quarter, generally contain the same information as customs passenger lists.

Immigration and Naturalization Service Passenger Lists

Immigration and Naturalization Service passenger lists include the names of U.S. citizens returning from abroad, foreign visitors, and immigrants. The lists usually also contain names of vessels and shipmasters, ports of arrival and embarkation, dates of arrival, and the following information about each passenger: full name; age; sex; marital status; occupation; last residence; port of arrival and final destination in the United States; if the passenger had been in the United States before, when, and where; and if the passenger were going to join a relative, the relative's name and address, and relationship. Beginning in 1903, race was included; in 1906, personal description and birthplace; in 1907, the name and address of the alien's nearest relative in country from which he or she came.

Crew Lists

Crew lists may include the names of both American and alien seamen. Information about each crew member may include his length of service at sea, position in the ship's company, when and where the seaman joined the vessel's crew, whether he was to be discharged at the port of arrival, literacy, age, race, nationality, height, and weight.

Obtaining Single Copies of Passenger Lists

For a researcher who doesn't wish to buy an entire roll of film to look for a single name, the National Archives will provide, for a fee, copies of single pages of passenger lists. If the list is indexed, the Reference Services Branch will consult the index to find the correct page of the passenger list to copy. The minimum information required for a search of the index is the full name of the person being researched, the port of arrival, and the approximate date of arrival. Additional information such as age of passenger and names of accompanying passengers can be useful. More specific information, however, is needed to search unindexed lists. In addition to the facts listed above, it is necessary to provide either the exact date of arrival or the name of the ship on which the person arrived.

Requests for these copies must be made on NATF Form 81, "Order for Copies of Passenger Arrival Records." The fee for this service is $10, payable only when the records requested are found. If it is not possible to find records, no payment is required. The order form can be obtained from the Reference Service Branch (NNRS), National Archives, Washington, DC 20408.

This catalog was compiled by Constance Potter with assistance from Anne DeLong.

Records of the U.S. Customs Service, 1820–ca. 1891 Record Group 36

Atlantic, Gulf, and Great Lakes Ports

A Supplemental Index to Passenger Lists of Vessels Arriving at Atlantic and Gulf Coast Ports (Excluding New York), 1820–1874. M334. 188 rolls. 16mm. DP.

This publication indexes the passenger lists included under the alphabetical listing of ports in M575, which follows.

Roll	Range
1	A–Ak
2	Al–Amf
3	Amg–Aq
4	Ar–At
5	Au–Bak
6	Bal–Barm
7	Barn–Barz
8	Bas–Beb
9	Bec–Bem
10	Ben–Ber
11	Bes–Bk
12	Bl–Bob
13	Boc–Boq
14	Bor–Boyk
15	Boyl–Bran
16	Brao–Brif
17	Brig–Brov
18	Brow–Brum
19	Brun–Buj
20	Buk–Burm
21	Burn–Byrm
22	Byrn–Call
23	Calm–Canm
24	Cann–Carp
25	Carr–Carz
26	Cas–Caz
27	Cea–Chp
28	Chr–Clar
29	Clas–Coe
30	Cof–Coll
31	Colm–Connel
32	Connen–Conz
33	Coo–Cors
34	Cort–Crah
35	Crai–Cror
36	Cros–Cum
37	Cun–Dah
38	Dai–Dar
39	Das–Deam
40	Dean–Del
41	Dem–Devi
42	Devl–Diu
43	Div–Dold
44	Dole–Donn
45	Dono–Doug
46	Douh–Drir
47	Dris–Duk
48	Dul–Dus
49	Dut–Ed
50	Ee–El
51	Em–Eu
52	Ev–Fam
53	Fan–Fee
54	Fef–Fil
55	Fim–Fitzg
56	Fitzh–Fll
57	Flo–Ford
58	Fore–Fran
59	Frap–Frn
60	Fro–Galk
61	Gall–Gark
62	Garl–Gem
63	Gen–Gilc
64	Gild–Gll
65	Glo–Gord
66	Gore–Gral
67	Gram–Greg
68	Greh–Gro
69	Gru–Hab
70	Hac–Halk
71	Hall–Ham
72	Han–Harf
73	Harg–Hars
74	Hart–Hauk
75	Haul–Heap
76	Hear–Hel
77	Hem–Herb
78	Herc–Hic
79	Hid–His
80	Hit–Hok
81	Hol–Hop
82	Hoq–Hub
83	Huc–Hun
84	Huo–In
85	Io–Janr
86	Jans–Johnse
87	Johnso–Jones, J.
88	Jones, K.–Kak
89	Kal–Kea
90	Keb–Kellw
91	Kelly–Kem
92	Ken–Kerp
93	Kerr–Kinga
94	Kingb–Kna
95	Knc–Kraf
96	Krag–Kw
97	Ky–Land
98	Lane–Lat
99	Lau–Lear
100	Leas–Lenf
101	Leng–Lif
102	Lig–Loc
103	Lod–Lou
104	Lov–Lym
105	Lyn–Mac
106	Mad–Mah
107	Mai–Mann
108	Mano–Mars
109	Mart–Math
110	Mati–McA
111	McB–McCarthy, H.
112	McCarthy, I.–McCn
113	McCo–McCy

Roll	Range
114	McD–McDo
115	McDr–McGim
116	McGin–McGr
117	McGu–McKem
118	McKen–McLA
119	McLe–McMt
120	McMu–McR
121	McS–Mel
122	Mem–Mez
123	Mi–Mim
124	Min–Mom
125	Mon–Moo
126	Mop–Morr
127	Mors–Muller, A.
128	Muller, B.–Murphy, B.
129	Murphy, C.–Murpy
130	Murr–Nc
131	Ne–Nichm
132	Nicho–Nortm
133	Norto–Ob
134	Oc–Olh
135	Oli–Oss
136	Ost–Pari
137	Park–Pc
138	Pe–Pes
139	Pet–Pid
140	Pie–Pom
141	Pon–Pra
142	Prc–Quh
143	Qui–Ral
144	Ram–Rea
145	Reb–Reill
146	Reilm–Rib
147	Ric–Ril
148	Rim–Robe
149	Robi–Rog
150	Roh–Ros
151	Rot–Ruo
152	Rup–Rya
153	Ryb–Saq
154	Sar–Scha
155	Schb–Schm
156	Schn–Schuk
157	Schul–Sco
158	Scr–Sge
159	Sha–Shec
160	Shed–Sho
161	Shr–Sit
162	Siv–Smith, F.
163	Smith, G.–Smitz
164	Smo–Spen
165	Speo–Star
166	Stas–Stev
167	Stew–Sto
168	Str–Sullivan, C.
169	Sullivan, D.–Sum
170	Sun–Tag
171	Tah–Tep
172	Ter–Thomp
173	Thoms–Tom
174	Ton–Tro
175	Trr–Um
176	Un–Vez
177	Via–Wagm
178	Wagn–Wall

Roll	Range
179	Walm–Warda
180	Wardb–Web
181	Wec–Weng
182	Wenh–Whitc
183	White–Wig
184	Wih–Willia
185	Willib–Wins
186	Wint–Woode
187	Woodf–Yal
188	Yam–Zyn

Copies of Lists of Passengers Arriving at Miscellaneous Ports on the Atlantic and Gulf Coasts and at Ports on the Great Lakes, 1820–1873. M575. 16 rolls.

Roll	Description	Dates
1	Alexandria, VA	1820–65
	Annapolis, MD	1849
	Bangor, ME	1848
	Barnstable, MA	1820–26
	Bath, ME	1825–67
	Beaufort, NC	1865
	Belfast, ME	1820–51
	Bridgeport, CT	1870
	Bristol and Warren, RI	1820–71
	Cape May, NJ	1828
2	Charleston, SC	1820–28
	Darien, GA	1823–25
	Dighton, MA	1820–36
	East River, VA	1830
	Edenton, NC	1820
	Edgartown, MA	1820–70
	Fairfield, CT	1820–21
	Fall River, MA	1837–65
	Frenchman's Bay, ME	1821–27
3	Galveston, TX	1846–71
4	Georgetown, DC	1820–21
	Gloucester, MA	1820–70
	Hampton, VA	1820–21
	Hartford, CT	1837
	Havre de Grace, MD	1820
	Hingham, MA	1852
	Kennebunk, ME	1820–42
	Key West, FL	1837–68
	Little Egg Harbor, NJ	1831
	Marblehead, MA	1820–49
	Mobile, AL	1832–52
5	Nantucket, MA	1820–62
	Newark, NJ	1836
	New Bedford, MA	1826–52
	New Berne, NC	1820–65
	Newburyport, MA	1821–39
	New Haven, CT	1820–73
6	New London, CT	1820–47
	Newport, RI	1820–57
	Norfolk and Portsmouth, VA	1820–57
	Oswegatchie, NY	1821–23
7	Passamaquoddy, ME (pt.)	1820–44
8	Passamaquoddy, ME (pt.)	1845–59
	Penobscot, ME	1851
	Perth Amboy, NJ	1820–32
	Petersburg, VA	1820–21
	Plymouth, MA	1821–44
	Plymouth, NC	1820–40
9	Portland and Falmouth, ME	1820–47
10	Portland and Falmouth, ME	1848–58

Roll	Description	Dates		Roll	Range
11	Portland and Falmouth, ME	1859–62		34	F-260—F-416
12	Portland and Falmouth, ME	1863–65		35	F-420—F-466
13	Portland and Falmouth, ME	Jan. 1866–		36	F-500—F-620
		Sept. 1867		37	F-621—F-636
14	Portland and Falmouth, ME	Oct. 1867–		38	F-640—F-666
		Mar. 1868		39	G-000—G-231
15	Port Royal, SC	1865		40	G-232—G-340
	Portsmouth, NH	1820–61		41	G-341—G-425
	Providence, RI	1820–49		42	G-426—G-516
16	Providence, RI	1850–67		43	G-520—G-611
	Richmond, VA	1820–44		44	G-612—G-620
	Rochester, NY	1866		45	G-621—G-632
	Sag Harbor, NY	1829–34		46	G-633—G-652
	St. Augustine, FL	1821–70		47	G-653—H-126
	St. Johns, FL	1865		48	H-130—H-156
	Salem, MA	1865–66		49	H-160—H-200
	Sandusky, OH	1820		50	H-210—H-254
	Savannah, GA	1820–68		51	H-255—H-351
	Saybrook, CT	1820		52	H-352—H-420
	Waldeboro, ME	1820–33		53	H-421—H-455
	Washington, NC	1820–48		54	H-456—H-516
	Wilmington, DE	1820–48		55	H-520—H-524
	Yarmouth, ME	1820		56	H-525—H-551
				57	H-552—H-616
				58	H-620—H-634
				59	H-635—H-665

Baltimore, Maryland

Index (Soundex) to Passenger Lists of Vessels Arriving at Baltimore, MD, (Federal Passenger Lists), 1820–1897. M327. 171 rolls. 16mm. DP.

Roll	Range		Roll	Range
1	A-000—A-336		60	I-100—J-200
2	A-340—A-451		61	J-210—J-316
3	A-452—A-543		62	J-320—J-520
4	A-545—B-162		63	J-521—J-525
5	B-163—B-216		64	J-526—J-662
6	B-220—B-250		65	K-000—K-145
7	B-251—B-264		66	K-146—K-200
8	B-265—B-355		67	K-210—K-241
9	B-356—B-420		68	K-242—K-261
10	B-421—B-452		69	K-262—K-356
11	B-453—B-520		70	K-360—K-416
12	B-521—B-556		71	K-420—K-425
13	B-560—B-616		72	K-426—K-451
14	B-620—B-621		73	K-452—K-461
15	B-622—B-625		74	K-462—K-516
16	B-626—B-633		75	K-520—K-526
17	B-634—B-650		76	K-530—K-561
18	B-651—B-652		77	K-562—K-616
19	B-653—B-656		78	K-620
20	B-660—C-252		79	K-621—K-625
21	C-253—C-500		80	K-626—K-633
22	C-510—C-623		81	K-634—K-652
23	C-624—D-121		82	K-653—L-121
24	D-122—D-236		83	L-122—L-166
25	D-240—D-355		84	L-200—L-226
26	D-356—D-465		85	L-230—L-266
27	D-500—D-541		86	L-300—L-351
28	D-542—D-621		87	L-352—L-516
29	D-622—D-665		88	L-520—L-523
30	E-000—E-256		89	L-524—L-546
31	E-260—E-520		90	L-550—L-665
32	E-521—E-663		91	M-000—M-216
33	F-000—F-256		92	M-220—M-241
			93	M-242—M-255
			94	M-256—M-321
			95	M-322—M-416
			96	M-420—M-456
			97	M-460—M-461
			98	M-462—M-524

Roll	Range
99	M-525—M-566
100	M-600
101	M-610—M-624
102	M-625—M-666
103	N-000—N-200
104	N-210—N-323
105	N-324—N-522
106	N-523—N-666
107	O-000—O-265
108	O-300—O-435
109	O-436—P-141
110	P-142—P-220
111	P-221—P-266
112	P-300—P-361
113	P-362—P-400
114	P-410—P-425
115	P-426—P-522
116	P-523—P-620
117	P-621—P-636
118	P-640—R-100
119	R-110—R-165
120	R-200
121	R-210—R-241
122	R-242—R-255
123	R-256—R-316
124	R-320—R-340
125	R-341—R-400
126	R-410—R-520
127	R-521—R-663
128	S-000—S-131
129	S-132—S-156
130	S-160—S-163
131	S-164—S-226
132	S-230—S-264
133	S-265—S-316
134	S-320—S-325
135	S-326—S-346
136	S-350—S-356
137	S-360—S-363
138	S-364—S-416
139	S-420
140	S-421—S-432
141	S-433—S-466
142	S-500—S-520
143	S-521—S-530, C
144	S-530, D–Z
145	S-531—S-536
146	S-540—S-552
147	S-553—S-615
148	S-616—S-634
149	S-635—S-666
150	T-000—T-242
151	T-243—T-450
152	T-452—T-546
153	T-550—T-634
154	T-635—U-515
155	U-516—V-240
156	V-241—V-545
157	V-550—W-166
158	W-200—W-231
159	W-232—W-252
160	W-253—W-266
161	W-300—W-350
162	W-351—W-414
163	W-415—W-425

Roll	Range
164	W-426—W-452
165	W-453—W-524
166	W-525—W-562
167	W-563—W-651
168	W-652—Z-166
169	Z-200—Z-364
170	Z-365—Z-524
171	Z-525—Z-666

Index (Soundex) to Passenger Lists of Vessels Arriving at Baltimore, MD, (City Passenger Lists), 1833–1866. M326. 22 rolls. 16mm. DP.

Under a Maryland State law of March 22, 1833, effective from September 1833 until October 1866, the masters of vessels were required to submit lists of passengers arriving at Baltimore to the mayor of that city. The law required that these "city lists" report the age and occupation of the passengers, and that the lists be sworn to by the master of the vessel in the presence of the mayor.

The lists for the period 1833–1866 to which the index relates were borrowed from the city of Baltimore and were filmed as part of Passenger Lists of Vessels Arriving at Baltimore, 1820–91 (M255).

Roll	Range
1	A-000—B-330
2	B-340—B-625
3	B-626—C-665
4	D-000—E-240
5	E-241—F-622
6	F-623—G-616
7	G-620—H-251
8	H-252—H-546
9	H-550—J-655
10	K-000—K-465
11	K-500—K-662
12	L-000—L-655
13	M-000—M-520
14	M-521—N-546
15	N-550—P-616
16	P-620—R-365
17	R-400—S-260
18	S-261—S-426
19	S-430—S-552
20	S-553—U-465
21	U-500—W-365
22	W-400—Z-656

Passenger Lists of Vessels Arriving at Baltimore, MD, 1820–1891. M255. 50 rolls. DP.

Roll	Dates
1	Sept. 2, 1820–Mar. 30, 1837
2	Apr. 7, 1837–July 31, 1840
3	Aug. 3, 1840–Dec. 21, 1842
4	Jan. 3, 1843–Aug. 29, 1845
5	Sept. 1, 1845–June 28, 1847
6	July 2, 1847–Dec. 20, 1848
7	Jan. 2, 1849–June 28, 1850
8	July 3, 1850–May 28, 1852
9	June 2, 1852–Aug. 29, 1853
10	Sept. 5, 1853–Dec. 30, 1854
11	Feb. 5, 1855–June 22, 1858
12	July 6, 1858–Sept. 28, 1860
13	Oct. 8, 1860–Sept. 24, 1863
14	Oct. 7, 1863–July 31, 1866

Roll	Dates
15	Aug. 3, 1866–Oct. 30, 1867
16	Nov. 5, 1867–Mar. 31, 1869
17	Apr. 3, 1869–June 27, 1870
18	July 2, 1870–May 30, 1871
19	June 1, 1871–Feb. 29, 1872
20	Mar. 4–Sept. 30, 1872
21	Oct. 4, 1872–June 28, 1873
22	July 2, 1873–Apr. 27, 1874
23	May 4–Dec. 30, 1874
24	Jan. 2–Sept. 25, 1875
25	Oct. 1, 1875–June 30, 1876
26	July 1, 1876–Mar. 31, 1877
27	Apr. 2–Dec. 29, 1877
28	Jan. 2–Aug. 30, 1878
29	Sept. 2, 1878–Apr. 28, 1879
30	May 2–Sept. 29, 1879
31	Oct. 1, 1879–May 14, 1880
32	May 15–Dec. 22, 1880
33	Jan. 3–June 30, 1881
34	July 2–Dec. 26, 1881
35	Jan. 6–July 26, 1882
36	Aug. 1, 1882–Feb. 24, 1883
37	Mar. 1–Aug. 29, 1883
38	Sept. 8, 1883–May 31, 1884
39	June 3, 1884–Feb. 28, 1885
40	Mar. 6–Dec. 24, 1885
41	Jan. 4–Sept. 30, 1886
42	Oct. 2, 1886–May 31, 1887
43	June 4–Dec. 30, 1887
44	Jan. 3–July 27, 1888
45	Aug. 7, 1888–May 30, 1889
46	June 1–Dec. 31, 1889
47	Jan. 11–July 31, 1890
48	Aug. 5, 1890–Mar. 25, 1891
49	Apr. 2–June 29, 1891
50	July 1–Dec. 28, 1891

Quarterly Abstracts of Passenger Lists of Vessels Arriving at Baltimore, MD, 1820–1869. M596. 6 rolls. DP.

Roll	Dates
1	Jan. 1, 1820–Dec. 31, 1829
2	Jan. 1, 1830–Dec. 31, 1833
3	Jan. 1, 1834–Dec. 31, 1837
4	Jan. 1, 1838–Dec. 31, 1845
5	July 1, 1848–Dec. 31, 1859
6	Jan. 1, 1860–June 30, 1869

Boston, Massachusetts

Index to Passenger Lists of Vessels Arriving at Boston, MA, 1848–1891. M265. 282 rolls. 16mm. DP.

Roll	Range
1	A–Aherm
2	Ahern–Allen, E.
3	Allen, F.–Am
4	An–Anderson, E.
5	Anderson, F.–Andreu
6	Andrew–Aq
7	Ar–Ashu
8	Ashw–Az
9	B–Baker, L.
10	Baker, M.–Bara

Roll	Range
11	Barb–Barrett, O.
12	Barrett, P.–Bas
13	Bat–Beat
14	Beau–Bengs
15	Bengt–Bergr
16	Bergs–Biel
17	Bien–Biz
18	Bj–Blin
19	Blio–Bonn
20	Bono–Bowd
21	Bowe–Brac
22	Brad–Bras
23	Brat–Brh
24	Bri–Brodo
25	Brodr–Brown, E.
26	Brown, F.–Brown, Z.
27	Browna–Buckley, I.
28	Buckley, J.–Burke, A.
29	Burke, B.–Burns, D.
30	Burns, E.–Butler, I.
31	Butler, J.–Cag
32	Cah–Callahan, F.
33	Callahan, G.–Campbell, C.
34	Campbell, D.–Cann, L.
35	Cann, M.–Carlson, A.
36	Carlson, B.–Carr, S.
37	Carr, T.–Cart
38	Caru–Catn
39	Cato–Charl
40	Charm–Christia
41	Christie–Clark, D.
42	Clark, E.–Clear
43	Cleas–Cob
44	Coc–Cold
45	Cole–Collins, J.
46	Collins, K.–Conc
47	Cond–Connelly, D.
48	Connelly, E.–Connor, I.
49	Connor, J.–Conway, I.
50	Conway, J.–Cop
51	Cora–Corz
52	Cos–Cours
53	Court–Cram
54	Cran–Croe
55	Crof–Crosb
56	Crosc–Crowle
57	Crowli–Cunm
58	Cunn–Curs
59	Curt–Daley, J.
60	Daley, K.–Darc
61	Dard–Davis, M.
62	Davis, N.–Ded
63	Dee–Denm
64	Denn–Devine, M.
65	Devine, N.–Dillon, L.
66	Dillon, M.–Dod
67	Doe–Donaho
68	Donahu–Donoh
69	Donol–Dorg
70	Dorh–Downes, M.
71	Downes, N.–Dre
72	Dri–Duffy, B.
73	Duffy, C.–Dunk
74	Dunl–Dw
75	Dy–Edm

Roll	Range
76	Edn–Elliott, I.
77	Elliott, J.–Enm
78	Enn–Evans, F.
79	Evans, G.–Falli
80	Fallo–Far
81	Fas–Ferguson, C.
82	Ferguson, D.–Finn, E.
83	Finn, F.–Fitzgerald, K.
84	Fitzgerald, L.–Fland
85	Flane–Flv
86	Fly–Foley, L.
87	Foley, M.–Form
88	Forn–Fow
89	Fox–Fraser, M.
90	Fraser, N.–Fre
91	Fri–Fz
92	G–Gal
93	Gam–Gar
94	Gas–Gep
95	Ger–Gile
96	Gilf–Gj
97	Gl–Gok
98	Gol–Gordon, A.
99	Gordon, B.–Goz
100	Gr–Grant, T.
101	Grant, U.–Green, T.
102	Green, W.–Griffiths, L.
103	Griffiths, M.–Gun
104	Guo–Hag
105	Hah–Halla
106	Hallb–Haml
107	Hamm–Hanr
108	Hans–Harg
109	Harh–Harris, F.
110	Harris, G.–Haru
111	Harv–Hawki
112	Hawkn–Healey, M.
113	Healey, N.–Hel
114	Hem–Henr
115	Hens–Hickey, M.
116	Hickey, N.–Hilli
117	Hillm–Hoe
118	Hof–Holl
119	Holm–Hopkins, L.
120	Hopkins, M.–Howard, L.
121	Howard, M.–Hughes, M.
122	Hughes, N.–Hurley, I.
123	Hurley, J.–Ik
124	Il–Jackson, C.
125	Jackson, D.–Janson, C.
126	Janson, D.–Jer
127	Jes–Johanson, C.
128	Johanson, D.–Johnson, C.
129	Johnson, D.–Johnston, L.
130	Johnston, M.–Jones, V.
131	Jones, W.–Joyce, J.
132	Joyce, K.–Kar
133	Kas–Keefe, M.
134	Keefe, N.–Kelley, E.
135	Kelley, F.–Kelly, Mart
136	Kelly, Mary–Kennedy, E.
137	Kennedy, F.–Kep
138	Ker–Kill
139	Kilm–Kinney, M.
140	Kinney, N.–Kn

Roll	Range
141	Ko–Lag
142	Lah–Lane, M.
143	Lane, N.–Larsen, C.
144	Larsen, D.–Lavil
145	Lavin–Leah
146	Leai–Lee, Ja
147	Lee, Je–Leonard, C.
148	Leonard, D.–Lex
149	Ley–Lir
150	Lis–Loge
151	Logg–Lot
152	Lou–Luk
153	Lul–Lynch, L.
154	Lynch, M.–Macd
155	Mace–Magn
156	Mago–Mahony, C.
157	Mahony, D.–Maloney, J.
158	Maloney, K.–Map
159	Maq–Marshall, E.
160	Marshall, F.–Martin, T.
161	Martin, V.–Mats
162	Matt–McArd
163	McAre–McCal
164	McCam–McCarthy, Mart
165	McCarthy, Mary–McClur
166	McClus–McCui
167	McCul–McDonald, Ale
168	McDonald, Alf–McDonald, Jh
169	McDonald, Jo–McDonl
170	McDonn–McEv
171	McEw–McGinnis, I.
172	McGinnis, J.–McGrath, P.
173	McGrath, R.–McIm
174	McIn–McKay, J.
175	McKay, K.–McKenzie, H.
176	McKenzie, I.–McLag
177	McLai–McLean, K.
178	McLean, L.–McLeod, S.
179	McLeod, T.–McMo
180	McMr–McNie
181	McNif–McSha
182	McShe–Mek
183	Mel–Merr
184	Mers–Miller, D.
185	Miller, E.–Miq
186	Mir–Monag
187	Monah–Moore, J.
188	Moore, K.–Moran, H.
189	Moran, I.–Morrison, D.
190	Morrison, E.–Moses, F.
191	Moses, G.–Mulc
192	Muld–Mulln
193	Mullo–Murphy, Bo
194	Murphy, Br–Murphy, K.
195	Murphy, L.–Murray, A.L.
196	Murray, Am–Muz
197	My–Nee, L.
198	Nee, M.–Neve
199	Nevi–Nicken
200	Nicker–Nilson, G.
201	Nilson, H.–Noona
202	Noonb–Ny
203	O–O'Brien, P.
204	O'Brien, R.–O'Donnell, Je
205	O'Donnell, Jo–Old

Roll	Range
206	Ole–Olson, L.
207	Olson, M.–Ord
208	Ore–Oz
209	P–Parker, M.
210	Parker, N.–Patterson, B.
211	Patterson, C.–Pedersi
212	Pederso–Perp
213	Perr–Petersen, D.
214	Petersen, E.–Pha
215	Phe–Pij
216	Pik–Pom
217	Pon–Pov
218	Pow–Prens
219	Prent–Purim
220	Purin–Quinn, O.
221	Quinn, P.–Randa
222	Randb–Reag
223	Reai–Regan, J.
224	Regan, K.–Reyng
225	Reyno–Richa
226	Richb–Riop
227	Rior–Roberts, D.
228	Roberts, E.–Robinson, J.
229	Robinson, K.–Rogers, E.
230	Rogers, F.–Rosd
231	Rose–Rov
232	Row–Russell, G.
233	Russell, H.–Ryan, P.
234	Ryan, R.–Sam
235	San–Savage, L.
236	Savage, M.–Schn
237	Scho–Scully, K.
238	Scully, M.–Se
239	Sg–Sha
240	She–Sheh
241	Shei–Shy
242	Si–Simon, J.
243	Simon, K.–Slattery, L.
244	Slattery, M.–Smith, B.
245	Smith, C.–Smith, Joh
246	Smith, Jon–Smith, S.
247	Smith, T.–Som
248	Son–Spil
249	Spim–Stanley, E.
250	Stanley, F.–Step
251	Ster–Stib
252	Stic–Stron
253	Stroo–Sullivan, Ha
254	Sullivan, He–Sullivan, Min
255	Sullivan, Mit–Svensk
256	Svenso–Swees
257	Sweet–Tat
258	Tau–Tell
259	Tem–Thomo
260	Thomp–Thorn
261	Thoro–Tod
262	Toe–Trac
263	Trad–Tuch
264	Tuck–Tw
265	Ty–Va
266	Ve–Wac
267	Wad–Walk
268	Wall–Walsh, J.
269	Walsh, K.–Ward, I.
270	Ward, J.–Watr

Roll	Range
271	Wats–Wed
272	Wee–Welsh, S.
273	Welsh, T.–Whed
274	Whee–White, Ja
275	White, Je–Whitta
276	Whitte–Willh
277	Willi–Willr
278	Wills–Wils
279	Wilt–Wood, D.
280	Wood, E.–Worr
281	Wors–Yen
282	Yoe–Zy

Passenger Lists of Vessels Arriving at Boston, MA, 1820–1891. M277. 115 rolls.

Roll	Dates
1	Sept. 22–25, 1820 (list nos. 1–2)
	Jan. 11–Dec. 31, 1821 (list nos. 1–89)
	Jan. 2–Dec. 21, 1822 (list nos. 1–163)
	Mar. 29–Nov. 22, 1823 (list nos. 1–2)
	Apr. 5–Dec. 27, 1824 (list nos. 1–128)
	Jan. 14–Mar. 30, 1825 (list nos. 1–32)
2	Apr. 4–Dec. 31, 1825 (list nos. 33–211)
	Apr. 3–June 30, 1826 (list nos. 1–101)
3	July 3–Dec. 27, 1826 (list nos. 102–234)
	Jan. 5–Dec. 26, 1827 (list nos. 1–132)
	Jan. 4–Mar. 29, 1828 (list nos. 1–21)
4	Apr. 2–June 30, 1828 (list nos. 22–70)
	Jan. 8–Dec. 28, 1829 (list nos. 1–200)
	Jan. 2–Mar. 31, 1830 (list nos. 1–24)
5	Apr. 1–Dec. 29, 1830 (list nos. 25–191)
	Jan. 1–July 30, 1831 (list nos. 1–122)
6	Aug. 2–Dec. 31, 1831 (list nos. 123–231)
	Jan. 3–Sept. 29, 1832 (list nos. 1–175)
7	Feb. 7–Dec. 27, 1833 (list nos. 1–317)
8	Jan. 1–Dec. 29, 1834 (list nos. 1–244)
	Apr. 2–30, 1835 (list nos. 1–37)
9	May 1–Sept. 30, 1835 (list nos. 38–285)
10	Oct. 1–Dec. 31, 1835 (list nos. 286–393)
	July 1–Dec. 29, 1836 (list nos. 1–211)
	Jan. 1–Mar. 30, 1837 (list nos. 1–40)
11	Apr. 1–Dec. 28, 1837 (list nos. 41–244)
	Jan. 1–Aug. 31, 1838 (list nos. 1–222)
12	Sept. 1–Dec. 31, 1838 (list nos. 223–340)
	Jan. 1–Aug. 31, 1839 (list nos. 1–294)
13	Sept. 2–Dec. 24, 1839 (list nos. 295–432)
	Jan. 2–Aug. 10, 1840 (list nos. 1–104) and
	Jan. 4–Apr. 28, 1841 (list nos. 1–75)
14	May 1–Aug. 31, 1841 (list nos. 76–330)
15	Sept. 1–Dec. 30, 1841 (list nos. 331–486) and
	Jan. 3–June 29, 1842 (list nos. 1–119)
16	July 1–Sept. 30, 1842 (list nos. 120–281) and
	Jan. 4–Aug. 31, 1843 (list nos. 1–133)
17	Sept. 1–Dec. 27, 1843 (list nos. 134–303) and
	Jan. 5–June 28, 1844 (list nos. 1–157)
18	Oct. 1–Dec. 28, 1844 (list nos. 158–265) and
	Jan. 1–May 31, 1845 (list nos. 1–219)
19	June 2–Sept. 30, 1845 (list nos. 220–547)
20	Oct. 1–Dec. 30, 1845 (list nos. 548–690) and
	Jan. 14–May 29, 1846 (list nos. 1–180)
21	June 1–Aug. 31, 1846 (list nos. 181–409)
22	Sept. 1–30, 1846 (list nos. 410–484) and
	Jan. 1–May 31, 1847 (list nos. 1–209)
23	June 1–Oct. 12, 1847 (list nos. 210–427)

Roll	Dates
24	Nov. 4–Dec. 31, 1847 (list nos. 428–512) and Apr. 1–May 19, 1848 (list nos. 1–169)
25	May 20–July 10, 1848 (list nos. 170–429)
26	July 11–Sept. 30, 1848 (list nos. 430–727)
27	Oct. 2–Dec. 29, 1848 (list nos. 728–954)
28	Jan. 2–Apr. 30, 1849 (list nos. 1–202)
29	May 1–June 7, 1849 (list nos. 203–395)
30	June 8–July 17, 1849 (list nos. 396–607)
31	July 19–Sept. 15, 1849 (list nos. 608–831)
32	Sept. 17–Nov. 30, 1849 (list nos. 832–1077)
33	Dec. 1–31, 1849 (list nos. 1078–1116) and Jan. 2–Apr. 30, 1850 (list nos. 1–180)
34	May 1–June 19, 1850 (list nos. 181–402)
35	June 20–Aug. 31, 1850 (list nos. 403–727)
36	Sept. 2–Dec. 30, 1850 (list nos. 673–1031)
37	Jan. 4–May 20, 1851 (list nos. 1–275)
38	May 21–Aug. 20, 1851 (list nos. 276–567)
39	Aug. 21–Nov. 13, 1851 (list nos. 568–862)
40	Jan. 1–May 31, 1852 (list nos. 1–313)
41	June 1–Aug. 19, 1852 (list nos. 314–634)
42	Aug. 20–Dec. 31, 1852 (list nos. 635–921)
43	Jan. 3–May 31, 1853 (list nos. 1–302)
44	June 1–Aug. 19, 1853 (list nos. 303–613)
45	Aug. 20–Nov. 10, 1853 (list nos. 614–902)
46	Nov. 11–Dec. 27, 1853 (list nos. 903–1009) and Jan. 2–June 14, 1854 (list nos. 1–186)
47	June 16–Aug. 14, 1854 (list nos. 187–444)
48	Aug. 15–Oct. 31, 1854 (list nos. 445–761)
49	Nov. 1–Dec. 30, 1854 (list nos. 762–878) and Jan. 1–May 9, 1857 (list nos. 1–188)
50	May 11–Aug. 19, 1857 (list nos. 189–481)
51	Aug. 20–Dec. 31, 1857 (list nos. 482–807)
52	Jan. 4–July 16, 1858 (list nos. 1–344)
53	July 17–Nov. 30, 1858 (list nos. 345–711)
54	Dec. 1–30, 1858 (list nos. 712–742) and Jan. 3–June 30, 1859 (list nos. 1–337)
55	July 1–Nov. 10, 1859 (list nos. 338–715)
56	Nov. 11–Dec. 31, 1859 (list nos. 716–795) and Jan. 2–June 15, 1860 (list nos. 1–298)
57	June 16–Sept. 29, 1860 (list nos. 299–660)
58	Oct. 1–Dec. 31, 1860 (list nos. 661–857) and Jan. 2–May 31, 1861 (list nos. 1–160)
59	June 1–Dec. 30, 1861 (list nos. 161–520) and Jan. 9–Feb. 25, 1862 (list nos. 1–27)
60	Mar. 4–Aug. 19, 1862 (list nos. 28–416)
61	Aug. 20–Dec. 29, 1862 (list nos. 417–693) and Jan. 2–May 9, 1863 (list nos. 1–116)
62	May 11–Sept. 18, 1863 (list nos. 117–497)
63	Sept. 21–Dec. 30, 1863 (list nos. 498–737) and Jan. 6–May 31, 1864 (list nos. 1–144)
64	June 1–Sept. 29, 1864 (list nos. 145–522)
65	Oct. 1–Dec. 24, 1864 (list nos. 523–701) and Jan. 2–June 15, 1865 (list nos. 1–208)
66	June 16–Oct. 31, 1865 (list nos. 209–548)
67	Nov. 1–Dec. 30, 1865 (list nos. 549–674) and Feb. 2–May 25, 1866 (list nos. 1–177)
68	May 26–Sept. 10, 1866 (list nos. 178–513)
69	Sept. 11–Dec. 31, 1866 (list nos. 514–791) and Jan. 3–Mar. 28, 1867 (list nos. 1–54)
70	Apr. 1–July 19, 1867 (list nos. 55–383)
71	July 20–Oct. 30, 1867 (list nos. 384–717)
72	Nov. 1–Dec. 30, 1867 (list nos. 718–791) and Jan. 2–July 18, 1868 (list nos. 1–243)
73	July 20–Sept. 29, 1868 (list nos. 244–559)
74	Oct. 1–Dec. 31, 1868 (list nos. 560–782) and Jan. 1–July 6, 1869 (list nos. 1–108)
75	July 7–Sept. 10, 1869 (list nos. 109–377)
76	Sept. 13–Dec. 31, 1869 (list nos. 378–647)
77	Apr. 2–June 20, 1870 (list nos. 1–291)
78	June 21–Sept. 10, 1870 (list nos. 292–605)
79	Sept. 12–Dec. 30, 1870 (list nos. 606–837) and Jan. 2–Mar. 31, 1871 (list nos. 1–54)
80	Apr. 1–July 10, 1871 (list nos. 55–350)
81	July 11–Oct. 20, 1871 (list nos. 351–634)
82	Oct. 23–Dec. 30, 1871 (list nos. 635–740) and Jan. 2–May 20, 1872 (list nos. 1–159)
83	May 21–Sept. 24, 1872 (list nos. 160–518)
84	Sept. 25–Dec. 31, 1872 (list nos. 519–654) and Jan. 1–May 22, 1873 (list nos. 1–147)
85	May 23–July 31, 1873 (list nos. 148–307)
86	Aug. 1–Oct. 31, 1873 (list nos. 308–515)
87	Nov. 3–Dec. 31, 1873 (list nos. 516–565) Jan. 5–Mar. 31, 1874 (list nos. 1–35) and Jan. 1–Apr. 6, 1883 (list nos. 1–120)
88	Apr. 7–May 15, 1883 (list nos. 121–241)
89	May 16–July 18, 1883 (list nos. 242–384)
90	July 21–Sept. 20, 1883 (list nos. 385–543)
91	Sept. 1–Dec. 31, 1883 (list nos. 544–718)
92	Jan. 1–May 6, 1884 (list nos. 1–186)
93	May 7–July 8, 1884 (list nos. 187–353)
94	July 10–Sept. 20, 1884 (list nos. 354–544)
95	Sept. 22–Dec. 31, 1884 (list nos. 545–729)
96	Jan. 1–May 20, 1885 (list nos. 1–204)
97	May 21–July 31, 1885 (list nos. 205–407)
98	Aug. 1–Sept. 30, 1885 (list nos. 408–588)
99	Oct. 1–Dec. 31, 1885 (list nos. 589–749) and Jan. 1–Feb. 26, 1886 (list nos. 1–44)
100	Mar. 1–May 15, 1886 (list nos. 45–228)
101	May 17–Aug. 9, 1886 (list nos. 229–381)
102	Aug. 11–Dec. 31, 1886 (list nos. 382–502) and Jan 1–31, 1887 (list nos. 1–25)
103	Feb. 2–May 31, 1887 (list nos. 26–142)
104	June 1–Sept. 15, 1887 (list nos. 143–259)
105	Sept. 16–Dec. 31, 1887 (list nos. 260–348) and Jan. 2–Feb. 29, 1888 (list nos. 1–47)
106	Mar. 2–June 12, 1888 (list nos. 48–155)
107	June 16–Sept. 28, 1888 (list nos. 156–262)
108	Oct. 1–31, 1888 (list nos. 263–293) and Jan. 1–Apr. 29, 1889 (list nos. 1–103)
109	May 1–Aug. 9, 1889 (list nos. 104–205)
110	Aug. 12–Dec. 31, 1889 (list nos. 206–318)
111	Jan. 1–May 19, 1890 (list nos. 1–128)
112	May 21–Sept. 10, 1890 (list nos. 129–254)
113	Sept. 12–Dec. 31, 1890 (list nos. 255–351) and Jan. 1–Feb. 28, 1891 (list nos. 1–43)
114	Mar. 2–May 29, 1891 (list nos. 44–152)
115	June 1–July 29, 1891 (list nos. 153–230)

New Orleans, Louisiana

Index to Passenger Lists of Vessels Arriving at New Orleans, LA, before 1900. T527. 32 rolls. 16mm.

This index covers the period 1853–1899. The original records were transferred to the Immigration and Naturalization Service and are part of Record Group 85. The publication is described with the records of the U.S. Customs Service for the convenience of the researcher.

Roll	Contents
1	Aab, Mr. and Mrs. Aug.–Bannerman, Mrs. W.
2	Bannico, Concetta–Bertucca, R. Lattanta
3	Bertucci, Agata–Brem, Sophia
4	Bremen, Catherine–Cathicot, Elie
5	Cahil, Honora–Claude, Jean Baptiste
6	Claude, Joseph–Dallu, L.
7	Dalma, N.–Doniedo, Marie
8	Doning, Friederich–Engle, Paul
9	Englehardt, Cath.–Fontana, Giovanni
10	Fontana, Guiliana–Garot, Catherine
11	Garot, Eugenie–Graywelding, Carl
12	Grazia, Leonardo–Harding, C.F.
13	Hardiman, Abraham–Hincks, T.
14	Hind, Gridget–Iszig, Rosalia
15	Italia, Francesca–Johse, Carl
16	Joice, Mary Ann–Kleekamp, Francis
17	Kleekamp, Louise–Lacosse, Michel
18	Lacoste, Angelo–Lewandowsky, Franz
19	Leweling, Angela–Malony, Wm.
20	Malodec, Franz–Mickey, Maria
21	McKibborin, George–Moone, Matt.
22	Mooney, Ann–Nipote, Arcommano F.
23	Nipp, A. Maria–Penlington, James
24	Penn, Cohn–Rageio, Fortuna
25	Ragge, August–Rolwess, Franz
26	Roma, Horatis–Schapani, Stefano
27	Schape, Caroline–Schuter, A.
28	Schuth, Angela–Sparr, Robt.
29	Sparraguirra, Migel–Taylor, Wm. H.
30	Tazo, Christesa–Veronique, Ketterer
31	Veroz, Benito–Wertermann, Wilhelm
32	Werth, E.–Zyricki, Caspar

Passenger Lists of Vessels Arriving at New Orleans, LA, 1820–1902. M259. 93 rolls. DP.

Roll	Inclusive Dates
1	Jan. 1, 1820–Mar. 31, 1821
2	Apr. 1, 1821–Dec. 26, 1822
3	Jan. 3, 1823–Jan. 28, 1824
4	Feb. 9, 1824–May 30, 1825
5	June 1, 1825–Oct. 30, 1826
6	Nov. 1, 1826–Sept. 25, 1827
7	Oct. 3, 1827–Mar. 31, 1829
8	Apr. 3, 1829–Feb. 27, 1830
9	Mar. 8, 1830–Feb. 28, 1831
10	Mar. 1, 1831–Jan. 31, 1832
11	Feb. 6, 1832–July 24, 1833
12	Aug. 5, 1833–May 30, 1835
13	June 1, 1835–Apr. 30, 1836
14	May 1, 1836–Feb. 28, 1837
15	Mar. 2–Dec. 30, 1837
16	Jan. 3–June 30, 1838
17	July 2, 1838–Jan. 29, 1839
18	Feb. 1–July 31, 1839
19	Aug. 1, 1839–Jan. 30, 1840
20	Feb. 1–June 29, 1840
21	July 1, 1840–Oct. 20, 1841
22	Nov. 2, 1841–Aug. 31, 1843
23	Sept. 4, 1843–Dec. 31, 1844
24	Jan. 1–Dec. 30, 1845
25	Jan. 1–Nov. 30, 1846
26	Dec. 4, 1846–June 14, 1847
27	June 16–Dec. 31, 1847
28	Jan. 1–Oct. 31, 1848
29	Nov. 6, 1848–Feb. 6, 1849
30	Feb. 7–May 29, 1849
31	June 3–Dec. 31, 1849
32	Jan. 1–Oct. 31, 1850
33	Nov. 1, 1850–Mar. 21, 1851
34	Mar. 22–Dec. 15, 1851
35	Dec. 16, 1851–Apr. 30, 1852
36	May 1–Oct. 30, 1852
37	Nov. 1, 1852–Apr. 25, 1853
38	Apr. 26–Nov. 30, 1853
39	Dec. 1, 1853–Apr. 29, 1854
40	May 1–Nov. 22, 1854
41	Nov. 23, 1854–May 3, 1855
42	May 4, 1855–Apr. 28, 1856
43	Apr. 29, 1856–Mar. 3, 1857
44	Mar. 4–Nov. 5, 1857
45	Nov. 6, 1857–May 19, 1858
46	May 20–Dec. 29, 1858
47	Jan. 1–July 27, 1859
48	Aug. 4, 1859–Feb. 29, 1860
49	Mar. 1–Nov. 30, 1860
50	Dec. 1, 1860–Mar. 31, 1866
51	Apr. 2, 1866–Feb. 25, 1867
52	Mar. 1, 1867–Feb. 29, 1868
53	Mar. 4, 1868–Mar. 31, 1869
54	Apr. 1, 1869–Apr. 28, 1870
55	May 2, 1870–July 31, 1871
56	Aug. 14, 1871–Oct. 31, 1872
57	Nov. 5, 1872–Feb. 26, 1874
58	Mar. 2, 1874–Sept. 27, 1875
59	Oct. 4, 1875–Feb. 28, 1877
60	Mar. 3, 1877–May 30, 1878
61	June 1, 1878–Nov. 30, 1879
62	Dec. 2, 1879–Nov. 15, 1880
63	Nov. 16, 1880–Oct. 31, 1881
64	Nov. 1, 1881–Nov. 20, 1882
65	Nov. 21, 1882–Oct. 31, 1883
66	Nov. 1, 1883–Aug. 30, 1884
67	Sept. 3, 1884–Apr. 29, 1885
68	May 1, 1885–Feb. 27, 1886
69	Mar. 1–Dec. 31, 1886
70	Jan. 4–Dec. 30, 1887
71	Jan. 2–Oct. 30, 1888
72	Nov. 1, 1888–Sept. 21, 1889
73	Oct. 2, 1889–June 25, 1890
74	July 5, 1890–Feb. 27, 1891
75	Mar. 2–Nov. 14, 1891
76	Nov. 16, 1891–Apr. 27, 1892
77	May 1, 1892–Feb. 28, 1893
78	Mar. 1–Nov. 15, 1893
79	Nov. 20, 1893–July 30, 1894
80	Aug. 1, 1894–Mar. 30, 1895
81	Apr. 1–Dec. 31, 1895
82	Jan. 1–July 10, 1896
83	July 13, 1896–Feb. 20, 1897
84	Feb. 22–Sept. 10, 1897
85	Sept. 11, 1897–Mar. 31, 1898
86	Apr. 1–Oct. 31, 1898
87	Nov. 1, 1898–June 28, 1899
88	July 5, 1899–Feb. 28, 1900
89	Mar. 2–Aug. 28, 1900
90	Sept. 4, 1900–Mar. 15, 1901
91	Mar. 15–Dec. 31, 1901
92	Jan. 1–Sept. 29, 1902
93	Oct. 1, 1902–Jan. 31, 1903

Quarterly Abstracts of Passenger Lists of Vessels Arriving at New Orleans, LA, 1820–1875. M272. 17 rolls. DP.

Roll	Dates
1	Jan. 1, 1820–Dec. 30, 1837
2	Jan. 2, 1838–Sept. 30, 1845
3	Oct. 6, 1845–Dec. 31, 1846
4	Jan. 1–Dec. 31, 1847
5	Jan. 3, 1848–Mar. 31, 1849
6	Apr. 2, 1849–Sept. 28, 1850
7	Oct. 2, 1850–Mar. 31, 1851
8	Apr. 1–Dec. 29, 1851
9	Apr. 1, 1852–Mar. 31, 1853
10	Apr. 1–Dec. 29, 1853
11	Jan. 2–June 30, 1854
12	July 7, 1854–June 30, 1857
13	Oct. 1, 1857–Sept. 21, 1866
14	Oct. 2, 1866–Dec. 30, 1867
15	Jan. 1, 1868–Dec. 31, 1869
16	Jan. 4, 1870–Sept. 25, 1872
17	Oct. 1, 1872–June 30, 1875

New York, New York

Index to Passenger Lists of Vessels Arriving at New York, NY, 1820–1846. M261. 103 rolls. 16mm. DP.

Roll	Range	Roll	Range
1	A–Alo	39	Grt–Hai
2	Alp–Art	40	Haj–Hanr
3	Aru–Bal	41	Hans–Harv
4	Ball–Bas	42	Harw–Heh
5	Bass–Bel	43	Hei–Hern
6	Bell–Bex	44	Hero–Hir
7	Bey–Blum	45	His–Hoo
8	Blum–Box	46	Hop–Hug
9	Boy–Bree	47	Huh–Irw
10	Bref–Browl	48	Is–Jog
11	Brown–Buckl	49	Joh–Jon
12	Buckm–Buts	50	Joo–Keem
13	Butt–Cam	51	Keen–Kennd
14	Can–Cart	52	Kenne–Kim
15	Caru–Cha	53	Kin–Kob
16	Che–Cla	54	Koc–Ky
17	Cle–Coll	55	L–Lau
18	Colm–Cook	56	Lav–Leo
19	Cooke–Coy	57	Lep–Loa
20	Coz–Cul	58	Lob–Lur
21	Cum–Dan	59	Lus–Mahn
22	Dao–Deh	60	Maho–Mark
23	Dei–Did	61	Marl–Mat
24	Die–Dona	62	Mau–McCap
25	Donb–Dox	63	McCar–McCu
26	Doy–Dunm	64	McD–McGi
27	Dunn–Ed	65	McGl–McKem
28	Ee–Er	66	McKen–McNa
29	Es–Farq	67	McNd–Me
30	Farr–Fil	68	Mi–Mok
31	Fim–Fle	69	Mol–Morh
32	Fli–Fo	70	Mori–Muller, G.
33	Fr–Fus	71	Muller, H.–Murp
34	Fut–Gar	72	Murr–Neu
35	Gas–Gilb	73	Nev–Ny
36	Gilc–Gom	74	O–On
37	Gon–Grau	75	Op–Par
38	Grav–Gro	76	Pas–Pet
		77	Peu–Poq
		78	Por–Qug
		79	Qui–Rea
		80	Reb–Rex
		81	Rey–Ril
		82	Rim–Rof
		83	Rog–Ruf
		84	Rug–Sap
		85	Sar–Schl
		86	Schm–Schv
		87	Schw–Shap
		88	Shar–Simo
		89	Simp–Smith, K.
		90	Smith, L.–Spi
		91	Spl–Ste
		92	Stf–Su
		93	Sv–Tha
		94	The–Til
		95	Tim–Turl
		96	Turm–Vi
		97	Vl–Walse
		98	Walsh–Waz
		99	Wes–Wer
		100	Wes–Wile
		101	Wilf–Wily
		102	Wim–Wri
		103	Wro–Z

Passenger Lists of Vessels Arriving at New York, NY, 1820–1897. M237. 675 rolls. DP. (★ A complete list of rolls has been added).

Roll	Dates
1	Jan. 7, 1820–June 30, 1821
2	July 2, 1821–May 17, 1822
3	May 18, 1822–Mar. 26, 1823
4	Apr. 3–Nov. 17, 1823
5	Nov. 18, 1823–Aug. 11, 1824
6	Aug. 12, 1824–Apr. 30, 1825
7	May 2–Dec. 29, 1825
8	Jan. 2–Aug. 31, 1826
9	Sept. 2, 1826–May 30, 1827
10	June 1, 1827–Nov. 16, 1827
11	Nov. 21, 1827–June 30, 1828
12	July 1, 1828–Feb. 28, 1829
13	Mar. 4, 1829–Apr. 30, 1830
14	May 1, 1830–June 30, 1831
15	July 2, 1831–Jan. 31, 1832
16	Feb. 1–June 12, 1832
17	June 13–Sept. 29, 1832
18	Oct. 1, 1832–Apr. 12, 1833
19	Apr. 13–June 21, 1833
20	June 22–Aug. 27, 1833
21	Aug. 28, 1833–Feb. 10, 1834
22	Feb. 14–May 20, 1834
23	May 21–July 19, 1834
24	July 21–Oct. 12, 1834
25	Oct. 13–Mar. 25, 1835
26	Mar. 26–June 22, 1835
27	June 23–Aug. 31, 1835
28	Sept. 1, 1835–Jan. 19, 1836
29	Jan. 20–May 17, 1836
30	May 18–July 25, 1836
31	July 26–Oct. 14, 1836
32	Oct. 15, 1836–Mar. 14, 1837
33	Mar. 16–June 11, 1837
34	June 12–Aug. 21, 1837
35	Aug. 22, 1837–Feb. 26, 1838
36	Mar. 1–June 30, 1838
37	July 1–Dec. 31, 1838
38	Jan. 2–June 29, 1839
39	July 1–Sept. 5, 1839
40	Sept. 6–Dec. 31, 1839
41	Jan. 4–May 18, 1840
42	May 19–July 13, 1840
43	July 14–Sept. 15, 1840
44	Sept. 16, 1840–May 10, 1841
45	May 11–June 28, 1841
46	June 29–Sept. 11, 1841
47	Sept. 13, 1841–Jan. 31, 1842
48	Feb. 1–May 31, 1842
49	June 1–July 30, 1842
50	Aug. 1–Oct. 25, 1842
51	Oct. 26, 1842–June 15, 1843
52	June 16–Aug. 31, 1843
53	Sept. 1, 1843–Mar. 30, 1844
54	Apr. 1–June 18, 1844
55	June 19–Aug. 31, 1844
56	Sept. 2–Dec. 31, 1844
57	Jan. 2–May 31, 1845
58	June 2–July 15, 1845
59	July 16–Sept. 15, 1845
60	Sept. 16, 1845–Mar. 31, 1846
61	Apr. 1–May 30, 1846
62	June 1–July 10, 1846

Roll	Dates
63	July 11–Aug. 31, 1846
64	Sept. 1–Nov. 30, 1846
65	Dec. 2, 1846–Apr. 7, 1847
66	Apr. 8–May 20, 1847
67	May 21–June 24, 1847
68	June 25–Aug. 31, 1847
69	Sept. 1–Oct. 30, 1847
70	Nov. 1, 1847–Feb. 29, 1848
71	Mar. 1–May 8, 1848
72	May 9–31, 1848
73	June 1–July 10, 1848
74	July 11–August 24, 1848
75	Aug. 25–Oct. 16, 1848
76	Oct. 17–Dec. 30, 1848
77	Jan. 1–Mar. 31, 1849
78	Apr. 1–May 3, 1849
79	May 4–June 4, 1849
80	June 5–July 2, 1849
81	July 3–26, 1849
82	July 27–Aug. 23, 1849
83	Aug. 24–Sept. 25, 1849
84	Sept. 26–Oct. 31, 1849
85	Nov. 1, 1849–Jan. 12, 1850
86	Jan. 14–Apr. 8, 1850
87	Apr. 9–May 14, 1850
88	May 15–25, 1850
89	May 26–June 30, 1850
90	July 1–23, 1850
91	July 24–Aug. 31, 1850
92	Sept. 2–30, 1850
93	Oct. 1–25, 1850
94	Oct. 28–Dec. 18, 1850
95	Dec. 20, 1850–Feb. 22, 1851
96	Feb. 23–Apr. 10, 1851
97	Apr. 11–30, 1851
98	May 1–26, 1851
99	May 27–June 10, 1851
100	June 11–30, 1851
101	July 1–16, 1851
102	July 17–Aug. 4, 1851
103	Aug. 5–22, 1851
104	Aug. 23–Sept. 13, 1851
105	Sept. 15–30, 1851
106	Oct.1–31, 1851
107	Nov. 1–26, 1851
108	Nov. 28, 1851–Jan. 5, 1852
109	Jan. 6–Feb. 24, 1852
110	Feb. 25–Mar. 31, 1852
111	Apr. 1–23, 1852
112	Apr. 24–May 11, 1852
113	May 12–31, 1852
114	June 1–19, 1852
115	June 21–July 5, 1852
116	July 6–22, 1852
117	July 23–Aug. 10, 1852
118	Aug. 11–31, 1852
119	Sept. 1–25, 1852
120	Sept. 27–Oct. 21, 1852
121	Oct. 22–Nov. 30, 1852
122	Dec. 1, 1852–Jan. 22, 1853
123	Jan. 24–Mar. 8, 1853
124	Mar. 9–Apr. 21, 1853
125	Apr. 22–May 21, 1853
126	May 23–June 3, 1853
127	June 4–17, 1853

Roll	Dates
128	June 18–July 16, 1853
129	July 18–Aug. 12, 1853
130	Aug. 13–31, 1853
131	Sept. 1–19, 1853
132	Sept. 20–Oct. 21, 1853
133	Oct. 22–Nov. 17, 1853
134	Nov. 18–Dec. 12, 1853
135	Dec. 13, 1853–Jan. 18, 1854
136	Jan. 19–Apr. 3, 1854
137	Apr. 4–21, 1854
138	Apr. 22–May 15, 1854
139	May 16–22, 1854
140	May 23–June 11, 1854
141	June 12–31 [sic], 1854
142	July 1–24, 1854
143	July 25–Aug. 13, 1854
144	Aug. 14–28, 1854
145	Aug. 29–Sept. 19, 1854
146	Sept. 20–Oct. 16, 1854
147	Oct. 17–Nov. 11, 1854
148	Nov. 13–Dec. 14, 1854
149	Dec. 15, 1854–Jan. 11, 1855
150	Jan. 20–Mar. 24, 1855
151	Mar. 26–May 7, 1855
152	May 8–31, 1855
153	June 1–23, 1855
154	June 24–July 20, 1855
155	July 21–Aug. 22, 1855
156	Aug. 23–Sept. 24, 1855
157	Sept. 25–Oct. 25, 1855
158	Oct. 26–Dec. 15, 1855
159	Dec. 17, 1855–Jan. 31, 1856
160	Feb. 1–Mar. 31, 1856
161	Apr. 1–May 14, 1856
162	May 15–June 9, 1856
163	June 10–30, 1856
164	July 1–25, 1856
165	July 26–Aug. 21, 1856
166	Aug. 22–Sept. 18, 1856
167	Sept. 19–Oct. 18, 1856
168	Oct. 20–Nov. 17, 1856
169	Nov. 18–Dec. 31, 1856
170	Jan. 2–Feb. 10, 1857
171	Feb. 11–Mar. 23, 1857
172	Mar. 24–Apr. 22, 1857
173	Apr. 23–May 19, 1857
174	May 20–June 4, 1857
175	June 5–July 1, 1857
176	July 2–21, 1857
177	July 22–Aug. 24, 1857
178	Aug. 25–Sept. 16, 1857
179	Sept. 17–Oct. 22, 1857
180	Oct. 23–Nov. 24, 1857
181	Nov. 25, 1857–Jan. 28, 1858
182	Feb. 1–Apr. 12, 1858
183	Apr. 13–May 18, 1858
184	May 19–June 19, 1858
185	June 21–July 19, 1858
186	July 20–Aug. 27, 1858
187	Aug. 28–Oct. 2, 1858
188	Oct. 3–Nov. 9, 1858
189	Nov. 10, 1858–Jan. 18, 1859
190	Jan. 19–Apr. 13, 1859
191	Apr. 14–May 14, 1859
192	May 16–June 13, 1859

Roll	Dates
193	June 14–July 14, 1859
194	July 15–Aug. 19, 1859
195	Aug. 20–Sept. 30, 1859
196	Oct. 1–Nov. 11, 1859
197	Nov. 12–Dec. 21, 1859
198	Dec. 22, 1859–Feb. 29, 1860
199	Mar. 1, 1860–Apr. 13, 1860
200	Apr. 14–May 11, 1860
201	May 12–June 18, 1860
202	June 19–July 16, 1860
203	July 18–Aug. 15, 1860
204	Aug. 16–Sept. 17, 1860
205	Sept. 18–Oct. 18, 1860
206	Oct. 19–Nov. 21, 1860
207	Nov. 22–Dec. 31, 1860
208	Jan. 1–Mar. 14, 1861
209	Mar. 15–Apr. 17, 1861
210	Apr. 18–May 10, 1861
211	May 11–June 5, 1861
212	June 6–July 8, 1861
213	July 9–Aug. 10, 1861
214	Aug. 12–Sept. 27, 1861
215	Sept. 28–Nov. 11, 1861
216	Nov. 12, 1861–Jan. 14, 1862
217	Jan. 15–Mar. 26, 1862
218	Mar. 27–May 5, 1862
219	May 6–June 8, 1862
220	June 9–July 7, 1862
221	July 7–Aug. 8, 1862
222	Aug. 9–Sept. 10, 1862
223	Sept. 11–Oct. 16, 1862
224	Oct. 17–Dec. 19, 1862
225	Dec. 20, 1862–Jan. 9, 1863
226	Feb. 10–Apr. 8, 1863
227	Apr. 9–May 4, 1863
228	May 5–25, 1863
229	May 26–June 16, 1863
230	June 17–July 9, 1863
231	July 10–30, 1863
232	July 31–Sept. 2, 1863
233	Sept. 3–Oct. 3, 1863
234	Oct. 5–27, 1863
235	Oct. 28–Nov. 30, 1863
236	Dec. 1, 1863–Jan. 8, 1864
237	Jan. 9–Feb. 27, 1864
238	Feb. 29–Apr. 4, 1864
239	Apr. 5–May 4, 1864
240	May 5–25, 1864
241	May 26–June 15, 1864
242	June 16–July 12, 1864
243	July 13–Aug. 5, 1864
244	Aug. 6–29, 1864
245	Aug. 30–Oct. 2, 1864
246	Oct. 3–27, 1864
247	Oct. 28–Dec. 4, 1864
248	Dec. 5, 1864–Jan. 31, 1865
249	Feb. 1–Mar. 29, 1865
250	Apr. 1–May 3, 1865
251	May 4–26, 1865
252	May 27–June 19, 1865
253	June 20–July 17, 1865
254	July 18–Aug. 11, 1865
255	Aug. 12–Sept. 6, 1865
256	Sept. 7–30, 1865
257	Oct. 2–27, 1865

Roll	Dates
258	Oct. 28–Nov. 13, 1865
259	Nov. 14–Dec. 8, 1865
260	Dec. 9, 1865–Jan. 15, 1866
261	Jan. 16–Feb. 22, 1866
262	Feb. 23–Mar. 31, 1866
263	Apr. 2–20, 1866
264	Apr. 20–May 10, 1866
265	May 11–25, 1866
266	May 26–June 7, 1866
267	June 8–23, 1866
268	June 24–July 17, 1866
269	July 18–Aug. 2, 1866
270	Aug. 3–31, 1866
271	Sept. 1–28, 1866
272	Sept. 29–Oct. 26, 1866
273	Oct. 27–Nov. 21, 1866
274	Nov. 22–Dec. 31, 1866
275	Jan. 2–Feb. 11, 1867
276	Feb. 12–Mar. 20, 1867
277	Mar. 21–Apr. 22, 1867
278	Apr. 23–May 12, 1867
279	May 13–25, 1867
280	May 26–June 7, 1867
281	June 8–22, 1867
282	June 23–July 12, 1867
283	July 13–31, 1867
284	Aug. 1–21, 1867
285	Aug. 22–Sept. 12, 1867
286	Sept. 13–Oct. 4, 1867
287	Oct. 5–25, 1867
288	Oct. 26–Nov. 15, 1867
289	Nov. 16–Dec. 16, 1867
290	Dec. 17, 1867–Jan. 31, 1868
291	Feb. 1–Mar. 19, 1868
292	Mar. 20–Apr. 10, 1868
293	Apr. 11–May 4, 1868
294	May 5–18, 1868
295	May 19–June 2, 1868
296	June 3–19, 1868
297	June 20–July 7, 1868
298	July 8–27, 1868
299	July 28–Aug. 15, 1868
300	Aug. 16–Sept. 7, 1868
301	Sept. 8–25, 1868
302	Sept. 26–Oct. 20, 1868
303	Oct. 21–Nov. 18, 1868
304	Nov. 19–Dec. 17, 1868
305	Dec. 18, 1868–Jan. 20, 1969
306	Jan. 21–Mar. 2, 1869
307	Mar. 3–31, 1869
308	Apr. 1–21, 1869
309	Apr. 22–May 5, 1869
310	May 6–17, 1869
311	May 18–31, 1869
312	June 1–14, 1869
313	June 15–29, 1869
314	June 30–July 17, 1869
315	July 19–Aug. 5, 1869
316	Aug. 6–23, 1869
317	Aug. 24–Sept. 10, 1869
318	Sept. 11–27, 1869
319	Sept. 28–Oct. 18, 1869
320	Oct. 19–Nov. 9, 1869
321	Nov. 10–Dec. 6, 1869
322	Dec. 7, 1869–Jan. 11, 1870

Roll	Dates
323	Jan. 12–Feb. 21, 1870
324	Feb. 22–Mar. 28, 1870
325	Mar. 29–Apr. 18, 1870
326	Apr. 19–May 3, 1870
327	May 4–17, 1870
328	May 18–28, 1870
329	May 30–June 9, 1870
330	June 10–25, 1870
331	June 27–July 9, 1870
332	July 11–Aug. 1, 1870
333	Aug. 2–29, 1870
334	Aug. 30–Sept. 26, 1870
335	Sept. 27–Oct. 18, 1870
336	Oct. 19–Nov. 14, 1870
337	Nov. 15–Dec. 15, 1870
338	Dec. 17, 1870–Jan. 20, 1871
339	Jan. 21–Mar. 15, 1871
340	Mar. 16–Apr. 15, 1871
341	Apr. 17–May 4, 1871
342	May 5–19, 1871
343	May 20–June 8, 1871
344	June 9–28, 1871
345	June 29–July 20, 1871
346	July 21–Aug. 15, 1871
347	Aug. 16–Sept. 4, 1871
348	Sept. 5–25, 1871
349	Sept. 26–Oct. 17, 1871
350	Oct. 18–Nov. 13, 1871
351	Nov. 14–Dec. 19, 1871
352	Dec. 21, 1871–Feb. 6, 1872
353	Feb. 7–Mar. 20, 1872
354	Mar. 21–Apr. 8, 1872
355	Apr. 9–20, 1872
356	Apr. 22–May 3, 1872
357	May 4–13, 1872
358	May 14–21, 1872
359	May 22–June 3, 1872
360	June 4–15, 1872
361	June 17–July 2, 1872
362	July 3–23, 1872
363	July 24–Aug. 13, 1872
364	Aug. 14–31, 1872
365	Sept. 2–17, 1872
366	Sept. 18–Oct. 4, 1872
367	Oct. 5–18, 1872
368	Oct. 19–Nov. 6, 1872
369	Nov. 7–30, 1872
370	Dec. 2–31, 1872
371	Jan. 1–Feb. 20, 1873
372	Feb. 21–Apr. 7, 1873
373	Apr. 8–24, 1873
374	Apr. 25–May 14, 1873
375	May 15–31, 1873
376	June 2–11, 1873
377	June 12–27, 1873
378	June 28–July 16, 1873
379	July 17–Aug. 7, 1873
380	Aug. 8–25, 1873
381	Aug. 26–Sept. 13, 1873
382	Sept. 15–30, 1873
383	Oct. 1–21, 1873
384	Oct. 22–Nov. 13, 1873
385	Nov. 14–Dec. 10, 1873
386	Dec. 11, 1873–Jan. 31, 1874
387	Feb. 2–Mar. 22, 1874

Roll	Dates	Roll	Dates
388	Mar. 23–Apr. 25, 1874	453	June 7–23, 1882
389	Apr. 27–May 23, 1874	454	June 24–July 18, 1882
390	May 25–June 17, 1874	455	July 19–Aug. 12, 1882
391	June 18–July 17, 1874	456	Aug. 14–Sept. 9, 1882
392	July 18–Aug. 21, 1874	457	Sept. 11–Oct. 5, 1882
393	Aug. 22–Sept. 28, 1874	458	Oct. 6–21, 1882
394	Sept. 29–Nov. 12, 1874	459	Oct. 23–Nov. 22, 1882
395	Nov. 13–Dec. 31, 1874	460	Nov. 23–Dec. 30, 1882
396	Jan. 1–Mar. 10, 1875	461	Jan. 1–Feb 12, 1883
397	Mar. 11–May 3, 1875	462	Feb. 13–Mar. 27, 1883
398	May 4–June 26, 1875	463	Mar. 28–Apr. 21, 1883
399	June 28–Aug. 31, 1875	464	Apr. 23–May 8, 1883
400	Sept. 1–Dec. 31, 1875	465	May 9–25, 1883
401	Jan. 3–Mar. 7, 1876	466	May 26–June 13, 1883
401	Mar. 8–May 1, 1876	467	June 14–July 7, 1883
403	May 1–June 3, 1876	468	July 9–Aug. 7, 1883
404	June 5–July 25, 1876	469	Aug. 8–Sept. 7, 1883
405	July 26–Sept. 23, 1876	470	Sept. 8–29, 1883
406	Sept. 26–Dec. 30, 1876	471	Sept. 30–Nov. 12, 1883
407	Jan. 1–Mar. 26, 1877	472	Nov. 14–Dec. 31, 1883
408	Mar. 28–June 13, 1877	473	Jan. 2–Mar. 10, 1884
409	June 14–Aug. 30, 1877	474	Mar. 11–Apr. 12, 1884
410	Aug. 31–Dec. 31, 1877	475	Apr. 14–May 6, 1884
411	Jan. 1–Mar. 30, 1878	476	May 2–27, 1884
412	Mar. 31–May 28, 1878	477	May 28–June 23, 1884
413	May 29–July 13, 1878	478	June 24–July 25, 1884
414	July 15–Sept. 13, 1878	479	July 26–Sept. 2, 1884
415	Sept. 14–Dec. 31, 1878	480	Sept. 3–Oct. 4, 1884
416	Jan. 1–Apr. 1, 1879	481	Oct. 6–Nov. 15, 1884
417	Apr. 2–May 27, 1879	482	Nov. 17–Dec. 31, 1884
418	May 28–July 18. 1879	483	Jan. 1–Mar. 16, 1885
419	July 19–Sept. 12, 1879	484	Mar. 17–Apr. 13, 1885
420	Sept. 15–Nov. 5, 1879	485	Apr. 14–May 9, 1885
421	Nov. 6–Dec. 31, 1879	486	May 11–30, 1885
422	Jan. 2–Feb. 24, 1880	487	June 1–27, 1885
423	Feb. 25–Apr. 4, 1880	488	June 29–Aug. 7, 1885
424	Apr. 7–27, 1880	489	Aug. 8–Sept. 17, 1885
425	Apr. 28–May 12, 1880	490	Sept. 18–Oct. 27, 1885
426	May 13–24, 1880	491	Oct. 28–Dec. 31, 1885
427	May 25–June 17, 1880	492	Jan. 1–Mar. 10, 1886
428	June 18–July 21, 1880	493	Mar. 11–Apr. 20, 1886
429	July 22–Aug. 26, 1880	494	Apr. 21–May 17, 1886
430	Aug. 27–Sept. 25, 1880	495	May 18–June 16, 1886
431	Sept. 27–Oct. 28, 1880	496	June 17–July 27, 1886
432	Oct. 29–Dec. 30, 1880	497	July 28–Aug. 27, 1886
433	Jan. 1–Mar. 8, 1881	498	Aug. 28–Sept. 23, 1886
434	Mar. 9–Apr. 11, 1881	499	Sept. 24–Oct. 14, 1886
435	Apr. 12–30, 1881	500	Oct. 15–Nov. 3, 1886
436	May 2–18, 1881	501	Nov. 14–Dec. 11, 1886
437	May 19–June 3, 1881	502	Dec. 13–31, 1886
438	June 4–24, 1881	503	Jan. 3–Feb. 27, 1887
439	June 25–July 18, 1881	504	Feb. 28–Mar. 31, 1887
440	July 19–Aug. 18, 1881	505	Apr. 1–30, 1887
441	Aug. 19–Sept. 13, 1881	506	May 2–17, 1887
442	Sept. 14–Oct. 10, 1881	507	May 19–June 6, 1887
443	Oct. 11–25, 1881	508	June 7–29, 1887
444	Oct. 26–Nov. 21, 1881	509	June 30–Aug. 1, 1887
445	Nov. 22–Dec. 31, 1881	510	Aug. 2–Sept. 3, 1887
446	Jan. 2–21, 1882	511	Sept. 5–19, 1887
447	Jan. 23–Mar. 8, 1882	512	Sept. 20–Oct. 10, 1887
448	Mar. 9–Apr. 8, 1882	513	Oct. 11–Nov. 11, 1887
449	Apr. 10–24, 1882	514	Nov. 12–Dec. 31, 1887
450	Apr. 25–May 10, 1882	515	Jan. 2–Feb. 16, 1888
451	May 11–22, 1882	516	Feb. 17–Mar. 28, 1888
452	May 23–June 6, 1882	517	Mar. 29–Apr. 19, 1888

Roll	Dates
518	Apr. 20–May 4, 1888
519	May 5–18, 1888
520	May 19–June 4, 1888
521	June 5–20, 1880
522	June 21–July 14, 1888
523	July 16–Aug. 10, 1888
524	Aug. 11–Sept. 7, 1888
525	Sept. 8–Oct. 6, 1888
526	Oct. 8–Nov. 9, 1888
527	Nov. 10–30, 1888
528	Dec. 1–31, 1888
529	Jan. 1–Feb. 16, 1889
530	Feb. 18–Mar. 25, 1889
531	Mar. 26–Apr. 20, 1889
532	Apr. 22–May 10, 1889
533	May 11–June 1, 1889
534	June 3–22, 1889
535	June 24–July 19, 1889
536	July 20–Aug. 12, 1889
537	Aug. 13–Sept. 3, 1889
538	Sept. 4–21, 1889
539	Sept. 23–Oct. 12, 1889
540	Oct. 14–Nov. 2, 1889
541	Nov. 4–26, 1889
542	Nov. 27–Dec. 31, 1889
543	Jan. 2–Feb. 20, 1890
544	Feb. 21–Mar. 22, 1890
545	Mar. 24–Apr. 10, 1890
546	Apr. 11–25, 1890
547	Apr. 26–May 8, 1890
548	May 9–26, 1890
549	May 27–June 12, 1890
550	June 13–July 2, 1890
551	July 3–19, 1890
552	July 21–Aug. 11, 1890
553	Aug. 12–20, 1890
554	Aug. 21–Sept. 6, 1890
555	Sept. 8–22, 1890
556	Sept. 23–Oct. 8, 1890
557	Oct. 9–28, 1890
558	Oct. 29–Nov. 17, 1890
559	Nov. 18–Dec. 8, 1890
560	Dec. 9–31, 1890
561	Jan. 2–Feb. 11, 1891
562	Feb. 12–Mar. 11, 1891
563	Mar. 12–27, 1891
564	Mar. 28–Apr. 11, 1891
565	Apr. 13–24, 1891
566	Apr. 25–May 5, 1891
567	May 6–16, 1891
568	May 18–29, 1891
569	May 30–June 10, 1891
570	June 11–25, 1891
571	June 26–July 13, 1891
572	July 14–Aug. 1, 1891
573	Aug. 3–17, 1891
574	Aug. 18–Sept. 3, 1891
575	Sept. 4–15, 1891
576	Sept. 16–30, 1891
577	Oct. 1–13, 1891
578	Oct. 14–31, 1891
579	Nov. 2–23, 1891
580	Nov. 24–Dec. 31, 1891
581	Jan. 2–Feb. 8, 1892
582	Feb. 9–Mar. 1, 1892

Roll	Dates
583	Mar 2–22, 1892
584	Mar. 23–Apr. 6, 1892
585	Apr. 7–19, 1892
586	Apr. 20–29, 1892
587	Apr. 30–May 9, 1892
588	May 10–18, 1892
589	May 19–30, 1892
590	May 31–June 11, 1892
591	June 13–25, 1892
592	June 27–July 11, 1892
593	July 12–19, 1892
594	July 20–Aug. 3, 1892
595	Aug. 4–22, 1892
596	Aug. 23–Sept. 7, 1892
597	Sept. 8–23, 1892
598	Sept. 24–Oct. 18, 1892
599	Oct. 19–Nov. 19, 1892
600	Nov. 21–Dec. 13, 1892
601	Dec. 15–31, 1892
602	Jan. 1–Feb. 11, 1893
603	Feb. 13–Mar. 13, 1893
604	Mar. 14–27, 1893
605	Mar. 28–Apr. 10, 1893
606	Apr. 11–24, 1893
607	Apr. 25–May 5, 1893
608	May 6–15, 1893
609	May 16–26, 1893
610	May 27–June 5, 1893
611	June 6–14, 1893
612	June 15–26, 1893
613	June 27–July 7, 1893
614	July 8–22, 1893
615	July 24–Aug. 8, 1893
616	Aug. 9–24, 1893
617	Aug. 25–Sept. 9, 1893
618	Sept. 11–26, 1893
619	Sept. 27–Oct. 18, 1893
620	Oct. 19–Nov. 14, 1893
621	Nov. 15–Dec. 30, 1893
622	Jan. 1–Feb. 11, 1894
623	Feb. 12–Mar. 16, 1894
624	Mar. 17–Apr. 9, 1894
625	Apr. 10–27, 1894
626	Apr. 28–May 17, 1894
627	May 18–June 7, 1894
628	June 8–July 5, 1894
629	July 6–Aug. 3, 1894
630	Aug. 4–28, 1894
631	Aug. 29–Sept. 17, 1894
632	Sept. 18–Oct. 6, 1894
633	Oct. 8–29, 1894
634	Oct. 30–Nov. 29, 1894
635	Nov. 30–Dec. 31, 1894
636	Jan. 2–Feb. 2, 1895
637	Feb. 4–Mar. 12, 1895
638	Mar. 13–Apr. 5, 1895
639	Apr. 6–22, 1895
640	Apr. 23–May 11, 1895
641	May 13–24, 1895
642	May 25–June 11, 1895
643	June 12–28, 1895
644	June 29–July 18, 1895
645	July 19–Aug. 10, 1895
646	Aug. 12–30, 1895
647	Aug. 31–Sept. 13, 1895

Roll	Dates
648	Sept. 14–30, 1895
649	Oct. 1–18, 1895
650	Oct. 19–Nov. 4, 1895
651	Nov. 5–Dec. 5, 1895
652	Dec. 6–31, 1895
653	Jan. 1–Feb. 10, 1896
654	Feb. 11–Mar. 9, 1896
655	Mar. 10–27, 1896
656	Mar. 28–Apr. 14, 1896
657	Apr. 15–29, 1896
657	Apr. 30–May 12, 1896
659	May 13–27, 1896
660	May 28–June 18, 1896
661	June 19–July 9, 1896
662	July 10–30, 1896
663	July 31–Aug. 22, 1896
664	Aug. 24–Sept. 11, 1896
665	Sept. 12–26, 1896
666	Sept. 28–Oct. 6, 1896
667	Oct. 7–31, 1896
668	Nov. 1–30, 1896
669	Dec. 1–31, 1896
670	Jan. 2–Feb. 6, 1897
671	Feb. 8–Mar. 24, 1897
672	Mar. 25–Apr. 20, 1897
673	Apr. 21–May 17, 1897
674	May 18–June 5, 1897
675	June 5–17, 1897

Registers of Vessels Arriving at the Port of New York from Foreign Ports, 1789–1919. M1066. 27 rolls. DP.

The records in this publication are grouped in two series. The volumes that make up the first series, reproduced on rolls 1–22, cover the period from August 5, 1789, to December 30, 1899, except for the following gaps: September 1, 1796–September 25, 1798; July 19, 1801–December 31, 1804; and October 14, 1811–December 31, 1815. These volumes originally were maintained by the offices of the collector, naval officer, and surveyor of the Port of New York. Because the records were created by these offices for different purposes, the volumes vary in internal arrangement, dates covered, and information recorded. The volumes have been combined as a single series because they all record the arrival of vessels from foreign ports and, as such, provide the most complete record available of these vessel arrivals at New York. The volumes have been arranged and filmed in chronological order, although there is frequent overlapping of dates among the volumes.

The entries in the volumes filmed on rolls 1–22 are arranged either chronologically, alphabetically by the name of vessel, alphabetically by the name of owner, or alphabetically by the type of rig of the vessel. The most frequent arrangement is alphabetical by the name of vessel. Most of the volumes contain at least the date of entry; the name, country of origin, and type of rig of the vessel; the master's name; and the last port of embarkation. A few volumes also contain information about tonnage, duties, cargo, consignees, number of crew and passengers, owners' names, manifest numbers, clearances, bond releases, and officers' returns.

The volumes that make up the second series, reproduced on rolls 23–27, cover the period from January 3, 1860, to December 31, 1919. This series was created at a later date as a standard index to vessel arrivals from foreign ports. Within each volume the entries are arranged alphabetically by the name of vessel and thereunder chronologically.

Roll	Inclusive Dates	Arrangement
1	Aug. 5, 1789–Mar. 31, 1795	Chronological
	Jan. 1, 1795–Aug. 31, 1796	,,
	Sept. 26, 1798–July 18, 1801	,,
	Jan. 2, 1805–Mar. 30, 1807	,,
	June 2, 1806–Oct. 13, 1811	,,
	Jan. 2, 1808–Oct. 30, 1809	,,
	Jan. 2, 1816–Dec. 31, 1825	Alphabetical by name of owner
	Jan. 2, 1819–Dec. 31, 1822	Alphabetical by name of vessel
2	July 19, 1819–Mar. 30, 1821	Chronological
	Apr. 2, 1821–July 1, 1822	,,
	Jan. 3, 1823–Dec. 31, 1824	Alphabetical by name of vessel
	Jan. 3, 1825–Dec. 27, 1826	,,
	Jan. 3, 1825–Dec. 27, 1826	,,
	Oct. 1, 1825–Mar. 31, 1827	Chronological
	Apr. 1, 1826–Mar. 30, 1831	Alphabetical by name of vessel
	Jan. 2, 1827–Dec. 30, 1828	,,
	Apr. 2, 1827–Aug. 30, 1828	Chronological
3	Aug. 1, 1828–Nov. 27, 1832, and Jan. 2–May 10, 1834	Alphabetical by name of vessel
	Jan. 2, 1829–Dec. 31, 1830	,,
	May 1, 1829–Dec. 9, 1831	,,
	Sept. 6, 1830–July 31, 1835	Chronological
	Jan. 3, 1831–Oct. 10, 1832	Alphabetical by name of vessel
	Jan. 3–July 13, 1831	,,
	Apr. 1, 1831–Dec. 31, 1833	,,
	Jan. 3–Dec. 31, 1832	,,
	Jan. 2, 1833–Dec. 31, 1835	,,
	Jan. 2, 1834–Dec. 31, 1835	,,
	Jan. 2, 1834–Dec. 31, 1835	,,
	Jan. 2–Dec. 23, 1834	,,
	July 1, 1835–Dec. 31, 1837	Chronological
4	Jan. 2, 1836–Dec. 31, 1837	Alphabetical by name of vessel
	Jan. 2–Dec. 31, 1836	,,
	Jan. 2–Dec. 31, 1836	,,
	Jan. 5, 1836–Sept. 30, 1837	,,
	Jan. 3, 1837–Apr. 13, 1838	,,
	Jan. 3–Dec. 30, 1837	,,
	Jan. 3–Dec. 30, 1837	,,
	Sept. 5, 1837–Jan. 6, 1840	,,
	Jan. 2, 1838–Dec. 31, 1840	,,
	Jan. 2, 1838–Dec. 31, 1839	Alphabetical by name of vessel
	Jan. 2, 1838–Dec. 31, 1839	,,
	May 27–Oct. 21, 1839	Chronological
	Jan. 3, 1840–Dec. 31, 1842	,,
5	Jan. 3–Dec. 31, 1840	Alphabetical by name of vessel
	Jan. 3–Dec. 31, 1840	,,
	Jan. 2, 1841–July 6, 1844	,,
	Jan. 2, 1841–Dec. 31, 1842	,,
	Jan. 2, 1841–Jan. 31, 1842	,,
	Jan. 2–Dec. 31, 1841	,,
	Mar. 23, 1841–Dec. 31, 1844	,,
	Jan. 2, 1842–Dec. 30, 1843	,,
	Jan. 3–Dec. 31, 1842	,,
	Jan. 2, 1843–Dec. 31, 1843	Chronological

Roll	Inclusive Dates	Arrangement
	Jan. 2–Dec. 30, 1843	Alphabetical by name of vessel
	July 8, 1844–June 17, 1847	,,
6	Jan. 2, 1845–Oct. 30, 1846	Alphabetical by name of vessel
	July 1, 1845–Dec. 31, 1846	,,
	Aug. 23, 1845–Sept. 14, 1847	,,
	Nov. 1, 1845–Dec. 31, 1846	,,
	Jan. 2–Dec. 31, 1847	,,
	Apr. 1, 1847–Sept. 30, 1851	Chronological
	Jan. 3–Dec. 28, 1848	Alphabetical by name of vessel
	Jan. 1, 1849–June 30, 1852	,,
	Jan. 1, 1849–Dec. 31, 1850	,,
7	Jan. 1–Dec. 31, 1849	Alphabetical by name of vessel
	Jan. 1–Dec. 31, 1849	,,
	Jan. 2, 1850–Apr. 30, 1852	Chronological
	Jan. 2, 1850–Jan. 14, 1851	Alphabetical by name of vessel
	June 1, 1850–Dec. 31, 1852	,,
	Jan. 2, 1851–June 21, 1852	,,
	Jan. 2–Dec. 31, 1851	,,
	Jan. 2–Dec. 31, 1852	,,
	Jan. 3, 1853–Apr. 30, 1855	,,
	Jan. 3–Dec. 31, 1853	,,
	Jan. 2–Dec. 30, 1854	,,
	Jan. 2–Dec. 30, 1854	,,
8	Jan. 1–Dec. 31, 1855	Alphabetical by name of vessel
	Jan. 2–Dec. 31, 1856	,,
	Jan. 2–Dec. 31, 1857	,,
	July 1, 1857–Dec. 31, 1859	,,
	July 1, 1857–Dec. 16, 1859	,,
	Jan. 3, 1859–Dec. 31, 1863	Chronological
	Jan. 3–Dec. 31, 1859	Alphabetical by name of vessel
9	Jan. 3–Dec. 31, 1860	Alphabetical by name of vessel
	June 1, 1860–Dec. 18, 1863	Chronological
	May 1–July 31, 1861	Alphabetical by name of vessel
	Aug. 1–Dec. 31, 1861	,,
	Jan. 2, 1862–May 31, 1864	,,
	Jan. 2–Dec. 31, 1862	,,
	Jan. 2, 1863–Apr. 30, 1864	Chronological
	Jan. 2, 1863–Apr. 21, 1864	Alphabetical by name of vessel
	Jan. 2–Dec. 31, 1863	,,
10	Jan. 2–Mar. 31, 1863	Alphabetical by name of vessel
	Dec. 18, 1863–July 31, 1865	Chronological
	Jan. 2–Dec. 31, 1864	Alphabetical by name of vessel
	May 2, 1864–Oct. 31, 1865	Chronological
	Jan. 2–Dec. 30, 1865	Alphabetical by name of vessel
	Jan. 2–Dec. 30, 1865	,,
	June 7, 1865–Oct. 29, 1867	Chronological
	Aug. 1, 1865–July 31, 1866	Alphabetical by name of vessel
	Oct. 2, 1865–May 24, 1867	Alphabetical by name of owner

Roll	Inclusive Dates	Arrangement
11	Nov. 1, 1865–May 27, 1867	Chronological
	Jan. 2–Dec. 31, 1866	Alphabetical by name of vessel
	Jan. 2–Dec. 31, 1866	,,
	July 2, 1866–May 31, 1867	,,
	Aug. 1, 1866–Apr. 30, 1867	,,
	Jan. 2–June 29, 1867	,,
	May 1–Oct. 4, 1867	,,
	May 28, 1867–June 7, 1869	Chronological
	June 1, 1867–Dec. 9, 1869	,,
	June 1, 1867–Dec. 9, 1869	,,
	July 1, 1867–June 30, 1868	Alphabetical by name of vessel
12	Oct. 5, 1867–Sept. 14, 1868	Alphabetical by name of vessel
	Dec. 2, 1867–Feb. 28, 1871	Chronological
	Jan. 2–Dec. 31, 1868	Alphabetical by name of vessel
	Sept. 12, 1868–Apr. 28, 1869	,,
	Jan. 2–Dec. 31, 1869	Alphabetical by name of vessel
	Jan. 2–Dec. 31, 1869	,,
	Apr. 29, 1869–June 11, 1870	,,
	June 8, 1869–Mar. 30, 1872	Chronological
13	Dec. 10, 1869–Jan. 3, 1877	Chronological
	Dec. 10, 1869–Nov. 18, 1874	,,
	Jan. 1–Dec. 31, 1870	Alphabetical by name of vessel
	Apr. 1, 1870–Dec. 31, 1872	Chronological
	Jan. 2–Dec. 30, 1871	Alphabetical by name of vessel
	Mar. 1, 1871–Jan. 31, 1876	Chronological
14	Feb. 1–Dec. 31, 1872	Alphabetical by name of vessel
	Apr. 1, 1872–Dec. 10, 1873	Chronological
	Jan. 1–Dec. 31, 1873	Alphabetical by name of vessel
	Jan. 1–Dec. 31, 1873	,,
	Jan. 2–June 30, 1873	,,
	July 1–Dec. 31, 1873	,,
	Dec. 11, 1873–Feb. 28, 1877	Chronological
	Jan. 1–Dec. 31, 1874	Alphabetical by name of vessel
	Jan. 2–Dec. 31, 1874	,,
15	Jan. 2–June 30, 1874	Alphabetical by name of vessel
	May 4, 1874–Mar. 31, 1875	,,
	July 1–Dec. 31, 1874	,,
	Jan. 1–Dec. 31, 1875	,,
	Jan. 1–Dec. 31, 1875	,,
	June 1, 1875–July 27, 1876	Chronological
	Jan. 3, 1876–Jan. 2, 1877	Alphabetical by name of vessel
	Feb. 1, 1876–Oct. 31, 1879	Chronological
	Jan. 1, 1877–Dec. 31, 1879	,,
	Jan. 1–Dec. 31, 1877	Alphabetical by name of vessel
16	Mar. 1, 1877–May 31, 1879	Chronological
	Jan. 3–July 1, 1878	Alphabetical by name of vessel
	June 2, 1879–Oct. 31, 1881	Chronological
	Nov. 1, 1879–Mar. 31, 1884	,,
	Jan. 2–Dec. 31, 1880	Alphabetical by name of vessel
	Jan. 2–Dec. 31, 1880	,,

Roll	Inclusive Dates	Arrangement
	Jan. 2–Dec. 31, 1881	Alphabetical by name of vessel
	Jan. 2–Dec. 31, 1881	Alphabetical by name of vessel
17	Jan. 2–Dec. 30, 1882	Alphabetical by name of vessel
	Jan. 2–Dec. 30, 1882	,,
	Jan. 1–Dec. 1, 1883	,,
	Jan. 1–Dec. 31, 1884	,,
	Apr. 1, 1884–Sept. 30, 1888	Chronological
	Jan. 1, 1885–June 30, 1890	Alphabetical by type of rig of vessel
	Jan. 1–Dec. 31, 1886	Alphabetical by name of vessel
18	Jan. 1–Dec. 31, 1886	Alphabetical by name of vessel
	Jan. 1–Dec. 31, 1886	,,
	Jan. 3–Dec. 31, 1887	,,
	Jan. 3–Dec. 31, 1887	,,
	Jan. 2–Dec. 31, 1888	,,
	Jan. 2–Dec. 31, 1888	,,
	Oct. 31, 1888–Dec. 31, 1892	Chronological
	Jan. 1–Dec. 31, 1889	Alphabetical by name of vessel
19	Jan. 1–Dec. 31, 1889	Alphabetical by name of vessel
	Jan. 2–Dec. 31, 1890	,,
	Jan. 2–Dec. 31, 1890	,,
	Jan. 2–Dec. 31, 1891	,,
	Jan. 2–Dec. 31, 1891	,,
	Jan. 2–Dec. 31, 1891	,,
	Jan. 2–Dec. 31, 1892	,,
	Jan. 2–Dec. 31, 1892	,,
	Jan. 2–Dec. 31, 1892	,,
20	Jan. 2–Dec. 30, 1893	Alphabetical by name of vessel
	Jan. 2–Dec. 30, 1893	,,
	Jan. 2–Dec. 30, 1893	,,
	Jan. 3–Dec. 30, 1893	,,
	Oct. 6, 1893–Oct. 30, 1901	Chronological
	Jan. 1–Dec. 31, 1894	Alphabetical by name of vessel
	Jan. 1–Dec. 31, 1894	,,
	Jan. 1–Dec. 31, 1894	,,
	Jan. 2–Dec. 31, 1895	,,
	Jan. 2–Dec. 31, 1895	,,
21	Jan. 2–Dec. 31, 1895	Alphabetical by name of vessel
	Jan. 2–Dec. 31, 1895	,,
	Jan. 2, 1896–Dec. 31, 1900	,,
	Jan. 2–Dec. 31, 1896	Alphabetical by name of vessel
	Jan. 2–Dec. 31, 1896	,,
	Jan. 2–Dec. 31, 1896	,,
	Jan. 2–Dec. 31, 1896	,,
	Jan. 2–Dec. 31, 1897	,,
22	Jan. 2–Dec. 31, 1897	Alphabetical by name of vessel
	Jan. 2–Dec. 31, 1897	,,
	Jan. 2–Dec. 31, 1897	,,
	Jan. 3–Dec. 31, 1898	,,
	Jan. 3–Dec. 31, 1898	,,
	Jan. 3–Dec. 31, 1898	,,
	Jan. 2–Dec. 30, 1899	,,
	Jan. 2–Dec. 30, 1899	,,

Roll	Inclusive Dates	Arrangement
	Jan. 2–Dec. 30, 1899	Alphabetical by name of vessel
23	Jan. 3–Dec. 31, 1860	Alphabetical by name of vessel
	Jan. 2–Dec. 31, 1861	,,
	Jan. 2–Dec. 31, 1862	,,
	Jan. 2–Dec. 31, 1863	,,
	Jan. 2–Dec. 31, 1864	,,
	Jan. 2–Dec. 30, 1865	,,
	Jan. 2–Dec. 31, 1866	,,
24	Jan. 2–Dec. 31, 1867	Alphabetical by name of vessel
	Jan. 2–Dec. 31, 1868	,,
	Jan. 2–Dec. 31, 1869	,,
	Jan. 1–Dec. 31, 1870	,,
	Jan. 2–Dec. 30, 1871	,,
	Jan. 2–Dec. 31, 1872	,,
	Jan. 2–Dec. 31, 1873	,,
25	Jan. 2–Dec. 31, 1874	Alphabetical by name of vessel
	Jan. 1–Dec. 30, 1875	,,
	Jan. 3–Dec. 30, 1876	,,
	Jan. 2–Dec. 31, 1877	,,
	Jan. 1–Dec. 31, 1878	,,
	Jan. 2–Dec. 31, 1879	,,
	Jan. 2, 1880–Dec. 31, 1881	,,
26	Jan. 3, 1882–Dec. 31, 1883	Alphabetical by name of vessel
	Jan. 2, 1884–Dec. 31, 1885	,,
	Jan. 2, 1886–Dec. 31, 1887	,,
	Jan. 2, 1888–Dec. 31, 1889	,,
	Jan. 2, 1890–Dec. 31, 1891	,,
	Jan. 2, 1892–Dec. 31, 1893	,,
	Jan. 1, 1894–Dec. 31, 1895	,,
	Jan. 2, 1896–Dec. 31, 1897	Alphabetical by name of vessel
	Jan. 2, 1898–Dec. 30, 1899	,,
	Jan. 2, 1900–Dec. 31, 1901	,,
27	Jan. 2, 1902–Dec. 31, 1903	Alphabetical by name of vessel
	Jan. 2, 1904–Dec. 30, 1905	,,
	Jan. 2, 1906–Dec. 31, 1907	,,
	Jan. 2, 1908–Dec. 31, 1909	,,
	Jan. 3, 1910–Dec. 30, 1911	,,
	Jan. 2, 1912–Dec. 31, 1913	,,
	Jan. 2, 1914–Dec. 31, 1919	,,

Philadelphia, Pennsylvania

Index to Passenger Lists of Vessels Arriving at Philadelphia, PA, 1800–1906. M360. 151 rolls. 16mm. DP.

Roll	Range
1	A–Alk
2	All–Anderson, I.
3	Anderson, J.–Arl
4	Arm–Bae
5	Baf–Bark
6	Barl–Bat
7	Bau–Belk
8	Bell–Bern
9	Bero–Bj
10	Bl–Boe

Roll	Range	Roll	Range
11	Bof–Bov	76	Kio–Kn
12	Bow–Bradley, M.	77	Ko–Krf
13	Bradley, N.–Bren	78	Kri–Laj
14	Brer–Brown, C.	79	Lak–Larsen, I.
15	Brown, D.–Buckles	80	Larsen, J.–Lean
16	Buckley–Burn	81	Leap–Ler
17	Buro–Cak	82	Les–Lind
18	Cal–Cam	83	Lins–Long
19	Can–Car	84	Longacre–Lum
20	Carr–Casso	85	Lun–Mac
21	Cassoc–Chetf	86	Mad–Malk
22	Cheth–Clark, M.	87	Mall–Marl
23	Clark, N.–Cof	88	Marm–Mas
24	Cog–Conm	89	Mat–McAn
25	Conn–Conz	90	McAp–McCan
26	Coo–Cot	91	McCap–McCl
27	Cou–Crg	92	McCn–McCw
28	Cri–Cul	93	McD–McE
29	Cum–Dak	94	McF–McGi
30	Dal–Davies, J.	95	McGl–McGy
31	Davies, K.–Def	96	McH–McKen
32	Deg–Deven	97	McKeo–McL
33	Dever–Diven	98	McM–McN
34	Diver–Dol	99	McO–Mek
35	Dom–Doo	100	Mel–Mic
36	Dop–Dra	101	Mid–Mis
37	Dre–Dunk	102	Mit–Mon
38	Dunl–Ec	103	Moo–Morg
39	Ed–Ellis, G.	104	Morh–Muk
40	Ellis, H.–Es	105	Mui–Mup
41	Et–Faq	106	Mur–Muz
42	Far–Fep	107	Mv–Nelson, I.
43	Fer–Fisher, L.	108	Nelson, J.–Nilsh
44	Fisher, M.–Fir	109	Nilsi–Nz
45	Flu–Fox	110	O–Ok
46	Foy–Frk	111	Ol
47	Frl–Gallagher, I.	112	Om–Ov
48	Gallagher, J.–Gar	113	Ow–Par
49	Gas–Gh	114	Pas–Ped
50	Gi–Giz	115	Pee–Pet
51	Gj–Gop	116	Peu–Pn
52	Gor–Gram	117	Po–Prg
53	Gran–Grh	118	Pri–Q
54	Gri–Gui	119	R–Rd
55	Gul–Hah	120	Re–Rel
56	Hai–Ham	121	Rem–Rik
57	Han–Hard	122	Ril–Rob
58	Hare–Hart	123	Roc–Rosr
59	Haru–Hd	124	Ross–Rus
60	He–Hend	125	Rut–Saq
61	Hene–Hes	126	Sar–Sche
62	Het–Hi	127	Schi–Scht
63	Hj–Holm	128	Schu–Sel
64	Holn–Hov	129	Sem–Shep
65	How–Huns	130	Sher–Sim
66	Hunt–Ir	131	Sin–Smith, G.
67	Is–Jano	132	Smith, H.–Sn
68	Janp–Jog	133	So–Ss
69	Joh–Johnson, S.	134	St–Stet
70	Johnson, T.–Jones	135	Steu–Sto
71	Jonet–Kam	136	Str–Su
72	Kan–Kea	137	Sy–Tal
73	Keb–Kelly, Martin	138	Tam–Tg
74	Kelly, Mary–Kern	139	Th–Thop
75	Kero–Kin	140	Thor–Too

Roll	Range
141	Top–Tu
142	Tv–Ve
143	Vi–Walk
144	Wall–Ward
145	Warde–Weh
146	Wel–Whe
147	Whi–Wili
148	Wilk–Wilsom
149	Wilson–Wn
150	Wo–Ws
151	Wu–Z and miscellaneous cards

Passenger Lists of Vessels Arriving at Philadelphia, PA, 1800–1882. M425. 108 rolls. DP.

Roll	Inclusive Dates	Lists
1	Jan. 1–Dec. 30, 1800	1–223
2	Jan. 5–Dec. 31, 1801	1–246
3	Jan. 2–Aug. 30, 1802	1–173
4	Sept. 1–Dec. 31, 1802	174–278
5	Jan. 1–Dec. 27, 1803	1–255
6	Jan. 3–Aug. 31, 1804	1–222
7	Sept. 4–Dec. 31, 1804	223–300
8	Jan. 1–Aug. 31, 1805	1–178
9	Sept. 4–Dec. 31, 1805	179–269
10	Jan. 7–July 31, 1806	1–201
11	Aug. 2–Dec. 30, 1806	202–365
12	Feb. 16–Aug. 31, 1807	1–190
13	Sept. 1–Dec. 31, 1807	191–297
14	Jan. 1–Dec. 29, 1808	1–162
15	Jan. 2–Dec. 29, 1809	1–206
16	Jan. 2–Aug. 31, 1810	1–172
17	Sept. 15–Dec. 31, 1810	173–276
18	Jan. 2–Dec. 31, 1811	1–267
19	Feb. 10–Dec. 15, 1812	1–169
	Feb. 15–Apr. 15, 1813	1–20
	Jan. 14–Dec. 3, 1814	1–26
20	Jan. 6–Sept. 30, 1815	1–154
21	Oct. 2–Dec. 27, 1815	155–244
22	Jan. 1–July 29, 1816	1–164
23	Aug. 1–Dec. 27, 1816	165–307
24	Jan. 6–Aug. 29, 1817	1–160
25	Sept. 1–Dec. 26, 1817	161–288
26	Jan. 1–July 31, 1818	1–159
27	Aug. 1–Dec. 23, 1818	160–281
28	Jan. 1–Aug. 30, 1819	1–188
29	Sept. 1–Dec. 27, 1819	189–288
30	Jan. 1–Dec. 26, 1820	1–270
31	Jan. 4–Dec. 24, 1821	1–236
32	Feb. 14–Dec. 31, 1822	1–246
33	Jan. 14–Dec. 30, 1823	1–248
34	Jan. 3–July 31, 1824	1–148
35	Aug. 2–Dec. 27, 1825	149–275
36	Jan. 1–June 27, 1826	1–116
37	July 1–Dec. 27, 1825	117–277
38	Jan. 7–July 31, 1826	1–159
39	Aug. 2–Dec. 27, 1826	160–287
40	Jan. 15–July 30, 1827	1–144
41	Aug. 2–Dec. 31, 1827	145–287
42	Jan. 1–July 31, 1828	1–171
43	Aug. 1–Dec. 31, 1828	172–293
44	Jan. 10–Dec. 26, 1829	1–215
45	Jan. 4–Dec. 30, 1830	1–229
46	Jan. 1–Dec. 6, 1831	1–231
47	Jan. 12–Dec. 31, 1832	1–228
48	Jan. 1–Dec. 31, 1833	1–233

Roll	Inclusive Dates	Lists
49	Jan. 14–Dec. 29, 1834	1–200
50	Jan. 22–Dec. 29, 1836	1–193
51	Jan. 1–Dec. 29, 1836	1–196
52	Feb. 3–Dec. 31, 1837	1–195
53	Jan. 2–Dec. 24, 1838	1–157
54	Jan. 14–July 31, 1839	1–147
55	Aug. 1–Dec. 30, 1839	148–238
56	Jan. 16–July 31, 1840	1–94
57	Aug. 3–Dec. 23, 1840	95–178
58	Jan. 13–Dec. 23, 1841	1–175
59	Jan. 3–Dec. 31, 1842	1–200
60	Jan. 11–Dec. 22, 1843	1–140
61	Jan. 4–Dec. 31, 1844	1–198
62	Jan. 1–Dec. 20, 1845	1–183
63	Jan. 3–Dec. 26, 1846	1–197
64	Jan. 1–July 31, 1847	1–159
65	Aug. 1–Dec. 30, 1847	160–246
66	Jan. 3–July 31, 1848	1–146
67	Aug. 1–Dec. 28, 1848	147–257
68	Jan. 2–July 28, 1849	1–161
69	Aug. 1–Dec. 31, 1849	162–251
70	Jan. 5–July 31, 1850	1–127
71	Aug. 3–Dec. 23, 1850	128–209
72	Jan. 3–June 28, 1851	1–114
73	July 1–Dec. 31, 1851	115–230
74	Jan. 2–June 30, 1852	1–130
75	July 3–Dec. 25, 1852	131–235
76	Jan. 3–Dec. 30, 1853	1–198
77	Jan. 2–Dec. 23, 1854	1–198
78	Jan. 1–Dec. 28, 1855	1–147
79	Jan. 1–Dec. 22, 1856	1–140
80	Jan. 2–Dec. 27, 1857	1–102
81	Jan. 4–Dec. 20, 1858	1–122
82	Jan. 4–Dec. 28, 1859	1–120
83	Jan. 12–Dec. 10, 1860	1–123
84	Jan. 3–Dec. 24, 1861	1–107
85	Jan. 13–Dec. 31, 1862	1–112
86	Jan. 2–Dec. 29, 1863	1–104
87	Jan. 2–Dec. 31, 1864	1–93
	Jan. 11–Dec. 19, 1865	1–74
88	Jan. 31–Dec. 21, 1866	1–106
	Jan. 8–Dec. 31, 1867	1–64
89	Jan. 8–Dec. 23, 1868	1–85
	Jan. 19–Dec. 29, 1869	1–46
90	Jan. 7–Dec. 30, 1870	1–64
	Jan. 12–Dec. 27, 1871	1–77
91	Jan. 11–Dec. 31, 1872	1–72
	Jan. 7–Dec. 30, 1873	1–93
92	Jan. 15–Dec. 30, 1874	1–128
93	Jan. 7–Aug. 23, 1875	1–93
94	Jan. 3–Dec. 29, 1876	1–129
95	Jan. 4–Dec. 29, 1877	1–134
96	Jan. 2–Dec. 31, 1878	1–102
97	Jan. 9–June 25, 1879	1–49
98	July 2–Dec. 28, 1879	50–111
99	Jan. 3–May 31, 1880	1–53
100	June 2–Aug. 30, 1880	54–101
101	Sept. 1–Dec. 29, 1880	102–132
102	Jan. 3–Apr. 30, 1881	1–26
103	May 3–June 30, 1881	27–46
104	July 4–Sept. 27, 1881	47–72
105	Oct. 1–Dec. 30, 1881	73–94
106	Jan. 3–Apr. 29, 1882	1–35
107	May 5–June 27, 1882	36–66
108	July 3–Dec. 29, 1882	67–121

Records of the Immigration and Naturalization Service, 1891–1957, Record Group 85

Alabama, Florida, Georgia, and South Carolina

Index to Passenger Lists of Vessels Arriving at Ports in Alabama, Florida, Georgia, and South Carolina, 1890–1924. T517. 26 rolls. 16mm.

Roll	Contents
1	Aabott–Anderson
2	Andersson–Basora
3	Basque–Brito
4	Bro–Carrascale
5	Carrasco–Collymore
6	Colma–Delayto
7	Delfin–Escay
8	Escenazi–Fernandez, Roq
9	Fernandez, Ros–Garcia, Jose
10	Garcia, Jose Maria–Gonzalez, Lor
11	Gonzalez, Lou–Hernandez, F.
12	Hernandez, G.–Johnson, S.
13	Johnson–L'Heme
14	Li–Marban
15	March–Menike
16	Mena–Moss
17	Moss–Padron, H.
18	Padron, I.–Piedno
19	Peidra–Rayneri, El
20	Rayneri, Eu–Rodriquez, Ramon
21	Rodriguez, Ramon–Snachez, M.
22	Snachez–Soldevilla
23	Sole–Thompson, R.
24	Thompson, S.–Vega, J.
25	Vega, L.–Young, R.
26	Young, S.–Zygand

Baltimore, Maryland

Index (Soundex) to Passenger Lists of Vessels Arriving at Baltimore, MD, 1897–1952. T520. 43 rolls. 16mm.

Roll	Contents
1	A-000 Abe—A-210 Zelig
2	A-213 Szwajka—A-651 Zann
3	A-652 Abraham—B-320 Alice K.
4	B-320 Alma—B-526 Francisco
5	B-526 Franz—B-645 Zirel
6	B-650 See—C-410 Zuza
7	C-412 Adam—D-165 Zsuzsa
8	D-200 Achim—D-560 Elizabeth
9	D-560 Emilie—F-260 Sarah
10	F-260 Scheie—G-176 Leia
11	G-165 Lieb—G-532 Jent
12	G-532 Jerelim—G-653 Konstanto
13	G-653 Laura Theiza—H-520 Fuadbey
14	H-520 Gafia—J-120 Wojciech
15	J-121 Adam—J-621 Jordan, V.
16	J-621 Josef—K-233 Zelesko

Roll	Contents
17	K-234 Afanasy—K-420 Juzapas
18	K-420 Kalarzyna—K-536 Juro
19	K-536 Kamedi—K-640 Jan
20	K-640 Jan—L-222 Stanislaw
21	L-222 Stanilaw—M-100 Agostino
22	M-100 Alexander—M-260 Jozsef
23	M-260 Jozsef—M-452 Vukasin
24	M-452 Waciaw—M-625 Bude
25	M-625 Casimir—N-520 Josef
26	N-520 Josef—P-122 Ivan
27	P-122 Ivan—P-361 Pusaw
28	P-361 Efim, Tarosovich—P-615 Ivo
29	P-615 Jan—R-215 Juro
30	R-215 Karl—R-357 Hija
31	R-351 Hinde—S-152 Claus Emil
32	S-152 Creszens—S-262 P. Justyna
33	S-262 P. Kalin—S-360 Auram
34	S-360 Babette—S-455 Sydney
34a	S-455 Sydney H.—S-460 Sophia
35	S-460 Sophie—S-552 Piotr
36	S-552 Piotr—T-242 Simo
37	T-245 Simon—T-632 Nicolae
38	T-632 Niecislaw—V-500 Jan
39	V-500 Jan—Janssen—W-322 Milhor
40	W-322 Mizzi—Y-400 Noel
41	Y-331 Norman—Z-620 Mile
42	Z-620 Mile—Z-662 Minne

Passenger Lists of Vessels Arriving at Baltimore, MD, 1891–1909. T844. 150 rolls. (★ Rolls 78-150 are new listings.)

The manifests were filmed as they appeared in bound volumes. Date spans may overlap.

Roll	Volumes	Dates
1	116–118	June 2, 1892–Aug. 31, 1892
2	119–121	Dec. 12, 1891–Dec. 27, 1892
3	122–123	Jan. 6, 1893–June 27, 1893
4	124–125	July 3, 1893–Dec. 28, 1893
5	126–127	Jan. 4, 1894–Aug. 21, 1894
6	128–130	Sept. 5, 1894–Dec. 28, 1895
7	131	Jan. 1, 1896–Apr. 30, 1896
8	132–133	Jan. 20, 1896–Feb. 13, 1897
9	134–136	Mar. 1, 1897–Mar. 21, 1898
10	137	Apr. 15, 1898–June 30, 1898
11	138–139	July 6, 1898–Oct. 3, 1898
12	140–141	Jan. 20, 1899–May 28, 1899
13	142–143	June 5, 1899–Aug. 5, 1899
14	144–145	Aug. 24, 1899–Dec. 20, 1899
15	146	Nov. 1, 1899–Nov. 26, 1899
16	147	Jan. 5, 1900–Mar. 28, 1900
17	148	Apr. 8, 1900–Apr. 25, 1900
18	149	July 8, 1900–May 31, 1900 *
19	150–151	June 7, 1900–Feb. 25, 1901
20	152	Mar. 2, 1901–Mar. 29, 1901
21	153	Apr. 18, 1901–May 15, 1901
22	154–155	May 9, 1901–Aug. 31, 1901
23	156–157	Sept. 11, 1901–Nov. 20, 1901
24	158–159	Dec. 1, 1901–Mar. 31, 1902
25	160	Mar. 4, 1902–Mar. 29, 1902
26	161	Apr. 4, 1902–Apr. 28, 1902
27	162	Apr. 24, 1902–May 9, 1902
28	163	May 14, 1902–May 5, 1902 *
29	164	June 4, 1902–June 30, 1902
30	165	July 1, 1902–Aug. 4, 1902

Roll	Volumes	Dates
31	166	Aug. 20, 1902–Sept. 27, 1902
32	167	Oct. 15, 1902–Oct 20, 1902
33	168	Nov. 21, 1902–Dec. 29, 1902
34	169–170	Feb. 1, 1903–Mar. 14, 1903
35	171–172	Mar. 26, 1903–May 3, 1903
36	173–174	May 2, 1903–June 30, 1903
37	175–176	June 9, 1903–July 28, 1903
38	177–178	Aug. 12, 1903–Sept. 30, 1903
39	179–180	Oct. 2, 1903–Nov. 22, 1903
40	181–182	Dec. 4, 1903–Mar. 23, 1904
41	183–184	Apr. 5, 1904–May 5, 1904
42	185–186	June 2, 1904–Aug. 31, 1904
43	187	Sept. 2, 1904–Oct. 20, 1904
44	188–189	Nov. 1, 1904–Dec. 24, 1904
45	190–191	Feb. 7, 1905–Mar. 14, 1905
46	192–193	Mar. 1, 1905–Apr. 12, 1905
47	194–195	Apr. 2, 1905–May 25, 1905
48	196	June 1, 1905–June 7, 1905
49	197–198	June 5, 1905–July 31, 1905
50	199–201	Aug. 8, 1905–Aug. 30, 1905
51	202–203	Nov. 11, 1905–Feb. 26, 1906
52	204	Mar. 3, 1906–Mar. 31, 1906
53	205	Apr. 1, 1906–apr. 30, 1906
54	206	May 4, 1906–May 30, 1906
55	207–208	June 8, 1906–July 30, 1906
56	209–210	Aug. 1, 1906–Sept. 20, 1906
57	211–212	Aug. 25, 1906–Sept. 30, 1906
58	213–214	Oct. 18, 1906–Dec. 29, 1906
59	1–2	Jan. 1, 1907–Feb. 26, 1907
60	3	Mar. 1, 1907–Mar. 31, 1907
61	4	Mar. 19, 1907–Mar. 30, 1907
62	5–6	Apr. 1, 1907–Apr. 30, 1907
63	7–8	May 1, 1907–May 18, 1907
64	9–10	May 11, 1907–June 25, 1907
65	11–12	June 14, 1907–July 20, 1907
66	13–14	July 26, 1907–Aug. 28, 1907
67	15–16	Sept. 4, 1907–Oct. 4, 1907
68	17–18	Oct. 9, 1907–Oct. 17, 1907
69	19–20	Nov. 6, 1907–Dec. 2, 1907
70	21–22	Dec. 10, 1907–Dec. 30, 1907
71	23–24	Jan. 5, 1908–June 29, 1908
72	25–26	July 9, 1908–Dec. 28, 1908
73	27–28	Jan. 6, 1909–Mar. 28, 1909
74	29	Apr. 2, 1909–May 31, 1909
75	30	June 5, 1909–June 28, 1909
76	31	July 3, 1909–Aug. 30, 1909
77	32–33	Sept. 9, 1909–Nov. 30, 1909
78	34–35	Dec. 2, 1909–Jan. 16, 1910
79	36–37	Feb. 28, 1910–Mar. 31, 1910
80	38	Apr. 13, 1910–May 15, 1910
81	39	May 25, 1910–June 28, 1910
82	40	July 7, 1910–Aug. 31, 1910
83	41–41	Sept. 1, 1910–Oct. 31, 1910
84	43–44	Nov. 9, 1910–Feb. 27, 1911
85	45	Mar. 4, 1911–Apr. 28, 1911
86	46–47	May 11, 1911–Sept. 3, 1911
87	48–49	Sept. 4, 1911–Dec. 27, 1911
88	50	Jan. 8, 1912–Mar. 20, 1912
89	51	Mar. 30, 1912–Apr. 28, 1912
90	52	May 10, 1912–May 31, 1912
91	53–54	June 6, 1912–July 31, 1912
92	54a–55	Aug. 4, 1912–Sept. 12, 1912
93	56–57	Oct. 8, 1912–Dec. 28, 1912
94	58–59	Jan. 6, 1913–Apr. 1, 1913
95	60	Apr. 8, 1913–Apr. 29, 1913

Roll	Volumes	Dates
96	61	May 5, 1913–May 31, 1913
97	62	June 6, 1913–June 19, 1913
98	63	June 29, 1913–July 25, 1913
99	64	July 25, 1913–Aug. 16, 1913
100	65	Aug. 28, 1913–Sept. 17, 1913
101	66	Sept. 25, 1913–Oct. 20, 1913
102	67	Sept. 30, 1913–Nov. 30, 1913
103	68	Dec. 1, 1913–Dec. 29, 1913
104	69–70	Jan. 4, 1914–Mar. 29, 1914
105	71	Apr. 2, 1914–Apr. 30, 1914
106	72–73	May 3, 1914–June 30, 1914
107	74	July 1, 1914–Aug. 31, 1914
108	75	Sept. 1, 1914–June 28, 1915
109	76	July 1, 1915–June 28, 1916
110	77	July 1, 1916–Feb. 26, 1917
111	78	Feb. 26, 1917–Sept. 20, 1917
112	79	Oct. 2, 1917–May 28, 1918
113	80	June 5, 1918–Dec. 29, 1918
114	81	Jan. 1, 1919–May 23, 1919
115	82	June 3, 1919–Jan. 21, 1920
116	83	Feb. 3, 1920–June 30, 1920
117	84	July 1, 1920–Oct. 31, 1920
118	85	Nov. 1, 1920–Feb. 28, 1921
119	86	Mar. 2, 1921–June 30, 1921
120	87	July 4, 1921–Nov. 24, 1921
121	88–89	Jan. 9, 1922–Dec. 31, 1922
122	90	Jan. 1, 1923–June 30, 1923
123	91	July 2, 1923–Dec. 27, 1923
124	92–93	Dec. 31, 1923–June 29, 1925
125	94–95	July 13, 1925–June 29, 1927
126	96–97	July 10, 1927–June 29, 1929
127	98–99	July 1, 1929–June 28, 1931
128	100	June 29, 1921–Feb. 29, 1932
129	101–102	Mar. 2, 1932–July 27, 1933
130	103–104	Aug. 1, 1933–Apr. 30, 1934
131	105–106	May 1, 1934–Dec. 29, 1934
132	107–108	Jan. 10, 1935–Nov. 25, 1935
133	109–110	Dec. 2, 1935–Dec. 29, 1936
134	111–112	Jan. 6, 1937–Dec. 30, 1937
135	113–114	Jan. 3, 1938–June 29, 1939
136	115–116	July 1, 1939–June 30, 1941
137	117–118	July 1, 1941–Sept. 28, 1942
138	119–120	Oct. 1, 1942–Jan. 30, 1944
139	121–122	Feb. 3, 1944–Mar. 31, 1945
140	123–126	Apr. 1, 1945–Nov. 30, 1945
141	127–128	Dec. 2, 1945–Mar. 5, 1946
142	129–130	Mar. 7, 1946–June 23, 1946
143	131–133	June 23, 1946–Oct. 24, 1946
144	134–135	Oct. 24, 1946–Dec. 23, 1946
145	136–137	Dec. 24, 1946–Apr. 9, 1947
146	138–139	Apr. 9, 1947–May 31, 1947
147	140–141	June 1, 1947–July 31, 1947
148	142–143	Aug. 1, 1947–Sept. 30, 1947
149	144–146	Oct. 1, 1947–Jan. 30, 1948
150	147–148	Feb. 3, 1948–June 30, 1948

*Lists filmed in reverse order by INS.

Passenger Lists of Vessels Arriving at Baltimore, MD, 1954–1957. M1477. 34 rolls.

Roll	Contents
1	Dec. 1, 1954, AMERSEA–Jan. 17, 1955, SUZANNE
2	Jan. 18, 1955, CITY OF DONCASTER–Feb. 23, 1955, SEA COMET
3	Feb. 24, 1955, ANNITSA L.–Apr. 2, 1955, SANTORE

Roll	Contents
4	Apr. 3, 1955, ATHELBEACH–Apr. 20, 1955, SIXAOLA
5	Apr. 21, 1955, BIRTE HUGO STINNES–May 14, 1955, TORR HEAD
6	May 15, 1955, AXTEC–June 9, 1955, VENORE
7	June 10, 1955, AEQUITAS II–July 3, 1955, FELTORE
8	July 4, 1955, ARAGON–July 26, 1955, VENORE
9	July 27, 1955, PLANE U. S. N. FLT. 50852–Aug. 18, 1955, PROBITAS
10	Aug. 20, 1955, FREDERICKSBURG–Sept. 6, 1955, SANTA CLARA
11	Sept. 11, 1955, ARAGON–Sept. 30, 1955, STELLA
12	Oct. 1, 1955, U. S. N. FLT. 125–Oct. 25, 1955, PILOT
13	Oct. 26, 1955, BOSTON–Nov. 27, 1955, TRANSATLANTA
14	Nov. 28, 1955, PLANE U. S. N. FLT. 56535–Dec. 17, 1955, REXTON KENT
15	Dec. 18, 1955, VALENCIA–Jan. 6, 1956, V. E. RAYMOND
16	Jan. 7, 1956, CHILORE–Feb. 13, 1956, VIGLANDO
17	Feb. 14, 1956, AQUANTE–Mar. 16, 1956, YAKA
18	Mar. 17, 1956, BOAC FLT. 656/629–Apr. 11, 1956, YARACUAY
19	Apr. 13, 1956, MATS FLT. AE 426/12–May 9, 1956, MICHAEL
20	May 9, 1956, REMORVAH–June 1, 1956, TARFALA
21	June 2, 1956, M. V. VERGELEGEN–June 25, 1956, UNION POWER
22	June 26, 1956, ALCOA ROAMER–July 3, 1956, TRUDVANG
23	July 4, 1956, ASPROMONTE–July 25, 1956, VALBORG NIELSEN
24	July 26, 1956, ANDREAS K.–Aug. 19, 1956, OMNIUM FREIGHTER
25	Aug. 20, 1956, ALCOA ROAMER–Sept. 11, 1956, WORLD LORE
26	Sept. 12, 1956, CIBAC–Oct. 5, 1956, MARORE
27	Oct. 6, 1956, ATLANTIC AIR–Oct. 28, 1956, RCAF FLT. SPL. 397
28	Oct. 29, 1956, ALCOA ROAMER–Nov. 18, 1956, SOYA PACIFIC
29	Nov. 19, 1956, ATLANTICO–Dec. 12, 1956, YARACUY
30	Dec. 13, 1956, ARTEMIS–Jan. 10, 1957, USN FLT. N(SPL.)
31	Jan. 11, 1957, ALBERTA–Feb. 1, 1957, MORMACPINE
32	Feb. 2, 1957, ANDROS VENTURE–Mar. 5, 1957, CUBORE
33	Mar. 6, 1957, ARGOBEC–Apr. 3, 1957, OREMAR
34	Apr. 4, 1957, ANNA C.–May 7, 1957, VIRGINIA G.

Boston, Massachusetts

Index to Passenger Lists of Vessels Arriving at Boston, MA, Jan. 1, 1902–June 30, 1906. T521. 11 rolls. 16mm.

Roll	Contents
1	Aakvik, Emil, J.–Bradley, Jos.
2	Bradshaw–Crodin, Cornelius
3	Cronshaw–Ferrante, Ignazio
4	Ferranti–Harris
5	Harris, Raymond–Keene, Mary

Roll	Contents
6	Keene, Mary–McDuff, James
7	McDuff, Hugh–Nilson, C. Paulrna
8	Nilsson, Ernst–Quinlan, Mary
9	Quist, Joseph F.–Solimene, Sabath
10	Sollitto, Gaetano–Wechsler, Nissen
11	Weeder, John R.–Zullo, Sabato

Index to Passenger Lists of Vessels Arriving at Boston, MA, July 1, 1906–December 31, 1920. T617. 11 rolls. 16mm.

This index is arranged in rough alphabetical order.

Roll	Contents
1	AA–Degrandis, Eduando
2	De Gregroio–Fiorentini, Gennar
3	Fiori–Halle, Max
4	Hallessy–Karlborn, Niles Olof
5	Karlberg–McDonough (for Lu–Ly, see roll 6)
6	MacDov–Pano, Marianna (also Lu–Ly)
7	Mong–Pardo, Benio
8	Pardo, Vincenzo–Ritari, Jaakko
9	Rita, Henry–Slarve, Boonch
10	Slavin–Tygielski, Michal
11	Tylmann, Hanislaw–Zyhaluls, Mytro

Book Indexes to Boston Passenger Lists, 1899–1940. T790. 107 rolls.

There are no book indexes for 1901.

Roll	Dates
1	Apr. 1, 1899–Aug. 25, 1899
2	Aug. 26, 1899–June 30, 1900
3	July 5, 1900–Dec. 28, 1900
4	Jan. 17, 1902–May 2, 1902
5	May 16, 1902–Aug. 13, 1902
6	Aug. 17, 1902–Nov. 13, 1902
7	Nov. 27, 1902–Apr. 7, 1903
8	Apr. 15, 1903–June 13, 1903
9	June 16, 1903–Sept. 2, 1903
10	Sept. 5, 1903–Nov. 15, 1903
11	Nov. 17, 1903–Mar. 27, 1904
12	Apr. 4, 1904–June 11, 1904
13	June 13, 1904–Sept. 8, 1904
14	Sept. 10, 1904–Nov. 14, 1904
15	Nov. 23, 1904–Apr. 13, 1905
16	Apr. 18, 1905–June 19, 1905
17	June 25, 1905–Sept. 20, 1905
18	Sept. 30, 1905–Dec. 14, 1905
19	Dec. 24, 1905–Mar. 29, 1906
20	Apr. 4, 1906–May 24, 1906
21	May 31, 1906–Aug. 6, 1906
22	Aug. 16, 1906–Oct. 1906
23	Oct. 7, 1906–Dec. 23, 1906
24	Jan. 1, 1907–Apr. 5, 1907
25	Apr. 7, 1907–May 27, 1907
26	June 1, 1907–July 25, 1907
27	Aug. 1, 1907–Sept. 30, 1907
28	Oct. 1, 1907–Dec. 19, 1907
29	Jan. 1, 1908–May 19, 1908
30	May 19, 1908–Aug. 27, 1908
31	Sept. 3, 1908–Dec. 11, 1908
32	Dec. 19, 1908–Apr. 1, 1909
33	Apr. 4, 1909–June 10, 1909
34	June 15, 1909–Sept. 13, 1909
35	Sept. 15, 1909–Nov. 29, 1909
36	Dec. 1, 1909–Mar. 29, 1910

Roll	Dates
37	Mar. 29, 1910–May 19, 1910
38	May 23, 1910–July 28, 1910
39	Aug. 1, 1910–Sept. 25, 1910
40	Sept. 25, 1910–Dec. 2, 1910
41	Dec. 13, 1910–Jan. 20, 1911
42	Apr. 21, 1911–June 21, 1911
43	June 26, 1911–Sept. 14, 1911
44	Sept. 14, 1911–Nov. 16, 1911
45	Nov. 24, 1911–Apr. 3, 1912
46	Jan. 3, 1912–June 6, 1912
47	June 10, 1912–July 31, 1912
48	Aug. 6, 1912–Sept. 23, 1912
49	Sept. 25, 1912–Dec. 4, 1912
50	Dec. 9, 1912–Mar. 17, 1913
51	Mar. 20, 1913–May 22, 1913
52	May 23, 1913–June 26, 1913
53	July 1, 1913–Aug. 26, 1913
54	Aug. 18, 1913–Sept. 29, 1913
55	Sept. 30, 1913–Nov. 4, 1913
56	Nov. 14, 1913–Feb. 10, 1914
57	Feb. 14, 1914–Apr. 11, 1914
58	Apr. 16, 1914–May 24, 1914
59	May 28, 1914–July 9, 1914
60	July 13, 1914–Aug. 30, 1914
61	Sept. 3, 1914–Mar. 10, 1915
62	Mar. 25, 1915–Apr. 7, 1916
63	Apr. 15, 1916–Oct. 8, 1917
64	Oct. 16, 1917–Dec. 24, 1919
65	Jan. 6, 1920–Oct. 17, 1920
66	Oct. 20, 1920–Mar. 2, 1921
67	Mar. 4, 1921–May 21, 1921
68	May 23, 1921–May 26, 1922
69	June 2, 1922–Nov. 12, 1922
70	Nov. 25, 1922–May 21, 1923
71	June 6, 1923–Aug. 5, 1923
72	Aug. 13, 1923–Oct. 1, 1923
73	Oct. 4, 1923–June 1, 1924
74	June 2, 1924–Mar. 16, 1925
75	Mar. 21, 1925–Aug. 31, 1925
76	Sept. 5, 1925–Mar. 7, 1926
77	Mar. 3, 1926–Aug. 16, 1926
78	Aug. 14, 1926–Oct. 11, 1926
79	Oct. 17, 1926–Apr. 4, 1927
80	Apr. 11, 1927–July 24, 1927
81	July 28, 1927–Oct. 20, 1927
82	Oct. 23, 1928–Apr. 1, 1928
83	Apr. 2, 1928–June 1, 1928
84	June 4, 1928–Sept. 11, 1928
85	Sept. 2, 1928–Nov. 19, 1928
86	Nov. 26, 1928–June 6, 1929
87	June 9, 1929–July 29, 1929
88	Aug. 4, 1929–Oct. 7, 1929
89	Oct. 9, 1929–Apr. 8, 1930
90	Apr. 14, 1930–July 20, 1930
91	July 23, 1930–Oct. 19, 1930
92	Oct. 21, 1930–July 5, 1931
93	July 12, 1931–Dec. 28, 1931
94	Jan. 19, 1832–Sept. 25, 1932
95	Oct. 1, 1932–July 6, 1933
96	July 9, 1933–Nov. 27, 1933
97	Dec. 4, 1933–Aug. 29, 1934
98	Sept. 1, 1934–Dec. 31, 1934
99	Jan. 8, 1935–Sept. 5, 1935
100	Sept. 8, 1935–Apr. 12, 1936
101	Apr. 19, 1936 –Aug. 15, 1936

Roll	Dates
102	Aug. 16, 1936–Dec. 29, 1936
103	Jan. 11, 1937–July 31, 1937
104	Aug. 6, 1937–Nov. 1, 1937
105	Nov. 7, 1937–July 17, 1938
106	July 18, 1938–Dec. 5, 1938
107	Dec. 6, 1938–Sept. 14, 1940

Passenger Lists of Vessels Arriving at Boston, MA, 1891–1943. T843. 454 rolls. (★A complete list of rolls has been added.)

These records were filmed by the Immigration and Naturalization Service as they appeared in volumes. The volumes do not necessarily end on December 31 of the year. There may be two volumes bearing the same date span.

Roll	Volumes	Dates
1	1–2	Aug. 1–Dec. 31, 1891
2	3–4	Jan. 1–June 30, 1892
3	5	July 1–Aug. 31, 1892
4	6	Sept. 1–Oct. 31, 1892
5	7–8	Nov. 1, 1892–Mar. 31, 1893
6	9	Apr. 1–May 31, 1893
7	10–11	May 1–July 31, 1893
8	12	Aug. 1–Sept. 30, 1893
9	13–15	Sept. 1, 1893–Mar. 31, 1894
10	16–17	Jan. 1–June 30, 1894
11	18–20	June 1–Aug. 31, 1894
12	21–23	Sept. 1–Dec. 31, 1894
13	24–25	Oct. 1, 1894–Apr. 30, 1895
14	26–27	Jan. 1–June 30, 1895
15	28–29	May 1–Aug. 31, 1895
16	30–30A	July 1–Sept. 30, 1895
17	31–32	Sept. 1–Dec. 31, 1895
18	33–34	Oct. 1, 1895–Apr. 30, 1896
19	34A–35	Jan. 1–June 30, 1896
20	36–37	May 1–Aug. 31, 1896
21	38–39	July 1–Sept. 30, 1896
22	40–42	Sept. 1–Dec. 31, 1896
23	43–45	Jan. 1–June 30, 1897
24	46–49	May 1–Aug. 31, 1897
25	50–52	Sept. 1–Dec. 31, 1897
26	53–54	Oct. 1, 1897–July 31, 1898
27	55–57	Jan. 1–May 31, 1898
28	58–59	June 1–Aug. 1, 1898
29	59A–60	Aug. 1–Dec. 1, 1898
30	61–63	Oct. 1, 1898–Feb. 28, 1899
31	64–66	Mar. 1–May 31, 1899
32	67–68	June 1–July 31, 1899
33	69	Aug. 1–Aug. 31, 1899
34	70–71	Sept. 1–Sept. 30, 1899
35	72–73	Oct. 1–Dec. 31, 1899
36	74–75	Jan. 1, 1899–Mar. 31, 1900
37	76–78	Apr. 1–June 30, 1900
38	79	Jan. 1–Dec. 31, 1900
39	80–81	July 1–Aug. 15, 1900
40	82–83	Aug. 16–Sept. 30, 1900
41	84–86	Sept. 1–Oct. 12, 1900
42	87–88	Nov. 1, 1900–June 30, 1901
43	89–90	Jan. 1–Feb. 28, 1901 and July 1–Dec. 31, 1901
44	91–92	Mar. 1–Apr. 30, 1901
45	93–94	May 1–June 30, 1901
46	95–97	July 1–Aug. 31, 1901
47	98–99	Sept. 1–Sept. 30, 1901
48	100–102	Oct. 1–Dec. 31, 1901

Roll	Volumes	Dates	Roll	Volumes	Dates
49	103–104	Jan. 1–Mar. 31, 1902	114	199	Sept. 12–Sept. 19, 1907
50	105–106	Apr. 1–Apr. 30, 1902	115	200	Sept. 20–Sept. 30, 1907
51	107–108	May 1–May 31, 1902	116	201–202	Oct. 1–Oct. 24, 1907
52	109–110	June 1–July 31, 1902	117	203–204	Oct. 25–Nov. 17, 1907
53	111–112	July 1–Aug. 15, 1902	118	205–206	Nov. 18–Dec. 31, 1907
54	113–114	Aug. 16–Sept. 15, 1902	119	207–208	Jan. 1–Feb. 29, 1908
55	115–116	Sept. 16–Oct. 11, 1902	120	209	Mar. 1–Mar. 31, 1908
56	117–118	Oct. 12–Nov. 30, 1902	121	210–211	Apr. 1–Apr. 30, 1908
57	119–120	Dec. 1, 1902–Feb. 28, 1903	122	212–213	May 1–May 31, 1908
58	121	Mar. 1–Mar. 31, 1903	123	214–215	June 1–June 30, 1908
59	122	Apr. 1–Apr. 30, 1903	124	216–217	July 1–Aug. 20, 1908
60	123	May 1–May 15, 1903	125	218–219	Aug. 21–Sept. 17, 1908
61	124	May 16–May 31, 1903	126	220–221	Sept. 18–Oct. 18, 1908
62	125	June 1–June 30, 1903	127	222–223	Oct. 19–Nov. 17, 1908
63	126–127	July 1–July 31, 1903	128	224–225	Nov. 18–Dec. 31, 1908
64	128	Aug. 1–Aug. 19, 1903	129	226–227	Jan. 1–Feb. 9, 1909
65	129–130	Aug. 20–Sept. 10, 1903	130	228–229	Feb. 10–Mar. 17, 1909
66	131	Sept. 11–Sept. 19, 1903	131	230–231	Mar. 18–Apr. 31, 1909
67	132–133	Sept. 20–Oct. 14, 1903	132	232	Apr. 13–Apr. 26, 1909
68	134–135	Oct. 15–Nov. 30, 1903	133	233–234	Apr. 27–May 13, 1909
69	136–137	Dec. 1, 1903–Jan. 31, 1904	134	235–236	May 14–May 31, 1909
70	138	Feb. 1–Mar. 10, 1904	135	237–238	June 1–June 30, 1909
71	139–140	Mar. 11–Apr. 20, 1904	136	239–240	July 1–July 31, 1909
72	141	Apr. 21–Apr. 30, 1904	137	241–242	Aug. 1–Aug. 31, 1909
73	142	May 1–May 31, 1904	138	243–244	Sept. 1–Sept. 26, 1909
74	142	June 1–June 30, 1904	139	245	Sept. 27–Sept. 30, 1909
75	144–145	July 1–Aug. 31, 1904	140	246–247	Oct. 1–Oct. 31, 1909
76	146	Sept. 1–Sept. 12, 1904	141	248	Nov. 1–Nov. 11, 1909
77	147	Sept. 13–Sept. 30, 1904	142	249–250	Nov. 12–Dec. 31, 1909
78	148–149	Oct. 1–Oct. 31, 1904	143	251–252	Jan. 1–Feb. 28, 1910
79	150–150a	Nov. 1–Dec. 31, 1904	144	253	Mar. 1–Mar. 11, 1910
80	151	Jan. 1–Feb. 28, 1905	145	254–255	Mar. 12–Mar. 31, 1910
81	152	Mar. 1–Mar. 31, 1905	146	256	Apr. 1–Apr. 15, 1910
82	153	Apr. 1–Apr. 30, 1905	147	257–258	Apr. 16–Apr. 30, 1910
83	154–155	May 1–May 31, 1905	148	259–260	May 1–May 18, 1910
84	156	June 1–June 30, 1905	149	261–262	May 19–June 9, 1910
85	157	July 1–July 31, 1905	150	263	June 9–June 16, 1910
86	158–159	Aug. 1–Sept. 9, 1905	151	264–265	June 17–July 14, 1910
87	160	Sept. 10–Sept. 30, 1905	152	266–267	July 15–Aug. 10, 1910
88	161–162	Oct. 1–Oct. 31, 1905	153	268–269	Aug. 11–Aug. 31, 1910
89	163–164	Nov. 1–Dec. 31, 1905	154	270	Sept. 1–Sept. 8, 1910
90	165	Jan. 1–Feb. 28, 1906	155	271–272	Sept. 9–Sept. 30, 1910
91	166	Mar. 1–Mar. 31, 1906	156	273	Oct. 1–Oct. 19, 1910
92	167–168	Apr. 1–Apr. 30, 1906	157	274	Oct. 20–Oct. 31, 1910
93	169	May 1–May 19, 1906	158	275–276	Nov. 1–Dec. 31, 1910
94	170	May 20–May 31, 1906	159	277–278	Jan. 1–Feb. 28, 1911
95	171–171a	June 1–June 30, 1906	160	279	Mar. 1–Mar. 31, 1911
96	171b	July 1–July 31, 1906	161	280	Apr. 1–Apr. 15, 1911
97	171c–172	Aug. 1–Aug. 31, 1906	162	281	Apr. 16–Apr. 30, 1911
98	173–174	Sept. 1–Sept. 30, 1906	163	282	May 1–May 15, 1911
99	175	Oct. 1–Oct. 13, 1906	164	283	May 16–May 31, 1911
100	176	Oct. 14–Oct. 31, 1906	165	284–285	June 1–June 22, 1911
101	177–178	Nov. 1–Nov. 30, 1906	166	286–287	June 23–July 31, 1911
102	179	Dec. 1–Dec. 31, 1906	167	288–289	Aug. 1–Aug. 31, 1911
103	180–181	Jan. 1–Feb. 28, 1907	168	290	Sept. 1–Sept. 14, 1911
104	182	Mar. 1–Mar. 15, 1907	169	291	Sept. 15–Sept. 30, 1911
105	183–184	Mar. 16–Apr. 20, 1907	170	292	Oct. 1–Oct. 15, 1911
106	185–186	Apr. 21–May 7, 1907	171	293	Oct. 16–Oct. 31, 1911
107	187–189	May 8–May 31, 1907	172	294–295	Nov. 1–Nov. 30, 1911
108	190–191	June 1–June 14, 1907	173	296–297	Dec. 1, 1911–Feb. 29, 1912
109	192	June 15–June 30, 1907	174	298–299	Mar. 1–Mar. 31, 1912
110	193	July 1–July 11, 1907	175	300	Apr. 1–Apr. 15, 1912
111	194–195	July 12–Aug. 8, 1907	176	301	Apr. 16–Apr. 30, 1912
112	196–197	Aug. 9–Aug. 31, 1907	177	302–303	May 1–May 22, 1912
113	198	Sept. 1–Sept. 12, 1907	178	304–305	May 23–June 9, 1912

Roll	Volumes	Dates	Roll	Volumes	Dates
179	306–307	June 10–June 30, 1912	244	397	Jan. 1–Feb. 8, 1917
180	308–309	July 1–July 22, 1912	245	398	Mar. 1–Apr. 16, 1917
181	310–311	July 23–Aug. 11, 1912	246	399–400	Apr. 16–August, 1917
182	312–313	Aug. 12–Aug. 31, 1912	247	401–402	September, 1917–February, 1918
183	314	Sept. 1–Sept. 11, 1912	248	403–404	March–December, 1918
184	315	Sept. 11–Sept. 20, 1912	249	405–406	January–August, 1919
185	316	Sept. 21–Sept. 30, 1912	250	407–408	September–November, 1919
186	317	Oct. 1–Oct. 10, 1912	251	409–410	Nov. 16, 1919–February, 1920
187	318–319	Oct. 11–Oct. 31, 1912	252	411–412	Mar. 1–Apr. 27, 1920
188	320–321	Nov. 1–Nov. 30, 1912	253	413	Apr. 28–May 30, 1920
189	322	Dec. 1–Dec. 31, 1912	254	414–415	June–July, 1920
190	323–324	Jan. 1–Feb. 28, 1913	255	416–417	August–September, 1920
191	325–326	Mar. 1–Mar. 31, 1913	256	418	Oct. 1–Oct. 31, 1920
192	327–328	Apr. 1–Apr. 30, 1913	257	419	Nov. 1–Dec. 10, 1920
193	329	May 1–May 12, 1913	258	420–421	Dec. 11, 1920–Feb. 11, 1921
194	330–331	May 13–May 31, 1913	259	422–423	Feb. 12–Feb. 20, 1921
195	332	June 1–June 14, 1913	260	424	Feb. 12–Feb. 28, 1921
196	333–334	June 15–June 30, 1913	261	425	Feb. 27–Mar. 1, 1921
197	335	July 1–July 11, 1913	262	426–427	Mar. 2–Mar. 17, 1921
198	336	July 12–July 23, 1913	263	428–429	Mar. 18–Apr. 2, 1921
199	337	July 23–July 31, 1913	264	430	Apr. 3–Apr. 11, 1921
200	338–339	Aug. 1–Aug. 21, 1913	265	431	Apr. 12–Apr. 19, 1921
201	340–341	Aug. 22–Sept. 3, 1913	266	432–433	Apr. 20–May 22, 1921
202	342	Sept. 4–Sept. 9, 1913	267	434–435	May 23–June 6, 1921
203	343	Sept. 10–Sept. 16, 1913	268	436–438	June 7–Sept. 30, 1921
204	344	Sept. 16–Sept. 23, 1913	269	439–440	Oct. 1–Dec. 31, 1921
205	345	Sept. 24–Sept. 30, 1913	270	441	Jan. 1–Apr. 30, 1922
206	346–347	Oct. 1–Oct. 17, 1913	271	442–443	May 1–July 31, 1922
207	348–349	Oct. 18–Oct. 31, 1913	272	444–445	Aug. 1–Sept. 30, 1922
208	350	Nov. 1–Nov. 16, 1913	273	446	Oct. 1–Oct. 31, 1922
209	351	Nov. 17–Nov. 30, 1913	274	447	Nov. 1–Nov. 30, 1922
210	352–353	Dec. 1–Dec. 31, 1913	275	448–449	Dec. 3, 1922–Feb. 28, 1923
211	354	January, 1914	276	450	March 1923
212	355	Feb. 1–Feb. 28, 1914	277	451	April 1923
213	356	Mar. 1–Mar. 15, 1914	278	452	May 1–June 24, 1923
214	357	Mar. 16–Mar. 31, 1914	279	453	June 26–July 1, 1923
215	358	Apr. 1–Apr. 15, 1914	280	454	July 2–July, 1923
216	359	Apr. 16–Apr. 30, 1914	281	455–456	July 15–Aug. 4, 1923
217	361	May 1–May 9, 1914	282	457–458	Aug. 5–Sept. 2, 1923
218	362–363	May 10–May 31, 1914	283	459	Sept. 3–Sept. 1923
219	364	June 1–June 8, 1914	284	460	Sept. 14–Oct. 1, 1923
220	365	June 9–June 21, 1914	285	461	Oct. 1–Oct. 2, 1923
221	366	June 22–June 30, 1914	286	462–463	Oct. 3–November, 1923
222	367	July 1–July 11, 1914	287	464	November 1, 1923
223	368	July 12–July 23, 1914	288	465–466	Nov. 2–Dec. 28, 1923
224	369	July 24–July 31, 1914	289	467	January–February, 1924
225	370	Aug. 1–Aug. 16, 1914	290	468	March–May, 1924
226	371	Aug. 17–Aug. 31, 1914	291	469	June–July, 1924
227	372	Sept. 1–Sept. 20, 1914	292	470	August, 1924
228	373	Sept. 21–Sept. 30, 1914	293	471	September, 1924
229	374	Oct. 1–Oct. 31, 1914	294	472	October, 1924
230	375–376	November–December, 1914	295	473	November–December, 1924
231	377	January–February, 1915	296	474	Nov. 29, 1924–Feb. 28, 1925
232	378–379	March–April, 1915	297	475	Mar. 1–Mar. 31, 1925
233	380	May 1–June 14, 1915	298	476	April, 1925
234	381–382	June 15–August, 1915	299	477	May, 1925
235	383	September–October, 1915	300	478–479	June 1–July 16, 1925
236	384	Nov. 1–Dec. 16, 1915	301	480	June 16–Aug. 13, 1925
237	385–386	Dec. 17, 1915–Feb. 10, 1916	302	481	August–September, 1925
238	387	Feb. 11–Feb. 29, 1916	303	482	Sept. 2–Sept. 21, 1925
239	388	Mar. 1–Apr. 7, 1916	304	483	Sept. 21–Oct. 4, 1925
240	389–390	Apr. 8–May 30, 1916	305	484	Oct. 12–Oct. 31, 1925
241	391–392	June–July, 1916	306	485	Nov. 2–Nov. 30, 1925
242	393–394	August–September, 1916	307	486	December, 1925–January, 1926
243	395–396	October–December, 1916	308	487	Feb. 1–Mar. 31, 1926

Roll	Volumes	Dates	Roll	Volumes	Dates
309	488	Apr. 2–Apr. 28, 1926	374	570	Nov. 1–Nov. 30, 1931
310	489	May 1–May 31, 1926	375	571–572	Dec. 1, 1931–Jan. 31, 1932
311	490	June 1–June 30, 1926	376	573–574	Feb. 1–Mar. 31, 1932
312	491	July 1–July 31, 1926	377	575–576	Apr. 1–May 31, 1932
313	492	Aug. 2–Aug. 31, 1926	378	577	June 1–June 30, 1932
314	493	Sept. 2–Sept. 11, 1926	379	578	July 1–July 22, 1932
315	493a	Sept. 12–Sept. 30, 1926	380	579–580	July 23–Aug. 15, 1932
316	494	Sept. 29–Oct. 17, 1926	381	581–582	Aug. 16–Sept. 13, 1932
317	495	Oct. 17–Nov. 15, 1926	382	583	Sept. 13–Sept. 30, 1932
318	496	Nov. 17–Dec. 30, 1926	383	584	Oct. 1–Oct. 31, 1932
319	497	Jan. 2–Feb. 18, 1927	384	585–586	Nov. 1–Dec. 31, 1932
320	498	Feb. 17–Mar. 15, 1927	385	587–588	Jan. 1–Feb. 28, 1933
321	499	Mar. 16–Apr. 18, 1927	386	589–590	Mar. 1–Apr. 30, 1933
322	500	Apr. 19–May 16, 1927	387	591	May 1–May 31, 1933
323	501	May 16–May 30, 1927	388	592	June 1–June 30, 1933
324	502	June 2–June 30, 1927	389	593	July 1–July 31, 1933
325	503	July 2–July 26, 1927	390	594–595	Aug. 1–Aug. 31, 1933
326	504	July 28–Aug. 14, 1927	391	596–597	Sept. 1–Sept. 30, 1933
327	505	Aug. 14–Sept. 4, 1927	392	598–599	Oct. 1–Oct. 31, 1933
328	506	Sept. 5–Sept. 30, 1927	393	600–601	Nov. 1–Dec. 31, 1933
329	507	Oct. 1–Oct. 21, 1927	394	602–603	Jan. 1–Feb. 28, 1934
330	508a–508b	Oct. 23–Nov. 30, 1927	395	604–605	Mar. 1–Apr. 30, 1934
331	509	Dec. 2, 1927–Jan. 31, 1928	396	606	May 1–May 31, 1934
332	510	Feb. 1–Mar. 11, 1928	397	607	June 1–June 30, 1934
333	511	Mar. 12–Apr. 10, 1928	398	608	July 1–July 15, 1934
334	512	Apr. 11–Apr. 30, 1928	399	609–610	July 16–Aug. 22, 1934
335	513	May 1–May 30, 1928	400	611–612	Aug. 22–Sept. 15, 1934
336	514	June 1–June 14, 1928	401	613	Sept. 16–Sept. 30, 1934
337	514a–515	June 14–July 28, 1928	402	614	Oct. 1–Oct. 31, 1934
338	516	Aug. 1–Aug. 30, 1928	403	615–616	Nov. 1–Dec. 31, 1934
339	517–518	Sept. 1–Sept. 30, 1928	404	617–619	Jan. 1–Mar. 31, 1935
340	519–519a	Oct. 1–Oct. 31, 1928	405	620–621	Apr. 1–May 31, 1935
341	520–521	Nov. 1–Dec. 31, 1928	406	622	June 1–June 30, 1935
342	522	Jan. 1–Jan. 31, 1929	407	623	July 1–July 23, 1935
343	523–524	Feb. 1–Mar. 31, 1929	408	624	Aug. 1–Aug. 31, 1935
344	525–526	Apr. 1–Apr. 30, 1929	409	625	Sept. 1–Sept. 15, 1935
345	527–528	May 1–May 31, 1929	410	626	Sept. 16–Sept. 30, 1935
346	529	June 1–June 30, 1929	411	627–628	Oct. 1–Nov. 30, 1935
347	530–531	July 1–July 31, 1929	412	629–630	Dec. 1, 1935–Jan. 31, 1936
348	532	Aug. 1–Aug. 18, 1929	413	631–632	Feb. 1–Mar. 31, 1936
349	533	Aug. 18–Aug. 31, 1929	414	633	Apr. 1–Apr. 30, 1936
350	534	Sept. 1–Sept. 10, 1929	415	634–635	May 1, June 20, 1936
351	535	Sept. 11–Sept. 20, 1929	416	636–637	June 21–July 31, 1936
352	536	Sept. 21–Sept. 30, 1929	417	638	Aug. 1–Aug. 15, 1936
353	537–538	Oct. 1–Oct. 31, 1929	418	639	Aug. 16–Aug. 31, 1936
354	539–540	Nov. 1–Dec. 30, 1929	419	640–641	Sept. 1–Sept. 30, 1936
355	541	Jan. 1–Jan. 31, 1929	420	642	Oct. 1–Oct. 31, 1936
356	542–543	Feb. 1–Mar. 31, 1930	421	643–644	Nov. 1–Dec. 31, 1936
357	544–545	Apr. 1–Apr. 30, 1930	422	645–647	Jan. 1–Mar. 31, 1937
358	546	May 1–May 31, 1930	423	648	Apr. 1–Apr. 30, 1937
359	547–548	June 1–June 30, 1930	424	649	May 1–May 31, 1937
360	549–550	July 1–July 31, 1930	425	650–651	June 1–July 14, 1937
361	551	Aug. 1–Aug. 17, 1930	426	652	July 15–July 31, 1937
362	552	Aug. 17–Aug. 31, 1930	427	653	Aug. 1–Aug. 15, 1937
363	553–554	Sept. 1–Sept. 30, 1930	428	654	Aug. 16–Aug. 31, 1937
364	555–556	Oct. 1–Oct. 31, 1930	429	655	Sept. 1–Sept. 15, 1937
365	557–558	Nov. 1–Dec. 31, 1930	430	656	Sept. 16–Sept. 30, 1937
366	559	Jan. 1–Feb. 28, 1931	431	657	Oct. 1–Oct. 31, 1937
367	560	Mar. 1–Mar. 31, 1931	432	658–659	Nov. 1–Dec. 31, 1937
368	561	Apr. 1–Apr. 30, 1931	433	660–662	Jan. 1–Mar. 31, 1938
369	562	May 1–May 31, 1931	434	663	Apr. 1–Apr. 30, 1938
370	563–564a	June 1–July 18, 1931	435	664	May 1–May 31, 1938
371	564b–565	July 18–Aug. 16, 1931	436	665–666	June 1–July 15, 1938
372	566–567	Aug. 17–Sept. 15, 1931	437	666a–667	July 16–Aug. 15, 1938
373	568–569	Sept. 16–Oct. 31, 1931	438	668–669	Aug. 16–Sept. 14, 1938

Roll	Volumes	Dates
439	670	Sept. 15–Sept. 30, 1938
440	671–672	Oct. 1–Oct. 30, 1938
441	673–675	Nov. 1, 1938–Jan. 31, 1939
442	676–677	Feb. 1–Mar. 31, 1939
443	678	Apr. 1–May 31, 1939
444	679	May 1–May 31, 1939
445	680	June 1–June 30, 1939
446	681–682	July 1–Aug. 17, 1939
447	683–684	Aug. 18–Sept. 30, 1939
448	685–687	Oct. 1, 1939–Feb. 28, 1940
449	688–689	Mar. 1–June 30, 1940
450	690–691	July 1–Oct. 31, 1940
451	692–695	Nov. 1, 1940–June 30, 1941
452	696–698	July 1–Dec. 30, 1941
453	699–700	Jan. 1–Nov. 30, 1942
454	701–703	Dec. 1, 1942–December, 1943

Crew Lists of Vessels Arriving at Boston, MA, 1917–1943. T938. 269 rolls.

Roll	Volumes	Dates
1	1–2	May 1, 1917–Aug. 31, 1917
2	3–4	Sept. 1, 1917–Dec. 31, 1917
3	5–7	Jan. 1, 1918–Apr. 30, 1918
4	8	May 1, 1918–June 30, 1918
5	9	July 1, 1918–Aug. 31, 1918
6	10–11	Sept. 1, 1918–Dec. 31, 1918
7	12	Jan. 1, 1919–Apr. 30, 1919
8	13	May 1, 1919–June 30, 1919
9	14	July 1, 1919 –Aug. 31, 1919
10	15	Sept. 1, 1919–Oct. 31, 1919
11	16	Nov. 1, 1919–Dec. 31, 1919
12	17	Jan. 1, 1920–Feb. 29, 1920
13	18	Mar. 1, 1920–Apr. 30, 1920
14	19	May 1, 1920–June 30, 1920
15	20	July 1, 1920–Aug. 31, 1920
16	21	Sept. 1, 1920–Oct. 31, 1920
17	22	Nov. 1, 1920–Dec. 31, 1920
18	23	Jan. 1, 1921–Feb. 28, 1921
19	24	Mar. 1, 1921–Mar. 31, 1921
20	25–26	Apr. 1, 1921–May 30, 1921
21	27–28	June 1, 1921–July 31, 1921
22	29–30	Aug. 1, 1921–Sept. 30, 1921
23	31–32	Oct. 1, 1921–Nov. 30, 1921
24	33–34	Dec. 1, 1921–Jan. 31, 1922
25	35	Feb. 1, 1922–Feb. 28, 1922
26	36	Mar. 1, 1922–Mar. 31, 1922
27	37	Apr. 1, 1922–Apr. 30, 1922
28	38	May 1, 1922–May 31, 1922
29	39	June 1, 1922–June 30, 1922
30	40	July 1, 1922–July 31, 1922
31	41	Aug. 1, 1922–Aug. 31, 1922
32	42	Sept. 1, 1922–Sept. 30, 1922
33	43	Oct. 1, 1922–Oct. 31, 1922
34	44	Nov. 1, 1922–Nov. 30, 1922
35	45	Dec. 1, 1922–Dec. 31, 1922
36	46	Jan. 1, 1923–Jan. 31, 1923
37	47	Feb. 1, 1923–Feb. 28, 1923
38	48	Mar. 1, 1923–Mar. 31, 1923
39	49	Apr. 1, 1923–Apr. 30, 1923
40	50	May 1, 1923–May 31, 1923
41	51	June 1, 1923–June 30, 1923
42	52	July 1, 1923–July 31, 1923
43	53	Aug. 1, 1923–Aug. 31, 1923
44	54	Sept. 1, 1923–Sept. 30, 1923
45	55	Oct. 1, 1923–Oct. 31, 1923
46	56	Nov. 1, 1923–Nov. 30, 1923
47	57	Dec. 1, 1923–Dec. 31, 1923
48	58	Jan. 1, 1924–Jan. 31, 1924
49	59	Feb. 1, 1924–Feb. 29, 1924
50	60	Mar. 1, 1924–Mar. 31, 1924
51	61	Apr. 1, 1924–Apr. 30, 1924
52	62	May 1, 1924–May 31, 1924
53	63	June 1, 1924–June 30, 1924
54	64	July 1, 1924–July 31, 1924
55	65	Aug. 1, 1924–Aug. 31, 1924
56	66	Sept. 1, 1924–Sept. 30, 1924
57	67	Oct. 1, 1924–Oct. 31, 1924
58	68	Nov. 1, 1924–Nov. 30, 1924
59	69	Dec. 1, 1924–Dec. 31, 1924
60	70	Jan. 1, 1925–Jan. 30, 1925
61	71	Feb. 1, 1925–Feb. 28, 1925
62	72	Mar. 1, 1925–Mar. 31, 1925
63	73	Apr. 1, 1925–Apr. 30, 1925
64	74	May 1, 1925–May 31, 1925
65	75	June 1, 1925–June 30, 1925
66	76	July 1, 1925–July 31, 1924
67	77	Aug. 1, 1925–Aug. 31, 1925
68	78	Sept. 1, 1929–Sept. 30, 1929
69	79	Oct. 1, 1925–Oct. 31, 1925
70	80	Nov. 1, 1925–Nov. 30, 1925
71	81	Dec. 1, 1925–Dec. 31, 1925
72	82	Jan. 1, 1926–Jan. 31, 1926
73	83	Feb. 1, 1926–Feb. 28, 1926
74	84	Mar. 1, 1926–Mar. 31, 1926
75	85	Apr. 1, 1926–Apr. 30, 1926
76	86	May 1, 1926–May 31, 1926
77	87	June 1, 1926–June 30, 1926
78	88	July 1, 1926–July 31, 1926
79	89	Aug. 1, 1926–Aug. 31, 1926
80	90	Sept. 1, 1926–Sept. 30, 1926
81	91	Oct. 1, 1926–Oct. 31, 1926
82	92	Nov. 1, 1926–Nov. 30, 1926
83	93	Dec. 1, 1926–Dec. 31, 1926
84	94	Jan. 1, 1927–Jan. 31, 1927
85	95	Feb. 1, 1927–Feb. 28, 1927
86	96	Mar. 1, 1927–Mar. 31, 1927
87	97	Apr. 1, 1927–Apr. 30, 1927
88	98	May 1, 1927–May 31, 1927
89	99	June 1, 1927–June 30, 1927
90	100	July 1, 1927–July 31, 1927
91	101	Aug. 1, 1927–Aug. 31, 1927
92	102	Sept. 1, 1927–Sept. 30, 1927
93	103	Oct. 1, 1927–Oct. 31, 1927
94	104	Nov. 1, 1927–Nov. 30, 1927
95	105	Dec. 1, 1927–Dec. 31, 1927
96	106	Jan. 1, 1928–Jan. 31, 1928
97	107	Feb. 1, 1928–Feb. 29, 1928
98	108	Mar. 1, 1928–Mar. 31, 1928
99	109	Apr. 1, 1928–Apr. 30, 1928
100	110	May 1, 1928–May 31, 1928
101	111	June 1, 1928–June 30, 1928
102	112	July 1, 1928–July 31, 1928
103	113	Aug. 1, 1928–Aug. 31, 1928
104	114	Sept. 1, 1928–Sept. 30, 1928
105	115	Oct. 1, 1928–Oct. 31, 1928
106	116	Nov. 1, 1928–Nov. 30, 1928
107	117	Dec. 1, 1928–Dec. 31, 1928
108	118	Jan. 1, 1929–Jan. 31, 1929
109	119	Feb. 1, 1929–Feb. 28, 1929
110	120	Mar. 1, 1929–Mar. 31, 1929

Roll	Volumes	Dates	Roll	Volumes	Dates
111	121	Apr. 1, 1929–Apr. 30, 1929	176	186	Sept. 1, 1934–Sept. 30, 1934
112	122	May 1, 1929–May 31, 1929	177	187	Oct. 1, 1934–Oct. 31, 1934
113	123	June 1, 1929–June 30, 1929	178	188	Nov. 1, 1934–Nov. 31, 1934
114	124	July 1, 1929–July 31, 1929	179	189	Dec. 1, 1934–Dec. 31, 1934
115	125	Aug. 1, 1929–Aug. 31, 1929	180	190	Jan. 1, 1934–Jan. 31, 1935
116	126	Sept. 1, 1929–Sept. 30, 1929	181	191	Feb. 1, 1935–Feb. 38, 1935
117	127	Oct. 1, 1929–Oct. 31, 1929	182	192	Mar. 1, 1935–Mar. 31, 1935
118	128	Nov. 1, 1929–Nov. 30, 1929	183	193	Apr. 1, 1935–Apr. 31, 1935
119	129	Dec. 1, 1929–Dec. 31, 1929	184	194	May 1, 1935–May 31, 1935
120	130	Jan. 1, 1930–Jan. 31, 1930	185	195	June 1, 1935–June 30, 1935
121	131	Feb. 1, 1930–Feb. 28, 1930	186	196	July 1, 1935–July 31, 1935
122	132	Mar. 1, 1930–Mar. 31, 1930	187	197	Aug. 1, 1935–Aug. 31, 1935
123	133	Apr. 1, 1930–Apr. 30, 1930	188	198	Sept. 1, 1935–Sept. 30, 1935
124	134	May 1, 1930–May 30, 1930	189	199	Oct. 1, 1935–Oct. 31, 1935
125	135	June 1, 1930–June 30, 1930	190	200	Nov. 1, 1935–Nov. 30, 1935
126	136	July 1, 1930–July 31, 1930	191	201	Dec. 1, 1935–Dec. 31, 1935
127	137	Aug. 1, 1930–Aug. 31, 1930	192	202	Jan. 1, 1936–Jan. 31, 1936
128	138	Sept. 1, 1930–Sept. 30, 1930	193	203	Feb. 1, 1936–Feb. 29, 1936
129	139	Oct. 10, 1930–Oct. 31, 1930	194	204	Mar. 1, 1936–Mar. 31, 1936
130	140	Nov. 1, 1930–Nov. 30, 1930	195	205	Apr. 1, 1936–Apr. 30, 1936
131	141	Dec. 1, 1930–Dec. 31. 1930	196	206–207	May 1, 1936–May 31, 1936
132	142	Jan. 1, 1931–Jan. 31, 1931	197	208	June 1, 1936–June 30, 1936
133	143	Feb. 1, 1931–Feb. 28, 1931	198	209	July 1, 1936–July 31, 1936
134	144	Mar. 1, 1931–Mar. 31, 1931	199	210–211	Aug. 1, 1936–Aug. 31, 1936
135	145	Apr. 1, 1931–Apr. 30, 1931	200	212	Sept. 1, 1936–Sept. 31, 1936
136	146	May 1, 1931–May 31, 1931	201	213	Oct. 1, 1936–Oct. 31, 1936
137	147	June 1, 1931–June 30, 1931	202	213a	Nov. 1, 1936–Nov. 30, 1936
138	148	July 1, 1931–July 31, 1931	203	214	Dec. 1, 1936–Dec. 31, 1936
139	149	Aug. 1, 1931–Aug. 31, 1931	*204	215	Feb. 1, 1937–Feb. 28, 1937
140	150	Sept. 1, 1931–Sept. 30, 1931	205	216	Jan. 1, 1937–Jan. 31, 1937
141	151	Oct. 1, 1931–Oct. 31, 1931	206	217	Mar. 1, 1937–Mar. 31, 1937
142	152	Nov. 1, 1931–Nov. 30, 1931	207	218	Apr. 1, 1937–Apr. 30, 1937
143	153	Dec. 1, 1931–Dec. 31, 1931	208	219	May 1, 1937–May 31, 1937
144	154	Jan. 1, 1932–Jan. 31, 1932	209	220	June 1, 1937–June 30, 1937
145	155	Feb. 1, 1932–Feb. 29, 1932	210	221	June 16, 1937–June 30, 1937
146	156	Mar. 1, 1932–Mar. 31, 1932	211	222	July 1, 1937–July 15, 1937
147	157	Apr. 1, 1932–Apr. 30, 1932	212	223	July 16, 1937–July 31, 1937
148	158	May 1, 1932–May 31, 1932	213	224	Aug. 1, 1937–Aug. 15, 1937
149	159	June 1, 1932–June 30, 1932	214	225	Aug. 16, 1937–Aug. 31, 1937
150	160	July 1, 1932–July 31, 1932	215	226	Sept. 1, 1937–Sept. 14, 1937
151	161	Aug. 1, 1932–Aug. 31, 1932	216	227	Sept. 15, 1937–Sept. 30, 1937
152	162	Sept. 1, 1932–Sept. 30, 1932	217	228	Oct. 1, 1937–Oct. 31, 1937
153	163	Oct. 1, 1932–Oct. 31, 1932	218	229	Nov. 1, 1937–Nov. 30, 1937
154	164	Nov. 1, 1932–Nov. 31, 1932	219	230	Dec. 1, 1937–Dec. 31, 1937
155	165	Dec. 1, 1932–Dec. 31, 1932	220	231	Jan. 1, 1938–Jan. 31, 1938
156	166	Jan. 1, 1933–Jan. 31, 1933	221	232	Feb. 1, 1938–Feb. 28, 1938
157	167	Feb. 1, 1933–Feb. 28, 1933	222	233	Mar. 1, 1938–Mar. 31, 1938
158	168	Mar. 1, 1933–Mar. 31, 1933	223	234	Apr. 1, 1938–Apr. 30, 1938
159	169	Apr. 1, 1933–Apr. 30, 1933	224	235	May 1, 1938–May 31, 1938
160	170	May 1, 1933–May 31, 1933	225	236	June 1, 1938–June 30, 1938
161	171	June 1, 1933–June 30, 1933	226	237	July 1, 1938–July 31, 1938
162	172	July 1, 1933–July 31, 1933	227	238	Aug. 1, 1938–Aug. 31, 1938
163	173	Aug. 1, 1933–Aug. 31, 1933	228	239	Sept. 1, 1938–Sept. 30, 1938
164	174	Sept. 1, 1933–Sept. 30, 1933	229	240	Oct. 1, 1938–Oct. 31, 1938
165	175	Oct. 1, 1933–Oct. 31, 1933	230	241	Nov. 1, 1938–Nov. 30, 1938
166	176	Nov. 1, 1933–Nov. 31, 1933	231	242	Dec. 1, 1938–Dec. 31, 1938
167	177	Dec. 1, 1933–Dec. 31, 1933	232	243	Jan. 1, 1939–Jan. 31, 1939
168	178	Jan. 1, 1934–Jan. 31, 1934	233	244	Feb. 1, 1939–Feb. 28, 1939
169	179	Feb. 1, 1934–Feb. 38, 1934	234	245	Mar. 1, 1939–Mar. 31, 1939
170	180	Mar. 1, 1934–Mar. 31, 1934	235	246	Apr. 1, 1939–Apr. 30, 1939
171	181	Apr. 1, 1934–Apr. 31, 1934	236	247	May 1, 1939–May 31, 1939
172	182	May 1, 1934–May 31, 1934	237	248	June 1, 1939–June 30, 1939
173	183	June 1, 1934–June 30, 1934	238	249	July 1, 1939–July 31, 1939
174	184	July 1, 1934–July 31, 1934	239	250	Aug. 1, 1939–Aug. 31, 1939
175	185	Aug. 1, 1934–Aug. 31, 1934	240	251	Sept. 1, 1939–Sept. 30, 1939

Roll	Volumes	Dates
241	252	Oct. 1, 1939–Oct. 31, 1939
242	253	Nov. 1, 1939–Nov. 30, 1939
243	254	Dec. 1, 1939–Dec. 31, 1939
244	255	Jan. 1, 1940–Jan. 31, 1940
245	256	Feb. 1, 1940–Feb. 29, 1940
246	257	Mar. 1, 1940–Mar. 31, 1940
247	258	Apr. 1, 1940–Apr. 30, 1940
248	259	May 1, 1940–May 31, 1940
249	260	June 1, 1940–June 30, 1940
250	261	July 1, 1940–July 31, 1940
251	262–263	Aug. 1, 1940–Sept. 30, 1940
252	264	Oct. 1, 1940–Oct. 31, 1940
253	265–266	Nov. 1, 1940–Dec. 31, 1940
254	267–268	Jan. 1, 1941–Feb. 28, 1941
255	269	Mar. 1, 1941–Mar. 31, 1941
256	270	Apr. 1, 1941–Apr. 30, 1941
257	271	May 1, 1941–May 31, 1941
258	272–273	June 1, 1941–July 31, 1941
259	274–275	Aug. 1, 1941–Sept. 30, 1941
260	276–277	Oct. 1, 1941–Nov. 30, 1941
261	278	Dec. 1, 1941–Dec. 31, 1941
262	279–281	Jan. 1, 1942–Mar. 31, 1942
263	282–286	Apr. 1, 1942–July 31, 1942
264	287–291	Aug. 1, 1942–Dec. 31, 1942
265	292–294	Jan. 1, 1943–Apr. 30, 1943
266	295–297	May 1, 1943–July 31, 1943
267	298–300	Aug. 1, 1943–Oct. 31, 1943
268	301–302	Nov. 1, 1943–Dec. 31, 1943
**269	302a	Aug. 1919–Oct. 1930

*February listed before January here.

**Miscellaneous listings.

Detroit, Michigan

★ **Card Manifests (Alphabetical) of Entries through the Port of Detroit, MI, 1906-1954. M1478. 117 rolls.**

Roll	Contents
1	Aaeng, Egil Akers–Anderson, Wilhelmina
2	Anderson, William–Bacon, Eva
3	Bacon, Frank Wilfred–Battersy, Joseph
4	Battersy, Mary C.–Bennett, Marion May
5	Bennett, Marjorie Leon–Blake, Blanche
6	Blake, Charles A.–Bott, John
7	Boudreau, Elsie–Bristol, Hillard
8	Bristol, Ida Maud H.–Bryan, John Francis
9	Bryan, John Henry–Cairns, Peter J.
10	Cairns, Peter–Carson, Agnes
11	Carson, Alexander–Chowen, Victor Wilfred
12	Chowen, William–Collier, Leah
13	Collier, Leah G.–Cotman, George Henry
14	Cotnam, Agnes Stella–Cupryniak, Jacob
15	Cupryniak, Jacob–Dawson, Edward Wesley
16	Dawson, Edwin–Diakopoulos, Georgios Michail
17	Diakow, Karoline–Dowse, Percy
18	Dowse, Thomas–Edelstine, Celia
19	Eden, Agnes F.–Everly, Albert Edward
20	Everly, Emily Jeanette–Fischer, Anne
21	Fischer, Anthony–Fortin, Marie M.B.
22	Fortin, Mary–Gainforth, John
23	Gainley, Theresa–Geroux, Louis
24	Geroux, Margaret Anne–Golden, Ruth Elizabeth
25	Golden, Sophie–Gravelle, Aline

Roll	Contents
26	Gravelle, Andy–Haelewyn, Gustaaf
27	Haelewyn, Mary–Harkness, Jean C.
28	Harkness, Jennie–Hegan, Robert James
29	Hegarty, Annie–Hillman, Milton
30	Hillman, Heward–Howard, Gladys D.
31	Howard, Gloria P.–Hyatt, Barbara J.
32	Hyatt, Beatrice I–Jackson, Hilda N.
33	Jackson, Hilda Nora–Johnson, Kenneth James
34	Johnson, Kittie–Jongsma, Tjeerd
35	Jonic, Frank–Kangas, Helmi
36	Kangas, Helmi S.–Keith, Marion
37	Keith, Marion–Keovas, Jim
38	Keown, Annie–Kinueh, Paul
39	Kinueton, Harold P.–Knister, William A.
40	Knistoft, Antonas–Kowalczyk, Jozef
41	Kowalczyk, Leon S.–Kundig, Indah H.
42	Kundes, Martin–Lahood, Tom
43	Lahood, Victoria–Lang, Mary Frances
44	Lang, Mary T.–Laurier, Francais
45	Laurier, Francis–Lechiara, Estherina
46	Lechiara, Esther Mary–Lenartowicz, Felix
47	Lenartowicz, Harry–Lewin, Samuel
48	Lewin, Sara–Littleton, Alice
49	Littleton, Arthur–Lotherington, Mosey
50	Lotherman, Harry–Lynch, John Simon
51	Lynch, John Walter–Mackey, Kenzie Colin
52	MacKay, Constance–Mahoney, Eileen Marcella
53	Mahoney, Eileen Marcella–Mann, Annie
54	Mann, Annie L.–Marsh, Arthur
55	Marsh, Arthur H.–Mason, Fay Haroline
56	Mason, Filomena S.–Mazurkiewcz, Roman
57	Mazurkiewicz, Rose–McClenahan, George
58	McCleneghan, Arthur Riggs–McDonald, Stephen Noel
59	McDonald, Stewart–McGregor, Joseen
60	McGregor, Kate–McKeough, John
61	McKeough, Mabel Annie–McMahon, Julie
62	McMahon, June Eileen–McVeigh, James
63	McVeigh, James Henry–Merivale, June Iris
64	Merivalia, Mart–Miller, Audrey Isabella
65	Miller, Augusta Louise–Mirocznik, Szejna
66	Mirocznik, Taube–Montigny, Joseph Alfred
67	Montigue, Richard James Bruce–Moroney, Cornelius
68	Moroney, Earl–Muir, Mary Brown
69	Mur, Nora–Murray, Susan Vivian
70	Murray, Sybil Audrey Geraldine–Nelson, Carol
71	Nelson, Carrie Edna–Nielson, Deborah
72	Nielson, Edward K.–O'Brien, Martin
73	O'Brien, Martin J.–Onches, Juliana
74	Onci, Adam–Pace, Joseph F.
75	Pace, Josephine–Parent, Stanley L.
76	Parent, Susanne–Patzalek, Sophie
77	Patzer, Adele–Penn, Ralph
78	Penn, Samuel–Pfeffer, Grace
79	Pfeifer, George Francis–Pisani, Canille Ferri
80	Pisani, Carmel–Possobon, Alfonso
81	Possobon, Francesca–Prior, Robert C.
82	Prior, Ruby Estelle–Raczin, Anna
83	Raczinski, Franciczek–Rayment, Cortland
84	Rayment, Cortland B.–Renaud, Joseph
85	Renaud, Joseph A.–Rickeard, Dorothy J.
86	Rickeard, Elizabeth D.–Robertson, Gordon
87	Robertson, Grace–Rogatko, Harry
88	Rogatko, Issie–Rossi, Antonia
89	Rossi, Antonio–Russell, Madge
90	Ruselvan, Barbara–Samet, Isaac

Roll	Contents
91	Samet, Nathan–Schwattz, Rose
92	Schweisheimer, Erich L.–Sergison, Rosabelle D.
93	Sergison, Virginia K.C.–Sheffield, Jessie
94	Sheffield, Jessie–Silk, Joseph E.
95	Silk, Margaret P.–Sitarz, Pauline
96	Sitarz, Theodora–Smith, Doris
97	Smith, Doris Doreen–Smith, William John
98	Smith, William John–Spearing, Alice E.
99	Spearing, Alice M.–Standon, Leta
100	Standon, Leta May–Stevenson, Evelyn J.
101	Stevenson, Everett E.–Stover, Emma F.
102	Stover, Esther Jean–Sutton, John
103	Sutton, John–Talbot, George E.
104	Talbot, George Elmer–Tenenbaum, Henry
105	Tenenbaum, Israel–Thompson, James
106	Thompson, James–Tofflemire, Douglas
107	Tofflemire, Edgar J.–Trevelyan, Beatrice E.
108	Treven, Joseph H.–Tyas, Dorothy Grange
109	Tyas, Joseph–Van Elswyk, Cornelia
110	Van Elswyk, Kryn–Vinette, Alice
111	Vinette, Anita–Walker, John David
112	Walker, John Donald–Warren, Robert Charles
113	Warren, Robert Charles–Webster, Opal
114	Webster, Patricia–White, Rita Hope
115	White, Robert–Wilson, Arnold
116	Wilson, Arnold L.–Wroblewski, Frank
117	Wroblewski, Josephine–Zyzys, Anna K.

★ **Passenger and Alien Crew Lists of Vessels Arriving at the Port of Detroit, MI, 1946–1957. M1479. 23 rolls.**

Roll	Contents
1	Jan. 29, 1946, OREGON–Sept. 12, 1946, MITSCHFIBRE
2	Sept. 13, 1946, NORONIC–June 4, 1947, COLUMBIA
3	June 5, 1947, STE. CLAIRE–Oct. 26, 1947, PRINS FREDERIC HENDRIK
4	Sept. 27, 1947, SULPHITE–July, 5, 1948, SULPHITE
5	July 5, 1948, TUG RACEY–Oct. 24, 1948, SHIRLEY G. TAYLOR
6	Oct. 24, 1948, IMPERIAL WHITTY–July 8, 1949, CITY OF CLEVELAND
7	July 8, 1949, NORONIC–Nov. 7, 1949, HARRY T. EWIG
8	Nov. 8, 1949, BROWN BEAVER–Sept. 12, 1950, TERNEFJELL
9	Sept. 13, 1950, FAIRMONT–July 15, 1951, BLANCHE HENDMAN
10	July 16, 1951, CITY OF HAMILTON–May 2. 1952, ATOMIC
11	May 3, 1952, SABADASH I–Aug. 24, 1952, CHARLES R. RONDLE SR.
12	Aug. 25, 1952, COLLINGWOOD–June 25, 1953, KIMMOUNT
13	June 25, 1953, BRO–Dec. 2, 1953, WYANDOTTE
14	Dec. 3, 1953, ALGORAIL–Aug. 30, 1954, MARTIAN!
15	Aug. 31, 1954, YANKCANUCK–Nov. 29, 1954, MARTIAN
16	Dec. 2, 1954, PRESCODOC–July 13, 1955, CLEOPATRA
17	July 15, 1955, PAN AM Flight 55/14–Nov. 6. 1955, RAGNEBORG
18	Nov. 7, 1955, AUGUST SARTORI–Jan. 31, 1956, SABADASH I
19	Feb. 26, 1956, EVERETTON–June 15, 1956, MARTIAN

Roll	Contents
20	June 15, 1956, PAN AM Flight 59/15–July 28, 1956, HELEN HINDMAN
21	July 29, 1956, PAN AM Flight 59/28–Sept. 16, 1956, TEAKBAY
22	Sept. 17, 1956, CHARLES DICK–Nov. 18, 1956, R.O. PETMAN
23	Nov. 19, 1956, CITY OF WINDSOR–Mar. 31, 1957, IMPERIAL WELLAND

Galveston, Texas

★ **Indexes to Passenger Lists of Vessels Arriving at Galveston, TX, 1896–1906. M1357. 3 rolls. 16mm.**

Roll	Content
1	Aab, Heinrich–Kraus, Piotr
2	Kraus, Albert–Polyak, Maria
3	Pitsch, Franz–Zytekiewcz, Stanislaw

★ **Index to Passenger Lists of Vessels Arriving at Galveston, TX, 1906–1951. M1358. 7 rolls. 16mm.**

This is an alphabetical index to the names of passengers arriving at Galveston and the subports of Houston and Brownsville, Texas beginning in October 1906.

Roll	Content
1	Aab, Maria–Duquesne, Isidro Ariosa
2	Duran, Carlos–Inglis, Elizabeth
3	Ingram, Joseph–Lavitjanz, Arschak
4	Lawenda, Joel–Papurlieff
5	Paracheroff, Dimitar–Schriever
6	Schrobenhauser, Anni–Weigert, Jacques
7	Weiger, Georg–Zyzora, Wasyi

★ **Passenger Lists of Vessels Arriving at Galveston, TX, 1896–1951. M1359. 36 rolls.**

This microfilm publication reproduces passenger manifests of vessels arriving at Galveston and the subports of Houston, Brownsville, Port Arthur, Sabine, and Texas City, Texas. The early lists are shipping company manifests. The later lists are on Immigration and Naturalization Service forms. The lists are arranged chronologically by date of arrival beginning in January 1896.

Some lists are annotated to show the date of admission as a resident alien or date of naturalization. Some entries are stamped "debarred" if the alien was not allowed to enter the United States. Some of the lists include names of U.S. citizens returning from abroad.

Roll 1 includes several lists from 1893, but none from 1894 or 1895. Roll 14 contains one list for September 16, 1911, and both rolls 32 and 33 include lists for 1938. On rolls 24 and 29, the first list was filmed out of order. Roll 24 includes several lists that are very difficult to read due to poor focus having been used during the filming process.

Roll	Content
1	January 14, 1896–January 13, 1902
2	February 1902–December 10, 1904
3	December 4, 1904–April 20, 1906
4	April 20, 1906–February 13, 1907
5	February 13, 1907–August 6, 1907
6	August 6, 1907–October 25, 1907
7	October 26, 1907–June 13, 1908
8	June 18, 1908–June 8, 1909
9	June 11, 1909–April 2, 1910

Roll	Content
10	April 2, 1910–November 12, 1910
11	November 12, 1910–July 20, 1911
12	July 20, 1911–March 27, 1912
13	March 29, 1912–September 26, 1912
14	September 26, 1912–May 18, 1913
15	May 22, 1913–October 19, 1913
16	October 19, 1913–April 6, 1914
17	March 28, 1914–January 5, 1915
18	July 28, 1914–July 14, 1917
19	October 8, 1917–April 16, 1920
20	April 2, 1920–April 1, 1921
21	April 4, 1921–December 15, 1922
22	December 17, 1922–June 22, 1923
23	April 11, 1924–September 14, 1925
24	September 14, 1925–October 28, 1926
25	October 31, 1926–October 13, 1927
26	October 13, 1927–November 11, 1928
27	November 11, 1928–November 29, 1929
28	November 29, 1929–January 12, 1931
29	January 18, 1931–September 22, 1931
30	September 22, 1931–July 2, 1932
31	July 2, 1932–May 19, 1934
32	May 31, 1934–November 17, 1938
33	December 6, 1936–November 29, 1939
34	December 29, 1939–September 24, 1946
35	September 24, 1946–July 27, 1947
36	July 29, 1947–October 25, 1948

Gloucester, Massachusetts

Crew Lists of Vessels Arriving at Gloucester, MA, 1918–1943. T941. 13 rolls.

Roll	Dates
1	Mar. 1918–June 1919
2	July 1919–Dec. 1920
3	Jan. 1921–Dec. 1923
4	Jan. 1924–Nov. 1928
5	Jan. 1929–Apr. 1932
6	May 1932–June 1934
7	July 1934–June 1935
8	July 1935–July 1936
9	July 1936–Jan. 1938
10	Jan. 1, 1938–Jan. 1, 1940
11	Jan. 1, 1940–July 1, 1940
12	July 1, 1941–Oct. 1, 1942
13	Oct. 1942–Dec. 1943

Gulfport and Pascagoula, Mississippi

Index to Passengers Arriving at Gulfport, MS, August 27, 1904–August 28, 1954; and at Pascagoula, MS, July 15, 1903–May 21, 1935. T523. 1 roll. 16mm.

Key West, Florida

Passenger Lists of Vessels Arriving at Key West, FL, 1898–1945. T940. 122 rolls.

Roll	Volumes	Dates
1	1–3	Nov. 2, 1898–Dec. 20, 1902
2	4	Jan. 1, 1903–Dec. 31, 1903
3	5	Jan. 2, 1904–July 18, 1904
4	6–7	July 19, 1904–Mar. 30, 1905
5	8–9	Apr. 1, 1905–Dec. 30, 1905
6	10	Jan. 1, 1906–May 26, 1906
7	11–12	May 28, 1906–Dec. 31, 1906
8	13–14	Jan. 25, 1907–June 29, 1907
9	15	July 1, 1907–Dec. 31, 1907
10	16	Jan. 1, 1908–June 30, 1908
11	17	July 1, 1908–Dec. 31, 1908
12	18	Jan. 2, 1909–Apr. 30, 1909
13	19	May 1, 1909–Aug. 31, 1909
14	20	Sept. 3, 1909–Dec. 30, 1909
15	21	Jan. 1, 1910–Apr. 30, 1910
16	22	May 3, 1910–July 30, 1910
17	23	Aug. 2, 1910–Nov. 14, 1910
18	24	Nov. 15, 1910–Feb. 28, 1911
19	25	Mar. 1, 1911–May 31, 1911
20	26	June 1, 1911–Aug. 31, 1911
21	27	Sept. 1, 1911–Dec. 31, 1911
22	28	Jan. 1, 1912–Feb. 29, 1912
23	29	Mar. 1, 1912–Apr. 30, 1912
24	30	May 1, 1912–June 29, 1912
25	31	July 1, 1912–Sept. 30, 1912
26	32–33	Oct. 1, 1912–Jan. 30, 1913
27	34	Feb. 1, 1913–Mar. 31, 1913
28	35	Apr. 1, 1913–May 31, 1913
29	36	June 2, 1913–Aug. 31, 1913
30	37–38	Sept. 1, 1913–Mar. 15, 1914
31	39–40	Mar. 16, 1914–Sept. 14, 1914
32	41–42	Sept. 15, 1914–Apr. 30, 1915
33	43–44	May 1, 1915–Feb. 29, 1916
34	45–46	Mar. 1, 1916–Aug. 27, 1916
35	47–48	Aug. 28, 1916–Feb. 17, 1917
36	49–50	Feb. 18, 1917–July 15, 1917
37	51–52	July 16, 1917–Dec. 31, 1917
38	53–54	Jan. 1, 1918–July 31, 1918
39	55	Aug. 2, 1918–Nov. 21, 1918
40	56–57	Nov. 22, 1918–June 6, 1919
41	58–59	June 7, 1919–Oct. 8, 1919
42	60–61	Oct. 8, 1919–Apr. 5, 1920
43	62	Apr. 6, 1920–May 31, 1920
44	63	June 1, 1920–July 14, 1920
45	64	July 15, 1920–Sept. 6, 1920
46	65	Sept. 6, 1920–Nov. 16, 1920
47	66	Nov. 17, 1920–Feb. 3, 1921
48	67	Feb. 4, 1921–Apr. 15, 1921
49	68	Apr. 15, 1921–June 17, 1921
50	69	June 20, 1921–Aug. 29, 1921
51	70	Aug. 20, 1921–Nov. 30, 1921
52	71	Dec. 1, 1921–Feb. 28, 1922
53	72	Mar. 1, 1922–May 31, 1922
54	73–74	June 2, 1922–Nov. 29, 1922
55	75	Dec. 1, 1922–Feb. 28, 1923
56	76–77	Mar. 1, 1923–June 30, 1923
57	78	July 1, 1923–Aug. 18, 1923
58	79	Aug. 20, 1923–Oct. 13, 1923
59	80	Oct. 15, 1923–Dec. 22, 1923
60	81	Dec. 24, 1923–Feb. 24, 1924
61	82	Feb. 25, 1924–Apr. 18, 1924
62	83	Apr. 19, 1924–June 16, 1924
63	84–85	June 17, 1924–Sept. 30, 1924
64	86	Oct. 1, 1924–Dec. 3, 1924
65	87	Dec. 5, 1924–Jan. 31, 1925

Roll	Volumes	Dates
66	88	Feb. 1, 1925–Mar. 31, 1925
67	89	Apr. 1, 1925–May 31, 1925
68	90	June 1, 1925–July 15, 1925
69	91	July 17, 1925–Aug. 31, 1925
70	92	Sept. 1, 1925–Oct. 14, 1925
71	93	Oct. 16, 1925–Nov. 30, 1925
72	94	Dec. 1, 1925–Jan. 20, 1926
73	95	Jan. 21, 1926–Feb. 27, 1926
74	96	Mar. 1, 1926–Apr. 17, 1926
75	97	Apr. 19, 1926–June 11, 1926
76	98	June 12, 1926–Aug. 4, 1926
77	99	Aug. 5, 1926–Sept. 29, 1926
78	100	Oct. 1, 1926–Dec. 6, 1926
79	101	Dec. 7, 1926–Feb. 14, 1927
80	102	Feb. 15, 1927–Apr. 16, 1927
81	103	Apr. 18, 1927–June 17, 1927
82	104	June 18, 1927–Aug. 23, 1927
83	105	Aug. 24, 1927–Nov. 4, 1927
84	106	Nov. 5, 1927–Jan. 14, 1928
85	107	Jan. 15, 1928–Mar. 15, 1928
86	108	Mar. 16, 1928–May 5, 1928
87	109	May 6, 1928–June 11, 1928
88	110	June 12, 1928–July 14, 1928
89	111	July 16, 1928–Aug. 27, 1928
90	112	Aug. 28, 1928–Oct. 5, 1928
91	113	Oct. 6, 1928–Nov. 24, 1928
92	114	Nov. 25, 1928–Jan. 18, 1929
93	115	Jan. 18, 1929–Mar. 14, 1929
94	116	Mar. 15, 1929–Apr. 30, 1929
95	117	May 1, 1929–July 5, 1929
96	119	July 6, 1929–Aug. 10, 1929
97	120	Aug. 11, 1929–Sept. 24, 1929
98	121	Sept. 25, 1929–Nov. 30, 1929
99	122	Dec. 1, 1929–Jan. 31, 1930
100	123	Feb. 1, 1930–Mar. 31, 1930
101	124	Apr. 1, 1930–May 31, 1930
102	125	June 1, 1930–July 31, 1930
103	126	Aug. 1, 1930–Sept. 30, 1930
104	127	Oct. 1, 1930–Dec. 31, 1930
105	128	Jan. 1, 1931–Feb. 28, 1931
106	129	Mar. 1, 1931–Apr. 30, 1931
107	130	May 1, 1931–June 30, 1931
108	131	July 1, 1931–Sept. 18, 1931
109	132	Sept. 19, 1931–Dec. 31, 1931
110	133	Jan. 1, 1932–Mar. 31, 1932
111	134	Apr. 1, 1932–June 30, 1932
112	135	July 1, 1932–Sept. 30, 1932
113	136	Oct. 1, 1932–Jan. 31, 1933
114	137–138	Feb. 1, 1933–July 31, 1933
115	139–141	Aug. 2, 1933–Apr. 30, 1934
116	142–143	May 1, 1934–Sept. 30, 1934
117	144–145	Oct. 1, 1934–Apr. 30, 1935
118	146	May 1, 1935–July 31, 1935
119	147–148	Aug. 1, 1935–Sept. 30, 1936
120	149–151	Oct. 2, 1936–Aug. 31, 1938
121	152–153	Sept. 2, 1938–July 31, 1940
122	154–155	Aug. 1, 1940–Dec. 14, 1945

New Bedford, Massachusetts

Index to Passengers Arriving at New Bedford, MA, July 1, 1902–November 18, 1954. T522. 2 rolls. 16mm.

Roll	Contents
1	Abalo–Simas, Marie Da
2	Simas, Maria Da–Zuzarte

Passenger Lists of Vessels Arriving at New Bedford, MA, 1902–1942. T944. 8 rolls.

Roll	Volumes	Dates
1	1–2	July 1, 1902–Nov. 24, 1903
2	3–4	Mar. 6, 1904–Sept. 6, 1905
3	5–6	Sept. 6, 1905–June 21, 1907
4	7–8	Aug. 10, 1907–Aug. 20, 1910
5	9–10	Feb. 11, 1911–Oct. 6, 1914
6	11–12	May 16, 1915–July 15, 1920
7	13	Aug. 4, 1920–June 22, 1921
8	14–15	July 1921–July 1942

Crew Lists of Vessels Arriving at New Bedford, MA, 1917–1943. T942. 2 rolls.

Roll	Volumes	Dates
1	1	May 1917–Dec. 1924
	2	May 1924–Dec. 1932
2	3	Dec. 1932–Dec. 1943

New Orleans, Louisiana

Index to Passenger Lists of Vessels Arriving at New Orleans, LA, 1900–1952. T618. 22 rolls. 16mm.

Roll	Contents
1	Aaberg, Vendel–Arias, Josefina
2	Arias, Magdalena–Bellini, Nazzareno
3	Bellino, Amalia–Brown, Arthur Andrew
4	Brown, Ashton–Carteni, Catelena
5	Carter, Mrs. A.B.–Coope, Anna
6	Cooper, Mr.–DeBenedetto, Viola
7	DeBeneditto, Horace–Fernandex, Avelino
8	Fernandez, Bartolo–Gardley, Bernard
9	Gardner, Alex. Golfie–Gutierres, Rafael
10	Gutman, David–Iris, Jose Maria
11	Irish, Thomas L.–LaCassin, Theresa
12	LaCava, Domenica–Lopez, Evaristo
13	Lopez, Miss F.–Matters, R.
14	Mattes, Claudio Duarte–Morenier, Josefa
15	Moreno, A.–Ottley, Clarence Eldridge
16	Otto, Bessie–Pleikys, Else
17	Pleisner, Franz–Robertson, Florence
18	Robertson, A.–Scamone, Jose
19	Scandalis, Joseph–Stilinovic, Ante
20	Stillone, Guiseppe–Vakoff, Stanko
21	Valade, Henry Etienne–Woo Sai, Young
22	Wood, Alexander–Zyromski, Wladyslaw

Passenger and Crew Lists of Vessels Arriving at New Orleans, LA, 1910–1945. T905. 189 rolls.

Roll	Volumes	Dates
1	1	Jan. 8, 1903–July 3, 1903
2	2	July 4, 1903–Dec. 31, 1903
3	3	Jan. 1, 1904–May 31, 1904
4	4	June 1, 1904–Oct. 16, 1904
5	5	Oct. 17, 1904–Dec. 31, 1904
6	6	Jan. 1, 1905–Apr. 1, 1905
7	7	Apr. 2, 1905–June 30, 1905
8	8	July 1, 1905–Dec. 31, 1905
9	9	Jan. 1, 1906–Feb. 28, 1906
10	10	Mar. 1, 1906–May 31, 1906
11	11, 11a	June 1, 1906–Oct. 31, 1906

Roll	Volumes	Dates
12	12, 12a, 13	Nov. 1, 1906–Feb. 7, 1907
13	13a, 14, 14a	Feb. 8, 1907–Apr. 30, 1907
14	15, 15a	May 1, 1907–June 30, 1907
15	16	July 1, 1907–Sept. 8, 1907
16	17	Sept. 9, 1907–Oct. 20, 1907
17	18	Oct. 21, 1907–Nov. 18, 1907
18	19	Nov. 19, 1907–Jan. 8, 1908
19	20	Jan. 9, 1908–Mar. 16, 1908
20	21	Mar. 17, 1908–May 11, 1908
21	22	May 12, 1908–Aug. 7, 1908
22	23	Aug. 9, 1908–Sept. 30, 1908
23	24, 25	Oct. 1, 1908–Jan. 31, 1909
24	26	Feb. 1, 1909–Apr. 12, 1909
25	27	Apr. 13, 1909–June 14, 1909
26	28	June 15, 1909–Aug. 31, 1909
27	29	Sept. 1, 1909–Oct. 30, 1909
28	30, 31	Oct. 31, 1909–Feb. 28, 1910
29	32	Mar. 1, 1910–Apr. 30, 1910
30	33	May 1, 1910–June 30, 1910
31	34	July 1, 1910–Aug. 31, 1910
32	35	Sept. 1, 1910–Oct. 31, 1910
33	36	Nov. 1, 1910–Dec. 31, 1910
34	37, 38	Jan. 2, 1911–Mar. 31, 1911
35	39	Apr. 1, 1911–June 9, 1911
36	40	June 10, 1911–Aug. 7, 1911
37	41	Aug. 8, 1911–Sept. 30, 1911
38	42	Oct. 1, 1911–Nov. 30, 1911
39	43, 44	Dec. 1, 1911–Feb. 29, 1912
40	45, 46	Mar. 2, 1912–Apr. 30, 1912
41	47 48	May 1, 1912–July 31, 1912
42	49, 50	Aug. 1, 1912–Nov. 30, 1912
43	51, 52	Dec. 1, 1912–Feb. 28, 1913
44	53, 54	Mar. 1, 1913–Apr. 30, 1913
45	55, 56, 57	May 1, 1913–July 31, 1913
46	58, 59	Aug. 1, 1913–Sept. 30, 1913
47	60, 61	Oct. 1, 1913–Nov. 30, 1913
48	61, 63, 64	Dec. 1, 1913–Feb. 28, 1914
49	65, 66	Mar. 1, 1914–Apr. 30, 1914
50	67, 68	May 1, 1914–June 30, 1914
51	69, 70	July 1, 1914–Aug. 31, 1914
52	71, 72, 73	Sept. 1, 1914–Nov. 30, 1914
53	74, 75, 76	Dec. 1, 1914–Feb. 28, 1915
54	77, 78, 79	Mar. 1, 1915–May 31, 1915
55	80, 81, 82	June 1, 1915–Aug. 31, 1915
56	83, 84, 85	Sept. 1, 1915–Nov. 30, 1915
57	86, 87, 88	Dec. 1, 1915–Feb. 29, 1918
58	89, 90, 91	Mar. 1, 1916–May 31, 1916
59	92, 93, 94	June 1, 1916–Aug. 31, 1916
60	95, 96, 97	Sept. 1, 1916–Nov. 30, 1916
61	98, 99, 100	Dec. 1, 1916–Feb. 28, 1917
62	101, 102	Mar. 1, 1917–Apr. 30, 1917
63	103, 104, 105	May 1, 1917–July 31, 1917
64	106, 107, 108	Aug. 1, 1917–Oct. 31, 1917
65	109, 110, 111	Nov. 1, 1917–Jan. 31, 1918
66	112, 113, 114	Feb. 1, 1918–Apr. 30, 1918
67	115, 116, 117	May 1, 1918–July 31, 1918
68	118, 119, 120	Aug. 1, 1918–Oct. 31, 1918
69	121–124	Nov. 1, 1918–Feb. 28, 1919
70	125, 126	Mar. 1, 1919–Apr. 30, 1919
71	127, 128, 129	May 1, 1919–July 3, 1919
72	130, 131, 132	Aug. 1, 1919–Oct. 31, 1919
73	133, 134, 135	Nov. 1, 1919–Jan. 31, 1920
74	136, 137	Feb. 1, 1920–May 31, 1920
75	138, 139	Apr. 1, 1920–May 3, 1920
76	140, 141	June 1, 1920–July 31, 1920

Roll	Volumes	Dates
77	142, 143, 144	Aug. 1, 1920–Oct. 31, 1920
78	145, 146	Nov. 1, 1920–Dec. 31, 1920
79	147, 148	Jan. 1, 1921–Feb. 28, 1921
80	149	Mar. 1, 1921–Mar. 31, 1921
81	150, 151	Apr. 1, 1921–May 31, 1921
82	152, 153	June 1, 1921–July 31, 1921
83	154, 155	Aug. 1, 1921–Sept. 30, 1921
84	156, 157	Oct. 1, 1921–Nov. 30, 1921
85	158, 159, 160	Dec. 1, 1921–Feb. 28, 1922
86	161, 162	Mar. 1, 1922–Apr. 30, 1922
87	163, 164	May 1, 1922–June 30, 1922
88	165, 166	July 1, 1922–Aug. 31, 1922
89	167, 168	Sept. 1, 1922–Oct. 31, 1922
90	169, 179	Nov. 1, 1922–Dec. 31, 1922
91	171, 172	Jan. 1, 1923–Feb. 28, 1923
92	173, 174	Mar. 1, 1923–Apr. 30, 1923
93	175, 176	May 1, 1923–June 30, 1923
94	177, 178	July 1, 1923–Aug. 31, 1923
95	179, 180	Sept. 1, 1923–Oct. 31, 1923
96	181, 182	Nov. 1, 1923–Dec. 31, 1923
97	183, 184	Jan. 1, 1924–Feb. 29, 1924
98	185, 186	Mar. 1, 1924–Apr. 30, 1924
99	187, 188	May 1, 1924–June 30, 1924
100	189, 190	July 1, 1924–Aug. 31, 1924
101	191, 192	Sept. 1, 1924–Oct. 31, 1924
102	193, 194	Nov. 1, 1924–Dec. 31, 1924
103	195, 196	Jan. 1, 1925–Feb. 28, 1925
104	197, 198	Mar. 1, 1925–Apr. 30, 1925
105	199, 200	May 1, 1925–Aug. 31, 1925
106	201, 202	July 1, 1925–Aug. 31, 1925
107	203, 204	Sept. 1, 1925–Oct. 31, 1925
108	205, 206	Nov. 1, 1925–Dec. 31, 1925
109	207, 208	Jan. 1, 1926–Feb. 28, 1926
110	209, 210	Mar. 1, 1926–Apr. 30, 1926
111	211, 212	May 1, 1926–June 30, 1926
112	213, 214	July 1, 1926–Aug. 31, 1926
113	215, 216	Sept. 1, 1926–Oct. 31, 1926
114	217, 218	Nov. 1, 1926–Dec. 31, 1926
115	219, 220	Jan. 1, 1927–Feb. 28, 1927
116	221, 222	Mar. 1, 1927–Apr. 30, 1927
117	223, 224	May 1, 1927–Jun. 30, 1927
118	225, 226	July 1, 1927–Aug. 31, 1927
119	227, 228	Sept. 1, 1927–Oct. 31, 1927
120	229, 230	Nov. 1, 1927–Dec. 3, 1927
121	231, 232	Jan. 1, 1928–Feb. 29, 1928
122	233, 234	Mar. 1, 1928–Apr. 30, 1928
123	235, 236	May 1, 1928–June 30, 1928
124	237, 238	July 1, 1928–Aug. 31, 1928
125	239, 240	Sept. 1, 1928–Oct. 31, 1928
126	241, 242	Nov. 1, 1928–Dec. 31, 1928
127	243, 244	Jan. 1, 1929–Feb. 28, 1929
128	245, 246	Mar. 1, 1929–Apr. 30, 1929
129	247, 248	May 1, 1929–June 30, 1929
130	249, 250	July 1, 1929–Aug. 31, 1929
131	251, 252	Sept. 1, 1929–Oct. 31, 1929
132	253, 254	Nov. 1, 1929–Dec. 31, 1929
133	255, 256	Jan. 1, 1930–Feb. 28, 1930
134	257, 258	Mar. 1, 1930–Apr. 30, 1930
135	259, 260	May 1, 1930–June 30, 1930
136	261, 262	July 1, 1930–Aug. 31, 1930
137	263, 264	Sept. 1, 1930–Oct. 31, 1930
138	265–267	Nov. 1, 1930–Jan. 31, 1931
139	268–270	Feb. 1, 1931–Apr. 30, 1931
140	271, 272	May 1, 1931–June 30, 1931
141	273–275	July 1, 1931–Sept. 30, 1931

Roll	Volumes	Dates
142	276–278	Oct. 1, 1931–Dec. 31, 1931
143	279–281	Jan. 1, 1931–Mar. 31, 1932
144	282–284	Apr. 1, 1932–June 30, 1932
145	285–287	July 1, 1932–Sept. 30, 1932
146	288–290	Oct. 1, 1932–Dec. 31, 1932
147	291–294	Jan. 1, 1933–Apr. 30, 1933
148	295–297	May 1, 1933–July 31, 1933
149	298–300	Aug. 1, 1933–Oct. 31, 1933
150	301–304	Nov. 1, 1933–Feb. 28, 1934
151	305–307	Mar. 1, 1934–May 31, 1934
152	308–310	June 1, 1934–Aug. 31, 1934
153	311–313	Sept. 1, 1934–Nov. 30, 1934
154	314–316	Dec. 1, 1934–Feb. 29, 1935
155	317–320	Mar. 1, 1935–June 30, 1935
156	321–323	July 1, 1935–Sept. 30, 1935
157	324–326	Oct. 1, 1935–Dec. 31, 1935
158	327–329	Jan. 1, 1936–Mar. 31, 1936
159	330–332	Apr. 1, 1936–June 30, 1936
160	333–335	July 1, 1936–Sept. 30, 1936
161	336–338	Oct. 1, 1936–Dec. 31, 1936
162	339–341	Jan. 1, 1937–Mar. 31, 1937
163	342–344	Apr. 1, 1937–June 30, 1937
164	345–347	July 1, 1937–Sept 31, 1937
165	348–350	Oct. 1, 1937–Dec. 31, 1937
166	351–354	Jan. 1, 1938–Apr. 30, 1938
167	355–357	May 1, 1938–July 31, 1938
168	358–360	Aug. 1, 1938–Oct. 31, 1938
169	361–364	Nov. 1, 1938–Feb. 28, 1939
170	365–367	Mar. 1, 1939–May 31, 1939
171	368–370	June 1, 1939–Aug. 31, 1939
172	371–374	Sept. 1, 1939–Dec. 31, 1939
173	375–378	Jan. 1, 1940–Apr. 30, 1940
174	379–381	May 1, 1940–July 31, 1940
175	382–385	Aug. 1, 1940–Nov. 30, 1940
176	386–389	Dec. 1, 1940–Mar. 31, 1941
177	390–392	Apr. 1, 1941–June 30, 1941
178	393–395	July 1, 1941–Sept. 30, 1941
179	396–399	Oct. 1, 1941–Jan. 31, 1942
180	400–402	Feb. 1, 1942–Apr. 30, 1942
181	403–405	May 1, 1942–Aug. 31, 1942
182	406–409	Sept. 1, 1942–Feb. 28, 1943
183	410–412	Mar. 2, 1943–Apr. 29, 1943
184	413, 414	Apr. 30, 1943–June 30, 1943
185	415, 416	July 4, 1943–Dec. 31, 1943
186	417–420	Jan. 5, 1943–July 31, 1943
187	421–426	Aug. 1, 1944–Jan. 31, 1945
188	427–431	Feb. 1, 1945–June 30, 1945
189	432–437	July 1, 1945–Dec. 31, 1945

Crew Lists of Vessels Arriving at New Orleans, LA, 1910–1945. T939. 311 rolls. (★A complete list of rolls has been added.)

Roll	Volumes	Dates
1	1–3	January–June, 1910
2	4–5	July–October, 1910
3	6–7	November, 1910–February, 1911
4	8–9	March–June, 1911
5	10–11	July–October, 1911
6	12–13	November, 1911–February, 1912
7	14–15	March–June, 1912
8	16–17	July–October, 1912
9	18–19	November, 1912–February, 1913
10	20–21	March–June, 1913
11	22–23	July–October, 1913
12	24–25	November, 1913–February, 1914

Roll	Volumes	Dates
13	26	March–April, 1914
14	27	May–June, 1914
15	28–29	July–October, 1914
16	30–31	November, 1914–February, 1915
17	32	March–April, 1915
18	33	May–June, 1915
19	34–35	July–October, 1915
20	36–37	November, 1915–February, 1916
21	38–39	March–June, 1916
22	40–41	July–October, 1916
23	42–43	November, 1916–February, 1917
24	44	March–April, 1917
25	45	May–June, 1917
26	46	July–August, 1917
27	47	September–October, 1917
28	48	November–December, 1917
29	49–50	Jan. 1–Mar. 15, 1918
30	51–53	Mar. 16–Apr. 30, 1918
31	56–59	June 1–Aug. 15, 1918
32	60–64	Aug. 16–Oct. 31, 1918
33	65–69	Nov. 1, 1918–Jan. 15, 1919
34	70–73	Jan. 16–Mar. 31, 1919
35	74–77	April–May, 1919
36	78–79	June–July, 1919
37	80–81	August–September, 1919
38	82–83	October–November, 1919
39	84–85	December, 1919–January, 1920
40	86–87	February–March, 1920
41	88–89	April–May, 1920
42	90	June, 1920
43	91	July, 1920
44	92	August, 1920
45	93	September, 1920
46	94	October, 1920
47	95–96	November, 1920
48	97–98	December, 1920
49	99–100	Jan. 1–Feb. 15, 1921
50	101–102	Feb. 16–Mar. 31, 1921
51	103–104	April, 1921
52	105	May, 1921
53	106	June, 1921
54	107–108	July 1–Aug. 15, 1921
55	109–110	Aug. 16–Sept. 15, 1921
56	111–112	Sept. 16–Oct. 31, 1921
57	113	November, 1921
58	114	December, 1921
59	115–116	January–February, 1922
60	117	March, 1922
61	118	April, 1922
62	119	May, 1922
63	120	June, 1922
64	121	July, 1922
65	122–123	August–September, 1922
66	124–125	October–November, 1922
67	126–127	December, 1922–January, 1923
68	128–129	February–March, 1923
69	130	April, 1923
70	131	May, 1923
71	132	June, 1923
72	133	July, 1923
73	134	August, 1923
74	135–136	September–October, 1923
75	137–138	November–December, 1923
76	139–140	January–February, 1924
77	141	March, 1924

Roll	Volumes	Dates
78	142	April, 1924
79	143	May, 1924
80	144	June, 1924
81	145	July, 1924
82	146	August, 1924
83	147	September, 1924
84	148	October, 1924
85	149	November, 1924
86	150	December, 1924
87	151	January, 1925
88	152	February, 1925
89	153	March, 1925
90	154	April, 1925
91	155	May, 1925
92	156	June, 1925
93	157	July, 1925
94	158	August, 1925
95	159	September, 1925
96	160	October, 1925
97	161	November, 1925
98	162	December, 1925
99	163	January, 1926
100	164	February, 1926
101	165	March, 1926
102	166	April, 1926
103	167	May, 1926
104	168	June, 1926
105	169	July, 1926
106	170	August, 1926
107	171–172	September–October, 1926
108	173	November, 1926
109	174	December, 1926
110	175	January, 1927
111	176	February, 1927
112	177	March, 1927
113	178	April, 1927
114	179	May, 1927
115	180	June, 1927
116	181	July, 1927
117	182	August, 1927
118	183	September, 1927
119	184	October, 1927
120	185	November, 1927
121	186	December, 1927
122	187	January, 1928
123	188	February, 1928
124	189	March, 1928
125	190	April, 1928
126	191	May, 1928
127	192–193	June 1–July 15, 1928
128	194–195	July 16–Aug. 15, 1928
129	196–197	Aug. 16–Sept. 15, 1928
130	198–199	Sept. 16–Oct. 15, 1928
131	200	Oct. 16–31, 1928
132	201–202	November, 1928
133	203	Dec. 1–15, 1928
134	204–205	Dec. 16, 1928–Jan. 15, 1929
135	206–207	Jan. 16–Feb. 15, 1929
136	208–209	Feb. 16–Mar. 15, 1929
137	210	Mar. 15–31, 1929
138	211	Apr. 1–15, 1929
139	212–213	Apr. 16–May 15, 1929
140	214	May 16–31, 1929
141	215	June 1–15, 1929
142	216	June 16–30, 1929

Roll	Volumes	Dates
143	217	July, 1929
144	218	Aug. 1–21, 1929
145	218 (cont'd)	Aug. 22–31, 1929
146	219	September, 1929
147	220	October, 1929
148	221	November, 1929
149	222	December, 1929
150	223	January, 1930
151	224	February, 1930
152	225	March, 1930
153	226	April, 1930
154	227	May, 1930
155	228	June, 1930
156	229	July, 1930
157	230	August, 1930
158	231	September, 1930
159	232	October, 1930
160	233	November, 1930
161	234	December, 1930
162	235	January, 1931
163	236	February, 1931
164	237	March, 1931
165	238	April, 1931
166	239	May, 1931
167	240	June, 1931
168	241	July, 1931
169	242	August, 1931
170	243	September, 1931
171	244	October, 1931
172	245	November, 1931
173	246	December, 1931
174	247	January, 1932
175	248	February, 1932
176	249	March, 1932
177	250	April, 1932
178	251	May, 1932
179	252	June, 1932
180	253	July, 1932
181	254	August, 1932
182	255–256	September–October, 1932
183	257–258	November–December, 1932
184	259–260	January–February, 1933
185	261–262	March–April, 1933
186	263	May, 1933
187	264	June, 1933
188	265–266	July–August, 1933
189	267–268	September–October, 1933
190	269–270	November–December, 1933
191	271–272	January–February, 1934
192	273–274	March–April, 1934
193	275	May, 1934
194	276	June, 1934
195	277	July, 1934
196	278	August, 1934
197	279	September, 1934
198	280–281	October–November, 1934
199	282	December, 1934
200	283–284	January–February, 1935
201	285	March, 1935
202	286	April, 1935
203	287	May, 1935
204	288	June, 1935
205	289	July, 1935
206	290	August, 1935
207	291	September, 1935

Roll	Volumes	Dates
208	292–293	October–November, 1935
209	294	December, 1935
210	295–296	January–February, 1936
211	297	March, 1936
212	298	April, 1936
213	299	May, 1936
214	300	June, 1936
215	301	July, 1936
216	302	August, 1936
217	303	September, 1936
218	304	October, 1936
219	305	November, 1936
220	306	December, 1936
221	307	January, 1937
222	308	February, 1937
223	309	March, 1937
224	310	April, 1937
225	311	May, 1937
226	312	June, 1937
227	313	July, 1937
228	314	August, 1937
229	315	September, 1937
230	316	October, 1937
231	317	November, 1937
232	318	December, 1937
233	319	January, 1938
234	320	February, 1938
235	321	March, 1938
236	322	April, 1938
237	323	May, 1938
238	324	June, 1938
239	325	July, 1938
240	326	August, 1938
241	327	September, 1938
242	328	October, 1938
243	329	November, 1938
244	330	December, 1938
245	331	January, 1939
246	332	February, 1939
247	333	March, 1939
248	334	April, 1939
249	335	May, 1939
250	336	June, 1939
251	337	July, 1939
252	338	August, 1939
253	339	September, 1939
254	340	October, 1939
255	341	November, 1939
256	342	December, 1939
257	343	January, 1940
258	344	February, 1940
259	345	March, 1940
260	346	April, 1940
261	347	May, 1940
262	348	June, 1940
263	349	July, 1940
264	350	August, 1940
265	351	September, 1940
266	352–353	October–November, 1940
267	354–355	December, 1940–January, 1941
268	356	February, 1941
269	357	March, 1941
270	358	April, 1941
271	359	May, 1941
272	360	June, 1941

Roll	Volumes	Dates
273	361	July, 1941
274	362	August, 1941
275	363	September, 1941
276	364	October, 1941
277	365	November, 1941
278	366	December, 1941
279	367	January, 1942
280	368	February, 1942
281	369	March, 1942
282	370	April, 1942
283	371	May, 1942
284	372–373	June–July, 1942
285	374–377	August–November, 1942
286	378–380	December, 1942–February, 1943
287	381–383	March–May, 1943
288	384–385	June–July, 1943
289	386–387	August–September, 1943
290	388	October, 1943
291	389	November, 1943
292	390–391	December, 1943–January, 1944
293	392–393	February–March, 1944
294	394	April, 1944
295	395–396	May–June, 1944
296	397	July, 1944
297	398	August, 1944
298	399	September, 1944
299	400	October, 1944
300	401–402	November–December, 1944
301	403–404	January–February, 1945
302	405	March, 1945
303	406	April, 1945
304	407	May, 1945
305	408	June, 1945
306	409	July, 1945
307	410	August, 1945
308	411	September, 1945
309	412	October, 1945
310	413	November, 1945
311	414	December, 1945

New York, New York

Index to Passenger Lists of Vessels Arriving at New York, NY, June 16, 1897–June 30, 1902. T519. 115 rolls. 16mm.

Roll	Contents
1	Aab–Adduceteo, A.
2	Adduceteo, D.–Albrakoszky
3	Albramo–Amato, Vincenzo
4	Amato, Vincenzo–Anderson, D.
5	Anderson, E.–Andrulis, E.
6	Andrulis, F.–Apsoi
7	Apte–Aslyian
8	Asma–Bacci, F.
9	Bacci, G.–Balezunas
10	Balewitz–Barbero, E.
11	Barbero, E.–Bartolomei, Gi
12	Bartolomei, Gu–Beattie, Jas.
13	Beattie, Je–Beltestad
14	Beltin–Bergamino
15	Bergamini, D.–Bertolletti, O.
16	Bertolletti, P.–Bies, M.
17	Bies, P.–Blahot, J.

Roll	Contents
18	Blahot, M.–Bochzdiswitz
19	Bocian–Bonaficlia
20	Bonafiglia–Borosky, F.
21	Borosky, J.–Boyadjian, D.
22	Boyadjian, E.–Braun, Aro
23	Braun, Arp–Brindle, Jos.
24	Brindle, P.–Brunello, Ang
25	Brunello, Ant–Buczok, Mih
26	Buczok, Mik–Burkhard, P.
27	Burkhard, S.–Campbell, A.
28	Campbell, A.–Carlson, H.
29	Carlson, J.–Cavanna, D.
30	Cavanna, D.–Chrissopoulos, G.
31	Chrissopoulos, J.–Cnosfen, D.
32	Cnosfen, J.–Corazza, V.
33	Corazzo–Csecsnek
34	Csecsovszki–Dahas
35	Daher–Davidsen, Anna
36	Davidsen, Anna–De Luca, D.
37	De Luca, D.–Dialessandria, F.
38	Dialessandria, V.–Di Mezzo
39	Dimic–Dombrowsky, Victor
40	Dombrowsky, Victoria–Duffy, Lizzie
41	Duffy, Lizzie–Ellingsen, An
42	Ellingsen, As–Falduto, G.
43	Falduto, G.–Fenczik, H.
44	Fenczik, J.–Fiorentino
45	Fiorio–Francavilla, Gio
46	Francavilla, Giu–Furist
47	Furjak–Gargarella, Al
48	Gargarella, An–Ghiraldi
49	Ghirardanj–Glik, A.
50	Glik, C.–Graff, Je
51	Graff, Je–Gruber, Cha
52	Gruber, Chu–Gyuskin
53	Gyutavico–Harczin
54	Hard–Herling, Sara
55	Herling, Sarah–Hood, S.
56	Hood, T.–Lanello, F.
57	Lannello, G.–Jacorone
58	Jacot–Jerzykiewicz
59	Jeschelnik–Josefek
60	Josefer–Kapinos, Jad
61	Kapinos, Jan–Kelly, Barb
62	Kelly, Bart–Klein, Jol
63	Klein, Jon–Konefat, Ja
64	Konefat, Jo–Kraems
65	Kraemer–Kuenzle
66	Kuetko–Lakowitz, D.
67	Lakowitz, J.–Laurilsen, H.A.
68	Laurilsen, Hans–Leto, Giuseppa
69	Leto, Giuseppa–Litwin, Men
70	Litwin, Mey–Luhtala, M.
71	Luhtala, S.–Maguino, D.
72	Maguino, P.–Manniello, F.
73	Manniello, G.–Marsalisi, C.
74	Marsalisi, F.–Matulka, A.
75	Matulka, C.–McLuskin
76	McMacken–Mevik
77	Meviloinen–Miranti, Ma. Rosalia
78	Miranti, S.–Mordkowitz
79	Morea–Murin, Maria
80	Murin, Maria–Neizl
81	Nej–Nolan, Sa
82	Nolan, St–Olawinska

Roll	Contents
83	Olbadjian–Osowska, L.
84	Osowska, R.–Panek, Wladyslaw
85	Panek, Wladyslaw–Paul, Alf
86	Paul, Alm–Perri, N.
87	Perri, P.–Phillips, George
88	Phillips, George–Platek
89	Plaster,–Poznic, F.
90	Poznic, N.–Quinn, Da
91	Quinn, De–Rech, V.
92	Rech, W.–Rigone
93	Rigoni–Ronuondo
94	Ronyak–Ruffini, Le
95	Ruffini, Li–Sakowicz
96	Sakowitz, Adolf–Sartori, M.
97	Sartori, Maria(25)–Schinied
98	Schinilovitz–Schweyer, J.
99	Schweyer, P.–Shahin, Ann
100	Shahin, Ant–Siservic
101	Sisger–Solowicz
102	Solowinski–Stanajtis
103	Stanakiewicz–Stranizza
104	Stranizzo–Swenson, Ali
105	Swenson, Alm–Tadolena
106	Tadolenci–Theodoropocilos
107	Theodoropoulas–Tosonotto, P.
108	Tosonotto, P.–Twomey, Mar
109	Twomey, Mat–Varso, I.
110	Varso, J.–Vitarella, F.
111	Vitarella, G.–Warninski, J.
112	Warninski, W.–Wiedelgurt, D.
113	Wiedelgurt, S.–Wozisk
114	Woziwoda–Zelt, G.
115	Zelt, J.–Zzidor

Index (Soundex) to Passenger Lists of Vessels Arriving at New York, NY, July 1, 1902–December 31, 1943. T621. 755 rolls. 16mm.

Roll	Contents
1	A-000–A-140 Abrahamm
2	A-140 Allesandro–A-162 Remigio
3	A-162 Rosalia–A-214 Ernst A.
4	A-214 Emanuel–A-232 Nella
5	A-232 Pasquale–A-250 Hannah
6	A-250 Helena–A-262 Selma
7	A-262 Torsten A.–A-346 Beni J.
8	A-346 Chaie–A-353 Francesco
9	A-353 Francesco–A-415 Emilia
10	A-415 Eustachio–A-416 Richard
11	A-416 Ricardo A.–A-425 Jenny
12	A-425 Jennie S.–A-450 Albert
13	A-450 Alexander–A-500 Juan
14	A-500 Kate–A-523 Moische
15	A-523 Maria–A-525 Ezio
16	A-525 Fiorindo–A-534 Pietro
17	A-534 Pavel–A-536 Anders
18	A-536 Anders–A-536 Frans
19	A-536 Franz–A-536 Lawrence R.
20	A-536 Lauritz M.–A-536 William
21	A-536 Wm Henry–A-600 Rudolph
22	A-600 Rosalie–A-624 Manuel
23	A-624 Miguel–A-640 Virgilia
24	A-640 Vincenzo–A-653 Sore
25	A-653 S. Agnes–B-120 Josef
26	B-120 Josef–B-162 Anna
27	B-162 Adam–B-200 Gaetano

Roll	Contents	Roll	Contents
28	B-200 Gabriel–B-200 Michele	93	C-263 Eugenia–C-320 Athanassius
29	B-200 Michele–B-215 Gideon W.	94	C-320 Anna–C-342 Elias
30	B-215 Hanze–B-220 Theodoros	95	C-342 Eva–C-360 Mary
31	B-220 Terezia–B-232 Razolina	96	C-360 Mary–C-400 Luigi
32	B-232 Robert–B-240 Michele	97	C-400 Luigi–C-416 Annie
33	B-240 Michal–B-250 George W.	98	C-416 Annie–C-420 Rosaria
34	B-250 Giovanni–B-253 Carlo	99	C-420 Rosaria–C-430 Antonio
35	B-253 Cilie–B-260 Honore	100	C-430 Antonio–C-440 Stephano
36	B-260 Ilie–B-263 Rosa	101	C-440 Sabatino–C-452 Leopardo
37	B-263 Robert–B-300 Wilhelm	102	C-452 Leon–C-460 Antonio
38	B-300 William S.–B-324 Jessie K.	103	C-460 Bentivolio–C-500 Abdo
39	B-324 Jolanda–B-350 Henry J.	104	C-500 Adolfina–C-500 Pietro
40	B-350 H.–B-360 Riphat	105	C-500 Peter–C-514 Charles, B.
41	B-360 Ruggero–B-400 Jan	106	C-514 Ciriaco–C-516 Mary, I.
42	B-400 John–B-420 Alexander	107	C-516 Maria, F.–C-522 Vincenzo
43	B-420 Alice–B-420 Laszlo	108	C-522 Zorfia–C-530 Amodio
44	B-420 Lauria–B-422 Kazimaras	109	C-530 Angelo–C-533 Porfirio
45	B-422 Katerina–B-426 Donato	110	C-533 Rocco–C-540 Fred
46	B-426 Dobe–B-435 C.	111	C-540 Frederick–C-552 Achillefs
47	B-435 Constance–B-450 Vincenza	112	C-552 Adelaide–C-563 Cateno
48	B-450 Vazul–B-453 Nadine	113	C-563 Carl–C-600 Mary V.
49	B-453 Oscar–B-500 F.S.	114	C-600 Maria–C-613 John H.
50	B-500 Felici–B-515 Giuseppe	115	C-613 Josef–C-616 Elisabeth L.
51	B-515 Giuseppe–B-520 Marjorie	116	C-616 Elias–C-620 Izrail
52	B-520 Matt–B-525 Angela	117	C-620 Jakob–C-622 Alfonso
53	B-525 Amalie–B-530 Lucia	118	C-622 Alvaro–C-623 Henrietta
54	B-530 Louis–B-535 F.D.	119	C-623 Henry, L.–C-624 Ines
55	B-535 Rosa–B-552 Joanna	120	C-624 James Wm.–C-630 Antonio
56	B-522 Karolia–B-600 Harry	121	C-630 Antonia, A.–C-632 Patrick
57	B-600 Hans–B-612 Erzsi	122	C-632 Paul–C-636 Fanny
58	B-612 Euthihia–B-620 Afanseos	123	C-636 Flora–C-640 Patrick
59	B-620 Alberdina–B-620 G. Jorgje	124	C-640 Paulina–C-642 Vito
60	B-620 Giuseppe–B-620 Maurice de	125	C-642 Vincenzo–C-650 Maria
61	B-620 Maurice–B-622 Adam	126	C-650 Mayer–C-652 Marton
62	B-622 Adam–B-623 Andree	127	C-652 Marya–C-655 Pavel
63	B-623 Angelo–B-624 Joseph	128	C-655 Philip–D-100 Nicola
64	B-624 Juliska–B-625 Lina	129	D-100 Nellie–D-120 Joseph
65	B-625 Lorenzo–B-626 Mave M.	130	D-120 Jozsef–D-126 Francis
66	B-626 Matthias–B-630 Maurice	130a	D-126 Francoise–D-130 Emilie
67	B-630 Michael–B-632 Maria	131	D-130 Emanuel–D-140 Christina
68	B-632 Marya–B-634 Maria	132	D-140 Cornelius–D-145 Angelo
69	B-634 Marco–B-636 Guillaume	133	D-145 Angela–D-152 Matteo
70	B-636 Hans–B-646 Viktor	134	D-152 Nicola–D-161 Yves
71	B-650 Mr.–B-650 Gladys E.	135	D-162 Adam–D-164 Stefan
72	B-650 Gorden–B-650 Pierina	136	D-164 Thomas–D-200 Cornelius
73	B-650 Pila–B-652 Cora Lee	137	D-200 Daniel–D-200 Robert
74	B-652 Davis–B-652 Piotr	138	D-200 Rosa–D-220 Ana
75	B-652 Petrone–B-653 Louis S.	139	D-220 Anadina–D-223 Antonio
76	B-653 Lucrezia, M.–B-655 Patrick	140	D-223 Antonio–D-230 Marthe
77	B-655 Patrick–B-663 Centanni	141	D-230 Matheus–D-236 Karl
78	B-663 Bolisario–C-120 Arturo	142	D-236 Luigi–D-242 Leslie
79	C-120 Antonio–C-130 Rosae	143	D-242 Marko–D-250 Patrick
80	C-130 Salvatore–C-140 Vincenzo	144	D-250 Pietro–D-253 Argerio
81	C-140 Vincenzo–C-150 Paul	145	D-253 Benedetto–D-256 Helmut
82	C-150 Pietro–C-162 Francis	146	D-256 Josef–D-262 Maddalena
83	C-162 Gerardo–C-200 Arthur	147	D-262 Maria–D-300 Albert
84	C-200 Arthur–C-200 Maria	148	D-300 Aniar–D-320 Peter
85	C-200 Maria, A.–C-220 Antonio, F.	149	D-320 Rasche–D-352 Marie
86	C-220 Augustin–C-230 Gioacchino	150	D-352 Nicola–D-400 Daniel
87	C-230 Gertie, B.–C-234 Domenico	151	D-400 Dorothea–D-411 Bortold
88	C-234 Domenico–C-236 Antonio	152	D-411 Cesare–D-416 Leopoldo
89	C-236 Artun, F.–C-241 Muriel, E.	153	D-416 Mandel–D-420 Robert
90	C-241 Michl–C-250 John	154	D-420 Rosa–D-425 G.J.
91	C-250 Jan–C-253 Weronika	155	D-425 Giovanni–D-440 Adelaide
92	C-253 Vincenzo–C-263 Emily	156	D-440 Camillo–D-453 Barbara

Roll	Contents
157	D-453 Carmela–D-500 Alf
158	D-500 Alfred–D-500 Moira
159	D-500 Moritz–D-516 Carmine
160	D-516 Chaim–D-520 Gilberto
161	D-520 Giovanni–D-521 Norman
162	D-521 Totros–D-524 Lucia
163	D-524 Luigi–D-530 Carmela
164	D-530 Caterina–D-535 Pietro
165	D-535 Pierre, Mrs.–D-540 Giovanni
166	D-540 Giovanni–D-550 Angel
167	D-550 Angela–D-552 Patricio
168	D-552 Patrick–D-560 Patrick
169	D-560 Paul–D-563 Nicodemo
170	D-563 Nicola–D-612 Antoinette
171	D-612 Anton–D-620 Dora
172	D-620 Doris–D-620 Virgilio
173	D-620 Virginia–D-624 Tzchok
174	D-624 Van–D-631 Zivan
175	D-632 A.D.–D-651 Rywka
176	D-651 S.–D-666 Marie
177	E-000 Aarne–E-152 Thomas
178	E-152 William–E-214 Alejandro
179	E-214 Alejandro–E-242 Gilda
180	E-242 Gilke–E-256 Volkeline
181	E-256 Walli–E-350 Lysbeth
182	E-350 McKay–E-420 Helani
183	E-420 Helen–E-452 Gyorgy
184	E-452 H. Enrigue–E-524 Martan
185	E-524 Martha–E-616 Zenta
186	E-620 Abram–E-625 Syverto
187	E-625 T.–F-000 John
188	F-000 John–F-162 Gyorgy
189	F-162 Hans–F-200 Lucci
190	F-200 Lucia–F-230 Ewa
191	F-230 F. Paola–F-245 Bume
192	F-245 Calogero–F-260 Elma
193	F-260 Elna–F-300 Michelangelo
194	F-300 Michele–F-351 Vicha
195	F-352 Achille–F-400 Pietrina
196	F-400 Pietro–F-420 Enrichetta
197	F-420 Enrico–F-425 Chas
198	F-425 Charles–F-432 Jwan
199	F-432 Kalena–F-452 John Peter
200	F-452 John Theodore–F-463 Myles
201	F-463 Nancy–F-520 Vojtech
202	F-520 W.–F-532 Mutro
203	F-532 Nachman–F-563 Rose
204	F-563 Ruth–F-612 Antonina
205	F-612 Antonio–F-620 Mari
206	F-620 Maria–F-623 Elia
207	F-623 Elias–F-625 Quirino
207a	F-625 R.–F-630 Kyriakoula
208	F-630 L. Gerald–F-635 Carolina M.
209	F-635 Carolina M.–F-636 Sara Jane
210	F-636 Scheindle–F-650 Jose S.
211	F-650 John–F-652 Franzo
212	F-652 Fred–F-652 Pietro
213	F-652 Politrini–F-654 Vituccio
214	F-654 Walenty–F-656 Francesco
215	F-656 Francesco–F-660 Vincenzina
216	F-660 Vincenzo–G-130 Martins
217	G-130 Mary–G-160 Pecovic
218	G-160 Pedro–G-200 Jose S.
219	G-200 Jose F.–G-220 Mariana
220	G-220 Marianna–G-234 Giuseppa
221	G-234 Giuseppe–G-245 Ronald
222	G-245 Rosa–G-255 Nieves
223	G-255 Nikola–G-300 Pioter
224	G-300 Piotr–G-325 Arminia
225	G-325 Arnold–G-352 Norma E.
226	G-352 Norman–G-400 Cornelius
227	G-400 Cornelius–G-410 Izeren
228	G-410 J. Leib–G-420 Davis
229	G-420 Dawid–G-422 Margueritte
230	G-422 Maria–G-426 Vsevolod
231	G-426 W.–G-432 Beila
232	G-432 Aristide–G-435 Moise
233	G-435 Moische–G-451 August
234	G-451 Balars–G-460 Ryszla
235	G-460 Sabina–G-514 Constantino
236	G-514 Constantinos–G-520 Nella
237	G-520 Nellie–G-524 Pedro N.
238	G-524 Pedro P.–G-534 Giuseppe
239	G-534 Giuseppe–G-550 Theodore
240	G-550 Thomas–G-600 Mary Clemency
241	G-600 Mary D.–G-612 Juli
242	G-612 Julia–G-615 Petres
243	G-615 Peter–G-620 Carolina T.
244	G-620 Caroline–G-620 Johann
245	G-620 Johann–G-620 Phatim
246	G-620 Philip–G-622 Christina
247	G-622 Christine–G-624 Franjo
248	G-624 Frank–G-625 Petris
249	G-625 Petro–G-630 Mancel
250	G-630 Manuel–G-635 Chail
251	G-635 Chaim–G-640 Ella
252	G-640 Ellen–G-650 Elizabeth
253	G-650 Elizabeth–G-651 Feiga
254	G-651 Feige–G-652 Ozik
255	G-652 P.A.–G-653 William
256	G-653 William–G-660 Humberto
257	G-660 Juni–H-120 Lydia S.
258	H-120 M.I.–H-155 Catherine
259	H-155 Catherine–H-163 Johannes
260	H-163 John–H-200 John
261	H-200 John–H-216 Ewald
262	H-216 Fajgaesters–H-232 Kurtl
263	H-232 Ladislaus–H-246 Szymon
264	H-246 T.–H-252 William R.
265	H-252 William R.–H-300 Emilia
266	H-300 Emily–H-324 Zuzana
267	H-325 A.–H-355 Johanne
268	H-355 Johannes–H-400 Mary
269	H-400 Mary–H-420 Alftanas
270	H-420 Alice–H-422 Brynjulf
271	H-422 C. Marie–H-432 Justyne
272	H-432 K. Albert–H-452 Joel
273	H-452 Johan–H-500 Alfons
274	H-500 Alfred–H-516 Johannus
275	H-516 John–H-522 Prokop
276	H-522 R.W.–H-525 Hendrick A.A.
277	H-525 Hendrick–H-530 Fyzoo
278	H-530 G.–H-536 Myrtle
279	H-536 N. George–H-550 Wilfrid
280	H-550 Wilhelm–H-562 Otto
281	H-562 P. Emils–H-613 Gyorgj
282	H-613 Gyorgy–H-620 Gyuro
283	H-620 H.–H-622 Syzman
284	H-622 Tacyaneva–H-630 Axel R.
285	H-630 B.R.J.–H-632 Windsor

Roll	Contents	Roll	Contents
286	H-632 Winifred–H-650 Bulko A.	350	K-620 Ella–K-620 Theresia
287	H-650 Cato F.–I-143 Francesco	351	K-620 Theresie–K-622 Paleologos
288	I-143 G. Antonio–I-212 Bosko	352	K-622 Palne–K-624 Konstantin
289	I-212 Caim–I-250 Dung	353	K-624 Konstantina–K-625 Vaclaw
290	I-250 Eberhardt–I-362 Augusto	354	K-625 Vadil–K-632 Marie
291	I-362 Balac F.–I-514 D. Elias	355	K-632 Marie E.–K-642 Charlotta O.
292	I-514 Dante–I-525 Bulino	356	K-642 Charlotte–K-650 Katarina
293	I-525 C. Buffoni–I-560 Brigida G.	357	K-650 Katerine–K-653 Isidor
294	I-560 Calla A.–J-100 Magnus	358	K-653 Isidore–L-000 Corneluis H.D.
295	J-100 Max–J-200 Czili	359	L-000 Cornelius–L-100 George R.
296	J-200 Daba–J-210 Ousem	360	L-100 George T.–L-120 Dyny
297	J-210 P.–J-212 Nilola	361	L-120 E.–L-122 Minia
298	J-212 Nils–J-225 Szpasoja	362	L-122 Minna–L-132 Moische L.
299	J-225 Tekla–J-250 Jame	363	L-132 Moise–L-150 Kussiel
300	J-250 James–J-300 Gustav	364	L-150 L.–L-160 Gaetano
301	J-300 H.–J-450 Mysche	365	L-160 Gaetana–L-163 Leonardo
302	J-450 N.–J-520 Charles H.M.	366	L-163 Leoncio–L-200 Charlia
303	J-520 Charles J.–J-520 Ludweiki	367	L-200 Charlotte–L-200 Julia
304	J-520 Ludmila–J-522 Alzbeta	368	L-200 Julia–L-200 Vincenzo
305	J-522 Amalia–J-525 Alfred	369	L-200 Vincenzo–L-220 Ignazio
306	J-525 Alfred–J-525 Edith	370	L-220 Ignio–L-222 Wawrzyniec
307	J-525 Edith–J-525 Herania	371	L-222 Wazlaw–L-232 Serafin
308	J-525 Herbert–J-525 Karl	372	L-232 Serafina–L-250 Berta
309	J-525 Karl W.–J-525 Rorghild J.	373	L-250 Bertha–L-252 Pawel
310	J-525 Rosa–J-542 Ludwig	374	L-252 Pawet–L-260 Mauro
311	J-534 Pasquale–J-620 Janos	375	L-260 Max–L-265 Renne
311a	J-620 Janos–J-620 Mihal	376	L-265 Repeka–L-320 Janos
312	J-620 Mihaly–J-626 Wtasylstan	377	L-320 Janos–L-350 Giuseppe
313	J-630 A.–K-100 Fred G.	378	L-350 Giuseppe–L-362 Leie
314	K-100 Frederick–K-120 Lajos	379	L-362 Leif I.–L-454 Yenork
315	K-120 Lajos–K-125 Ovsanna	380	L-455 Adla–L-500 Lydia de
316	K-125 P.–K-145 Ezra	381	L-500 Lyla M.–L-516 Antonina
317	K-145 F.–K-155 Jentze	382	L-516 Antonina–L-520 Anna
318	K-155 Jerome–K-165 Szymon J.	383	L-520 Anna–L-520 Rosa
319	K-165 Tadeus–K-200 Karini	384	L-520 M. Teresa–L-523 Edvin A.
320	K-200 Karl–K-213 Zose	385	L-523 Edward–L-526 Olga
321	K-214 Abram–K-220 Ludwica	386	L-526 Olgier–L-534 Leonard
322	K-220 Ludwig–K-231 Dragica	387	L-534 Leonhard–L-550 Elmar
323	K-231 Eduard–K-240 Berty	388	L-550 Elsa–L-563 Barrett H.
324	K-240 Bessie–K-243 Rudolf	389	L-563 Barte–I-616 Emil
325	K-243 Sabina–K-250 Thekla	390	L-616 Emile–L-625 Ernfrid
326	K-250 Theodor–K-255 Alesea	391	L-625 Ernst–L-632 Hans
327	K-255 Alex–K-260 Lydia	392	L-632 Hans–L-656 Leil
328	K-260 M.–K-300 Willem	393	L-656 Leiser–M-150 Frits
329	K-300 William–K-320 Uzen	394	M-150 G. Ewald–M-200 Elfrida
330	K-320 V. Angelica–K-325 Kyriak	395	M-200 Elsa–M-200 Jozco
331	K-325 Lajos–K-360 Anton	396	M-200 Jozef–M-200 Tommaso
332	K-360 Antoni–K-400 Marinus J.	397	M-200 Tommaso–M-216 Don
333	K-400 Mario G.–K-414 Szymon	398	M-216 Donald–M-220 Igdrzej
334	K-414 Tamas–K-420 Kate A.	399	M-220 Ignac–M-221 Karoline
335	K-420 Katerina–K-422 Roman	400	M-221 Karoly–M-230 Maria
336	K-422 Romela–K-430 Zygfryde	401	M-230 Maria–M-235 Alice T.
337	K-431 Aage–K-450 Julia S.	402	M-235 Alicia–M-236 Ciacoumis
338	K-450 Julian–K-452 Magdalena	403	M-236 Giambattista–M-240 Arsenio
339	K-452 Magdalene–K-456 Johanne	404	M-240 Arthur–M-240 Katarzyna
340	K-456 Johannes–K-500 Benno	405	M-240 Kate–M-241 Francette
341	K-500 Benny–K-500 Siegfried	406	M-241 Frederick–M-242 Janos
342	K-500 Siegmund–K-520 Abraham W.	407	M-242 Janos–M-242 Stanislaw
343	K-520 Abrahm–K-520 Simonas	408	M-242 Stanislawa–M-245 Eliza R.
344	K-520 Simone–K-525 Josef	409	M-245 Elizabeth–M-246 James
345	K-530 Josip F.–K-532 Oscar V.	410	M-246 James–M-250 Franyo
346	K-532 Oscher–K-550 Ester	411	M-250 Franz–M-250 Owen Leonard
347	K-550 Esther–K-505 Janos	412	M-250 Mason P.–M-252 Dysart
348	K-565 Janosne–K-612 Menasche	413	M-252 ''E''–M-252 Stavroula
349	K-612 Mendel–K-620 Elkune	414	M-252 Stefan–M-254 John

Roll	Contents	Roll	Contents
415	M-254 John–M-255 Ronald	479	N-242 Rosario–N-260 Azra
416	M-255 Rosa–M-260 Francesco	480	N-260 B. Jakab–N-314 August
417	M-260 Francesco–M-260 Philippine	481	N-314 Battista–N-350 Jaroslaw
418	M-260 Phoebe–M-262 Josef	482	N-350 Jesus–N-420 Ann
419	M-262 Josef–M-263 Lydia A.	483	N-420 Anna–N-425 Johan M.
420	M-263 M.–M-265 Maria	484	N-425 Johan N.–N-450 Anne A.
421	M-265 Maria–M-300 Mariantonio	485	N-450 Annie–N-520 Staza
422	M-300 Marie–M-320 Fusajiro	486	N-520 Stefan–N-550 Mia
423	M-320 Matthews G.–M-321 Izzet	487	N-550 Michael–N-622 Juzopas
424	M-321 J. Albertine–M-324 Lucas	488	N-622 Kachadour–N-642 Lukacz
425	M-324 Lucia–M-326 Marguerite	489	N-642 M. Henry–O-155 Aysig
426	M-326 Maria–M-346 Gustave A.	490	O-155 Barbetta–O-200 Joseph B.
427	M-346 Hanna–M-360 Jose Silva	491	O-200 Josephine–O-235 Thinasi
428	M-360 Josef–M-400 Andon	492	O-235 Thomas–O-250 Jasuka
429	M-400 Andras–M-400 Petri	493	O-250 Jean–O-263 James O.
430	M-400 Petro–M-420 Antonina	494	O-263 Jan–O-354 Mary
431	M-420 Antonio–M-420 Milna	495	O-354 Mary–O-416 Joaquim M.
432	M-420 Milo–M-423 Czipre	496	O-416 John–O-425 Charles
433	M-423 Danilo–M-430 Christina J.	497	O-425 Charles–O-425 Ole
434	M-430 Christine–M-436 Hendrich	498	O-425 Ole–O-500 Henry
435	M-436 Handrik–M-450 Lucette Y.	499	O-500 Henry–O-550 Sventure
436	M-450 Lucia–M-452 Johannis	500	O-550 Tanel–O-624 Fre.
437	M-452 John–M-456 Froim	501	O-624 Gaetano–O-645 Vittorio E.
438	M-456 Milner G.–M-460 Elizabeth	502	O-645 Wassia–P-100 Margaretha
439	M-460 Elizabeth–M-460 Marcedea	503	P-100 Margarethe–P-122 Hyre
440	M-460 Marcel–M-465 Stylianos	504	P-122 Ignac–P-140 Maria O.
441	M-465 Teoronia–M-500 Nicol	505	P-140 Maria R.–P-153 Rudolph
442	M-500 Nicola–M-520 Conceszia	506	P-153 S. Amatia–P-200 Dominic A.
443	M-520 Concetta–M-520 Paufilo	507	P-200 Domenica–P-200 Mietle
444	M-520 Paul–M-522 Saveria	508	P-200 Miguel–P-200 Dimitr
445	M-522 Saverio–M-525 Antonio	509	P-220 Domitri–P-226 Zuzanna
446	M-525 Antonio–M-525 Willem R.	510	P-230 Abram A.–P-234 Michelangelo
447	M-525 William–M-530 Pezelj	511	P-234 Tommaso–P-240 Giovanni
448	M-530 Philip–M-532 Maria	512	P-240 Giovanni–P-242 Xenophen
449	M-532 Maria–M-534 Maria	513	P-242 Yvonne–P-250 Mansueto
450	M-534 Maria–M-536 James	514	P-250 Manuel–P-254 Lucien H.
451	M-536 Jan–M-550 Mary	515	P-254 Luigi–P-262 Myo
452	M-550 Mary–M-560 Carmen R.	516	P-262 Nachama–P-300 Massimino
453	M-560 Carmina–M-563 Henri L.	517	P-300 Matthew–P-322 Johannis
454	M-563 Henrietta–M-600 Florence	518	P-322 John–P-340 William I.
455	M-600 Florence–M-600 Louis	519	P-340 Wincet–P-360 Eduardo G.
456	M-600 Louis–M-600 Willis	520	P-360 Edward–P-362 Anicha
457	M-600 William–M-614 Maria B.	521	P-362 Aniela–P-362 Giuseppe
458	M-614 Maria C.–M-620 Giovanni	522	P-362 Giuseppe–P-362 Maria
458a	M-620 Giovanni–M-620 Giuseppe	523	P-362 Maria–P-362 Wasurryniec
459	M-620 Giuseppe–M-620 Rosa	524	P-362 Wasyl–P-366 Bruno
460	M-620 Rosa–M-622 Franciszek	525	P-366 Camillo–P-400 Rayalio
461	M-622 Franciszek–M-623 Efrimo	526	P-400 Reginald W.–P-420 Aaro
462	M-623 Efthimios–M-624 Maryanna	527	P-420 Aaron–P-420 Janos
463	M-624 Maryen–M-625 Jessel	528	P-420 Janos–P-420 Wojciech
464	M-625 Jessie–M-626 Snowden	529	P-420 Wojciech–P-425 Carin
465	M-626 Sofia–M-632 Moritz	530	P-425 Carl–P-426 Serafina
466	M-632 Morris–M-635 Erig	531	P-426 Serafino–P-435 Elizabeth M.
467	M-635 Erik–M-635 Mary	532	P-435 Ellen–P-450 Petro
468	M-635 Mary–M-640 Francesco	533	P-450 Petronila–P-453 Kyriakon I.
469	M-640 Francesco–M-650 Carlemal	534	P-453 L. Harry–P-465 Rosa M.
470	M-650 Carlo–M-650 Radomente	535	P-465 Rosalia–P-515 Giuseppe
471	M-650 Rafael–M-653 Szava	536	P-515 Giuseppe–P-521 Szymon
472	M-653 Tadate–N-120 Czerna	537	P-521 Tasos–P-526 Rosa
473	N-120 Dal–N-143 Frode	538	P-526 Rosa M–P-534 Fejga
474	N-143 G. Battista–N-200 Dimitrio	539	P-534 Felice–P-552 Maria
475	N-200 Domenico–N-200 Petar	540	P-552 Maria–P-600 Maria
476	N-200 Peter–N-220 Zynokiti	541	P-600 Maria–P-615 John
477	N-221 Agop–N-240 Francisek	542	P-615 Joseph A.–P-620 George
478	N-240 Franciska–N-242 Rosaria	543	P-620 George–P-620 Pietro

Roll	Contents	Roll	Contents
544	P-620 Pietro–P-622 Domenico	608	S-236 Julia–S-242 Czirla
545	P-622 Domenico–P-623 Sore	609	S-242 Dabrotil–S-250 Samuel A.
546	P-623 Susan–P-625 Ida	610	S-250 Sandor–S-260 Fermin
547	P-625 Ida–P-630 Alina	611	S-260 Ferencz–S-360 Catherin
548	P-630 Aline–P-632 Antonio	612	S-300 Cath–S-310 Dzole
549	P-632 Birisch–P-636 Erna	613	S-310 Earl–S-315 Fera
550	P-636 Ernest–P-650 Armand L.	614	S-315 Ferdinand–S-316 Maria
551	P-650 Armando–P-652 Marian M.	615	S-316 Maria–S-320 Salomon N.
552	P-652 Mario–Q-000 Lam	616	S-320 Salvatore–S-325 Anton
553	Q-000 Lars. L.–Q-640 Beseilde	617	S-325 Antoni–S-334 Frusiana
554	Q-640 Blanca A.–R-100 Giovanni	618	S-334 Steidel, G.–S-342 Heinrich
555	R-100 Giovanni–R-120 Maria	619	S-342 Heinrich–S-350 Emillo
556	R-120 Maria–R-140 Elly	620	S-350 Emily P.–S-351 Petri
557	R-140 Elmer–R-150 Vincenza	621	S-351 Petro–S-352 Rudolf Von
558	R-150 Vincenza–R-156 Izak	622	S-352 Rudolph–S-356 Petar
559	R-156 Jacob–R-163 John V.	623	S-356 Peter–S-361 Pavao
560	R-163 John W.–R-200 Antonio	624	S-361 Pavel–S-362 Ludwina
561	R-200 Antonio–R-200 Elvira	625	S-362 Luigi–S-363 Leonardus
562	R-200 Elvira–R-200 Giuseppe	626	S-363 Leonida–S-365 Giuseppe
563	R-200 Giuseppe–R-200 Luigi	627	S-365 Giuseppe–S-400 Emilian
564	R-200 Luigi–R-200 Pietro	628	S-400 Emilie–S-410 Giovanni
565	R-200 Pietro–R-212 Anica	629	S-410 Giovanni–S-413 Demetrio
566	R-212 Aniela–R-220 Iwan	630	S-413 Demetrios–S-416 Guri
567	R-220 Iwan–R-230 Anna	631	S-416 Gussie–S-420 Indya
568	R-230 Anna–R-234 Arne, I.B.	632	S-420 Ines–S-422 Franjo
569	R-234 Arnold–R-240 Louis	633	S-422 Frank–S-430 Anna Liese
570	R-240 Louis–R-250 Emma	634	S-430 Anna–S-435 Gregoire
571	R-250 Emmanuel–R-251 Jacob	635	S-435 Gregorio–S-452 Andrzei
572	R-251 Jacob–R-252 Leie	636	S-452 Andrzej–S-455 Janku
573	R-252 Leonard–R-255 Kusti	637	S-455 Janos–S-463 Ewa
574	R-255 Ladislas–R-262 Ginendun	638	S-463 Fanny–S-500 Menasche
575	R-262 Giulio–R-300 Beila	639	S-500 Mendel–S-514 Owschia
576	R-300 Beile–R-300 Emma	640	S-514 Pablo L.–S-520 Jan
577	R-300 Emma–R-300 Wilhelm	640a	S-520 Jan–S-520 Jose
578	R-300 Wilhelma–R-320 Szymon	641	S-520 Jose–S-522 Jonos
578a	R-320 Tacka–R-320 Wladinier	642	S-522 Jons–S-525 Emiliano
579	R-320 Wladislaw–R-326 Ivy M.L.	643	S-525 Emilie–S-530 Anna
580	R-326 Izabel–R-351 Erich	644	S-530 Anna–S-530 Helen
581	R-351 Erik G.–R-360 Jacab	645	S-530 Helen–S-530 Nicolaos
582	R-360 Jack–R-365 Edla	646	S-530 Nicolae–S-532 Chaja R.
583	R-365 Edwin–R-430 Gustav	647	S-532 Chaje–S-534 Eveline
584	R-430 H.W. Leopold–R-500 Jose	648	S-534 Evelyn–S-536 Angel
585	R-500 Jose M.–R-520 Annie	649	S-536 Angela–S-536 Minni
586	R-520 Annie–R-522 Mario	650	S-536 Minnie–S-542 Ludvik
587	R-522 Marion–R-532 Emil	651	S-542 Ludwig–S-550 Lizzi
588	R-532 Emile–R-543 Patrick	652	S-550 Lizzie–S-552 Willi
589	R-543 Patrick J.–R-552 Pelagja	653	S-552 William–S-562 Jose R.
590	R-552 Pellegrino–R-563 Riwke	654	S-562 Josef–S-600 Josef
591	R-563 Roald A.–S-100 Andras	655	S-600 Josef–S-612 M. Rosa
592	S-100 Andras–S-100 Micael	656	S-612 Maria–S-620 Arthur M.
593	S-100 Michael–S-120 Josef	657	S-620 Arthur W.–S-620 Petar
594	S-120 Josef–S-123 Owsey	658	S-620 Peter–S-625 Franjo
595	S-123 Pacifico–S-130 Ruzena	659	S-625 Frank–S-632 Josep
596	S-130 Sabastiana–S-140 Alois	660	S-632 Joseph–S-640 Giuseppa
597	S-140 Alois–S-143 Jennie	661	S-640 Giuseppe–S-652 Ellef
598	S-143 Jenny–S-150 Pietrantonic	662	S-652 Ellen–S-660 Estelle
599	S-150 Pietro–S-152 Ottilie	662a	S-660 Ester–S-666 Willy
600	S-152 Otto–S-160 Eliza G.	663	T-000 Tea Tsai–Tan–T-140 Josel
601	S-160 Elizabeth–S-162 Alexandre	664	T-140 Joseph–T-162 Mortiz
602	S-162 Alexandros–S-163 Kristoph	665	T-162 Morris–T-200 Sebastiana
603	S-163 Kristos–S-200 Alberico	666	T-200 Sebastiano–T-224 Rosa
604	S-200 Albert–S-200 Jesica	667	T-224 Salomon–T-242 Rosa
605	S-200 Jessie–S-200 Wiktorya	668	T-242 Evangelos–T-242 Vusilios
606	S-200 Wilhelm–S-225 Ottaviano	669	T-252 Waclaw–T-265 Lydia
607	S-225 Paasqualina–S-236 Jules F.	670	T-265 M. Grazia–T-300 Zuza

Roll	Contents
671	T-300 Zuza–T-360 Frank
672	T-360 Frank–T-416 Ivy
673	T-416 J.E.V.–T-460 Albert P.C.
674	T-460 Albert R.–T-500 Johann
675	T-500 Johann–T-516 Emilia
676	T-516 Emilia–T-520 Maricic
677	T-520 Marie–T-524 Justine
678	T-524 K.–T-530 Secondo
679	T-530 Secondo–T-560 Ewa
680	T-560 Bertha–T-610 May Helen
681	T-610 Mechoidje–T-615 Maria Sofia
682	T-615 Maria–T-620 Maria
683	T-620 Maria–T-623 Marie
684	T-623 Marie–T-626 Dora
685	T-626 Doris–T-640 Berardino
686	T-640 Berardino–T-651 Alessandro
687	T-651 Alessandro–T-653 Charles
688	T-653 Charles–T-660 Leonie
689	T-660 Leonilda–U-420 Melina
690	U-420 Mendel–U-615 Giuseppe
691	U-615 Giuseppe–V-160 Stefan
692	V-160 Stefan–V-210 Szlobodan
693	V-210 Tanios–V-232 Lydie
694	V-232 Maarten–V-243 Antonio
695	V-243 Antonio–V-260 Eleni
696	V-260 Elias–V-322 Bozo
697	V-322 Caroline–V-365 Mariantonia
698	V-365 Marie–V-420 Edvards
698a	V-420 Edward–V-432 Clodomiro
698b	V-432 Concepcion–V-453 Giuseppe
698c	V-453 Giuseppe–V-511 Lucienne
698d	V-511 Maatje–V-523 Geert
698e	V-523 Geert–V-523 Willemine
699	V-523 Willem–V-532 Laurens
700	V-532 Laurent–V-536 Johanna
701	V-536 Johanna–V-536 Henrique
—	*National Archives does not hold roll 702.*
703	V-563 Henry–V-620 Lajos
704	V-620 Lajos–V-632 Francesco
705	V-632 Francesco–V-650 Qyintino
706	V-656 Rachel–W-162 Iwan
707	W-162 J.O.–W-200 Rvart P.
708	W-200 Rubin–W-222 Awrum
709	W-222 Balbina–W-235 Gworge H.
710	W-235 H. Karel–W-242 Werona
711	W-242 Weronika–W-252 Pronciskas
712	W-252 R.–W-256 Louis A.
713	W-256 Louisa–W-300 Elizabeth
714	W-300 Elizabeth–W-320 Erich
715	W-320 Erik–W-325 Juvencio
716	W-325 K. May–W-352 Zofia
717	W-353 Abraham–W-400 Ewalt
718	W-400 Will F.–W-412 Anilian
719	W-412 Anna–W-420 Hart
720	W-420 Harvey–W-420 Werran
721	W-420 Werner–W-425 Elizabeta
722	W-425 Elisabeth–W-426 Emilie
723	W-426 Emily–W-435 Sergej
724	W-435 Serla–W-452 David
725	W-452 David–W-453 Kasis
726	W-453 Kata–W-520 Ion Fon
727	W-520 Iren–W-526 Juzas
728	W-526 Kadesch–W-560 Alfonso
729	W-560 Alfred–W-620 Stanislawa
730	W-620 Stanely T.–W-630 Karl

Roll	Contents
731	W-630 Karl–W-653 Moses
732	W-653 Natalia–Y-436 Maria
733	Y-440 Isabella–Z-100 Lotta
734	Z-100 Louis–Z-152 Franjo
735	Z-152 Frank–Z-200 Nicol
736	Z-200 Nicola–Z-242 Amanda
737	Z-242 Anastasios–Z-262 Josef
738	Z-262 Josef–Z-356 Veron
739	Z-356 W. Raymond–Z-425 Johanna
740	Z-425 John–Z-500 Hussein
741	Z-500 Ian–Z-523 Azriel
742	Z-523 Bara–Z-552 Zeigmund
743	Z-552 Simion–Z-620 Nykola
744	Z-620 Obrad–Z-665 Wasin

Book Indexes to New York Passenger Lists, 1906–1942. T612. 807 rolls. (★ A complete list of rolls has been added.)

These alphabetical indexes to passenger manifests are grouped by shipping line and arranged chronologically by date of arrival in the Port of New York. There is an index for each vessel.

Roll	Shipping Lines	Beginning Dates
1	Italian; Insular	Jan. 10, 1906
2	Italian; Insular	Apr. 23, 1906
3	Italian; Insular	June 23, 1906
4	Austrian; Greek; Russian; Scandinavian; miscellaneous	Jan. 2, 1906
5	Austrian; Greek; Russian; Scandinavian; miscellaneous	May 5, 1906
6	Austrian; Greek; Russian; Scandinavian; miscellaneous	Sept. 14, 1906
7	Hamburg-American	Jan. 5, 1905
8	Hamburg-American	Apr. 24, 1906
9	Hamburg-American	July 15, 1906
10	Hamburg-American	Oct. 20, 1906
11	North German Lloyd	Jan. 4, 1906
12	North German Lloyd	Apr. 20, 1906
13	North German Lloyd	July 18, 1906
14	North German Lloyd	Nov. 1, 1906
15	Red Star; Holland-American	Jan. 3, 1906
16	Red Star; Holland-American	May 29, 1906
17	Red Star; Holland-American	Sept. 4, 1906
18	Cunard; Anchor	Jan. 1, 1906
19	Cunard; Anchor	Apr. 17, 1906
20	Cunard; Anchor	June 19, 1906
21	Cunard; Anchor	Sept. 1, 1906
22	Cunard; Anchor	Nov. 7, 1906
23	White Star; American	Jan. 1, 1906
24	White Star; American	May 10, 1906
25	White Star; American	July 19, 1906
26	White Star; American	Oct. 12, 1906
27	French; Fabre	Jan. 1, 1906
28	French; Fabre	May 19, 1906
29	French; Fabre	Sept. 8, 1906
30	Italian; Prince	Jan. 16, 1907
31	Italian; Prince	May 8, 1907
32	Italian; Prince	Aug. 2, 1907
33	Italian; Prince	Nov. 23, 1907
34	Russian; Greek; Austro-Americana	Jan. 2, 1907
35	Russian; Greek; Austro-Americana	May 10, 1907
36	Russian; Greek; Austro-Americana	Sept. 5, 1907
37	Scandinavian-American; Spanish; miscellaneous	Jan. 12, 1907

Roll	Shipping Lines	Beginning Dates	Roll	Shipping Lines	Beginning Dates
38	Scandinavian-American; Spanish; miscellaneous	July 23, 1907	97	Hamburg-American	Jan. 8, 1909
39	Hamburg-American	Jan. 6, 1907	98	Hamburg-American	Jan. 11, 1909
40	Hamburg-American	May 5, 1907	99	Hamburg-American	May 2, 1909
41	Hamburg-American	June 30, 1907	100	Hamburg-American	Aug. 26, 1909
42	Hamburg-American	Sept. 5, 1907	101	North German Lloyd	Jan. 3, 1909
43	Red Star; Holland-American	Jan. 9, 1907	102	North German Lloyd	Mar. 30, 1909
44	Red Star; Holland-American	Mar. 28, 1907	103	North German Lloyd	June 2, 1909
45	Red Star; Holland-American	June 4, 1907	104	North German Lloyd	Sept. 14, 1909
46	Red Star; Holland-American	Sept. 24, 1907	105	Red Star; Holland-American	Jan. 5, 1909
47	North German Lloyd	Jan. 4, 1907	106	Red Star; Holland-American	Apr. 13, 1909
48	North German Lloyd	Apr. 7, 1907	107	Red Star; Holland-American	Aug. 2, 1909
49	North German Lloyd	June 6, 1907	108	Cunard; Anchor	Jan. 2, 1909
50	North German Lloyd	Aug. 21, 1907	109	Cunard; Anchor	Mar. 27, 1909
51	North German Lloyd	Nov. 6, 1907	110	Cunard; Anchor	June 7, 1909
52	Cunard; Anchor	Jan. 4, 1907	111	Cunard; Anchor	Sept. 8, 1909
53	Cunard; Anchor	Apr. 13, 1907	112	White Star; American	Jan. 2, 1909
54	Cunard; Anchor	June 19, 1907	113	White Star; American	Mar. 31, 1909
55	Cunard; Anchor	Sept. 4, 1907	114	White Star; American	June 27, 1909
56	Cunard; Anchor	Nov. 11, 1907	115	White Star; American	Sept. 26, 1909
57	White Star; American	Jan. 3, 1907	116	French; Fabre	Jan. 4, 1909
58	White Star; American	Mar. 3, 1907	117	French; Fabre	May 8, 1909
59	White Star; American	May 19, 1907	118	French; Fabre	Aug. 31, 1909
60	White Star; American	Aug. 3, 1907	119	Italian	Jan. 11, 1910
61	White Star; American	Oct. 26, 1907	120	Italian	Apr. 15, 1910
62	French; Fabre	Jan. 7, 1907	121	Italian	June 29, 1910
63	French; Fabre	May 10, 1907	122	Austrian; Greek; Russian	Jan. 4, 1910
64	French; Fabre	Aug. 17, 1907	123	Austrian; Greek; Russian	June 9, 1910
65	Italian; Prince	Jan. 8, 1908	124	Austrian; Greek; Russian	Oct. 22, 1910
66	Italian; Prince	Apr. 23, 1908	125	Scandinavian-American; Spanish; miscellaneous	Jan. 10, 1910
67	Italian; Prince	Oct. 18, 1908	126	Scandinavian-American; Spanish; miscellaneous	July 12, 1910
68	Austrian; Greek; Russian	Jan. 3, 1908	127	Hamburg-American	Jan. 8, 1910
69	Austrian; Greek; Russian	Dec. 12, 1908	128	Hamburg-American	Feb. 20, 1910
70	Scandinavian-American; Spanish; miscellaneous	Nov. 21, 1908	129	Hamburg-American	June 6, 1910
71	Hamburg-American	Jan. 4, 1908	130	Hamburg-American	Sept. 13, 1910
72	Hamburg-American	June 18, 1908	131	North German Lloyd	Jan. 3, 1910
73	North German Lloyd	Jan. 3, 1908	132	North German Lloyd	May 4, 1910
74	North German Lloyd	Mar. 30, 1908	133	North German Lloyd	July 5, 1910
75	North German Lloyd	July 21, 1908	134	North German Lloyd	Sept. 23, 1910
76	North German Lloyd and Red Star; Holland-American	Nov. 17, 1908 Jan. 2, 1908	135	Red Star; Uranium; Holland-American	Jan. 6, 1910
77	Red Star; Holland-American	Apr. 29, 1908	136	Red Star; Uranium; Holland-American	Apr. 27, 1910
78	Red Star; Holland-American	Oct. 13, 1908	137	Red Star; Uranium; Holland-American	Aug. 26, 1910
79	Cunard; Anchor	Jan. 4, 1908	138	Cunard; Anchor	Jan. 2, 1910
80	Cunard; Anchor	Mar. 9, 1908	139	Cunard; Anchor	May 2, 1910
81	Cunard; Anchor	June 1, 1908	140	Cunard; Anchor	July 2, 1910
82	Cunard; Anchor	Sept. 1, 1908	141	Cunard; Anchor	Oct. 1, 1910
83	White Star; American	Jan. 4, 1908	142	White Star; American	Jan. 7, 1910
84	White Star; American	Apr. 6, 1908	143	White Star; American	May 1, 1910
85	White Star; American	July 16, 1908	144	White Star; American	Aug. 1, 1910
86	White Star; American	Oct. 30, 1908	145	White Star; American	Nov. 3, 1910
87	French; Fabre	Jan. 6, 1908	146	French; Fabre	Jan. 3, 1910
88	French; Fabre	Apr. 11, 1908	147	French; Fabre	Mar. 26, 1910
89	Italian; Insular	Jan. 13, 1909	148	French; Fabre	July 13, 1910
90	Italian; Insular	Mar. 5, 1909	149	French; Fabre	Nov. 9, 1910
91	Italian; Insular	Apr. 22, 1909	150	Italian	Jan. 17, 1911
92	Italian; Insular	June 14, 1909	151	Italian	Apr. 12, 1911
93	Italian; Insular	Oct. 1, 1909	152	Italian	July 28, 1911
94	Austrian; Greek; Russian; Scandinavian; miscellaneous	Jan. 7, 1909	153	Austrian; Greek; Russian	Jan. 4, 1911
95	Austrian; Greek; Russian; Scandinavian; miscellaneous	July 21, 1909	154	Austrian; Greek; Russian	June 12, 1911
96	Scandinavian-American; Spanish; miscellaneous	Jan. 20, 1909	155	Austrian; Greek; Russian	Dec. 6, 1911

Roll	Shipping Lines	Beginning Dates	Roll	Shipping Lines	Beginning Dates
156	Scandinavian; Spanish; miscellaneous	Jan. 4, 1911	214	Italian	Sept. 3, 1913
157	Scandinavian; Spanish; miscellaneous	Aug. 29, 1911	215	Austrian; Greek; Russian; Scandinavian; Spanish; miscellaneous	Jan. 4, 1913
158	Hamburg-American	Jan. 11, 1911	216	Austrian; Greek; Russian; Scandinavian; Spanish; miscellaneous	May 1, 1913
159	Hamburg-American	Apr. 6, 1911			
160	Hamburg-American	Aug. 7, 1911	217	Austrian; Greek; Russian; Scandinavian; Spanish; miscellaneous	Aug. 4, 1913
161	Hamburg-American	Dec. 21, 1911			
162	Red Star; Holland-American	Jan. 3, 1911	218	Austrian; Greek; Russian; Scandinavian; Spanish; miscellaneous	Nov. 8, 1913
163	Red Star; Holland-American	June 5, 1911			
164	Red Star; Holland-American	Sept. 5, 1911	219	Hamburg-American	Jan. 6, 1913
165	North German Lloyd	Jan. 3, 1911	220	Hamburg-American	May 9, 1913
166	North German Lloyd	Apr. 3, 1911	221	Hamburg-American	Aug. 1, 1913
167	North German Lloyd	Aug. 1, 1911	222	Hamburg-American	Oct. 2, 1913
168	North German Lloyd	Nov. 1, 1911	223	Red Star; Uranium; Holland-American	Jan. 2, 1913
169	Cunard; Anchor	Jan. 3, 1911			
170	Cunard; Anchor	May 2, 1911	224	Red Star; Uranium; Holland-American	May 3, 1913
171	Cunard; Anchor	Aug. 4, 1911			
172	White Star; American	Jan. 1, 1911	225	Red Star; Uranium; Holland-American	Aug. 4, 1913
173	White Star; American	Mar. 3, 1911			
174	White Star; American	June 1, 1911	226	Red Star; Uranium; Holland-American	Nov. 3, 1913
175	White Star; American	Sept. 3, 1911			
176	French; Fabre	Jan. 7, 1911	227	North German Lloyd	Jan. 4, 1913
177	French; Fabre	Apr. 3, 1911	228	North German Lloyd	Apr. 1, 1913
178	French; Fabre	Aug. 4, 1911	229	North German Lloyd	June 1, 1913
179	Austrian; Greek; Russian; Scandinavian; Spanish	Jan. 3, 1912	230	North German Lloyd	Aug. 5, 1913
			231	North German Lloyd	Oct. 1, 1913
180	Austrian; Greek; Russian; Scandinavian; Spanish	May 1, 1912	232	Cunard; Anchor	Jan. 7, 1913
			233	Cunard; Anchor	Mar. 1, 1913
181	Austrian; Greek; Russian; Scandinavian; Spanish	June 2, 1912	234	Cunard; Anchor	June 2, 1913
			235	Cunard; Anchor	Sept. 4, 1913
182	Austrian; Greek; Russian; Scandinavian; Spanish	Aug. 3, 1912	236	Cunard; Anchor	Nov. 12, 1913
			237	White Star; American	Jan. 1, 1913
183	Austrian; Greek; Russian; Scandinavian; Spanish	Nov. 6, 1912	238	White Star; American	Apr. 4, 1913
			239	White Star; American	June 5, 1913
184	Italian	Jan. 1, 1912	240	White Star; American	Aug. 2, 1913
185	Italian	May 4, 1912	241	White Star; American	Oct. 2, 1913
186	Italian	July 27, 1912	242	French; Fabre	Jan. 3, 1913
187	Italian	Nov. 12, 1912	243	French; Fabre	Apr. 2, 1913
188	Hamburg-American	Jan. 5, 1912	244	French; Fabre	July 2, 1913
189	Hamburg-American	Feb. 28, 1912	245	French; Fabre	Sept. 4, 1913
190	Hamburg-American	June 23, 1912	246	Italian	Jan. 12, 1914
191	Hamburg-American	Oct. 10, 1912	247	Italian	Mar. 27, 1914
192	Red Star; Holland-American	Jan. 3, 1912	248	Italian	July 27, 1914
193	Red Star; Holland-American	May 14, 1912	249	Austrian; Greek; Russian	Jan. 5, 1914
194	Red Star; Holland-American	Oct. 1, 1912	250	Austrian; Greek; Russian	May 2, 1914
195	North German Lloyd	Jan. 2, 1912	251	Scandinavian; Spanish; miscellaneous	Jan. 5, 1914
196	North German Lloyd	Apr. 7, 1912			
197	North German Lloyd	June 5, 1912	252	Scandinavian; Spanish; miscellaneous	July 5, 1914
198	North German Lloyd	Aug. 28, 1912			
199	North German Lloyd	Oct. 24, 1912	253	Hamburg-American	Jan. 2, 1914
200	Cunard; Anchor	Jan. 2, 1912	254	Hamburg-American	Apr. 19, 1914
201	Cunard; Anchor	Feb. 11, 1912	255	Hamburg-American	July 11, 1914
202	Cunard; Anchor	May 29, 1912	256	North German Lloyd	Jan. 2, 1914
203	Cunard; Anchor	Sept. 1, 1912	257	North German Lloyd	Mar. 26, 1914
204	White Star; American	Jan. 4, 1912	258	North German Lloyd	June 11, 1914
205	White Star; American	Mar. 10, 1912	259	Red Star; Holland-American	Jan. 8, 1914
206	White Star; American	June 29, 1912	260	Red Star; Holland-American	Mar. 18, 1914
207	White Star; American	Sept. 19, 1912	261	Red Star; Holland-American	July 1, 1914
208	French; Fabre	Jan. 1, 1912	262	Cunard; Anchor	Jan. 4, 1914
209	French; Fabre	Apr. 12, 1912	263	Cunard; Anchor	Apr. 25, 1914
210	French; Fabre	Aug. 18, 1912	264	Cunard; Anchor	Aug. 6, 1914
211	Italian	Jan. 13, 1913			
212	Italian	Apr. 4, 1913			
213	Italian	July 1, 1913			

Roll	Shipping Lines	Beginning Dates	Roll	Shipping Lines	Beginning Dates
265	White Star; American	Jan. 2, 1914	307	White Star; American; Cunard; Anchor; French; Scandinavian	Dec. 1, 1919
266	White Star; American	Apr. 3, 1914	308	Italian; Greek	Jan. 3, 1920
267	White Star; American	May 21, 1914	309	Italian; Greek	Mar. 22, 1920
268	White Star; American	Aug. 12, 1914	310	Italian; Greek	July 2, 1920
269	White Star; American	Oct. 22, 1914	311	Italian; Greek	Nov. 1, 1920
270	French; Fabre	Jan. 3, 1914	312	Red Star; American	Jan. 15, 1920
271	French; Fabre	Mar. 14, 1914	313	Red Star; American	Aug. 22, 1920
272	French; Fabre	June 15, 1914	314	White Star	Jan. 1, 1920
273	Italian; Greek; Russian	Jan. 5, 1915	315	White Star	Apr. 19, 1920
274	Italian; Greek; Russian	May 2, 1915	316	White Star	Aug. 3, 1920
275	Italian; Greek; Russian	Sept. 3, 1915	317	White Star	Sept. 8, 1920
276	Scandinavian; Spanish; miscellaneous	Jan. 2, 1915	318	White Star	Oct. 27, 1920
277	Scandinavian; Spanish; miscellaneous	Aug. 3, 1915	319	French; Fabre	Jan. 7, 1920
278	Red Star; Holland-American; French; Fabre	Jan. 2, 1915	320	French; Fabre	May 4, 1920
279	Red Star; Holland-American; French; Fabre	Aug. 2, 1915	321	French; Fabre	Aug. 12, 1920
280	Cunard; Anchor	Jan. 7, 1915	322	French; Fabre	Nov. 8, 1920
281	White Star; American	Jan. 4, 1915	323	Scandinavian; Spanish; miscellaneous	Jan. 2, 1920
282	White Star; American	July 2, 1915	324	Scandinavian; Spanish; miscellaneous	Apr. 23, 1920
283	Italian; Greek; Russian	Jan. 3, 1916	325	Scandinavian; Spanish; miscellaneous	Aug. 6, 1920
284	Italian; Greek; Russian	May 2, 1916	326	Italian; Greek; Russian	Jan. 2, 1921
285	Italian; Greek; Russian	Oct. 2, 1916	327	Italian; Greek; Russian	Feb. 3, 1921
286	Scandinavian; Spanish; miscellaneous	Jan. 2, 1916	328	Italian; Greek; Russian	June 3, 1921
287	Scandinavian; Spanish; miscellaneous	July 3, 1916	329	Italian; Greek; Russian	Aug. 2, 1921
288	Red Star; Holland-American; French; Fabre	Jan. 2, 1916	330	Italian; Greek; Russian	Nov. 1, 1921
289	Red Star; Holland-American; French; Fabre	June 1, 1916	331	Red Star; Holland-American, North German Line; Royal Mail	Jan. 3, 1921
290	Cunard; Anchor; White Star; American	Jan. 2, 1916	332	Red Star; Holland-American, North German Line; Royal Mail	July 7, 1921
291	Cunard; Anchor; White Star; American	June 4, 1916	333	Red Star; Holland-American, North German Line; Royal Mail	Nov. 1, 1921
292	Cunard; Anchor; White Star; American	Oct. 1, 1916	334	Cunard; Anchor; U.S.T.S.	Jan. 3, 1921
293	Italian; Greek; Spanish; miscellaneous	Jan. 1, 1917	335	Cunard; Anchor; U.S.T.S.	June 4, 1921
294	Italian; Greek; Spanish; miscellaneous	Oct. 22, 1917	336	Cunard; Anchor; U.S.T.S.	Oct. 2, 1921
295	Holland-American; Cunard; Anchor; Scandinavian	Jan. 3, 1917	337	White Star; American; U.S.T.S.; U.S. Mail	Jan. 6, 1921
296	Holland-American; Cunard; Anchor; Scandinavian	Aug. 2, 1917	338	White Star; American; U.S.T.S.; U.S. Mail	July 1, 1921
297	White Star; American; French; Fabre	Jan. 2, 1917	339	White Star; American; U.S.T.S.; U.S. Mail	Aug. 1, 1921
298	White Star; American; French; Fabre	Sept. 8, 1917	340	White Star; American; U.S.T.S.; U.S. Mail	Oct. 11, 1921
299	All lines	Jan. 2, 1918	341	French; Fabre; Baltic	Jan. 3, 1921
300	All lines	Mar. 10, 1918	342	French; Fabre; Baltic	June 3, 1921
301	All lines	June 27, 1918	343	French; Fabre; Baltic	Sept. 10, 1921
302	Italian; Spanish; Greek; miscellaneous	Mar. 2, 1919	344	Scandinavian; Spanish; miscellaneous	Jan. 1, 1921
303	Italian; Spanish; Greek; miscellaneous	Sept. 5, 1919	345	Scandinavian; Spanish; miscellaneous	Sept. 6, 1921
304	White Star; American; Cunard; Anchor; French; Scandinavian	Jan. 1, 1919	346	Italian; Greek	Jan. 2, 1922
305	White Star; American; Cunard; Anchor; French; Scandinavian	June 1, 1919	347	Italian; Greek	May 29, 1922
306	White Star; American; Cunard; Anchor; French; Scandinavian	Sept. 6, 1919	348	Italian; Greek	Aug. 5, 1922
			349	Italian; Greek	Oct. 1, 1922
			350	Red Star; North German Lloyd; Holland-American; Hamburg-American; Royal Mail; American	Jan. 3, 1922
			351	Red Star; North German Lloyd; Holland-American; Hamburg-American; Royal Mail; American	Mar. 23, 1922
			352	Red Star; North German Lloyd; Holland-American; Hamburg-American; Royal Mail; American	June 17, 1922

Roll	Shipping Lines	Beginning Dates
353	Red Star; North German Lloyd; Holland-American; Hamburg-American; Royal Mail; American	Aug. 21, 1922
354	Red Star; North German Lloyd; Holland-American; Hamburg-American; Royal Mail; American	Oct. 26, 1922
355	White Star; Canada-Pacific; American; Cunard; Anchor	Jan. 3, 1922
356	White Star; Canada-Pacific; American; Cunard; Anchor	Apr. 6, 1922
357	White Star; Canada-Pacific; American; Cunard; Anchor	June 5, 1922
358	White Star; Canada-Pacific; American; Cunard; Anchor	July 23, 1922
359	White Star; Canada-Pacific; American; Cunard; Anchor	Aug. 29, 1922
360	White Star; Canada-Pacific; American; Cunard; Anchor	Oct. 9, 1922
361	White Star; Canada-Pacific; American; Cunard; Anchor	Nov. 15, 1922
362	French; Fabre	Jan. 3, 1922
363	French; Fabre	Aug. 11, 1922
364	Scandinavian; Spanish; miscellaneous	Jan. 10, 1922
365	Scandinavian; Spanish; miscellaneous	June 23, 1922
366	Scandinavian; Spanish; miscellaneous	Oct. 21, 1922
367	Italian; Greek	Jan. 19, 1923
368	Italian; Greek	Jan. 9, 1923
369	Italian; Greek	July 1, 1923
370	Italian; Greek	Sept. 5, 1923
371	Italian; Greek	Oct. 1, 1923
372	Red Star; Holland-American; Royal Mail	Jan. 2, 1923
373	Red Star; Holland-American; Royal Mail	June 4, 1923
374	Red Star; Holland-American; Royal Mail	Oct. 1, 1923
375	Hamburg-American; United American; North German Lloyd; Baltic-American	Jan. 1, 1923
376	Hamburg-American; United American; North German Lloyd; Baltic-American	June 7, 1923
377	Hamburg-American; United American; North German Lloyd; Baltic-American	Sept. 1, 1923
378	Cunard; Anchor; Canada-Pacific	Jan. 3, 1923
379	Cunard; Anchor; Canada-Pacific	Apr. 4, 1923
380	Cunard; Anchor; Canada-Pacific	Aug. 1, 1923
381	Cunard; Anchor; Canada-Pacific	Oct. 1, 1923
382	White Star; American; Canada-Pacific	Jan. 1, 1923
383	White Star; American; Canada-Pacific	Apr. 3, 1923
384	White Star; American; Canada-Pacific	July 4, 1923
385	White Star; American; Canada-Pacific	Oct. 3, 1923
386	French; Fabre	Jan. 4, 1923
387	French; Fabre	Aug. 2, 1923
388	Scandinavian; Spanish; miscellaneous	Jan. 3, 1923

Roll	Shipping Lines	Beginning Dates
389	Scandinavian; Spanish; miscellaneous	June 5, 1923
391	Italian; Greek	Jan. 2, 1924
392	Italian; Greek	Feb. 26, 1924
393	Italian; Greek	May 24, 1924
394	Italian; Greek	Aug. 18, 1924
395	Italian; Greek	Oct. 31, 1924
396	Holland-American; Red Star; Royal Mail	Jan. 2, 1924
397	Holland-American; Red Star; Royal Mail	June 14, 1924
398	Hamburg-American	Jan. 1, 1924
399	Hamburg-American	June 21, 1924
400	Hamburg-American	Oct. 9, 1924
401	French; Fabre	Jan. 1, 1924
402	French; Fabre	Oct. 14, 1924
403	Cunard; Anchor; U.S.	Jan. 3, 1924
404	Cunard; Anchor; U.S.	Mar. 6, 1924
405	Cunard; Anchor; U.S.	June 21, 1924
406	Cunard; Anchor; U.S.	Sept. 2, 1924
407	Cunard; Anchor; U.S.	Nov. 19, 1924
408	White Star; American	Jan. 1, 1924
409	White Star; American	Mar. 24, 1924
410	White Star; American	July 9, 1924
411	White Star; American	Sept. 23, 1924
412	White Star; American	Dec. 1, 1924
413	Scandinavian; Spanish; miscellaneous	Jan. 8, 1924
414	Scandinavian; Spanish; miscellaneous	Apr. 14, 1924
415	Scandinavian; Spanish; miscellaneous	Sept. 1, 1924
416	Italian; Greek	Jan. 5, 1925
417	Italian; Greek	May 2, 1925
418	Italian; Greek	Aug. 3, 1925
419	Italian; Greek	Oct. 6, 1925
420	Holland-American; Red Star; Royal Mail	Jan. 12, 1925
421	Holland-American; Red Star; Royal Mail	July 2, 1925
422	Holland-American; Red Star; Royal Mail	Nov. 2, 1925
423	White Star; Canada-Pacific; American	Jan. 6, 1925
424	White Star; Canada-Pacific; American	June 2, 1925
425	Duplicate of Roll #424	
426	White Star; Canada-Pacific; American	Sept. 3, 1925
427	Cunard; Anchor; U.S.T.S.	Jan. 4, 1925
428	Cunard; Anchor; U.S.T.S.	Mar. 4, 1925
429	Cunard; Anchor; U.S.T.S.	May 2, 1925
430	Cunard; Anchor; U.S.T.S.	July 1, 1925
431	Cunard; Anchor; U.S.T.S.	Sept. 1, 1925
432	Cunard; Anchor; U.S.T.S.	Nov. 4, 1925
433	French; Fabre	Jan. 2, 1925
434	French; Fabre	June 1, 1925
435	Hamburg-American; North German Lloyd	Jan. 7, 1925
436	Hamburg-American; North German Lloyd	May 3, 1925
437	Hamburg-American; North German Lloyd	Aug. 3, 1925
438	Hamburg-American; North German Lloyd	Oct. 2, 1925

Roll	Shipping Lines	Beginning Dates
439	Scandinavian; Spanish; miscellaneous	Jan. 3, 1925
440	Scandinavian; Spanish; miscellaneous	June 2, 1925
441	Italian; Greek	Jan. 12, 1926
442	Italian; Greek	Apr. 29, 1926
443	Italian; Greek	July 11, 1926
444	Italian; Greek	Oct. 6, 1926
445	Red Star; Holland-American	Jan. 12, 1926
446	Red Star; Holland-American	June 18, 1926
447	White Star	Jan. 2, 1926
448	White Star	Mar. 29, 1926
449	White Star	July 6, 1926
450	White Star	Sept. 21, 1926
451	Cunard; Anchor; U.S.T.S.	Jan. 7, 1926
452	Cunard; Anchor; U.S.T.S.	Apr. 13, 1926
453	Cunard; Anchor; U.S.T.S.	June 14, 1926
454	Cunard; Anchor; U.S.T.S.	Aug. 16, 1926
455	Cunard; Anchor; U.S.T.S.	Sept. 24, 1926
456	Cunard; Anchor; U.S.T.S.	Nov. 1, 1926
457	French; Fabre	Jan. 2, 1926
458	French; Fabre	July 30, 1926
459	Scandinavian; miscellaneous; Spanish; Baltic-American; Royal Mail	Jan. 5, 1926
460	Scandinavian; miscellaneous; Spanish; Baltic-American; Royal Mail	May 19, 1926
461	Scandinavian; miscellaneous; Spanish; Baltic-American; Royal Mail	Aug. 24, 1926
462	Scandinavian; miscellaneous; Spanish; Baltic-American; Royal Mail	Nov. 5, 1926
463	Hamburg-American; United American; North German Lloyd	Jan. 16, 1926
464	Hamburg-American; United American; North German Lloyd	Mar. 11, 1926
465	Hamburg-American; United American; North German Lloyd	June 8, 1926
466	Hamburg-American; United American; North German Lloyd	Aug. 21, 1926
467	Hamburg-American; United American; North German Lloyd	Oct. 18, 1926
468	Italian; Greek	Jan. 13, 1927
469	Italian; Greek	Mar. 5, 1927
470	Italian; Greek	May 1, 1927
471	Italian; Greek	June 7, 1927
472	Italian; Greek	July 1, 1927
473	Italian; Greek	Sept. 3, 1927
474	Italian; Greek	Nov. 5, 1927
475	Scandinavian; Spanish; French; Fabre	Jan. 5, 1927
476	Scandinavian; Spanish; French; Fabre	Apr. 5, 1927
477	Scandinavian; Spanish; French; Fabre	June 1, 1927
478	Scandinavian; Spanish; French; Fabre	July 5, 1927
479	Scandinavian; Spanish; French; Fabre	Sept. 6, 1927
480	Scandinavian; Spanish; French; Fabre	Nov. 4, 1927
481	Hamburg-American; North German Lloyd	Jan. 3, 1927
482	Hamburg-American; North German Lloyd	Apr. 3, 1927
483	Hamburg-American; North German Lloyd	June 3, 1927
484	Hamburg-American; North German Lloyd	Sept. 1, 1927
485	Hamburg-American; North German Lloyd	Oct. 3, 1927
486	Hamburg-American; North German Lloyd	Oct. 31, 1927
487	White Star; Red Star	Jan. 3, 1927
488	White Star; Red Star	Apr. 13, 1927
489	White Star; Red Star	June 20, 1927
490	White Star; Red Star	Aug. 3, 1927
491	White Star; Red Star	Nov. 2, 1927
492	Cunard; Anchor; U.S.	Jan. 3, 1927
493	Cunard; Anchor; U.S.	Apr. 13, 1927
494	Cunard; Anchor; U.S.	June 13, 1927
495	Cunard; Anchor; U.S.	Aug. 16, 1927
496	Cunard; Anchor; U.S.	Oct. 3, 1927
497	Cunard; Anchor; U.S.	Nov. 21, 1927
498	Italian; Greek	Jan. 1, 1928
499	Italian; Greek	Apr. 7, 1928
500	Italian; Greek	May 19, 1928
501	Italian; Greek	July 10, 1928
502	Italian; Greek	Aug. 18, 1928
503	Italian; Greek	Sept. 29, 1928
504	Italian; Greek	Nov. 10, 1928
505	Spanish; Scandinavian; French; miscellaneous	Jan. 3, 1928
506	Spanish; Scandinavian; French; miscellaneous	Mar. 12, 1928
507	Spanish; Scandinavian; French; miscellaneous	May 9, 1928
508	Spanish; Scandinavian; French; miscellaneous	July 5, 1928
509	Spanish; Scandinavian; French; miscellaneous	Aug. 30, 1928
510	Spanish; Scandinavian; French; miscellaneous	Oct. 16, 1928
511	Holland-American; Hamburg-American; North German Lloyd	Jan. 3, 1928
512	Holland-American; Hamburg-American; North German Lloyd	Mar. 8, 1928
513	Holland-American; Hamburg-American; North German Lloyd	May 14, 1928
514	Holland-American; Hamburg-American; North German Lloyd	July 3, 1928
515	Holland-American; Hamburg-American; North German Lloyd	Aug. 25, 1928
516	Holland-American; Hamburg-American; North German Lloyd	Sept. 11, 1928
517	Holland-American; Hamburg-American; North German Lloyd	Nov. 5, 1928
518	White Star; Red Star	Jan. 3, 1928
519	White Star; Red Star	Apr. 4, 1928
520	White Star; Red Star	June 5, 1928
521	White Star; Red Star	Aug. 14, 1928
522	White Star; Red Star	Oct. 8, 1928
523	Cunard; Anchor; U.S.	Jan. 3, 1928
524	Cunard; Anchor; U.S.	Mar. 20, 1928
525	Cunard; Anchor; U.S.	May 28, 1928
526	Cunard; Anchor; U.S.	Aug. 6, 1928
527	Cunard; Anchor; U.S.	Sept. 14, 1928
528	Cunard; Anchor; U.S.	Oct. 22, 1928

Roll	Shipping Lines	Beginning Dates
529	Italian; Greek	Jan. 5, 1929
530	Italian; Greek	Feb. 13, 1929
531	Italian; Greek	Apr. 6, 1929
532	Italian; Greek	May 21, 1929
533	Italian; Greek	July 8, 1929
534	Italian; Greek	Aug. 27, 1929
535	Italian; Greek	Oct. 15, 1929
536	Italian; Greek	Nov. 19, 1929
537	Scandinavian; Spanish; French; Fabre	Jan. 2, 1929
538	Scandinavian; Spanish; French; Fabre	Apr. 3, 1929
539	Scandinavian; Spanish; French; Fabre	June 3, 1929
540	Scandinavian; Spanish; French; Fabre	July 30, 1929
541	Scandinavian; Spanish; French; Fabre	Sept. 11, 1929
542	Scandinavian; Spanish; French; Fabre	Nov. 4, 1929
543	Holland-American; Hamburg-American	Jan. 2, 1929
544	Holland-American; Hamburg-American	Mar. 26, 1929
545	Holland-American; Hamburg-American	May 5, 1929
546	Holland-American; Hamburg-American	June 30, 1929
547	Holland-American; Hamburg-American	Aug. 19, 1929
548	Holland-American; Hamburg-American	Sept. 16, 1929
549	Holland-American; Hamburg-American	Oct. 20, 1929
550	Holland-American; Hamburg-American	Dec. 2, 1929
551	White Star; Red Star	Jan. 2, 1929
552	White Star; Red Star	Feb. 20, 1929
553	White Star; Red Star	May 9, 1929
554	White Star; Red Star	July 10, 1929
555	White Star; Red Star	Sept. 3, 1929
556	White Star; Red Star	Oct. 14, 1929
557	Cunard; Anchor; U.S.	Jan. 2, 1929
558	Cunard; Anchor; U.S.	Mar. 5, 1929
559	Cunard; Anchor; U.S.	May 4, 1929
560	Cunard; Anchor; U.S.	June 26, 1929
561	Cunard; Anchor; U.S.	Aug. 22, 1929
562	Cunard; Anchor; U.S.	Sept. 30, 1929
563	Cunard; Anchor; U.S.	Nov. 9, 1929
564–570	*See 1931	
571	Italian; Greek	Jan. 2, 1930
572	Italian; Greek	Feb. 19, 1930
573	Italian; Greek	Apr. 15, 1930
574	Italian; Greek	May 19, 1930
575	Italian; Greek	June 17, 1930
576	Italian; Greek	Aug. 11, 1930
577	Italian; Greek	Sept. 24, 1930
578	Italian; Greek	Nov. 7, 1930
579	Italian; Greek	Dec. 6, 1930
580	Spanish; Scandinavian; French; miscellaneous	Jan. 1, 1930
581	Spanish; Scandinavian; French; miscellaneous	Feb. 18, 1930
582	Spanish; Scandinavian; French; miscellaneous	Apr. 28, 1930
583	Spanish; Scandinavian; French; miscellaneous	June 30, 1930
584	Spanish; Scandinavian; French; miscellaneous	Aug. 24, 1930
585	Spanish; Scandinavian; French; miscellaneous	Oct. 7, 1930
586	Spanish; Scandinavian; French; miscellaneous	Dec. 2, 1930
587	Hamburg-American; Holland-American; North German Lloyd	Jan. 2, 1930
588	Hamburg-American; Holland-American; North German Lloyd	Feb. 19, 1930
589	Duplicate of Roll #588	
590	Hamburg-American; Holland-American; North German Lloyd	May 18, 1930
591	Hamburg-American; Holland-American; North German Lloyd	July 3, 1930
592	Hamburg-American; Holland-American; North German Lloyd	Aug. 2, 1930
593	Hamburg-American; Holland-American; North German Lloyd	Sept. 5, 1930
594	Hamburg-American; Holland-American; North German Lloyd	Oct. 2, 1930
595	Hamburg-American; Holland-American; North German Lloyd	Nov. 3, 1930
596	White Star; Red Star	Jan. 2, 1930
597	White Star; Red Star	Apr. 3, 1930
598	White Star; Red Star	July 2, 1930
599	White Star; Red Star	Sept. 2, 1930
600	White Star; Red Star	Oct. 6, 1930
601	Cunard; Anchor	Jan. 2, 1930
602	Cunard; Anchor	Apr. 1, 1930
603	Cunard; Anchor	May 3, 1930
604	Cunard; Anchor	June 30, 1930
605	Cunard; Anchor	Aug. 24, 1930
606	Cunard; Anchor	Oct. 2, 1930
564	Italian; Greek	Jan. 4, 1931
565	Italian; Greek	Jan. 31, 1931
566	Italian; Greek	Mar. 30, 1931
567	Italian; Greek	May 18, 1931
568	Italian; Greek	July 21, 1931
569	Italian; Greek	Sept. 8, 1931
570	Italian; Greek	Oct. 24, 1931
607	Scandinavian; Spanish; French; miscellaneous	Jan. 2, 1931
608	Scandinavian; Spanish; French; miscellaneous	Apr. 3, 1931
609	Scandinavian; Spanish; French; miscellaneous	June 29, 1931
610	Scandinavian; Spanish; French; miscellaneous	Sept. 9, 1931
611	Holland-American; Hamburg-American; North German Lloyd	Jan. 2, 1931
612	Holland-American; Hamburg-American; North German Lloyd	Mar. 13, 1931
613	Holland-American; Hamburg-American; North German Lloyd	May 11, 1931
614	Holland-American; Hamburg-American; North German Lloyd	June 29, 1931
615	Holland-American; Hamburg-American; North German Lloyd	Aug. 11, 1931
616	Holland-American; Hamburg-American; North German Lloyd	Sept. 11, 1931
617	Holland-American; Hamburg-American; North German Lloyd	Oct. 19, 1931

Roll	Shipping Lines	Beginning Dates
618	Cunard; U.S.; Red Star; White Star	Jan. 5, 1931
619	Cunard; U.S.; Red Star; White Star	Feb. 18, 1931
620	Cunard; U.S.; Red Star; White Star	Apr. 14, 1931
621	Cunard; U.S.; Red Star; White Star	May 31, 1931
622	Cunard; U.S.; Red Star; White Star	July 9, 1931
623	Cunard; U.S.; Red Star; White Star	Aug. 18, 1931
624	Cunard; U.S.; Red Star; White Star	Sept. 14, 1931
625	Cunard; U.S.; Red Star; White Star	Nov. 14, 1931
626	Italian; Greek	Jan. 3, 1932
627	Italian; Greek	Feb. 23, 1932
628	Italian; Greek	May 10, 1932
629	Italian; Greek	July 5, 1932
630	Italian; Greek	Sept. 6, 1932
631	Italian; Greek	Oct. 31, 1932
632	Scandinavian; Spanish; French; miscellaneous	Jan. 11, 1932
633	Scandinavian; Spanish; French; miscellaneous	Apr. 19, 1932
634	Scandinavian; Spanish; French; miscellaneous	July 14, 1932
635	Scandinavian; Spanish; French; miscellaneous	Sept. 19, 1932
636	Hamburg-American; Holland-American; North German Lloyd	Jan. 2, 1932
637	Hamburg-American; Holland-American; North German Lloyd	Mar. 12, 1932
638	Hamburg-American; Holland-American; North German Lloyd	June 4, 1932
639	Hamburg-American; Holland-American; North German Lloyd	July 14, 1932
640	Hamburg-American; Holland-American; North German Lloyd	Aug. 26, 1932
641	Hamburg-American; Holland-American; North German Lloyd	Sept. 26, 1932
642	Hamburg-American; Holland-American; North German Lloyd	Nov. 10, 1932
643	Cunard; Anchor; U.S.; White Star; Red Star	Jan. 2, 1932
644	Cunard; Anchor; U.S.; White Star; Red Star	Feb. 3, 1932
645	Cunard; Anchor; U.S.; White Star; Red Star	Apr. 25, 1932
646	Cunard; Anchor; U.S.; White Star; Red Star	July 3, 1932
647	Cunard; Anchor; U.S.; White Star; Red Star	Aug. 25, 1932
648	Cunard; Anchor; U.S.; White Star; Red Star	Sept. 29, 1932
649	Italian; Greek	Feb. 8, 1933
650	Italian; Greek	Jan. 4, 1933
651	Italian; Greek	Apr. 6, 1933
652	Italian; Greek	May 22, 1933
653	Italian; Greek	July 4, 1933
654	Italian; Greek	Aug. 31, 1933
655	Italian; Greek	Nov. 2, 1933
656	Scandinavian; Spanish; French; miscellaneous	Jan. 4, 1933
657	Scandinavian; Spanish; French; miscellaneous	Apr. 24, 1933
658	Scandinavian; Spanish; French; miscellaneous	July 20, 1933
659	Scandinavian; Spanish; French; miscellaneous	Oct. 2, 1933
660	Holland-American; Hamburg-American	Jan. 3, 1933
661	Holland-American; Hamburg-American	Apr. 14, 1933
662	Holland-American; Hamburg-American	June 20, 1933
663	Holland-American; Hamburg-American	Aug. 12, 1933
664	Holland-American; Hamburg-American	Sept. 15, 1933
665	Holland-American; Hamburg-American	Dec. 3, 1933
666	Cunard; U.S.; Red Star; White Star	Jan. 1, 1933
667	Cunard; U.S.; Red Star; White Star	Mar. 6, 1933
668	Cunard; U.S.; Red Star; White Star	May 31, 1933
669	Cunard; U.S.; Red Star; White Star	Aug. 7, 1933
670	Cunard; U.S.; Red Star; White Star	Oct. 13, 1933
671	Italian; Greek	Jan. 3, 1934
672	Italian; Greek	Feb. 28, 1934
673	Italian; Greek	May 3, 1934
674	Italian; Greek	June 7, 1934
675	Italian; Greek	Aug. 2, 1934
676	Italian; Greek	Sept. 27, 1934
677	Italian; Greek	Nov. 11, 1934
678	Scandinavian; Spanish; French; miscellaneous	Jan. 4, 1934
679	Scandinavian; Spanish; French; miscellaneous	May 16, 1934
680	Scandinavian; Spanish; French; miscellaneous	Aug. 2, 1934
681	Scandinavian; Spanish; French; miscellaneous	Nov. 5, 1934
682	Holland-American; Hamburg-American; North German Lloyd	Jan. 4, 1934
683	Holland-American; Hamburg-American; North German Lloyd	May 8, 1934
684	Holland-American; Hamburg-American; North German Lloyd	June 26, 1934
685	Holland-American; Hamburg-American; North German Lloyd	Sept. 2, 1934
686	Holland-American; Hamburg-American; North German Lloyd	Nov. 2, 1934
687	Cunard; Anchor; U.S.; White Star; Red Star	Feb. 20, 1934
688	Cunard; Anchor; U.S.; White Star; Red Star	Jan. 3, 1934
689	Cunard; Anchor; U.S.; White Star; Red Star	May 1, 1934
690	Cunard; Anchor; U.S.; White Star; Red Star	July 12, 1934
691	Cunard; Anchor; U.S.; White Star; Red Star	Sept. 3, 1934
692	Cunard; Anchor; U.S.; White Star; Red Star	Oct. 15, 1934
693	Scandinavian; Spanish; French; miscellaneous	Jan. 8, 1935
694	Scandinavian; Spanish; French; miscellaneous	Apr. 1, 1935
695	Scandinavian; Spanish; French; miscellaneous	June 29, 1935
696	Scandinavian; Spanish; French; miscellaneous	Sept. 16, 1935
697	Italian; Greek	Jan. 3, 1935
698	Italian; Greek	Mar. 14, 1935
699	Italian; Greek	May 23, 1935
700	Italian; Greek	July 20, 1935
701	Italian; Greek	Sept. 7, 1935

Roll	Shipping Lines	Beginning Dates	Roll	Shipping Lines	Beginning Dates
702	Italian; Greek	Oct. 3, 1935	740	Scandinavian; Spanish; French; miscellaneous	July 2, 1937
703	Holland-American; Hamburg-American; North German Lloyd	Jan. 1, 1935	741	Scandinavian; Spanish; French; miscellaneous	Sept. 10, 1937
704	Holland-American; Hamburg-American; North German Lloyd	Apr. 18, 1935	742	Holland-American; Hamburg-American; North German Lloyd	Jan. 3, 1937
705	Holland-American; Hamburg-American; North German Lloyd	June 21, 1935	743	Holland-American; Hamburg-American; North German Lloyd	Feb. 24, 1937
706	Holland-American; Hamburg-American; North German Lloyd	July 5, 1935	744	Holland-American; Hamburg-American; North German Lloyd	Apr. 10, 1937
707	Holland-American; Hamburg-American; North German Lloyd	Sept. 22, 1935	745	Holland-American; Hamburg-American; North German Lloyd	June 25, 1937
708	Holland-American; Hamburg-American; North German Lloyd	Nov. 29, 1935	746	Holland-American; Hamburg-American; North German Lloyd	Aug. 3, 1937
709	Cunard; Anchor; Red Star; White Star	Jan. 1, 1935	747	Holland-American; Hamburg-American; North German Lloyd	Sept. 20, 1937
710	Cunard; Anchor; Red Star; White Star	Feb. 25, 1935	748	Holland-American; Hamburg-American; North German Lloyd	Nov. 1, 1937
711	Cunard; Anchor; Red Star; White Star	May 26, 1935	749	Cunard; Anchor; Red Star; White Star	Jan. 1, 1937
712	Cunard; Anchor; Red Star; White Star	Aug. 16, 1935	750	Cunard; Anchor; Red Star; White Star	Apr. 13, 1937
713	Cunard; Anchor; Red Star; White Star	Oct. 6, 1935	751	Cunard; Anchor; Red Star; White Star	June 29, 1937
714	Italian; Greek	Jan. 4, 1936	752	Cunard; Anchor; Red Star; White Star	Aug. 19, 1937
715	Italian; Greek	May 7, 1936	753	Cunard; Anchor; Red Star; White Star	Sept. 26, 1937
716	Italian; Greek	July 30, 1936	754	Cunard; Anchor; Red Star; White Star	Nov. 29, 1937
717	Italian; Greek	Oct. 1, 1936	755	Italian; Greek	Jan. 5, 1938
718	Scandinavian; Spanish; French; miscellaneous	Jan. 5, 1936	756	Italian; Greek	Mar. 10, 1938
719	Scandinavian; Spanish; French; miscellaneous	Mar. 20, 1936	757	Italian; Greek	Apr. 7, 1938
720	Scandinavian; Spanish; French; miscellaneous	Aug. 11, 1936	758	Italian; Greek	June 2, 1938
721	Scandinavian; Spanish; French; miscellaneous	Oct. 6, 1936	759	Italian; Greek	Aug. 4, 1938
722	Holland-American; Hamburg-American; North German Lloyd	Jan. 1, 1936	760	Italian; Greek	Oct. 7, 1938
723	Holland-American; Hamburg-American; North German Lloyd	June 3, 1936	761	Italian; Greek	Nov. 10, 1938
724	Holland-American; Hamburg-American; North German Lloyd	July 31, 1936	762	Scandinavian; Spanish; French; miscellaneous	Jan. 2, 1938
725	Holland-American; Hamburg-American; North German Lloyd	Sept. 6, 1936	763	Scandinavian; Spanish; French; miscellaneous	June 7, 1938
726	Holland-American; Hamburg-American; North German Lloyd	Oct. 15, 1936	764	Scandinavian; Spanish; French; miscellaneous	Aug. 26, 1938
727	Cunard; U.S.; White Star; Red Star; Anchor	Jan. 1, 1936	765	Scandinavian; Spanish; French; miscellaneous	Oct. 1, 1938
728	Cunard; U.S.; White Star; Red Star; Anchor	May 11, 1936	766	Hamburg-American; Holland-American; North German Lloyd	Jan. 2, 1938
729	Cunard; U.S.; White Star; Red Star; Anchor	Aug. 2, 1936	767	Hamburg-American; Holland-American; North German Lloyd	Feb. 3, 1938
730	Cunard; U.S.; White Star; Red Star; Anchor	Sept. 27, 1936	768	Hamburg-American; Holland-American; North German Lloyd	May 1, 1938
731	Italian; Greek	Jan. 4, 1937	769	Hamburg-American; Holland-American; North German Lloyd	July 1, 1938
732	Italian; Greek	Mar. 4, 1937	770	Hamburg-American; Holland-American; North German Lloyd	Aug. 19, 1938
733	Italian; Greek	May 13, 1937	771	Hamburg-American; Holland-American; North German Lloyd	Sept. 28, 1938
734	Italian; Greek	June 3, 1937	772	Hamburg-American; Holland-American; North German Lloyd	Nov. 3, 1938
735	Italian; Greek	July 29, 1937	773	Cunard; U.S.; White Star; Anchor	Jan. 1, 1938
736	Italian; Greek	Sept. 16, 1937	774	Cunard; U.S.; White Star; Anchor	Apr. 25, 1938
737	Italian; Greek	Oct. 28, 1937	775	Cunard; U.S.; White Star; Anchor	July 18, 1938
738	Scandinavian; Spanish; French; miscellaneous	Jan. 7, 1937	776	Cunard; U.S.; White Star; Anchor	Sept. 11, 1938
739	Scandinavian; Spanish; French; miscellaneous	Mar. 25, 1937	777	Cunard; U.S.; White Star; Anchor	Nov. 3, 1938
			778	Italian; Greek	Jan. 2, 1939

Roll	Shipping Lines	Beginning Dates
779	Italian; Greek	Feb. 13, 1939
780	Italian; Greek	Apr. 27, 1939
781	Italian; Greek	July 6, 1939
782	Italian; Greek	Aug. 24, 1939
783	Italian; Greek	Nov. 9, 1939
784	Scandinavian; Spanish; French; miscellaneous	Jan. 2, 1939
785	Scandinavian; Spanish; French; miscellaneous	May 9, 1939
786	Scandinavian; Spanish; French; miscellaneous	Aug. 2, 1939
787	Scandinavian; Spanish; French; miscellaneous	Oct. 14, 1939
788	Holland-American; Hamburg-American; North German Lloyd	Jan. 1, 1939
789	Holland-American; Hamburg-American; North German Lloyd	Feb. 17, 1939
790	Holland-American; Hamburg-American; North German Lloyd	May 12, 1939
791	Holland-American; Hamburg-American; North German Lloyd	July 4, 1939
792	Holland-American; Hamburg-American; North German Lloyd	Sept. 2, 1939
793	Cunard; U.S.; Anchor; White Star	Jan. 1, 1939
794	Cunard; U.S.; Anchor; White Star	Feb. 13, 1939
795	Cunard; U.S.; Anchor; White Star	May 1, 1939
796	Cunard; U.S.; Anchor; White Star	July 14, 1939
797	Cunard; U.S.; Anchor; White Star	Aug. 29, 1939
798	Italian; Greek	Jan. 1, 1940
799	Italian; Greek	Feb. 1, 1940
800	Italian; Greek	Apr. 2, 1940
801	Miscellaneous	Jan. 1, 1940
802	Miscellaneous	Apr. 14, 1940
803	Miscellaneous	Sept. 23, 1940
804	All lines	Jan. 1, 1941
805	All lines	Apr. 11, 1941
806	All lines	Sept. 27, 1941
807	All lines	Jan. 4, 1942

Passenger and Crew Lists of Vessels Arriving at New York, NY, 1897–1957. T715. 8,892 rolls. (★Rolls 6675–8892 are new listings, and a complete list of rolls has been added.)

Roll	Volumes	Beginning Dates
1	1–2	June 16, 1897
2	3–4	July 1, 1897
3	5–6	July 22, 1897
4	7–8	Aug. 12, 1897
5	9–11	Sept. 1, 1897
6	12–13	Sept. 19, 1897
7	14–15	Oct. 11, 1897
8	16–17	Oct. 13, 1897
9	18–20	Oct. 27, 1897
10	21–22	Nov. 18, 1897
11	23–25	Dec. 1, 1897
12	26–27	Jan. 19, 1898
13	28	Feb. 1, 1898
14	29–30	Feb. 11, 1898
15	31–33	Mar. 2, 1898
16	34–35	Mar. 22, 1898
17	36–37	Apr. 1, 1898
18	38–39	Apr. 12, 1898
19	40–41	Apr. 22, 1898
20	42–43	Apr. 28, 1898
21	44–45	May 6, 1898

Roll	Volumes	Beginning Dates
22	46–48	May 15, 1898
23	49–50	June 1, 1898
24	51–52	June 13, 1898
25	53–54	July 1, 1898
26	55	July 24, 1898
27	56–57	July 26, 1898
28	58–59	Aug. 12, 1898
29	60	Aug. 24, 1898
30	61	Sept. 1, 1898
31	62	Sept. 12, 1898
32	63	Sept. 19, 1898
33	64	Sept. 24, 1898
34	65–66	Sept. 30, 1898
35	67–68	Oct. 6, 1898
36	69	Oct. 18, 1898
37	70	Oct. 21, 1898
38	71–72	Oct. 27, 1898
39	74	Nov. 6, 1898
40	75–76	Nov. 14, 1898
41	77	Nov. 25, 1898
42	78–79	Dec. 2, 1898
43	80	Dec. 16, 1898
44	81–82	Dec. 19, 1898
45	83–84	Jan. 1, 1899
46	85	Jan. 29, 1899
47	86–87	Feb. 17, 1899
48	88–89	Feb. 19, 1899
49	90	Mar. 1, 1899
50	91–92	Mar. 8, 1899
51	93–94	Mar. 17, 1899
52	95	Mar. 26, 1899
53	96–97	Mar. 28, 1899
54	98	Apr. 4, 1899
55	99–100	Apr. 8, 1899
56	101–102	Apr. 15, 1899
57	103	Apr. 22, 1899
58	104	Apr. 24, 1899
59	105	Apr. 29, 1898
60	106–107	May 1, 1899
61	108	May 6, 1899
62	109–110	May 9, 1899
63	111	May 14, 1899
64	112	May 17, 1899
65	113–114	May 19, 1899
66	115	May 25, 1899
67	116–117	May 29, 1899
68	118	June 4, 1899
69	119	June 8, 1899
70	120–121	June 12, 1899
71	122	June 18, 1899
72	123	June 23, 1899
73	124–125	June 27, 1899
74	126	July 8, 1899
75	127–128	July 13, 1899
76	129–130	July 26, 1899
77	131	Aug. 7, 1899
78	132–133	Aug. 11, 1899
79	134–135	Aug. 22, 1899
80	136	Sept. 1, 1899
81	137–138	Sept. 5, 1899
82	139–140	Sept. 13, 1899
83	141–142	Sept. 21, 1899
84	143	Oct. 1, 1899
85	144–145	Oct. 4, 1899
86	146	Oct. 12, 1899

Roll	Volumes	Beginning Dates	Roll	Volumes	Beginning Dates
87	147–148	Oct. 13, 1899	152	250–251	Oct. 3, 1900
88	149–150	Oct. 22, 1899	153	252	Oct. 8, 1900
89	151	Oct. 29, 1899	154	253	Oct. 16, 1900
90	152–153	Nov. 2, 1899	155	254–255	Oct. 19, 1900
91	154–155	Nov. 9, 1899	156	256–257	Oct. 25, 1900
92	156	Nov. 17, 1899	157	258	Nov. 1, 1900
93	157–158	Nov. 20, 1899	158	259	Nov. 5, 1900
94	159–160	Nov. 28, 1899	159	260–261	Nov. 10, 1900
95	161	Dec. 5, 1899	160	262	Nov. 19, 1900
96	162	Dec. 10, 1899	161	263–264	Nov. 26, 1900
97	163	Dec. 18, 1899	162	265–266	Nov. 28, 1900
98	164–165	Dec. 21, 1899	163	267–268	Dec. 6, 1900
99	166	Jan. 2, 1900	164	269–270	Dec. 17, 1900
100	167–168	Jan. 12, 1900	165	271	Dec. 22, 1900
101	169–170	Jan. 26, 1900	166	272	Dec. 27, 1900
102	171	Feb. 7, 1900	167	273	Jan. 2, 1901
103	172–173	Feb 12, 1900	168	274–275	Jan. 8, 1901
104	174–175	Feb. 24, 1900	169	276	Jan. 25, 1901
105	176	Mar. 5, 1900	170	277–278	Feb. 2, 1901
106	177–178	Mar. 7, 1900	171	279–280	Feb. 10, 1901
107	179–180	Mar. 12, 1900	172	281–282	Feb. 21, 1901
108	181	Mar. 19, 1900	173	283–284	Feb. 27, 1901
109	182–183	Mar. 23, 1900	174	285–286	Mar. 4, 1901
110	184	Mar. 28, 1900	175	287	Mar. 13, 1901
111	184–185	Apr. 2, 1900	176	288–289	Mar. 15, 1901
112	187	Apr. 5, 1900	177	290–291	Mar. 20, 1901
113	188–189	Apr. 7, 1900	178	292	Mar. 26, 1901
114	190–191	Apr. 13, 1900	179	293–294	Mar. 28, 1901
115	192	Apr. 17, 1900	180	295–296	Apr. 1, 1901
116	193	Apr. 20, 1900	181	297–298	Apr. 5, 1901
117	194–195	Apr. 23, 1900	182	299–300	Apr. 8, 1901
118	196	Apr. 28, 1900	183	301–302	Apr. 11, 1901
119	197–198	May 1, 1900	184	303	Apr. 14, 1901
120	199	MAy 10, 1900	185	304	Apr. 18, 1901
121	200–201	May 12, 1900	186	305–306	Apr. 22, 1901
122	203	May 16, 1900	187	307	Apr. 24, 1901
123	204–205	May 17, 1900	188	308–309	Apr. 27, 1901
124	206	May 20, 1900	189	310	Apr. 30, 1901
125	207	May 25, 1900	190	311–312	May 1, 1901
126	207	May 26, 1900	191	313	May 5, 1901
127	208	May 29, 1900	192	314–315	May 6, 1901
128	209	May 31, 1900	193	316	May 9, 1901
129	210–211	June 2, 1900	194	317–318	May 11, 1901
130	212–213	June 5, 1900	195	319–320	May 14, 1901
131	214	June 9, 1900	196	321	May 17, 1901
132	215	June 12, 1900	197	322–323	May 19, 1901
133	216–217	June 14, 1900	198	324	May 23, 1901
134	218–219	June 20, 1900	199	325–326	May 25, 1901
135	220	June 26, 1900	200	327	May 28, 1901
136	221–222	July 1, 1900	201	328–330	May 29, 1901
137	223–224		202	331	June 5, 1901
138	225	July 11, 1900	203	332–333	June 8, 1901
139	226–227	July 16, 1900	204	334	June 11, 1901
140	228–229	July 21, 1900	205	335	June 13, 1901
141	230	Aug. 1, 1900	206	336–337	June 16, 1901
142	231–232	Aug. 3, 1900	207	338	June 21, 1901
143	233–235	Aug. 9, 1900	208	339–340	June 23, 1901
144	236–237	Aug. 17, 1900	209	341–342	June 27, 1901
145	238	Aug. 26, 1900	210	343–344	July 7, 1901
146	239	Aug. 29, 1900	211	345	July 11, 1901
147	241–242	Sept. 5, 1900	212	346–347	July 14, 1901
148	243	Sept. 13, 1900	213	348–349	July 22, 1901
149	244–245	Sept. 16, 1900	214	350	July 28, 1901
150	246–247	Sept. 22, 1900	215	351–352	Aug. 1, 1901
151	248–249	Sept. 27, 1900	216	353	Aug. 9, 1901

Roll	Volumes	Beginning Dates	Roll	Volumes	Beginning Dates
217	354–355	Aug. 13, 1901	282	471–473	June 3, 1902
218	356–357	Aug. 22, 1901	283	474–475	June 11, 1902
219	358	Aug. 29, 1901	284	476–477	June 14, 1902
220	359–360	Sept. 1, 1901	285	477a–478	June 19, 1902
221	361	Sept. 7, 1901	286	480–482	June 22, 1902
222	362	Sept. 11, 1901	287	483–484	June 29, 1902
223	363–364	Sept. 13, 1901	288	485–486	July 5, 1902
224	365–366	Sept. 18, 1901	289	487–488	July 10, 1902
225	367–368	Sept. 24, 1901	290	489–490	July 17, 1902
226	369	Oct. 1, 1901	291	491–492	July 22, 1902
227	370–371	Oct. 4, 1901	292	493–494	Aug. 1, 1902
228	372–373	Oct. 11, 1901	293	495–497	Aug. 6, 1902
229	374–375	Oct. 17, 1901	294	498–499	Aug. 17, 1902
230	376	Oct. 23, 1901	295	500–501	Aug. 23, 1902
231	377–378	Oct. 26, 1901	296	502–504	Aug. 30, 1902
232	379	Nov. 1, 1901	297	505–507	Sept. 6, 1902
233	380	Nov. 4, 1901	298	508–510	Sept. 13, 1902
234	381–382	Nov. 6, 1901	299	511–513	Sept. 20, 1902
235	383	Nov. 13, 1901	300	514–515	Sept. 27, 1902
236	384	Nov. 17, 1901	301	516–518	Oct. 1, 1902
237	385	Nov. 18, 1901	302	519–520	Oct. 8, 1902
238	386	Nov. 20, 1901	303	521–523	Oct. 12, 1902
239	387	Nov. 25, 1901	304	524–525	Oct. 19, 1902
240	388	Nov. 26, 1901	305	526–527	Oct. 22, 1902
241	389–390	Dec. 1, 1901	306	528–530	Oct. 30, 1902
242	391	Dec. 7, 1901	307	531–532	Nov. 5, 1902
243	392–393	Dec, 10, 1901	308	533–535	Nov. 14, 1902
244	394	Dec. 18, 1901	309	536–537	Nov. 17, 1902
245	395–396	Dec. 21, 1901	310	538–539	Nov. 20, 1902
246	397	Dec. 28, 1901	311	540–541	Nov. 28, 1902
247	398	Jan. 1, 1902	312	542–544	Dec. 3, 1902
248	399–400	Jan. 9, 1902	313	545–546	Dec. 14, 1902
249	401–402	Jan. 17, 1902	314	547–549	Dec. 18, 1902
250	403–404	Jan. 23, 1902	315	550	Dec. 29, 1902
251	405–406	Feb. 13, 1902	316	551	Jan. 2, 1903
252	407	Feb. 7, 1902	317	552–554	Jan. 7, 1903
253	408–409	Feb. 12, 1902	318	555–556	Jan. 19, 1903
254	410–411	Feb. 19, 1902	319	557	Jan. 27, 1903
255	412–413	Feb. 27, 1902	320	558	Jan. 30, 1903
256	414	Mar. 1, 1902	321	559–560	Feb. 1, 1903
257	415–416	Mar. 4, 1902	322	561–562	Feb. 11, 1903
258	417	Mar. 10, 1902	323	563–564	Feb. 16, 1903
259	418–419	Mar. 11, 1902	324	565	Feb. 20, 1903
260	420–421	Mar. 17, 1902	325	566–567	Feb. 24, 1903
261	422–424	Mar. 19, 1902	326	568	Mar. 1, 1903
262	425–426	Mar. 25, 1902	327	569–570	Mar. 3, 1903
263	427–429	Mar. 27, 1902	328	571–572	Mar. 11, 1903
264	430–431	Apr. 1, 1902	329	573	Mar. 14, 1903
265	432–433	Apr. 5, 1902	330	574–575	Mar. 17, 1903
266	434–435	Apr. 6, 1902	331	576–577	Mar. 22, 1903
267	436–438	Apr. 10, 1902	332	578–579	Mar. 26, 1903
268	439–440	Apr. 15, 1902	333	580	Mar. 29, 1903
269	441–443	Apr. 19, 1902	334	581	Apr. 1, 1903
270	444–445	Apr. 24, 1902	335	582	Apr. 2, 1903
271	446–447	Apr. 28, 1902	336	583–584	Apr. 3, 1903
272	448–450	May 1, 1902	337	585–586	Apr. 8, 1903
273	451–452	May 4, 1902	338	587	Apr. 9, 1903
274	453–455	May 9, 1902	339	588–589	Apr. 9, 1903
275	456–457	May 13, 1902	340	590	Apr. 12, 1903
276	458–459	May 15, 1902	341	591	Apr. 13, 1903
277	460–461	May 19, 1902	342	592	Apr. 15, 1903
278	462–463	May 22, 1902	343	593–594	Apr. 16, 1903
279	464–465	May 26, 1902	344	595–596	Apr. 18, 1903
280	466–467	May 28, 1902	345	597	Apr. 21, 1903
281	468–470	May 31, 1902	346	598–599	Apr. 22, 1903

Roll	Volumes	Beginning Dates	Roll	Volumes	Beginning Dates
347	600	Apr. 26, 1903	411	755–756	Nov. 4, 1903
348	601–602	Apr. 27, 1903	412	757–759	Nov. 7, 1903
349	603–604	Apr. 30, 1903	413	760–762	Nov. 11, 1903
350	605–606	May 2, 1903	414	763–764	Nov. 15, 1903
351	607–608	May 5, 1903	415	765–767	Nov. 18, 1903
352	609–610	May 7, 1903	416	768–770	Nov. 23, 1903
353	611–612	May 9, 1903	417	771–772	Nov. 27, 1903
354	613–614	May 11, 1903	418	773–775	Dec. 1, 1903
355	615–616	May 13, 1903	419	776–778	Dec. 5, 1903
356	617–618	May 16, 1903	420	779–781	Dec. 9, 1903
357	619–621	May 17, 1903	421	782–784	Dec. 17, 1903
358	622–624	May 20, 1903	422	785–787	Dec. 22, 1903
359	625–627	May 22, 1903	423	788–789	Dec. 26, 1903
360	628–629	May 25, 1903	424	790–792	Jan. 1, 1904
361	630–631	May 26, 1903	425	793–796	Jan. 6, 1904
362	632–633a	May 29, 1903	426	797–799	Jan. 14, 1904
363	634–634a	June 2, 1903	427	800–803	Jan. 21, 1904
364	635–635a	June 2, 1903	428	804–806	Jan. 30, 1904
365	636–638	June 8, 1903	429	807–809	Feb. 6, 1904
366	639–640	June 10, 1903	430	810–812	Feb. 14, 1904
367	641–643	June 14, 1903	431	813–815	Feb. 21, 1904
368	644–646	June 17, 1903	432	816–817	Feb. 26, 1904
369	647–648	June 22, 1903	433	818–819	Mar. 1, 1904
370	649–652	June 24, 1903	434	820–822	Mar. 5, 1904
371	653–654,		435	823–825	Mar. 8, 1904
	658–659	June 29, 1903	436	826–827	Mar. 12, 1904
372	660–661	July 4, 1903	437	828–830	Mar. 15, 1904
373	662–663	July 7, 1903	438	831–833	Mar. 18, 1904
374	664–666	July 9, 1903	439	834–835	Mar. 24, 1904
375	667–668	July 13, 1903	440	836–838	Mar. 27, 1904
376	669–671	July 16, 1903	441	839–840	Mar. 28, 1904
377	672–674	July 21, 1903	442	841–843	Mar. 31, 1904
378	675–676	July 27, 1903	443	844–845	Apr. 4, 1904
379	677–678	July 30, 1903	444	846–847	Apr. 6, 1904
380	679–681	Aug. 2, 1903	445	848–850	Apr. 10, 1904
381	682–683	Aug. 7, 1903	446	851–853	Apr. 11, 1904
382	684–685	Aug. 11, 1903	447	854–855	Apr. 16, 1904
383	686–687	Aug. 15, 1903	448	856–858	Apr. 18, 1904
384	688–690	Aug. 18, 1903	449	859–861	Apr. 21, 1904
385	691–693	Aug. 20, 1903	450	862–863	Apr. 24, 1904
386	694–696	Aug. 25, 1903	451	864–866	Apr. 27, 1904
387	697–698	Aug. 27, 1903	452	867–868	Apr. 28, 1904
388	699–701	Aug. 30, 1903	453	869–871	May 1, 1904
389	702–703	Sept. 3, 1903	454	872–874	May 4, 1904
390	704–705	Sept. 5, 1903	455	875–876	May 6, 1904
391	706–708	Sept. 8, 1903	456	877–879	May 9, 1904
392	709–710	Sept. 11, 1903	457	880–881	May 11, 1904
393	711–712	Sept. 12, 1903	458	882–884	May 14, 1904
394	713–714	Sept. 14, 1903	459	885–886	May 17, 1904
395	715–717	Sept. 18, 1903	460	887–889	May 20, 1904
396	718–719	Sept. 22, 1903	461	890–891	May 22, 1904
397	720–721	Sept. 24, 1903	462	892–894	May 24, 1904
398	722–723	Sept. 27, 1903	463	895–897	May 28, 1904
399	724–726	Sept. 29, 1903	464	898–900	June 2, 1904
400	727–729	Oct. 4, 1903	465	901–904	June 4, 1904
401	730–731	Oct. 6, 1903	466	905–907	June 8, 1904
402	732–733	Oct. 8, 1903	467	908–911	June 11, 1904
403	734–736	Oct. 11, 1903	468	912–913	June 15, 1904
404	737–739	Oct. 13, 1903	469	914–916	June 16, 1904
405	740–742	Oct. 15, 1903	470	917–919	June 20, 1904
406	743–744	Oct. 20, 1903	471	920–923	June 23, 1904
407	745–747	Oct. 22, 1903	472	924–927	June 28, 1904
408	748–750	Oct. 27, 1903	473	928–929	July 2, 1904
409	751–752	Oct. 31, 1903	474	930–932	July 5, 1904
410	753–754	Nov. 2, 1903	475	933–934	July 9, 1904

Roll	Volumes	Beginning Dates	Roll	Volumes	Beginning Dates
476	935–937	July 13, 1904	541	1106–1108	Mar. 3, 1905
477	938–940	July 17, 1904	542	1109–1111	Mar. 9, 1905
478	941–942	July 20, 1904	543	1112–1113	Mar. 12, 1905
479	943–944	July 24, 1904	544	1114–1117	Mar. 14, 1905
480	945–947	July 27, 1904	545	1118–1120	Mar. 17, 1905
481	948–950	Aug. 2, 1904	546	1121–1122	Mar. 20, 1905
482	951–952	Aug. 6, 1904	547	1123–1125	Mar. 21, 1905
483	953–956	Aug. 8, 1904	548	1126–1128	Mar. 23, 1905
484	957–958	Aug. 14, 1904	549	1129–1131	Mar. 25, 1905
485	959–961	Aug. 16, 1904	550	1132–1134	Mar. 27, 1905
486	962–964	Aug. 21, 1904	551	1135–1136	Mar. 28, 1905
487	965–967	Aug. 24, 1904	552	1138–1140	Mar. 30, 1905
488	968–969	Aug. 27, 1904	553	1141–1143	Apr. 1, 1905
489	970–971	Aug. 30, 1904	554	1144–1146	Apr. 3, 1905
490	972–973	Sept. 2, 1904	555	1147–1149	Apr. 5, 1905
491	974–975	Sept. 6, 1904	556	1150–1152	Apr. 6, 1905
492	976–977	Sept. 7, 1904	557	1153–1154	Apr. 9, 1905
493	978–980	Sept. 12, 1904	558	1155–1157	Apr. 11, 1905
494	981–982	Sept. 14, 1904	559	1158–1160	Apr. 13, 1905
495	983–984	Sept. 18, 1904	560	1161–1162	Apr. 15, 1905
496	985–986	Sept. 20, 1904	561	1163–1165	Apr. 17, 1905
497	987–988	Sept. 22, 1904	562	1166–1168	Apr. 19, 1905
498	989–990	Spet. 26, 1904	563	1169–1171	Apr. 22, 1905
499	991–992	Sept. 30, 1904	564	1172–1174	Apr. 24, 1905
500	993–994	Oct. 1, 1904	565	1175–1176	Apr. 25, 1905
501	995–997	Oct. 4, 1904	566	1177–1179	Apr. 27, 1905
502	998–1000	Oct. 8, 1904	567	1180–1182	Apr. 30, 1905
503	1001–1002	Oct. 11, 1904	568	1183–1184	May 2, 1905
504	1003–1005	Oct. 13, 1904	569	1185–1187	May 4, 1905
505	1006–1008	Oct. 17, 1904	570	1188–1190	May 8, 1905
506	1009–1010	Oct. 20, 1904	571	1191–1193	May 9, 1905
507	1011–1013	Oct. 24, 1904	572	1194–1195	May 11, 1905
508	1014–1016	Oct. 26, 1904	573	1196–1198	May 12, 1905
509	1017–1019	Oct. 29, 1904	574	1199–1201	May 15, 1905
510	1020–1021	Nov. 1, 1904	575	1202–1204	May 18, 1905
511	1022–1024	Nov. 5, 1904	576	1205–1206	May 20, 1905
512	1025–1027	Nov. 9, 1904	577	1207–1209	May 22, 1905
513	1028–1029	Nov. 12, 1904	578	1210–1212	May 23, 1905
514	1030–1032	Nov. 15, 1904	579	1213–1214	May 26, 1905
515	1033–1035	Nov. 19, 1904	580	1215–1217	May 27, 1905
516	1036–1038	Nov. 23, 1904	581	1218–1221	May 30, 1905
517	1039–1041	Nov. 26, 1904	582	1222–1224	June 1, 1905
518	1042–1044	Dec. 2, 1904	583	1225–1226	June 3, 1905
519	1045–1047	Dec. 5, 1904	584	1227	June 5, 1905
520	1048–1050	Dec. 9, 1904	585	1228–1230	June 5, 1905
521	1051–1054	Dec. 12, 1904	586	1231–1232	June 7, 1905
522	1055–1057	Dec. 16, 1904	587	1233–1235	June 8, 1905
523	1058–1060	Dec. 22, 1904	588	1236–1237	June 11, 1905
524	1061–1062	Dec. 25, 1904	589	1238–1240	June 12, 1905
525	1063–1064	Dec. 29, 1904	590	1241	June 16, 1905
526	1065–1067	Jan. 1, 1905	591	1242–1244	June 18, 1905
527	1068–1070	Jan. 5, 1905	592	1245–1247	June 20, 1905
528	1071–1073	Jan. 10, 1905	593	1248–1250	June 24, 1905
529	1074–1075	Jan. 18, 1905	594	1251–1253	June 27, 1905
530	1076–1078	Jan. 22, 1905	595	1254–1255	June 30, 1905
531	1079–1081	Jan. 28, 1905	596	1256–1258	July 2, 1905
532	1082–1084	Jan. 31, 1905	597	1259–1261	July 5, 1905
533	1085–1086	Feb. 3, 1905	598	1262–1264	July 6, 1905
534	1087–1089	Feb. 7, 1905	599	1265–1267	July 11, 1905
535	1090–1091	Feb. 13, 1905	600	1268–1270	July 14, 1905
536	1092–1094	Feb. 15, 1905	601	1271–1272	July 18, 1905
537	1095–1097	Feb. 19, 1905	602	1273–1276	July 21, 1905
538	1098–1099	Feb. 23, 1905	603	1277–1278	July 25, 1905
539	1100–1102	Feb. 25, 1905	604	1279–1280	July 27, 1905
540	1103–1105	Mar. 1, 1905	605	1281–1283	July 30, 1905

Roll	Volumes	Beginning Dates	Roll	Volumes	Beginning Dates
606	1284–1285	Aug. 2, 1905	671	1463–1465	Mar. 5, 1906
607	1286–1289	Aug. 6, 1905	672	1466–1468	Mar. 7, 1906
608	1290–1292	Aug. 10, 1905	673	1469–1471	Mar. 10, 1906
609	1293–1294	Aug. 14, 1905	674	1472–1473	Mar. 14, 1906
610	1295–1297	Aug. 15, 1905	675	1474–1476	Mar. 15, 1906
611	1298–1300	Aug. 18, 1905	676	1477–1479	Mar. 16, 1906
612	1301–1303	Aug. 22, 1905	677	1480–1482	Mar. 19, 1906
613	1304–1306	Aug. 27, 1905	678	1483–1485	Mar. 21, 1906
614	1307–1309	Aug. 30, 1905	679	1486–1488	Mar. 22, 1906
615	1310–1312	Sept. 2, 1905	680	1489–1491	Mar. 24, 1906
616	1313–1314	Sept. 5, 1905	681	1492–1494	Mar. 25, 1906
617	1315–1317	Sept. 6, 1905	682	1495–1497	Mar. 27, 1906
618	1318–1320	Sept. 9, 1905	683	1498–1500	Mar. 29, 1906
619	1321–1323	Sept. 12, 1905	684	1501–1053	Mar. 31, 1906
620	1324–1325	Sept. 15, 1905	685	1504–1506	Apr. 1, 1906
621	1326–1328	Sept. 16, 1905	686	1507–1508	Apr. 3, 1906
622	1329–1331	Sept. 19, 1905	687	1509–1511	Apr. 4, 1906
623	1332–1334	Sept. 23, 1905	688	1512–1514	Apr. 6, 1906
624	1335–1337	Sept. 25, 1905	689	1515–1517	Apr. 8, 1906
625	1338–1340	Sept. 27, 1905	690	1518–1519	Apr. 11, 1906
626	1341–1343	Sept. 30, 1905	691	1520–1522	Apr. 12, 1906
627	1344–1345	Oct. 3, 1905	692	1523–1525	Apr. 15, 1906
628	1346–1348	Oct. 5, 1905	693	1526–1527	Apr. 17, 1906
629	1349–1351	Oct. 7, 1905	694	1528–1530	Apr. 18, 1906
630	1352–1353	Oct. 10, 1905	695	1531–1533	Apr. 19, 1906
631	1354–1356	Oct. 13, 1905	696	1534–1536	Apr. 20, 1906
632	1357–1359	Oct. 16, 1905	697	1537–1539	Apr. 22, 1906
633	1360–1362	Oct. 20, 1905	698	1540–1543	Apr. 24, 1906
634	1363–1364	Oct. 23, 1905	699	1544–1545	Apr. 26, 1906
635	1365–1367	Oct. 25, 1905	700	1546–1548	Apr. 27, 1906
636	1368–1370	Oct. 28, 1905	701	1549–1550	Apr. 29, 1906
637	1371–1373	Oct. 30, 1905	702	1551–1553	May 2, 1906
638	1374–1376	Nov. 2, 1905	703	1554–1556	May 3, 1906
639	1377–1378	Nov. 8, 1905	704	1557–1558	May 5, 1906
640	1379–1381	Nov. 9, 1905	705	1559–1561	May 6, 1906
641	1382–1384	Nov. 13, 1905	706	1562–1564	May 7, 1906
642	1385–1387	Nov. 15, 1905	707	1565–1567	May 10, 1906
643	1388–1389	Nov. 21, 1905	708	1568–1570	May 12, 1906
644	1390–1392	Nov. 23, 1905	709	1571–1573	May 14, 1906
645	1393–1395	Nov. 28, 1905	710	1574–1576	May 15, 1906
646	1396–1398	Dec. 1, 1905	711	1577–1579	May 17, 1906
647	1399–1400	Dec. 5, 1905	712	1580–1582	May 18, 1906
648	1401–1403	Dec. 8, 1905	713	1583–1585	May 20, 1906
649	1404–1406	Dec. 14, 1905	714	1586–1588	May 22, 1906
650	1407–1408	Dec. 17, 1905	715	1586–1588	May 24, 1906
651	1409–1411	Dec. 19, 1905	716	1591–1593	May 26, 1906
652	1412–1414	Dec. 21, 1905	717	1594–1596	May 27, 1906
653	1415–1416	Dec. 27, 1905	718	1597–1599	May 29, 1906
654	1417–1418	Jan. 1, 1906	719	1600–1602	May 31, 1906
655	1419–1421	Jan. 4, 1906	720	1603–1605	June 2, 1906
656	1422–1423	Jan. 9, 1906	721	1606–1607	June 3, 1906
657	1424–1426	Jan. 14, 1906	722	1608–1610	June 5, 1906
658	1427–1428	Jan. 19, 1906	723	1611	June 7, 1906
659	1429–1431	Jan. 24, 1906	724	1612–1614	June 7, 1906
660	1432–1434	Jan. 27, 1906	725	1615–1616	June 10, 1906
661	1435–1437	Jan. 30, 1906	726	1617–1619	June 11, 1906
662	1438–1440	Feb. 5, 1906	727	1620–1622	June 13, 1906
663	1441–1443	Feb. 9, 1906	728	1623–1625	June 14, 1906
664	1444–1445	Feb. 12, 1906	729	1626–1628	June 18, 1906
665	1446–1448	Feb. 14, 1906	730	1629–1631	June 20, 1906
666	1449–1451	Feb. 19, 1906	731	1632–1633	June 22, 1906
667	1452–1453	Feb. 23, 1906	732	1634–1636	June 24, 1906
668	1454–1456	Feb. 26, 1906	733	1637–1638	June 27, 1906
669	1457–1459	Feb. 28, 1906	734	1639–1641	June 28, 1906
670	1460–1462	Mar. 2, 1906	735	1642–1644	June 30, 1906

Roll	Volumes	Beginning Dates	Roll	Volumes	Beginning Dates
736	1645–1647	July 1, 1906	801	1812–1814	Nov. 23, 1906
737	1648–1650	July 5, 1906	802	1815–1816	Nov. 26, 1906
738	1651–1652	July 8, 1906	803	1817–1819	Nov. 29, 1906
739	1653–1655	July 9, 1906	804	1820–1821	Dec. 1, 1906
740	1656–1658	July 12, 1906	805	1822–1823	Dec. 2, 1906
741	1659	July 15, 1906	806	1824–1826	Dec. 3, 1906
742	1660–1662	July 16, 1906	807	1827–1828	Dec. 7, 1906
743	1663	July 19, 1906	808	1829–1831	Dec. 10, 1906
744	1664–1666	July 20, 1906	809	1832–1833	Dec. 11, 1906
745	1667–1669	July 23, 1906	810	1834–1836	Dec. 13, 1906
746	1670–1672	July 25, 1906	811	1837–1838	Dec. 16, 1906
747	1673–1675	July 28, 1906	812	1839–1841	Dec. 20, 1906
748	1676–1677	Aug. 1, 1906	813	1842–1843	Dec. 23, 1906
749	1678–1680	Aug. 3, 1906	814	1844–1845	Dec. 24, 1906
750	1681–1683	Aug. 6, 1906	815	1846–1848	Dec. 29, 1906
751	1684–1686	Aug. 8, 1906	816	1849	Jan. 1, 1907
752	1687–1689	Aug. 11, 1906	817	1850–1851	Jan. 4, 1907
753	1690–1692	Aug. 14, 1906	818	1852–1853	Jan. 7, 1907
754	1693–1695	Aug. 16, 1906	819	1854–1855	Jan. 12, 1907
755	1696–1697	Aug. 21, 1906	820	1856–1857	Jan. 15, 1907
756	1698–1700	Aug. 22, 1906	821	1858–1859	Jan. 19, 1907
757	1701–1703	Aug. 25, 1906	822	1860–1861	Jan. 21, 1907
758	1704–1706	Aug. 28, 1906	823	1862–1863	Jan. 30, 1907
759	1707–1709	Aug. 30, 1906	824	1864–1865	Jan. 30, 1907
760	1710–1711	Sept. 2, 1906	825	1866–1867	Feb. 1, 1907
761	1712–1714	Sept. 4, 1906	826	1868–1869	Feb. 4, 1907
762	1715–1717	Sept. 5, 1906	827	1870–1871	Feb. 9, 1907
763	1718–1720	Sept. 7, 1906	828	1872–1873	Feb. 10, 1907
764	1721–1722	Sept. 10, 1906	829	1874–1875	Feb. 13, 1907
765	1723–1725	Sept. 11, 1906	830	1876–1877	Feb. 16, 1907
766	1726–1728	Sept. 13, 1906	831	1878–1879	Feb. 18, 1907
767	1729–1731	Spet. 16, 1906	832	1880–1882	Feb. 21, 1907
768	1732–1733	Sept. 19, 1906	833	1883–1884	Feb. 25, 1907
769	1734–1737	Sept. 20, 1906	834	1885–1886	Feb. 27, 1907
770	1738–1739	Sept. 22, 1906	835	1887–1888	Mar. 1, 1907
771	1740–1742	Sept. 24, 1906	836	1889–1890	Mar. 3, 1907
772	1743–1744	Sept. 26, 1906	837	1891–1892	Mar. 5, 1907
773	1745–1747	Sept. 27, 1906	838	1893–1894	Mar. 5, 1907
774	1748–1750	Sept. 30, 1906	839	1895–1896	Mar. 7, 1907
775	1751–1752	Oct. 2, 1906	840	1897–1898	Mar. 10, 1907
776	1753–1754	Oct. 2, 1906	841	1899–1900	Mar. 11, 1907
777	1755–1757	Oct. 5, 1906	842	1901–1902	Mar. 13, 1907
778	1758–1759	Oct. 6, 1906	843	1903–1904	Mar. 15, 1907
779	1760–1761	Oct. 9, 1906	844	1905–1906	Mar. 16, 1907
780	1762–1763	Oct. 9, 1906	845	1907–1908	Mar. 17, 1907
781	1764–1766	Oct. 12, 1906	846	1909–1910	Mar. 18, 1907
782	1767–1769	Oct. 15, 1906	847	1911–1912	Mar. 19, 1907
783	1770–1771	Oct. 18, 1906	848	1913–1914	Mar. 20, 1907
784	1772–1773	Oct. 18, 1906	849	1915–1916	Mar. 21, 1907
785	1774–1776	Oct. 20, 1906	850	1917–1918	Mar. 23, 1907
786	1777–1778	Oct. 22, 1906	851	1919–1920	Mar. 24, 1907
787	1779–1780	Oct. 23, 1906	852	1921–1922	Mar. 25, 1907
788	1781–1782	Oct. 25, 1906	853	1923–1924	Mar. 26, 1907
789	1783–1785	Oct. 28, 1906	854	1925–1926	Mar. 27, 1907
790	1786–1787	Oct. 31, 1906	855	1927–1928	Mar. 28, 1907
791	1788–1790	Nov. 1, 1906	856	1929–1930	Mar. 30, 1907
792	1791–1792	Nov. 3, 1906	857	1931–1932	Mar. 31, 1907
793	1793–1795	Nov. 7, 1906	858	1933–1935	Apr. 1, 1907
794	1796–1797	Nov. 8, 1906	859	1936–1937	Apr. 3, 1907
795	1798–1800	Nov. 10, 1906	860	1938	Apr. 4, 1907
796	1801–1802	Nov. 12, 1906	861	1939–1941	Apr. 4, 1907
797	1803–1804	Nov. 14, 1906	862	1942–1943	Apr. 6, 1907
798	1805–1806	Nov. 16, 1906	863	1944–1945	Apr. 7, 1907
799	1807–1089	Nov. 18, 1906	864	1946–1947	Apr. 8, 1907
800	1810–1811	Nov. 21, 1906	865	1948–1949	Apr. 10, 1907

Roll	Volumes	Beginning Dates	Roll	Volumes	Beginning Dates
866	1950–1951	Apr. 12, 1907	931	2084–2085	June 27, 1907
867	1952–1953	Apr. 13, 1907	932	2086–2087	June 28, 1907
868	1954–1955	Apr. 14, 1907	933	2088–2089	June 29, 1907
869	1956–1958	Apr. 15, 1907	934	2090	June 30, 1907
870	1959–1961	Apr. 17, 1907	935	2091–2092	July 1, 1907
871	1962–1963	Apr. 19, 1907	936	2093–2095	July 2, 1907
872	1964–1965	Apr. 20, 1907	937	2096–2098	July 5, 1907
873	1966–1967	Apr. 21, 1907	938	2099–2101	July 6, 1907
874	1968–1969	Apr. 21, 1907	939	2102–2103	July 7, 1907
875	1970–1972	Apr. 25, 1907	940	2104–2106	July 8, 1907
876	1973–1974	Apr. 26, 1907	941	2107–2108	July 10, 1907
877	1975	Apr. 27, 1907	942	2109–2110	July 10, 1907
878	1976–1978	Apr. 27, 1907	943	2111–2112	July 12, 1907
879	1979–1980	Apr. 29, 1907	944	2113–2114	July 14, 1907
880	1981–1983	Apr. 30, 1907	945	2115–2116	July 15, 1907
881	1984–1985	May 1, 1907	946	2117–2119	July 17, 1907
882	1986–1988	May 1, 1907	947	2120	July 19, 1907
883	1989	May 2, 1907	948	2121–2122	July 21, 1907
884	1990–1991	May 4, 1907	949	2123–2124	July 21, 1907
885	1992–1993	May 5, 1907	950	2125–2126	July 24, 1907
886	1994–1995	May 4, 1907	951	2127–2129	July 25, 1907
887	1996–1998	May 7, 1907	952	2130–2131	July 27, 1907
888	1999–2000	May 9, 1907	953	2132–2133	July 27, 1907
889	2001–2002	May 10, 1907	954	2134–2135	July 30, 1907
890	2003–2004	May 10, 1907	955	2136–2137	Aug. 1, 1907
891	2005–2006	May 11, 1907	956	2138–2139	Aug. 1, 1907
892	2007	May 11, 1907	957	2140–2142	Aug. 3, 1907
893	2008–2009	May 12, 1907	958	2143	Aug. 4, 1907
894	2010–2011	May 14, 1907	959	2144–2145	Aug. 5, 1907
895	2012	May 14, 1907	960	2146	Aug. 6, 1907
896	2013–2014	May 15, 1907	961	2147–2148	Aug. 7, 1907
897	2015–2017	May 16, 1907	962	2149–2150	Aug. 9, 1907
898	2018–2019	May 17, 1907	963	2151–2152	Aug. 10, 1907
899	2020–2021	May 18, 1907	964	2153–2154	Aug. 12, 1907
900	2022–2023	May 20, 1907	965	2155–2156	Aug. 14, 1907
901	2024–2025	May 21, 1907	966	2157–2158	Aug. 15, 1907
902	2026–2027	May 21, 1907	967	2159	Aug. 17, 1907
903	2028–2029	May 23, 1907	968	2160–2161	Aug. 17, 1907
904	2030–2031	May 24, 1907	969	2162–2163	Aug. 18, 1907
905	2032–2033	May 26, 1907	970	2164–2165	Aug. 20, 1907
906	2034–2035	May 27, 1907	971	2166–2167	Aug. 21, 1907
907	2036	May 29, 1907	972	2168–2169	Aug. 23, 1907
908	2037–2038	May 29, 1907	973	2170–2171	Aug. 24, 1907
909	2039	May 30, 1907	974	2172–2173	Aug. 27, 1907
910	2040–2042	May 31, 1907	975	2174	Aug. 28, 1907
911	2043–2044	June 1, 1907	976	2175–2176	Aug. 29, 1907
912	2045–2047	June 3, 1907	977	2177–2178	Aug. 30, 1907
913	2048–2049	June 5, 1907	978	2179–2180	Aug. 31, 1907
914	2050	June 6, 1907	979	2181–2182	Sept. 1, 1907
915	2051–2052	June 8, 1907	980	2183–2184	Sept. 3, 1907
916	2053–2055	June 9, 1907	981	2185	Sept. 4, 1907
917	2056–2057	June 10, 1907	982	2186–2187	Sept. 4, 1907
918	2058–2059	June 11, 1907	983	2188	Sept. 5, 1907
919	2060–2061	June 12, 1907	984	2189–2190	Sept. 5, 1907
920	2062–2063	June 14, 1907	985	2191–2193	Sept. 7, 1907
921	2064–2065	June 14, 1907	986	2194	Sept. 10, 1907
922	2066–2067	June 15, 1907	987	2195–2196	Sept. 10, 1907
923	2068–2070	June 15, 1907	988	2197–2198	Sept. 13, 1907
924	2071–2072	June 16, 1907	989	2199	Sept. 14, 1907
925	2073–2074	June 17, 1907	990	2200–2201	Sept. 14, 1907
926	2075–2076	June 20, 1907	991	2202–2203	Sept. 14, 1907
927	2077	June 22, 1907	992	2204–2205	Sept. 17, 1907
928	2078–2079	June 22, 1907	993	2206–2207	Sept. 18, 1907
929	2080–2081	June 24, 1907	994	2208–2209	Sept. 18, 1907
930	2082–2083	June 26, 1907	995	2210–2211	Sept. 19, 1907

Roll	Volumes	Beginning Dates	Roll	Volumes	Beginning Dates
996	2212	Sept. 20, 1907	1061	2333–2334	Dec. 16, 1907
997	2213–2214	Sept. 21, 1907	1062	2335–2336	Dec. 20, 1907
998	2215–2216	Sept. 23, 1907	1063	2337	Dec. 21, 1907
999	2217–2218	Sept. 25, 1907	1064	2338–2339	Dec. 22, 1907
1000	2219–2220	Sept. 25, 1907	1065	2340–2341	Dec. 24, 1907
1001	2221	Sept. 27, 1907	1066	2342	Dec. 28, 1907
1002	2222–2223	Sept. 28, 1907	1067	2343–2344	Dec. 29, 1907
1003	2224–2225	Sept. 28, 1907	1068	2345–2346	Jan. 1, 1908
1004	2226	Oct. 1, 1907	1069	2347–2348	Jan. 4, 1908
1005	2227–2228	Oct. 1, 1907	1070	2349–2350	Jan. 11, 1908
1006	2229–2230	Oct. 2, 1907	1071	2351–2352	Jan. 18, 1908
1007	2231–2232	Oct. 3, 1907	1072	2353–2354	Jan. 25, 1908
1008	2233–2234	Oct. 3, 1907	1073	2355–2356	Jan. 26, 1908
1009	2235	Oct. 5, 1907	1074	2357–2358	Feb. 1, 1908
1010	2236–2237	Oct. 6, 1907	1075	2359–2360	Feb. 6, 1908
1011	22387–2239	Oct. 8, 1907	1076	2361–2362	Feb. 11, 1908
1012	2240–2241	Oct. 9, 1907	1077	2363–2364	Feb. 16, 1908
1013	2242–2243	Oct. 11, 1907	1078	2365–2366	Feb. 21, 1908
1014	2244	Oct. 12, 1907	1079	2367–2369	Feb. 26, 1908
1015	2245–2246	Oct. 12, 1907	1080	2370–2371	Mar. 1, 1908
1016	2247–2248	Oct. 13, 1907	1081	2372–2374	Mar. 5, 1908
1017	2249–2250	Oct. 10, 1907	1082	2375–2376	Mar. 11, 1908
1018	2251–2252	Oct. 16, 1907	1083	2377–2378	Mar. 15, 1908
1019	2253–2254	Oct. 18, 1907	1804	2379–2381	Mar. 20, 1908
1020	2255–2256	Oct. 19, 1907	1085	2382–2383	Mar. 24, 1908
1021	2257	Oct. 20, 1907	1086	2384–2385	Mar. 26, 1908
1022	2258–2259	Oct. 21, 1907	1087	2386–2387	Mar. 30, 1908
1023	2260	Oct. 23, 1907	1088	2388–2389	Apr. 1, 1908
1024	2261–2262	Oct. 24, 1907	1089	2390–2392	Apr. 3, 1908
1025	2263–2264	Oct. 26, 1907	1090	2393–2394	Apr. 8, 1908
1026	2265–2266	Oct. 26, 1907	1091	2395–2396	Apr. 8, 1908
1027	2267–2268	Oct. 28, 1907	1092	2397–2398	Apr. 11, 1908
1028	2269	Oct. 28, 1907	1093	2399–2401	Apr. 15, 1908
1029	2270–2271	Oct. 30, 1907	1094	2402–2403	Apr. 17, 1908
1030	2272–2273	Oct. 31, 1907	1095	2404–2405	Apr. 20, 1908
1031	2274–2275	Nov. 2, 1907	1096	2406–2407	Apr. 23, 1908
1032	2276–2277	Nov. 2, 1907	1097	2408–2409	Apr. 26, 1908
1033	2278–2279	Nov. 3, 1907	1098	2410–2411	Apr. 29, 1908
1034	2280–2281	Nov. 5, 1907	1099	2412–2413	May 2, 1908
1035	2282–2283	Nov. 7, 1907	1100	2414–2415	May 5, 1908
1036	2284–2285	Nov. 9, 1907	1101	2416–2418	May 8, 1908
1037	2286–2287	Nov. 9, 1907	1102	2419–2420	May 13, 1908
1038	2288–2289	Nov. 10, 1907	1103	2421–2422	May 16, 1908
1039	2290–2291	Nov. 12, 1907	1104	2423–2424	May 18, 1908
1040	2292–2293	Nov. 13, 1907	1105	2425–2426	May 22, 1908
1041	2294–2295	Nov. 15, 1907	1106	2427–2429	May 24, 1908
1042	2296–2297	Nov. 16, 1907	1107	2430–2431	May 27, 1908
1043	2298–2299	Nov. 18, 1907	1108	2432–2433	May 31, 1908
1044	2300–2301	Nov. 19, 1907	1109	2434–2436	June 2, 1908
1045	2302	Nov. 21, 1907	1110	2437–2438	June 7, 1908
1046	2304–2305	Nov. 21, 1907	1111	2439–2440	June 10, 1908
1047	2305–2306	Nov. 23, 1907	1112	2441–2442	June 12, 1908
1048	2307–2308	Nov. 24, 1907	1113	2443–2444	June 16, 1908
1049	2309–2311	Nov. 25, 1907	1114	2445–2446	June 18, 1908
1050	2312–2313	Nov. 27, 1907	1115	2447–2448	June 23, 1908
1051	2314–2315	Nov. 29, 1907	1116	2449–2450	June 27, 1908
1052	2316–2317	Nov. 30, 1907	1117	2451–2453	June 30, 1908
1053	2318–2319	Dec. 1, 1907	1118	2454–2455	July 4, 1908
1054	2320–2321	Dec. 3, 1907	1119	2456–2457	July 8, 1908
1055	2322–2323	Dec. 4, 1907	1120	2458–2460	July 10, 1908
1056	2324–2325	Dec. 7, 1907	1121	2461–2462	July 16, 1908
1057	2326–2327	Dec. 9, 1907	1122	2463–2464	July 18, 1908
1058	2328	Dec. 11, 1907	1123	2465–2466	July 22, 1908
1059	2329–2330	Dec. 16, 1907	1124	2467–2469	July 25, 1908
1060	2331–2332	Dec. 16, 1907	1125	2470–2471	July 30, 1908

Roll	Volumes	Beginning Dates	Roll	Volumes	Beginning Dates
1126	2472–2473	Aug. 1, 1908	1191	2619–2621	Jan. 26, 1909
1127	2474–2475	Aug. 6, 1908	1192	2622–2623	Jan. 29, 1909
1128	2476–2477	Aug. 7, 1908	1193	2624–2625	Feb. 1, 1909
1129	2478–2480	Aug. 10, 1908	1194	2626–2627	Feb. 2, 1909
1130	2481–2482	Aug. 15, 1908	1195	2628–2630	Feb. 3, 1909
1131	2483–2484	Aug. 17, 1908	1196	2631	Feb. 7, 1909
1132	2485–2486	Aug. 19, 1908	1197	2632–2633	Feb. 8, 1909
1133	2487–2489	Aug. 22, 1908	1198	2634–2636	Feb. 10, 1909
1134	2490–2491	Aug. 26, 1908	1199	2637–2638	Feb. 13, 1909
1135	2492–2494	Aug. 27, 1908	1200	2639–2640	Feb. 15, 1909
1136	2495–2496	Sept. 1, 1908	1201	2641–2643	Feb. 16, 1909
1137	2497–2498	Sept. 2, 1908	1202	2644–2645	Feb. 17, 1909
1138	2499–2501	Sept. 4, 1908	1203	2646–2648	Feb. 19, 1909
1139	2502–2503	Sept. 8, 1908	1204	2649–2650	Feb. 22, 1909
1140	2504–2505	Sept. 8, 1908	1205	2651–2652	Feb. 25, 1909
1141	2506–2507	Sept. 11, 1908	1206	2653–2655	Feb. 25, 1909
1142	2508–2509	Sept. 12, 1908	1207	2656–2657	Feb. 28, 1909
1143	2510–2512	Sept. 14, 1908	1208	2658–2659	Mar. 1, 1909
1144	2513–2514	Sept. 17, 1908	1209	2660–2661	Mar. 2, 1909
1145	2515–2517	Sept. 19, 1908	1210	2662–2664	Mar. 3, 1909
1146	2518–2519	Sept. 22, 1908	1211	2665–2667	Mar. 5, 1909
1147	2520–2522	Sept. 25, 1908	1212	2668–2669	Mar. 8, 1909
1148	2523–2524	Sept. 26, 1908	1213	2670–2672	Mar. 8, 1909
1149	2525–2526	Sept. 28, 2908	1214	2673–2674	Mar. 12, 1909
1150	2527–2528	Sept. 30, 1908	1215	2675–2676	Mar. 13, 1909
1151	2529–2531	Oct. 2, 1908	1216	2677–2679	Mar. 15, 1909
1152	2532–2533	Oct. 5, 1908	1217	2680–2681	Mar. 16, 1909
1153	2534–2535	Oct. 7, 1908	1218	2682–2684	Mar. 18, 1909
1154	2536–2537	Oct. 9, 1908	1219	2685–2686	Mar. 19, 1909
1155	2538–2539	Oct. 10, 1908	1220	2687–2689	Mar. 20, 1909
1156	2540–2541	Oct. 13, 1908	1221	2690–2691	Mar. 21, 1909
1157	2542–2543	Oct. 16, 1908	1222	2692	Mar. 23, 1909
1158	2544–2545	Oct. 17, 1908	1223	2693–2694	Mar. 23, 1909
1159	2546–2547	Oct. 20, 1908	1224	2695–2697	Mar. 24, 1909
1160	2548–2549	Oct. 22, 1908	1225	2698–2699	Mar. 26, 1909
1161	2550–2551	Oct. 24, 1908	1226	2700–2701	Mar. 27, 1909
1162	2552–2554	Oct. 27, 1908	1227	2702,	
1163	2555–2556	Oct. 30, 1908		2704–2705	Mar. 27, 1909
1164	2557–2559	Nov. 1, 1908	1228	2703	Mar. 28, 1909
1165	2560–2561	Nov. 4, 1908	1229	2706–2707	Mar. 30, 1909
1166	2562–2563	Nov. 7, 1908	1230	2708–2710	Mar. 30, 1909
1167	2564–2565	Nov. 9, 1908	1231	2711–2712	Apr. 1, 1909
1168	2566–2567	Nov. 12, 1908	1232	2713–2715	Apr. 1, 1909
1169	2568–2570	Nov. 15, 1908	1233	2716–2717	Apr. 3, 1909
1170	2571–2572	Nov. 21, 1908	1234	2718–2720	Apr. 4, 1909
1171	2573–2574	Nov. 24, 1908	1235	2721–2722	Apr. 7, 1909
1172	2575–2577	Nov. 27, 1908	1236	2723–2724	Apr. 8, 1909
1173	2578–2579	Dec. 1, 1908	1237	2725–2726	Apr. 8, 1909
1174	2580–2581	Dec. 3, 1908	1238	2727–2728	Apr. 9, 1909
1175	2582–2584	Dec. 5, 1908	1239	2729–2730	Apr. 10, 1909
1176	2585–2586	Dec. 8, 1908	1240	2731–2732	Apr. 11, 1909
1177	2587–2588	Dec. 9, 1908	1241	2733–2735	Apr. 12, 1909
1178	2589–2590	Dec. 12, 1908	1242	2736–2737	Apr. 14, 1909
1179	2591–2592	Dec. 18, 1908	1243	2738–2740	Apr. 15, 1909
1180	5293–2595	Dec. 23, 1908	1244	2741–2742	Apr. 16, 1909
1181	2596–2597	Dec. 23, 1908	1245	2743–2745	Apr. 17, 1909
1182	2598–2599	Dec. 24, 1908	1246	2746–2747	Apr. 19, 1909
1183	2600–2602	Dec. 26, 1908	1247	2748–2749	Apr. 21, 1909
1184	2603–2605	Jan. 1, 1909	1248	2750	Apr. 21, 1909
1185	2606–2607	Jan. 4, 1909	1249	2751–2752	Apr. 22, 1909
1186	2608–2609	Jan. 8, 1909	1250	2753–2755	Apr. 23, 1909
1187	2610–2611	Jan. 12, 1909	1251	2756–2757	Apr. 24, 1909
1188	2612–2614	Jan. 14, 1909	1252	2758–2759	Apr. 26, 1909
1189	2615–2616	Jan. 19, 1909	1253	2760–2762	Apr. 28, 1909
1190	2617–2618	Jan. 25, 1909	1254	2763–2765	Apr. 30, 1909

Roll	Volumes	Beginning Dates	Roll	Volumes	Beginning Dates
1255	2766–2767	Apr. 30, 1909	1320	2909–2910	Aug. 20, 1909
1256	2768–2770	May 3, 1909	1321	2911–2913	Aug. 23, 1909
1257	2771–2773	May 4, 1909	1322	2914–2915	Aug. 25, 1909
1258	2774–2775	May 6, 1909	1323	2916–2917	Aug. 25, 1909
1259	2776–2777	May 6, 1909	1324	2918–2919	Aug. 28, 1909
1260	2778–2779	May 7, 1909	1325	2920–2921	Aug. 30, 1909
1261	2780	May 9, 1909	1326	2922–2924	Sept. 1, 1909
1262	2781–2783	May 9, 1909	1327	2925–2926	Sept. 2, 1909
1263	2784	May 11, 1909	1328	2927–2928	Sept. 3, 1909
1264	2785–2786	May 11, 1909	1329	2929–2930	Sept. 5, 1909
1265	2787–2788	May 12, 1909	1330	2931–2932	Sept. 7, 1909
1266	2789–2791	May 14, 1909	1331	2933–2934	Sept. 8, 1909
1267	2792–2793	May 16, 1909	1332	2935–2936	Sept. 9, 1909
1268	2794–2795	May 16, 1909	1333	2937–2938	Sept. 10, 1909
1269	2796–2798	May 17, 1909	1334	2939–2940	Sept. 13, 1909
1270	2799–2800	May 20, 1909	1335	2941–2942	Sept. 14, 1909
1271	2801–2802	May 21, 1909	1336	2943–2944	Sept. 15, 1909
1272	2803–2804	May 23, 1909	1337	2945–2947	Sept. 16, 1909
1273	2805–2806	May 24, 1909	1338	2948–2949	Sept. 18, 1909
1274	2807–2809	May 26, 1909	1339	2950	Sept. 20, 1909
1275	2810–2811	May 27, 1909	1340	2951–2953	Sept. 20, 1909
1276	2812–2813	May 29, 1909	1341	2954–2955	Sept. 22, 1909
1277	2814–2815	May 30, 1909	1342	2956–2957	Sept. 24, 1909
1278	2816–2818	June 1, 1909	1343	2958–2959	Sept. 26, 1909
1279	2819–2820	June 2, 1909	1344	2960–2961	Sept. 27, 1909
1280	2821–2822	June 3, 1909	1345	2962–2964	Sept. 28, 1909
1281	2823–2825	June 4, 1909	1346	2965–2966	Oct. 1, 1909
1282	2826–2827	June 7, 1909	1347	2967–2968	Oct. 3, 1909
1283	2828–2829	June 9, 1909	1348	2969–2970	Oct. 4, 1909
1284	2830–2831	June 9, 1909	1349	2971–2972	Oct. 5, 1909
1285	2832–2833	June 11, 1909	1350	2973–2974	Oct. 6, 1909
1286	2834–2835	June 13, 1909	1351	2975–2977	Oct. 8, 1909
1287	2836–2838	June 14, 1909	1352	2978–2979	Oct. 10, 1909
1288	2839–2840	June 16, 1909	1353	2980–2981	Oct. 11, 1909
1289	2841–2842	June 19, 1909	1354	2982–2983	Oct. 13, 1909
1290	2843–2844	June 21, 1909	1355	2984–2985	Oct. 14, 1909
1291	2845–2847	June 22, 1909	1356	2986–2987	Oct. 16, 1909
1292	2848–2849	June 24, 1909	1357	2988–2989	Oct. 18, 1909
1293	2850–2851	June 26, 1909	1358	2990–2991	Oct. 19, 1909
1294	2852–2853	June 28, 1909	1359	2992–2993	Oct. 21, 1909
1295	2854–2856	June 30, 1909	1360	2994–2995	Oct. 23, 1909
1296	2857–2858	July 2, 1909	1361	2996–2998	Oct. 25, 1909
1297	2859–2860	July 4, 1909	1362	2999–3000	Oct. 27, 1909
1298	2861–2862	July 7, 1909	1363	3001–3002	Oct. 29, 1909
1299	2863–2864	July 8, 1909	1364	3003–3004	Oct. 30, 1909
1300	2865–2866	July 11, 1909	1365	3005–3006	Nov. 1, 1909
1301	2867–2869	July 12, 1909	1366	3007–3008	Nov. 1, 1909
1302	2870–2871	July 14, 1909	1367	3009–3011	Nov. 3, 1909
1303	2872–2873	July 15, 1909	1368	3012–3013	Nov. 4, 1909
1304	2874–2875	July 18, 1909	1369	3014–3015	Nov. 8, 1909
1305	2876–2877	July 20, 1909	1370	3016–3017	Nov. 9, 1909
1306	2878–2880	July 22, 1909	1371	3018–3019	Nov. 11, 1909
1307	2881–2882	July 26, 1909	1372	3020–3021	Nov. 12, 1909
1308	2883–2884	July 27, 1909	1373	3022–3023	Nov. 14, 1909
1309	2885–2886	July 29, 1909	1374	3024–3025	Nov. 16, 1909
1310	2887–2889	July 31, 1909	1375	3026–3027	Nov. 18, 1909
1311	2890–2891	Aug. 2, 1909	1376	3028–3029	Nov. 20, 1909
1312	2892–2893	Aug. 3, 1909	1377	3030–3032	Nov. 21, 1909
1313	2894–2895	Aug. 6, 1909	1378	3033–3034	Nov. 23, 1909
1314	2896–2898	Aug. 8, 1909	1379	3035–3036	Nov. 25, 1909
1315	2899–2900	Aug. 11, 1909	1380	3037–3038	Nov. 26, 1909
1316	2901–2902	Aug. 12, 1909	1381	3039–3041	Nov. 29, 1909
1317	2903–2904	Aug. 15, 1909	1382	3042–3043	Dec. 1, 1909
1318	2905–2906	Aug. 16, 1909	1383	3044–3045	Dec. 3, 1909
1319	2907–2908	Aug. 18, 1909	1384	3046–3047	Dec. 5, 1909

Roll	Volumes	Beginning Dates	Roll	Volumes	Beginning Dates
1385	3048–3050	Dec. 6, 1909	1450	3191–3193	Apr. 12, 1910
1386	3051–3052	Dec. 9, 1909	1451	3194–3195	Apr. 13, 1910
1387	3053	Dec. 11, 1909	1452	3196–3197	Apr. 13, 1910
1388	3054–3055	Dec. 12, 1909	1453	3198–3199	Apr. 14, 1910
1389	3056–3057	Dec. 16, 1909	1454	3200–3202	Apr. 15, 1910
1390	3058–3060	Dec. 17, 1909	1455	3203–3204	Apr. 17, 1910
1391	3061–3062	Dec. 20, 1909	1456	3205–3206	Apr. 19, 1910
1392	3063–3064	Dec. 21, 1909	1457	3207–3209	Apr. 19, 1910
1393	3065–3066	Dec. 23, 1909	1458	3210–3211	Apr. 21, 1910
1394	3067–3068	Dec. 27, 1909	1459	3212–3214	Apr. 22, 1910
1395	3069–3070	Dec. 28, 1909	1460	3215–3216	Apr. 23, 1910
1396	3071	Jan. 1, 1910	1461	3217–3218	Apr. 24, 1910
1397	3072–3073	Jan. 2, 1910	1462	3219–3221	Apr. 25, 1910
1398	3074–3076	Jan. 6, 1910	1463	3222–3223	Apr. 26, 1910
1399	3077–3078	Jan. 11, 1910	1464	3224–3225	Apr. 27, 1910
1400	3079–3080	Jan. 15, 1910	1465	3226–3228	Apr. 28, 1910
1401	3081–3082	Jan. 18, 1910	1466	3229–3230	Apr. 29, 1910
1402	3083–3085	Jan. 19, 1910	1467	3231–3232	May 1, 1910
1403	3086–3087	Jan. 24, 1910	1468	3233–3234	May 2, 1910
1404	3088–3090	Jan. 26, 1910	1469	3235–3237	May 3, 1910
1405	3091–3092	Jan. 28, 1910	1470	3238	May 4, 1910
1406	3093–3094	Feb. 1, 1910	1471	3239–3241	May 4, 1910
1407	3095–3096	Feb. 2, 1910	1472	3242	May 6, 1910
1408	3097–3098	Feb. 4, 1910	1473	3243–3245	May 6, 1910
1409	3099–3101	Feb. 5, 1910	1474	3246–3247	May 10, 1910
1410	3102–3103	Feb. 10, 1910	1475	3248–3249	May 10, 1910
1411	3104–3105	Feb. 14, 1910	1476	3250	May 11, 1910
1412	3106–3108	Feb. 15, 1910	1477	3251–3252	May 12, 1910
1413	3109–3110	Feb. 17, 1910	1478	3253–3255	May 12, 1910
1414	3111–3113	Feb. 18, 1910	1479	3256–3257	May 14, 1910
1415	3114–3115	Feb. 23, 1910	1480	3258–3259	May 16, 1910
1416	3116–3117	Feb. 25, 1910	1481	3260–3261	May 17, 1910
1417	3118–3120	Feb. 28, 1910	1482	3262–3264	May 18, 1910
1418	3121–3122	Mar. 2, 1910	1483	3265–3266	May 22, 1910
1419	3123–3124	Mar. 3, 1910	1484	3267–3268	May 23, 1910
1420	3125–3127	Mar. 4, 1910	1485	3269–3270	May 24, 1910
1421	3128–3129	Mar. 5, 1910	1486	3271–3273	May 25, 1910
1422	3130–3131	Mar. 6, 1910	1487	3274–3275	May 27, 1910
1423	3132–3133	Mar. 9, 1910	1488	3276–3278	May 27, 1910
1424	3134–3135	Mar. 10, 1910	1489	3279–3280	May 29, 1910
1425	3136–3137	Mar. 11, 1910	1490	3281–3282	May 31, 1910
1426	3138–3139	Mar. 13, 1910	1491	3283–3285	June 1, 1910
1427	3140–3142	Mar. 14, 1910	1492	3286–3287	June 2, 1910
1428	3143–3144	Mar. 15, 1910	1493	3288–3289	June 4, 1910
1429	3145	Mar. 16, 1910	1494	3290–3292	June 6, 1910
1430	3146–3147	Mar. 16, 1910	1495	3293–3294	June 7, 1910
1431	3148–3149	Mar. 17, 1910	1496	3295–3296	June 8, 1910
1432	3150–3151	Mar. 18, 1910	1497	3297–3299	June 9, 1910
1433	3152–3153	Mar. 20, 1910	1498	3300–3301	June 11, 1910
1434	3154–3156	Mar. 21, 1910	1499	3302–3303	June 13, 1910
1435	3157–3158	Mar. 22, 1910	1500	3304–3305	June 14, 1910
1436	3159–3160	Mar. 23, 1910	1501	3306–3308	June 16, 1910
1437	3161–3163	Mar. 25, 1910	1502	3309–3310	June 18, 1910
1438	3164–3165	Mar. 26, 1910	1503	3311–3312	June 20, 1910
1439	3166–3167	Mar. 28, 1910	1504	3313–3314	June 21, 1910
1440	3168–3170	Mar. 29, 1910	1505	3315–3317	June 23, 1910
1441	3171–3172	Mar. 30, 1910	1506	3318–3319	June 24, 1910
1442	3173–3174	Mar. 31, 1910	1507	3320–3321	June 26, 1910
1443	3175–3177	Apr. 1, 1910	1508	3322–3324	June 28, 1910
1444	3178–3179	Apr. 3, 1910	1509	3325–3326	June 30, 1910
1445	3180–3181	Apr. 4, 1910	1510	3327–3328	July 2, 1910
1446	3182–3184	Apr. 6, 1910	1511	3329–3330	July 4, 1910
1447	3185–3186	Apr. 7, 1910	1512	3331–3332	July 4, 1910
1448	3187–3188	Apr. 9, 1910	1513	3333–3335	July 6, 1910
1449	3189–3190	Apr. 11, 1910	1514	3336–3337	July 8, 1910

Roll	Volumes	Beginning Dates	Roll	Volumes	Beginning Dates
1515	3338–3339	July 11, 1910	1580	3481–3483	Oct. 20, 1910
1516	3340–3342	July 12, 1910	1581	3484–3485	Oct. 22, 1910
1517	3343–3344	July 15, 1910	1582	3486–3487	Oct. 24, 1910
1518	3345–3346	July 17, 1910	1583	3488–3489	Oct. 25, 1910
1519	3347–3348	July 19, 1910	1584	3490–3491	Oct. 26, 1910
1520	3349–3350	July 20, 1910	1585	3492–3494	Oct. 29, 1910
1521	3351–3352	July 23, 1910	1586	3495–3496	Oct. 31, 1910
1522	3353–3355	July 25, 1910	1587	3497–3498	Nov. 1, 1910
1523	3356–3357	July 26, 1910	1588	3499–3501	Nov. 3, 1910
1524	3358–3360	July 29, 1910	1589	3502–3503	Nov. 5, 1910
1525	3361–3362	Aug. 1, 1910	1590	3504–3505	Nov. 7, 1910
1526	3363–3364	Aug. 2, 1910	1591	3506–3507	Nov. 9, 1910
1527	3365–3366	Aug. 3, 1910	1592	3508–3509	Nov. 12, 1910
1528	3367–3368	Aug. 4, 1910	1593	3510–3511	Nov. 14, 1910
1529	3369–3370	Aug. 6, 1910	1594	3512–3514	Nov. 14, 1910
1530	3371–3372	Aug. 8, 1910	1595	3515–3516	Nov. 18, 1910
1531	3373–3374	Aug. 10, 1910	1596	3517–3518	Nov. 21, 1910
1532	3375–3377	Aug. 12, 1910	1597	3519–3520	Nov. 22, 1910
1533	3378–3379	Aug. 14, 1910	1598	3521–3522	Nov. 23, 1910
1534	3380–3381	Aug. 16, 1910	1599	3523–3524	Nov. 25, 1910
1535	3382–3383	Aug. 16, 1910	1600	3525–3526	Nov. 26, 1910
1536	3384–3386	Aug. 18, 1910	1601	3527–3528	Nov. 28, 1910
1537	3387–3388	Aug. 21, 1910	1602	3529–3531	Nov. 29, 1910
1538	3389–3390	Aug. 23, 1910	1603	3532–3533	Dec. 3, 1910
1539	3391–3392	Aug. 23, 1910	1604	3534–3535	Dec. 4, 1910
1540	3393–3394	Aug. 25, 1910	1605	3536–3537	Dec. 6, 1910
1541	3395–3396	Aug. 27, 1910	1606	3538–3539	Dec. 8, 1910
1542	3397–3399	Aug. 28, 1910	1607	3540–3541	Dec. 11, 1910
1543	3400–3401	Aug. 29, 1910	1608	3542–3543	Dec. 13, 1910
1544	3402–3403	Aug. 31, 1910	1609	3544–3545	Dec. 17, 1910
1545	3404–3405	Sept. 1, 1910	1610	3546–3547	Dec. 19, 1910
1546	3406–3408	Sept. 2, 1910	1611	3548–3549	Dec. 21, 1910
1547	3409–3410	Sept. 4, 1910	1612	3550–3551	Dec. 22, 1910
1548	3411–3412	Sept. 4, 1910	1613	3552–3553	Dec. 23, 1910
1549	3413–3414	Sept. 6, 1910	1614	3554–3545	Dec. 29, 1910
1550	3415–3416	Sept. 8, 1910	1615	3546–3547	Dec. 30, 1910
1551	3417–3419	Sept. 10, 1910	1616	3548–3549	Jan. 1, 1911
1552	3420–3421	Sept. 11, 1910	1617	3560–3561	Jan. 5, 1911
1553	3422–3423	Sept. 13, 1910	1618	3562–3563	Jan. 10, 1911
1554	3424–3425	Sept. 14, 1910	1619	3564–3566	Jan. 16, 1911
1555	3426–3428	Sept. 15, 1910	1620	3567–3568	Jan. 19, 1911
1556	3429–3430	Sept. 16, 1910	1621	3569–3570	Jan. 23, 1911
1557	3431–3432	Sept. 18, 1910	1622	3571–3572	Jan. 26, 1911
1558	3433–3434	Sept. 19, 1910	1623	3573–3575	Jan. 28, 1911
1559	3435–3437	Sept. 20, 1910	1624	3576–3577	Feb. 1, 1911
1560	3438–3439	Sept. 22, 1910	1625	3578–3579	Feb. 4, 1911
1561	3440–3441	Sept. 23, 1910	1626	3580–3581	Feb. 6, 1911
1562	3442–3443	Sept. 26, 1910	1627	3582–3584	Feb. 9, 1911
1563	3444–3445	Sept. 26, 1910	1628	3585–3586	Feb. 13, 1911
1564	3446–3447	Sept. 27, 1910	1629	3587–3588	Feb. 16, 1911
1565	3448–3449	Sept. 28, 1910	1630	3589–3591	Feb. 17, 1911
1566	3450–3452	Sept. 28, 1910	1631	3592–3593	Feb. 21, 1911
1567	3453–3454	Oct. 2, 1910	1632	3594–3595	Feb. 25, 1911
1568	3455–3456	Oct. 3, 1910	1633	3596–3598	Feb. 26, 1911
1569	3457–3458	Oct. 4, 1910	1634	3599–3601	Mar. 1, 1911
1570	3459–3460	Oct. 5, 1910	1635	3602–3603	Mar. 3, 1911
1571	3461–3462	Oct. 5, 1910	1636	3604–3605	Mar. 7, 1911
1572	3463–3464	Oct. 9, 1910	1637	3606–3607	Mar. 9, 1911
1573	3465–3467	Oct. 10, 1910	1638	3608–3610	Mar. 10, 1911
1574	3468–3469	Oct. 11, 1910	1639	3611–3162	Mar. 14, 1911
1575	3470–3472	Oct. 12, 1910	1640	3613–3614	Mar. 15, 1911
1576	3473–3474	Oct. 13, 1910	1641	3615–3616	Mar. 16, 1911
1577	3475–3476	Oct. 13, 1910	1642	3617–3619	Mar. 18, 1911
1578	3477–3478	Oct. 16, 1910	1643	3620–3621	Mar. 20, 1911
1579	3479–3480	Oct. 18, 1910	1644	3622–3623	Mar. 21, 1911

Roll	Volumes	Beginning Dates	Roll	Volumes	Beginning Dates
1645	3624–3626	Mar. 22, 1911	1710	3777–3778	July 17, 1911
1646	3627–3628	Mar. 25, 1911	1711	3779–3781	July 19, 1911
1647	3629–3631	Mar. 27, 1911	1712	3782–3783	July 24, 1911
1648	3632–3633	Mar. 27, 1911	1713	3784–3785	July 26, 1911
1649	3634–3635	Mar. 29, 1911	1714	3786–3788	July 28, 1911
1650	3636–3638	Mar. 30, 1911	1715	3789–3790	July 31, 1911
1651	3639–3641	Apr. 1, 1911	1716	3791–3792	Aug. 2, 1911
1652	3642–3643	Apr. 3, 1911	1717	3793–3795	Aug. 3, 1911
1653	3644–3646	Apr. 4, 1911	1718	3796–3797	Aug. 7, 1911
1654	3647–3648	Apr. 6, 1911	1719	3798–3799	Aug. 9, 1911
1655	3649–3651	Apr. 7, 1911	1720	3800–3801	Aug. 10, 1911
1656	3652–3653	Apr. 9, 1911	1721	3802–3803	Aug. 14, 1911
1657	3654–3656	Apr. 10, 1911	1722	3804–3806	Aug. 15, 1911
1658	3657–3658	Apr. 11, 1911	1723	3807–3808	Aug. 18, 1911
1659	3659–3660	Apr. 12, 1911	1724	3809–3810	Aug. 21, 1911
1660	3661–3663	Apr. 13, 1911	1725	3811–3813	Aug. 22, 1911
1661	3664–3665	Apr. 17, 1911	1726	3814–3815	Aug. 24, 1911
1662	3666–3668	Apr. 17, 1911	1727	3816–3818	Aug. 27, 1911
1663	3669–3670	Apr. 18, 1911	1728	3819–3820	Aug. 29, 1911
1664	3671–3672	Apr. 19, 1911	1729	3821–3823	Aug. 29, 1911
1665	3673–3675	Apr. 21, 1911	1730	3824–3825	Sept. 2, 1911
1666	3676–3677	Apr. 24, 1911	1731	3826–3827	Sept. 3, 1911
1667	3678–3679	Apr. 24, 1911	1732	3828–3829	Sept. 5, 1911
1668	3680–3682	Apr. 26, 1911	1733	3830–3832	Sept. 5, 1911
1669	3683–3684	Apr. 28, 1911	1734	3833–3834	Sept. 7, 1911
1670	3685–3687	May 1, 1911	1735	3835–3836	Sept. 8, 1911
1671	3688–3689	May 3, 1911	1736	3837–3839	Sept. 9, 1911
1672	3690–3691	May 4, 1911	1737	3840–3841	Sept. 12, 1911
1673	3692–3693	May 5, 1911	1738	3842–3843	Sept. 13, 1911
1674	3694–3696	May 6, 1911	1739	3844–3846	Sept. 14, 1911
1675	3697–3698	May 8, 1911	1740	3847–3848	Sept. 17, 1911
1676	3699–3700	May 9, 1911	1741	3849–3850	Sept. 19, 1911
1677	3701–3703	May 11, 1911	1742	3851–3852	Sept. 20, 1911
1678	3704–3705	May 14, 1911	1743	3853–3855	Sept. 21, 1911
1679	3706–3707	May 15, 1911	1744	3856–3857	Sept. 23, 1911
1680	3708–3710	May 17, 1911	1745	3858–3859	Sept. 25, 1911
1681	3711–3712	May 20, 1911	1746	3860–3862	Sept. 26, 1911
1682	3713–3715	May 22, 1911	1747	3863	Sept. 29, 1911
1683	3716–3717	May 24, 1911	1748	3864–3865	Sept. 29, 1911
1684	3718–3719	May 25, 1911	1749	3866–3868	Oct. 2, 1911
1685	3720–3721	May 27, 1911	1750	3869–3870	Oct. 4, 1911
1686	3722–3724	May 29, 1911	1751	3871–3872	Oct. 5, 1911
1687	3725–3727	May 31, 1911	1752	3873–3875	Oct. 7, 1911
1688	3728–3729	June 1, 1911	1753	3876–3877	Oct. 9, 1911
1689	3730–3731	June 3, 1911	1754	3878–3880	Oct. 10, 1911
1690	3732–3733	June 5, 1911	1755	3881–3882	Oct. 13, 1911
1691	3734–3736	June 6, 1911	1756	3883–3884	Oct. 13, 1911
1692	3737–3738	June 9, 1911	1757	3885–3886	Oct. 16, 1911
1693	3739–3741	June 9, 1911	1758	3887–3888	Oct. 18, 1911
1694	3742–3743	June 12, 1911	1759	3889–3890	Oct. 19, 1911
1695	3744–3745	June 14, 1911	1760	3891–3893	Oct. 21, 1911
1696	3746–3747	June 17, 1911	1761	3894–3895	Oct. 24, 1911
1697	3748–3750	June 19, 1911	1762	3896–3898	Oct. 24, 1911
1698	3751–3752	June 21, 1911	1763	3899–3900	Oct. 27, 1911
1699	3753–3754	June 24, 1911	1764	3901–3903	Oct. 29, 1911
1700	3755–3756	June 27, 1911	1765	3904–3905	Oct. 31, 1911
1701	3757–3759	June 28, 1911	1766	3906–3907	Nov. 2, 1911
1702	3760–3761	June 30, 1911	1767	3908–3910	Nov. 4, 1911
1703	3762–3763	July 2, 1911	1768	3911–3912	Nov. 6, 1911
1704	3764–3765	July 3, 1911	1769	3913–3914	Nov. 8, 1911
1705	3766–3767	July 5, 1911	1770	3915–3916	Nov. 10, 1911
1706	3768–3769	July 8, 1911	1771	3917–3919	Nov. 12, 1911
1707	3770–3772	July 11, 1911	1772	3920–3921	Nov. 14, 1911
1708	3773–3774	July 13, 1911	1773	3922–3923	Nov. 16, 1911
1709	3775–3776	July 16, 1911	1774	3924–3926	Nov. 18, 1911

Roll	Volumes	Beginning Dates	Roll	Volumes	Beginning Dates
1775	3927–3928	Nov. 22, 1911	1840	4077–4078	Apr. 12, 1912
1776	3929–3930	Nov. 24, 1911	1841	4079–4081	Apr. 16, 1912
1777	3931–3932	Nov. 26, 1911	1842	4082–4083	Apr. 17, 1912
1778	3933–3935	Nov. 28, 1911	1843	4084–4086	Apr. 18, 1912
1779	3936–3938	Dec. 1, 1911	1844	4087–4088	Apr. 20, 1912
1780	3939–3940	Dec. 5, 1911	1845	4089–4090	Apr. 22, 1912
1781	3941–3942	Dec. 6, 1911	1846	4091–4093	Apr. 24, 1912
1782	3943–3944	Dec. 6, 1911	1847	4094–4095	Apr. 26, 1912
1783	3945–3947	Dec. 7, 1911	1848	4096–4098	Apr. 26, 1912
1784	3948–3949	Dec. 12, 1911	1849	4099–4100	Apr. 29, 1912
1785	3950–3952	Dec. 14, 1911	1850	4101–4103	Apr. 29, 1912
1786	3953–3954	Dec. 19, 1911	1851	4104–4105	May 1, 1912
1787	3955–3956	Dec. 21, 1911	1852	4106–4108	May 2, 1912
1788	3957–3958	Dec. 22, 1911	1853	4109–4110	May 4, 1912
1789	3959–3960	Dec. 23, 1911	1854	4111–4113	May 6, 1912
1790	3961–3962	Dec. 26, 1911	1855	4114–4115	May 8, 1912
1791	3963–3964	Dec. 28, 1911	1856	4116–4118	May 8, 1912
1792	3965	Jan. 1, 1912	1857	4119–4120	May 10, 1912
1793	3966–3967	Jan. 2, 1912	1858	4121–4122	May 12, 1912
1794	3968–3969	Jan. 4, 1912	1859	4123–4125	May 12, 1912
1795	3970–3972	Jan. 8, 1912	1860	4126–4127	May 13, 1912
1796	3973–3974	Jan. 14, 1912	1861	4128–4129	May 14, 1912
1797	3975–3976	Jan. 17, 1912	1862	4130–4132	May 15, 1912
1798	3977–3978	Jan. 18, 1912	1863	4133–4134	May 17, 1912
1799	3979–3981	Jan. 22, 1912	1864	4135–4136	May 19, 1912
1800	3982–3983	Jan. 25, 1912	1865	4137–4139	May 20, 1912
1801	3984–3985	Jan. 29, 1912	1866	4140–4142	May 21, 1912
1802	3986–3987	Feb. 4, 1912	1867	4143–4144	May 23, 1912
1803	3988–3990	Feb. 6, 1912	1868	4145–4146	May 25, 1912
1804	3991–3992	Feb. 8, 1912	1869	4147–4149	May 26, 1912
1805	3993–3994	Feb. 10, 1912	1870	4150–4151	May 29, 1912
1806	3995–3997	Feb. 14, 1912	1871	4152–4154	May 29, 1912
1807	3998–3999	Feb. 17, 1912	1872	4155–4157	May 31, 1912
1808	4000–4002	Feb. 20, 1912	1873	4158–4159	June 1, 1912
1809	4003–4004	Feb. 23, 1912	1874	4160–4162	June 2, 1912
1810	4005	Feb. 25, 1912	1875	4163–4164	June 4, 1912
1811	4006–4007	Feb. 27, 1912	1876	4165–4167	June 5, 1912
1812	4008–4010	Feb. 28, 1912	1877	4168–4169	June 8, 1912
1813	4011–4012	Mar. 1, 1912	1878	4170–4171	June 8, 1912
1814	4013–4015	Mar. 3, 1912	1879	4172–4174	June 10, 1912
1815	4016–4017	Mar. 6, 1912	1880	4175–4176	June 11, 1912
1816	4018–4019	Mar. 8, 1912	1881	4177–4178	June 12, 1912
1817	4020–4022	Mar. 10, 1912	1882	4179–4181	June 14, 1912
1818	4023–4024	Mar. 13, 1912	1883	4182–4183	June 17, 1912
1819	4025–4026	Mar. 15, 1912	1884	4184–4185	June 19, 1912
1820	4027–4029	Mar. 16, 1912	1885	4186–4188	June 19, 1912
1821	4030–4031	Mar. 18, 1912	1886	4189–4191	June 22, 1912
1822	4032–4033	Mar. 19, 1912	1887	4192–4193	June 25, 1912
1823	4034–4036	Mar. 20, 1912	1888	4194–4196	June 26, 1912
1824	4037–4038	Mar. 22, 1912	1889	4197–4198	June 27, 1912
1825	4039–4041	Mar. 23, 1912	1890	4199–4201	June 28, 1912
1826	4042–4043	Mar. 27, 1912	1891	4202–4203	July 1, 1912
1827	4044–4044	Mar. 28, 1912	1892	4204–4206	July 2, 1912
1828	4045–4048	Mar. 28, 1912	1893	4207–4209	
1829	4049–4050	Mar. 29, 1912	1894	4210–4211	July 8, 1912
1830	4051–4054	Mar. 30, 1912	1895	4212–4214	July 8, 1912
1831	4055–4056	Apr. 1, 1912	1896	4215–4217	July 10, 1912
1832	4057–4059	Apr. 2, 1912	1897	4218–4219	July 12, 1912
1833	4060–4062	Apr. 3, 1912	1898	4220–4222	July 14, 1912
1834	4063–4064	Apr. 6, 1912	1899	4223–4225	July 16, 1912
1835	4065–4066	Apr. 7, 1912	1900	4226–4228	July 19, 1912
1836	4067–4069	Apr. 8, 1912	1901	4229–4231	July 21, 1912
1837	4070–4071	Apr. 9, 1912	1902	4232–4233	July 23, 1912
1838	4072–4073	Apr. 9, 1912	1903	4234–4236	July 23, 1912
1839	4074–4076	Apr. 11. 1912	1904	4237–4239	July 27, 1912

Roll	Volumes	Beginning Dates	Roll	Volumes	Beginning Dates
1905	4240–4241	July 30, 1912	1970	4424–4425	Nov. 6, 1912
1906	4242–4244	July 31, 1912	1971	4426–4428	Nov. 7, 1912
1907	4245–4246	Aug. 3, 1912	1972	4429–4430	Nov. 9, 1912
1908	4247–4249	Aug. 4, 1912	1973	4431–4433	Nov. 10, 1912
1909	4250–4251	Aug. 6, 1912	1974	4434–4435	Nov. 12, 1912
1910	4253–4254	Aug. 7, 1912	1975	4436–4438	Nov. 13, 1912
1911	4255–4257	Aug. 9, 1912	1976	4439–4440	Nov. 14, 1912
1912	4258–4260	Aug. 12, 1912	1977	4441–4443	Nov. 15, 1912
1913	4261–4263	Aug. 13, 1912	1978	4444–4446	Nov. 18, 1912
1914	4264–4266	Aug. 14, 1912	1979	4447–4449	Nov. 20, 1912
1915	4267–4269	Aug. 16, 1912	1980	4450–4451	Nov. 22, 1912
1916	4270–4271	Aug. 17, 1912	1981	4452–4454	Nov. 24, 1912
1917	4272–4274	Aug. 19, 1912	1982	4455–4456	Nov. 26, 1912
1918	4275–4277	Aug. 21, 1912	1983	4457–4459	Nov. 28, 1912
1919	4278–4280	Aug. 22, 1912	1984	4460–4462	Nov. 30, 1912
1920	4281–4282	Aug. 24, 1912	1985	4463–4464	Dec. 3, 1912
1921	4283–4285	Aug. 26, 1912	1986	4465–4467	Dec. 4, 1912
1922	4286–4287	Aug. 28, 1912	1987	4468–4469	Dec. 5, 1912
1923	4288–4290	Aug. 28, 1912	1988	4470–4472	Dec. 6, 1912
1924	4291–4293	Aug. 31, 1912	1989	4473–4475	Dec. 9, 1912
1925	4294–4296	Sept. 2, 1912	1990	4476–4477	Dec. 12, 1912
1926	4297–4299	Sept. 3, 1912	1991	4478–4480	Dec. 14, 1912
1927	4300–4302	Sept. 4, 1912	1992	4481–4482	Dec. 16, 1912
1928	4303–4305	Sept. 5, 1912	1993	4483–4485	Dec. 19, 1912
1929	4306–4308	Sept. 6, 1912	1994	4486–4487	Dec. 21, 1912
1930	4309–4311	Sept. 8, 1912	1995	4488–4490	Dec. 23, 1912
1931	4312–4314	Sept. 10, 1912	1996	4491–4493	Dec. 26, 1912
1932	4315–4317	Sept. 11, 1912	1997	4494–4495	Dec. 28, 1912
1933	4318–4320	Sept. 13, 1912	1998	4496	Dec. 31, 1912
1934	4321–4324	Sept. 14, 1912	1999	4497	Jan. 2, 1913
1935	4325–4326	Sept. 16, 1912	2000	4498–4500	Jan. 3, 1913
1936	4327–4329	Sept. 17, 1912	2001	4501–4502	Jan. 8, 1913
1937	4330–4333	Sept. 18, 1912	2002	4503–4505	Jan. 10, 1913
1938	4334–4336	Sept. 20, 1912	2003	4506–4507	Jan. 14, 1913
1939	4337–4339	Sept. 21, 1912	2004	4508–4510	Jan. 16, 1913
1940	4340–4342	Sept. 22, 1912	2005	4511–4512	Jan. 20, 1913
1941	4343–4345	Sept. 23, 1912	2006	4513–4515	Jan. 22, 1913
1942	4346–4348	Sept. 26, 1912	2007	4516–4518	Jan. 25, 1913
1943	4349–4352	Sept. 27, 1912	2008	4519–4521	Jan. 29, 1913
1944	4353–4355	Sept. 28, 1912	2009	4522–4523	Feb. 1, 1913
1945	4356–4358	Sept. 30, 1912	2010	4524–4526	Feb. 3, 1913
1946	4359–4360	Oct. 1, 1912	2011	4527–4529	Feb. 5, 1913
1947	4361–4363	Oct. 1, 1912	2012	4530–4532	Feb. 8, 1913
1948	4364–4366	Oct. 3, 1912	2013	4533–4535	Feb. 14, 1913
1949	4367–4369	Oct. 5, 1912	2014	4536–4537	Feb. 16, 1913
1950	4370–4372	Oct. 7, 1912	2015	4538–4540	Feb. 16, 1913
1951	4373–4375	Oct. 9, 1912	2016	4541–4543	Feb. 19, 1913
1952	4376–4377	Oct. 10, 1912	2017	4544–4546	Feb. 21, 1913
1953	4378–4380	Oct. 12, 1912	2018	4547–4548	Feb. 23, 1913
1954	4381–4382	Oct. 13, 1912	2019	4549–4551	Feb. 25, 1913
1955	4383–4385	Oct. 14, 1912	2020	4552–4554	Feb. 27, 1913
1956	4386–4388	Oct. 17, 1912	2021	4555–4556	Mar. 1, 1913
1957	4389–4391	Oct. 18, 1912	2022	4557–4559	Mar. 2, 1913
1958	4392–4394	Oct. 18, 1912	2023	4560–4561	Mar. 5, 1913
1959	4395–4396	Oct. 21, 1912	2024	4562–4564	Mar. 6, 1913
1960	4397–4399	Oct. 22, 1912	2025	4565–4566	Mar. 8, 1913
1961	4400–4401	Oct. 23, 1912	2026	4567–4569	Mar. 9, 1913
1962	4402–4404	Oct. 24, 1912	2027	4570–4572	Mar. 12, 1913
1963	4405–4407	Oct. 26, 1912	2028	4573–4575	Mar. 13, 1913
1964	4408–4409	Oct. 28, 1912	2029	4576–4577	Mar. 15, 1913
1965	4410–4412	Oct. 29, 1912	2030	4578–4580	Mar. 17, 1913
1966	4413–4415	Oct. 30, 1912	2031	4581–4582	Mar. 18, 1913
1967	4416–4418	Oct. 31, 1912	2032	4583–4585	Mar. 19, 1913
1968	4419–4421	Nov. 3, 1912	2033	4586–4587	Mar. 20, 1913
1969	4422–4423	Nov. 6, 1912	2034	4588–4590	Mar. 21, 1913

Roll	Volumes	Beginning Dates	Roll	Volumes	Beginning Dates
2035	4591–4592	Mar. 21, 1913	2100	4753–4754	June 10, 1913
2036	4593–4595	Mar. 25, 1913	2101	4755–4757	June 11, 1913
2037	4596–4598	Mar. 27, 1913	2102	4758–4759	June 12, 1913
2038	4599–4601	Mar. 28, 1913	2103	4760–4761	June 12, 1913
2039	4602–4603	Mar. 31, 1913	2104	4762–4764	June 13, 1913
2040	4604–4606	Apr. 1, 1913	2105	4765–4766	June 15, 1913
2041	4607–4608	Apr. 2, 1913	2106	4767–4769	June 16, 1913
2042	4609–4610	Apr. 2, 1913	2107	4770–4771	June 17, 1913
2043	4611–4613	Apr. 3, 1913	2108	4772–4774	June 17, 1913
2044	4614–4615	Apr. 4, 1913	2109	4775–4776	June 18, 1913
2045	4616–4618	Apr. 7, 1913	2110	4777–4778	June 19, 1913
2046	4619–4621	Apr. 8, 1913	2111	4779–4781	June 21, 1913
2047	4622–4623	Apr. 10, 1913	2112	4782–4783	June 23, 1913
2048	4624–4626	Apr. 11, 1913	2113	4784–4785	June 23, 1913
2049	4627–4628	Apr. 12, 1913	2114	4786–4787	June 24, 1913
2050	4629–4631	Apr. 14, 1913	2115	4788–4790	June 25, 1913
2051	4632–4633	Apr. 14, 1913	2116	4791–4792	June 27, 1913
2052	4634–4635	Apr. 16, 1913	2117	4793–4795	June 27, 1913
2053	4636–4638	Apr. 16, 1913	2118	4796–4798	June 29, 1913
2054	4639–4641	Apr. 17, 1913	2119	4799–4800	July 1, 1913
2055	4642–4643	Apr. 19, 1913	2120	4801–4803	July 1, 1913
2056	4644–4646	Apr. 19, 1913	2121	4804–4806	July 2, 1913
2057	4647–4648	Apr. 21, 1913	2122	4807–4808	July 5, 1913
2058	4649–4651	Apr. 22, 1913	2123	4809–4811	July 5, 1913
2059	4652–4653	Apr. 24, 1913	2124	4812–4813	July 7, 1913
2060	4654–4655	Apr. 24, 1913	2125	4814–4815	July 8, 1913
2061	4656–4658	Apr. 26, 1913	2126	4816–4818	July 9, 1913
2062	4659–4660	Apr. 27, 1913	2127	4819–4820	July 11, 1913
2063	4661–4663	Apr. 28, 1913	2128	4821–4823	July 12, 1913
2064	4664–4665	Apr. 29, 1913	2129	4824–4825	July 14, 1913
2065	4666–4668	Apr. 29, 1913	2130	4826–4828	July 15, 1913
2066	4669–4071	May 1, 1913	2131	4829–4830	July 17, 1913
2067	4672–4673	May 2, 1913	2132	4831–4833	July 18, 1913
2068	4674–4676	May 4, 1913	2133	4834–4835	July 20, 1913
2069	4677–4678	May 5, 1913	2134	4836–4838	July 21, 1913
2070	4679–4681	May 6, 1913	2135	4839–4840	July 23, 1913
2071	4682–4683	May 7, 1913	2136	4841–4842	July 24, 1913
2072	4684–4685	May 8, 1913	2137	4843–4844	July 25, 1913
2073	4686–4688	May 8, 1913	2138	4845–4847	July 25, 1913
2074	4689–4690	May 9, 1913	2139	4848–4849	July 27, 1913
2075	4691–4693	May 11, 1913	2140	4850–4852	July 28, 1913
2076	4694–4695	May 12, 1913	2141	4853–4854	July 30, 1913
2077	4696–4698	May 13, 1913	2142	4855–4857	July 30, 1913
2078	4699–4700	May 15, 1913	2143	4858–4859	Aug. 2, 1913
2079	4701–4703	May 16, 1913	2144	4860–4862	Aug. 2, 1913
2080	4704–4705	May 17, 1913	2145	4863–4864	Aug. 4, 1913
2081	4706–4708	May 18, 1913	2146	4865–4867	Aug. 5, 1913
2082	4709–4710	May 19, 1913	2147	4868–4869	Aug. 7, 1913
2083	4711–4713	May 21, 1913	2148	4870–4871	Aug. 8, 1913
2084	4714–4715	May 22, 1913	2149	4872–4874	Aug. 8, 1913
2085	4716–4718	May 23, 1913	2150	4875–4876	Aug. 11, 1913
2086	4719–4720	May 25, 1913	2151	4877–4879	Aug. 12, 1913
2087	4721–4722	May 26, 1913	2152	4880–4881	Aug. 15, 1913
2088	4723–4725	May 27, 1913	2153	4882–4884	Aug. 16, 1913
2089	4726–4727	May 28, 1913	2154	4885–4886	Aug. 16, 1913
2090	4728–4730	May 29, 1913	2155	4887–4889	Aug. 17, 1913
2091	4731–4733	May 31, 1913	2156	4890–4093	Aug. 19, 1913
2092	4734–4735	June 2, 1913	2157	4894–4896	Aug. 20, 1913
2093	4736–4738	June 3, 1913	2158	4897–4899	Aug. 22, 1913
2094	4739–4740	June 4, 1913	2159	4900–4902	Aug. 25, 1913
2095	4741–4743	June 5, 1913	2160	4903–4904	Aug. 26, 1913
2096	4744–4745	June 6, 1913	2161	4905–4907	Aug. 26, 1913
2097	4746–4748	June 7, 1913	2162	4908–4909	Aug. 27, 1913
2098	4749–4750	June 8, 1913	2163	4910–4912	Aug. 28, 1913
2099	4751–4752	June 9, 1913	2164	4913–4915	Aug. 30, 1913

Roll	Volumes	Beginning Dates
2165	4916–4918	Aug. 31, 1913
2166	4919–4921	Sept. 2, 1913
2167	4922–4924	Sept. 3, 1913
2168	4925–4927	Sept. 4, 1913
2169	4928–4929	Sept. 6, 1913
2170	4930–4932	Sept. 8, 1913
2171	4933–4935	Sept. 9, 1913
2172	4936–4937	Sept. 10, 1913
2173	4938–4940	Sept. 10, 1913
2174	4941–4942	Sept. 12, 1913
2175	4943–4945	Sept. 13, 1913
2176	4946–4947	Sept. 14, 1913
2177	4948–4950	Sept. 15, 1913
2178	4951–4952	Sept. 17, 1913
2179	4953–4955	Sept. 17, 1913
2180	4956–4957	Sept. 19, 1913
2181	4958–4960	Sept. 20, 1913
2182	4961–4963	Sept. 23, 1913
2183	4964–4965	Sept. 24, 1913
2184	4966–4968	Sept. 25, 1913
2185	4969–4971	Sept. 26, 1913
2186	4972–4974	Sept. 27, 1913
2187	4975–4976	Sept. 28, 1913
2188	4977–4979	Sept. 29, 1913
2189	4980–4981	Oct. 1, 1913
2190	4982–4984	Oct. 2, 1913
2191	4985–4987	Oct. 4, 1913
2192	4988–4990	Oct. 5, 1913
2193	4991–4922	Oct. 6, 1913
2194	4993–4995	Oct. 7, 1913
2195	4996–4998	Oct. 8, 1913
2196	4999–5000	Oct. 9, 1913
2197	5001–5003	Oct. 10, 1913
2198	5004–5006	Oct. 12, 1913
2199	5007–5009	Oct. 14, 1913
2200	5010–5011	Oct. 16, 1913
2201	5012–5014	Oct. 17, 1913
2202	5015–5017	Oct. 18, 1913
2203	5018–5019	Oct. 20, 1913
2204	5020–5022	Oct. 20, 1913
2205	5023–5024	Oct. 22, 1913
2206	5025–5026	Oct. 22, 1913
2207	5027–5029	Oct. 22, 1913
2208	5030–5031	Oct. 25, 1913
2209	5032–5034	Oct. 26, 1913
2210	5035–5036	Oct. 27, 1913
2211	5037–5039	Oct, 28, 1913
2212	5040–5041	Oct. 29, 1913
2213	5042–5044	Oct. 31, 1913
2214	5045–5047	Nov. 3, 1913
2215	5048–5049	Nov. 5, 1913
2216	5050–5052	Nov. 6, 1913
2217	5053–5054	Nov. 8, 1913
2218	5055–5057	Nov. 11, 1913
2219	5058–5059	Nov. 12, 1913
2220	5060–5061	Nov. 13, 1913
2221	5062–5064	Nov. 13, 1913
2222	5065–5066	Nov. 15, 1913
2223	5067–5069	Nov. 16, 1913
2224	5070–5071	Nov. 18, 1913
2225	5072–5073	Nov. 20, 1913
2226	5074–5076	Nov. 21, 1913
2227	5077–5078	Nov. 24, 1913
2228	5079–5081	Nov. 25, 1913
2229	5082–5083	Nov. 28, 1913

Roll	Volumes	Beginning Dates
2230	5084–5086	Nov. 29, 1913
2231	5087–5088	Dec. 2, 1913
2232	5089–5091	Dec. 2, 1913
2233	5092–5093	Dec. 4, 1913
2234	5094–5096	Dec. 5, 1913
2235	5097–5098	Dec. 7, 1913
2236	5099–5101	Dec. 8, 1913
2237	5102–5103	Dec. 9, 1913
2238	5104–5106	Dec. 9, 1913
2239	5107–5108	Dec. 13, 1913
2240	5109–5111	Dec. 16, 1913
2241	5112–5114	Dec. 19, 1913
2242	5115–5116	Dec. 21, 1913
2243	5117–5119	Dec. 22, 1913
2244	5120–5121	Dec. 24, 1913
2245	5122–5124	Dec. 26, 1913
2246	5125–5126	Dec. 28, 1913
2247	5127–5129	Jan. 1, 1914
2248	5130–5131	Jan. 5, 1914
2249	5132–5134	Jan. 9, 1914
2250	5135–5136	Jan. 12, 1914
2251	5137–5139	Jan. 15, 1914
2252	5140–5142	Jan. 20, 1914
2253	5143–5144	Jan. 22, 1914
2254	5145–5147	Jan. 24, 1914
2255	5148–5149	Jan. 28, 1914
2256	5150–5152	Jan. 29, 1914
2257	5153–5154	Feb. 3, 1914
2258	5155–5156	Feb. 5, 1914
2259	5157–5159	Feb. 7, 1914
2260	5160–5162	Feb. 11, 1914
2261	5163–5164	Feb. 16, 1914
2262	5165–5167	Feb. 18, 1914
2263	5168–5170	Feb. 20, 1914
2264	5171–5172	Feb. 24, 1914
2265	5173–5175	Feb. 25, 1914
2266	5176–5177	Mar. 1, 1914
2267	5178–5180	Mar. 3, 1914
2268	5181–5182	Mar. 4, 1914
2269	5183–5185	Mar. 5, 1914
2270	5186–5187	Mar. 6, 1914
2271	5188–5190	Mar. 8, 1914
2272	5191–5192	Mar. 11, 1914
2273	5193–5195	Mar. 13, 1914
2274	5196–5197	Mar. 15, 1914
2275	5198–5200	Mar. 16, 1914
2276	5201–5203	Mar. 18, 1914
2277	5204–5205	Mar. 19, 1914
2278	5206–5207	Mar. 20, 1914
2279	5208–5210	Mar. 23, 1914
2280	5211–5212	Mar. 25, 1914
2281	5213–5215	Mar. 26, 1914
2282	5216–5217	Mar. 27, 1914
2283	5218–5220	Mar. 28, 1914
2284	5221–5222	Mar. 29, 1914
2285	5223–5225	Apr. 1, 1914
2286	5226–5227	Apr. 3, 1914
2287	5228–5229	Apr. 4, 1914
2288	5230–5232	Apr. 5, 1914
2289	5233–5234	Apr. 6, 1914
2290	5235–5237	Apr. 7, 1914
2291	5238–5239	Apr. 8, 1914
2292	5240–5242	Apr. 9, 1914
2293	5243–5244	Apr. 11, 1914
2294	5245–5247	Apr. 11, 1914

Roll	Volumes	Beginning Dates	Roll	Volumes	Beginning Dates
2295	5248–5250	Apr. 13, 1914	2360	5408–5410	Aug. 12, 1914
2296	5251–5252	Apr. 14, 1914	2361	5411–5413	Aug. 15, 1914
2297	5253–5254	Apr. 15, 1914	2362	5414–5416	Aug. 19, 1914
2298	5255–5257	Apr. 16, 1914	2363	5417–5419	Aug. 23, 1914
2299	5258–5259	Apr. 18, 1914	2364	5420–5423	Aug. 24, 1914
2300	5260–5262	Apr. 19, 1914	2365	5424–5426	Aug. 30, 1914
2301	5263–5264	Apr. 21, 1914	2366	5427–5430	Sept. 2, 1914
2302	5265–5267	Apr. 23, 1914	2367	5431–5435	Sept. 5, 1914
2303	5268–5269	Apr. 24, 1914	2368	5436–5438	Sept. 11, 1914
2304	5270–5272	Apr. 26, 1914	2369	5439–5441	Sept. 13, 1914
2305	5273–5275	Apr. 26, 1914	2370	5442–5444	Sept. 16, 1914
2306	5276–5277	Apr. 30, 1914	2371	5445–5447	Sept. 19, 1914
2307	5278–5279	Apr. 30, 1914	2372	5448–5451	Sept. 23, 1914
2308	5280–5282	May 2, 1914	2373	5452–5453	Sept. 27, 1914
2309	5283–5285	May 4, 1914	2374	5454–5457	Oct. 1, 1914
2310	5286–5287	May 7, 1914	2375	5458–5460	Oct. 4, 1914
2311	5288–5289	May 8, 1914	2376	5461–5463	Oct. 9, 1914
2312	5290–5292	May 11, 1914	2377	5464–5466	Oct. 13, 1914
2313	5293–5294	May 11, 1914	2378	5467–5468	Oct. 16, 1914
2314	5295–5296	May 12, 1914	2379	5469–5472	Oct. 21, 1914
2315	5297–5299	May 13, 1914	2380	5473–5475	Oct. 26, 1914
2316	5300–5301	May 14, 1914	2381	5476–5478	Oct. 31, 1914
2317	5302–5304	May 16, 1914	2382	5479–5480	Nov. 4, 1914
2318	5305–5306	May 18, 1914	2383	5481–5483	Nov. 7, 1914
2319	5307–5309	May 18, 1914	2384	5484–5486	Nov. 13, 1914
2320	5310–5311	May 20, 1914	2385	5487–5488	Nov. 19, 1914
2321	5312–5314	May 21, 1914	2386	5489–5491	Nov. 21, 1914
2322	5315–5316	May 22, 1914	2387	5492–5494	Nov. 28, 1914
2323	5317–5319	May 25, 1914	2388	5495–5497	Dec. 4, 1914
2324	5320–5321	May 26, 1914	2389	5498–5500	Dec. 10, 1914
2325	5322–5324	May 27, 1914	2390	5501–5502	Dec. 19, 1914
2326	5325–5326	May 29, 1914	2391	5503–5505	Dec. 23, 1914
2327	5327–5328	May 31, 1914	2392	5506–5508	Jan. 1, 1915
2328	5329–5331	June 1, 1914	2393	5509–5511	Jan. 12, 1915
2329	5332–5333	June 3, 1914	2394	5512–5513	Jan. 19, 1915
2330	5334–5336	June 4, 1914	2395	5514–5516	Jan. 24, 1915
2331	5337–5339	June 7, 1914	2396	5517–5519	Feb. 3, 1915
2332	5340–5341	June 9, 1914	2397	5520–5522	Feb. 13, 1915
2333	5342–5344	June 10, 1914	2398	5523–5525	Feb. 20, 1915
2334	5345–5346	June 13, 1914	2399	5526–5528	Mar. 1, 1915
2335	5347–5349	June 15, 1914	2400	5529–5530	Mar. 9, 1915
2336	5350–5351	June 18, 1914	2401	5531–5533	Mar. 13, 1915
2337	5352–5354	June 21, 1914	2402	5534–5536	Mar. 20, 1915
2338	5355–5356	June 23, 1914	2403	5537–5539	Mar. 23, 1915
2339	5357–5359	June 25, 1914	2404	5540–5542	Apr. 1, 1915
2340	5360–5361	June 26, 1914	2405	5543–5545	Apr. 7, 1915
2341	5362–5364	June 29, 1914	2406	5546–5548	Apr. 12, 1915
2342	5365–5366	July 2, 1914	2407	5549–5551	Apr. 19, 1915
2343	5367–5369	July 3, 1914	2408	5552–5554	Apr. 24, 1915
2344	5370–5372	July 6, 1914	2409	5555–5557	Apr. 28, 1915
2345	5373–5374	July 8, 1914	2410	5558–5559	May 4, 1915
2346	5375–5377	July 10, 1914	2411	5560–5562	May 9, 1915
2347	5378–5380	July 14, 1914	2412	5563–5565	May 12, 1915
2348	5381–5382	July 16, 1914	2413	5566–5567	May 19, 1915
2349	5383–5385	July 18, 1914	2414	5568–5570	May 25, 1915
2350	5386–5388	July 21, 1914	2415	5571–5573	June 1, 1915
2351	5389	July 23, 1914	2416	5574–5575	June 6, 1915
2352	5390–5391	July 24, 1914	2417	5576–5578	June 11, 1915
2353	5392–5394	July 27, 1914	2418	5579–5581	June 18, 1915
2354	5395–5396	July 30, 1914	2419	5582–5585	June 24, 1915
2355	5397–5398	July 31, 1914	2420	5586–5587	July 6, 1915
2356	5399–5400	Aug. 2, 1914	2421	5588–5590	July 10, 1915
2357	5401–5403	Aug. 3, 1914	2422	5591–5593	July 15, 1915
2358	5404–5405	Aug. 5, 1914	2423	5594–5596	July 21, 1915
2359	5406–5407	Aug. 10, 1914	2424	5597–5599	July 30, 1915

Roll	Volumes	Beginning Dates	Roll	Volumes	Beginning Dates
2425	5600–5602	Aug. 6, 1915	2490	5785–5787	Sept. 19, 1916
2426	5603–5605	Aug. 12, 1915	2491	5788–5790	Sept. 25, 1916
2427	5606–5608	Aug. 20, 1915	2492	5791–5792	Sept. 29, 1916
2428	5609–5611	Aug. 26, 1915	2493	5793–5795	Oct. 1, 1916
2429	5612–5614	Sept. 2, 1915	2494	5796–5797	Oct. 7, 1916
2430	5615–5616	Sept. 7, 1915	2495	5798–5800	Oct. 10, 1916
2431	5617–5620	Sept. 12, 1915	2496	5801–5803	Oct. 16, 1916
2432	5621–5622	Sept. 20, 1915	2497	5804–5806	Oct. 23, 1916
2433	5623–5625	Sept. 24, 1915	2498	5807–5809	Oct. 27, 1916
2434	5626–5628	Oct. 1, 1915	2499	5810–5811	Nov. 4, 1916
2435	5629–5631	Oct. 6, 1915	2500	5812–5814	Nov. 8, 1916
2436	5632–5634	Oct. 13, 1915	2501	5815–5817	Nov. 15, 1916
2437	5635–5637	Oct. 19, 1915	2502	5818–5820	Nov. 22, 1916
2438	5638–5640	Oct. 26, 1915	2503	5821–5823	Nov. 27, 1916
2439	5641–5642	Nov. 1, 1915	2504	5824–5826	Dec. 4, 1916
2440	5643–5645	Nov. 8, 1915	2505	5827–5828	Dec. 11, 1916
2441	5646–5648	Nov. 13, 1915	2506	5829–5831	Dec. 17, 1916
2442	5649–5650	Nov. 23, 1915	2507	5832–5834	Dec. 19, 1916
2443	5651–5654	Nov. 27, 1915	2508	5835–5836	Dec. 26, 1916
2444	5655–5657	Dec. 7, 1915	2509	5837	Jan. 2, 1917
2445	5658–5659	Dec. 19, 1915	2510	5838–5840	Jan. 10, 1917
2446	5660–5661	Dec. 24, 1915	2511	5841–5843	Jan. 14, 1917
2447	5662–5664	Jan. 2, 1916	2512	5844–5846	Jan. 22, 1917
2448	5665–5667	Jan. 7, 1916	2513	5847–5849	Jan. 29, 1917
2449	5668–5670	Jan. 18, 1916	2514	5850–5852	Feb. 8, 1917
2450	5671–5672	Jan. 29, 1916	2515	5853–5855	Feb. 14, 1917
2451	5673–5675	Feb. 2, 1916	2516	5856–5858	Feb. 25, 1917
2452	5676–5678	Feb. 11, 1916	2517	5859–5861	Mar. 10, 1917
2453	5679–5681	Feb. 23, 1916	2518	5862–5865	Mar. 23, 1917
2454	5682–5684	Feb. 26, 1916	2519	5866–5868	Apr. 5, 1917
2455	5685–5687	Mar. 7, 1916	2520	5869–5871	Apr. 16, 1917
2456	5688–5690	Mar. 10, 1916	2521	5872–5874	Apr. 25, 1917
2457	5691–5693	Mar. 16, 1916	2522	5875–5877	May 4, 1917
2458	5694–5696	Mar. 21, 1916	2523	5878–5881	May 10, 1917
2459	5697–5699	Mar. 27, 1916	2524	5882–5884	May 17, 1917
2460	5700–5702	Apr. 4, 1916	2525	5885–5887	May 22, 1917
2461	5703–5706	Apr. 10, 1916	2526	5888–5890	May 29, 1917
2462	5707–5708	Apr. 17, 1916	2527	5891–5894	June 3, 1917
2463	5709–5711	Apr. 19, 1916	2528	5895–5897	June 11, 1917
2464	5712–5714	Apr. 25, 1916	2529	5898–5901	June 16, 1917
2465	5715–5717	May 1, 1916	2530	5902–5904	June 23, 1917
2466	5718–5719	May 4, 1916	2531	5905–5908	June 29, 1917
2467	5720–5722	May 6, 1916	2532	5909–5911	July 5, 1917
2468	5723–5725	May 12, 1916	2533	5912–5914	July 12, 1917
2469	5726–5728	May 23, 1916	2534	5915–5917	July 17, 1917
2470	5729–5731	May 29, 1916	2535	5918–5920	July 23, 1917
2471	5732–5734	June 1, 1916	2536	5921–5924	July 28, 1917
2472	5735–5736	June 8, 1916	2537	5925–5927	Aug. 6, 1917
2473	5737–5739	June 12, 1916	2538	5928–5930	Aug. 10, 1917
2474	5740–5741	June 19, 1916	2539	5931–5934	Aug. 16, 1917
2475	5742–5744	June 21, 1916	2540	5935–5937	Aug. 26, 1917
2476	5745–5747	June 26, 1916	2541	5938–5940	Sept. 1, 1917
2477	5748–5750	July 6, 1916	2542	5941–5943	Sept. 7, 1917
2478	5751–5753	July 12, 1916	2543	5944–5946	Sept. 14, 1917
2479	5754–5755	July 17, 1916	2544	5947–5948	Sept. 20, 1917
2480	5756–5758	July 23, 1916	2545	5949–5951	Sept. 26, 1917
2481	5759–5761	July 31, 1916	2546	5952–5954	Oct. 3, 1917
2482	5762–5764	Aug. 5, 1916	2547	5955–5956	Oct. 10, 1917
2483	5765–5767	Aug. 10, 1916	2548	5957–5959	Oct. 15, 1917
2484	5768–5769	Aug. 14, 1916	2549	5960–5962	Oct. 22, 1917
2485	5770–5772	Aug. 20, 1916	2550	5963–5964	Oct. 28, 1917
2486	5773–5776	Aug. 25, 1916	2551	5965–5967	Nov. 4, 1917
2487	5777–5778	Sept. 5, 1916	2552	5968–5970	Nov. 11, 1917
2488	5779–5781	Sept. 6, 1916	2553	5971–5973	Nov. 19, 1917
2489	5782–5784	Sept. 15, 1916	2554	5974–5976	Nov. 28, 1917

Roll	Volumes	Beginning Dates	Roll	Volumes	Beginning Dates
2555	5977–5978	Dec. 7, 1917	2620	6124–6125	Jan. 19, 1919
2556	5979–5981	Dec. 12, 1917	2621	6126–6128	Jan. 25, 1919
2557	5982–5984	Dec. 19, 1917	2622	6129–6131	Jan. 30, 1919
2558	5985–5986	Dec. 26, 1917	2623	6132–6134	Feb. 4, 1919
2559	5987–5989	Jan. 1, 1918	2624	6135–6136	Feb. 11, 1919
2560	5990–5991	Jan. 11, 1918	2625	6137–6138	Feb. 17, 1919
2561	5992–5994	Jan. 18, 1918	2626	6139–6141	Feb. 21, 1919
2562	5995–5996	Feb. 1, 1918	2627	6142–6144	Feb. 27, 1919
2563	5997–5998	Feb. 7, 1918	2628	6145–6146	Mar. 3, 1919
2564	5999–6000	Feb. 13, 1918	2629	6147–6149	Mar. 8, 1919
2565	6001–6003	Feb. 21, 1918	2630	6150–6151	Mar. 14, 1919
2566	6004–6005	Mar. 4, 1918	2631	6152–6153	Mar. 19, 1919
2567	6006–6008	Mar. 9, 1918	2632	6154–6155	Mar. 24, 1919
2568	6009–6010	Mar. 21, 1918	2633	6156–6158	Mar. 29, 1919
2569	6011–6012	Mar. 27, 1918	2634	6159–6160	Apr. 3, 1919
2570	6013–6015	Apr. 3, 1918	2635	6161–6162	Apr. 7, 1919
2571	6016–6017	Apr. 12, 1918	2636	6163–6165	Apr. 9, 1919
2572	6018–6020	Apr. 18, 1918	2637	6166–6167	Apr. 14, 1919
2573	6021–6022	Apr. 26, 1918	2638	6168–6170	Apr. 18, 1919
2574	6023–6025	May 1, 1918	2639	6171–6172	Apr. 23, 1919
2575	6026–6027	May 7, 1918	2640	6173–6174	Apr. 26, 1919
2576	6028–6030	May 13, 1918	2641	6175–6177	Apr. 29, 1919
2577	6031–6032	May 20, 1918	2642	6178–6179	May 5, 1919
2578	6033–6035	May 26, 1918	2643	6180–6182	May 9, 1919
2579	6036–6037	June 3, 1918	2644	6183–6184	May 14, 1919
2580	6038–6040	June 9, 1918	2645	6185–6187	May 17, 1919
2581	6041–6042	June 15, 1918	2646	6188–6189	May 22, 1919
2582	6043–6045	June 21, 1918	2647	6190–6191	May 25, 1919
2583	6046–6047	June 27, 1918	2648	6192–6194	May 29, 1919
2584	6048–6049	July 3, 1918	2649	6195–6196	June 3, 1919
2585	6050–6052	July 8, 1918	2650	6197–6198	June 6, 1919
2586	6053–6055	July 17, 1918	2651	6199–6201	June 9, 1919
2587	6056–6057	July 22, 1918	2652	6202–6203	June 12, 1919
2588	6058	Aug. 1, 1918	2653	6204–6205	June 16, 1919
2589	6059–6060	Aug. 3, 1918	2654	6206–6207	June 19, 1919
2590	6061	Aug. 7, 1918	2655	6208–6210	June 22, 1919
2591	6062–6063	Aug. 10, 1918	2656	6211–6212	June 27, 1919
2592	6064–6065	Aug. 14, 1918	2657	6213–6214	July 1, 1919
2593	6066–6067	Aug. 20, 1918	2658	6215–6216	July 5, 1919
2594	6068	Aug. 24, 1918	2659	6217–6218	July 8, 1919
2595	6069–6070	Aug. 27, 1918	2660	6219–6221	July 13, 1919
2596	6071–6072	Sept. 1, 1918	2661	6222–6223	July 16, 1919
2597	6073–6074	Sept. 4, 1918	2662	6224–6225	July 21, 1919
2598	6075–6076	Sept. 10, 1918	2663	6226–6228	July 23, 1919
2599	6077	Sept. 17, 1918	2664	6229–6230	July 29, 1919
2600	6078–6079	Sept. 20, 1918	2665	6231–6232	Aug. 3, 1919
2601	6080–6081	Sept. 27, 1918	2666	6233–6234	Aug. 7, 1919
2602	6082–6083	Oct. 2, 1918	2667	6235–6236	Aug. 10, 1919
2603	6084–6086	Oct. 8, 1918	2668	6237–6239	Aug. 12, 1919
2604	6087–6088	Oct. 15, 1918	2669	6240–6241	Aug. 18, 1919
2605	6089–6090	Oct. 20, 1918	2670	6242–6244	Aug. 20, 1919
2606	6091–6092	Oct. 26, 1918	2671	6245–6246	Aug. 25, 1919
2607	6093–6095	Nov. 1, 1918	2672	6247–6248	Aug. 26, 1919
2608	6096–6098	Nov. 7, 1918	2673	6249–6250	Aug. 29, 1919
2609	6099–6101	Nov. 12, 1918	2674	6251–6252	Sept. 2, 1919
2610	6102–6103	Nov. 19, 1918	2675	6253–6254	Sept. 5, 1919
2611	6104–6106	Nov. 23, 1918	2676	6255–6256	Sept. 7, 1919
2612	6107–6108	Dec. 1, 1918	2677	6257–6258	Sept. 12, 1919
2613	6109–6111	Dec. 7, 1918	2678	6259–6260	Sept. 14, 1919
2614	6112–6113	Dec. 16, 1918	2679	6261–6263	Sept. 16, 1919
2615	6114–6116	Dec. 21, 1918	2680	6264–6265	Sept. 20, 1919
2616	6117	Dec. 28, 1918	2681	6266–6267	Sept. 23, 1919
2617	6118	Jan. 1, 1919	2682	6268–6269	Sept. 26, 1919
2618	6119–6120	Jan. 3, 1919	2683	6270–6271	Oct. 1, 1919
2619	6121–6123	Jan. 10, 1919	2684	6272	Oct. 2, 1919

Roll	Volumes	Beginning Dates	Roll	Volumes	Beginning Dates
2685	6273–6275	Oct. 4, 1919	2751	6402–6403	Apr. 13, 1920
2686	6276	Oct. 8, 1919	2752	6404	Apr. 16, 1920
2687	6277–6278	Oct. 10, 1919	2753	6405–6406	Apr. 16, 1920
2688	6279–6281	Oct. 13, 1919	2754	6407–6408	Apr. 19, 1920
2689	6282–6283	Oct. 17, 1919	2755	6409–6410	Apr. 22, 1920
2690	6284–6285	Oct. 20, 1919	2756	6411–6412	Apr. 23, 1920
2691	6286–6287	Oct. 22, 1919	2757	6413–6414	Apr. 28, 1920
2692	6288–6289	Oct. 27, 1919	2758	6415	Apr. 30, 1920
2693	6290–6291	Oct. 27, 1919	2759	6416–6417	May 1, 1920
2694	6292–6293	Nov. 1, 1919	2760	6418–6419	May 3, 1920
2625	6294–6295	Nov. 3, 1919	2761	6420–6421	May 5, 1920
2696	6296–6297	Nov. 7, 1919	2762	6422	May 10, 1920
2697	6298	Nov. 10, 1919	2763	6423–6424	May 12, 1920
2698	6299–6300	Nov. 12, 1919	2764	6425	May 14, 1920
2699	6301–6302	Nov. 18, 1919	2765	6426–6427	May 15, 1920
2700	6303–6305	Nov. 22, 1919	2766	6428–6429	May 17, 1920
2701	6306–6307	Nov. 26, 1919	2767	6430–6431	May 17, 1920
2702	6308	Dec. 1, 1919	2768	6432–6433	May 21, 1920
2703	6309–6310	Dec. 1, 1919	2769	6434	May 24, 1920
2704	6311–6312	Dec. 4, 1919	2770	6435–6436	May 24, 1920
2705	6313–6314	Dec. 7, 1919	2771	6437–6438	May 27, 1920
2706	6315–6316	Dec. 10, 1919	2772	6439–6440	May 29, 1920
2707	6317–6318	Dec. 15, 1919	2773	6441	May 30, 1920
2708	6319–6320	Dec. 18, 1919	2774	6442–6443	May 31, 1920
2709	6321–6322	Dec. 19, 1919	2775	6444–6445	June 2, 1920
2710	6323–6324	Dec. 21, 1919	2776	6446–6447	June 5, 1920
2711	6325–6326	Dec. 23, 1919	2777	6448–6449	June 7, 1920
2712	6327–6328	Dec. 25, 1919	2778	6450–6451	June 9, 1920
2713	6329–6330	Dec. 26, 1919	2779	6452–6453	June 10, 1920
2714	6331–6332	Dec. 29, 1919	2780	6454–6455	June 12, 1920
2715	6333–6334	Jan. 2, 1920	2781	6456–6457	June 15, 1920
2716	6335–6336	Jan. 5, 1920	2782	6458	June 17, 1920
2718	6338–6339	Jan. 9, 1920	2783	6459–6460	June 19, 1920
2719	6340–6341	Jan. 15, 1920	2784	6461–6462	June 20, 1920
2720	6342–6343	Jan. 19, 1920	2785	6463–6464	June 21, 1920
2721	6344–6345	Jan. 22, 1920	2786	6465–6466	June 22, 1920
2722	6346–6347	Jan. 24, 1920	2787	6467–6468	June 25, 1920
2723	6348–6349	Jan. 27, 1920	2788	6469–6470	June 28, 1920
2724	6350–6351	Jan. 29, 1920	2789	6471	June 29, 1920
2725	6352–6353	Feb. 1, 1920	2790	6472–6473	July 1, 1920
2726	6354–6355	Feb. 4, 1920	2791	6474	July 2, 1920
2727	6356–6357	Feb. 8, 1920	2792	6475–6476	July 3, 1920
2728	6358–6359	Feb. 11, 1920	2793	6477–6478	July 6, 1920
2729	6360	Feb. 14, 1920	2794	6479	July 7, 1920
2730	6361–6362	Feb. 15, 1920	2795	6480–6481	July 9, 1920
2731	6363–6364	Feb. 19, 1920	2796	6482–6483	July 12, 1920
2732	6365–6366	Feb. 22, 1920	2797	6484–6485	July 13, 1920
2733	6367–6368	Feb. 24, 1920	2798	6486–6487	July 15, 1920
2734	6369–6370	Feb. 28, 1920	2799	6488	July 18, 1920
2735	6371–6372	Mar. 2, 1920	2800	6489–6490	July 17, 1920
2736	6373–6374	Mar. 4, 1920	2801	6491	July 20, 1920
2737	6375–6376	Mar. 6, 1920	2802	6492–6493	July 21, 1920
2738	6377–6378	Mar. 9, 1920	2803	6494–6495	July 23, 1920
2739	6379	Mar. 13, 1920	2804	6496	July 27, 1920
2740	6380–6381	Mar. 14, 1920	2805	6497–6498	July 28, 1920
2741	6382–6383	Mar. 18, 1920	2806	6499–6500	July 29, 1920
2742	6384–6385	Mar. 22, 1920	2807	6501–6502	Aug. 1, 1920
2743	6386	Mar. 23, 1920	2808	6503	Aug. 4, 1920
2744	6387–6388	Mar. 24, 1920	2809	6504–6505	Aug. 4, 1920
2745	6389–6391	Mar. 27, 1920	2810	6506–6507	Aug. 8, 1920
2746	6392–6393	Apr. 1, 1920	2811	6508–6509	Aug. 9, 1920
2747	6394–6395	Apr. 3, 1920	2812	6510	Aug. 11, 1920
2748	6396–6397	Apr. 6, 1920	2813	6511–6512	Aug. 12, 1920
2749	6398–6399	Apr. 9, 1920	2814	6513	Aug. 13, 1920
2750	6400–6401	Apr. 10, 1920	2815	6514–6515	Aug. 14, 1920

Roll	Volumes	Beginning Dates	Roll	Volumes	Beginning Dates
2816	6516–6517	Aug. 16, 1920	2881	6631	Nov. 26, 1920
2817	6518–6519	Aug. 20, 1920	2882	6632–6633	Nov. 27, 1920
2818	6520–6521	Aug. 21, 1920	2883	6634	Nov. 29, 1920
2819	6522	Aug. 22, 1920	2884	6635–6636	Nov. 29, 1920
2820	6523–6524	Aug. 23, 1920	2885	6637	Dec. 2, 1920
2821	6525–6526	Aug. 25, 1920	2886	6638–6639	Dec. 2, 1920
2822	6527–6528	Aug. 27, 1920	2887	6640–6641	Dec. 4, 1920
2823	6529	Aug. 28, 1920	2888	6642	Dec. 7, 1920
2824	6530–6532	Aug. 29, 1920	2889	6643–6644	Dec. 10, 1920
2825	6533–6534	Sept. 4, 1920	2890	6645–6646	Dec. 13, 1920
2826	6535	Sept. 4, 1920	2891	6647	Dec. 13, 1920
2827	6536–6537	Sept. 4, 1920	2892	6648–6649	Dec. 14, 1920
2828	6538–6539	Sept. 6, 1920	2893	6650	Dec. 16, 1920
2829	6540–6541	Sept. 7, 1920	2894	6651–6652	Dec. 17, 1920
2830	6542	Sept. 8, 1920	2895	6653–6654	Dec. 18, 1920
2831	6543–6544	Sept. 9, 1920	2896	6655	Dec. 20, 1920
2832	6545–6546	Sept. 10, 1920	2897	6656–6657	Dec. 20, 1920
2833	6547–6548	Sept. 12, 1920	2898	6658	Dec. 20, 1920
2834	6549–6550	Sept. 14, 1920	2899	6659–6660	Dec. 21, 1920
2835	6551–6552	Sept. 16, 1920	2900	6661–6662	Dec. 26, 1920
2836	6553–6554	Sept. 17, 1920	2901	6663–6664	Dec. 28, 1920
2837	6555	Sept. 18, 1920	2902	6665	Dec. 31, 1920
2838	6556–6557	Sept. 19, 1920	2903	6666–6667	Jan. 1, 1921
2839	6558–6559	Sept. 20, 1920	2904	6668–6669	Jan. 4, 1921
2840	6560–6561	Sept. 22, 1920	2905	6670	Jan. 1, 1921
2841	6562	Sept. 25, 1920	2906	6671–6672	Jan. 6, 1921
2842	6563–6564	Sept. 25, 1920	2907	6673	Jan. 8, 1921
2843	6565–6566	Sept. 27, 1920	2908	6674–6675	Jan. 10, 1921
2844	6567–6568	Sept. 30, 1920	2909	6676–6677	Jan. 13, 1921
2845	6569–6570	Oct. 2, 1920	2910	6678	Jan. 16, 1921
2846	6571–6572	Oct. 4, 1920	2911	6679–6680	Jan. 18, 1921
2847	6573	Oct. 5, 1920	2912	6681–6682	Jan. 19, 1921
2848	6574–6575	Oct. 5, 1920	2913	6683–6684	Jan. 20, 1921
2849	6576–6577	Oct. 6, 1920	2914	6685	Jan. 21, 1921
2850	6578–6579	Oct. 9, 1920	2915	6686–6687	Jan. 22, 1921
2851	6580–6581	Oct. 11, 1920	2916	6688–6689	Jan. 24, 1921
2852	6582	Oct. 12, 1920	2917	6690–6691	Jan. 28, 1921
2853	6583–6584	Oct. 13, 1920	2918	6692	Jan. 31, 1921
2854	6585–6586	Oct. 16, 1920	2919	6693–6694	Jan. 31, 1921
2855	6587	Oct. 17, 1920	2920	6695–6696	Feb. 2, 1921
2856	6588–6589	Oct. 18, 1920	2921	6697–6698	Feb. 3, 1921
2857	6590–6591	Oct. 19, 1920	2922	6699	Feb. 7, 1921
2858	6592	Oct. 22, 1920	2923	6700–6701	Feb. 8, 1921
2859	6593–6594	Oct. 23, 1920	2924	6702–6703	Feb. 11, 1921
2860	6595–6596	Oct. 23, 1920	2925	6704	Feb. 14, 1921
2861	6597–6598	Oct. 26, 1920	2926	6705–6706	Feb. 16, 1921
2862	6599	Oct. 27, 1920	2927	6707–6708	Feb. 18, 1921
2863	6600–6601	Oct. 27, 1920	2928	6709	Feb. 21, 1921
2864	6602–6603	Oct. 28, 1920	2929	6710–6711	Feb. 22, 1921
2865	6604	Oct. 30, 1920	2930	6712–6713	Feb. 24, 1921
2866	6605–6606	Oct. 30, 1920	2931	6714–6715	Mar. 1, 1921
2867	6607–6608	Nov. 2, 1920	2932	6716–6717	Mar. 3, 1921
2868	6609–6610	Nov. 3, 1920	2933	6718–6719	Mar. 6, 1921
2869	6611	Nov. 6, 1920	2934	6720	Mar. 10, 1921
2870	6612–6613	Nov. 8, 1920	2935	6721–6722	Mar. 10, 1921
2871	6614–6615	Nov. 9, 1920	2936	6723–6724	Mar. 13, 1921
2872	6616	Nov. 12, 1920	2937	6725–6726	Mar. 16, 1921
2873	6617–6618	Nov. 13, 1920	2938	6727–6728	Mar. 19, 1921
2874	6619–6620	Nov. 13, 1920	2939	6729–6730	Mar. 20, 1921
2875	6621	Nov. 15, 1920	2940	6731–6732	Mar. 22, 1921
2876	6622–6623	Nov. 15, 1920	2941	6733	Mar. 25, 1921
2877	6624–6625	Nov. 19, 1920	2942	6734–6735	Mar. 28, 1921
2878	6626	Nov. 20, 1920	2943	6736–6737	Mar. 28, 1921
2879	6627–6628	Nov. 22, 1920	2944	6738–6739	Mar. 31, 1921
2880	6629–6630	Nov. 24, 1920	2945	6740–6741	Apr. 2, 1921

Roll	Volumes	Beginning Dates	Roll	Volumes	Beginning Dates
2946	6742	Apr. 2, 1921	3011	6859–6860	Aug. 19, 1921
2947	6743–6744	Apr. 5, 1921	3012	6861–6863	Aug. 21, 1921
2948	6745–6746	Apr. 7, 1921	3013	6864–6865	Aug. 24, 1921
2949	6747–6748	Apr. 9, 1921	3014	6866–6877	Aug. 28, 1921
2950	6749–6750	Apr. 13, 1921	3015	6868–6869	Aug. 29, 1921
2951	6751–6752	Apr. 14, 1921	3016	6870–6871	Aug. 30, 1921
2952	6753	Apr. 16, 1921	3017	6872–6873	Sept. 1, 1921
2593	6754–6755	Apr. 17, 1921	3018	6874–6876	Sept. 4, 1921
2954	6756–6757	Apr. 19, 1921	3019	6877–6878	Sept. 5, 1921
2955	6758	Apr. 23, 1921	3020	6879–6881	Sept. 10, 1921
2956	6759–6760	Apr. 24, 1921	3021	6882–6883	Sept. 11, 1921
2957	6761–6762	Apr. 25, 1921	3022	6884–6885	Sept. 13, 1921
2958	6763–6764	Apr. 29, 1921	3023	6886–6888	Sept. 16, 1921
2959	6765–6766	May 1, 1921	3024	6889–6890	Sept. 18, 1921
2960	6767	May 2, 1921	3025	6891–6893	Sept. 19, 1921
2961	6768–6769	May 3, 1921	3026	6894–6895	Sept. 22, 1921
2962	6770–6771	May 7, 1921	3027	6896–6898	Sept. 23, 1921
2963	6772	May 9, 1921	3028	6899–6900	Sept. 26, 1921
2964	6773–6774	May 10, 1921	3029	6901–6902	Sept. 27, 1921
2965	6775–6776	May 11, 1921	3030	6903–6905	Sept. 30, 1921
2966	6777–6778	May 12, 1921	3031	6906–6907	Oct. 1, 1921
2967	6779	May 14, 1921	3032	6908–6910	Oct. 3, 1921
2968	6780–6781	May 15, 1921	3033	6911–6912	Oct. 5, 1921
2969	6782–6783	May 18, 1921	3034	6913–6914	Oct. 7, 1921
2970	6784	May 21, 1921	3035	6915–6916	Oct. 10, 1921
2971	6785–6786	May 21, 1921	3036	6917–6919	Oct. 12, 1921
2972	6787–6788	May 22, 1921	3037	6920–6921	Oct. 16, 1921
2973	6789–6790	May 25, 1921	3038	6922–6923	Oct. 17, 1921
2974	6791–6792	May 27, 1921	3039	6924–6925	Oct. 17, 1921
2975	6793–6794	June 1, 1921	3040	6926–6928	Oct. 21, 1921
2976	6795–6796	June 2, 1921	3041	6929–6930	Oct. 24, 1921
2977	6797–6798	June 4, 1921	3042	6931–6933	Oct. 25, 1921
2978	6799	June 5, 1921	3043	6934–6935	Oct. 29, 1921
2979	6800–6801	June 6, 1921	3044	6936–6937	Nov. 1, 1921
2980	6802–6803	June 10, 1921	3045	6938–6939	Nov. 1, 1921
2981	6804–6805	June 12, 1921	3046	6940–6942	Nov. 3, 1921
2982	6806	June 13, 1921	3047	6943–6944	Nov. 6, 1921
2983	6807–6808	June 15, 1921	3048	6945–6947	Nov. 8, 1921
2984	6809–6810	June 18, 1921	3049	6948–6949	Nov. 11, 1921
2985	6811–6812	June 21, 1921	3050	6950–6951	Nov. 12, 1921
2986	6813	June 24, 1921	3051	6952–6953	Nov. 14, 1921
2987	6814–6815	June 25, 1921	3052	6954–6955	Nov. 17, 1921
2988	6816–6817	June 28, 1921	3053	6956–6958	Nov. 20, 1921
2989	6818–6819	July 1, 1921	3054	6959–6960	Nov. 22, 1921
2990	6820–6821	July 2, 1921	3055	6961–6963	Nov. 25, 1921
2991	6822–6823	July 4, 1921	3056	6964–6965	Nov. 28, 1921
2992	6824	July 6, 1921	3057	6966–6967	Dec. 1, 1921
2993	6825–6826	July 9, 1921	3058	6968–6969	Dec. 2, 1921
2994	6827–6828	July 11, 1921	3059	6970–6971	Dec. 5, 1921
2995	6829–6830	July 13, 1921	3060	6972–6974	Dec. 7, 1921
2996	6831–6832	July 16, 1921	3061	6975–6976	Dec. 12, 1921
2997	6833–6834	July 19, 1921	3062	6977–6978	Dec. 14, 1921
2998	6835–6836	July 22, 1921	3063	6979–6980	Dec. 17, 1921
2999	6837–6838	July 24, 1921	3064	6981–6983	Dec. 19, 1921
3000	6839–6840	July 27, 1921	3065	6984–6985	Dec. 23, 1921
3001	6841	Aug. 1, 1921	3066	6986–6988	Dec. 24, 1921
3002	6842–6843	Aug. 1, 1921	3067	6989–6990	Dec. 28, 1921
3003	6844–6845	Aug. 2, 1921	3068	6991–6993	Jan. 1, 1922
3004	6846–6847	Aug. 6, 1921	3069	6994–6995	Jan. 6, 1922
3005	6848–6849	Aug. 8, 1921	3070	6996–6997	Jan. 10, 1922
3006	6850–6851	Aug. 10, 1921	3071	6998–7000	Jan. 13, 1922
3007	6852	Aug. 12, 1921	3072	7001–7002	Jan. 16, 1922
3008	6853–6854	Aug. 13, 1921	3073	7003–7004	Jan. 18, 1922
3009	6855–6856	Aug. 14, 1921	3074	7005–7007	Jan. 21, 1922
3010	6857–6858	Aug. 16, 1921	3075	7008–7009	Jan. 26, 1922

Roll	Volumes	Beginning Dates	Roll	Volumes	Beginning Dates
3076	7010–7012	Jan. 30, 1922	3141	7170–7172	July 10, 1922
3077	7013–7015	Feb. 1, 1922	3142	7173–7174	July 14, 1922
3078	7016–7017	Feb. 5, 1922	3143	7175–7176	July 15, 1922
3079	7018–7019	Feb. 8, 1922	3144	7177–7179	July 18, 1922
3080	7020–7022	Feb. 11, 1922	3145	7180–7181	July 21, 1922
3081	7023–7025	Feb. 14, 1922	3146	7182–7183	July 22, 1922
3082	7026–7027	Feb. 17, 1922	3147	7184–7186	July 24, 1922
3083	7028–7030	Feb. 20, 1922	3148	7187–7188	July 26, 1922
3084	7031–7032	Feb. 25, 1922	3149	7189	July 29, 1922
3085	7033–7034	Mar. 1, 1922	3150	7190–7192	July 30, 1922
3086	7035–7037	Mar. 3, 1922	3151	7193–7194	July 31, 1922
3087	7038–7039	Mar. 7, 1922	3152	7195–7196	Aug. 1, 1922
3088	7040–7042	Mar. 13, 1922	3153	7197–7198	Aug. 3, 1922
3089	7043–7044	Mar. 8, 1922	3154	7199–7200	Aug. 4, 1922
3090	7045–7047	Mar. 18, 1922	3155	7202–7203	Aug. 6, 1922
3091	7048–7049	Mar. 19, 1922	3156	7204–7205	Aug. 8, 1922
3092	7050–7052	Mar. 20, 1922	3157	7206–7208	Aug. 11, 1922
3093	7053–7054	Mar. 23, 1922	3158	7209–7210	Aug. 13, 1922
3094	7055–7057	Mar. 26, 1922	3159	7211–7212	Aug. 14, 1922
3095	7058–7060	Mar. 29, 1922	3160	7213–7215	Aug. 16, 1922
3096	7061–7063	Apr. 1, 1922	3161	7216–7217	Aug. 18, 1922
3097	7064–7065	Apr. 4, 1922	3162	7218–7219	Aug. 19, 1922
3098	7066–7068	Apr. 7, 1922	3163	7220–7222	Aug. 20, 1922
3099	7069–7070	Apr. 9, 1922	3164	7223–7224	Aug. 22, 1922
3100	7071–7072	Apr. 11, 1922	3165	7225–7227	Aug. 24, 1922
3101	7073–7075	Apr. 13, 1922	3166	7228–7229	Aug. 26, 1922
3102	7076–7077	Apr. 17, 1922	3167	7230–7232	Aug. 28, 1922
3103	7078–7080	Apr. 17, 1922	3168	7233–7234	Aug. 30, 1922
3104	7081–7083	Apr. 21, 1922	3169	7235–7236	Sept. 1, 1922
3105	7084–7085	Apr. 24, 1922	3170	7237–7239	Sept. 1, 1922
3106	7086–7088	Apr. 26, 1922	3171	7240–7241	Sept. 2, 1922
3107	7089–7091	Apr. 29, 1922	3172	7242–7244	Sept. 3, 1922
3108	7092–7093	May 2, 1922	3173	7245–7246	Sept. 5, 1922
3109	7094–7096	May 5, 1922	3174	7247–7249	Sept. 7, 1922
3110	7097–7098	May 8, 1922	3175	7250–7251	Sept. 8, 1922
3111	7099–7100	May 9, 1922	3176	7252–7253	Sept. 9, 1922
3112	7101–7103	May 12, 1922	3177	7254–7256	Sept. 10, 1922
3113	7104–7105	May 13, 1922	3178	7257–7259	Sept. 11, 1922
3114	7106–7108	May 16, 1922	3179	7260–7261	Sept. 14, 1922
3115	7109–7110	May 19, 1922	3180	7262–7263	Sept. 16, 1922
3116	7111–7113	May 20, 1922	3181	7264	Sept. 17, 1922
3117	7114–7115	May 23, 1922	3182	7265–7266	Sept. 18, 1922
3118	7116–7118	May 27, 1922	3183	7267–7268	Sept. 19, 1922
3119	7119–7120	May 28, 1922	3184	7269–7271	Sept. 20, 1922
3120	7121–7123	May 29, 1922	3185	7272–7274	Sept. 24, 1922
3121	7124–7125	June 1, 1922	3186	7275–7276	Sept. 24, 1922
3122	7126–7127	June 3, 1922	3187	7277–7279	Sept. 26, 1922
3123	7128–7130	June 5, 1922	3188	7280–7281	Sept. 28, 1922
3124	7131–7132	June 8, 1922	3189	7282–7284	Sept. 30, 1922
3125	7133–7135	June 9, 1922	3190	7285–7286	Oct. 1, 1922
3126	7136–7137	June 12, 1922	3191	7287–7289	Oct. 2, 1922
3127	7138–7140	June 14, 1922	3192	7290–7291	Oct. 3, 1922
3128	7141–7142	June 17, 1922	3193	7292–7293	Oct. 4, 1922
3129	7143–7144	June 19, 1922	3194	7294–7296	Oct. 6, 1922
3130	7145–7147	June 21, 1922	3195	7297–7298	Oct. 9, 1922
3131	7148–7149	June 24, 1922	3196	7299–7300	Oct. 9, 1922
3132	7150–7151	June 26, 1922	3197	7301–7303	Oct. 11, 1922
3133	7152–7153	June 29, 1922	3198	7304–7305	Oct. 13, 1922
3134	7154–7156	July 1, 1922	3199	7306–7307	Oct. 15, 1922
3135	7157–7158	July 1, 1922	3200	7308–7310	Oct. 16, 1922
3136	7159–7160	July 2, 1922	3201	7311–7312	Oct. 18, 1922
3137	7161–7163	July 3, 1922	3202	7313–7315	Oct. 20, 1922
3138	7164–7165	July 7, 1922	3203	7316–7317	Oct. 22, 1922
3139	7166–7167	July 8, 1922	3204	7318–7320	Oct. 23, 1922
3140	7168–7169	July 10, 1922	3205	7321–7323	Oct. 25, 1922

Roll	Volumes	Beginning Dates	Roll	Volumes	Beginning Dates
3206	7324–7325	Oct. 28, 1922	3271	7477–7479	Mar. 25, 1923
3207	7326–7328	Oct. 30, 1922	3272	7480–7481	Mar. 27, 1923
3208	7329–7330	Oct. 31, 1922	3273	7482–7483	Mar. 29, 1923
3209	7331–7332	Nov. 1, 1922	3274	7484–7485	Mar. 31, 1923
3210	7333–7334	Nov. 1, 1922	3275	7486–7487	Apr. 1, 1923
3211	7335–7336	Nov. 3, 1922	3276	7488–7490	Apr. 3, 1923
3212	7337–7338	Nov. 3, 1922	3277	7491–7492	Apr. 6, 1923
3213	7339–7341	Nov. 6, 1922	3278	7493–7949	Apr. 6, 1923
3214	7342–7343	Nov. 8, 1922	3279	7495–7497	Apr. 9, 1923
3215	7344–7345	Nov. 10, 1922	3280	7498–7499	Apr. 11, 1923
3216	7346–7348	Nov. 12, 1922	3281	7500–7502	Apr. 12, 1923
3217	7349–7350	Nov. 14, 1922	3282	7503–7504	Apr. 15, 1923
3218	7351–7353	Nov. 15, 1922	3283	7505–7507	Apr. 16, 1923
3219	7354–7355	Nov. 18, 1922	3284	7508–7509	Apr. 19, 1923
3220	7356–7358	Nov. 20, 1922	3285	7510–7511	Apr. 22, 1923
3221	7359–7360	Nov. 22, 1922	3286	7512–7514	Apr. 23, 1923
3222	7361–7363	Nov. 25, 1922	3287	7515–7517	Apr. 25, 1923
3223	7364–7365	Nov. 27, 1922	3288	7518–7519	Apr. 29, 1923
3224	7366–7368	Nov. 28, 1922	3289	7520–7522	Apr. 30, 1923
3225	7369–7370	Dec. 1, 1922	3290	7523–7524	May 1, 1923
3226	7371–7372	Dec. 1, 1922	3291	7525–7526	May 2, 1923
3227	7373–7374	Dec. 3, 1922	3292	7527–7529	May 4, 1923
3228	7375–7377	Dec. 5, 1922	3293	7530–7531	May 7, 1923
3229	7378–7380	Dec. 8, 1922	3294	7532–7534	May 7, 1923
3230	7381–7382	Dec. 11, 1922	3295	7535–7536	May 11, 1923
3231	7383–7384	Dec. 12, 1922	3296	7537–7539	
3232	7385–7387	Dec. 14, 1922	3297	7540–7541	May 14, 1923
3233	7388–7389	Dec. 18, 1922	3298	7542–7544	May 16, 1923
3234	7390–7392	Dec. 21, 1922	3299	7545–7546	May 19, 1923
3235	7393–7394	Dec. 23, 1922	3300	7547–7549	May 21, 1923
3236	7395–7397	Dec. 25, 1922	3301	7550–7551	May 25, 1923
3237	7398–7399	Dec. 29, 1922	3302	7552–7554	May 27, 1923
3238	7400–7402	Jan. 1, 1923	3303	7555–7556	May 29, 1923
3239	7403–7404	Jan. 3, 1923	3304	7557–7558	May 31, 1923
3240	7405–7406	Jan. 6, 1923	3305	7559–7561	June 2, 1923
3241	7407–7409	Jan. 8, 1923	3306	7562–7563	June 4, 1923
3242	7410–7411	Jan. 11, 1923	3307	7564–7565	June 5, 1923
3243	7412–7413	Jan. 14, 1923	3308	7566–7568	June 7, 1923
3244	7414–7416	Jan. 16, 1923	3309	7569–7571	June 9, 1923
3245	7417–7418	Jan. 18, 1923	3310	7572–7573	June 12, 1923
3246	7419–7420	Jan. 21, 1923	3311	7574–7576	June 14, 1923
3247	7421–7423	Jan. 25, 1923	3312	7577–7578	June 17, 1923
3248	7424–7425	Jan. 27, 1923	3313	7579–7581	June 19, 1923
3249	7426–7427	Jan. 30, 1923	3314	7582–7583	June 22, 1923
3250	7428–7429	Feb. 2, 1923	3315	7584–7586	June 23, 1923
3251	7430–7432	Feb. 5, 1923	3316	7587–7588	June 25, 1923
3252	7433–7434	Feb. 6, 1923	3317	7589–7591	June 27, 1923
3253	7435–7436	Feb. 8, 1923	3318	7592–7593	July 1, 1923
3254	7437–7438	Feb. 12, 1923	3319	7594–7595	July 1, 1923
3255	7439–7441	Feb. 14, 1923	3320	7596–7597	July 1, 1923
3256	7442–7443	Feb. 18, 1923	3321	7598–7599	July 2, 1923
3257	7444–7446	Feb. 19, 1923	3322	7600–7601	July 3, 1923
3258	7447–7448	Feb. 22, 1923	3323	7602–7603	July 3, 1923
3259	7449–7450	Feb. 25, 1923	3324	7604–7606	July 5, 1923
3260	7451–7453	Mar. 1, 1923	3325	7607	July 6, 1923
3261	7454–7455	Mar. 5, 1923	3326	7608–7610	July 7, 1923
3262	7456–7457	Mar. 6, 1923	3327	7611–7612	July 9, 1923
3263	7458–7459	Mar. 7, 1923	3328	7613–7614	July 10, 1923
3264	7460–7462	Mar. 8, 1923	3329	7615–7617	July 13, 1923
3265	7463–7464	Mar. 11, 1923	3330	7618–7619	July 15, 1923
3266	7465–7466	Mar. 14, 1923	3331	7620–7621	July 17, 1923
3267	7467–7468	Mar. 15, 1923	3332	7622–7623	July 18, 1923
3268	7469–7471	Mar. 17, 1923	3333	7624–7625	July 19, 1923
3269	7472–7474	Mar. 19, 1923	3334	7626–7628	July 20, 1923
3270	7475–7476	Mar. 22, 1923	3335	7629–7630	July 23, 1923

Roll	Volumes	Beginning Dates	Roll	Volumes	Beginning Dates
3336	7631–7632	July 24, 1923	3401	7780–7782	Oct. 27, 1923
3337	7633–7635	July 26, 1923	3402	7783	Oct. 31, 1923
3338	7636–7637	Aug. 1, 1923	3403	7784–7785	Nov. 1, 1923
3339	7638–7639	Aug. 1, 1923	3404	7786–7787	Nov. 1, 1923
3340	7640–7641	Aug. 1, 1923	3405	7788–7790	Nov. 1, 1923
3341	7642–7643	Aug. 1, 1923	3406	7791	Nov. 2, 1923
3342	7644–7645	Aug. 2, 1923	3407	7792–7794	Nov. 2, 1923
3343	7646–7647	Aug. 3, 1923	3408	7795–7796	Nov. 4, 1923
3344	7648–7649	Aug. 4, 1923	3409	7797–7798	Nov. 6, 1923
3345	7650–7651	Aug. 6, 1923	3410	7799–7800	Nov. 9, 1923
3346	7652–7654	Aug. 7, 1923	3411	7801–7803	Nov. 9, 1923
3347	7655–7666	Aug. 9, 1923	3412	7804–7805	Nov. 11, 1923
3348	7657–7658	Aug. 11, 1923	3413	7806–7807	Nov. 12, 1923
3349	7659–7661	Aug. 13, 1923	3414	7808–7809	Nov. 15, 1923
3350	7662–7663	Aug. 15, 1923	3415	7810–7812	Nov. 18, 1923
3351	7664–7665	Aug. 16, 1923	3416	7813–7814	Nov. 19, 1923
3352	7667–7668	Aug. 17, 1923	3417	7815–7816	Nov. 21, 1923
3353	7669–7670	Aug. 18, 1923	3418	7817–7819	Nov. 23, 1923
3354	7671–7673	Aug. 20, 1923	3419	7820–7821	Nov. 26, 1923
3355	7674–7675	Aug. 22, 1923	3420	7822–7824	Nov. 27, 1923
3356	7676–7678	Aug. 24, 1923	3421	7825	Dec. 1, 1923
3357	7679–7681	Aug. 26, 1923	3422	7826–7827	Dec. 1, 1923
3358	7682–7683	Aug. 28, 1923	3423	7829–7830	Dec. 2, 1923
3359	7684–7685	Aug. 30, 1923	3424	7831–7832	Dec. 3, 1923
3360	7686–7687	Sept. 1, 1923	3425	7833–7834	Dec. 4, 1923
3361	7688–7690	Sept. 1, 1923	3426	7835–7837	Dec. 6, 1923
3362	7691–7692	Sept. 2, 1923	3427	7838–7839	Dec. 10, 1923
3363	7693–7694	Sept. 2, 1923	3428	7840–7841	Dec. 12, 1923
3364	7695–7696	Sept. 2, 1923	3429	7842–7843	Dec. 15, 1923
3365	7697–7699	Sept. 5, 1923	3430	7844–7846	Dec. 17, 1923
3366	7700–7701	Sept. 6, 1923	3431	7847–7848	Dec. 19, 1923
3367	7702–7703	Sept. 6, 1923	3432	7849–7850	Dec. 22, 1923
3368	7704–7706	Sept. 7, 1923	3433	7851–7853	Dec. 23, 1923
3369	7707–7708	Sept. 9, 1923	3434	7854–7855	Dec. 26, 1923
3370	7709–7710	Sept. 10, 1923	3435	7856	December, 1923
3371	7711–7713	Sept. 11, 1923	3436	7857–7858	Jan. 1, 1924
3372	7714–7715	Sept. 14, 1923	3437	7859–7860	Jan. 2, 1924
3373	7716–7718	Sept. 15, 1923	3438	7861–7862	Jan. 7, 1924
3374	7719–7720	Sept. 17, 1923	3439	7863–7864	Jan. 9, 1924
3375	7721–7723	Sept. 19, 1923	3440	7865–7866	Jan. 10, 1924
3376	7724–7725	Sept. 21, 1923	3441	7867–7869	Jan. 12, 1924
3377	7726–7727	Sept. 23, 1923	3442	7870–7871	Jan. 16, 1924
3378	7728–7730	Sept. 25, 1923	3443	7872–7873	Jan. 21, 1924
3379	7731–7732	Sept. 26, 1923	3444	7874–7876	Jan. 23, 1924
3380	7733–7734	Sept. 27, 1923	3445	7877–7878	Jan. 27, 1924
3381	7735–7737	Sept. 29, 1923	3446	7879–7881	Jan. 29, 1924
3382	7738–7739	Oct. 1, 1923	3447	7882–7883	Feb. 1, 1924
3383	7740–7741	Oct. 1, 1923	3448	7884–7885	Feb. 4, 1924
3384	7742–7743	Oct. 1, 1923	3449	7886–7888	Feb. 6, 1924
3385	7744–7745	Oct. 3, 1923	3450	7889–7890	Feb. 11, 1924
3386	7746–7747	Oct. 4, 1923	3451	7891–7892	Feb. 12, 1924
3387	7748–7749	Oct. 5, 1923	3452	7893–7895	Feb. 14, 1924
3388	7750–7752	Oct. 6, 1923	3453	7896–7897	Feb. 18, 1924
3389	7753–7754	Oct. 7, 1923	3454	7898–7899	Feb. 20, 1924
3390	7755–7756	Oct. 10, 1923	3455	7900–7902	Feb. 24, 1924
3391	7757–7759	Oct. 10, 1923	3456	7903–7904	Feb. 26, 1924
3392	7760–7761	Oct. 12, 1923	3457	7905–7906	Feb. 29, 1924
3393	7762–7763	Oct. 14, 1923	3458	7907–7908	Mar. 2, 1924
3394	7764–7765	Oct. 15, 1923	3459	7909–7911	Mar. 5, 1924
3395	7766–7768	Oct. 15, 1923	3460	7912–7913	Mar. 9, 1924
3396	7769–7770	Oct. 19, 1923	3461	7914–7915	Mar. 11, 1924
3397	7771–7772	Oct. 20, 1923	3462	7916–7918	Mar. 13, 1924
3398	7773–7775	Oct. 21, 1923	3463	7919–7920	Mar. 19, 1924
3399	7776–7777	Oct. 24, 1923	3464	7921–7923	Mar. 20, 1924
3400	7778–7779	Oct. 26, 1923	3465	7924–7925	Mar. 24, 1924

Roll	Volumes	Beginning Dates	Roll	Volumes	Beginning Dates
3466	7926–7928	Mar. 25, 1924	3531	8088–8089	Aug. 31, 1924
3467	7929–7930	Mar. 28, 1924	3532	8090–8092	Sept. 1, 1924
3468	7931–7932	Mar. 31, 1924	3533	8093–8094	Sept. 2, 1924
3469	7933–7934	Apr. 1, 1924	3534	8095–8097	Sept. 3, 1924
3470	7935–7937	Apr. 4, 1924	3535	8098–8099	Sept. 6, 1924
3471	7938–7940	Apr. 8, 1924	3536	8100–8102	Sept. 7, 1924
3472	7941–7942	Apr. 10, 1924	3537	8103–8104	Sept. 9, 1924
3473	7943–7944	Apr. 11, 1924	3538	8105–8107	Sept. 11, 1924
3474	7945–7947	Apr. 14, 1924	3539	8108–8109	Sept. 12, 1924
3475	7948–7949	Apr. 16, 1924	3540	8110–8112	Sept. 14, 1924
3476	7950–7951	Apr. 19, 1924	3541	8113–8114	Sept. 16, 1924
3477	7952–7954	Apr. 20, 1924	3542	8115–8116	Sept. 18, 1924
3478	7955–7956	Apr. 23, 1924	3543	8117–8119	Sept. 20, 1924
3479	7957–7959	Apr. 25, 1924	3544	8120–8122	Sept. 22, 1924
3480	7960–7961	Apr. 28, 1924	3545	8123–8124	Sept. 24, 1924
3481	7962–7964	Apr. 29, 1924	3546	8125–8126	Sept. 25, 1924
3482	7965–7966	May 2, 1924	3547	8127–8128	Sept. 28, 1924
3483	7967–7969	May 5, 1924	3548	8129	Sept. 29, 1924
3484	7970–7971	May 8, 1924	3549	8130–8132	Sept. 29, 1924
3485	7972–7974	May 10, 1924	3550	8133–8134	Oct. 1, 1924
3486	7975–7976	May 12, 1924	3551	8135–8137	Oct. 3, 1924
3487	7977–7978	May 15, 1924	3552	8138–8139	Oct. 6, 1924
3488	7979–7981	May 18, 1924	3553	8140–8141	Oct. 7, 1924
3489	7982–7983	May 19, 1924	3554	8142–8143	Oct. 9, 1924
3490	7984–7986	May 22, 1924	3555	8144–8146	Oct. 10, 1924
3491	7987–7988	May 25, 1924	3556	8147–8148	Oct. 13, 1924
3492	7989–7991	May 26, 1924	3557	8149–8150	Oct. 14, 1924
3493	7992–7994	May 30, 1924	3558	8151–8152	Oct. 16, 1924
3494	7995–7996	June 2, 1924	3559	8153–8154	Oct. 18, 1924
3495	7997–7999	June 3, 1924	3560	8155–8157	Oct. 21, 1924
3496	8000–8002	June 5, 1924	3561	8158–8159	Oct. 22, 1924
3497	8003–8004	June 8, 1924	3562	8160–8161	Oct. 25, 1924
3498	8005–8006	June 9, 1924	3563	8162–8163	Oct. 26, 1924
3499	8007–8009	June 12, 1924	3564	8164–8166	Oct. 28, 1924
3500	8010–8011	June 16, 1924	3565	8167–8168	Nov. 1, 1924
3501	8012–8013	June 17, 1924	3566	8169–8170	Nov. 2, 1924
3502	8014–8016	June 19, 1924	3567	8171–8172	Nov. 4, 1924
3503	8017–8018	June 22, 1924	3568	8173–8174	Nov. 7, 1924
3504	8019–8021	June 23, 1924	3569	8175–8177	Nov. 9, 1924
3505	8022–8023	June 27, 1924	3570	8178–8179	Nov. 11, 1924
3506	8024–8026	June 29, 1924	3571	8180–8181	Nov. 14, 1924
3507	8027–8028	July 1, 1924	3572	8182–8183	Nov. 18, 1924
3508	8029–8031	July 1, 1924	3573	8184–8185	Nov. 20, 1924
3509	8032–8033	July 4, 1924	3574	8186–8187	Nov. 22, 1924
3510	8034–8036	July 7, 1924	3575	8188–8189	Nov. 24, 1924
3511	8037–8038	July 11, 1924	3576	8190–8191	Nov. 25, 1924
3512	8039–8041	July 14, 1924	3577	8192–8193	Nov. 27, 1924
3513	8042–8043	July 18, 1924	3578	8194–8195	Nov. 29, 1924
3514	8044–8046	July 21, 1924	3579	8196–8197	Dec. 1, 1924
3515	8047–8049	July 23, 1924	3580	8198–8199	Dec. 3, 1924
3516	8050–8051	July 27, 1924	3581	8200–8201	Dec. 6, 1924
3517	8052–8054	July 29, 1924	3582	8202–8203	Dec. 8, 1924
3518	8055–8057	Aug. 1, 1924	3583	8204–8205	Dec. 10, 1924
3519	8058–8059	Aug. 3, 1924	3584	8206–8207	Dec. 15, 1924
3520	8060–8062	Aug. 5, 1924	3585	8208–8209	Dec. 16, 1924
3521	8063–8064	Aug. 9, 1924	3586	8210–8211	Dec. 21, 1924
3522	8065–8067	Aug. 11, 1924	3587	8212–8213	Dec. 23, 1924
3523	8068–8069	Aug. 12, 1924	3588	8214–8215	Dec. 23, 1924
3524	8070–8072	Aug. 14, 1924	3589	8216–8217	Dec. 25, 1924
3525	8073–8074	Aug. 18, 1924	3590	8218–8219	Dec. 29, 1924
3526	8075–8077	Aug. 19, 1924	3591	8220–8221	Jan. 1, 1925
3527	8078–8079	Aug. 24, 1924	3592	8222–8224	Jan. 5, 1925
3528	8080–8082	Aug. 25, 1924	3593	8225–8226	Jan. 10, 1925
3529	8083–8084	Aug. 27, 1924	3594	8227–8228	Jan. 13, 1925
3530	8085–8087	Aug. 29, 1924	3595	8229–8230	Jan. 14, 1925

Roll	Volumes	Beginning Dates	Roll	Volumes	Beginning Dates
3596	8231–8232	Jan. 18, 1925	3661	8357–8358	June 1, 1925
3597	8233–8234	Jan. 19, 1925	3662	8359–8360	June 2, 1925
3598	8235	Jan. 22, 1925	3663	8361–8362	June 4, 1925
3599	8236–8237	Jan. 24, 1925	3664	8363–8364	June 5, 1925
3600	8238–8239	Jan. 26, 1925	3665	8365–8366	June 7, 1925
3601	8240–8241	Jan. 28, 1925	3666	8367–8368	June 8, 1925
3602	8242–8243	Feb. 1, 1925	3667	8369–8371	June 10, 1925
3603	8244–8245	Feb. 2, 1925	3668	8372	June 13, 1925
3604	8246–8247	Feb. 4, 1925	3669	8373–8374	June 15, 1925
3605	8248–8249	Feb. 6, 1925	3670	8375–8376	June 16, 1925
3606	8250–8251	Feb. 9, 1925	3671	7377–8378	June 19, 1925
3607	8252–8253	Feb. 11, 1925	3672	8379–8380	June 21, 1925
3608	8254–8255	Feb. 14, 1925	3673	8381–8382	June 22, 1925
3609	8256–8257	Feb. 17, 1925	3674	8383–8384	June 23, 1925
3610	8258–8259	Feb. 18, 1925	3675	8385–8386	June 26, 1925
3611	8260–8262	Feb. 21, 1925	3676	8387–8388	June 28, 1925
3612	8263	Feb. 24, 1925	3677	8389–8390	June 29, 1925
3613	8264–8265	Feb. 24, 1925	3678	8391–8392	July 1, 1925
3614	8266–8267	Feb. 26, 1925	3679	8393–8394	July 2, 1925
3615	8268–8269	Mar. 3, 1925	3680	8395–8396	July 5, 1925
3616	8270–8271	Mar. 4, 1925	3681	8397–8398	July 7, 1925
3617	8272–8273	Mar. 6, 1925	3682	8399–8401	July 9, 1925
3618	8274–8275	Mar. 9, 1925	3683	8402	July 13, 1925
3619	8276–8277	Mar. 10, 1925	3684	8403–8404	July 13, 1925
3620	8278–8279	Mar. 12, 1925	3685	8405–8406	July 14, 1925
3621	8280–8281	Mar. 16, 1925	3686	8407–8408	July 18, 1925
3622	8282–8283	Mar. 17, 1925	3687	8409–8411	July 20, 1925
3623	8284–8285	Mar. 19, 1925	3688	8412–8413	July 23, 1925
3624	8286–8287	Mar. 22, 1925	3689	8414–8415	July 25, 1925
3625	8288–8289	Mar. 23, 1925	3690	8416–8417	July 27, 1925
3626	8290–8291	Mar. 24, 1925	3691	8418–8419	July 28, 1925
3627	8292–8293	Mar. 26, 1925	3692	8420–8421	July 31, 1925
3628	8294–8295	Mar. 27, 1925	3693	8422–8423	Aug. 2, 1925
3629	8296–8297	Mar. 31, 1925	3694	8424–8425	Aug. 4, 1925
3630	8298–8299	Apr. 2, 1925	3695	8426–8427	Aug. 6, 1925
3631	8300–8301	Apr. 4, 1925	3696	8428–8429	Aug. 7, 1925
3632	8302–8303	Apr. 6, 1925	3697	8430–8431	Aug. 9, 1925
3633	8304–8305	Apr. 6, 1925	3698	8432–8433	Aug. 10, 1925
3634	8306–8307	Apr. 9, 1925	3699	8434–8435	Aug. 12, 1925
3635	8308–8309	Apr. 11, 1925	3700	8436–8437	Aug. 14, 1925
3636	8310–8311	Apr. 13, 1925	3701	8438–8439	Aug. 16, 1925
3637	8312–8313	Apr. 15, 1925	3702	8440–8441	Aug. 17, 1925
3638	8314–8315	Apr. 18, 1925	3703	8442–8443	Aug. 19, 1925
3639	8316–8317	Apr. 20, 1925	3704	8444–8445	Aug. 21, 1925
3640	8318	Apr. 22, 1925	3705	8446–8447	Aug. 22, 1925
3641	8319–8320	Apr. 23, 1925	3706	8448–8449	Aug. 24, 1925
3642	8321–8322	Apr. 26, 1925	3707	8450–8452	Aug. 25, 1925
3643	8323–8324	Apr. 28, 1925	3708	8453–8454	Aug. 28, 1925
3644	8325–8326	Apr. 29, 1925	3709	8455–8456	Aug. 30, 1925
3645	8327–8328	May 2, 1925	3710	8457–8458	Aug. 31, 1925
3646	8329	May 3, 1925	3711	8459–8460	Sept. 1, 1925
3647	8330–8331	May 4, 1925	3712	8461–8463	Sept. 2, 1925
3648	8332–8334	May 6, 1925	3713	8464–8465	Sept. 4, 1925
3649	8335–8336	May 9, 1925	3714	8466–8467	Sept. 5, 1925
3650	8337–8338	May 11, 1925	3715	8468–8469	Sept. 7, 1925
3651	8339–8340	May 12, 1925	3716	8470–8472	Sept. 8, 1925
3652	8341–8342	May 14, 1925	3717	8473–8474	Sept. 9, 1925
3653	8343	May 16, 1925	3718	8475–8476	Sept. 10, 1925
3654	8344–8345	May 18, 1925	3719	8477–8478	Sept. 11, 1925
3655	8346–8347	May 18, 1925	3720	8479–8480	Sept. 14, 1925
3656	8348	May 20, 1925	3721	8481–8483	Sept. 15, 1925
3657	8349–8350	May 23, 1925	3722	8484–8485	Sept. 17, 1925
3658	8351–8352	May 24, 1925	3723	8486–8487	Sept. 18, 1925
3659	8353–8354	May 27, 1925	3724	8488–8489	Sept. 21, 1925
3660	8355–8356	May 29, 1925	3725	8490–8491	Sept. 21, 1925

Roll	Volumes	Beginning Dates	Roll	Volumes	Beginning Dates
3726	8492–8493	Sept. 22, 1925	3791	8611	Jan. 28, 1926
3727	8494–8495	Sept. 23, 1925	3792	8612–8613	Feb. 1, 1926
3728	8496–8497	Sept. 25, 1925	3793	8614–8615	Feb. 5, 1926
3729	8498–8499	Sept. 27, 1925	3794	8616–8617	Feb. 6, 1926
3730	8500–8502	Sept. 28, 1925	3795	8618–8619	Feb. 9, 1926
3731	8503–8504	Sept. 30, 1925	3796	8620	Feb. 10, 1926
3732	8505	Oct. 1, 1925	3797	8621–8622	Feb. 12, 1926
3733	8506–8507	Oct. 2, 1925	3798	8623–8624	Feb. 16, 1926
3734	8508–8509	Oct. 5, 1925	3799	8625	Feb. 18, 1926
3735	8510–8511	Oct. 5, 1925	3800	8626	Feb. 19, 1926
3736	8512–8513	Oct. 7, 1925	3801	8627	Feb. 21, 1926
3737	8514–8515	Oct. 12, 1925	3802	8628	Feb. 22, 1926
3738	8516–8517	Oct. 12, 1925	3803	8629–8630	Feb. 23, 1926
3739	8518	Oct. 13, 1925	3804	8631–8632	Feb. 23, 1926
3740	8519–8520	Oct. 14, 1925	3805	8633–8634	Feb. 25, 1926
3741	8521–8522	Oct. 16, 1925	3806	8635–8636	Mar. 2, 1926
3742	8523–8524	Oct. 17, 1925	3807	8637–8638	Mar. 3, 1926
3743	8525–8526	Oct. 19, 1925	3808	8639	Mar. 6, 1926
3744	8527–8528	Oct. 20, 1925	3809		
3745	8529–8530	Oct. 21, 1925	3810	8642–8643	Mar. 9, 1926
3746	8531–8532	Oct. 24, 1925	3811	8644	Mar. 10, 1926
3747	8533–8534	Oct. 26, 1925	3812	8645–8646	Mar. 12, 1926
3748	8535–8536	Oct. 29, 1925	3813	8647	Mar. 15, 1926
3749	8537	Nov. 1, 1925	3814	8648–8649	Mar. 16, 1926
3750	8538–8539	Nov. 2, 1925	3815	8650–8651	Mar. 18, 1926
3751	8540–8541	Nov. 3, 1925	3816	8652–8653	Mar. 22, 1926
3752	8542–8543	Nov. 4, 1925	3817	8654	Mar. 23, 1926
3753	8544–8545	Nov. 6, 1925	3818	8655–8656	Mar. 24, 1926
3754	8546	Nov. 9, 1925	3819	8657–8658	Mar. 26, 1926
3755	8547–8548	Nov. 10, 1925	3820	8659–8660	Mar. 27, 1926
3756	8549–8550	Nov. 11, 1925	3821	8661–8662	Mar. 29, 1926
3757	8551–8552	Nov. 14, 1925	3822	8663	Mar. 30, 1926
3758	8553–8554	Nov. 16, 1925	3823	8664–8665	Apr. 1, 1926
3759	8555–8557	Nov. 19, 1925	3824	8666	Apr. 2, 1926
3760	8558–8559	Nov. 20, 1925	3825	8667–8668	Apr. 5, 1926
3761	8560	Nov. 23, 1925	3826	8669–8670	Apr. 6, 1926
3762	8561–8562	Nov. 25, 1925	3827	8671–8672	Apr. 7, 1926
3763	8563–8564	Nov. 26, 1925	3828	8673–8674	Apr. 11, 1926
3764	8563–8564	Nov. 29, 1925	3829	8675–8676	Apr. 13, 1926
3765	8565–8566	Nov. 30, 1925	3830	8677–8678	Apr. 14, 1926
3766	8567	Dec. 1, 1925	3831	8679–8680	Apr. 17, 1926
3767	8568–8569	Dec. 2, 1925	3832	8681–8682	Apr. 19, 1926
3768	8570–8571	Dec. 4, 1925	3833	8683–8684	Apr. 20, 1926
3769	8572–8573	Dec. 7, 1925	3834	8685–8686	Apr. 21, 1926
3770	8574	Dec. 9, 1925	3835	8687–8688	Apr. 23, 1926
3771	8575–8576	Dec. 13, 1925	3836	8689	Apr. 26, 1926
3772	8577–8578	Dec. 15, 1925	3837	8690–8691	Apr. 26, 1926
3773	8579	Dec. 19, 1925	3838	8692–8693	Apr. 27, 1926
3774	8580–8581	Dec. 21, 1925	3839	8694–8695	Apr. 29, 1926
3775	8582–8583	Dec. 21, 1925	3840	8696	May 1, 1926
3776	8584–8585	Dec. 23, 1925	3841	8697–8698	May 2, 1926
3777	8586–8587	Dec. 28, 1925	3842	8699	May 3, 1926
3778	8588	Dec. 31, 1925	3843	8700–8701	May 3, 1926
3779	8589–8590	Jan. 1, 1926	3844	8702–8703	May 5, 1926
3780	8591–8592	Jan. 4, 1926	3845	8704–8705	May 8, 1926
3781	8593–8594	Jan. 8, 1926	3846	8706–8707	May 10, 1926
3782	8595	Jan. 11, 1926	3847	8708	May 12, 1926
3783	8596–8597	Jan. 13, 1926	3848	8709–8710	May 13, 1926
3784	8598–8599	Jan. 14, 1926	3849	8711–8712	May 15, 1926
3785	8600	Jan. 16, 1926	3850	8713–8714	May 17, 1926
3786	8601–8602	Jan. 19, 1926	3851	8715	May 18, 1926
3787	8603–8604	Jan. 19, 1926	3852	8716–8717	May 19, 1926
3788	8605–8606	Jan. 23, 1926	3853	8718	May 22, 1926
3789	8607–8608	Jan. 26, 1926	3854	8719–8720	May 23, 1926
3790	8609–8610	Jan. 27, 1926	3855	8721	May 24, 1926

Roll	Volumes	Beginning Dates	Roll	Volumes	Beginning Dates
3856	8722–8723	May 26, 1926	3921	8839–8841	Sept. 6, 1926
3857	8724–8725	May 28, 1926	3922	8842–8843	Sept. 7, 1926
3858	8726	May 30, 1926	3923	8844–8845	Sept. 9, 1926
3859	8727–8728	May 31, 1926	3924	8846–8847	Sept. 12, 1926
3860	8729–8730	June 1, 1926	3925	8848–8849	Sept. 13, 1926
3861	8731–8732	June 4, 1926	3926	8850–8851	Sept. 14, 1926
3862	8733	June 6, 1926	3927	8852–8853	Sept. 16, 1926
3863	8734–8735	June 7, 1926	3928	8854–8855	Sept. 18, 1926
3864	8736	June 8, 1926	3929	8856–8857	Sept. 20, 1926
3865	8737–8738	June 8, 1926	3930	8858–8859	Sept. 20, 1926
3866	8739–8740	June 10, 1926	3931	8860	Sept. 21, 1926
3867	8741	June 13, 1926	3932	8861–8862	Sept. 21, 1926
3868	8742	June 14, 1926	3933	8863–8865	Sept. 24, 1926
3869	8743–8744	June 14, 1926	3934	8866–8867	Sept. 26, 1926
3870	8745–8746	June 14, 1926	3935	8868–8869	Sept. 27, 1926
3871	8747–8748	June 18, 1926	3936	8870–8871	Sept. 28, 1926
3872	8749	June 21, 1926	3937	8872–8873	Sept. 29, 1926
3873	8750–8751	June 22, 1926	3938	8874–8875	Oct. 1, 1926
3874	8752–8753	June 24, 1926	3939	8876	Oct. 2, 1926
3875	8754–8755	June 26, 1926	3940	8877–8878	Oct. 3, 1926
3876	8756–8757	June 28, 1926	3941	8879–8880	Oct. 4, 1926
3877	8758	June 29, 1926	3942	8881–8882	Oct. 5, 1926
3878	8759–8760	June 30, 1926	3943	8883–8884	Oct. 7, 1926
3879	8761–8762	July 1, 1926	3944	8885–8886	Oct. 9, 1926
3880	8763	July 3, 1926	3945	8887–8888	Oct. 11, 1926
3881	8764–8765	July 4, 1926	3946	8889–8890	Oct. 12, 1926
3882	8766–8767	July 6, 1926	3947	8891–8892	Oct. 14, 1926
3883	8768–8769	July 9, 1926	3948	8893–8894	Oct. 15, 1926
3884	8770	July 11, 1926	3949	8895–8896	Oct. 18, 1926
3885	8771–8772	July 12, 1926	3950	8897	Oct. 18, 1926
3886	8773–8774	July 13, 1926	3951	8898–8899	Oct. 19, 1926
3887	8775–8776	July 16, 1926	3952	8900–8901	Oct. 22, 1926
3888	8777	July 18, 1926	3953	8902–8903	Oct. 23, 1926
3889	8778–8779	July 19, 1926	3954	8904–8905	Oct. 24, 1926
3890	8780–8781	July 20, 1926	3955	8906–8907	Oct. 26, 1926
3891	8782–8783	July 23, 1926	3956	8908–8909	Oct. 28, 1926
3892	8784	July 26, 1926	3957	8910–8911	Oct. 30, 1926
3893	8785–8786	July 26, 1926	3958	8912–8913	Nov. 1, 1926
3894	8787–8788	July 30, 1926	3959	8914	Nov. 3, 1926
3895	8789–8790	July 31, 1926	3960	8915–8916	Nov. 4, 1926
3896	8791–8792	Aug. 1, 1926	3961	8917–8918	Nov. 7, 1926
3897	8793–8794	Aug. 3, 1926	3962	8919	Nov. 8, 1926
3898	8795	Aug. 5, 1926	3963	8920–8921	Nov. 8, 1926
3899	8796–8797	Aug. 5, 1926	3964	8922–8923	Nov. 10, 1926
3900	8798–8799	Aug. 8, 1926	3965	8924–8925	Nov. 13, 1926
3901	8800	Aug. 9, 1926	3966	8926	Nov. 15, 1926
3902	8801–8802	Aug. 10, 1926	3967	8927–8928	Nov. 15, 1926
3903	8803–8804	Aug. 12, 1926	3968	8929–8930	Nov. 18, 1926
3904	8805–8806	Aug. 16, 1926	3969	8931–8932	Nov. 21, 1926
3905	8807–8808	Aug. 16, 1926	3970	8933–8934	Nov. 23, 1926
3906	8809–8810	Aug. 17, 1926	3971	8935–8936	Nov. 26, 1926
3907	8811–8812	Aug. 19, 1926	3972	8937–8938	Nov. 29, 1926
3908	8813–8814	Aug. 20, 1926	3973	8939–8940	Nov. 30, 1926
3909	8815–8816	Aug. 22, 1926	3974	8941	Dec. 1, 1926
3910	8817–8818	Aug. 23, 1926	3975	8942–8943	Dec. 3, 1926
3911	8819–8820	Aug. 25, 1926	3976	8944–8945	Dec. 6, 1926
3912	8821	Aug. 26, 1926	3977	8946	Dec. 7, 1926
3913	8822–8823	Aug. 27, 1926	3978	8947–8948	Dec. 7, 1926
3914	8824–8826	Aug. 28, 1926	3979	8949–8950	Dec. 10, 1926
3915	8827–8828	Aug. 30, 1926	3980	8951–8952	Dec. 14, 1926
3916	8829–8830	Aug. 31, 1926	3981	8953	Dec. 17, 1926
3917	8831–8832	Sept. 1, 1926	3982	8954–8955	Dec. 19, 1926
3918	8833–8834	Sept. 3, 1926	3983	8956–8957	Dec. 20, 1926
3919	8835–8836	Sept. 4, 1926	3984	8958–8959	Dec. 21, 1926
3920	8837–8838	Sept. 6, 1926	3985	8960	Dec. 24, 1926

Roll	Volumes	Beginning Dates	Roll	Volumes	Beginning Dates
3986	8961–8962	Dec. 27, 1926	4051	9081–9082	May 7, 1927
3987	8963–8964	Dec. 28, 1926	4052	9083–9084	May 9, 1927
3988	8965–8966	Jan. 1, 1927	4053	9085–9086	May 10, 1927
3989	8967–8968	Jan. 4, 1927	4054	9087–9088	May 13, 1927
3990	8969–8970	Jan. 6, 1927	4055	9089	May 15, 1927
3991	8971–8972	Jan. 10, 1927	4056	9090–9091	May 16, 1927
3992	8973	Jan. 12, 1927	4057	9092–9093	May 16, 1927
3993	8974–8975	Jan. 14, 1927	4058	9094	May 19, 1927
3994	8976–8977	Jan. 17, 1927	4059	9095–9096	May 19, 1927
3995	8978	Jan. 20, 1927	4060	9097–9098	May 22, 1927
3996	8979–8980	Jan. 21, 1927	4061	9099	May 23, 1927
3997	8981–8982	Jan. 24, 1927	4062	9100–9101	May 24, 1927
3998	8983–8984	Jan. 24, 1927	4063	9102–9103	May 27, 1927
3999	8985–8986	Jan. 27, 1927	4064	9104–9105	May 30, 1927
4000	8987–8988	Feb. 1, 1927	4065	9106	May 30, 1927
4001	8989–8990	Feb. 2, 1927	4066	9107–9108	May 31, 1927
4002	8991–8992	Feb. 5, 1927	4067	9109–9110	June 2, 1927
4003	8993	Feb. 8, 1927	4068	9111–9112	June 5, 1927
4004	8994–8995	Feb. 9, 1927	4069	9113–9114	June 6, 1927
4005	8996–8997	Feb. 11, 1927	4070	9115–9116	June 7, 1927
4006	8998–8999	Feb. 14, 1927	4071	9117	June 10, 1927
4007	9000–9001	Feb. 16, 1927	4072	9118–9119	June 11, 1927
4008	9002–9003	Feb. 21, 1927	4073	9120–9121	June 13, 1927
4009	9004–9005	Feb. 22, 1927	4074	9122–9123	June 14, 1927
4010	9006	Feb. 23, 1927	4075	9124–9125	June 16, 1927
4011	9007–9008	Feb. 23, 1927	4076	9126	June 19, 1927
4012	9009–9010	Feb. 26, 1927	4077	9127–9128	June 20, 1927
4013	9011–9012	Mar. 1, 1927	4078	9129–9130	June 21, 1927
4014	9013–9014	Mar. 3, 1927	4079	9131–9132	June 23, 1927
4015	9015–9016	Mar. 5, 1927	4080	9133–9134	June 25, 1927
4016	9017–9018	Mar. 8, 1927	4081	9135–9136	June 27, 1927
4017	9019	Mar. 9, 1927	4082	9137–9138	June 27, 1927
4018	9020–9021	Mar. 10, 1927	4083	9139–9140	June 29, 1927
4019	9022–9023	Mar. 13, 1927	4084	9141–9142	July 1, 1927
4020	9024–9025	Mar. 15, 1927	4085	9143–9144	July 4, 1927
4021	9026–9027	Mar. 16, 1927	4086	9145–9146	July 5, 1927
4022	9028–9029	Mar. 18, 1927	4087	9147–9148	July 8, 1927
4203	9030–9031	Mar. 22, 1927	4088	9149	July 10, 1927
4024	9032	Mar. 23, 1927	4089	9150–9151	July 11, 1927
4025	9033–9034	Mar. 23, 1927	4090	9152–9153	July 12, 1927
4026	9035–9036	Mar. 27, 1927	4091	9154–9155	July 15, 1927
4027	9037–9038	Mar. 29, 1927	4092	9156–9157	July 18, 1927
4028	9039–9040	Mar. 30, 1927	4093	9158–9159	July 20, 1927
4029	9041–9042	Apr. 1, 1927	4094	9160–9161	July 22, 1927
4030	9043–9044	Apr. 3, 1927	4095	9162–9163	July 24, 1927
4031	9045	Apr. 5, 1927	4096	9164–9165	July 25, 1927
4032	9046–9047	Apr. 5, 1927	4097	9166–9167	July 28, 1927
4033	9048–9049	Apr. 7, 1927	4098	9168–9169	July 29, 1927
4034	9050–9051	Apr. 10, 1927	4099	9170–9171	Aug. 1, 1927
4035	9052–9053	Apr. 11, 1927	4100	9172–9173	Aug. 2, 1927
4036	9054–9055	Apr. 12, 1927	4101	9174–9175	Aug. 4, 1927
4037	9056	Apr. 14, 1927	4102	9176	Aug. 5, 1927
4038	9057–9058	Apr. 15, 1927	4103	9177–9178	Aug. 7, 1927
4039	9059–9060	Apr. 16, 1927	4104	9179–9180	Aug. 8, 1927
4040	9061–9062	Apr. 18, 1927	4105	9181–9182	Aug. 9, 1927
4041	9063–9064	Apr. 20, 1927	4106	9183–9184	Aug. 12, 1927
4042	9065–9066	Apr. 22, 1927	4107	9185–9186	Aug. 15, 1927
4043	9067–9068	Apr. 24, 1927	4108	9187–9188	Aug. 15, 1927
4044	9069–9070	Apr. 25, 1927	4109	9189–9190	Aug. 16, 1927
4045	9071–9072	Apr. 27, 1927	4110	9191–9192	Aug. 18, 1927
4046	9073	May 1, 1927	4111	9193–9194	Aug. 20, 1927
4047	9074–9075	May 1, 1927	4112	9195–9196	Aug. 22, 1927
4048	9076–9077	May 2, 1927	4113	9197–9198	Aug. 23, 1927
4049	9078–9079	May 4, 1927	4114	9199–9200	Aug. 25, 1927
4050	9080	May 6, 1927	4115	9201	Aug. 26, 1927

Roll	Volumes	Beginning Dates	Roll	Volumes	Beginning Dates
4116	9202–9204	Aug. 28, 1927	4181	9326	Dec. 6, 1927
4117	9205–9206	Aug. 29, 1927	4182	9327–9328	Dec. 7, 1927
4118	9207–9208	Aug. 30, 1927	4183	9329–9330	Dec. 11, 1927
4119	9209–9210	Sept. 1, 1927	4184	9331	Dec. 14, 1927
4120	9211–9212	Sept. 2, 1927	4185	9332–9333	Dec. 14, 1927
4121	9213–9215	Sept. 4, 1927	4186	9334–9335	Dec. 16, 1927
4122	9216–9217	Sept. 5, 1927	4187	9336–9337	Dec. 20, 1927
4123	9218–9219	Sept. 6, 1927	4188	9338	Dec. 21, 1927
4124	9220–9221	Sept. 7, 1927	4189	9339–9340	Dec. 22, 1927
4125	9222–9223	Sept. 9, 1927	4190	9341–9342	Dec. 24, 1927
4126	9224–9225	Sept. 11, 1927	4191	9343–9344	Dec. 27, 1927
4127	9226–9227	Sept. 12, 1927	4192	9345–9346	Jan. 1, 1928
4128	9228–9229	Sept. 13, 1927	4193	9347–9348	Jan. 3, 1928
4129	9230–9231	Sept. 14, 1927	4194	9349–9350	Jan. 4, 1928
4130	9232–9233	Sept. 16, 1927	4195	9351–9352	Jan. 9, 1928
4131	9234–9235	Sept. 18, 1927	4196	9353–9354	Jan. 10, 1928
4132	9236–9237	Sept. 19, 1927	4197	9355	Jan. 14, 1928
4133	9238–9239	Sept. 19, 1927	4198	9356–9357	Jan. 16, 1928
4134	9240–9241	Sept. 20, 1927	4199	9358–9359	Jan. 18, 1928
4135	9242–9243	Sept. 22, 1927	4200	9360–9361	Jan. 21, 1928
4136	9244–9245	Sept. 24, 1927	4201	9362	Jan. 24, 1928
4137	9246–9247	Sept. 26, 1927	4202	9363–9364	Jan. 25, 1928
4138	9248–9249	Sept. 27, 1927	4203	9365–9366	Jan. 27, 1928
4139	9250–9251	Sept. 28, 1927	4204	9367–9368	Jan. 31, 1928
4140	9252–9253	Sept. 30, 1927	4205	9369–9370	Feb. 1, 1928
4141	9254–9255	Oct. 2, 1927	4206	9371	Feb. 2, 1928
4142	9256–9257	Oct. 3, 1927	4207	9372–9373	Feb. 3, 1928
4143	9258–9259	Oct. 4, 1927	4208	9374–9375	Feb. 6, 1928
4144	9260–9261	Oct. 5, 1927	4209	9376–9377	Feb. 8, 1928
4145	9262–9263	Oct. 7, 1927	4210	9378–9379	Feb. 11, 1928
4146	9264	Oct. 7, 1927	4211	9380	Feb. 14, 1928
4147	9265–9266	Oct. 9, 1927	4212	9381–9382	Feb. 14, 1928
4148	9267–9268	Oct. 10, 1927	4213	9383–9384	Feb. 16, 1928
4149	9269–9270	Oct. 11, 1927	4214	9385	Feb. 21, 1928
4150	9271–9272	Oct. 14, 1927	4215	9386–9387	Feb. 21, 1928
4151	9273–9274	Oct. 17, 1927	4216	9388–9389	Feb. 23, 1928
4152	9275–9276	Oct. 17, 1927	4217	9390–9391	Feb. 25, 1928
4153	9277–9278	Oct. 18, 1927	4218	9392–9393	Feb. 27, 1928
4154	9279	Oct. 20, 1927	4219	9394	Feb. 28, 1928
4155	9280–9281	Oct. 21, 1927	4220	9395–9396	Mar. 1, 1928
4156	9282–9283	Oct. 24, 1927	4221	9397–9398	Mar. 3, 1928
4157	9284–9285	Oct. 25, 1927	4222	9399–9400	Mar. 5, 1928
4158	9286–9287	Oct. 26, 1927	4223	9401–9402	Mar. 6, 1928
4159	9288–9289	Oct. 28, 1927	4224	9403	Mar. 7, 1928
4160	9290–9291	Oct. 30, 1927	4225	9404–9405	Mar. 9, 1928
4161	9292–9293	Nov. 1, 1927	4226	9406–9407	Mar. 12, 1928
4162	9294–9295	Nov. 3, 1927	4227	9408–9409	Mar. 13, 1928
4163	9296	Nov. 4, 1927	4228	9410–9411	Mar. 14, 1928
4164	9297–9298	Nov. 6, 1927	4229	9412	Mar. 18, 1928
4165	9299–9300	Nov. 7, 1927	4230	9413–9414	Mar. 19, 1928
4166	9301	Nov. 8, 1927	4231	9415–9416	Mar. 20, 1928
4167	9302–9303	Nov. 10, 1927	4232	9417	Mar. 22, 1928
4168	9304–9305	Nov. 11, 1927	4233	9419	Mar. 25, 1928
4169	9306–9307	Nov. 14, 1927	4234	9420–9421	Mar. 26, 1928
4170	9308	Nov. 15, 1927	4235	9422–9423	Mar. 28, 1928
4171	9309–9310	Nov. 16, 1927	4236	9424–9425	Mar. 29, 1928
4172	9311–9312	Nov. 20, 1927	4237	9426–9427	Apr. 1, 1928
4173	9313–9314	Nov. 22, 1927	4238	9428–9429	Apr. 2, 1928
4174	9315	Nov. 24, 1927	4239	9430–9431	Apr. 3, 1928
4175	9316–9317	Nov. 25, 1927	4240	9432–9433	Apr. 5, 1928
4176	9318–9319	Nov. 28, 1927	4241	9434	Apr. 7, 1928
4177	9320	Nov. 29, 1927	4242	9435–9436	Apr. 9, 1928
4178	9321–9322	Dec. 1, 1927	4243	9437–9438	Apr. 9, 1928
4179	9323	Dec. 4, 1927	4244	9439–9440	Apr. 9, 1928
4180	9324–9325	Dec. 5, 1927	4245	9441	Apr. 13, 1928

Roll	Volumes	Beginning Dates	Roll	Volumes	Beginning Dates
4246	9442–9443	Apr. 13, 1928	4311	9561–9563	July 31, 1928
4247	9444–9445	Apr. 16, 1928	4312	9564	Aug. 3, 1928
4248	9446–9447	Apr. 16, 1928	4313	9565–9566	Aug. 4, 1928
4249	9448–9449	Apr. 19, 1928	4314	9567–9568	Aug. 6, 1928
4250	9450	Apr. 20, 1928	4315	9569–9570	Aug. 7, 1928
4251	9451–9452	Apr. 21, 1928	4316	9571–9572	Aug. 8, 1928
4252	9453–9454	Apr. 23, 1928	4317	9573–9574	Aug. 11, 1928
4253	9455–9456	Apr. 25, 1928	4318	9575–9576	Aug. 13, 1928
4254	9457–9458	Apr. 26, 1928	4319	9577–9578	Aug. 13, 1928
4255	9459–9460	Apr. 29, 1928	4320	9579–9580	Aug. 15, 1928
4256	9461–9462	Apr. 30, 1928	4321	9581–9582	Aug. 17, 1928
4257	9463	May 1, 1928	4322	9583–9584	Aug. 19, 1928
4258	9464–9465	May 2, 1928	4323	9585–9586	Aug. 21, 1928
4259	9466–9467	May 4, 1928	4324	9587–9588	Aug. 21, 1928
4260	9468	May 7, 1928	4325	9589–9590	Aug. 22, 1928
4261	9469–9470	May 8, 1928	4326	9591–9593	Aug. 24, 1928
4262	9471–9472	May 9, 1928	4327	9594–9595	Aug. 26, 1928
4263	9473–9474	May 12, 1928	4328	9596–9597	Aug. 27, 1928
4264	9475	May 14, 1928	4329	9598–9599	Aug. 28, 1928
4265	9476–9477	May 14, 1928	4330	9600–9602	Aug. 29, 1928
4266	9478–9479	May 15, 1928	4331	9603–9604	Aug. 31, 1928
4267	9480–9481	May 18, 1928	4332	9605–9606	Sept. 2, 1928
4268	9482	May 21, 1928	4333	9607–9608	Sept. 3, 1928
4269	9483–9484	May 21, 1928	4334	9609–9610	Sept. 3, 1928
4270	9485–9486	May 22, 1928	4335	9611–9613	Sept. 5, 1928
4271	9487–9488	May 25, 1928	4336	9614–9615	Sept. 7, 1928
4272	9489	May 26, 1928	4337	9616–9617	Sept. 9, 1928
4273	9490–9491	May 28, 1928	4338	9618–9619	Sept. 9, 1928
4274	9492–9493	May 28, 1928	4339	9620–9621	Sept. 10, 1928
4275	9494–9495	May 30, 1928	4340	9622–9623	Sept. 11, 1928
4276	9496	June 2, 1928	4341	9624–9625	Sept. 12, 1928
4277	9497–9498	June 4, 1928	4342	9626–9627	Sept. 14, 1928
4278	9499–9500	June 4, 1928	4343	9628–9629	Sept. 17, 1928
4279	9501–9502	June 5, 1928	4344	9630–9631	Sept. 17, 1928
4280	9503–9504	June 8, 1928	4345	9632–9633	Sept. 18, 1928
4281	9505	June 10, 1928	4346	9634–9635	Sept. 20, 1928
4282	9506–9507	June 11, 1928	4347	9636–9637	Sept. 21, 1928
4283	9508–9509	June 13, 1928	4348	9638–9639	Sept. 23, 1928
4284	9510–9511	June 15, 1928	4349	9640–9641	Sept. 24, 1928
4285	9512–9513	June 18, 1928	4350	9642	Sept. 25, 1928
4286	9514–9515	June 18, 1928	4351	9643–9644	Sept. 26, 1928
4287	9516–9517	June 20, 1928	4352	9645–9646	Sept. 28, 1928
4288	9518	June 22, 1928	4353	9647–9648	Sept. 30, 1928
4289	9519–9520	June 24, 1928	4354	9649–9650	Oct. 1, 1928
4290	9521–9522	June 25, 1928	4355	9651–9652	Oct. 1, 1928
4291	9523–9525	June 27, 1928	4356	9653–9654	Oct. 2, 1928
4292	9526–9527	June 29, 1928	4357	9655	Oct. 4, 1928
4293	9528–9529	July 1, 1928	4358	9656–9657	Oct. 5, 1928
4294	9530–9531	July 2, 1928	4359	9658–9659	Oct. 7, 1928
4295	9532–9533	July 2, 1928	4360	9660–9661	Oct. 9, 1928
4296	9534	July 5, 1928	4361	9662–9663	Oct. 9, 1928
4297	9535–9536	July 6, 1928	4362	9664	Oct. 12, 1928
4298	9537–9538	July 9, 1928	4363	9665–9666	Oct. 13, 1928
4299	9539–9540	July 10, 1928	4364	9667–9668	Oct. 15, 1928
4300	9541–9542	July 12, 1928	4365	9669–9670	Oct. 16, 1928
4301	9543–9544	July 13, 1928	4366	9671–9672	Oct. 17, 1928
4302	9545–9546	July 16, 1928	4367	9673	Oct. 19, 1928
4303	9547–9548	July 17, 1928	4368	9674–9675	Oct. 21, 1928
4304	9549–9550	July 19, 1928	4369	9676–9677	Oct. 22, 1928
4305	9551	July 21, 1928	4370	9678–9679	Oct. 23, 1928
4306	9552–9553	July 23, 1928	4371	9680–9681	Oct. 26, 1928
4307	9554–9555	July 24, 1928	4372	9682	Oct. 28, 1928
4308	9556–9557	July 27, 1928	4373	9683–9684	Oct. 29, 1928
4309	9558–9559	July 29, 1928	4374	9685–9686	Oct. 30, 1928
4310	9560	July 30, 1928	4375	9687–9688	Nov. 1, 1928

Roll	Volumes	Beginning Dates	Roll	Volumes	Beginning Dates
4376	9689	Nov. 2, 1928	4441	9792–9793	Mar. 1, 1929
4377	9690–9691	Nov. 2, 1928	4442	9794–9795	Mar. 4, 1929
4378	9692–9693	Nov. 5, 1928	4443	9796	Mar. 5, 1929
4379	9694	Nov. 7, 1928	4444	9797–9798	Mar. 6, 1929
4380	9695–9696	Nov. 8, 1928	4445	9799–9800	Mar. 9, 1929
4381	9697–9698	Nov. 9, 1928	4446	9801	Mar. 11, 1929
4382	9699	Nov. 12, 1928	4447	9802–9803	Mar. 12, 1929
4383	9700–9701	Nov. 12, 1928	4448	9804–9805	Mar. 13, 1929
4384	9702	Nov. 14, 1928	4449	9806	Mar. 15, 1929
4385	9703–9704	Nov. 18, 1928	4450	9807	Mar. 17, 1929
4386	9705–9706	Nov. 19, 1928	4451	9808–9809	Mar. 18, 1929
4387	9707	Nov. 21, 1928	4452	9810	Mar. 19, 1929
4388	9708–9709	Nov. 24, 1928	4453	9811–9812	Mar. 19, 1929
4389	9710	Nov. 26, 1928	4454	9813	Mar. 22, 1929
4390	9711–9712	Nov. 27, 1928	4455	9814–9815	Mar. 23, 1929
4391	9713–9714	Nov. 29, 1928	4456	9816–9817	Mar. 25, 1929
4392	9715	Dec. 1, 1928	4457	9818–9819	Mar. 26, 1929
4393	9716–9717	Dec. 2, 1928	4458	9820–9821	Mar. 27, 1929
4394	9718–9719	Dec. 4, 1928	4459	9822–9823	Apr. 1, 1929
4395	9720–9721	Dec. 6, 1928	4460	9824	Apr. 2, 1929
4396	9722	Dec. 8, 1928	4461	9825–9826	Apr. 2, 1929
4397	9723–9724	Dec. 9, 1928	4462	9827	Apr. 3, 1929
4398	9725–9726	Dec. 12, 1928	4463	9828–9829	Apr. 5, 1929
4399	9727	Dec. 14, 1928	4464	9830	Apr. 6, 1929
4400	9728–9729	Dec. 17, 1928	4465	9831	Apr. 6, 1929
4401	9730–9731	Dec. 18, 1928	4466	9832–9833	Apr. 8, 1929
4402	9732	Dec. 19, 1928	4467	9834–9835	Apr. 10, 1929
4403	9733–9734	Dec. 20, 1928	4468	9836	Apr. 10, 1929
4404	9735–9736	Dec. 23, 1928	4469	9837–9838	Apr. 13, 1929
4405	9737–9738	Dec. 25, 1928	4470	9839	Apr. 13, 1929
4406	9739	Dec. 31, 1928	4471	9840–9841	Apr. 15, 1929
4407	9740–9741	Jan. 2, 1929	4472	9842–9843	Apr. 17, 1929
4408	9742	Jan. 3, 1929	4473	9844	Apr. 19, 1929
4409	9743–9744	Jan. 4, 1929	4474	9845	Apr. 21, 1929
4410	9745–9746	Jan. 7, 1929	4475	9846–9847	Apr. 22, 1929
4411	9747	Jan. 9, 1929	4476	9848	Apr. 23, 1929
4412	9748–9749	Jan. 11, 1929	4477	9849–9850	Apr. 23, 1929
4413	9750	Jan. 14, 1929	4478	9851	Apr. 24, 1929
4414	9751	Jan. 15, 1929	4479	9852–9853	Apr. 26, 1929
4415	9752–9753	Jan. 16, 1929	4480	9854	Apr. 29, 1929
4416	9754	Jan. 20, 1929	4481	9855–9856	Apr. 29, 1929
4417	9755–9756	Jan. 21, 1929	4482	9857–9858	Apr. 30, 1929
4418	9757	Jan. 22, 1929	4483	9859–9860	May 2, 1929
4419	9758–9759	Jan. 24, 1929	4484	9861	May 5, 1929
4420	9760	Jan. 26, 1929	4485	9862–9863	May 6, 1929
4421	9761	Jan. 26, 1929	4486	9864	May 6, 1929
4422	9762–9763	Jan. 28, 1929	4487	9865	May 7, 1929
4423	9764–9765	Jan. 29, 1929	4488	9866–9867	May 8, 1929
4424	9766–9767	Feb. 1, 1929	4489	9868	May 10, 1929
4425	9768	Feb. 4, 1929	4490	9869–9870	May 12, 1929
4426	9769	Feb. 4, 1929	4491	9871	May 13, 1929
4427	9770–9771	Feb. 5, 1929	4492	9872–9873	May 14, 1929
4428	9772	Feb. 7, 1929	4493	9874	May 16, 1929
4429	9773–9774	Feb. 7, 1929	4494	9875–9876	May 20, 1929
4430	9775	Feb. 11, 1929	4495	9877	May 20, 1929
4431	9776–9777	Feb. 12, 1929	4496	9878–9879	May 21, 1929
4432	9778	Feb. 14, 1929	4497	9880	May 21, 1929
4433	9779–9780	Feb. 17, 1929	4498	9881–9882	May 25, 1929
4434	9781	Feb. 19, 1929	4499	9883–9884	May 27, 1929
4435	9782–9783	Feb. 20, 1929	4500	9885	May 27, 1929
4436	9784–9785	Feb. 21, 1929	4501	9886	May 27, 1929
4437	9786	Feb. 25, 1929	4502	9887–9888	May 29, 1929
4438	9787–9788	Feb. 25, 1929	4503	9889–9890	May 31, 1929
4439	9789–9790	Feb. 26, 1929	4504	9891	June 1, 1929
4440	9791	Feb. 27, 1929	4505	9892–9893	June 3, 1929

Roll	Volumes	Beginning Dates
4506	9894	June 3, 1929
4507	9895–9896	June 4, 1929
4508	9897	June 4, 1929
4509	9898–9899	June 8, 1929
4510	9900–9901	June 10, 1929
4511	9902	June 10, 1929
4512	9903–9904	June 12, 1929
4513	9905	June 13, 1929
4514	9906–9907	June 14, 1929
4515	9908	June 17, 1929
4516	9909–9910	June 17, 1929
4517	9911	June 18, 1929
4518	9912–9913	June 20, 1929
4519	9914–9915	June 22, 1929
4520	9916	June 24, 1929
4521	9917–9918	June 24, 1929
4522	9919–9920	June 25, 1929
4523	9921	June 26, 1929
4524	9922–9923	June 27, 1929
4525	9924–9925	June 30, 1929
4526	9926	July 1, 1929
4527	9927–9928	July 2, 1929
4528	9929	July 3, 1929
4529	9930–9931	July 5, 1929
4530	9932	July 8, 1929
4531	9933–9934	July 8, 1929
4532	9935–9936	July 11, 1929
4533	9937	July 13, 1929
4534	9938–9939	July 14, 1929
4535	9940–9941	July 15, 1929
4536	9942	July 16, 1929
4537	9943–9944	July 18, 1929
4538	9945	July 20, 1929
4539	9946–9947	July 22, 1929
4540	9948	July 22, 1929
4541	9949–9950	July 24, 1929
4542	9951	July 25, 1929
4543	9952–9953	July 27, 1929
4544	9954–9955	July 29, 1929
4545	9956	July 29, 1929
4546	9957–9958	July 30, 1929
4547	9959–9960	Aug. 2, 1929
4548	9961–9962	Aug. 4, 1929
4549	9963–9964	Aug. 5, 1929
4550	9965–9966	Aug. 6, 1929
4551	9967	Aug. 7, 1929
4552	9968–9969	Aug. 10, 1929
4553	9970–9971	Aug. 12, 1929
4554	9972	Aug. 12, 1929
4555	9973–9974	Aug. 13, 1929
4556	9975	Aug. 15, 1929
4557	9976–9977	Aug. 16, 1929
4558	9978–9979	Aug. 18, 1929
4559	9980–9981	Aug. 19, 1929
4560	9982–9983	Aug. 20, 1929
4561	9984–9985	Aug. 20, 1929
4562	9986–9987	Aug. 22, 1929
4563	9988–9989	Aug. 23, 1929
4564	9990	Aug. 26, 1929
4565	9991–9992	Aug. 26, 1929
4566	9993–9994	Aug. 26, 1929
4567	9995–9996	Aug. 28, 1929
4568	9997–9998	Aug. 29, 1929
4569	9999	Sept. 1, 1929
4570	10000–10001	Sept. 1, 1929

Roll	Volumes	Beginning Dates
4571	10002–10003	Sept. 2, 1929
4572	10004–10006	Sept. 2, 1929
4573	10007–10008	Sept. 5, 1929
4574	10009	Sept. 7, 1929
4575	10010–10011	Sept. 8, 1929
4576	10012–10013	Sept. 9, 1929
4577	10014–10015	Sept. 10, 1929
4578	10016–10017	Sept. 10, 1929
4579	10018–10019	Sept. 12, 1929
4580	10020	Sept. 13, 1929
4581	10021–10022	Sept. 14, 1929
4582	10023–10024	Sept. 15, 1929
4583	10025	Sept. 16, 1929
4584	10026–10027	Sept. 17, 1929
4585	10028–10029	Sept. 18, 1929
4586	10030–10031	Sept. 19, 1929
4587	10032–10033	Sept. 23, 1929
4588	10034–10035	Sept. 23, 1929
4589	10036–10037	Sept. 24, 1929
4590	10038–10039	Sept. 24, 1929
4591	10040	Sept. 25, 1929
4592	10041–10042	Sept. 26, 1929
4593	10043–10044	Sept. 28, 1929
4594	10045	Sept. 30, 1929
4595	10046–10047	Sept. 30, 1929
4596	10048–10049	Oct. 1, 1929
4597	10050	Oct. 1, 1929
4598	10051–10052	Oct. 3, 1929
4599	10053–10054	Oct. 5, 1929
4600	10055–10056	Oct. 7, 1929
4601	10057	Oct. 7, 1929
4602	10058–10059	Oct. 8, 1929
4603	10060–10061	Oct. 9, 1929
4604	10062–10063	Oct. 12, 1929
4605	10064	Oct. 13, 1929
4606	10065–10066	Oct. 14, 1929
4607	10067	Oct. 14, 1929
4608	10068–10069	Oct. 15, 1929
4609	10070	Oct. 18, 1929
4610	10071–10072	Oct. 19, 1929
4611	10073–10074	Oct. 21, 1929
4612	10075	Oct. 21, 1929
4613	10076–10077	Oct. 22, 1929
4614	10078–10079	Oct. 23, 1929
4615	10080–10081	Oct. 25, 1929
4616	10082–10083	Oct. 28, 1929
4617	10084	Oct. 29, 1929
4618	10085–10086	Oct. 29, 1929
4619	10087	Nov. 1, 1929
4620	10088–10089	Nov. 3, 1929
4621	10090	Nov. 4, 1929
4622	10091–10092	Nov. 4, 1929
4623	10093	Nov. 7, 1929
4624	10094–10095	Nov. 8, 1929
4625	10096–10097	Nov. 11, 1929
4626	10098	Nov. 12, 1929
4627	10099–10100	Nov. 12, 1929
4628	10101–10102	Nov. 15, 1929
4629	10103–10104	Nov. 18, 1929
4630	10105–10106	Nov. 19, 1929
4631	10107	Nov. 20, 1929
4632	10108–10109	Nov. 20, 1929
4633	10110	Nov. 21, 1929
4634	10111–10112	Nov. 25, 1929
4635	10113	Nov. 26, 1929

Roll	Volumes	Beginning Dates	Roll	Volumes	Beginning Dates
4636	10114–10115	Nov. 27, 1929	4701	10224–10225	Mar. 25, 1930
4637	10116–10117	Nov. 28, 1929	4702	10226–10227	Mar. 26, 1930
4638	10118	Nov. 29, 1929	4703	10228	Mar. 29, 1930
4639	10119–10120	Nov. 29, 1929	4704	10229–10230	Mar. 30, 1930
4640	10121	Dec. 7, 1929	4705	10231–10232	Apr. 1, 1930
4641	10122–10123	Dec. 7, 1929	4706	10233–10234	Apr. 2, 1930
4642	10124–10125	Dec. 9, 1929	4707	10235	Apr. 5, 1930
4643	10126	Dec. 11, 1929	4708	10236–10237	Apr. 6, 1930
4644	10127–10128	Dec. 12, 1929	4709	10238–10239	Apr. 8, 1930
4645	10129	Dec. 14, 1929	4710	10240–10241	Apr. 8, 1930
4646	10130–10131	Dec. 16, 1929	4711	10242–10243	Apr. 9, 1930
4647	10132–10133	Dec. 18, 1929	4712	10244–10245	Apr. 10, 1930
4648	10134	Dec. 20, 1929	4713	10246	Apr. 14, 1930
4649	10135–10136	Dec. 20, 1929	4714	10247–10248	Apr. 14, 1930
4650	10137	Dec. 23, 1929	4715	10249–10250	Apr. 15, 1930
4651	10138–10139	Dec. 23, 1929	4716	10251–10252	Apr. 16, 1930
4652	10140–10141	Dec. 29, 1929	4717	10253–10254	Apr. 18, 1930
4653	10142	Dec. 31, 1929	4718	10255	Apr. 20, 1930
4654	10143	Jan. 1, 1930	4719	10256–10257	Apr. 21, 1930
4655	10144–10145	Jan. 1, 1930	4720	10258–10259	Apr. 22, 1930
4656	10146–10147	Jan. 4, 1930	4721	10260–10261	Apr. 22, 1930
4657	10148–10149	Jan. 8, 1930	4722	10262–10263	Apr. 24, 1930
4658	10150	Jan. 9, 1930	4723	10264–10265	Apr. 26, 1930
4659	10151	Jan. 10, 1930	4724	10266–10267	Apr. 28, 1930
4660	10152–10153	Jan. 12, 1930	4725	10268–10269	Apr. 29, 1930
4661	10154–10155	Jan. 14, 1930	4726	10270	Apr. 30, 1930
4662	10156–10157	Jan. 15, 1930	4727	10271–10272	May 1, 1930
4663	10158–10159	Jan. 20, 1930	4728	10273–10274	May 3, 1930
4664	10160	Jan. 21, 1930	4729	10275–10276	May 5, 1930
4665	10161–10162	Jan. 21, 1930	4730	10277–10278	May 6, 1930
4666	10163–10164	Jan. 24, 1930	4731	10279–10280	May 7, 1930
4667	10165	Jan. 27, 1930	4732	10281	May 10, 1930
4668	10166–10167	Jan. 27, 1930	4733	10282–10283	May 11, 1930
4669	10168–10169	Jan. 28, 1930	4734	10284–10285	May 12, 1930
4670	10170–10171	Jan. 30, 1930	4735	10286–10287	May 13, 1930
4671	10172–10173	Feb. 3, 1930	4736	10288–10289	May 14, 1930
4672	10174	Feb. 5, 1930	4737	10290	May 18, 1930
4673	10175–10176	Feb. 6, 1930	4738	10291–10292	May 18, 1930
4674	10177–10178	Feb. 7, 1930	4739	10293–10294	May 19, 1930
4675	10179	Feb. 11, 1930	4740	10295–10296	May 19, 1930
4676	10180–10181	Feb. 11, 1930	4741	10297–10298	May 21, 1930
4677	10182	Feb. 13, 1930	4742	10299–10300	May 24, 1930
4678	10183–10184	Feb. 14, 1930	4743	10301	May 26, 1930
4679	10185–10186	Feb. 17, 1930	4744	10302–10303	May 26, 1930
4680	10187–10188	Feb. 18, 1930	4745	10304–10305	May 27, 1930
4681	10189–10190	Feb. 19, 1930	4746	10306–10307	May 28, 1930
4682	10191	Feb. 22, 1930	4747	10308–10309	May 30, 1930
4683	10192–10193	Feb. 23, 1930	4748	10310–10311	June 1, 1930
4684	10194–10195	Feb. 24, 1930	4749	10312–10313	June 2, 1930
4685	10196–10197	Feb. 26, 1930	4750	10314–10315	June 3, 1930
4686	10198	Mar. 1, 1930	4751	10316–10317	June 3, 1930
4687	10199–10200	Mar. 3, 1930	4752	10318–10319	June 7, 1930
4688	10201–10202	Mar. 4, 1930	4753	10320–10321	June 9, 1930
4689	10203–10204	Mar. 5, 1930	4754	10322–10323	June 10, 1930
4690	10205–10206	Mar. 7, 1930	4755	10324–10325	June 13, 1930
4691	10207	Mar. 10, 1930	4756	10326–10327	June 14, 1930
4692	10208–10209	Mar. 11, 1930	4757	10328–10329	June 15, 1930
4693	10210–10211	Mar. 11, 1930	4758	10330	June 16, 1930
4694	10212–10213	Mar. 13, 1930	4759	10331–10332	June 17, 1930
4695	10214	Mar. 17, 1930	4760	10333–10334	June 18, 1930
4696	10215–10216	Mar. 17, 1930	4761	10335–10336	June 21, 1930
4697	10217–10218	Mar. 18, 1930	4762	10337–10338	June 22, 1930
4698	10219–10220	Mar. 21, 1930	4763	10339–10340	June 23, 1930
4699	10221	Mar. 24, 1930	4764	10341–10342	June 24, 1930
4700	10222–10223	Mar. 24, 1930	4765	10343–10344	June 26, 1930

Roll	Volumes	Beginning Dates
4766	10345–10346	June 28, 1930
4767	10347	June 30, 1930
4768	10348–10349	July 1, 1930
4769	10350–10351	July 2, 1930
4770	10352–10353	July 5, 1930
4771	10354–10355	July 5, 1930
4772	10356–10357	July 7, 1930
4773	10358–10359	July 7, 1930
4774	10360–10361	July 10, 1930
4775	10362–10363	July 12, 1930
4776	10364–10365	July 13, 1930
4777	10366–10367	July 14, 1930
4778	10368	July 15, 1930
4779	10369–10370	July 16, 1930
4780	10371–10372	July 18, 1930
4781	10373–10374	July 20, 1930
4782	10375–10376	July 21, 1930
4783	10377–10378	July 22, 1930
4784	10379–10380	July 24, 1930
4785	10381–10382	July 27, 1930
4786	10383–10384	July 28, 1930
4787	10385–10386	July 29, 1930
4788	10387–10388	July 30, 1930
4789	10389–10390	Aug. 1, 1930
4790	10391–10392	Aug. 3, 1930
4791	10393–10394	Aug. 4, 1930
4792	10395–10396	Aug. 4, 1930
4793	10397–10398	Aug. 6, 1930
4794	10399–10400	Aug. 7, 1930
4795	10401–10402	Aug. 10, 1930
4796	10403–10404	Aug. 11, 1930
4797	10405–10406	Aug. 11, 1930
4798	10407–10408	Aug. 13, 1930
4799	10408–10409	Aug. 15, 1930
4800	10410–10412	Aug. 16, 1930
4801	10413–10414	Aug. 17, 1930
4802	10415–10416	Aug. 18, 1930
4803	10417–10418	Aug. 19, 1930
4804	10419–10420	Aug. 21, 1930
4805	10421–10422	Aug. 22, 1930
4806	10423	Aug. 24, 1930
4807	10424	Aug. 24, 1930
4808	10425–10426	Aug. 25, 1930
4809	10427–10428	Aug. 25, 1930
4810	10429–10430	Aug. 26, 1930
4811	10431–10433	Aug. 28, 1930
4812	10434–10435	Aug. 29, 1930
4813	10436–10437	Aug. 31, 1930
4814	10438–10439	Sept. 1, 1930
4815	10440–10441	Sept. 1, 1930
4816	10442–10444	Sept. 3, 1930
4817	10445–10446	Sept. 4, 1930
4818	10447–10448	Sept. 5, 1930
4819	10449–10450	Sept. 7, 1930
4820	10451–10452	Sept. 7, 1930
4821	10453–10454	Sept. 8, 1930
4822	10455–10456	Sept. 9, 1930
4823	10457–10458	Sept. 10, 1930
4824	10459–10460	Sept. 12, 1930
4825	10461–10462	Sept. 13, 1930
4826	10463–10464	Sept. 14, 1930
4827	10465–10466	Sept. 15, 1930
4828	10467–10468	Sept. 16, 1930
4829	10469–10470	Sept. 16, 1930
4830	10471–10472	Sept. 19, 1930

Roll	Volumes	Beginning Dates
4831	10473–10474	Sept. 20, 1930
4832	10475–10476	Sept. 22, 1930
4833	10477–10478	Sept. 22, 1930
4834	10479–10480	Sept. 23, 1930
4835	10481–10482	Sept. 25, 1930
4836	10483–10484	Sept. 27, 1930
4837	10485–10486	Sept. 28, 1930
4838	10487–10488	Sept. 29, 1930
4839	10489–10490	Sept. 30, 1930
4840	10491	Oct. 1, 1930
4841	10492–10493	Oct. 2, 1930
4842	10494–10495	Oct. 3, 1930
4843	10496–10497	Oct. 4, 1930
4844	10498–10499	Oct. 5, 1930
4845	10500–10501	Oct. 6, 1930
4846	10502–10503	Oct. 7, 1930
4847	10504–10505	Oct. 9, 1930
4848	10506	Oct. 10, 1930
4849	10507–10508	Oct. 12, 1930
4850	10509–10510	Oct. 13, 1930
4851	10511–10512	Oct. 13, 1930
4852	10513–10514	Oct. 15, 1930
4853	10515–10516	Oct. 18, 1930
4854	10517–10518	Oct. 20, 1930
4855	10519–10520	Oct. 21, 1930
4856	10521–10522	Oct. 22, 1930
4857	10523–10524	Oct. 24, 1930
4858	10525	Oct. 27, 1930
4859	10526–10527	Oct. 27, 1930
4860	10528–10529	Oct. 28, 1930
4861	10530–10531	Oct. 31, 1930
4862	10532–10533	Nov. 1, 1930
4863	10534	Nov. 3, 1930
4864	10535–10536	Nov. 3, 1930
4865	10537–10538	Nov. 4, 1930
4866	10539–10540	Nov. 7, 1930
4867	10541–10542	Nov. 9, 1930
4868	10543–10544	Nov. 10, 1930
4869	10545–10546	Nov. 11, 1930
4870	10547	Nov. 15, 1930
4871	10548–10549	Nov. 17, 1930
4872	10550–10551	Nov. 18, 1930
4873	10552	Nov. 20, 1930
4874	10553–10554	Nov. 22, 1930
4875	10555	Nov. 24, 1930
4876	10556–10557	Nov. 24, 1930
4877	10558–10559	Nov. 28, 1930
4878	10560–10561	Nov. 30, 1930
4879	10562–10563	Dec. 1, 1930
4880	10564–10565	Dec. 3, 1930
4881	10566	Dec. 5, 1930
4882	10567–10568	Dec. 6, 1930
4883	10569–10570	Dec. 8, 1930
4884	10571–10572	Dec. 10, 1930
4885	10573–10574	Dec. 13, 1930
4886	10575–10576	Dec. 15, 1930
4887	10577–10578	Dec. 17, 1930
4888	10579–10580	Dec. 20, 1930
4889	10581–10582	Dec. 22, 1930
4890	10583–10584	Dec. 23, 1930
4891	10585–10586	Dec. 26, 1930
4892	10587–10588	Dec. 30, 1930
4893	10589	Jan. 1, 1931
4894	10590–10592	Jan. 3, 1931
4895	10593–10594	Jan. 5, 1931

Roll	Volumes	Beginning Dates	Roll	Volumes	Beginning Dates
4896	10595	Jan. 6, 1931	4961	10724–10725	May 15, 1931
4897	10596–10597	Jan. 9, 1931	4962	10726–10727	May 17, 1931
4898	10598–10599	Jan. 11, 1931	4963	10728–10729	May 18, 1931
4899	10600–10601	Jan. 13, 1931	4964	10730–10731	May 20, 1931
4900	10602–10603	Jan. 15, 1931	4965	10732–10733	May 22, 1931
4901	10604	Jan. 19, 1931	4966	10734–10735	May 24, 1931
4902	10605–10606	Jan. 20, 1931	4967	10736–10737	May 25, 1931
4903	10607–10608	Jan. 22, 1931	4968	10738	May 27, 1931
4904	10609–10610	Jan. 24, 1931	4969	10739–10740	May 28, 1931
4905	10611–10612	Jan. 27, 1931	4970	10741–10742	May 30, 1931
4906	10613–10614	Jan. 27, 1931	4971	10743–10744	June 1, 1931
4907	10615–10616	Jan. 29, 1931	4972	10745–10746	June 1, 1931
4908	10617–10618	Feb. 2, 1931	4973	10747–10748	June 2, 1931
4909	10619–10620	Feb. 3, 1931	4974	10749–10750	June 5, 1931
4910	10621–10622	Feb. 6, 1931	4975	10751–10752	June 7, 1931
4911	10623–10624	Feb. 9, 1931	4976	10753–10754	June 9, 1931
4912	10625–10626	Feb. 10, 1931	4977	10755–10756	June 11, 1931
4913	10627–10628	Feb. 13, 1931	4978	10757–10758	June 12, 1931
4914	10629–10630	Feb. 16, 1931	4979	10759–10760	June 14, 1931
4915	10631–10633	Feb. 17, 1931	4980	10761–10762	June 15, 1931
4916	10634–10635	Feb. 22, 1931	4981	10763–10764	June 17, 1931
4917	10636–10637	Feb. 23, 1931	4982	10765–10766	June 19, 1931
4918	10638–10639	Feb. 24, 1931	4983	10767–10768	June 21, 1931
4919	10640–10641	Feb. 27, 1931	4984	10769–10770	June 22, 1931
4920	10642–10643	Mar. 2, 1931	4985	10771–10772	June 23, 1931
4921	10644–10645	Mar. 3, 1931	4986	10773–10774	June 26, 1931
4922	10646–10647	Mar. 5, 1931	4987	10775–10776	June 28, 1931
4923	10648–10649	Mar. 9, 1931	4988	10777–10778	June 29, 1931
4924	10650–10651	Mar. 10, 1931	4989	10779–10780	July 1, 1931
4925	10652–10653	Mar. 11, 1931	4990	10781–10782	July 2, 1931
4926	10654–10655	Mar. 13, 1931	4991	10783–10784	July 3, 1931
4927	10656–10657	Mar. 15, 1931	4992	10785–10786	July 6, 1931
4928	10658–10659	Mar. 17, 1931	4993	10787–10788	July 7, 1931
4929	10660–10661	Mar. 19, 1931	4994	10789–10790	July 9, 1931
4930	10662–10663	Mar. 24, 1931	4995	10791–10792	July 11, 1931
4931	10664–10665	Mar. 24, 1931	4996	10793–10794	July 13, 1931
4932	10666–10667	Mar. 24, 1931	4997	10795–10796	July 14, 1931
4933	10668–10669	Mar. 27, 1931	4998	10797–10799	July 16, 1931
4934	10670–10671	Mar. 29, 1931	4999	10800–10801	July 20, 1931
4935	10672–10673	Mar. 31, 1931	5000	10802–10803	July 20, 1931
4936	10674–10675	Apr. 2, 1931	5001	10804–10805	July 21, 1931
4937	10676–10677	Apr. 3, 1931	5002	10806–10807	July 24, 1931
4938	10678–10679	Apr. 6, 1931	5003	10808–10809	July 25, 1931
4939	10680–10681	Apr. 7, 1931	5004	10810–10812	July 27, 1931
4940	10682–10683	Apr. 9, 1931	5005	10813–10814	July 28, 1931
4941	10684–10686	Apr. 11, 1931	5006	10815–10816	July 31, 1931
4942	10687	Apr. 13, 1931	5007	10817–10818	Aug. 2, 1931
4943	10688–10689	Apr. 13, 1931	5008	10820–10821	Aug. 3, 1931
4944	10690–10691	Apr. 14, 1931	5009	10822–10823	Aug. 4, 1931
4945	10692–10693	Apr. 17, 1931	5010	10824–10825	Aug. 6, 1931
4946	10694–10695	Apr. 20, 1931	5011	10826–10827	Aug. 7, 1931
4947	10696–10697	Apr. 21, 1931	5012	10828–10830	Aug. 10, 1931
4948	10698–10699	Apr. 22, 1931	5013	10831–10832	Aug. 10, 1931
4949	10700–10701	Apr. 24, 1931	5014	10833–10834	Aug. 12, 1931
4950	10702–10703	Apr. 27, 1931	5015	10835–10836	Aug. 14, 1931
4951	10704–10705	Apr. 28, 1931	5016	10837–10839	Aug. 15, 1931
4952	10706–10707	Apr. 30, 1931	5017	10840–10841	Aug. 17, 1931
4953	10708–10709	May 1, 1931	5018	10842–10843	Aug. 18, 1931
4954	10710–10711	May 2, 1931	5019	10844–10846	Aug. 19, 1931
4955	10712–10713	May 4, 1931	5020	10847–10848	Aug. 20, 1931
4956	10714–10715	May 5, 1931	5021	10849–10851	Aug. 23, 1931
4957	10716–10717	May 8, 1931	5022	10852–10853	Aug. 24, 1931
4958	10718–10719	May 10, 1931	5023	10854–10855	Aug. 24, 1931
4959	10720–10721	May 11, 1931	5024	10856–10858	Aug. 26, 1931
4960	10722–10723	May 12, 1931	5025	10859–10860	Aug. 28, 1931

Roll	Volumes	Beginning Dates	Roll	Volumes	Beginning Dates
5026	10861–10862	Aug. 30, 1931	5091	11001	Jan. 1, 1932
5027	10863	Aug. 31, 1931	5092	11002	Jan. 2, 1932
5028	10864–10865	Aug. 31, 1931	5093	11003–11005	Jan. 3, 1932
5029	10866–10868	Sept. 2, 1931	5094	11006–11007	Jan. 5, 1932
5030	10869–10870	Sept. 3, 1931	5095	11008–11009	Jan. 7, 1932
5031	10871–10872	Sept. 4, 1931	5096	11010–11011	Jan. 11, 1932
5032	10873–10875	Sept. 5, 1931	5097	11012	Jan. 13, 1932
5033	10876–10877	Sept. 7, 1931	5098	11013–11014	Jan. 13, 1932
5034	10878–10880	Sept. 8, 1931	5099	11015–11016	Jan. 17, 1932
5035	10881–10883	Sept. 8, 1931	5100	11017–11018	Jan. 20, 1932
5036	10884–10885	Sept. 10, 1931	5101	11019–11020	Jan. 22, 1932
5037	10886–10887	Sept. 11, 1931	5102	11021–11022	Jan. 25, 1932
5038	10888–10889	Sept. 13, 1931	5103	11023–11024	Jan. 26, 1932
5039	10890–10891	Sept. 14, 1931	5104	11025–11026	Jan. 27, 1932
5040	10892–10894	Sept. 15, 1931	5105	11027–11029	Feb. 1, 1932
5041	10895–10896	Sept. 17, 1931	5106	11030–11031	Feb. 2, 1932
5042	10897–10898	Sept. 18, 1931	5107	11032–11033	Feb. 5, 1932
5043	10899–10901	Sept. 20, 1931	5108	11034	Feb. 8, 1932
5044	10902–10903	Sept. 21, 1931	5109	11035–11036	Feb. 9, 1932
5045	10904–10905	Sept. 22, 1931	5110	11037–11038	Feb. 10, 1932
5046	10906–10907	Sept. 25, 1931	5111	11039–11040	Feb. 13, 1932
5047	10908–10909	Sept. 25, 1931	5112	11041–11042	Feb. 16, 1932
5048	10910–10912	Sept. 28, 1931	5113	11043–11044	Feb. 17, 1932
5049	10913–10914	Sept. 29, 1931	5114	11045–11046	Feb. 19, 1932
5050	10915–10916	Sept. 30, 1931	5115	11047–11048	Feb. 22, 1932
5051	10917–10918	Oct. 2, 1931	5116	11049–11050	Feb. 23, 1932
5052	10919–10920	Oct. 3, 1931	5117	11051–11052	Feb. 26, 1932
5053	10921–10922	Oct. 5, 1931	5118	11053–11054	Feb. 29, 1932
5054	10923–10924	Oct. 7, 1931	5119	11055–11056	Mar. 1, 1932
5055	10925–10926	Oct. 9, 1931	5120	11057–11058	Mar. 4, 1932
5056	10927–10928	Oct. 9, 1931	5121	11059–11061	Mar. 6, 1932
5057	10929–10931	Oct. 12, 1931	5122	11062–11063	Mar. 9, 1932
5058	10932–10933	Oct. 13, 1931	5123	11064–11065	Mar. 11, 1932
5059	10934–10935	Oct. 16, 1931	5124	11066–11067	Mar. 13, 1932
5060	10936–10937	Oct. 18, 1931	5125	11068–11069	Mar. 15, 1932
5061	10938–10939	Oct. 19, 1931	5126	11070–11071	Mar. 17, 1932
5062	10940–10941	Oct. 22, 1931	5127	11072–11073	Mar. 20, 1932
5063	10942–10943	Oct. 23, 1931	5128	11074–11075	Mar. 21, 1932
5064	10944–10945	Oct. 26, 1931	5129	11076–11077	Mar. 22, 1932
5065	10946–10947	Oct. 27, 1931	5130	11078–11079	Mar. 24, 1932
5066	10948–10950	Oct. 30, 1931	5131	11080–11081	Mar. 26, 1932
5067	10951–10952	Nov. 1, 1931	5132	11082–11083	Mar. 29, 1932
5068	10953–10954	Nov. 3, 1931	5133	11084–11085	Mar. 30, 1932
5069	10955–10956	Nov. 6, 1931	5134	11086–11087	Apr. 2, 1932
5070	10957–10958	Nov. 8, 1931	5135	11088–11089	Apr. 3, 1932
5071	10959–10960	Nov. 10, 1931	5136	11090–11091	Apr. 4, 1932
5072	10961–10962	Nov. 12, 1931	5137	11092–11093	Apr. 5, 1932
5073	10963–10964	Nov. 16, 1931	5138	11094–11095	Apr. 8, 1932
5074	10965–10966	Nov. 17, 1931	5139	11096–11097	Apr. 11, 1932
5075	10967–10969	Nov. 21, 1931	5140	11098–11099	Apr. 11, 1932
5076	10970–10971	Nov. 24, 1931	5141	11100–11101	Apr. 14, 1932
5077	10972–10973	Nov. 27, 1931	5142	11102–11103	Apr. 17, 1932
5078	10974–10976	Nov. 30, 1931	5143	11104–11105	Apr. 18, 1932
5079	10977–10978	Dec. 2, 1931	5144	11106	Apr. 20, 1932
5080	10979–10980	Dec. 4, 1931	5145	11107–11108	Apr. 22, 1932
5081	10981–10982	Dec. 6, 1931	5146	11109–11110	Apr. 24, 1932
5082	10983–10984	Dec. 9, 1931	5147	11111–11113	Apr. 26, 1932
5083	10985–10986	Dec. 10, 1931	5148	11114–11115	Apr. 29, 1932
5084	10987–10988	Dec. 13, 1931	5149	11116–11117	May 2, 1932
5085	10989–10991	Dec. 15, 1931	5150	11118–11119	May 3, 1932
5086	10992–10993	Dec. 19, 1931	5151	11120–11121	May 6, 1932
5087	10994–10995	Dec. 21, 1931	5152	11122	May 9, 1932
5088	10996–10997	Dec. 23, 1931	5153	11123–11125	May 9, 1932
5089	10998–10999	Dec. 25, 1931	5154	11126–11127	May 13, 1932
5090	11000	Dec. 29, 1931	5155	11128–11129	May 15, 1932

Roll	Volumes	Beginning Dates	Roll	Volumes	Beginning Dates
5156	11130	May 16, 1932	5221	11263–11264	Sept. 7, 1932
5157	11131–11132	May 18, 1932	5222	11265–11266	Sept. 9, 1932
5158	11133–11134	May 20, 1932	5223	11267–11268	Sept. 10, 1932
5159	11135–11136	May 23, 1932	5224	11269–11270	Sept. 12, 1932
5160	11137–11138	May 24, 1932	5225	11271–11272	Sept. 13, 1932
5161	11139–11140	May 26, 1932	5226	11273–11274	Sept. 14, 1932
5162	11141–11142	May 27, 1932	5227	11275–11277	Sept. 15, 1932
5163	11143–11144	May 30, 1932	5228	11278	Sept. 18, 1932
5164	11145–11146	June 1, 1932	5229	11279–11280	Sept. 19, 1932
5165	11147–11148	June 3, 1932	5230	11281–11282	Sept. 19, 1932
5166	11149–11150	June 5, 1932	5231	11283–11284	Sept. 21, 1932
5167	11151–11152	June 6, 1932	5232	11285–11287	Sept. 25, 1932
5168	11153–11154	June 8, 1932	5233	11288–11289	Sept. 25, 1932
5169	11155–11156	June 10, 1932	5234	11290–11291	Sept. 26, 1932
5170	11157–11158	June 13, 1932	5235	11292–11293	Sept. 28, 1932
5171	11159	June 15, 1932	5236	11294–11295	Sept. 29, 1932
5172	11160–11161	June 17, 1932	5237	11296–11297	Sept. 30, 1932
5173	11162–11163	June 18, 1932	5238	11298–11299	Oct. 1, 1932
5174	11164–11165	June 20, 1932	5239	11300–11301	Oct. 4, 1932
5175	11166–11167	June 21, 1932	5240	11302	Oct. 6, 1932
5176	11168–11170	June 23, 1932	5241	11303–11304	Oct. 7, 1932
5177	11171	June 26, 1932	5242	11305–11037	Oct. 7, 1932
5178	11172–11173	June 27, 1932	5243	11308–11309	Oct. 10, 1932
5179	11174–11175	June 28, 1932	5244	11310–11311	Oct. 11, 1932
5180	11176–11177	July 1, 1932	5245	11312–11313	Oct. 14, 1932
5181	11178–11179	July 2, 1932	5246	11314	Oct. 17, 1932
5182	11180–11181	July 5, 1932	5247	11315–11316	Oct. 17, 1932
5183	11182–11183	July 6, 1932	5248	11317–11318	Oct. 18, 1932
5184	11184–11185	July 8, 1932	5249	11319–11320	Oct. 22, 1932
5185	11186–11187	July 11, 1932	5250	11321–11322	Oct. 25, 1932
5186	11188–11189	July 13, 1932	5251	11323–11324	Oct. 27, 1932
5187	11190–11191	July 15, 1932	5252	11325–11326	Oct. 30, 1932
5188	11192–11193	July 16, 1932	5253	11327–11328	Nov. 1, 1932
5189	11194–11195	July 18, 1932	5254	11329–11330	Nov. 3, 1932
5190	11196–11197	July 18, 1932	5255	11331–11332	Nov. 6, 1932
5191	11198–11199	July 21, 1932	5256	11333–11334	Nov. 8, 1932
5192	11200–11201	July 24, 1932	5257	11335–11336	Nov. 10, 1932
5193	11202–11203	July 25, 1932	5258	11337	Nov. 13, 1932
5194	11204–11025	July 26, 1932	5259	11338–11339	Nov. 14, 1932
5195	11206–11207	July 29, 1932	5260	11340–11341	Nov. 18, 1932
5196	11208–11209	Aug. 1, 1932	5261	11342–11343	Nov. 21, 1932
5197	11210–11211	Aug. 1, 1932	5262	11344–11345	Nov. 22, 1932
5198	11212–11213	Aug. 3, 1932	5263	11346	Nov. 25, 1932
5199	11214–11216	Aug. 5, 1932	5264	11347–11348	Nov. 29, 1932
5200	11217–11218	Aug. 8, 1932	5265	11349–11350	Dec. 1, 1932
5201	11219–11220	Aug. 9, 1932	5266	11351–11352	Dec. 2, 1932
5202	11221–11222	Aug. 11, 1932	5267	11353–11354	Dec. 4, 1932
5203	11223–11224	Aug. 12, 1932	5268	11355–11356	Dec. 6, 1932
5204	11225–11226	Aug. 14, 1932	5269	11357–11358	Dec. 9, 1932
5205	11227–11228	Aug. 16, 1932	5270	11359–11360	Dec. 12, 1932
5206	11229–11230	Aug. 17, 1932	5271	11361–11362	Dec. 15, 1932
5207	11231–11232	Aug. 19, 1932	5272	11363–11364	Dec. 19, 1932
5208	11233–11234	Aug. 20, 1932	5273	11365	Dec. 21, 1932
5209	11235–11237	Aug. 22, 1932	5274	11366–11367	Dec. 22, 1932
5210	11238–11239	Aug. 23, 1932	5275	11368–11369	Dec. 23, 1932
5211	11240–11241	Aug. 26, 1932	5276	11370–11371	Dec. 28, 1932
5212	11242–11244	Aug. 26, 1932	5277	11371A–11372	Jan. 1, 1933
5213	11245–11246	Aug. 28, 1932	5278	11373–11374	Jan. 3, 1933
5214	11247–11248	Aug. 29, 1932	5279	11375–11376	Jan. 4, 1933
5215	11249–11250	Aug. 30, 1932	5280	11377–11378	Jan. 7, 1933
5216	11251–11252	Sept. 1, 1932	5281	11379–11380	Jan. 11, 1933
5217	11253–11254	Sept. 2, 1932	5282	11381–11383	Jan. 12, 1933
5218	11255–11257	Sept. 3, 1932	5283	11384–11385	Jan. 18, 1933
5219	11258–11259	Sept. 5, 1932	5284	11386–11387	Jan. 19, 1933
5220	11260–11262	Sept. 6, 1932	5285	11388–11389	Jan. 22, 1933

Roll	Volumes	Beginning Dates
5286	11390–11391	Jan. 25, 1933
5287	11392–11393	Jan. 27, 1933
5288	11394–11395	Jan. 30, 1933
5289	11396–11397	Feb. 2, 1933
5290	11398–11399	Feb. 4, 1933
5291	11400–11401	Feb. 7, 1933
5292	11403	Feb. 10, 1933
5293	11404–11405	Feb. 13, 1933
5294	11406–11408	Feb. 15, 1933
5295	11409–11410	Feb. 18, 1933
5296	11411–11412	Feb. 20, 1933
5297	11413–11414	Feb. 22, 1933
5298	11415–11416	Feb. 24, 1933
5299	11417–11418	Feb. 28, 1933
5300	11419–11420	Mar. 2, 1933
5301	11421–11422	Mar. 5, 1933
5302	11423–11424	Mar. 7, 1933
5303	11425–11427	Mar. 9, 1933
5304	11428–11429	Mar. 13, 1933
5305	11430–11431	Mar. 16, 1933
5306	11432–11433	Mar. 17, 1933
5307	11434–11435	Mar. 21, 1933
5308	11436–11437	Mar. 22, 1933
5309	11438–11439	Mar. 25, 1933
5310	11440–11441	Mar. 28, 1933
5311	11442–11443	Mar. 29, 1933
5312	11444–11446	Apr. 1, 1933
5313	11447–11448	Apr. 5, 1933
5314	11449–11450	Apr. 7, 1933
5315	11451–11452	Apr. 10, 1933
5316	11453–11454	Apr. 11, 1933
5317	11455–11456	Apr. 13, 1933
5318	11457–11458	Apr. 17, 1933
5319	11459–11460	Apr. 18, 1933
5320	11461–11463	Apr. 21, 1933
5321	11464–11465	Apr. 24, 1933
5322	11466–11467	Apr. 27, 1933
5323	11468–11469	May 1, 1933
5324	11470–11471	May 2, 1933
5325	11472–11473	May 3, 1933
5326	11474–11475	May 5, 1933
5327	11476–11477	May 9, 1933
5328	11478–11479	May 11, 1933
5329	11480–11481	May 13, 1933
5330	11482–11483	May 16, 1933
5331	11484–11485	May 19, 1933
5332	11486–11488	May 21, 1933
5333	11489–11490	May 23, 1933
5334	11491–11492	May 26, 1933
5335	11493–11494	May 29, 1933
5336	11495–11496	May 30, 1933
5337	11497–11498	June 1, 1933
5338	11499–11500	June 2, 1933
5339	11501–11502	June 5, 1933
5340	11503–11504	June 8, 1933
5341	11505–11506	June 11, 1933
5342	11507–11508	June 13, 1933
5343	11509–11510	June 15, 1933
5344	11511–11512	June 18, 1933
5345	11513–11514	June 19, 1933
5346	11515–11516	June 21, 1933
5347	11517–11518	June 24, 1933
5348	11519–11520	June 26, 1933
5349	11521–11522	June 28, 1933
5350	11523–11524	June 29, 1933
5351	11525–11526	July 2, 1933
5352	11527–11528	July 4, 1933
5353	11529–11530	July 6, 1933
5354	11531–11533	July 10, 1933
5355	11534–11535	July 11, 1933
5356	11536–11537	July 14, 1933
5357	11538–11539	July 17, 1933
5358	11540–11541	July 19, 1933
5359	11542–11544	July 20, 1933
5360	11545–11546	July 24, 1933
5361	11547	July 25, 1933
5362	11548–11549	July 26, 1933
5363	11550–11551	July 28, 1933
5364	11552–11553	Aug. 1, 1933
5365	11554–11556	Aug. 2, 1933
5366	11557–11558	Aug. 5, 1933
5367	11559–11560	Aug. 7, 1933
5368	11561–11562	Aug. 9, 1933
5369	11563–11565	Aug. 11, 1933
5370	11566–11567	Aug. 14, 1933
5371	11568–11569	Aug. 15, 1933
5372	11570–11571	Aug. 18, 1933
5373	11572–11574	Aug. 20, 1933
5374	11575–11576	Aug. 22, 1933
5375	11577–11578	Aug. 23, 1933
5376	11579–11581	Aug. 25, 1933
5377	11582–11583	Aug. 27, 1933
5378	11584–11585	Aug. 29, 1933
5379	11586–11587	Aug. 30, 1933
5380	11588–11589	Aug. 31, 1933
5381	11589–11592	Sept. 1, 1933
5382	11593–11594	Sept. 4, 1933
5383	11595–11596	Sept. 5, 1933
5384	11597	Sept. 6, 1933
5385	11598–11599	Sept. 7, 1933
5386	11600–11601	Sept. 8, 1933
5387	11602–11603	Sept. 8, 1933
5388	11604–11606	Sept. 11, 1933
5389	11607–11608	Sept. 13, 1933
5390	11609–11610	Sept. 15, 1933
5391	11611–11612	Sept. 18, 1933
5392	11613–11614	Sept. 19, 1933
5393	11615–11616	Sept. 20, 1933
5394	11617–11619	Sept. 22, 1933
5395	11620–11621	Sept. 25, 1933
5396	11622–11623	Sept. 27, 1933
5397	11624–11625	Sept. 29, 1933
5398	11626	Oct. 1, 1933
5399	11627–11628	Oct. 2, 1933
5400	11629–11631	Oct. 3, 1933
5401	11632–11633	Oct. 6, 1933
5402	11634–11635	Oct. 9, 1933
5403	11636–11637	Oct. 10, 1933
5404	11638–11639	Oct. 12, 1933
5405	11640–11641	Oct. 16, 1933
5406	11642–11643	Oct. 17, 1933
5407	11644–11645	Oct. 19, 1933
5408	11646–11647	Oct. 21, 1933
5409	11648–11649	Oct. 24, 1933
5410	11650–11651	Oct. 27, 1933
5411	11652–11653	Oct. 28, 1933
5412	11654–11655	Oct. 30, 1933
5413	11656–11657	Nov. 3, 1933
5414	11658–11659	Nov. 6, 1933
5415	11660–11661	Nov. 8, 1933

Roll	Volumes	Beginning Dates	Roll	Volumes	Beginning Dates
5416	11662–11663	Nov. 13, 1933	5481	11795–11796	Apr. 30, 1934
5417	11664–11665	Nov. 14, 1933	5482	11797–11798	May 2, 1934
5418	11665–11667	Nov. 17, 1933	5483	11799–11800	May 5, 1934
5419	11668–11669	Nov. 21, 1933	5484	11801–11082	May 8, 1934
5420	11670–11671	Nov. 23, 1933	5485	11803–11804	May 11, 1934
5421	11672–11673	Nov. 26, 1933	5486	11805–11806	May 14, 1934
5422	11674–11675	Nov. 28, 1933	5487	11807–11808	May 14, 1934
5423	11676–11677	Dec. 1, 1933	5488	11809–11810	May 16, 1934
5424	11678–11679	Dec. 4, 1933	5489	11811–11812	May 18, 1934
5425	11680–11681	Dec. 6, 1933	5490	11813–11814	May 21, 1934
5426	11682–11683	Dec. 9, 1933	5491	11815–11816	May 24, 1934
5427	11684–11685	Dec. 12, 1933	5492	11817–11818	May 25, 1934
5428	11686–11687	Dec. 14, 1933	5493	11819–11821	May 28, 1934
5429	11688–11689	Dec. 17, 1933	5494	11822–11823	May 31, 1934
5430	11690–11691	Dec. 20, 1933	5495	11824–11825	June 1, 1934
5431	11692–11693	Dec. 22, 1933	5496	11826–11827	June 4, 1934
5432	11694–11695	Dec. 25, 1933	5497	11828–11829	June 7, 1934
5433	11696	Dec. 28, 1933	5498	11830–11831	June 9, 1934
5434	11697	Jan. 1, 1934	5499	11832–11833	June 11, 1934
5435	11698–11700	Jan. 2, 1934	5500	11834–11836	June 14, 1934
5436	11701–11702	Jan. 4, 1934	5501	11837	June 18, 1934
5437	11703–11704	Jan. 7, 1934	5502	11838–11839	June 18, 1934
5438	11705–11706	Jan. 10, 1934	5503	11840–11841	June 21, 1934
5439	11707–11708	Jan. 16, 1934	5504	11842–11843	June 23, 1934
5440	11709–11710	Jan. 18, 1934	5505	11844–11845	June 25, 1934
5441	11711–11712	Jan. 20, 1934	5506	11846–11847	June 26, 1934
5442	11713–11714	Jan. 24, 1934	5507	11848–11850	June 28, 1934
5443	11715–11716	Jan. 25, 1934	5508	11851–11852	July 1, 1934
5444	11717–11718	Jan. 29, 1934	5509	11853–11854	July 2, 1934
5445	11719–11720	Feb. 1, 1934	5510	11855–11856	July 4, 1934
5446	11721–11722	Feb. 5, 1934	5511	11857–11858	July 6, 1934
5447	11723–11724	Feb. 7, 1934	5512	11859–11860	July 9, 1934
5448	11725–11726	Feb. 9, 1934	5513	11861–11862	July 12, 1934
5449	11727–11728	Feb. 12, 1934	5514	11863–11864	July 14, 1934
5450	11729–11730	Feb. 14, 1934	5515	11865–11866	July 16, 1934
5451	11731–11732	Feb. 16, 1934	5516	11867–11868	July 17, 1934
5452	11733–11734	Feb. 19, 1934	5517	11869–11871	July 20, 1934
5453	11735–11736	Feb. 21, 1934	5518	11872–11873	July 23, 1934
5454	11737–11739	Feb. 24, 1934	5519	11874–11875	July 24, 1934
5455	11740–11741	Feb. 28, 1934	5520	11876–11877	July 27, 1934
5456	11742–11743	Mar. 2, 1934	5521	11878–11879	July 29, 1934
5457	11744–11745	Mar. 5, 1934	5522	11880–11882	Aug. 1, 1934
5458	11746–11747	Mar. 6, 1934	5523	11883–11884	Aug. 3, 1934
5459	11748–11749	Mar. 8, 1934	5524	11885–11886	Aug. 4, 1934
5460	11750–11751	Mar. 12, 1934	5525	11887–11888	Aug. 6, 1934
5461	11752–11753	Mar. 14, 1934	5526	11889–11891	Aug. 8, 1934
5462	11754–11756	Mar. 15, 1934	5527	11892–11893	Aug. 10, 1934
5463	11757–11758	Mar. 19, 1934	5528	11894–11895	Aug. 11, 1934
5464	11759–11760	Mar. 21, 1934	5529	11896–11897	Aug. 14, 1934
5465	11761–11762	Mar. 23, 1934	5530	11898–11899	Aug. 15, 1934
5466	11763–11764	Mar. 27, 1934	5531	11900–11902	Aug. 17, 1934
5467	11765–11767	Mar. 29, 1934	5532	11903–11904	Aug. 20, 1934
5468	11768–11769	Apr. 1, 1934	5533	11905–11906	Aug. 22, 1934
5469	11770–11771	Apr. 3, 1934	5534	11907–11908	Aug. 23, 1934
5470	11772–11773	Apr. 4, 1934	5535	11909–11911	Aug. 24, 1934
5471	11774–11775	Apr. 6, 1934	5536	11912–11913	Aug. 27, 1934
5472	11776–11778	Apr. 8, 1934	5537	11914–11915	Aug. 28, 1934
5473	11779–11780	Apr. 10, 1934	5538	11916–11918	Aug. 29, 1934
5474	11781–11782	Apr. 16, 1934	5539	11919–11921	Aug. 31, 1934
5475	11783–11784	Apr. 17, 1934	5540	11922–11924	Sept. 2, 1934
5476	11785–11786	Apr. 19, 1934	5541	11925–11926	Sept. 4, 1934
5477	11787–11788	Apr. 21, 1934	5542	11927–11929	Sept. 4, 1934
5478	11789	Apr. 24, 1934	5543	11930–11931	Sept. 7, 1934
5479	11790–11791	Apr. 24, 1934	5544	11932–11933	Sept. 10, 1934
5480	11792–11794	Apr. 26, 1934	5545	11934–11935	Sept. 10, 1934

Roll	Volumes	Beginning Dates
5546	11936–11937	Sept. 13, 1934
5547	11938–11940	Sept. 14, 1934
5548	11941–11942	Sept. 16, 1934
5549	11943–11944	Sept. 17, 1934
5550	11945–11946	Sept. 19, 1934
5551	11947–11948	Sept. 20, 1934
5552	11949–11950	Sept. 21, 1934
5553	11951–11953	Sept. 24, 1934
5554	11954–11955	Sept. 27, 1934
5555	11956–11957	Sept. 28, 1934
5556	11958–11959	Oct. 1, 1934
5557	11960–11961	Oct. 3, 1934
5558	11962–11963	Oct. 4, 1934
5559	11964–11965	Oct. 5, 1934
5560	11966–11967	Oct. 7, 1934
5561	11968–11969	Oct. 10, 1934
5562	11970–11971	Oct. 12, 1934
5563	11972–11974	Oct. 15, 1934
5564	11975–11976	Oct. 16, 1934
5565	11977–11978	Oct. 19, 1934
5566	11979–11980	Oct. 22, 1934
5567	11981–11982	Oct. 24, 1934
5568	11983–11984	Oct. 26, 1934
5569	11985–11986	Oct. 29, 1934
5570	11987–11988	Nov. 1, 1934
5571	11989–11990	Nov. 2, 1934
5572	11991–11992	Nov. 6, 1934
5573	11993–11994	Nov. 6, 1934
5574	11995–11996	Nov. 10, 1934
5575	11997–11998	Nov. 13, 1934
5576	11999–12000	Nov. 16, 1934
5577	12001–12002	Nov. 20, 1934
5578	12003–12004	Nov. 23, 1934
5579	12005–12006	Nov. 27, 1934
5580	12007–12008	Nov. 28, 1934
5581	12009–12010	Dec. 1, 1934
5582	12011–12013	Dec. 4, 1934
5583	12014	Dec. 7, 1934
5584	12015–12017	Dec. 10, 1934
5585	12018–12019	Dec. 13, 1934
5586	12020–12021	Dec. 17, 1934
5587	12022–12023	Dec. 19, 1934
5588	12024–12025	Dec. 22, 1934
5589	12026	Dec. 24, 1934
5590	12027–12028	Dec. 25, 1934
5591	12029	Dec. 28, 1934
5592	12030–12032	Jan. 1, 1935
5593	12033–12034	Jan. 3, 1935
5594	12305–12036	Jan. 6, 1935
5595	12037–12038	Jan. 9, 1935
5596	12039–12040	Jan. 10, 1935
5597	12041–12042	Jan. 15, 1935
5598	12043–12044	Jan. 18, 1935
5599	12045–12046	Jan. 21, 1935
5600	12047–12048	Jan. 24, 1935
5601	12049–12050	Jan. 25, 1935
5602	12051–12053	Jan. 28, 1935
5603	12054–12055	Feb. 1, 1935
5604	12056–12057	Feb. 4, 1935
5605	12058–12059	Feb. 7, 1935
5606	12060–12061	Feb. 8, 1935
5607	12062–12063	Feb. 12, 1935
5608	12064–12066	Feb. 15, 1935
5609	12067–12068	Feb. 19, 1935
5610	12069–12070	Feb. 21, 1935

Roll	Volumes	Beginning Dates
5611	12071–12072	Feb. 24, 1935
5612	12073–12074	Feb. 26, 1935
5613	12075–12077	Mar. 1, 1935
5614	12078–12079	Mar. 5, 1935
5615	12080–12081	Mar. 7, 1935
5616	12082–12083	Mar. 8, 1935
5617	12084–12086	Mar. 11, 1935
5618	12087–12088	Mar. 14, 1935
5619	12089–12090	Mar. 16, 1935
5620	12091–12092	Mar. 19, 1935
5621	12093–12094	Mar. 21, 1935
5622	12095–12097	Mar. 25, 1935
5623	12098–12099	Mar. 27, 1935
5624	12100–12101	Mar. 28, 1935
5625	12102–12104	Mar. 30, 1935
5626	12105–12106	Apr. 3, 1935
5627	12107–12108	Apr. 4, 1935
5628	12109–12111	Apr. 7, 1935
5629	12112–12113	Apr. 9, 1935
5630	12114–12115	Apr. 11, 1935
5631	12116–12117	Apr. 15, 1935
5632	12118–12119	Apr. 16, 1935
5633	12120–12122	Apr. 18, 1935
5634	12123–12124	Apr. 21, 1935
5635	12125–12126	Apr. 23, 1935
5636	12127–12128	Apr. 24, 1935
5637	12129–12130	Apr. 27, 1935
5638	12132–12133	Apr. 29, 1935
5639	12134–12135	May 2, 1935
5640	12136–12137	May 6, 1935
5641	12138–12139	May 7, 1935
5642	12140–12141	May 9, 1935
5643	12142–12143	May 13, 1935
5644	12144–12145	May 14, 1935
5645	12146–12147	May 17, 1935
5646	12148–12150	May 20, 1935
5647	12151–12152	May 23, 1935
5648	12153–12154	May 25, 1935
5649	12155–12156	May 27, 1935
5650	12157–12158	May 29, 1935
5651	12159–12161	May 31, 1935
5652	12162–12163	June 3, 1935
5653	12164–12165	June 4, 1935
5654	12166–12167	June 7, 1935
5655	12168–12169	June 10, 1935
5656	12170–12171	June 12, 1935
5657	12172–12173	June 14, 1935
5658	12174–12175	June 17, 1935
5659	12176–12177	June 19, 1935
5660	12178	June 21, 1935
5661	12179–12180	June 23, 1935
5662	12181–12182	June 25, 1935
5663	12183–12184	June 27, 1935
5664	12185–12186	June 28, 1935
5665	12187–12189	June 30, 1935
5666	12190–12191	July 2, 1935
5667	12192–12193	July 5, 1935
5668	12194–12195	July 7, 1935
5669	12196–12197	July 9, 1935
5670	12198	July 11, 1935
5671	12199–12200	July 13, 1935
5672	12201–12202	July 15, 1935
5673	12203–12204	July 16, 1935
5674	12205–12207	July 19, 1935
5675	12208–12209	July 22, 1935

Roll	Volumes	Beginning Dates	Roll	Volumes	Beginning Dates
5676	12210–12211	July 24, 1935	5741	12356–12358	Dec. 11, 1935
5677	12212–12213	July 25, 1935	5742	12359–12360	Dec. 13, 1935
5678	12214–12216	July 29, 1935	5743	12361–12362	Dec. 18, 1935
5679	12217–12218	July 30, 1935	5744	12363–12364	Dec. 21, 1935
5680	12219–12220	Aug. 1, 1935	5745	12365–12366	Dec. 23, 1935
5681	12221–12223	Aug. 3, 1935	5746	12367–12368	Dec. 27, 1935
5682	12224–12225	Aug. 6, 1935	5747	12369	Jan. 1, 1936
5683	12226–12227	Aug. 8, 1935	5748	12370	Jan. 1, 1936
5684	12228–12229	Aug. 9, 1935	5749	12371–12372	Jan. 2, 1936
5685	12230–12232	Aug. 11, 1935	5750	12373–12374	Jan. 5, 1936
5686	12233–12334	Aug. 13, 1935	5751	12375–12376	Jan. 7, 1936
5687	12235–12237	Aug. 16, 1935	5752	12377–12378	Jan. 9, 1936
5688	12238–12239	Aug. 18, 1935	5753	12379–12380	Jan. 14, 1936
5689	12240–12242	Aug. 19, 1935	5754	12381–12382	Jan. 17, 1936
5690	12243–12244	Aug. 22, 1935	5755	12383–12384	Jan. 20, 1936
5691	12245–12246	Aug. 22, 1935	5756	12385–12386	Jan. 23, 1936
5692	12247–12248	Aug. 23, 1935	5757	12387–12388	Jan. 24, 1936
5693	12249–12251	Aug. 26, 1935	5758	12389–12390	Jan. 28, 1936
5694	12252–12253	Aug. 29, 1935	5759	12391–12392	Jan. 31, 1936
5695	12254–12256	Aug. 29, 1935	5760	12393–12394	Feb. 3, 1936
5696	12257–12259	Aug. 31, 1935	5761	12395–12396	Feb. 5, 1936
5697	12260–12261	Sept. 2, 1935	5762	12397–12398	Feb. 9, 1936
5698	12262–12264	Sept. 3, 1935	5763	12399–12401	Feb. 11, 1936
5699	12265–12266	Sept. 5, 1935	5764	12402	Feb. 16, 1936
5700	12267–12268	Sept. 7, 1935	5765	12403–12404	Feb. 17, 1936
5701	12269–12271	Sept. 8, 1935	5766	12405–12407	Feb. 18, 1936
5702	12272–12273	Sept. 9, 1935	5767	12408–12409	Feb. 21, 1936
5703	12274–12275	Sept. 11, 1935	5768	12410–12412	Feb. 25, 1936
5704	12276–12278	Sept. 13, 1935	5769	12413–12414	Feb. 27, 1936
5705	12279–12280	Sept. 16, 1935	5770	12415–12416	Mar. 1, 1936
5706	12281–12282	Sept. 17, 1935	5771	12417–12418	Mar. 2, 1936
5707	12283–12284	Sept. 18, 1935	5772	12419–12420	Mar. 5, 1936
5708	12285–12287	Sept. 20, 1935	5773	12421–12422	Mar. 8, 1936
5709	12288–12289	Sept. 23, 1935	5774	12423–12424	Mar. 10, 1936
5710	12290–12291	Sept. 24, 1935	5775	12425–12426	Mar. 13, 1936
5711	12292–12293	Sept. 26, 1935	5776	12427–12428	Mar. 16, 1936
5712	12294–12295	Sept. 27, 1935	5777	12429–12430	Mar. 17, 1936
5713	12296–12298	Sept. 30, 1935	5778	12431–12432	Mar. 19, 1936
5714	12299–12300	Oct. 1, 1935	5779	12433–12434	Mar. 20, 1936
5715	12301–12302	Oct. 3, 1935	5780	12435–12437	Mar. 25, 1936
5716	12303–12304	Oct. 4, 1935	5781	12438–12439	Mar. 27, 1936
5717	12305–12306	Oct. 7, 1935	5782	12440–12441	Mar. 30, 1936
5718	12307–12308	Oct. 8, 1935	5783	12442–12443	Apr. 1, 1936
5719	12310–12311	Oct. 13, 1935	5784	12444–12445	Apr. 2, 1936
5720	12312–12313	Oct. 14, 1935	5785	12446–12447	Apr. 5, 1936
5721	12314–12315	Oct. 16, 1935	5786	12448–12450	Apr. 7, 1936
5722	12316–12317	Oct. 18, 1935	5787	12451–12452	Apr. 8, 1936
5723	12318–12319	Oct. 21, 1935	5788	12453–12454	Apr. 12, 1936
5724	12320–12322	Oct. 22, 1935	5789	12455–12456	Apr. 14, 1936
5725	12323–12324	Oct. 25, 1935	5790	12457–12458	Apr. 17, 1936
5726	12325–12326	Oct. 28, 1935	5791	12459–12460	Apr. 19, 1936
5727	12327–12328	Oct. 30, 1935	5792	12461–12462	Apr. 21, 1936
5728	12329–12330	Nov. 1, 1935	5793	12463–12464	Apr. 23, 1936
5729	12331–12332	Nov. 4, 1935	5794	12465–12466	Apr. 27, 1936
5730	12333–12334	Nov. 7, 1935	5795	12467–12468	Apr. 29, 1936
5731	12335–12336	Nov. 9, 1935	5796	12469–12470	Apr. 30, 1936
5732	12337–12339	Nov. 12, 1935	5797	12471–12472	May 3, 1936
5733	12340–12341	Nov. 17, 1935	5798	12473–12474	May 5, 1936
5734	12342–12343	Nov. 21, 1935	5799	12475–12476	May 7, 1936
5735	12344–12345	Nov. 24, 1935	5800	12477–12478	May 10, 1936
5736	12346–12347	Nov. 27, 1935	5801	12479–12480	May 11, 1936
5737	12348–12349	Nov. 28, 1935	5802	12481–12482	May 14, 1936
5738	12350–12351	Dec. 3, 1935	5803	12483–12484	May 18, 1936
5739	12352–12353	Dec. 5, 1935	5804	12485–12486	May 19, 1936
5740	12354–12355	Dec. 9, 1935	5805	12487–12488	May 21, 1936

Roll	Volumes	Beginning Dates
5806	12489–12490	May 23, 1936
5807	12491–12492	May 25, 1936
5808	12493–12494	May 26, 1936
5809	12495–12496	May 28, 1936
5810	12497–12498	May 29, 1936
5811	12499–12500	June 1, 1936
5812	12501–12502	June 3, 1936
5813	12503–12504	June 5, 1936
5814	12505–12506	June 8, 1936
5815	12507–12508	June 9, 1936
5816	12509–12511	June 12, 1936
5817	12512–12513	June 15, 1936
5818	12514–12515	June 17, 1936
5819	12516–12517	June 19, 1936
5820	12518–12519	June 22, 1936
5821	12520–12521	June 24, 1936
5822	12522–12523	June 26, 1936
5823	12524–12526	June 27, 1936
5824	12527–12528	June 29, 1936
5825	12529–12530	July 1, 1936
5826	12531–12532	July 3, 1936
5827	12533–12534	July 5, 1936
5828	12535–12537	July 6, 1936
5829	12538–12539	July 9, 1936
5830	12540–12541	July 13, 1936
5831	12542–12543	July 14, 1936
5832	12544–12545	July 16, 1936
5833	12546–12547	July 19, 1936
5834	12548–12550	July 21, 1936
5835	12551–12552	July 23, 1936
5836	12553–12555	July 26, 1936
5837	12556–12557	July 28, 1936
5838	12558	July 31, 1936
5839	12559–12560	Aug. 1, 1936
5840	12561–12562	Aug. 2, 1936
5841	12563–12564	Aug. 3, 1936
5842	12565–12567	Aug. 6, 1936
5843	12568–12569	Aug. 8, 1936
5844	12570–12571	Aug. 11, 1936
5845	12572–12573	Aug. 11, 1936
5846	12574–12576	Aug. 14, 1936
5847	12577–12578	Aug. 16, 1936
5848	12579–12580	Aug. 17, 1936
5849	12581–12583	Aug. 18, 1936
5850	12584–12585	Aug. 20, 1936
5851	12586–12588	Aug. 21, 1936
5852	12589–12590	Aug. 24, 1936
5853	12591–12592	Aug. 26, 1936
5854	12593–12594	Aug. 27, 1936
5855	12595–12597	Aug. 28, 1936
5856	12598–12599	Aug. 31, 1936
5857	12600–12601	Aug. 31, 1936
5858	12602–12604	Sept. 1, 1936
5859	12605–12606	Sept. 3, 1936
5860	12607–12609	Sept. 4, 1936
5861	12610–12611	Sept. 5, 1936
5862	12612–12613	Sept. 7, 1936
5863	12614–12616	Sept. 8, 1936
5864	12617–12618	Sept. 9, 1936
5865	12619–12620	Sept. 11, 1936
5866	12621–12622	Sept. 12, 1936
5867	12623–12624	Sept. 14, 1936
5868	12625–12627	Sept. 15, 1936
5869	12628–12629	Sept. 17, 1936
5870	12630–12631	Sept. 19, 1936
5871	12632–12633	Sept. 20, 1936
5872	12634–12635	Sept. 21, 1936
5873	12636–12637	Sept. 22, 1936
5874	12638–12639	Sept. 24, 1936
5875	12640–12642	Sept. 26, 1936
5876	12643–12644	Sept. 28, 1936
5877	12645–12646	Sept. 28, 1936
5878	12647–12648	Oct. 1, 1936
5879	12649–12650	Oct. 2, 1936
5880	12651–12652	Oct. 5, 1936
5881	12653–12654	Oct. 6, 1936
5882	12655–12656	Oct. 8, 1936
5883	12657–12658	Oct. 9, 1936
5884	12659–12660	Oct. 11, 1936
5885	12661–12662	Oct. 13, 1936
5886	12663–12664	Oct. 13, 1936
5887	12665–12666	Oct. 16, 1936
5888	12667–12668	Oct. 18, 1936
5889	12669–12670	Oct. 19, 1936
5890	12671–12672	Oct. 22, 1936
5891	12673–12674	Oct. 23, 1936
5892	12675–12677	Oct. 26, 1936
5893	12678–12679	Oct. 29, 1936
5894	12680–12681	Oct. 30, 1936
5895	12682–12683	Nov. 2, 1936
5896	12684–12685	Nov. 5, 1936
5897	12686–12687	Nov. 5, 1936
5898	12688–12689	Nov. 9, 1936
5899	12690–12691	Nov. 10, 1936
5900	12692–12693	Nov. 13, 1936
5901	12694–12695	Nov. 17, 1936
5902	12696–12697	Nov. 20, 1936
5903	12698–12699	Nov. 21, 1936
5904	12700–12701	Nov. 24, 1936
5905	12702	Nov. 27, 1936
5906	12703–12704	Nov. 29, 1936
5907	12705–12707	Dec. 1, 1936
5908	12708	Dec. 4, 1936
5909	12709–12710	Dec. 6, 1936
5910	12711–12712	Dec. 9, 1936
5911	12713–12714	Dec. 10, 1936
5912	12715–12716	Dec. 14, 1936
5913	12717–12718	Dec. 17, 1936
5914	12719–12720	Dec. 21, 1936
5915	12721–12722	Dec. 23, 1936
5916	12723	Dec. 24, 1936
5917	12724–12726	Dec. 24, 1936
5918	12727	Dec. 30, 1936
5919	12728–12729	Jan. 1, 1937
5920	12730–12731	Jan. 3, 1937
5921	12732–12734	Jan. 4, 1937
5922	12735–12736	Jan. 8, 1937
5923	12737–12738	Jan. 12, 1937
5924	12739–12740	Jan. 14, 1937
5925	12741–12742	Jan. 15, 1937
5926	12743–12744	Jan. 20, 1937
5927	12745–12747	Jan. 21, 1937
5928	12748–12749	Jan. 25, 1937
5929	12750–12751	Jan. 28, 1937
5930	12752–12753	Jan. 30, 1937
5931	12754–12755	Feb. 1, 1937
5932	12756–12758	Feb. 4, 1937
5933	12759–12760	Feb. 7, 1937
5934	12761–12762	Feb. 9, 1937
5935	12763–12764	Feb. 12, 1937

Roll	Volumes	Beginning Dates
5936	12765–12767	Feb. 15, 1937
5937	12768–12769	Feb. 17, 1937
5938	12770–12771	Feb. 19, 1937
5939	12772–12774	Feb. 22, 1937
5940	12775–12776	Feb. 24, 1937
5941	12777–12778	Feb. 25, 1937
5942	12779–12781	Feb. 28, 1937
5943	12782–12783	Mar. 3, 1937
5944	12784–12785	Mar. 5, 1937
5945	12786–12787	Mar. 8, 1937
5946	12788	Mar. 10, 1937
5947	12789–12790	Mar. 11, 1937
5948	12791–12792	Mar. 12, 1937
5949	12793–12794	Mar. 15, 1937
5950	12795–12797	Mar. 16, 1937
5951	12798–12799	Mar. 18, 1937
5952	12800–12801	Mar. 20, 1937
5953	12802–12804	Mar. 22, 1937
5954	12805–12806	Mar. 25, 1937
5955	12807–12808	Mar. 26, 1937
5956	12809–12811	Mar. 30, 1937
5957	12812–12813	Apr. 1, 1937
5958	12814–12816	Apr. 2, 1937
5959	12817–12818	Apr. 5, 1937
5960	12819–12820	Apr. 6, 1937
5961	12821–12822	Apr. 9, 1937
5962	12823–12825	Apr. 11, 1937
5963	12826–12827	Apr. 12, 1937
5964	12828–12829	Apr. 15, 1937
5965	12830–12831	Apr. 17, 1937
5966	12832–12833	Apr. 19, 1937
5967	12834–12835	Apr. 21, 1937
5968	12836–12837	Apr. 22, 1937
5969	12838–12840	Apr. 26, 1937
5970	12841–12842	Apr. 27, 1937
5971	12843–12844	Apr. 29, 1937
5972	12845–12847	Apr. 30, 1937
5973	12848–12849	May 3, 1937
5974	12850–12851	May 6, 1937
5975	12852–12853	May 9, 1937
5976	12854–12856	May 10, 1937
5977	12856–12857	May 12, 1937
5978	12858–12859	May 14, 1937
5979	12860–12861	May 17, 1937
5980	12862–12863	May 19, 1937
5981	12864–12865	May 21, 1937
5982	12866–12868	May 23, 1937
5983	12869–12870	May 25, 1937
5984	12871–12872	May 27, 1937
5985	12873–12875	May 28, 1937
5986	12876–12877	June 1, 1937
5987	12878–12879	June 1, 1937
5988	12880–12881	June 3, 1937
5989	12882–12883	June 6, 1937
5990	12884–12885	June 7, 1937
5991	12886–12888	June 8, 1937
5992	12889–12890	June 11, 1937
5993	12891–12892	June 14, 1937
5994	12893–12894	June 16, 1937
5995	12895–12896	June 18, 1937
5996	12897–12898	June 21, 1937
5997	12899–12901	June 21, 1937
5998	12902–12903	June 24, 1937
5999	12904–12905	June 25, 1937
6000	12906–12907	June 28, 1937
6001	12908–12909	June 28, 1937
6002	12910–12912	June 30, 1937
6003	12913–12914	July 2, 1937
6004	12915–12916	July 5, 1937
6005	12917–12918	July 6, 1937
6006	12919–12920	July 8, 1937
6007	12921–12923	July 9, 1937
6008	12924–12925	July 13, 1937
6009	12926–12927	July 15, 1937
6010	12928–12929	July 16, 1937
6011	12930–12932	July 18, 1937
6012	12933–12934	July 22, 1937
6013	12935–12936	July 22, 1937
6014	12937–12939	July 25, 1937
6015	12940–12941	July 27, 1937
6016	12942–12943	July 29, 1937
6017	12944–12945	Aug. 1, 1937
6018	12946–12947	Aug. 2, 1937
6019	12948–12950	Aug. 2, 1937
6020	12951–12952	Aug. 6, 1937
6021	12953–12954	Aug. 9, 1937
6022	12955–12957	Aug. 9, 1937
6023	12958–12959	Aug. 12, 1937
6024	12960–12961	Aug. 14, 1937
6025	12962–12964	Aug. 15, 1937
6026	12965–12966	Aug. 17, 1937
6027	12967–12969	Aug. 18, 1937
6028	12970–12971	Aug. 20, 1937
6029	12972–12974	Aug. 20, 1937
6030	12975–12976	Aug. 23, 1937
6031	12977–12979	Aug. 24, 1937
6032	12980–12981	Aug. 26, 1937
6033	12982–12983	Aug. 26, 1937
6034	12984–12986	Aug. 29, 1937
6035	12987–12989	Aug. 30, 1937
6036	12990–12992	Sept. 2, 1937
6037	12993–12994	Sept. 2, 1937
6038	12995–12997	Sept. 3, 1937
6039	12998–12999	Sept. 6, 1937
6040	13000–13001	Sept. 7, 1937
6041	13002–13004	Sept. 8, 1937
6042	13005–13006	Sept. 10, 1937
6043	13007–13009	Sept. 11, 1937
6044	13010–13011	Sept. 13, 1937
6045	13012–13013	Sept. 14, 1937
6046	13014–13016	Sept. 16, 1937
6047	13017–13018	Sept. 20, 1937
6048	13019–13021	Sept. 20, 1937
6049	13022–13023	Sept. 23, 1937
6050	13024–13025	Sept. 24, 1937
6051	13026–13027	Sept. 25, 1937
6052	13028–13030	Sept. 26, 1937
6053	13031–13032	Sept. 28, 1937
6054	13033–13035	Sept. 30, 1937
6055	13036–13037	Oct. 1, 1937
6056	13038–13039	Oct. 4, 1937
6057	13040–13042	Oct. 4, 1937
6058	13043–13044	Oct. 6, 1937
6059	13045–13046	Oct. 7, 1937
6060	13047–13048	Oct. 10, 1937
6061	13049–13050	Oct. 11, 1937
6062	13051–13052	Oct. 12, 1937
6063	13053–13055	Oct. 14, 1937
6064	13056–13057	Oct. 16, 1937
6065	13058–13059	Oct. 18, 1937

Roll	Volumes	Beginning Dates	Roll	Volumes	Beginning Dates
6066	13060–13061	Oct. 21, 1937	6131	13197–13198	Mar. 25, 1938
6067	13062–13064	Oct. 22, 1937	6132	13199–13200	Mar. 27, 1938
6068	13065–13066	Oct. 25, 1937	6133	13201–13202	Mar. 29, 1938
6069	13067–13068	Oct. 26, 1937	6134	13203–13204	Apr. 1, 1938
6070	13069–13071	Oct. 28, 1937	6135	13205–13207	Apr. 1, 1938
6071	13072–13073	Nov. 1, 1937	6136	13208–13209	Apr. 5, 1938
6072	13074–13075	Nov. 1, 1937	6137	13210–13211	Apr. 7, 1938
6073	13076–13077	Nov. 4, 1937	6138	13212–13213	Apr. 10, 1938
6074	13078–13080	Nov. 6, 1937	6139	13214–13215	Apr. 11, 1938
6075	13081–13082	Nov. 8, 1937	6140	13216–13218	Apr. 13, 1938
6076	13083–13084	Nov. 11, 1937	6141	13219–13220	Apr. 15, 1938
6077	13085–13086	Nov. 12, 1937	6142	13221–13222	Apr. 18, 1938
6078	13087–13088	Nov. 15, 1937	6143	13223–13224	Apr. 21, 1938
6079	13089–13090	Nov. 18, 1937	6144	13225–13227	Apr. 23, 1938
6080	13091–13092	Nov. 21, 1937	6145	13228–13229	Apr. 25, 1938
6081	13093–13094	Nov. 22, 1937	6146	13230–13231	Apr. 27, 1938
6082	13095–13097	Nov. 25, 1937	6147	13232–13234	Apr. 28, 1938
6083	13098–13099	Nov. 29, 1937	6148	13235–13236	May 2, 1938
6084	13100–13101	Dec. 2, 1937	6149	13237–13238	May 3, 1938
6085	13102–13103	Dec. 5, 1937	6150	13239–13240	May 6, 1938
6086	13104–13105	Dec. 7, 1937	6151	13241–13242	May 9, 1938
6087	13106–13107	Dec. 10, 1937	6152	13243–13244	May 10, 1938
6088	13108–13110	Dec. 13, 1937	6153	13245–13246	May 13, 1938
6089	13111–13112	Dec. 16, 1937	6154	13247–13248	May 16, 1938
6090	13113–13114	Dec. 19, 1937	6155	13249–13250	May 17, 1938
6091	13115–13116	Dec. 20, 1937	6156	13251–13252	May 20, 1938
6092	13117–13118	Dec. 22, 1937	6157	13253–13255	May 23, 1938
6093	13119–13120	Dec. 23, 1937	6158	13256–13257	May 25, 1938
6094	13121–13122	Dec. 28, 1937	6159	13258–13259	May 26, 1938
6095	13123	Jan. 1, 1938	6160	13260–13261	May 30, 1938
6096	13124–13125	Jan. 2, 1938	6161	13262–13263	May 31, 1938
6097	13126–13127	Jan. 2, 1938	6162	13264–13265	June 2, 1938
6098	13128–13129	Jan. 5, 1938	6163	13266–13267	June 6, 1938
6099	13130–13131	Jan. 8, 1938	6164	13268–13269	June 6, 1938
6100	13132–13133	Jan. 11, 1938	6165	13270–13272	June 9, 1938
6101	13134–13135	Jan. 13, 1938	6166	13273–13274	June 12, 1938
6102	13136–13137	Jan. 17, 1938	6167	13275–13276	June 13, 1938
6103	13138–13139	Jan. 19, 1938	6168	13277–13278	June 16, 1938
6104	13140–13141	Jan. 21, 1938	6169	13279–13280	June 18, 1938
6105	13142–13143	Jan. 24, 1938	6170	13281–13282	June 20, 1938
6106	13144–13145	Jan. 26, 1938	6171	13283–13284	June 22, 1938
6107	13146–13148	Jan. 28, 1938	6172	13285–13287	June 24, 1938
6108	13149–13150	Feb. 2, 1938	6173	13288–13289	June 27, 1938
6109	13151–13152	Feb. 4, 1938	6174	13290–13291	June 29, 1938
6110	13153–13154	Feb. 6, 1938	6175	13292–13293	June 30, 1938
6111	13155–13156	Feb. 9, 1938	6176	13294–13295	July 1, 1938
6112	13157–13158	Feb. 10, 1938	6177	13296–13297	July 4, 1938
6113	13159–13160	Feb. 14, 1938	6178	13298–13300	July 5, 1938
6114	13161–13162	Feb. 15, 1938	6179	13301–13302	July 7, 1938
6115	13163–13164	Feb. 16, 1938	6180	13303–13304	July 10, 1938
6116	13165–13166	Feb. 18, 1938	6181	13305–13306	July 12, 1938
6117	13167–13168	Feb. 22, 1938	6182	13307–13308	July 14, 1938
6118	13169–13170	Feb. 23, 1938	6183	13309–13310	July 17, 1938
6119	13171–13173	Feb. 25, 1938	6184	13311–13312	July 18, 1938
6120	13174–13175	Feb. 28, 1938	6185	13313–13314	July 20, 1938
6121	13176–13177	Mar. 2, 1938	6186	13315–13317	July 21, 1938
6122	13178–13179	Mar. 6, 1938	6187	13318–13319	July 25, 1938
6123	13180–13181	Mar. 8, 1938	6188	13320–13321	July 27, 1938
6124	13182–13183	Mar. 10, 1938	6189	13322–13323	July 29, 1938
6125	13184–13186	Mar. 11, 1938	6190	13324–13325	July 31, 1938
6126	13187–13188	Mar. 15, 1938	6191	13326–13327	Aug. 1, 1938
6127	13189–13190	Mar. 17, 1938	6192	13328–13330	Aug. 3, 1938
6128	13191–13192	Mar. 19, 1938	6193	13331–13332	Aug. 5, 1938
6129	13193–13194	Mar. 21, 1938	6194	13333–13334	Aug. 8, 1938
6130	13195–13196	Mar. 23, 1938	6195	13335–13336	Aug. 9, 1938

Roll	Volumes	Beginning Dates	Roll	Volumes	Beginning Dates
6196	13337–13338	Aug. 11, 1938	6261	13479–13480	Dec. 15, 1938
6197	13339–13341	Aug. 12, 1938	6262	13481–13482	Dec. 17, 1938
6198	13342–13343	Aug. 15, 1938	6263	13483–13848	Dec. 21, 1938
6199	13344–13345	Aug. 16, 1938	6264	13485–13486	Dec. 22, 1938
6200	13346–13348	Aug. 18, 1938	6265	13487–13488	Dec. 23, 1938
6201	13349–13350	Aug. 19, 1938	6266	13489–13490	Dec. 25, 1938
6202	13351–13353	Aug. 22, 1938	6267	13491	Dec. 29, 1938
6203	13354–13355	Aug. 23, 1938	6268	13492–13493	Jan. 1, 1939
6204	13356–13357	Aug. 26, 1938	6269	13494–13496	Jan. 2, 1939
6205	13358–13360	Aug. 28, 1938	6270	13497–13498	Jan. 5, 1939
6206	13361–13362	Aug. 29, 1938	6271	13499–13500	Jan. 8, 1939
6207	13363–13365	Aug. 29, 1938	6272	13501–13503	Jan. 12, 1939
6208	13366–13367	Sept. 1, 1938	6273	13504–13505	Jan. 16, 1939
6209	13368–13370	Sept. 1, 1938	6274	13506–13507	Jan. 18, 1939
6210	13371–13372	Sept. 4, 1938	6275	13508–13510	Jan. 20, 1939
6211	13373–13374	Sept. 5, 1938	6276	13511–13512	Jan. 25, 1939
6212	13375–13377	Sept. 6, 1938	6277	13513–13514	Jan. 27, 1939
6213	13378–13379	Sept. 8, 1938	6278	13515–13516	Jan. 30, 1939
6214	13380–13382	Sept. 10, 1938	6279	13517–13518	Feb. 2, 1939
6215	13383–13384	Sept. 12, 1938	6280	13519–13520	Feb. 3, 1939
6216	13385–13386	Sept. 13, 1938	6281	13521–13523	Feb. 4, 1939
6217	13387–13388	Sept. 15, 1938	6282	13524–13526	Feb. 9, 1939
6218	13389	Sept. 15, 1938	6283	13527–13529	Feb. 11, 1939
6219	13390–13392	Sept. 16, 1938	6284	13530–13531	Feb. 15, 1939
6220	13393–13394	Sept. 19, 1938	6285	13532	Feb. 17, 1939
6221	13395–13396	Sept. 21, 1938	6286	13533–13534	Feb. 17, 1939
6222	13397–13398	Sept. 22, 1938	6287	13535–13537	Feb. 21, 1939
6223	13399–13400	Sept. 23, 1938	6288	13538–13539	Feb. 23, 1939
6224	13401–13402	Sept. 25, 1938	6289	13540–13541	Feb. 26, 1939
6225	13403–13404	Sept. 26, 1938	6290	13542–13543	Feb. 28, 1939
6226	13405–13407	Sept. 28, 1938	6291	13544–13545	Mar. 2, 1939
6227	13408–13409	Sept. 30, 1938	6292	13546–13548	Mar. 4, 1939
6228	13410–13411	Oct. 2, 1938	6293	13549–13550	Mar. 8, 1939
6229	13412–13413	Oct. 3, 1938	6294	13551–13552	Mar. 9, 1939
6230	13414–13415	Oct. 6, 1938	6295	13553–13554	Mar. 13, 1939
6231	13416–13417	Oct. 7, 1938	6296	13555–13556	Mar. 15, 1939
6232	13418–13419	Oct. 9, 1938	6297	13557–13558	Mar. 16, 1939
6233	13420–13421	Oct. 10, 1938	6298	13559–13560	Mar. 17, 1939
6234	13422–13423	Oct. 12, 1938	6299	13561–13562	Mar. 20, 1939
6235	13424–13425	Oct. 13, 1938	6300	13563–13564	Mar. 22, 1939
6236	13426–13427	Oct. 15, 1938	6301	13565–13566	Mar. 23, 1939
6237	13428–13429	Oct. 18, 1938	6302	13567–13568	Mar. 25, 1939
6238	13430–13431	Oct. 20, 1938	6303	13569–13570	Mar. 28, 1939
6239	13432–13433	Oct. 21, 1938	6304	13571–13572	Mar. 30, 1939
6240	13434–13435	Oct. 23, 1938	6305	13573–13574	Mar. 31, 1939
6241	13436–13437	Oct. 25, 1938	6306	13575–13576	Apr. 1, 1939
6242	13438–13439	Oct. 27, 1938	6307	13577–13578	Apr. 4, 1939
6243	13440–13441	Oct. 28, 1938	6308	13579	Apr. 5, 1939
6244	13442–13444	Oct. 31, 1938	6309	13580–13581	Apr. 6, 1939
6245	13445–13446	Nov. 3, 1938	6310	13582–13583	Apr. 7, 1939
6246	13447–13448	Nov. 4, 1938	6311	13584–13585	Apr. 9, 1939
6247	13449–13450	Nov. 7, 1938	6312	13586–13587	Apr. 11, 1939
6248	13451–13452	Nov. 10, 1938	6313	13588–13589	Apr. 14, 1939
6249	13453–13454	Nov. 12, 1938	6314	13590–13591	Apr. 15, 1939
6250	13455–13456	Nov. 15, 1938	6315	13592–13593	Apr. 16, 1939
6251	13457–13458	Nov. 17, 1938	6316	13594–13595	Apr. 19, 1939
6252	13459–13460	Nov. 20, 1938	6317	13596–13597	Apr. 20, 1939
6253	13461–13462	Nov. 24, 1938	6318	13598–13599	Apr. 23, 1939
6254	13463–13465	Nov. 25, 1938	6319	13600–13601	Apr. 25, 1939
6255	13466–13467	Nov. 29, 1938	6320	13602–13603	Apr. 27, 1939
6256	13468–13469	Dec. 1, 1938	6321	13604–13605	Apr. 28, 1939
6257	13470–13471	Dec. 4, 1938	6322	13606–13607	Apr. 29, 1939
6258	13472–13474	Dec. 7, 1938	6323	13608–13609	May 1, 1939
6259	13475–13476	Dec. 11, 1938	6324	13610–13611	May 3, 1939
6260	13477–13478	Dec. 14, 1938	6325	13612–13613	May 5, 1939

Roll	Volumes	Beginning Dates	Roll	Volumes	Beginning Dates
6326	13614–13615	May 8, 1939	6391	13755–13756	Aug. 29, 1939
6327	13616–13617	May 9, 1939	6392	13757–13758	Sept. 1, 1939
6328	13618–13619	May 11, 1939	6393	13759–13761	Sept. 4, 1939
6329	13620–13621	May 12, 1939	6394	13762–13763	Sept. 5, 1939
6330	13622–13623	May 15, 1939	6395	13764–13766	Sept. 6, 1939
6331	13624–13625	May 16, 1939	6396	13767–13768	Sept. 9, 1939
6332	13626–13627	May 19, 1939	6397	13769–13771	Sept. 11, 1939
6333	13628–13629	May 19, 1939	6398	13772–13773	Sept. 14, 1939
6334	13630–13631	May 22, 1939	6399	13774–13775	Sept. 16, 1939
6335	13632–13633	May 24, 1939	6400	13776–13778	Sept. 17, 1939
6336	13634–13635	May 25, 1939	6401	13779–13780	Sept. 21, 1939
6337	13636–13637	May 28, 1939	6402	13781–13782	Sept. 23, 1939
6338	13638–13639	May 30, 1939	6403	13783–13784	Sept. 25, 1939
6339	13640–13641	June 1, 1939	6404	13785–13787	Sept. 28, 1939
6340	13642–13643	June 2, 1939	6405	13788–13789	Oct. 1, 1939
6341	13644–13645	June 4, 1939	6406	13790–13792	Oct. 3, 1939
6342	13646–13647	June 6, 1939	6407	13793–13794	Oct. 10, 1939
6343	13648–13649	June 8, 1939	6408	13795–13796	Oct. 12, 1939
6344	13650–13651	June 10, 1939	6409	13797–13798	Oct. 15, 1939
6345	13652–13653	June 12, 1939	6410	13799–13800	Oct. 17, 1939
6346	13654–13655	June 13, 1939	6411	13801–13802	Oct. 21, 1939
6347	13656–13657	June 16, 1939	6412	13803–13804	Oct. 22, 1939
6348	13658–13659	June 18, 1939	6413	13805–13806	Oct. 26, 1939
6349	13660–13661	June 19, 1939	6414	13807–13808	Oct. 30, 1939
6350	13662–13663	June 21, 1939	6415	13809–13811	Oct. 31, 1939
6351	13664–13665	June 23, 1939	6416	13812–13813	Nov. 3, 1939
6352	13666–13667	June 26, 1939	6417	13814–13815	Nov. 7, 1939
6353	13668–13669	June 26, 1939	6418	13816–13817	Nov. 10, 1939
6354	13670–13671	June 28, 1939	6419	13818–13820	Nov. 14, 1939
6355	13672–13674	June 29, 1939	6420	13821–13822	Nov. 17, 1939
6356	13675–13676	July 1, 1939	6421	13823–13824	Nov. 21, 1939
6357	13677–13678	July 3, 1939	6422	13825–13826	Nov. 24, 1939
6358	13679–13680	July 4, 1939	6423	13827–13828	Nov. 28, 1939
6359	13681–13682	July 4, 1939	6424	13829–13830	Dec. 2, 1939
6360	13683–13684	July 7, 1939	6425	13831–13833	Dec. 5, 1939
6361	13685–13687	July 10, 1939	6426	13834–13835	Dec. 11, 1939
6362	13688–13689	July 12, 1939	6427	13836–13837	Dec. 16, 1939
6363	13690–13691	July 14, 1939	6428	13838–13840	Dec. 18, 1939
6364	13692–13693	July 15, 1939	6429	13841–13842	Dec. 23, 1939
6365	13694–13695	July 17, 1939	6430	13843–13845	Dec. 26, 1939
6366	13696–13698	July 19, 1939	6431	13846	Jan. 1, 1940
6367	13699–13700	July 21, 1939	6432	13847–13848	Jan. 2, 1940
6368	13701–13702	July 21, 1939	6433	13849–13850	Jan. 6, 1940
6369	13703–13704	July 24, 1939	6434	13851–13852	Jan. 11, 1940
6370	13705–13707	July 26, 1939	6435	13853–13854	Jan. 15, 1940
6371	13708–13709	July 28, 1939	6436	13855–13856	Jan. 19, 1940
6372	13710–13711	July 29, 1939	6437	13857–13858	Jan. 23, 1940
6373	13712–13714	July 30, 1939	6438	13859–13860	Jan. 25, 1940
6374	13715–13716	Aug. 1, 1939	6439	13861–13862	Feb. 1, 1940
6375	13717–13719	Aug. 2, 1939	6440	13863–13864	Feb. 3, 1940
6376	13720–13721	Aug. 5, 1939	6441	13865–13866	Feb. 7, 1940
6377	13722–13723	Aug. 7, 1939	6442	13867–13868	Feb. 10, 1940
6378	13724–13726	Aug. 10, 1939	6443	13869–13870	Feb. 15, 1940
6379	13727–13728	Aug. 11, 1939	6444	13871–13872	Feb. 19, 1940
6380	13729–13730	Aug. 12, 1939	6445	13873–13874	Feb. 21, 1940
6381	13731–13733	Aug. 14, 1939	6446	13875–13876	Feb. 25, 1940
6382	13734–13735	Aug. 17, 1939	6447	13877–13878	Feb. 29, 1940
6383	13736–13737	Aug. 17, 1939	6448	13879–13880	Mar. 4, 1940
6384	13738–13740	Aug. 18, 1939	6449	13881–13883	Mar. 7, 1940
6385	13741–13742	Aug. 21, 1939	6450	13884–13885	Mar. 13, 1940
6386	13743–13745	Aug. 22, 1939	6451	13886–13888	Mar. 16, 1940
6387	13746–13747	Aug. 24, 1939	6452	13889–13891	Mar. 20, 1940
6388	13748–13749	Aug. 25, 1939	6453	13892–13893	Mar. 25, 1940
6389	13750–13752	Aug. 27, 1939	6454	13894–13895	Mar. 28, 1940
6390	13753–13754	Aug. 29, 1939	6455	13896–13898	Apr. 1, 1940

Roll	Volumes	Beginning Dates	Roll	Volumes	Beginning Dates
6456	13899–13900	Apr. 3, 1940	6521	14033–14034	Jan. 16, 1941
6457	13901–13902	Apr. 8, 1940	6522	14035–14037	Jan. 23, 1941
6458	13903–13905	Apr. 11, 1940	6523	14038–14039	Jan. 29, 1941
6459	13906–13907	Apr. 16, 1940	6524	14040–14041	Feb. 4, 1941
6460	13908–13910	Apr. 26, 1940	6525	14042–14043	Feb. 10, 1941
6461	13911–13912	Apr. 25, 1940	6526	14044–14045	Feb. 13, 1941
6462	13913–13915	Apr. 26, 1940	6527	14046–14048	Feb. 19, 1941
6463	13915–13916	May 1, 1940	6528	14049–14050	Feb. 27, 1941
6464	13917–13918	May 5, 1940	6529	14051–14053	Mar. 4, 1941
6465	13919–13920	May 9, 1940	6530	14054–14055	Mar. 10, 1941
6466	13921–13922	May 11, 1940	6531	14056–14057	Mar. 14, 1941
6467	13923–13924	May 14, 1940	6532	14058–14059	Mar. 19, 1941
6468	13925–13927	May 16, 1940	6533	14060–14061	Mar. 24, 1941
6469	13928–13929	May 23, 1940	6534	14062–14063	Mar. 28, 1941
6470	13930–13931	May 28, 1940	6535	14064–14065	Apr. 1, 1941
6471	13932–13933	May 29, 1940	6536	14066–14067	Apr. 6, 1941
6472	13934–13935	June 3, 1940	6537	14068–14069	Apr. 8, 1941
6473	13936–13937	June 8, 1940	6538	14070–14071	Apr. 13, 1941
6474	13938–13939	June 11, 1940	6539	14072–14073	Apr. 18, 1941
6475	13940–13941	June 16, 1940	6540	14074–14075	Apr. 21, 1941
6476	13942–13943	June 20, 1940	6541	14076–14078	Apr. 25, 1941
6477	13944–13945	June 22, 1940	6542	14079–14080	May 1, 1941
6478	13946–13947	June 27, 1940	6543	14081–14082	May 5, 1941
6479	13948–13949	July 1, 1940	6544	14083–14084	May 9, 1941
6480	13950–13951	July 6, 1940	6545	14085	May 15, 1941
6481	13952–13953	July 9, 1940	6546	14086–14087	May 18, 1941
6482	13954–13955	July 12, 1940	6547	14088–14089	May 22, 1941
6483	13956–13957	July 16, 1940	6548	14090–14091	May 26, 1941
6484	13958–13959	July 20, 1940	6549	14092–14093	May 29, 1941
6485	13960–13961	July 25, 1940	6550	14094–14095	June 2, 1941
6486	13962–13964	July 29, 1940	6551	14096–14097	June 3, 1941
6487	13965–13966	Aug. 3, 1940	6552	14098–14099	June 9, 1941
6488	13969–13970	Aug. 7, 1940	6553	14100–14101	June 13, 1941
6489	13971–13972	Aug. 11, 1940	6554	14102–14103	June 17, 1941
6490	13971–13972	Aug. 15, 1940	6555	14104–14105	June 21, 1941
6491	13973–13974	Aug. 19, 1940	6556	14106	June 25, 1941
6492	13975–13976	Aug. 22, 1940	6557	14107–14108	June 27, 1941
6493	13977–13978	Aug. 27, 1940	6558	14109–14110	July 1, 1941
6494	13979–13981	Sept. 1, 1940	6559	14111–14112	July 5, 1941
6495	13982–13983	Sept. 6, 1940	6560	14113–14114	July 9, 1941
6496	13984–13985	Sept. 10, 1940	6561	14115–14116	July 13, 1941
6497	13986–13987	Sept. 17, 1940	6562	14117–14118	July 16, 1941
6498	13988–13989	Sept. 20, 1940	6563	14119–14120	July 21, 1941
6499	13990–13991	Sept. 25, 1940	6564	14121–14122	July 25, 1941
6500	13992–13993	Oct. 1, 1940	6565	14123–14124	July 28, 1941
6501	13994–13995	Oct. 3, 1940	6566	14125–14126	Aug. 1, 1941
6502	13996–13997	Oct. 9, 1940	6567	14127–14128	Aug. 5, 1941
6503	13998	Oct. 14, 1940	6568	14129	Aug. 8, 1941
6504	13999–14000	Oct. 17, 1940	6569	14130–14131	Aug. 11, 1941
6505	14001–14002	Oct. 21, 1940	6570	14132–14133	Aug. 15, 1941
6506	14003–14004	Oct. 26, 1940	6571	14134–14135	Aug. 19, 1941
6507	14005–14007	Oct. 30, 1940	6572	14136–14137	Aug. 22, 1941
6508	14008–14009	Nov. 7, 1940	6573	14138–14140	Aug. 26, 1941
6509	14010–14011	Nov. 14, 1940	6574	14141–14142	Sept. 1, 1941
6510	14012–14013	Nov. 21, 1940	6575	14143–14144	Sept. 4, 1941
6511	14014–14015	Nov. 25, 1940	6576	14145–14146	Sept. 8, 1941
6512	14016–14017	Dec. 1, 1940	6577	14147	Sept. 12, 1941
6513	14018–14019	Dec. 5, 1940	6578	14148–14149	Sept. 14, 1941
6514	14020–14021	Dec. 11, 1940	6579	14150–14151	Sept. 17, 1941
6515	14022–14023	Dec. 17, 1940	6580	14152–14153	Sept. 21, 1941
6516	14024–14025	Dec. 23, 1940	6581	14154–14155	Sept. 24, 1941
6517	14026	Dec. 30, 1940	6582	14156–14157	Sept. 28, 1941
6518	14027–14028	Jan. 1, 1941	6583	14158–14159	Oct. 3, 1941
6519	14029–14030	Jan. 6, 1941	6584	14160–14161	Oct. 6, 1941
6520	14031–14032	Jan. 10, 1941	6585	14162–14163	Oct. 10, 1941

Roll	Volumes	Beginning Dates	Roll	Volumes	Beginning Dates
6586	14164–14165	Oct. 14, 1941	6651	14272–14273	Sept. 4, 1942
6587	14166–14167	Oct. 19, 1941	6652	14274–14275	Sept. 6, 1942
6588	14168–14169	Oct. 23, 1941	6653	14276–14277	Sept. 11, 1942
6589	14170–14171	Oct. 27, 1941	6654	14278	Sept. 15, 1942
6590	14172–14173	Nov. 1, 1941	6655	14279–14280	Sept. 19, 1942
6591	14174–14175	Nov. 5, 1941	6656	14281–14282	Sept. 25, 1942
6592	14176–14177	Nov. 11, 1941	6657	14283–14284	Oct. 1, 1942
6593	14178–14179	Nov. 15, 1941	6658	14285–14286	Oct. 6, 1942
6594	14180–14181	Nov. 19, 1941	6659	14287–14288	Oct. 11, 1942
6595	14182–14183	Nov. 24, 1941	6660	14289–14290	Oct. 16, 1942
6596	14184–14185	Nov. 28, 1941	6661	14291–14292	Oct. 24, 1942
6597	14186–14187	Dec. 2, 1941	6662	14293	Oct. 29, 1942
6598	14188–14189	Dec. 7, 1941	6663	14294–14295	Nov. 1, 1942
6599	14190–14191	Dec. 12, 1941	6664	14296–14297	Nov. 7, 1942
6600	14192–14193	Dec. 17, 1941	6665	14298–14299	Nov. 11, 1942
6601	14194–14196	Dec. 22, 1941	6666	14300–14301	Nov. 17, 1942
6602	14197	Dec. 29, 1941	6667	14302–14303	Nov. 23, 1942
6603	14198–14199	Jan. 1, 1942	6668	14304–14305	Nov. 29, 1942
6604	14200–14201	Jan. 6, 1942	6669	14306–14307	Dec. 4, 1942
6605	14202–14203	Jan. 12, 1942	6670	14308–14309	Dec. 9, 1942
6606	14204–14205	Jan. 18, 1942	6671	14310–14311	Dec. 13, 1942
6607	14206–14207	Jan. 26, 1942	6672	14312–14313	Dec. 19, 1942
6608	14208–14209	Feb. 1, 1942	6673	14314–14315	Dec. 25, 1942
6609	14210	Feb. 11, 1942	6674	14316	Dec. 31, 1942
6610	14211–14212	Feb. 15, 1942	6675	14317–14318	Jan. 1, 1943
6611	14213–14214	Feb. 23, 1942	6676	14319–14320	Jan. 5, 1943
6612	14215	Mar. 1, 1942	6677	14321–13422	Jan. 9, 1943
6613	14216–14217	Mar. 6, 1942	6678	14323–14325	Jan. 12, 1943
6614	14218	Mar. 14, 1942	6679	14326–14327	Jan. 21, 1943
6615	14219–14220	Mar. 18, 1942	6680	14327–14328	Jan. 25, 1943
6616	14221–14222	Mar. 25, 1942	6681	14329–14330	Jan. 28, 1943
6617	14223	Mar. 28, 1942	6682	14331–14332	Feb. 1, 1943
6618	14224	Apr. 1, 1942	6683	14333–14334	Feb. 6, 1943
6619	14225	Apr. 3, 1942	6684	14335–14337	Feb. 10, 1943
6620	14226–14227	Apr. 8, 1942	6685	14338–14339	Feb. 17, 1943
6621	14228	Apr. 16, 1942	6686	14340–14341	Feb. 21, 1943
6622	14229–14230	Apr. 20, 1942	6687	14342–14344	Feb. 26, 1943
6623	14231	Apr. 26, 1942	6688	14345–14346	Mar. 3, 1943
6624	14232	May 1, 1942	6689	14347–14348	Mar. 9, 1943
6625	14233	May 7, 1942	6690	14349–14350	Mar. 13, 1943
6626	14234	May 10, 1942	6691	14351–14352	Mar. 17, 1943
6627	14235	May 16, 1942	6692	14353–14354	Mar. 21, 1943
6628	14236	May 20, 1942	6693	14355–14357	Mar. 26, 1943
6629	14237	May 28, 1942	6694	14358–14359	Apr. 1, 1943
6630	14238	May 31, 1942	6695	14360–14361	Apr. 6, 1943
6631	14239	June 1, 1942	6696	14362–14364	Apr. 9, 1943
6632	14240	June 3, 1942	6697	14365–14367	Apr. 14, 1943
6633	14241–14242	June 7, 1942	6698	14368–14369	Apr. 19, 1943
6634	14243–14244	June 19, 1942	6699	14370–14371	Apr. 22, 1943
6635	14245	June 21, 1942	6700	14372–14374	Apr. 28, 1943
6636	14246–14247	June 25, 1942	6701	14375–14377	May 2, 1943
6637	14248–14249	June 28, 1942	6702	14378–14380	May 6, 1943
6638	14250–14251	July 1, 1942	6703	14381–14383	May 9, 1943
6639	14252	July 10, 1942	6704	14384–14385	May 14, 1943
6640	14253–14254	July 13, 1942	6705	14386–14387	May 17, 1943
6641	14255	July 23, 1942	6706	14388–14389	May 21, 1943
6642	14256–14257	July 25, 1942	6707	14390–14391	May 23, 1943
6643	14258–14260	July 27, 1942	6708	14392–14393	May 27, 1943
6644	14261	Aug. 1, 1942	6709	14394–14395	May 31, 1943
6645	14262–14263	Aug. 5, 1942	6710	14396–14397	June 4, 1943
6646	14264	Aug. 14, 1942	6711	14398–14400	June 7, 1943
6647	14265–14266	Aug. 16, 1942	6712	14401–14402	June 11, 1943
6648	14267	Aug. 22, 1942	6713	14403–14405	June 15, 1943
6649	14268–14269	Aug. 25, 1942	6714	14406–14407	June 18, 1943
6650	14270–14271	Aug. 30, 1942	6715	14408–14410	June 25, 1943

Roll	Volumes	Beginning Dates	Roll	Volumes	Beginning Dates
6716	14411–14412	July 1, 1943	6781	14571–14573	Feb. 29, 1944
6717	14413–14415	July 2, 1943	6782	14574–14576	Mar. 3, 1944
6718	14416–14417	July 9, 1943	6783	14577–14579	Mar. 8, 1944
6719	14418–14419	July 10, 1943	6784	14580–14582	Mar. 10, 1944
6720	14420–14421	July 15, 1943	6785	14583–14584	Mar. 14, 1944
6721	14422–14423	July 20, 1943	6786	14585–14586	Mar. 16, 1944
6722	14424–14425	July 22, 1943	6787	14587–14588	Mar. 18, 1944
6723	14426–14427	July 25, 1943	6788	14589–14590	Mar. 21, 1944
6724	14428–14429	July 28, 1943	6789	14591–14593	Mar. 23, 1944
6725	14430–14431	July 31, 1943	6790	14594–14596	Mar. 26, 1944
6726	14432–14434	Aug. 4, 1943	6791	14597–14599	Mar. 31, 1944
6727	14435–14436	Aug. 7, 1943	6792	14600–14602	Apr. 3, 1944
6728	14437–14439	Aug. 9, 1943	6793	14603–14604	Apr. 4, 1944
6729	14440–14442	Aug. 14, 1943	6794	14605–14607	Apr. 6, 1944
6730	14443–14444	Aug. 19, 1943	6795	14608–14610	Apr. 11, 1944
6731	14445–14446	Aug. 22, 1943	6796	14611–14612	Apr. 16, 1944
6732	14447–14448	Aug. 25, 1943	6797	14613–14614	Apr. 17, 1944
6733	14449–14451	Aug. 28, 1943	6798	14615–14617	Apr. 20, 1944
6734	14452–14453	Sept. 3, 1943	6799	14618–14619	Apr. 22, 1944
6735	14454–14455	Sept. 6, 1943	6800	14620–14621	Apr. 25, 1944
6736	14456–14458	Sept. 10, 1943	6801	14622–14624	Apr. 26, 1944
6737	14459–14460	Sept. 15, 1943	6802	14625–14627	Apr. 30, 1944
6738	14461–14463	Sept. 19, 1943	6803	14628–14630	May 2, 1944
6739	14464–14465	Sept. 24, 1943	6804	14631–14633	May 6, 1944
6740	14466–14468	Sept. 26, 1943	6805	14634–14636	May 9, 1944
6741	14469–14470	Oct. 1, 1943	6806	14637–14638	May 11, 1944
6742	14471–14473	Oct. 4, 1943	6807	14639–14641	May 12, 1944
6743	14474–14476	Oct. 9, 1943	6808	14642–14644	May 16, 1944
6744	14477–14478	Oct. 13, 1943	6809	14645–14647	May 20, 1944
6745	14479–14480	Oct. 15, 1943	6810	14648–14649	May 22, 1944
6746	14481–14482	Oct. 18, 1943	6811	14650–14651	May 27, 1944
6747	14483–14485	Oct. 23, 1943	6812	14652–14653	May 28, 1944
6748	14486–14487	Oct. 27, 1943	6813	14654–14655	May 30, 1944
6749	14488–14490	Oct. 29, 1943	6814	14656–14657	June 1, 1944
6750	14491–14492	Nov. 3, 1943	6815	14658–14660	June 4, 1944
6751	14493–14494	Nov. 6, 1943	6816	14661–14662	June 7, 1944
6752	14495–14497	Nov. 8, 1943	6817	14663–14664	June 9, 1944
6753	14498–14499	Nov. 12, 1943	6818	14665–14667	June 10, 1944
6754	14500–14501	Nov. 16, 1943	6819	14668–14670	June 16, 1944
6755	14502–14504	Nov. 19, 1943	6820	14671–14672	June 19, 1944
6756	14505–14506	Nov. 24, 1943	6821	14673–14675	June 22, 1944
6757	14507–14508	Nov. 27, 1943	6822	14676–14678	June 24, 1944
6758	14509–14511	Nov. 29, 1943	6823	14679–14680	June 28, 1944
6759	14512–14513	Dec. 2, 1943	6824	14681–14682	June 29, 1944
6760	14534–14516	Dec. 5, 1943	6825	14683–14685	July 1, 1944
6761	14517–14519	Dec. 8, 1943	6826	14686–14688	July 3, 1944
6762	14520–14521	Dec. 15, 1943	6827	14689–14691	July 7, 1944
6763	14522–14524	Dec. 18, 1943	6828	14692–14694	July 11, 1944
6764	14525–14526	Dec. 21, 1943	6829	14695–14696	July 12, 1944
6765	14527–14528	Dec. 26, 1943	6830	14697–14698	July 16, 1944
6766	14529–14530	Dec. 29, 1943	6831	14699–14701	July 18, 1944
6767	14531–14533	Jan. 1, 1944	6832	14702–14703	July 21, 1944
6768	14534–14536	Jan. 5, 1944	6833	14704–14706	July 23, 1944
6769	14537–14538	Jan. 9, 1944	6834	14707–14709	July 27, 1944
6770	14539–14540	Jan. 11, 1944	6835	14710	July 31, 1944
6771	14541–14543	Jan. 16, 1944	6836	14711–14712	Aug. 1, 1944
6772	14544–14546	Jan. 19, 1944	6837	14713–14715	Aug. 2, 1944
6773	14547–14549	Jan. 26, 1944	6838	14716–14718	Aug. 5, 1944
6774	14550–14552	Jan. 29, 1944	6839	14719–14720	Aug. 9, 1944
6775	14553–14555	Feb. 4, 1944	6840	14721–14723	Aug. 10, 1944
6776	14556–14558	Feb. 7, 1944	6841	14724–14725	Aug. 14, 1944
6777	14559–14561	Feb. 13, 1944	6842	14726–14727	Aug. 16, 1944
6778	14562–14564	Feb. 16, 1944	6843	14728–14730	Aug. 18, 1944
6779	14656–14567	Feb. 19, 1944	6844	14731–14733	Aug. 20, 1944
6780	14568–14570	Feb. 24, 1944	6845	14734–14736	Aug. 23, 1944

Roll	Volumes	Beginning Dates	Roll	Volumes	Beginning Dates
6846	14737–14739	Aug. 28, 1944	6911	14883–14885	Feb. 3, 1945
6847	14740–14741	Aug. 31, 1944	6912	14886–14888	Feb. 6, 1945
6848	14742–14743	Sept. 1, 1944	6913	14889–14890	Feb. 9, 1945
6849	14744–14745	Sept. 3, 1944	6914	14891–14892	Feb. 11, 1945
6850	14746–14748	Sept. 3, 1944	6915	14893–14895	Feb. 14, 1945
6851	14749–14750	Sept. 6, 1944	6916	14896–14897	Feb. 19, 1945
6852	14751–14752	Sept. 8, 1944	6917	14898–14899	Feb. 20, 1945
6853	14753–14755	Sept. 11, 1944	6918	14900–14901	Feb. 23, 1945
6854	14756–14757	Sept. 15, 1944	6919	14902–14904	Feb. 24, 1945
6855	14758–14759	Sept. 17, 1944	6920	14905–14906	Feb. 27, 1945
6856	14760–14761	Sept. 19, 1944	6921	14907–14909	Mar. 1, 1945
6857	14762–14763	Sept. 20, 1944	6922	14910–14911	Mar. 3, 1945
6858	14764–14765	Sept. 22, 1944	6923	14912–14914	Mar. 5, 1945
6859	14766–14768	Sept. 23, 1944	6924	14915–14916	Mar. 8, 1945
6860	14769–14770	Sept. 26, 1944	6925	14917–14919	Mar. 11, 1945
6861	14771–14772	Sept. 28, 1944	6926	14920–14921	Mar. 12, 1945
6862	14773–14774	Sept. 30, 1944	6927	14922–14924	Mar. 13, 1945
6863	14775–14776	Oct. 3, 1944	6928	14925–14926	Mar. 18, 1945
6864	14777–14778	Oct. 5, 1944	6929	14927–14928	Mar. 19, 1945
6865	14779–14781	Oct. 8, 1944	6930	14929–14931	Mar. 21, 1945
6866	14782–14783	Oct. 10, 1944	6931	14932–14933	Mar. 23, 1945
6867	14784–14785	Oct. 12, 1944	6932	14934–14935	Mar. 26, 1945
6868	14786–14788	Oct. 13, 1944	6933	14936–14938	Mar. 28, 1945
6869	14789–14790	Oct. 16, 1944	6934	14939–14941	Mar. 30, 1945
6870	14791–14793	Oct. 18, 1944	6935	14942–14944	Apr. 3, 1945
6871	14794–14795	Oct. 23, 1944	6936	14945–14946	Apr. 5, 1945
6872	14796–14798	Oct. 25, 1944	6937	14947–14948	Apr. 7, 1945
6873	14799–14801	Oct. 28, 1944	6938	14949–14950	Apr. 9, 1945
6874	14802–14803	Oct. 31, 1944	6939	14951–14953	Apr. 11, 1945
6875	14804–14805	Nov. 1, 1944	6940	14954–14955	Apr. 14, 1945
6876	14806–14807	Nov. 5, 1944	6941	14956–14957	Apr. 16, 1945
6877	14808–14810	Nov. 6, 1944	6942	14958–14960	Apr. 19, 1945
6878	14811–14812	Nov. 9, 1944	6943	14961–14962	Apr. 22, 1945
6879	14813–14814	Nov. 12, 1944	6944	14963–14964	Apr. 25, 1945
6880	14815–14816	Nov. 15, 1944	6945	14965–14966	Apr. 26, 1945
6881	14817–14818	Nov. 17, 1944	6946	14967–14969	Apr. 28, 1945
6882	14819–14820	Nov. 19, 1944	6947	14970–14972	Apr. 30, 1945
6883	14821–14822	Nov. 22, 1944	6948	14973–14974	May 2, 1945
6884	14823–14825	Nov. 24, 1944	6949	14975–14976	May 5, 1945
6885	14826–14827	Nov. 26, 1944	6950	14977–14978	May 7, 1945
6886	14828–14829	Nov. 30, 1944	6951	14979–14981	May 9, 1945
6887	14830–14832	Dec. 2, 1944	6952	14982–14983	May 13, 1945
6888	14833–14834	Dec. 5, 1944	6953	14984–14985	May 15, 1945
6889	14835–14836	Dec. 8, 1944	6954	14986–14988	May 18, 1945
6890	14837–14839	Dec. 10, 1944	6955	14988–14989	May 20, 1945
6891	14840–14841	Dec. 13, 1944	6956	14990–14992	May 22, 1945
6892	14842–14843	Dec. 15, 1944	6957	14993–14994	May 24, 1945
6893	14844–14845	Dec. 20, 1944	6958	14995–14997	May 27, 1945
6894	14846–14847	Dec. 22, 1944	6959	14998–14999	May 29, 1945
6895	14848–14849	Dec. 23, 1944	6960	15000–15001	June 1, 1945
6896	14850–14851	Dec. 27, 1944	6961	15002–15004	June 3, 1945
6897	14852–14854	Dec. 28, 1944	6962	15005–15006	June 5, 1945
6898	14855–14856	Jan. 1, 1945	6963	15007–15009	June 8, 1945
6899	14857–14858	Jan. 3, 1945	6964	15010–15011	June 11, 1945
6900	14858–14860	Jan. 5, 1945	6965	15012–15013	June 13, 1945
6901	14861–14862	Jan. 8, 1945	6966	15014–15015	June 15, 1945
6902	14863–14864	Jan. 11, 1945	6967	15016–15017	June 18, 1945
6903	14865–14867	Jan. 13, 1945	6968	15018–15019	June 20, 1945
6904	14868–14869	Jan. 18, 1945	6969	15020–15022	June 21, 1945
6905	14870–14871	Jan. 19, 1945	6970	15023–15024	June 23, 1945
6906	14872–14873	Jan. 21, 1945	6971	15025–15026	June 26, 1945
6907	14874–14875	Jan. 23, 1945	6972	15027–15028	June 29, 1945
6908	14876–14878	Jan. 27, 1945	6973	15029–15030	July 1, 1945
6909	14879–14880	Jan. 30, 1945	6974	15031–15032	July 3, 1945
6910	14881–14882	Feb. 1, 1945	6975	15033–15034	July 5, 1945

Roll	Volumes	Beginning Dates	Roll	Volumes	Beginning Dates
6976	15035–15036	July 9, 1945	7041	15173–15174	Dec. 19, 1945
6977	15037–15038	July 11, 1945	7042	15175–15176	Dec. 21, 1945
6978	15039–15040	July 11, 1945	7043	15177–15178	Dec. 24, 1945
6979	15041–15042	July 13, 1945	7044	15179–15180	Dec. 27, 1945
6980	15043–15044	July 17, 1945	7045	15181–15182	Dec. 28, 1945
6981	15045–15046	July 19, 1945	7046	15183–15184	Jan. 1, 1946
6982	15047–15048	July 20, 1945	7047	15185–15186	Jan. 2, 1946
6983	15049–15050	July 23, 1945	7048	15187–15188	Jan. 4, 1946
6984	15051–15053	July 25, 1945	7049	15189–15190	Jan. 7, 1946
6985	15054–15055	July 29, 1945	7050	15191–15192	Jan. 10, 1946
6986	15056–15057	Aug. 1, 1945	7051	15193–15194	Jan. 14, 1946
6987	15058–15060	Aug. 2, 1945	7052	15195–15196	Jan. 15, 1946
6988	15061–15062	Aug. 5, 1945	7053	15197–15198	Jan. 18, 1946
6989	15063–15065	Aug. 8, 1945	7054	15199–15200	Jan. 22, 1946
6990	15066–15067	Aug. 11, 1945	7055	15201–15202	Jan. 25, 1946
6991	15068–15069	Aug. 14, 1945	7056	15203–15204	Jan. 28, 1946
6992	15070–15071	Aug. 16, 1945	7057	15205–15207	Jan. 29, 1946
6993	15072–15073	Aug. 19, 1945	7058	15208–15210	Feb. 2, 1946
6994	15074–15075	Aug. 21, 1945	7059	15211–15212	Feb. 4, 1946
6995	15076–15078	Aug. 23, 1945	7060	15213–15214	Feb. 7, 1946
6996	15079–15080	Aug. 28, 1945	7061	15215–15216	Feb. 10, 1946
6997	15081–15082	Aug. 30, 1945	7062	15217–15218	Feb. 13, 1946
6998	15083–15084	Sept. 1, 1945	7063	15219–15220	Feb. 17, 1946
6999	15085–15086	Sept. 3, 1945	7064	15221–15222	Feb. 20, 1946
7000	15087–15088	Sept. 5, 1945	7065	15223–15224	Feb. 20, 1946
7001	15089–15090	Sept. 8, 1945	7066	15225–15226	Feb. 22, 1946
7002	15091–15092	Sept. 10, 1945	7067	15227–15228	Feb. 24, 1946
7003	15093–15094	Sept. 12, 1945	7068	15229–15230	Feb. 26, 1946
7004	15095–15096	Sept. 14, 1945	7069	15231–15232	Mar. 1, 1946
7005	15097–15098	Sept. 17, 1945	7070	15233–15234	Mar. 2, 1946
7006	15099–15100	Sept. 19, 1945	7071	15235–15236	Mar. 4, 1946
7007	15101–15102	Sept. 21, 1945	7072	15237–15238	Mar. 6, 1946
7008	15103	Sept. 24, 1945	7073	15239–15240	Mar. 8, 1946
7009	15104–15105	Sept. 26, 1945	7074	15241–15242	Mar. 11, 1946
7010	15106–15108	Sept. 28, 1945	7075	15243–15244	Mar. 14, 1946
7011	15109–15110	Oct. 1, 1945	7076	15245–15246	Mar. 17, 1946
7012	15111–15112	Oct. 3, 1945	7077	15247–15248	Mar. 19, 1946
7013	15113–15114	Oct. 5, 1945	7078a	15249–15250	Mar. 21, 1946
7014	15115–15116	Oct. 8, 1945	7078b	15251–15252	Mar. 23, 1946
7015	15117–15118	Oct. 9, 1945	7079	15253–15254	Mar. 25, 1946
7016	15119–15120	Oct. 11, 1945	7080	15255–15256	Mar. 26, 1946
7017	15121–15122	Oct. 15, 1945	7081	15257–15258	Mar. 28, 1946
7018	15123–15124	Oct. 17, 1945	7082	15259–15260	Apr. 1, 1946
7019	15125–15126	Oct. 21, 1945	7083	15261–15262	Apr. 3, 1946
7020	15127–15128	Oct. 24, 1945	7084	15263–15264	Apr. 4, 1946
7021	15129–15130	Oct. 26, 1945	7085	15265–15266	Apr. 6, 1946
7022	15131–15132	Oct. 30, 1945	7086	15267–15268	Apr. 8, 1946
7023	15133–15134	Nov. 2, 1945	7087	15269–15270	Apr. 10, 1946
7024	15135–15136	Nov. 5, 1945	7088	15271–15272	Apr. 12, 1946
7025	15137–15139	Nov. 8, 1945	7089	15273–15274	Apr. 15, 1946
7026	15140–15141	Nov. 10, 1945	7090	15275–15276	Apr. 17, 1946
7027	15142–15143	Nov. 13, 1945	7091	15277–15278	Apr. 19, 1946
7028	15144–15146	Nov. 16, 1945	7092	15279–15280	Apr. 21, 1946
7029	15147–15148	Nov. 21, 1945	7093	15281–15282	Apr. 23, 1946
7030	15149–15150	Nov. 24, 1945	7094	15283–15284	Apr. 24, 1946
7031	15151–15152	Nov. 26, 1945	7095	15285–15286	Apr. 26, 1946
7032	15153–15154	Nov. 27, 1945	7096	15287–15288	Apr. 29, 1946
7033	15155–15157	Nov. 28, 1945	7097	15289–15290	May 1, 1946
7034	15158–15159	Dec. 2, 1945	7098	15291–15292	May 2, 1946
7035	15160–15161	Dec. 4, 1945	7099	15293–15294	May 5, 1946
7036	15162–15163	Dec. 7, 1945	7100	15295–15296	May 7, 1946
7037	15164–15165	Dec. 8, 1945	7101	15297–15298	May 10, 1946
7038	15166–15167	Dec. 11, 1945	7102	15299–15300	May 12, 1946
7039	15168–15170	Dec. 14, 1945	7103	15301–15032	May 14, 1946
7040	15171–15172	Dec. 16, 1945	7104	15303–15304	May 16, 1946

Roll	Volumes	Beginning Dates	Roll	Volumes	Beginning Dates
7105	15305–15306	May 18, 1946	7170	15410–15411	Sept. 3, 1946
7106	15307–15308	May 20, 1946	7171	15412	Sept. 4, 1946
7107	15309	May 22, 1946	7172	15413	Sept. 5, 1946
7108	15310–15311	May 23, 1946	7173	15414–15415	Sept. 7, 1946
7109	15312–15313	May 25, 1946	7174	15416–15417	Sept. 8, 1946
7110	15314	May 27, 1946	7175	15418	Sept. 10, 1946
7111	15315–15316	May 27, 1946	7176	15419	Sept. 11, 1946
7112	15317	May 29, 1946	7177	15420–15421	Sept. 12, 1946
7113	15318	May 30, 1946	7178	15422–15423	Sept. 14, 1946
7114	15319	June 1, 1946	7179	15424–15425	Sept. 16, 1946
7115	15320	June 2, 1946	7180	15426	Sept. 17, 1946
7116	15321–15322	June 3, 1946	7181	15427	Sept. 18, 1946
7117	15323–15324	June 5, 1946	7182	15428	Sept. 19, 1946
7118	15325	June 8, 1946	7183	15429	Sept. 20, 1946
7119	15326–15327	June 9, 1946	7184	15430	Sept. 22, 1946
7120	15328	June 11, 1946	7185	15431–15432	Sept. 24, 1946
7121	15329	June 12, 1946	7186	15433–15434	Sept. 26, 1946
7122	15330	June 13, 1946	7187	15435–15436	Sept. 28, 1946
7123	15331	June 15, 1946	7188	15437–15438	Sept. 30, 1946
7124	15332–15333	June 16, 1946	7189	15439	Oct. 1, 1946
7125	15334	June 17, 1946	7190	15440	Oct. 2, 1946
7126	15335	June 18, 1946	7191	15441	Oct. 3, 1946
7127	15336–15337	June 20, 1946	7192	15442	Oct. 4, 1946
7128	15338	June 22, 1946	7193	15443	Oct. 6, 1946
7129	15339	June 24, 1946	7194	15444	Oct. 7, 1946
7130	15340	June 25, 1946	7195	15445	Oct. 8, 1946
7131	15341–15342	June 26, 1946	7196	15446	Oct. 9, 1946
7132	15343–15344	June 28, 1946	7197	15447	Oct. 11, 1946
7133	15345–15346	June 30, 1946	7198	15448	Oct. 12, 1946
7134	15347–15348	July 1, 1946	7199	15449–15450	Oct. 13, 1946
7135	15349	July 3, 1946	7200	15451	Oct. 14, 1946
7136	15350–15351	July 5, 1946	7201	15452	Oct. 16, 1946
7137	15352–15353	July 6, 1946	7202	15453	Oct. 17, 1946
7138	15354–15355	July 8, 1946	7203	15454	Oct. 18, 1946
7139	15356–15357	July 10, 1946	7204	15455–15456	Oct. 20, 1946
7140	15358–15359	July 12, 1946	7205	15457–15458	Oct. 21, 1946
7141	15360–15361	July 15, 1946	7206	15459–15460	Oct. 22, 1946
7142	15362–15363	July 17, 1946	7207	15461	Oct. 24, 1946
7143	15364	July 19, 1946	7208	15462–15463	Oct. 26, 1946
7144	15365	July 20, 1946	7209	15464–15466	Oct. 28, 1946
7145	15366–15367	July 22, 1946	7210	15467	Oct. 29, 1946
7146	15368–15369	July 24, 1946	7211	15468	Oct. 30, 1946
7147	15370–15371	July 27, 1946	7212	15469–15470	Nov. 1, 1946
7148	15372–15373	July 29, 1946	7213	15471	Nov. 2, 1946
7149	15374	July 30, 1946	7214	15472–15473	Nov. 4, 1946
7150	15375–15376	Aug. 1, 1946	7215	15474	Nov. 7, 1946
7151	15377–15378	Aug. 3, 1946	7216	15475	Nov. 9, 1946
7152	15379–15380	Aug. 5, 1946	7217	15476–15477	Nov. 10, 1946
7153	15381–15382	Aug. 6, 1946	7218	15478–15479	Nov. 11, 1946
7154	15383–15384	Aug. 8, 1946	7219	15480	Nov. 12, 1946
7155	15385–15386	Aug. 11, 1946	7220	15481	Nov. 14, 1946
7156	15387	Aug. 12, 1946	7221	15482	Nov. 15, 1946
7157	15388–15389	Aug. 13, 1946	7222	15483	Nov. 17, 1946
7158	15390–15391	Aug. 14, 1946	7223	15484–15485	Nov. 18, 1946
7159	15392–15393	Aug. 17, 1946	7224	15486	Nov. 20, 1946
7160	15394–15395	Aug. 19, 1946	7225	15487	Nov. 20, 1946
7161	15396–15397	Aug. 21, 1946	7226	15488	Nov. 21, 1946
7162	15398	Aug. 23, 1946	7227	15489	Nov. 23, 1946
7163	15399	Aug. 25, 1946	7228	15490–15491	Nov. 24, 1946
7164	15400–15401	Aug. 26, 1946	7229	15492–15494	Nov. 26, 1946
7165	15402	Aug. 27, 1946	7230	15495	Nov. 27, 1946
7166	15403–15404	Aug. 28, 1946	7231	15496–15497	Nov. 28, 1946
7167	15405–15406	Aug. 30, 1946	7232	15498–15499	Nov. 29, 1946
7168	15407	Sept. 1, 1946	7233	15500–15501	Dec. 1, 1946
7169	15408–15409	Sept. 2, 1946	7234	15502	Dec. 2, 1946

Roll	Volumes	Beginning Dates	Roll	Volumes	Beginning Dates
7235	15503	Dec. 4, 1946	7300	15608	Mar. 12, 1947
7236	15504	Dec. 5, 1946	7301	15609	Mar. 13, 1947
7237	15505	Dec. 6, 1946	7302	15610	Mar. 14, 1947
7238	15506	Dec. 7, 1946	7303	15611	Mar. 15, 1947
7239	15507–15508	Dec. 9, 1946	7304	15612–15613	Mar. 16, 1947
7240	15509–15511	Dec. 11, 1946	7305	15614	Mar. 17, 1947
7241	15512–15513	Dec. 12, 1946	7306	15615	Mar. 18, 1947
7242	15514	Dec. 13, 1946	7307	15616–15617	Mar. 20, 1947
7243	15515–15516	Dec. 15, 1946	7308	15618–15619	Mar. 21, 1947
7244	15517	Dec. 16, 1946	7309	15620–15621	Mar. 23, 1947
7245	15518	Dec. 17, 1946	7310	15622–15623	Mar. 25, 1947
7246	15519	Dec. 18, 1946	7311	15624–15625	Mar. 27, 1947
7247	15520–15521	Dec. 19, 1946	7312	15626	Mar. 28, 1947
7248	15522–15523	Dec. 21, 1946	7313	15627–15628	Mar. 29, 1947
7249	15524	Dec. 22, 1946	7314	15629	Mar. 31, 1947
7250	15525–15526	Dec. 24, 1946	7315	15630–15631	Apr. 1, 1947
7251	15527	Dec. 25, 1946	7316	15632–15633	Apr. 3, 1947
7252	15528–15529	Dec. 27, 1946	7317	15634–15635	Apr. 4, 1947
7253	15530	Dec. 30, 1946	7318	15636–15637	Apr. 6, 1947
7254	15531–15532	Jan. 1, 1947	7319	15638–15639	Apr. 7, 1947
7255	15533–15534	Jan. 1, 1947	7320	15640–15641	Apr. 7, 1947
7256	15535	Jan. 5, 1947	7321	15642–15643	Apr. 9, 1947
7257	15536	Jan. 5, 1947	7322	15644	Apr. 11, 1947
7258	15537–15538	Jan. 7, 1947	7323	15645	Apr. 12, 1947
7259	15539	Jan. 9, 1947	7324	15646–15647	Apr. 13, 1947
7260	15540	Jan. 10, 1947	7325	15648–15649	Apr. 14, 1947
7261	15541	Jan. 11, 1947	7326	15650–15651	Apr. 16, 1947
7262	15542–15543	Jan. 13, 1947	7327	15652	Apr. 17, 1947
7263	15544–15545	Jan. 14, 1947	7328	15653	Apr. 18, 1947
7264	15546–15547	Jan. 16, 1947	7329	15654	Apr. 19, 1947
7265	15548	Jan. 17, 1947	7330	15655–15656	Apr. 21, 1947
7266	15549	Jan. 17, 1947	7331	15657	Apr. 22, 1947
7267	15550–15551	Jan. 19, 1947	7332	15658	Apr. 22, 1947
7268	15552–15553	Jan. 22, 1947	7333	15659	Apr. 23, 1947
7269	15554	Jan. 23, 1947	7334	15660–15661	Apr. 24, 1947
7270	15555	Jan. 24, 1947	7335	15662–15663	Apr. 25, 1947
7271	15556–15557	Jan. 26, 1947	7336	15664	Apr. 26, 1947
7272	15558	Jan. 27, 1947	7337	15665–15666	Apr. 27, 1947
7273	15559	Jan. 29, 1947	7338	15667	Apr. 28, 1947
7274	15560–15561	Jan. 30, 1947	7339	15668	Apr. 29, 1947
7275	15562–15563	Feb. 1, 1947	7340	15669	Apr. 30, 1947
7276	15564–15565	Feb. 3, 1947	7341	15670–15671	May 1, 1947
7277	15566–15567	Feb. 4, 1947	7342	15672	May 2, 1947
7278	15568	Feb. 5, 1947	7343	15673	May 4, 1947
7279	15569–15570	Feb. 6, 1947	7344	15674–15675	May 5, 1947
7280	15571–15572	Feb. 9, 1947	7345	15676	May 6, 1947
7281	15573–15574	Feb. 11, 1947	7346	15677	May 6, 1947
7282	15575–15576	Feb. 13, 1947	7347	15678	May 8, 1947
7283	15577	Feb. 14, 1947	7348	15679–15680	May 9, 1947
7284	15578–15579	Feb. 16, 1947	7349	15681	May 9, 1947
7285	15580–15581	Feb. 18, 1947	7350	15682	May 10, 1947
7286	15582–15583	Feb. 19, 1947	7351	15683	May 11, 1947
7287	15584–15586	Feb. 21, 1947	7352	15684	May 12, 1947
7288	15587–15588	Feb. 23, 1947	7353	15685	May 13, 1947
7289	15589	Feb. 25, 1947	7354	15686	May 14, 1947
7290	15590–15591	Feb. 26, 1947	7355	15687	May 15, 1947
7291	15592–15593	Feb. 28, 1947	7356	15688–15689	May 16, 1947
7292	15594	Mar. 1, 1947	7357	15690	May 17, 1947
7293	15595–15596	Mar. 3, 1947	7358	15691–15692	May 19, 1947
7294	15597–15598	Mar. 4, 1947	7359	15693	May 19, 1947
7295	15599–15600	Mar. 5, 1947	7360	15694–15695	May 20, 1947
7296	15601–15602	Mar. 6, 1947	7361	15696	May 22, 1947
7297	15603	Mar. 8, 1947	7362	15697–15699	May 22, 1947
7298	15604–15605	Mar. 10, 1947	7363	15700–15701	May 23, 1947
7299	15606–15607	Mar. 11, 1947	7364	15702	May 24, 1947

Roll	Volumes	Beginning Dates
7365	15703–15704	May 24, 1947
7366	15705–15706	May 26, 1947
7367	15707	May 27, 1947
7368	15708	May 28, 1947
7369	15709	May 29, 1947
7370	15710	May 30, 1947
7371	15711	May 30, 1947
7372	15712	June 1, 1947
7373	15713–15714	June 1, 1947
7374	15715	June 2, 1947
7375	15716	June 3, 1947
7376	15717	June 4, 1947
7377	15718	June 4, 1947
7378	15719	June 5, 1947
7379	15720	June 6, 1947
7380	15721	June 7, 1947
7381	15722–15723	June 8, 1947
7382	15724–15725	June 9, 1947
7383	15726	June 10, 1947
7384	15727	June 11, 1947
7385	15728–15729	June 12, 1947
7386	15730	June 13, 1947
7387	15731	June 14, 1947
7388	15732	June 15, 1947
7389	15733–15734	June 16, 1947
7390	15735–15736	June 16, 1947
7391	15737	June 17, 1947
7392	15738	June 18, 1947
7393	15739	June 19, 1947
7394	15740	June 20, 1947
7395	15741–15742	June 21, 1947
7396	15743	June 22, 1947
7397	15744–15745	June 22, 1947
7398	15746	June 23, 1947
7399	15747–15748	June 24, 1947
7400	15749–15750	June 25, 1947
7401	15751	June 26, 1947
7402	15752	June 27, 1947
7403	15753	June 28, 1947
7404	15754	June 28, 1947
7405	15755–15757	June 29, 1947
7406	15758	June 30, 1947
7407	15759	July 1, 1947
7408	15760–15761	July 2, 1947
7409	15762	July 3, 1947
7410	15763–15764	July 4, 1947
7411	15765–15766	July 5, 1947
7412	15767–15768	July 7, 1947
7413	15769–15770	July 7, 1947
7414	15771–15772	July 7, 1947
7415	15773–15774	July 11, 1947
7416	15775	July 13, 1947
7417	15776	July 14, 1947
7418	15777–15778	July 15, 1947
7419	15779–15780	July 15, 1947
7420	15781–15782	July 16, 1947
7421	15783	July 17, 1947
7422	15784–15785	July 19, 1947
7423	15786–15787	July 20, 1947
7424	15788–15789	July 22, 1947
7425	15790–15791	July 22, 1947
7426	15792–15793	July 23, 1947
7427	15794	July 24, 1947
7428	15795–15796	July 25, 1947
7429	15797	July 27, 1947
7430	15798–15799	July 28, 1947
7431	15800–15801	July 29, 1947
7432	15802–15803	July 29, 1947
7433	15804–15805	July 30, 1947
7434	15806–15807	Aug. 1, 1947
7435	15808–15809	Aug. 3, 1947
7436	15810–15811	Aug. 4, 1947
7437	15812–15813	Aug. 5, 1947
7438	15814–15815	Aug. 6, 1947
7439	15816–15817	Aug. 8, 1947
7440	15818–15819	Aug. 9, 1947
7441	15820–15821	Aug. 11, 1947
7442	15822–15823	Aug. 12, 1947
7443	15824–15825	Aug. 14, 1947
7444	15826–15827	Aug. 14, 1947
7445	15828–15829	Aug. 16, 1947
7446	15830–15832	Aug. 18, 1947
7447	15833–15834	Aug. 18, 1947
7448	15835–15836	Aug. 20, 1947
7449	15837–15838	Aug. 21, 1947
7450	15839–15840	Aug. 23, 1947
7451	15841–15842	Aug. 24, 1947
7452	15843–15845	Aug. 25, 1947
7453	15846–15847	Aug. 27, 1947
7454	15848–15849	Aug. 29, 1947
7455	15850–15851	Aug. 30, 1947
7456	15852–15853	Sept. 1, 1947
7457	15854–15855	Sept. 1, 1947
7458	15856–15858	Sept. 3, 1947
7459	15859–15861	Sept. 5, 1947
7460	15862–15863	Sept. 7, 1947
7461	15864–15865	Sept. 8, 1947
7462	15866–15868	Sept. 9, 1947
7463	15869–15870	Sept. 10, 1947
7464	15871–15872	Sept. 11, 1947
7465	15873–15874	Sept. 13, 1947
7466	15875–15876	Sept. 15, 1947
7467	15877–15879	Sept. 15, 1947
7468	15880–15881	Sept. 16, 1947
7469	15882–15883	Sept. 18, 1947
7470	15884–15885	Sept. 19, 1947
7471	15886–15887	Sept. 21, 1947
7472	15888–15890	Sept. 22, 1947
7473	15891–15892	Sept. 23, 1947
7474	15893–15894	Sept. 24, 1947
7475	15895–15896	Sept. 26, 1947
7476	15897–15898	Sept. 28, 1947
7477	15899–15901	Sept. 29, 1947
7478	15902–15904	Sept. 30, 1947
7479	15905–15906	Oct. 1, 1947
7480	15907–15909	Oct. 2, 1947
7481	15910–15911	Oct. 4, 1947
7482	15912–15914	Oct. 6, 1947
7483	15915–15917	Oct. 8, 1947
7484	15918–15919	Oct. 10, 1947
7485	15920–15922	Oct. 13, 1947
7486	15923–15924	Oct. 14, 1947
7487	15925–15927	Oct. 16, 1947
7488	15928–15929	Oct. 18, 1947
7489	15930–15932	Oct. 20, 1947
7490	15933–15935	Oct. 21, 1947
7491	15936–15937	Oct. 23, 1947
7492	15938–15940	Oct. 24, 1947
7493	15941–15942	Oct. 27, 1947
7494	15943–15945	Oct. 28, 1947

Roll	Volumes	Beginning Dates	Roll	Volumes	Beginning Dates
7495	15946–15948	Oct. 30, 1947	7560	16118–16120	Mar. 13, 1948
7496	15949–15950	Nov. 1, 1947	7561	16121–16123	Mar. 14, 1948
7497	15951–15953	Nov. 2, 1947	7562	16124–16126	Mar. 16, 1948
7498	15954–15956	Nov. 5, 1947	7563	16127–16129	Mar. 18, 1948
7499	15957–15959	Nov. 6, 1947	7564	16130–16132	Mar. 18, 1948
7500	15960–15962	Nov. 8, 1947	7565	16133–16134	Mar. 21, 1948
7501	15963–15964	Nov. 10, 1947	7566	16135–16137	Mar. 22, 1948
7502	15965–15967	Nov. 11, 1947	7567	16138–16140	Mar. 24, 1948
7503	15968–15970	Nov. 13, 1947	7568	16141–16143	Mar. 25, 1948
7504	15971–15973	Nov. 15, 1947	7569	16144–16146	Mar. 27, 1948
7505	15974–15976	Nov. 19, 1947	7570	16417–16148	Mar. 29, 1948
7506	15977–15978	Nov. 21, 1947	7571	16149–16151	Mar. 31, 1948
7507	15979–15980	Nov. 23, 1947	7572	16152–16154	Apr. 2, 1948
7508	15981–15982	Nov. 24, 1947	7573	16155–16156	Apr. 4, 1948
7509	15983–15985	Nov. 25, 1947	7574	16157–16159	Apr. 6, 1948
7510	15986–15988	Nov. 26, 1947	7575	16160–16161	Apr. 8, 1948
7511	15989–15991	Nov. 29, 1947	7576	16162–16164	Apr. 10, 1948
7512	15992–15994	Dec. 1, 1947	7577	16165–16167	Apr. 12, 1948
7513	15995–15997	Dec. 3, 1947	7578	16168–16169	Apr. 14, 1948
7514	15998–16000	Dec. 6, 1947	7579	16170–16171	Apr. 15, 1948
7515	16001–16003	Dec. 8, 1947	7580	16172–16173	Apr. 17, 1948
7516	16004–16005	Dec. 10, 1947	7581	16174–16176	Apr. 19, 1948
7517	16006–16007	Dec. 12, 1947	7582	16177–16178	Apr. 20, 1948
7518	16008–16010	Dec. 13, 1947	7583	16179–16180	Apr. 22, 1948
7519	16011–16013	Dec. 15, 1947	7584	16181–16182	Apr. 24, 1948
7520	16014–16016	Dec. 18, 1947	7585	16183–16184	Apr. 26, 1948
7521	16017–16019	Dec. 21, 1947	7586	16185–16187	Apr. 27, 1948
7522	16020–16021	Dec. 23, 1947	7587	16188–16189	Apr. 28, 1948
7523	16022–16024	Dec. 24, 1947	7588	16190–16191	Apr. 29, 1948
7524	16025–16026	Dec. 26, 1947	7589	16192–16193	May 1, 1948
7525	16027–16028	Dec. 29, 1947	7590	19194–16196	May 3, 1948
7526	16029–16030	Jan. 1, 1948	7591	16197–16198	May 4, 1948
7527	16031–16033	Jan. 3, 1948	7592	16199–16200	May 5, 1948
7528	16034–16036	Jan. 7, 1948	7593	16201–16202	May 8, 1948
7529	16037–16038	Jan. 8, 1948	7594	16203–16205	May 10, 1948
7530	16039–16040	Jan. 9, 1948	7595	16206–16207	May 12, 1948
7531	16041–16043	Jan. 9, 1948	7596	16208–16209	May 14, 1948
7532	16044–16045	Jan. 14, 1948	7597	16210–16211	May 15, 1948
7533	16046–16047	Jan. 15, 1948	7598	16212–16214	May 18, 1948
7534	16047a–16049	Jan. 16, 1948	7599	16215–16217	May 20, 1948
7535	16050–16052	Jan. 17, 1948	7600	16218–16219	May 21, 1948
7536	16053–16055	Jan. 20, 1948	7601	16220–16222	May 22, 1948
7537	16056–16057	Jan. 23, 1948	7602	16223–16224	May 24, 1948
7538	16508–16059	Jan. 24, 1948	7603	16225–16226	May 27, 1948
7539	16060–16061	Jan. 27, 1948	7604	16227–16228	May 27, 1948
7540	16062–16064	Jan. 28, 1948	7605	16229–16230	May 29, 1948
7541	16065–16067	Feb. 1, 1948	7606	16231–16233	May 31, 1948
7542	16068–16069	Feb. 4, 1948	7607	16234–16235	June 2, 1948
7543	16070–16072	Feb. 6, 1948	7608	16236–16237	June 4, 1948
7544	16073–16075	Feb. 8, 1948	7609	16238–16239	June 6, 1948
7545	16076–16078	Feb. 9, 1948	7610	16240–16241	June 7, 1948
7546	16079–16081	Feb. 11, 1948	7611	16242–16243	June 8, 1948
7547	16082–16084	Feb. 14, 1948	7612	16244–16245	June 11, 1948
7548	16085–16087	Feb. 17, 1948	7613	16246–16247	June 13, 1948
7549	16088–16089	Feb. 18, 1948	7614	16248–16250	June 14, 1948
7550	16090–16091	Feb. 20, 1948	7615	16251–16252	June 16, 1948
7551	16092–16094	Feb. 21, 1948	7616	16253–16254	June 17, 1948
7552	16095–16097	Feb. 22, 1948	7617	16255–16256	June 19, 1948
7553	16098–16100	Feb. 24, 1948	7618	16257–16258	June 21, 1948
7554	16101–16103	Feb. 26, 1948	7619	16259–16260	June 22, 1948
7555	16104–16106	Feb. 29, 1948	7620	16261–16262	June 25, 1948
7556	16107–16109	Mar. 3, 1948	7621	16263–16264	June 27, 1948
7557	16110–16111	Mar. 4, 1948	7622	16265–16266	June 28, 1948
7558	16112–16114	Mar. 8, 1948	7623	16267–16268	June 30, 1948
7559	16115–16117	Mar. 10, 1948	7624	16269–16271	July 2, 1948

Roll	Volumes	Beginning Dates	Roll	Volumes	Beginning Dates
7625	16272–16273	July 5, 1948	7690	16453–16455	Dec. 21, 1948
7626	16274–16276	July 7, 1948	7691	16456–16458	Dec. 22, 1948
7627	16277–16278	July 10, 1948	7692	16459–16461	Dec. 25, 1948
7628	16279–16280	July 12, 1948	7693	16462–16463	Dec. 29, 1948
7629	16281–16283	July 14, 1948	7694	16464–16470	Jan. 1, 1949
7630	16284–16286	July 16, 1948	7695	16471–16476	Jan. 10, 1949
7631	16287–16289	July 19, 1948	7696	16477–16481	Jan. 16, 1949
7632	16290–16291	July 23, 1948	7967	16481–16486	Jan. 21, 1949
7633	16292–19294	July 25, 1948	7698	16487–16491	Jan. 27, 1949
7634	16295–16296	July 28, 1948	7699	16492–16496	Feb. 2, 1949
7635	16297–16299	July 29, 1948	7700	16497–16500	Feb. 8, 1949
7636	16300–16302	Aug. 2, 1948	7701	16501–16507	Feb. 12, 1949
7637	16303–16304	Aug. 5, 1948	7702	16508–16514	Feb. 19, 1949
7638	16305–16307	Aug. 7, 1948	7703	16515–16521	Feb. 26, 1949
7639	16308–16310	Aug. 9, 1948	7704	16522–16529	Mar. 5, 1949
7640	16311–16313	Aug. 12, 1948	7705	16529–16535	Mar. 13, 1949
7641	16314–16315	Aug. 14, 1948	7706	16536–16542	Mar. 20, 1949
7642	16316–16318	Aug. 17, 1948	7707	16543–16550	Mar. 25, 1949
7643	16319–16321	Aug. 19, 1948	7708	16551–16558	Apr. 1, 1949
7644	16322–16323	Aug. 22, 1948	7709	16558–16565	Apr. 9, 1949
7645	16324–16326	Aug. 24, 1948	7710	16566–16572	Apr. 16, 1949
7646	16327–16329	Aug. 27, 1948	7711	16573–16582	Apr. 22, 1949
7647	16330–16332	Aug. 29, 1948	7712	16583–16587	Apr. 30, 1949
7648	16333–16335	Sept. 1, 1948	7713	16587–16595	May 4, 1949
7649	16336–16338	Sept. 3, 1948	7714	16596–16601	May 12, 1949
7650	16339–16341	Sept. 6, 1948	7715	16602–16609	May 17, 1949
7651	16342–16344	Sept. 7, 1948	7716	16610–16618	May 24, 1949
7652	16345–16347	Sept. 9, 1948	7717	16618–16625	May 30, 1949
7653	16348–16350	Sept. 12, 1948	7718	16626–16634	June 6, 1949
7654	16351–16353	Sept. 14, 1948	7719	16635–16641	June 13, 1949
7655	16354–16356	Sept. 17, 1948	7720	16642–16650	June 18, 1949
7656	16357–16359	Sept. 19, 1948	7721	16651–16660	June 25, 1949
7657	16360–16362	Sept. 21, 1948	7722	16661–16667	July 2, 1949
7658	16363–16365	Sept. 23, 1948	7723	16668–16676	July 8, 1949
7659	16366–16367	Sept. 26, 1948	7724	16676–16683	July 15, 1949
7660	16368–16370	Sept. 28, 1948	7725	16684–16690	July 21, 1949
7661	16371–16373	Oct. 1, 1948	7726	16691–16700	July 27, 1949
7662	16374–16376	Oct. 3, 1948	7727	16700–16706	Aug. 4, 1949
7663	16377–16379	Oct. 5, 1948	7728	16707–16716	Aug. 9, 1949
7664	16380–16382	Oct. 8, 1948	7729	16716–16723	Aug. 16, 1949
7665	16383–16385	Oct. 11, 1948	7730	16724–16732	Aug. 22, 1949
7666	16386–16388	Oct. 13, 1948	7731	16733–16742	Aug. 29, 1949
7667	16389–16391	Oct. 18, 1948	7732	16743–16749	Sept. 4, 1949
7668	16392–16394	Oct. 18, 1948	7733	16750–16757	Sept. 9, 1949
7669	16395–16397	Oct. 21, 1948	7734	16758–16763	Sept. 14, 1949
7670	16398–16399	Oct. 23, 1948	7735	16764–16766	Sept. 18, 1949
7671	16400–16402	Oct. 25, 1948	7736	16767–16769	Sept. 20, 1949
7672	16403–16405	Oct. 27, 1948	7737	16770–16772	Sept. 22, 1949
7673	16406–16408	Oct. 30, 1948	7738	16773–16775	Sept. 24, 1949
7674	16409–16411	Nov. 2, 1948	7739	16776–16778	Sept. 27, 1949
7675	16412–14613	Nov. 6, 1948	7740	16779–16781	Sept. 29, 1949
7676	16414–16416	Nov. 7, 1948	7741	16782–16784	Oct. 1, 1949
7677	16417–16419	Nov. 11, 1948	7742	16785–16787	Oct. 4, 1949
7678	16420–16422	Nov. 14, 1948	7743	16788–16789	Oct. 6, 1949
7679	16423–16425	Nov. 17, 1948	7744	16790–16792	Oct. 7, 1949
7680	16426–16427	Nov. 21, 1948	7745	16793–16794	Oct. 10, 1949
7681	16428–16430	Nov. 24, 1948	7746	16795–16797	Oct. 11, 1949
7682	16431–16432	Nov. 28, 1948	7747	16798–16800	Oct. 13, 1949
7683	16433–16435	Nov. 30, 1948	7748	16801–16803	Oct. 15, 1949
7684	16436–16438	Dec. 3, 1948	7749	16804–16806	Oct. 19, 1949
7685	16439–16441	Dec. 6, 1948	7750	16807–16809	Oct. 22, 1949
7686	16442–16444	Dec. 8, 1948	7751	16810–16812	Oct. 24, 1949
7687	16445–16447	Dec. 11, 1948	7752	16813–16814	Oct. 26, 1949
7688	16448–16450	Dec. 15, 1948	7753	16815–16817	Oct. 28, 1949
7689	16451–16452	Dec. 19, 1948	7754	16818–16820	Oct. 31, 1949

Roll	Volumes	Beginning Dates	Roll	Volumes	Beginning Dates
7755	16821–16823	Nov. 3, 1949	7820	16977–16979	Apr. 19, 1950
7756	16824–16825	Nov. 5, 1949	7821	16980–16981	Apr. 21, 1950
7757	16826–16827	Nov. 7, 1949	7822	16982–16983	Apr. 23, 1950
7758	16828–16829	Nov. 9, 1949	7823	16984–16986	Apr. 25, 1950
7759	16830–16832	Nov. 11, 1949	7824	16987–16989	Apr. 27, 1950
7760	16833–16835	Nov. 14, 1949	7825	16990–16991	May 1, 1950
7761	16836–16838	Nov. 17, 1949	7826	16992–16993	May 2, 1950
7762	16839–16841	Nov. 20, 1949	7827	16994–16996	May 4, 1950
7763	16842–16844	Nov. 23, 1949	7828	16997–16999	May 7, 1950
7764	16845–16846	Nov. 27, 1949	7829	17000–17001	May 10, 1950
7765	16847–16848	Nov. 29, 1949	7830	17002–17004	May 12, 1950
7766	16849–16851	Nov. 30, 1949	7831	17005–17006	May 15, 1950
7767	16852–16853	Dec. 3, 1949	7832	17007–17008	May 16, 1950
7768	16854–16856	Dec. 5, 1949	7833	17009–17011	May 17, 1950
7769	16857–16859	Dec. 7, 1949	7834	17012–17013	May 20, 1950
7770	16860–16861	Dec. 11, 1949	7835	17014–17016	May 22, 1950
7771	16862–16863	Dec. 14, 1949	7836	17017–17019	May 25, 1950
7772	16864–16866	Dec. 15, 1949	7837	17020–17021	May 28, 1950
7773	16867–16869	Dec. 18, 1949	7838	17022–17024	May 30, 1950
7774	16870–16871	Dec. 21, 1949	7839	17025–17027	June 2, 1950
7775	16872–16874	Dec. 22, 1949	7840	17028–17029	June 4, 1950
7776	16875–16876	Dec. 25, 1949	7841	17030–17031	June 6, 1950
7777	16877–16879	Dec. 28, 1949	7842	17032–17034	June 7, 1950
7778	16880–16881	Jan. 1, 1950	7843	17035–17036	June 9, 1950
7779	16882–16884	Jan. 3, 1950	7844	17037–17039	June 11, 1950
7780	16885–16886	Jan. 7, 1950	7845	17040–17041	June 14, 1950
7781	16887–16888	Jan. 10, 1950	7846	17042–17044	June 15, 1950
7782	16889–16891	Jan. 12, 1950	7847	17045–17046	June 17, 1950
7783	16892–16893	Jan. 16, 1950	7848	17047–17049	June 19, 1950
7784	16894–16895	Jan. 18, 1950	7849	17050–17052	June 22, 1950
7785	16896–16897	Jan. 21, 1950	7850	17053–17054	June 24, 1950
7786	16898–16899	Jan. 23, 1950	7851	17055–17057	June 26, 1950
7787	16900–16901	Jan. 25, 1950	7852	17058–17060	June 28, 1950
7788	16902–16904	Jan. 27, 1950	7853	17061–17063	June 30, 1950
7789	16905–16906	Feb. 1, 1950	7854	17064–17066	July 2, 1950
7790	16907–16909	Feb. 3, 1950	7855	17067–17069	July 5, 1950
7791	16910–16911	Feb. 7, 1950	7856	17070–17071	July 7, 1950
7792	16912–16913	Feb. 9, 1950	7857	17072–17074	July 8, 1950
7793	16914–16915	Feb. 12, 1950	7858	17075–17077	July 11, 1950
7794	16916–16917	Feb. 14, 1950	7859	17078–17080	July 13, 1950
7795	16918–16919	Feb. 16, 1950	7860	17081–17083	July 15, 1950
7796	16920–16921	Feb. 18, 1950	7861	17084–17086	July 18, 1950
7797	16922–16923	Feb. 20, 1950	7862	17087–17089	July 20, 1950
7798	16924–16925	Feb. 21, 1950	7863	17090–17092	July 24, 1950
7799	16926–16928	Feb 24, 1950	7864	17093–17095	July 25, 1950
7800	16929–16930	Mar. 1, 1950	7865	17096–17099	July 27, 1950
7801	16931–16932	Mar. 2, 1950	7866	17100–17102	July 29, 1950
7802	16933–16935	Mar. 5, 1950	7867	17103–17105	Aug. 1, 1950
7803	16936–16937	Mar. 8, 1950	7868	17106–17108	Aug. 2, 1950
7804	16938–16939	Mar. 10, 1950	7869	17109–17111	Aug. 5, 1950
7805	16940–16941	Mar. 12, 1950	7870	17112–17114	Aug. 7, 1950
7806	16942–16943	Mar. 15, 1950	7871	17115–17118	Aug. 9, 1950
7807	16944–16946	Mar. 17, 1950	7872	17119–17121	Aug. 12, 1950
7808	16947–16949	Mar. 21, 1950	7873	17122–17124	Aug. 15, 1950
7809	16950–16952	Mar. 23, 1950	7874	17125–17127	Aug. 17, 1950
7810	16953–16954	Mar. 27, 1950	7875	17128–17130	Aug. 18, 1950
7811	16955–16956	Mar. 28, 1950	7876	17131–17133	Aug. 21, 1950
7812	16957–16959	Mar. 30, 1950	7877	17134–17135	Aug. 23, 1950
7813	16960–16961	Apr. 2, 1950	7878	17136–17138	Aug. 23, 1950
7814	16962–16963	Apr. 4, 1950	7879	17139–17141	Aug. 26, 1950
7815	16964–16966	Apr. 5, 1950	7880	17142–17144	Aug. 28, 1950
7816	16967–16968	Apr. 9, 1950	7881	17145–17147	Aug. 31, 1950
7817	16969–16971	Apr. 11, 1950	7882	17148–17150	Sept. 2, 1950
7818	16972–16974	Apr. 13, 1950	7883	17151–17153	Sept. 4, 1950
7819	16975–16976	Apr. 16, 1950	7884	17154–17156	Sept. 5, 1950

Roll	Volumes	Beginning Dates
7885	17157–17160	Sept. 7, 1950
7886	17161–17163	Sept. 10, 1950
7887	17164–17166	Sept. 12, 1950
7888	17167–17169	Sept. 13, 1950
7889	17170–17172	Sept. 10, 1950
7890	17173–17175	Sept. 18, 1950
7891	17176–17178	Sept. 20, 1950
7892	17179–17181	Sept. 23, 1950
7893	17182–17183	Sept. 25, 1950
7894	17184–17186	Sept. 27, 1950
7895	17187–17189	Sept. 28, 1950
7896	17190–17192	Sept. 30, 1950
7897	17193–17195	Oct. 3, 1950
7898	17196–17198	Oct. 5, 1950
7899	17199–17201	Oct. 8, 1950
7900	17202–17203	Oct. 10, 1950
7901	17204–17206	Oct. 11, 1950
7902	17207–17209	Oct. 14, 1950
7903	17210–17211	Oct. 17, 1950
7904	17212–17213	Oct. 19, 1950
7905	17214–17216	Oct. 21, 1950
7906	17217–17219	Oct. 23, 1950
7907	17220–17221	Oct. 26, 1950
7908	17222–17224	Oct. 28, 1950
7909	17225–17226	Oct. 30, 1950
7910	17227–17229	Nov. 1, 1950
7911	17230–17232	Nov. 5, 1950
7912	17233–17235	Nov. 7, 1950
7913	17236–17238	Nov. 10, 1950
7914	17239–17240	Nov. 13, 1950
7915	17241–17242	Nov. 15, 1950
7916	17243–17245	Nov. 17, 1950
7917	17246–17248	Nov. 20, 1950
7918	17249–17251	Nov. 23, 1950
7919	17252–17253	Nov. 27, 1950
7920	17254–17256	Nov. 29, 1950
7921	17257–17259	Dec. 2, 1950
7922	17260–17262	Dec. 6, 1950
7923	17263–17265	Dec. 8, 1950
7924	17266–17267	Dec. 11, 1950
7925	17268–17270	Dec. 13, 1950
7926	17271–17273	Dec. 16, 1950
7927	17274–17275	Dec. 19, 1950
7928	17276–17278	Dec. 21, 1950
7929	17279–17281	Dec. 23, 1950
7930	17282–17284	Dec. 27, 1950
7931	17285	Dec. 30, 1950
7932	17286–17288	Jan. 1, 1951
7933	17289–17291	Jan. 2, 1951
7934	17292–17293	Jan. 17, 1951
7935	17294–17296	Jan. 9, 1951
7936	17297–17299	Jan. 13, 1951
7937	17300–17302	Jan. 17, 1951
7938	17303–17304	Jan. 20, 1951
7939	17305–17307	Jan. 21, 1951
7940	17308–17310	Jan. 24, 1951
7941	17311–17313	Jan. 28, 1951
7942	17314–17315	Feb. 1, 1951
7943	17316–17318	Feb. 3, 1951
7944	17319–17321	Feb. 5, 1951
7945	17322–17323	Feb. 9, 1951
7946	17324–17326	Feb. 11, 1951
7947	17327–17328	Feb. 13, 1951
7948	17329–17331	Feb. 15, 1951
7949	17332–17334	Feb. 18, 1951
7950	17335–17337	Feb. 22, 1951
7951	17338–17339	Feb. 24, 1951
7952	17340–17342	Feb. 26, 1951
7953	17343–17345	Mar. 2, 1951
7954	17346–17347	Mar. 5, 1951
7955	17348–17350	Mar. 7, 1951
7956	17351–17353	Mar. 11, 1951
7957	17354–17355	Mar. 13, 1951
7958	17356–17358	Mar. 15, 1951
7959	17359–17361	Mar. 18, 1951
7960	17362–17364	Mar. 21, 1951
7961	17365–17366	Mar. 23, 1951
7962	17367–17369	Mar. 26, 1951
7963	17370–17372	Mar. 28, 1951
7964	17373–17375	Apr. 1, 1951
7965	17376–17378	Apr. 3, 1951
7966	17379–17381	Apr. 5, 1951
7967	17382–17384	Apr. 8, 1951
7968	17385–17386	Apr. 11, 1951
7969	17387–17389	Apr. 13, 1951
7970	17390–17392	Apr. 16, 1951
7971	17393–17395	Apr. 19, 1951
7972	17396–17398	Apr. 21, 1951
7973	17399–17400	Apr. 25, 1951
7974	17401–17403	Apr. 26, 1951
7975	17404–17406	Apr. 29, 1951
7976	17407–17409	May 2, 1951
7977	17410–17411	May 4, 1951
7978	17412–17414	May 6, 1951
7979	17415–17417	May 9, 1951
7980	17418–17419	May 12, 1951
7981	17420–17421	May 14, 1951
7982	17422–17424	May 15, 1951
7983	17425–17427	May 17, 1951
7984	17428–17430	May 20, 1951
7985	14731–17433	May 23, 1951
7986	17434–17436	May 25, 1951
7987	17437–17439	May 28, 1951
7988	17440–17442	May 29, 1951
7989	17443–17445	June 1, 1951
7990	17446–17448	June 4, 1951
7991	17449–17450	June 7, 1951
7992	17451–17453	June 7, 1951
7993	17454–17456	June 10, 1951
7994	17457–17459	June 12, 1951
7995	17460–17462	June 15, 1951
7996	17463–17465	June 17, 1951
7997	17466–17468	June 20, 1951
7998	17469–17471	June 23, 1951
7999	17472–17474	June 25, 1951
8000	17475–17477	June 27, 1951
8001	17478–17480	June 29, 1951
8002	17481–17843	July 1, 1951
8003	17484–17486	July 3, 1951
8004	17487–17489	July 6, 1951
8005	17490–17492	July 8, 1951
8006	17493–17495	July 10, 1951
8007	17496–17499	July 12, 1951
8008	17500–17502	July 16, 1951
8009	17503–17505	July 18, 1951
8010	17506–17508	July 20, 1951
8011	17509–17511	July 23, 1951
8012	17512–17514	July 25, 1951
8013	17515–17517	July 28, 1951
8014	17518–17520	July 30, 1951

Roll	Volumes	Beginning Dates
8015	17521–17523	Aug. 1, 1951
8016	17524–17526	Aug. 2, 1951
8017	17527–17529	Aug. 4, 1951
8018	17530–17532	Aug. 6, 1951
8019	17533–17535	Aug. 9, 1951
8020	17536–17538	Aug. 11, 1951
8021	17539–17540	Aug. 14, 1951
8022	17541–17543	Aug. 15, 1951
8023	17544–17546	Aug. 17, 1951
8024	17547–17549	Aug. 20, 1951
8025	17550–17552	Aug. 22, 1951
8026	17553–17555	Aug. 24, 1951
8027	17556–17557	Aug. 27, 1951
8028	17558–17559	Aug. 27, 1951.
8029	17560–17562	Aug. 28, 1951
8030	17563–17565	Aug. 31, 1951
8031	17566–17567	Sept. 2, 1951
8032	17568–17569	Sept. 4, 1951
8033	17570–17572	Sept. 4, 1951
8034	17573–17575	Sept. 6, 1951
8035	17576–17578	Sept. 8, 1951
8036	17579–17581	Sept. 11, 1951
8037	17582–17584	Sept. 12, 1951
8038	17585–17587	Sept. 15, 1951
8039	17588–17590	Sept. 17, 1951
8040	17591–17593	Sept. 19, 1951
8041	17594–17595	Sept. 21, 1951
8042	17596–17598	Sept. 23, 1951
8043	17599–17600	Sept. 25, 1951
8044	17601–17603	Sept. 26, 1951
8045	17604–17605	Sept. 29, 1951
8046	17606–17608	Oct. 1, 1951
8047	17609–17611	Oct. 2, 1951
8048	17612–17614	Oct. 5, 1951
8049	17615–17616	Oct. 8, 1951
8050	17617–17619	Oct. 9, 1951
8051	17620–17622	Oct. 11, 1951
8052	17623–17624	Oct. 14, 1951
8053	17625–17627	Oct. 15, 1951
8054	17628–17629	Oct. 18, 1951
8055	17630–17632	Oct. 20, 1951
8056	17633–17635	Oct. 22, 1951
8057	17636–17637	Oct. 25, 1951
8058	17638–17640	Oct. 27, 1951
8059	17641–17643	Oct. 29, 1951
8060	17644–17646	Nov. 1, 1951
8061	17647–17648	Nov. 4, 1951
8062	17649–17651	Nov. 6, 1951
8063	17652–17654	Nov. 8, 1951
8064	17655–17656	Nov. 12, 1951
8065	17657–17659	Nov. 13, 1951
8066	17660–17661	Nov. 17, 1951
8067	17662–17663	Nov. 19, 1951
8068	17664–17665	Nov. 21, 1951
8069	17666–17667	Nov. 23, 1951
8070	17668–17669	Nov. 25, 1951
8071	17670–17672	Nov. 27, 1951
8072	17673–17674	Dec. 1, 1951
8073	17675–17676	Dec. 3, 1951
8074	17677–17678	Dec. 5, 1951
8075	17679–17680	Dec. 7, 1951
8076	17681–17682	Dec. 10, 1951
8077	17683–17684	Dec. 11, 1951
8078	17685–17687	Dec. 14, 1951
8079	17688–17689	Dec. 18, 1951
8080	17690–17691	Dec. 20, 1951
8081	17692–17693	Dec. 22, 1951
8082	17694–17695	Dec. 24, 1951
8083	17696–17697	Dec 26, 1951
8084	17698–17699	Dec 29, 1951
8085	17700	Jan. 1, 1952
8086	17701	Jan. 2, 1952
8087	17702–17703	Jan. 3, 1952
8088	17704–17706	Jan. 5, 1952
8089	17707–17708	Jan. 9, 1952
8090	17709–17710	Jan. 11, 1952
8091	17711–17712	Jan. 14, 1952
8092	17713–17714	Jan. 16, 1952
8093	17715–17716	Jan. 19, 1952
8094	17717–17718	Jan. 21, 1952
8095	17719–17720	Jan. 24, 1952
8096	17721–17722	Jan. 27, 1952
8097	17723–17724	Jan. 29, 1952
8098	17725–17726	Feb. 1, 1952
8099	17727–17728	Feb. 3, 1952
8100	17729–17730	Feb. 6, 1952
8101	17731	Feb. 7, 1952
8102	17732–17733	Feb. 8, 1952
8103	17734–17735	Feb. 11, 1952
8104	17736–17737	Feb. 14, 1952
8105	17738–17739	Feb. 17, 1952
8106	17740–17741	Feb. 18, 1952
8107	17742–17743	Feb. 21, 1952
8108	17744–17745	Feb. 24, 1952
8109	17746–17747	Feb. 26, 1952
8110	17748–17749	Feb. 28, 1952
8111	17750–17751	Mar. 2, 1952
8112	17752	Mar. 4, 1952
8113	17753	Mar. 5, 1952
8114	17754–17755	Mar. 6, 1952
8115	17756–17757	Mar. 9, 1952
8116	17758–17759	Mar. 11, 1952
8117	17760–17761	Mar. 12, 1952
8118	17762–17764	Mar. 15, 1952
8119	17765–17766	Mar. 19, 1952
8120	17767–17768	Mar. 20, 1952
8121	17769–17770	Mar. 23, 1952
8122	17771–17772	Mar. 25, 1952
8123	17773–17774	Mar. 28, 1952
8124	17775–17776	Mar. 30, 1952
8125	17777–17778	Apr. 1, 1952
8126	17779–17780	Apr. 3, 1952
8127	17781–17782	Apr. 5, 1952
8128	17783–17784	Apr. 7, 1952
8129	17785–17786	Apr. 9, 1952
8130	17787–17789	Apr. 11, 1952
8131	17790–17791	Apr. 14, 1952
8132	17792–17793	Apr. 16, 1952
8133	17794–17795	Apr. 18, 1952
8134	17796–17797	Apr. 20, 1952
8135	17798–17799	Apr. 21, 1952
8136	17800–17801	Apr. 24, 1952
8137	17802–17803	Apr. 26, 1952
8138	17804–17805	Apr. 28, 1952
8139	17806–17807	Apr. 29, 1952
8140	17808–17809	May 1, 1952
8141	17810–17811	May 3, 1952
8142	17812–17813	May 5, 1952
8143	17814–17815	May 6, 1952
8144	17816–17817	May 8, 1952

Roll	Volumes	Beginning Dates	Roll	Volumes	Beginning Dates
8145	17818–17819	May 11, 1952	8210	17966–17967	Sept. 13, 1952
8146	17820–17821	May 13, 1952	8211	17968–17969	Sept. 15, 1952
8147	17822–17824	May 14, 1952	8212	17970–17972	Sept. 16, 1952
8148	17825–17826	May 17, 1952	8213	17973–17974	Sept. 19, 1952
8149	17827–17828	May 19, 1952	8214	17975–17976	Sept. 21, 1952
8150	17829–17830	May 21, 1952	8215	17977–17978	Sept. 22, 1952
8151	17831–17833	May 24, 1952	8216	17979–17981	Sept. 23, 1952
8152	17834–17835	May 26, 1952	8217	17982–17983	Sept. 27, 1952
8153	17836–17838	May 28, 1952	8218	17984–17985	Sept. 29, 1952
8154	17839–17840	May 31, 1952	8219	17986–17987	Sept. 30, 1952
8155	17841–17842	June 2, 1952	8220	17988–17990	Oct. 2, 1952
8156	17843–17844	June 3, 1952	8221	17991–17992	Oct. 6, 1952
8157	17845–17846	June 4, 1952	8222	17993–17995	Oct. 7, 1952
8158	17847–17849	June 6, 1952	8223	17996–17997	Oct. 10, 1952
8159	17850–17851	June 10, 1952	8224	17998–17999	Oct. 12, 1952
8160	17852–17853	June 11, 1952	8225	18000–18001	Oct. 13, 1952
8161	17854–17855	June 13, 1952	8226	18002–18003	Oct. 14, 1952
8162	17856–17857	June 14, 1952	8227	18004–18006	Oct. 16, 1952
8163	17858–17859	June 16, 1952	8228	18007–18008	Oct. 19, 1952
8164	17860–17862	June 17, 1952	8229	18009–18010	Oct. 21, 1952
8165	17863–17864	June 20, 1952	8230	18011–18013	Oct. 23, 1952
8166	17865–17866	June 22, 1952	8231	18014–18015	Oct. 27, 1952
8167	17867–17868	June 24, 1952	8232	18016–18017	Oct. 28, 1952
8168	17869–17870	June 25, 1952	8233	18018–18019	Oct. 30, 1952
8169	17871–17873	June 27, 1952	8234	18020–18021	Nov. 2, 1952
8170	17874–17875	June 30, 1952	8235	18022–18023	Nov. 3, 1952
8171	17876–17877	July 1, 1952	8236	18024–18025	Nov. 6, 1952
8172	17878–17879	July 2, 1952	8237	18026–18027	Nov. 9, 1952
8173	17880–17882	July 4, 1952	8238	18028–18029	Nov. 11, 1952
8174	17883–17884	July 7, 1952	8239	18030–18031	Nov. 13, 1952
8175	17885–17886	July 8, 1952	8240	18032–18033	Nov. 15, 1952
8176	17887–17888	July 10, 1952	8241	18034–18035	Nov. 17, 1952
8177	17889–17890	July 12, 1952	8242	18036–18037	Nov. 20, 1952
8178	17891–17893	July 13, 1952	8243	18038–18039	Nov. 23, 1952
8179	17894–17996	July 16, 1952	8244	18040–18041	Nov. 26, 1952
8180	17897–17898	July 19, 1952	8245	18042–18043	Nov. 26, 1952
8181	17899–17900	July 20, 1952	8246	18044–18045	Nov. 30, 1952
8182	17901–17903	July 22, 1952	8247	18046–18047	Dec. 2, 1952
8183	17904–17905	July 24, 1952	8248	18048–18049	Dec. 5, 1952
8184	17906–17907	July 26, 1952	8249	18050–18051	Dec. 7, 1952
8185	17908–17909	July 28, 1952	8250	18052–18053	Dec. 9, 1952
8186	17910–17911	July 29, 1952	8251	18054–18055	Dec. 12, 1952
8187	17912–17914	July 31, 1952	8252	18056–18057	Dec. 14, 1952
8188	17915–17916	Aug. 3, 1952	8253	18058–18059	Dec. 18, 1952
8189	17917–17919	Aug. 4, 1952	8254	18060–18061	Dec. 19, 1952
8190	17920–17921	Aug. 7, 1952	8255	18062–18063	Dec. 21, 1952
8191	17922–17924	Aug. 8, 1952	8256	18064–18065	Dec. 23, 1952
8192	17925–17926	Aug. 11, 1952	8257	18066–18067	Dec. 26, 1952
8193	17927–17928	Aug. 12, 1952	8258	18068	Dec. 30, 1952
8194	17929–17931	Aug. 14, 1952	8259	18069–18070	Jan. 1, 1953
8195	17932–17933	Aug. 17, 1952	8260	18071–18072	Jan. 4, 1953
8196	17934–17935	Aug. 18, 1952	8261	18073–18074	Jan. 5, 1953
8197	17936–17937	Aug. 19, 1952	8262	18075–18076	Jan. 8, 1953
8198	17938–17939	Aug. 22, 1952	8263	18077–18078	Jan. 11, 1953
8199	17940–17941	Aug. 24, 1952	8264	18079–18080	Jan. 14, 1953
8200	17942–17944	Aug. 26, 1952	8265	18081–18082	Jan. 17, 1953
8201	17945–17946	Aug. 27, 1952	8266	18083–18084	Jan. 20, 1953
8202	17947–17949	Aug. 29, 1952	8267	18085–18086	Jan. 22, 1953
8203	17950–17951	Sept. 1, 1952	8268	18087–18088	Jan. 25, 1953
8204	17952–17954	Sept. 2, 1952	8269	18089–18090	Jan. 28, 1953
8205	17955–17956	Sept. 3, 1952	8270	18091–18092	Jan. 30, 1953
8206	17957–17958	Sept. 6, 1952	8271	18093–18094	Feb. 2, 1953
8207	17959–17960	Sept. 8, 1952	8272	18095–18096	Feb. 5, 1953
8208	17961–17963	Sept. 9, 1952	8273	18097–18098	Feb. 8, 1953
8209	17964–17965	Sept. 11, 1952	8274	18099–18100	Feb. 11, 1953

Roll	Volumes	Beginning Dates	Roll	Volumes	Beginning Dates
8275	18101–18102	Feb. 14, 1953	8340	18236–18237	July 24, 1953
8276	18103–18104	Feb. 16, 1953	8341	18238–18239	July 26, 1953
8277	18105–18106	Feb. 19, 1953	8342	18240–18242	July 27, 1953
8278	18107–18108	Feb. 22, 1953	8343	18243–18244	Aug. 1, 1953
8279	18109–18110	Feb. 24, 1953	8344	18245–18246	Aug. 3, 1953
8280	18111–18112	Feb. 27, 1953	8345	18247–18248	Aug. 4, 1953
8281	18113–18114	Mar. 2, 1953	8346	18249–18250	Aug. 7, 1953
8282	18115–18116	Mar. 5, 1953	8347	18251–18252	Aug. 9, 1953
8283	18117–18118	Mar. 7, 1953	8348	18253–18254	Aug. 11, 1953
8284	18119–18120	Mar. 10, 1953	8349	18255–18256	Aug. 12, 1953
8285	18121–18122	Mar. 12, 1953	8350	18257–18258	Aug. 14, 1953
8286	18123–18124	Mar. 15, 1953	8351	18259–18260	Aug. 16, 1953
8287	18125–18126	Mar. 17, 1953	8352	18261–18262	Aug. 18, 1953
8288	18127–18128	Mar. 19, 1953	8353	18263–18265	Aug. 19, 1953
8289	18129–18130	Mar. 22, 1953	8354	18266–18267	Aug. 23, 1953
8290	18131–18132	Mar. 24, 1953	8355	18268–18269	Aug. 25, 1953
8291	18133–18134	Mar. 27, 1953	8356	18270–18272	Aug. 27, 1953
8292	18135–18137	Mar. 29, 1953	8357	18273–18275	Aug. 30, 1953
8293	18138–18140	Apr. 1, 1953	8358	18276–18278	Sept. 1, 1953
8294	18141–18142	Apr. 6, 1953	8359	18279–18280	Sept. 4, 1953
8295	18143–18144	Apr. 7, 1953	8360	18281–18282	Sept. 5, 1953
8296	18145–18146	Apr. 9, 1953	8361	18283–18284	Sept. 8, 1953
8297	18147–18148	Apr. 12, 1953	8362	18285–18286	Sept. 9, 1953
8298	18149–18150	Apr. 14, 1953	8363	18287–18288	Sept. 10, 1953
8299	18151–18152	Apr. 17, 1953	8364	18289–18290	Sept. 12, 1953
8300	18153–18154	Apr. 20, 1953	8365	18291–18292	Sept. 14, 1953
8301	18155–18156	Apr. 21, 1953	8366	18293–18294	Sept. 15, 1953
8302	18157–18158	Apr. 24, 1953	8367	18295–18297	Sept. 17, 1953
8303	18159–18160	Apr. 27, 1953	8368	18298–18299	Sept. 20, 1953
8304	18161–18162	Apr. 29, 1953	8369	18300–18301	Sept. 22, 1953
8305	18163–18164	May 2, 1953	8370	18302–18304	Sept. 24, 1953
8306	18165–18166	May 5, 1953	8371	18305–18306	Sept. 28, 1953
8307	18167–18168	May 7, 1953	8372	18307–18308	Sept. 29, 1953
8308	18169–18170	May 10, 1953	8373	18309–18311	Oct. 1, 1953
8309	18171–18172	May 12, 1953	8374	18312–18313	Oct. 5, 1953
8310	18173–18174	May 15, 1953	8375	18314–18315	Oct. 7, 1953
8311	18175–18176	May 17, 1953	8376	18316–18317	Oct. 10, 1953
8312	18177–18178	May 19, 1953	8377	18318–18319	Oct. 12, 1953
8313	18179–18180	May 20, 1953	8378	18320–18321	Oct. 14, 1953
8314	18181–18182	May 24, 1953	8379	18322–18323	Oct. 16, 1953
8315	18183–18185	May 26, 1953	8380	18324–18325	Oct. 18, 1953
8316	18186–18187	May 30, 1953	8381	18326–18327	Oct. 20, 1953
8317	18188–18189	June 2, 1953	8382	18328–18329	Oct. 23, 1953
8318	18190–18192	June 3, 1953	8383	18330–18331	Oct. 26, 1953
8319	18193–18194	June 7, 1953	8384	18332–18334	Oct. 28, 1953
8320	18195–18196	June 9, 1953	8385	18335–18336	Nov. 1, 1953
8321	18197–18198	June 11, 1953	8386	18337–18338	Nov. 2, 1953
8322	18199–18200	June 13, 1953	8387	18339–18341	Nov. 4, 1953
8323	18201–18202	June 16, 1953	8388	18342–18343	Nov. 9, 1953
8324	18203	June 17, 1953	8389	18344–18345	Nov. 11, 1953
8325	18204–18206	June 18, 1953	8390	18346–18347	Nov. 14, 1953
8326	18207–18208	June 22, 1953	8391	18348–18349	Nov. 16, 1953
8327	18209–18210	June 25, 1953	8392	18350–18351	Nov. 20, 1953
8328	18211–18212	June 27, 1953	8393	18352–18353	Nov. 23, 1953
8329	18213–18214	June 29, 1953	8394	18354–18355	Nov. 26, 1953
8330	18215–18216	July 1, 1953	8395	18356–18358	Nov. 29, 1953
8331	18217–18218	July 2, 1953	8396	18359–18360	Dec. 2, 1953
8332	18219–18220	July 6, 1953	8397	18361–18362	Dec. 4, 1953
8333	18221–18222	July 6, 1953	8398	18363–18364	Dec. 7, 1953
8334	18223–18225	July 9, 1953	8399	18365–18366	Dec. 11, 1953
8335	18226–18227	July 12, 1953	8400	18367–18368	Dec. 14, 1953
8336	18228–18229	July 15, 1953	8401	18369–18370	Dec. 16, 1953
8337	18230–18231	July 17, 1953	8402	18371–18372	Dec. 18, 1953
8338	18232–18233	July 20, 1953	8403	18373–18374	Dec. 21, 1953
8339	18234–18235	July 22, 1953	8404	18375–18376	Dec. 23, 1953

Roll	Volumes	Beginning Dates	Roll	Volumes	Beginning Dates
8405	18377–18378	Dec. 28, 1953	8470	18513–18514	June 25, 1954
8406	18379–18380	Jan. 1, 1954	8471	18515–18516	June 28, 1954
8407	18381–18382	Jan. 3, 1954	8472	18517–18519	June 29, 1954
8408	18383–18384	Jan. 5, 1954	8473	18520–18521	July 1, 1954
8409	18385–18386	Jan. 10, 1954	8474	18522–18523	July 3, 1954
8410	18387–18388	Jan. 13, 1954	8475	18524–18526	July 6, 1954
8411	18389–18390	Jan. 18, 1954	8476	18527–18528	July 9, 1954
8412	18391–18392	Jan. 21, 1954	8477	18529–18530	July 11, 1954
8413	18393–18394	Jan. 23, 1954	8478	18531–18532	July 13, 1954
8414	18395–18396	Jan. 25, 1954	8479	18533–18534	July 16, 1954
8415	18397–18398	Jan. 28, 1954	8480	18535–18536	July 19, 1954
8416	18399–18400	Feb. 1, 1954	8481	18537–18538	July 20, 1954
8417	18401–18402	Feb. 3, 1954	8482	18539–18541	July 22, 1954
8418	18403–18404	Feb. 6, 1954	8483	18542–18543	July 26, 1954
8419	18405–18406	Feb. 10, 1954	8484	18544–18545	July 28, 1954
8420	18407–18408	Feb. 13, 1954	8485	18546–18548	July 30, 1954
8421	18409–18410	Feb. 16, 1954	8486	18549–18550	Aug. 2, 1954
8422	18411–18412	Feb. 18, 1954	8487	18551–18552	Aug. 4, 1954
8423	18413–18414	Feb. 22, 1954	8488	18553–18554	Aug. 6, 1954
8424	18415–18416	Feb. 24, 1954	8489	18555–18556	Aug. 8, 1954
8425	18417–18418	Feb. 26, 1954	8490	18557–18558	Aug. 10, 1954
8426	18419–18420	Mar. 1, 1954	8491	18559–18560	Aug. 13, 1954
8427	18421–18422	Mar. 4, 1954	8492	18561–18562	Aug. 15, 1954
8428	18423–18424	Mar. 7, 1954	8493	18563–18564	Aug. 17, 1954
8429	18425–18426	Mar. 10, 1954	8494	18565–18566	Aug. 19, 1954
8430	18427–18428	Mar. 12, 1954	8495	18567–18568	Aug. 21, 1954
8431	18429–18430	Mar. 16, 1954	8496	18569–18570	Aug. 23, 1954
8432	18431–18432	Mar. 19, 1954	8497	18571–18572	Aug. 25, 1954
8433	18433–18434	Mar. 22, 1954	8498	18573–18574	Aug. 27, 1954
8434	18435–18436	Mar. 24, 1954	8499	18575–18576	Aug. 30, 1954
8435	18437–18438	Mar. 27, 1954	8500	18577–18578	Aug. 31, 1954
8436	18439–18441	Mar. 30, 1954	8501	18579–18580	Sept. 2, 1954
8437	18442–18443	Apr. 3, 1954	8502	18581–18582	Sept. 3, 1954
8438	18444–18445	Apr. 6, 1954	8503	18583–18584	Sept. 5, 1954
8439	18446–18447	Apr. 8, 1954	8504	18585–18586	Sept. 7, 1954
8440	18448–18449	Apr. 11, 1954	8505	18587–18588	Sept. 9, 1954
8441	18450–18451	Apr. 14, 1954	8506	18589–18590	Sept. 12, 1954
8442	18452–18453	Apr. 16, 1954	8507	18591–18592	Sept. 14, 1954
8443	18454–18455	Apr. 19, 1954	8508	18593–18594	Sept. 15, 1954
8444	18456–18457	Apr. 21, 1954	8509	18595–18597	Sept. 17, 1954
8445	18458–18460	Apr. 24, 1954	8510	18598–18599	Sept. 21, 1954
8446	18461–18462	Apr. 28, 1954	8511	18600–18601	Sept. 23, 1954
8447	18463–18464	May 1, 1954	8512	18602–18603	Sept. 25, 1954
8448	18465–18466	May 3, 1954	8513	18604–18605	Sept. 27, 1954
8449	18467–18468	May 5, 1954	8514	18606–18607	Sept. 28, 1954
8450	18469–18470	May 8, 1954	8515	18608–18609	Oct. 1, 1954
8451	18471–18472	May 10, 1954	8516	18610–18611	Oct. 4, 1954
8452	18473–18474	May 11, 1954	8517	18612–18613	Oct. 5, 1954
8453	18475–18476	May 14, 1954	8518	18614–18615	Oct. 8, 1954
8454	18477–18479	May 16, 1954	8519	18616–18617	Oct. 11, 1954
8455	18480–18482	May 20, 1954	8520	18618–18619	Oct. 12, 1954
8456	18483–18484	May 24, 1954	8521	18620–18621	Oct. 15, 1954
8457	18485–18487	May 25, 1954	8522	18622–18623	Oct. 18, 1954
8458	18488–18489	May 29, 1954	8523	18624–18625	Oct. 20, 1954
8459	18490–18491	June 1, 1954	8524	18626–18627	Oct. 22, 1954
8460	18492–18493	June 3, 1954	8525	18628–18629	Oct. 26, 1954
8461	18494–18495	June 5, 1954	8526	18630–18631	Oct. 28, 1954
8462	18496–18497	June 8, 1954	8527	18632–18633	Oct. 30, 1954
8463	18498–18499	June 9, 1954	8528	18634–18635	Nov. 2, 1954
8464	18500–18501	June 11, 1954	8529	18636–18637	Nov. 4, 1954
8465	18502–18503	June 14, 1954	8530	18638–18639	Nov. 6, 1954
8466	18504–18505	June 16, 1954	8531	18640–18641	Nov. 9, 1954
8467	18506–18508	June 18, 1954	8532	18642–18643	Nov. 11, 1954
8468	18509–18510	June 22, 1954	8533	18644–18645	Nov. 14, 1954
8469	18511–18512	June 23, 1954	8534	18646–18647	Nov. 17, 1954

Roll	Volumes	Beginning Dates
8535	18648–18649	Nov. 20, 1954
8536	18650–18651	Nov. 24, 1954
8537	18652–18654	Nov. 27, 1954

Roll	Dates/Vessels
8538	Dec. 1, 1954, CAPE COD–Dec. 8, 1954, SAXONDALE
8539	Dec. 9, 1954, AMERICAN VETERAN–Dec. 14, 1954, VICTORIA MARU
8540	Dec. 14, 1954, BUNTENTOR–Dec. 21, 1954, FRANCONIA
8541	Dec. 21, 1954, ILE DE FRANCE–Dec. 28, 1954, SOLOR
8542	Dec. 29, 1954, ABBEDYK–Dec. 31, 1954, VASSILIS
8543	Jan. 1, 1955, ATLANTIC EARL–Jan. 3, 1955, SANTA MONICA
8544	Jan. 3, 1955, PLANE AF 070/0103–Jan. 7, 1955, PLANE TWA 975/06
8545	Jan. 8, 1955, AMERICAN SHIPPER–Jan. 12, 1955, QUEEN ELIZABETH
8546	Jan. 12, 1955, SOGNEFJELL–Jan. 17, 1955, AMERICA
8547	Jan. 17, 1955, ARKANSAS–Jan. 19, 1955, PATRICIA
8548	Jan. 19, 1955, SANTA PAULA–Jan. 24, 1955, QUEEN MARY
8549	Jan. 24, 1955, SANTA BARBARA–Jan. 26, 1955, T.W.A. FLT. 963/25
8550	Jan. 27, 1955, ATLANTIC DUKE–Jan. 29, 1955, RYNDAM
8551	Jan. 29, 1955, ROBERTO PARODI–Feb. 2, 1955, EXPEDITOR
8552	Feb. 2, 1955, ITALIA–Feb. 5, 1955, ANDREA DORIA
8553	Feb. 5, 1955, ANDROS SEA–Feb. 7, 1955, T.W.A. FLT. 997/06
8554	Feb. 8, 1955, AFRICAN STAR–Feb. 10, 1955, QUEEN OF BERMUDA
8555	Feb. 10, 1955, ROSEVILLE–Feb. 14, 1955, GUAPORE
8556	Feb. 14, 1955, ILE DE FRANCE–Feb. 16, 1955, MAURETANIA
8557	Feb. 16, 1955, NORTH DUKE–Feb. 20, 1955, MEDIA
8558	Feb. 20, 1955, NELLY–Feb. 23, 1955, CRISTOFORO COLOMBO
8559	Feb. 23, 1955, DARNIE–Feb. 26, 1955, VULCANIA
8560	Feb. 26, 1955, A.F. FLT. 071–Mar. 1, 1955, ILE DE FRANCE
8561	Mar. 1, 1955, MATARIPE–Mar. 4, 1955, K.L.M. FLT. 633
8562	Mar. 4, 1955, L.A.V. FLT. 252–Mar. 8, 1955, LUCKINEE
8563	Mar. 8, 1955, MARCHOVELETTE–Mar. 11, 1955, SIRIUS
8564	Mar. 11, 1955, STEEL CHEMIST–Mar. 11, 1955, FRANCONIA
8565	Mar. 15, 1955, KATHRYN–Mar. 18, 1955, NASSAU
8566	Mar. 18, 1955, PARISMINA–Mar. 21, 1955, NEA HELLAS
8567	Mar. 21, 1955, OCEAN MONARCH–Mar. 23, 1955, T.W.A. FLT. 963/22
8568	Mar. 24, 1955, AFRICAN ENDEAVOR–Mar. 25, 1955, S.W.A. FLT. 15
8569	Mar. 25, 1955, S.W.A. FLT. 1673–Mar. 30, 1955, CONSTITUTION
8570	Mar. 30, 1955, EXETER–Apr. 1, 1955, NASSAU
8571	Apr. 1, 1955, ULUA–Apr. 4, 1955, QUEEN ELIZABETH
8572	Apr. 4, 1955, QUIRIGUA–Apr. 7, 1955, VAMOS
8573	Apr. 7, 1955, A.F. FLT. 070/0407–Apr. 10, 1955, TWA FLT. 989/09

Roll	Dates/Vessels
8574	Apr. 11, 1955, DAYTONA–Apr. 13, 1955, LIBERTE
8575	Apr. 13, 1955, MANX KING–Apr. 16, 1955, WOLF CREER
8576	Apr. 16, 1955, A.F. 071/15–Apr. 19, 1955, QUEEN ELIZABETH
8577	Apr. 19, 1955, QUEEN FREDERICA–Apr. 22, 1955, TWA FLT. 975/21
8578	Apr. 23, 1955, ALPHACCA–Apr. 25, 1955, STAVAN-GERFJORD
8579	Apr. 25, 1955, SUSAN–Apr. 28, 1955, TWA FLT. 963/27
8580	Apr. 29, 1955, BILLETAL–May 2, 1955, LIBERTE
8581	May 2, 1955, NESTOR–May 4, 1955, MAURETANIA
8582	May 4, 1955, MORMACMAIL–May 7, 1955, OTTA
8583	May 7, 1955, PVT. JOSEF. VALDEZ–May 10, 1955, STEEL RECORDER
8584	May 10, 1955, A.F. FLT. 070/0510–May 13, 1955, ANCON
8585	May 13, 1955, ARCHANGELOS–May 16, 1955, TWA FLT. 997/15
8586	May 17, 1955, AMERICAN DEFENDER–May 18, 1955, OLYMPIA
8587	May 18, 1955, RAGNHILD BROVIG–May 22, 1955, TWA FLT. 989/21
8588	May 23, 1955, AMERICA–May 24, 1955, LOWLAND
8589	May 24, 1955, MARIANNA–May 26, 1955, TWA FLT. 8646/25
8590	May 27, 1955, AMERICAN CLIPPER–May 29, 1955, TWA FLT. 8657/28
8591	May 30, 1955, ANTIGUA–June 1, 1955, OLYMPIC ROCK
8592	June 1, 1955, ORSOLINA–June 4, 1955, GEN. R.E. CALLAM
8593	June 4, 1955, KIMIKAWA MARU–June 7, 1955, EROS
8594	June 7, 1955, FRANCES–June 9, 1955, TWA FLT. 8673/08
8595	June 10, 1955, ADRIAS–June 13, 1955, HORDO
8596	June 13, 1955, INDEPENDENCE–June 15, 1955, QUEEN ELIZABETH
8597	June 15, 1955, ROBERT WATT MILLER–June 18, 1955, RIO JACHAL
8598	June 18, 1955, SAN GIUSTO–June 20, 1955, TWA FLT. 977/19
8599	June 21, 1955, AMERICAN RANGER–June 23, 1955, SANTA PAULA
8600	June 23, 1955, SPENCER–June 27, 1955, FAIRPORT
8601	June 27, 1955, FORT HAMILTON–June 28, 1955, TWA FLT. 8677/27
8602	June 29, 1955, ACONCAGUA–June 30, 1955, TWA FLT. 8678/29
8603	July 1, 1955, CHUN AN–July 3, 1955, MAURETANIA
8604	July 3, 1955, PVT. JOHN R. TOWLE–July 5, 1955, UNITED STATES
8605	July 5, 1955, WESTERDAM–July 8, 1955, QUEEN OF BERMUDA
8606	July 8, 1955, STEENS MOUNTAIN–July 11, 1955, QUEEN FREDERICA
8607	July 11, 1955, SANTA ISABEL–July 13, 1955, ROMA
8608	July 13, 1955, SAINT MALO–July 16, 1955, GEN. R.E. CALLEN
8609	July 16, 1955, MEDIA–July 18, 1955, STEEL WORKER
8610	July 18, 1955, UNITED STATES–July 20, 1955, SANGAMON

Roll	Dates/Vessels
8611	July 20, 1955, SANTA PAULA–July 22, 1955, TWA FLT. 8711/21
8612	July 23, 1955, CHOLOMA–July 25, 1955, HEIDELBERG
8613	July 25, 1955, ILSE SCHULTE–July 27, 1955, MORMACLARK
8614	July 27, 1955, JOSE F. VALDEZ–July 30, 1955, CRISTOFORO COLOMBO
8615	July 30, 1955, DORESTAD–Aug. 1, 1955, OSLOFJORD
8616	Aug. 1, 1955, PVT. WILLIAM H. THOMAS–Aug. 3, 1955, UNITED STATES
8617	Aug. 3, 1955, A.A. FLT. 300/61–Aug. 6, 1955, NABOB
8618	Aug. 6, 1955, NEPTUNE–Aug. 6, 1955, TWA FLT. 977/07
8619	Aug. 9, 1955, BERLSTONE–Aug. 11, 1955, BIRGITTE TORM
8620	Aug. 11, 1955, CONCORDIA STAR–Aug. 14, 1955, ROW PLATE
8621	Aug. 14, 1955, BULKTRADER–Aug. 16, 1955, MORMACSAGA
8622	Aug. 16, 1955, NIGEL–Aug. 17, 1955, VARIG FLT. 850
8623	Aug. 18, 1955, APPENGEDYK–Aug. 20, 1955, CHOLOMA
8624	Aug. 20, 1955, CONTE BIANCAMANO–Aug. 22, 1955, USOA FLT. 444/45
8625	Aug. 23, 1955, ARGENTINIAN REEFER–Aug. 25, 1955, DAYTONA
8626	Aug. 25, 1955, DUNELMA–Aug. 27, 1955, SIBAJAK
8627	Aug. 25, 1955, A.F. FLT. 005–Aug. 30, 1955, GEN. W.C. LANGFITT
8628	Aug. 30, 1955, MYCENAE–Aug. 31, 1955, VARIG FLT. 850
8629	Sept. 1, 1955, AFRICAN ENDEAVOR–Sept. 2, 1955, TWA FLT. 987/01
8630	Sept. 3, 1955, BRITANNIC–Sept. 5, 1955, TWA FLT. 977/04
8631	Sept. 6, 1955, AMERICAN JURIST–Sept. 7, 1955, AMERICA
8632	Sept. 7, 1955, ATLANTIC VISCOUNTESS–Sept. 8, 1955, TWA FLT. 967/07
8633	Sept. 9, 1955, CASABLANCA–Sept. 12, 1955, EXETER
8634	Sept. 12, 1955, FINNTRADER–Sept. 13, 1955, UNITED STATES
8635	Sept. 13, 1955, A.F. FLT. 070/0913–Sept. 16, 1955, MAURETANIA
8636	Sept. 16, 1955, PAUL PIGOTT–Sept. 19, 1955, LAURA MAERSK
8637	Sept. 19, 1955, LIBERTE–Sept. 21, 1955, CARONIA
8638	Sept. 21, 1955, CONTE BIANCAMANO–Sept. 23, 1955, QUEEN OF BERMUDA
8639	Sept. 23, 1955, AF/045–Sept. 26, 1955, UNION TRADER
8640	Sept. 26, 1955, AIR FORCE FLT. 2133–Sept. 28, 1955, NABOB
8641	Sept. 28, 1955, SRBIJA–Oct. 1, 1955, BYKLEFJELL
8642	Oct. 1, 1955, BULKPETROL–Oct. 3, 1955, VULCANIA
8643	Oct. 3, 1955, A.F. FLT. 070/1003–Oct. 5, 1955, ROMA
8644	Oct. 5, 1955, SANTA ROSA–Oct. 7, 1955, MARGIT GORTHON

Roll	Dates/Vessels
8645	Oct. 8, 1955, MEDIA–Oct. 11, 1955, TWA FLT. 983/10
8646	Oct. 12, 1955, AFRICAN ENTERPRISE–Oct. 14, 1955, BOAC FLT. 509/639
8647	Oct. 14, 1955, BOAC FLT. 513/185–Oct. 17, 1955, ILE DE FRANCE
8648	Oct. 17, 1955, KERN HILLS–Oct. 19, 1955, FRANCES
8649	Oct. 19, 1955, GEIGER–Oct. 22, 1955, VILHELM TORKILDSEN
8650	Oct. 22, 1955, A.F. FLT. 078/1022–Oct. 25, 1955, QUEEN ELIZABETH
8651	Oct. 25, 1955, SANTA MARIA–Oct. 28, 1955, DOROTHY
8652	Oct. 28, 1955, GEN. W.C. LANGFITT–Oct. 29, 1955, BRITANNIC
8653	Oct. 29, 1955, CARROLL VICTORY–Oct. 31, 1955, A.F. SPECIAL
8654	Nov. 1, 1955, ANNISTON–Nov. 3, 1955, TUNGUS
8655	Nov. 3, 1955, A.F. FLT. 070/1103–Nov. 5, 1955, TWA FLT. 6005C
8656	Nov. 6, 1955, CARONIA–Nov. 8, 1955, TWA FLT. 983/07
8657	Nov. 9, 1955, AMERICAN CLIPPER–Nov. 11, 1955, TWA FLT. 933/10
8658	Nov. 12, 1955, A.N. KEMP–Nov. 15, 1955, MORMACLARK
8659	Nov. 15, 1955, QUEEN MARY–Nov. 16, 1955, VERA CRUZ
8660	Nov. 16, 1955, A.F. FLT. 070/11–Nov. 18, 1955, TWA FLT. 987/18
8661	Nov. 20, 1955, AFRICAN RAINBOW–Nov. 23, 1955, INUI SAN MARU
8662	Nov. 23, 1955, KONISTRA–Nov. 26, 1955, ESSO RICHMOND
8663	Nov. 26, 1955, GEN. WM. O. DARBY–Nov. 29, 1955, UNITED STATES
8664	Nov. 29, 1955, A.F. FLT. 070/1129–Dec. 1, 1955, VAR. FLT. 850/1
8665	Dec. 2, 1955, AKI MARU–Dec. 4, 1955, TWA FLT. 81502
8666	Dec. 5, 1955, ANNA MAERSK–Dec. 7, 1955, PERRY B.
8667	Dec. 7, 1955, ROMA–Dec. 10, 1955, ANDREA DORIA
8668	Dec. 10, 1955, CASABLANCA–Dec. 14, 1955, BOAC FLT. 521/307
8669	Dec. 14, 1955, BOAC FLT. 653–Dec. 17, 1955, NYLAND
8670	Dec. 17, 1955, OCEAN MONARCH–Dec. 20, 1955, GEN. A.M. PATCH
8671	Dec. 20, 1955, HADRIAN–Dec. 22, 1955, OCEAN MONARCH
8672	Dec. 22, 1955, OLYMPIC CLOUD–Dec. 26, 1955, NASSAU
8673	Dec. 26, 1955, SHETLAND–Dec. 30, 1955, PRESIDENT MADISON
8674	Dec. 30, 1955, A.F. FLT. 070/1230–Jan. 3, 1956, ILE DE FRANCE
8675	Jan. 3, 1956, JEANETTE–Jan. 5, 1956, KUNGSHOLM
8676	Jan. 5, 1956, MARIA STATHATOS–Jan. 9, 1956, TWA FLT. 1905/06
8677	Jan. 10, 1956, AMSTELVEEN–Jan. 14, 1956, MATHILDA THORDEN
8678	Jan. 14, 1956, MEMNON–Jan. 17, 1956, NIEUW AMSTERDAM
8679	Jan. 17, 1956, QUEEN MARY–Jan. 20, 1956, MASDAM

Roll	Dates/Vessels
8680	Jan. 20, 1956, MOUNT RHODOPE–Jan. 24, 1956, MUSKEGON
8681	Jan. 24, 1956, PVT. ELDEN H. JOHNSON–Jan. 27, 1956, HENRY GIBBINS
8682	Jan. 27, 1956, HOEGH RIDER–Jan. 30, 1956, QUEEN ELIZABETH
8683	Jan. 30, 1956, SANTA BARBARA–Feb. 3, 1956, CONTE BIANCAMANO
8684	Feb. 3, 1956, CRISTOBAL–Feb. 6, 1956, HOMERIC
8685	Feb. 6, 1956, ILE DE FRANCE–Feb. 9, 1956, OLYMPIC WIND
8686	Feb. 9, 1956, PVT. WM. H. THOMAS–Feb. 12, 1956, OCEAN JENNY
8687	Feb. 12, 1956, A.F. FLT. 070/0212–Feb. 15, 1956, ESSO RICHMOND
8688	Feb. 15, 1956, ESTRID TORM–Feb. 19, 1956, VDA FLT. R. G./850
8689	Feb. 20, 1956, ALLIANCE–Feb. 23, 1956, ITALIA
8690	Feb. 23, 1956, LUCKY STAR–Feb. 26, 1956, AMERICAN PLANTER
8691	Feb. 26, 1956, ANZOATEGUI–Feb. 29, 1956, INDEPENDENCE
8692	Feb. 29, 1956, LOIDE PANAMA–Mar. 3, 1956, AMERICAN CHIEF
8693	Mar. 3, 1956, ANGELIKI–Mar. 5, 1956, BEATRICE
8694	Mar. 5, 1956, BERLIN–Mar. 8, 1956, NABOB
8695	Mar. 8, 1956, NORDERHOLM–Mar. 12, 1956, PIONEER ISLE
8696	Mar. 12, 1956, QUEEN MARY–Mar. 15, 1956, NEW YORK
8697	Mar. 15, 1956, A.A. FLT. 300/R21–Mar. 19, 1956, AMERICA
8698	Mar. 19, 1956, ESSO CRISTOBAL–Mar. 21, 1956, GOLDEN EAGLE
8699	Mar. 21, 1956, GYPSUM KING–Mar. 24, 1956, AFRICAN DAWN
8700	Mar. 24, 1956, ALCEO–Mar. 27, 1956, QUEEN MARY
8701	Mar. 27, 1956, YAMAHARU MARU–Mar. 30, 1956, QUEEN OF BERMUDA
8702	Mar. 30, 1956, A.F. FLT. 045–Apr. 3, 1956, MARIANNE
8703	Apr. 3, 1956, MEXICO MARU–Apr. 5, 1956, UNITED STATES
8704	Apr. 5, 1956, A.F. FLT. 070/0405–Apr. 7, 1956, U.S.A.F. SPEC.
8705	Apr. 8, 1956, ALCOA PILGRIM–Apr. 10, 1956, ORIENTE
8706	Apr. 10, 1956, QUEEN MARY–Apr. 12, 1956, ILE DE FRANCE
8707	Apr. 12, 1956, OCEAN MONARCH–Apr. 14, 1956, BRITANNIC
8708	Apr. 14, 1956, CALI–Apr. 17, 1956, QUEEN ELIZABETH
8709	Apr. 17, 1956, REPUBLIC–Apr. 19, 1956, VARIG FLT. 850/18
8710	Apr. 20, 1956, AMERICAN MILLER–Apr. 21, 1956, TWA FLT. 8988/20
8711	Apr. 22, 1956, ADRIAS–Apr. 23, 1956, ALLIANCE
8712	Apr. 24, 1956, BLACK HERON–Apr. 26, 1956, GEN. G.M. RANDALL
8713	Apr. 26, 1956, HAVMANN–Apr. 29, 1956, LIBERATOR
8714	Apr. 29, 1956, SUCRE–Apr. 30, 1956, W&K FLT. SPL.

Roll	Dates/Vessels
8715	May 1, 1956, AFRICAN ENDEAVOR–May 3, 1956, VARIG FLT. R. G. 850
8716	May 4, 1956, AMERICAN CLIPPER–May 7, 1956, STOCKHOLM
8717	May 7, 1956, TOPA TOPA–May 10, 1956, LIBERTE
8718	May 10, 1956, MONTEVIDEO–May 13, 1956, GEORGE LYRAS
8719	May 13, 1956, GRIGORIOS C. III–May 15, 1956, QUEEN ELIZABETH
8720	May 15, 1956, JONAH E. KELLEY–May 17, 1956, AMERICAN PRESS
8721	May 17, 1956, AMES VICTORY–May 18, 1956, PRESIDENT JEFFERSON
8722	May 18, 1956, SAXON–May 22, 1956, GENERAL WILLIAM O. DARBY
8723	May 22, 1956, GYPSUM EXPRESS–May 23, 1956, AMERICA
8724	May 23, 1956, AMERICAN–May 25, 1956, NASSAU
8725	May 25, 1956, NICOLAOU ZOGRAFIA–May 28, 1956, FRANCONIA
8726	May 28, 1956, GENERAL S. B. BUCKNER–May 30, 1956, AMERICAN IMPORTER
8727	May 30, 1956, CLYDEWATER–June 1, 1956, SANTA INES
8728	June 1, 1956, AIR FRANCE RFLT. NO. AF-045–June 3, 1956, MAASDAM
8729	June 3, 1956, PARTHIA–June 5, 1956, QUEEN MARY
8730	June 5, 1956, QUEMADO LAKE–June 6, 1956, TWA FLT. 975/06
8731	June 7, 1956, AMERICAN SCOUT–June 9, 1956, ILE DE FRANCE
8732	June 9, 1956, MARIANNE–June 11, 1956, TWA FLT. 995/09
8733	June 12, 1956, AMAPA–June 13, 1956, SANTA ROSA
8734	June 13, 1956, AEROLINEA ARGENTINAS FLT. AR300/R47– June 15, 1956, LIBERTE
8735	June 15, 1956, CRAIG–June 17, 1956, VARIG FLT. RG850/16
8736	June 18, 1956, ALGOL–June 19, 1956, QUEEN MARY
8737	June 19, 1956, RHADAMES–June 21, 1956, FLANDRE
8738	June 21, 1956, GENERAL HARRY TAYLOR–June 23, 1956, TWA FLT. 969/22
8739	June 24, 1956, ALSATIA–June 25, 1956, TWA FLT. 995/23
8740	June 26, 1956, ANASTASIA–June 27, 1956, OSLOFJORD
8741	June 27, 1956, SANTA ROSA–June 29, 1956, OLYMPIA
8742	June 29, 1956, PLATIDIA–June 30, 1956, TWA FLT. 6939/29
8743	July 1, 1956, BOSWELL–July 3, 1956, ANDREA DORIA
8744	July 3, 1956, BURKHARD BROHAN–July 5, 1956, BERGENSFJORD
8745	July 5, 1956, BOLIVAR–July 7, 1956, TWA FLT. 985/06
8746	July 8, 1956, ALAMO VICTORY–July 10, 1956, FLANDRE
8747	July 10, 1956, GEN. H.F. HODGES–July 11, 1956, RHADAMES
8748	July 11, 1956, ROBERT WATT MILLER–July 14, 1956, VASSILIS
8749	July 14, 1956, WAVE PREMIER–July 17, 1956, CRISTOFORO COLOMBO

Roll	Dates/Vessels
8750	July 17, 1956, ESSO GENOVA–July 18, 1956, QUEEN MARY
8751	July 18, 1956, QUEEN OF BERMUDA–July 20, 1956, SATURNIA
8752	July 20, 1956, A.F. FLT. 045–July 23, 1956, QUEEN OF BERMUDA
8753	July 23, 1956, SAN ANGELO VICTORY–July 26, 1956, ESSO RICHMOND
8754	July 25, 1956, EXERMONT–July 28, 1956, MORMACMAIL
8755	July 28, 1956, MOTOMAR–July 30, 1956, UNITED STATES
8756	July 30, 1956, A.F. FLT. 029–Aug. 1, 1956, HOEGH SILVERSTREAM
8757	Aug. 1, 1956, KAREM REED–Aug. 3, 1956, QUEEN OF BERMUDA
8758	Aug. 3, 1956, YAMAHARU MARU–Aug. 6, 1956, LISTA
8759	Aug. 6, 1956, MICHAEL L.–Aug. 8, 1956, CRISTOFORO COLOMBO
8760	Aug. 8, 1956, GYPSUM KING–Aug. 10, 1956, NASSAU
8761	Aug. 10, 1956, OCEAN MONARCH–Aug. 13, 1956, CALLABEE
8762	Aug. 13, 1956, EXETER–Aug. 14, 1956, ZUIDERKRUIS
8763	Aug. 14, 1956, AF FLT. 070/0814–Aug. 16, 1956, MAURETANIA
8764	Aug. 16, 1956, SAGOLAND–Aug. 18, 1956, USN. FLT. SPL. 390
8765	Aug. 19, 1956, BASSANO–Aug. 20, 1956, TWA FLT. 983/19
8766	Aug. 21, 1956, ALCOA PEGASUS–Aug. 22, 1956, MONTE SAJA
8767	Aug. 22, 1956, NORWALK VICTORY–Aug. 24, 1956, NASSAU
8768	Aug. 24, 1956, NIMERTIS–Aug. 26, 1956, VARIG FLT. 850/25
8769	Aug. 27, 1956, AMERICAN HARVESTER–Aug. 28, 1956, QUEEN ELIZABETH
8770	Aug. 28, 1956, SANTA ELISA–Aug. 30, 1956, CONSTITUTION
8771	Aug. 30, 1956, GEN. HARRY TAYLOR–Aug. 31, 1956, OSLOFJORD
8772	Aug. 31, 1956, QUEEN OF BERMUDA–Sept. 2, 1956, ANGELITA
8773	Sept. 2, 1956, COVADONGA–Sept. 4, 1956, MAURETANIA
8774	Sept. 4, 1956, MELVIN H. BAKER–Sept. 5, 1956, NEW YORK
8775	Sept. 5, 1956, PLAGIOLA–Sept. 7, 1956, SIWANOY
8776	Sept. 7, 1956, ZUIDERKRUIS–Sept. 10, 1956, AMERICAN STARLING
8777	Sept. 10, 1956, AROSA KULM–Sept. 11, 1956, QUEEN ELIZABETH
8778	Sept. 11, 1956, QUEEN FREDERICA–Sept. 13, 1956, RIBCIRA GRANDE
8779	Sept. 13, 1956, SAN FELIPE–Sept. 15, 1956, TWA FLT. 6903/14
8780	Sept. 16, 1956, ALSATIA–Sept. 17, 1956, OLYMPIA
8781	Sept. 17, 1956, PIONEER MOOR–Sept. 19, 1956, FORT RICHE PANSE
8782	Sept. 19, 1956, USNS GEIGER–Sept. 21, 1956, LIBERTE
8783	Sept. 21, 1956, NORWALK VICTORY–Sept. 23, 1956, VARIG RG850/22

Roll	Dates/Vessels
8784	Sept. 24, 1956, AFRICAN RAINBOW–Sept. 25, 1956, QUEEN ELIZABETH
8785	Sept. 25, 1956, UNITED STATES–Sept. 27, 1956, REPUBLICA DE COLOMBIA
8786	Sept. 27, 1956, ROBIN TUXFORD–Sept. 30, 1956, VARIG RG850
8787	Oct. 1, 1956, ADRIAS–Oct. 3, 1956, INDEPENDENCE
8788	Oct. 3, 1956, JOAN–Oct. 5, 1956, EXBROOK
8789	Oct. 5, 1956, LIBURNIA–Oct. 8, 1956, LIBERTE
8790	Oct. 8, 1956, MAASDAM–Oct. 9, 1956, TWA FLT. 8234/08
8791	Oct. 10, 1956, ATLANTIC MARQUESS–Oct. 12, 1956, LYNN VICTORY
8792	Oct. 12, 1956, MAURETANIA–Oct. 15, 1956, AMERICA
8793	Oct. 15, 1956, ANGELITA–Oct. 17, 1956, GYPSUM EMPRESS
8794	Oct. 17, 1956, HAVFALK–Oct. 19, 1956, PERSIA MARU
8795	Oct. 19, 1956, PVT. WM. H. THOMAS–Oct. 21, 1956, VARIG FLT. 850/20
8796	Oct. 22, 1956, ALCOA PURITAN–Oct. 24, 1956, ETHEL B.
8797	Oct. 24, 1956, GENERAL H. TAYLOR–Oct. 27, 1956, BRITANNIC
8798	Oct. 27, 1956, CALI–Oct. 29, 1956, PIONEER MILL
8799	Oct. 29, 1956, PRESIDENT MONROE–Oct. 31, 1956, MONROE VICTORY
8800	Oct. 31, 1956, PANAMA MARU–Nov. 3, 1956, TWA FLT. 6947
8801	Nov. 4, 1956, ESSO RICHMOND–Nov. 6, 1956, WEBB KNAPP FLT. SPL.
8802	Nov. 7, 1956, AMERICAN MANUFACTURER–Nov. 8, 1956, VARIG FLT. 850
8803	Nov. 9, 1956, AMERICAN FORWARDER–Nov. 9, 1956, UNITED DYE & CHEMICAL
8804	Nov. 10, 1956, ANDROS VENTURE–Nov. 13, 1956, BERGENSFJORD
8805	Nov. 13, 1956, AMERICAN–Nov. 14, 1956, LEISE MAERSK
8806	Nov. 14, 1956, LOIDE BRASIL–Nov. 17, 1956, INDOCHINOIS
8807	Nov. 17, 1956, IRVINGWOOD–Nov. 20, 1956, WORLD LUCK
8808	Nov. 20, 1956, WORLD TRAVELLER–Nov. 23, 1956, OSLOFJORD
8809	Nov. 23, 1956, SANTA MONICA–Nov. 26, 1956, AFRICAN QUEEN
8810	Nov. 26, 1956, BOW HILL–Nov. 27, 1956, TWA FLT. 8282/26
8811	Nov. 28, 1956, ANGELBURG–Nov. 30, 1956, LEONIDAS
8812	Nov. 30, 1956, LOVLAND–Dec. 2, 1956, BERLANGA
8813	Dec. 2, 1956, GAUTHOID–Dec. 6, 1956, EROS
8814	Dec. 6, 1956, ESSO CRISTOBAL–Dec. 8, 1956, C. COLOMBO
8815	Dec. 8, 1956, ESSO COLOMBIA–Dec. 10, 1956, WILLMAR
8816	Dec. 10, 1956, A.F. FLT. 070/1210–Dec. 13, 1956, UNITED STATES
8817	Dec. 13, 1956, A.A. FLT. 300R115–Dec. 16, 1956, VARIG FLT. RG850
8818	Dec. 17, 1956, ALCOA PILGRIM–Dec. 19, 1956, MAASDAM
8819	Dec. 19, 1956, OTTA–Dec. 21, 1956, CARINTHIA

Roll	Dates/Vessels
8820	Dec. 21, 1956, CURRO–Dec. 23, 1956, CARIBIA
8821	Dec. 23, 1956, DOLORES–Dec. 27, 1956, GEN. HARRY TAYLOR
8822	Dec. 27, 1956, HEREDIA–Dec. 30, 1956, VARIG FLT. RG850/29
8823	Dec. 31, 1956, DOROTHY–Dec. 31, 1956, TWA FLT. 8306/30
8824	Jan. 1, 1957, AFRICAN ENDEAVOR–Jan. 3, 1957, TINI
8825	Jan. 3, 1957, UNITED STATES–Jan. 4, 1957, VARIG FLT. RG850
8826	Jan. 5, 1957, CAPE ANN–Jan. 7, 1957, TWA FLT. 1905/4
8827	Jan. 8, 1957, AMERICAN ARCHER–Jan. 11, 1957, ZION
8828	Jan. 11, 1957, A.F. FLT. 501SPL.–Jan. 14, 1957, EXOCHORDIA
8829	Jan. 14, 1957, FRANKLIN BERWIN–Jan. 17, 1957, QUEEN MARY
8830	Jan. 17, 1957, QUEEN OF BERMUDA–Jan. 20, 1957, COORANGA
8831	Jan. 20, 1957, KINDERDIJK–Jan. 24, 1957, GENERAL HARRY TAYLOR
8832	Jan. 24, 1957, GYPSUM DUCHESS–Jan. 28, 1957, CITY OF WINCHESTER
8833	Jan. 28, 1957, ESSO HUNTINGTON–Jan. 30, 1957, GENERAL LEROY ELTINGE
8834	Jan. 30, 1957, GIULIO CERSARE–Jan. 31, 1957, TWA FLT. 925–30
8835	Feb. 1, 1957, BLACK FALCON–Feb. 4, 1957, SAXONIA
8836	Feb. 4, 1957, SIBONEY–Feb. 7, 1957, VERAGUA
8837	Feb. 7, 1957, AIR FRANCE FLT. AF-031–Feb. 10, 1957, VARIG FLT. 850-09
8838	Feb. 11, 1957, AFRICAN ENTERPRISE–Feb. 14, 1957, QUEEN ELIZABETH
8839	Feb. 14, 1957, RONDO–Feb. 17, 1957, VARIG FLT. RG-850
8840	Feb. 18, 1957, AKIBASAN MARU–Feb. 20, 1957, GENERAL HARRY TAYLOR
8841	Feb. 20, 1957, ITAJI–Feb. 23, 1957, TWA FLT. 985/21
8842	Feb. 24, 1957, CONCORDIA FONN–Feb. 26, 1957, SCYTHIA
8843	Feb. 26, 1957, TILDA DAN–Feb. 28, 1957, TWA FLT. 1925/27
8844	Mar. 1, 1957, DALTON VICTORY–Mar. 2, 1957, KWNIKAWA MARU
8845	Mar. 2, 1957, LAGERFOSS–Mar. 4, 1957, TWA FLT. 1861/03
8846	Mar. 5, 1957, AMERICAN LEADER–Mar. 8, 1957, VARIG FLT. RG 850
8847	Mar. 9, 1957, ANDREW JACKSON–Mar. 11, 1957, TWA FLT. 983/10
8848	Mar. 12, 1957, AMERICA–Mar. 13, 1957, UNITED STATES
8849	Mar. 13, 1957, AER. ARF. FLT. 300/R41–Mar. 16, 1957, TWA FLT. 8341/15
8850	Mar. 17, 1957, ASAKASAN MARU–Mar. 18, 1957, SEATHUNDER
8851	Mar. 18, 1957, SIBENIK–Mar. 21, 1957, TROLLTIND
8852	Mar. 21, 1957, AIR FRANCE FLT. 031–Mar. 24, 1957, RYNDAM
8853	Mar. 24, 1957, VALMAR–Mar. 26, 1957, QUEEN MARY

Roll	Dates/Vessels
8854	Mar. 26, 1957, ROONAGH HEAD–Mar. 28, 1957, EMPRESS OF SCOTLAND
8855	Mar. 28, 1957, ESSO RICHMOND–Mar. 30, 1957, SAXONIA
8856	Mar. 30, 1957, TOPEKA–Apr. 2, 1957, PRESIDENT HAYES
8857	Apr. 2, 1957, QUEEN ELIZABETH–Apr. 4, 1957, OCEAN MONARCH
8858	Apr. 4, 1957, PERRY B.–Apr. 8, 1957, GYPSUM EMPRESS
8859	Apr. 8, 1957, LIBERTE 6527–Apr. 10, 1957, VULCANIA
8860	Apr. 10, 1957, AEROLINEAS ARGENTINAS–Apr. 13, 1957, TWA FLT. 985/11
8861	Apr. 14, 1957, BRITANNIC–Apr. 16, 1957, QUEEN ELIZABETH
8862	Apr. 16, 1957, SLOTERDIJK–Apr. 18, 1957, USAF FLT. SPL.
8863	Apr. 19, 1957, APURE–Apr. 21, 1957, VARIG FLT. 850/20
8864	Apr. 22, 1957, ARGENTINA–Apr. 23, 1957, QUEEN FREDERICA
8865	Apr. 23, 1957, QUEEN MARY–Apr. 25, 1957, NELLY
8866	Apr. 25, 1957, PIONEER MING–Apr. 28, 1957, VARIG FLT. RG/850
8867	Apr. 29, 1957, AMERICAN VETERAN–Apr. 30, 1957, QUEEN ELIZABETH
8868	Apr. 30, 1957, STROMBO–May 4, 1957, BOAC FLT. 495/018B
8869	May 4, 1957, BOAC FLT. 509/208–May 7, 1957, PVT. ELDEN H. JOHNSON
8870	May 7, 1957, QUEEN MARY–May 10, 1957, NEW YORK
8871	May 10, 1957, OCEAN EAGLE–May 13, 1957, BOAC FLT. 521/334
8872	May 13, 1957, CAPITAL FLT. 902/12–May 14, 1957, TWA FLT. 8486/13
8873	May 15, 1957, BLUE JACKET–May 18, 1957, QUEEN FREDERICKA
8874	May 18, 1957, RIO DE JANEIRO–May 21, 1957, CASTEL FELICE
8875	May 21, 1957, CRISTOBAL–May 24, 1957, ZION
8876	May 24, 1957, AIR FRANCE FLT. 003–May 27, 1957, SOESTDYK
8877	May 27, 1957, STEEL APPRENTICE–May 29, 1957, CONSTITUTION
8878	May 29, 1957, USNS GEIGER–May 31, 1957, TWA FLT. 981-30
8879	June 1, 1957, ALCOA RANGER–June 3, 1957, ILE DE FRANCE
8880	June 3, 1957, KRONOS–June 4, 1957, TWA FLT. 8394/03
8881	June 5, 1957, AMERICA–June 7, 1957, SPIRIT OF LIBERTY
8882	June 7, 1957, TAHSINIA–June 10, 1957, NOORDAM
8883	June 10, 1957, RHADAMES–June 12, 1957, UNITED STATES
8884	June 12, 1957, AEROARG. FLT. 300R-93–June 14, 1957, FLY. TIG. FLT. 924/13
8885	June 14, 1957, IBERIA FLT. 951–June 17, 1957, WEBB & KNAPP #1217337
8886	June 18, 1957, AMERICAN MERCHANT–June 20, 1957, AUGUSTUS
8887	June 20, 1957, BARBARA BROVIG–June 22, 1957, TWA FLT. 8506/21

Roll	Dates/Vessels
8888	June 23, 1957, BLACK OSPREY–June 25, 1957, GULF GLOW
8889	June 25, 1957, GYPSUM PRINCE–June 26, 1957, SANTA PAULA
8890	June 26, 1957, STATENDAM–June 29, 1957, HAI KWANG
8891	June 29, 1957, JOHN B. WATERMAN–July 1, 1957, YAMASKA
8892	July 1, 1957, AIR FRANCE FLT. 508SPL.–July 3, 1957, VARIG FLT. 850/02

★ **Index (Soundex) to Passenger Lists of Vessels Arriving at the Port of New York, 1944-48. M1417. 94 rolls. 16mm.**

Roll	Contents
1	A-000 Christian–A-210 Lilly Ellen
2	A-210 Jacques–A-410 Pietro
3	A-415 Salvatore–A-530 Pieriana
4	A-530 Perna–A-650 Alegria
5	A-650 Alice–B-230 Jose
6	B-230 Sidney–B-423 Maria
7	roll missing
8	B-423 Moische–B-520 Tranguillo
9	B-520 Theodoro–B-620 Charlie
10	B-620 Carol–B-626 Paul
11	B-626 Paul–B-650 Joan
12	B-650 Joan M–C-000 Hoo Shy
13	C-000 Hilda–C-220 Piotr
14	C-220 Pietro–C-360 Harvey S.
15	C-360 Enrique–C-462 Colin
16	C-462 Dimitrious–C-530 Vincent
17	C-530 Uriele–C-620 Zusana
18	C-620 Sophia–C-650 Kathleen
19	C-650 Ludmila–D145 Maria
20	D-145 Mendel–D-241 Giouanmi
21	D-241 Hannah–D-350 Maurice
22	D-350 Roberto–D-510 Joseph
23	D-510 Rosalia–D-562 Helen
24	D-562 Guarina–E-152 James L.
25	E-152 John–E-420 Edma
26	E-420 Ewa–F-200 Michael
27	F-200 Muriel I.–F-430 Colin N.
28	F-430 Brayan–F-620 Josephine
29	F-620 Josefa–F-652 Franco Tulio
30	F-652 Francis–G-164 Eduardo
31	G-164 Areti Jordan–G-363 Jean
32	G-363 John–G-452 Dora
33	G-452 Dunca–G-600 Lloyd
34	G-600 Luther–G-625 Marianne
35	roll missing
36	G-653 Karl H.–H-126 Dirk
37	H-126 Ernest–H-350 Jacqueline
38	H-350 Ida–H-516 David
39	H-516 Doreen–H-610 Winifred
40	H-610 Winifred–H-655 Beatrice Norma
41	H-655 Pedro Maria–J-212 Erling
42	J-212 Freidel–J-525 Aruid
43	J-525 Arnt–K-130 Gerda
44	K-130 Ebba Agnet–K-263 Frieda
45	K-263 Anna–K-452 Warwara
46	K-452 Tatiana–K-550 John
47	K-550 Jadau L.–K-645 Jacob
48	K-645 Elsbeth–L-140 Filomena
49	L-140 Francis–L-220 Pinkus
50	L-220 Pola–L-350 John H.

Roll	Contents
51	L-350 Henriquez–L-524 Umberto
52	L-524 Paul–L-635 Lucia
53	L-635 Marianna–M-222 Helena
54	M-222 Elisabeth–M-246 Joseph
55	M-246 Hersch–M-264 Elizabeth
56	M-264 Arthur–M-420 Issa Parvis
57	M-420 Margaret T–M-520 Angela
58	M-520 Angelina–M-563 Peter
59	M-363 Maria–M-623 Lars
60	M-623 Maria–M-650 Elvira
61	M-650 Elia–N-253 Maria Flavia
62	N-253 Rowena–N-635 Alice Betty
63	N-635 Clifford–O-425 John Kristian
64	O-425 John Valter–P-200 Helen
65	P-200 Helena–P-330 Gioditta
66	P-330 Luigi–P-420 Lina
67	P-420 Leopold–P-530 Jayne Leivas
68	P-530 Juda–P-620 Teresa
69	P-620 Teresa–P-655 Nicolina
70	P-655 Teodoro–R-163 Albert B.
71	R-163 Alfred–R-230 Andre
72	R-230 Antonio–R-300 Amy
73	R-300 Amanda–R-453 Emile Felix
74	R-453 Fernand–S-100 Dominco
75	S-140 Uvno–S-140 Salvatrice
76	S-160 Theodore–S-260 Heinrich
77	S-260 Herberto–S-340 Salo
78	S-340 Violet M–S-364 Hugh
79	S-364 Harold–S-430 Paul E.
80	S-430 Salvatore–S-520 Ting
81	S-520 Zai–S-534 Albert
82	S-524 Attilio–S-600 Tancher
83	S-600 Teresa–T-100 Angeles
84	T-100 Alles–T-400 Ella H.
85	T-400 Ernest G.–T-545 John D.
86	T-545 Helen–T-655 Concetta
87	T-655 Angela–V-345 Giuseppa
88	V-345 Pasqune–V-535 Dylvian
89	V-535 Elisabeth–W-200 Joan
90	W-200 Johanna–W-325 Margaret
91	W-325 Marjorie–W-426 Jossie
92	W-426 Jean–W-600 Albert H.
93	W-600 Alexa–Z-162 Leo
94	Z-162 Maria–Z-666 David

Philadelphia, Pennsylvania

Index (Soundex) to Passenger Lists of Vessels Arriving at Philadelphia, PA, January 1, 1883–June 28, 1948. T526. 61 rolls. 16mm.

Rolls	Contents
1	A-000 Andrew–A-522 Julian
2	A-522 Jurgis–B-200 Gertrud
3	B-200 Gertrude–B-340 Dr. Edw.
4	B-340 Dr. Edward–B-463 Herman
5	B-463 Ida–B-620 Ryvan
6	B-620 S–B-645 Child
7	B-645 Mrs.–C-142 Thomas
8	C-142 Valentin–C-365 Antonio
8a	C-365 Antonio–C-514 Norman J.
9	C-514 Mrs. Olive–C-623 Jens
10	C-623 Jens Char–D-120 Madeleine
11	D-120 Madeline–D-256 Elisabeth

Rolls	Contents
12	D-256 Lavainia–D-515 Nellie
13	D-515 Nellie B.–D-633 Raymond
14	D-633 Ricardo–E-625 Otto
15	E-625 P–F-452 Vincenzo
16	F-450 W–F-650 Julia
17	F-650 Kalman–G-341 Joseph
18	G-341 Kapel–G-513 Stefan
19	G-514 Mrs. A. Gamble–G-630 Susan
20	G-630 Syster–H-200 Gyura
21	H-200 H. Hayes–H-400 W. Holly
22	H-400 Walter–H-540 C. Hammel
23	H-540 Calliek–H-663 Roza
24	I-000 Joseif–J-520 Azubak
25	J-520 B. Janos–J-630 Zarol
26	J-634 Abmel–K-255 Jurke
27	K-255 Jorko–K-451 Zippe
28	K-452 Mrs. Kling–K-600 Myrs
29	K-600 Nadeem–L-000 Mary
30	L-000 Mary–L-230 Wladyslaw
31	L-230 Domenico–L-520 Josefine
32	L-520 Joseph–M-200 Marga
33	M-200 Margt.–M-242 Myehalina
34	M-242 N. Mikklesen–M-263 Anne
35	M-263 Annie–M-426 Zachie
36	M-430 Adelaide–M-550 Gje
37	M-550 Gladys–M-630 Suzanna
38	M-630 T. Moorehead–N-265 Wastil
39	N-300 Mr. Newitt–N-235 Amy
40	O-235 Dr. Andrew–O-653 Wilhelm
41	O-654 Jose Teixeirede–P-360 Ernst
42	P-360 Ernst–P-460 Wajeiech
43	P-462 A. Pollerk–P-640 Beile
44	P-640 Bendetto–R-200 Julia
45	R-200 Julia–R-300 Kunt
46	R-300 L. Reid–R-532 Wilhelmine
47	R-534 Infant–S-160 Lise
48	S-160 Lizette–S-313 Wasyl
49	S-313 Wm. Alfred–S-362 Anthony
50	S-362 Anton–S-435 Sydney
51	S-435 Master T.–S-530 James Gene
52	S-530 James A.–S-612 P. Serbsrak
53	S-612 Pal–T-262 Chaja
54	T-262 Chas.–T-614 Jurko
55	T-614 K.N. Tripple–V-420 Ottavio
56	V-420 Pal–W-260 Eve
57	W-260 Faiwill–W-425 Freak
58	W-425 Fred–W-623 John Graig
59	W-623 John Edward–Z-546 Mendel
60	Z-540 Menuche–Z-665 Peter

Book Indexes to Philadelphia Passenger Lists, 1906–1926. T791. 23 rolls.

Roll	Volumes	Dates
1	1–3	May 14, 1906–Dec. 26, 1906
2	4–5	Jan. 2, 1907–June 30, 1907
3	6–7	July 7, 1907–Dec. 25, 1907
4	8–9	Jan. 1, 1908–Oct. 16, 1908
5	10–12	Oct. 17, 1908–July 31, 1909
6	13–15	Aug. 8, 1909–May 3, 1910
7	16–17	May 4, 1910–Sept. 25, 1910
8	18–19a	Oct. 5, 1910–Mar. 5, 1911
9	20–21	Mar. 6, 1911–June 19, 1911
10	22–24	June 23, 1911–Nov. 25, 1911
11	24–25a	Nov. 29, 1911–Mar. 29, 1912
12	26–27	Apr. 1, 1912–July 9, 1912

Roll	Volumes	Dates
13	28–29	July 10, 1912–Oct. 21, 1912
14	30–31	Oct. 21, 1912–Mar. 8, 1913
15	32–33	Mar. 9, 1913–May 30, 1913
16	34–35	June 1, 1913–Aug. 30, 1913
17	36–37	Sept. 1, 1913–Nov. 23, 1913
18	38–39	Nov. 24, 1913–Mar. 9, 1914
19	40–41	Mar. 10, 1914–June 30, 1914
20	42–43	July 1, 1914–Jan. 31, 1915
21	44–45	Feb. 1, 1915–Dec. 9, 1920
22	46–48	Jan. 23, 1921–Nov. 30, 1921
23	49–51	June 5, 1922–June 17, 1926

Passenger Lists of Vessels Arriving at Philadelphia, PA, 1883–1945. T840. 181 rolls.

Roll	Volumes	Dates*
1	A	Jan. 1, 1883–Apr. 30, 1883
2	B	May 7, 1883–June 30, 1883
3	C	July 1, 1883–Dec. 31, 1883
4	D	Jan. 1, 1884–June 23, 1884
5	E–F	July 1, 1884–June 30, 1885
6	G	July 5, 1885–Dec. 28, 1886
7	H	Jan. 3, 1886–June 28, 1886
8	I–J	July 6, 1886–Apr. 26, 1887
9	K–L	May 3, 1887–Sept. 30, 1887
10	M–N	Oct. 3, 1887–Apr. 30, 1888
11	P	May 2, 1888–Dec. 30, 1888
12	Q	Jan. 5, 1889–June 25, 1889
13	R–S	July 3, 1889–June 30, 1890
14	T–U	July 6, 1890–Apr. 22, 1891
15	V–W	May 1, 1891–Dec. 20, 1891
16	X-1–X-2	Jan. 9, 1892–June 19, 1892
17	Y-1 Y-2m	July 8, 1892–Sept. 3, 1892
18	Z-1 Z-2	Jan. 5, 1893–May 31, 1893
19	1-1a-2-2a	May 18, 1893–Sept. 27, 1893
20	3–4	Oct. 2, 1893–May 30, 1894
21	5–6	June 1, 1894–Sept. 30, 1894
22	7-8-9	Oct. 1, 1894–Apr. 30, 1895
23	10-11-11a	May 1, 1895–July 31, 1895
24	12-12a-13-14	Aug. 1, 1895–Jan. 1, 1896
25	15-15a-16-16a	Apr. 1, 1896–Aug. 31,1896
26	17-17a-18-18a	Sept. 1, 1896–June 30, 1897
27	19-19a	July 1, 1897–Dec. 31, 1897
28	20-20a-21	Jan. 1, 1898–Oct. 21, 1898
29	21a-22-22a	Oct. 29, 1898–June 24, 1899
30	23-24-25-26-27	July 1, 1899–Nov. 29, 1899
31	28-29-30-31	Dec. 7, 1899–May 5, 1900
32	32-33-34-35	May 6, 1900–Sept. 17, 1900
33	36-37-38	Sept. 18, 1900–Feb. 28, 1901
34	39-40-41	Mar. 1, 1901–June 30, 1901
35	42-43	July 1, 1901–Sept. 8, 1901
36	44-45	Sept. 9, 1901–Nov. 10, 1901
37	46-47	Nov. 11, 1901–Feb. 13, 1902
38	48-49	Feb. 14, 1902–Apr. 24, 1902
39	50-51-52	Apr. 27, 1902–July 4, 1902
40	53m-54-55-56	July 5, 1902–Oct. 20, 1902
41	57-58-59-60	Oct. 12, 1902–Mar. 5, 1903
42	61-62-63	Mar. 6, 1903–Aug. 17, 1903
43	64-65-66	May 18, 1903–Aug. 22, 1903
44	67-68-69	Aug. 23, 1903–Dec. 8, 1903
45	70-71-72	Jan. 1, 1904–May 31, 1904
46	73-74-75	June 1, 1904–Sept. 30, 1904
47	76-77-78	Sept. 24, 1904–Jan. 22, 1905
48	79-80	Jan. 23, 1905–Apr. 12, 1905
49	81-82-83	Apr. 13, 1905–Aug. 14, 1905
50	84-85-86	Aug. 14, 1905–Dec. 31, 1905

Roll	Volumes	Dates*	Roll	Volumes	Dates*
51	87–88	Jan. 1, 1906–Apr. 9, 1906	116	181–182	June 12, 1913–July 4, 1913
52	89–90	Apr. 10, 1906–June 30, 1906	117	183–184	July 5, 1913–July 30, 1913
53	91–92	July 1, 1906–Sept. 24, 1906	118	185–186	Aug. 1, 1913–Aug. 20, 1913
54	93–94	Sept. 25, 1906–Dec. 31, 1906	119	187–188	Aug. 21, 1913–Sept. 17, 1913
55	95–96	Jan. 1, 1907–Apr. 13, 1907	120	189–190	Sept. 17, 1913–Oct. 15, 1913
56	97–98	Apr. 14, 1907–May 31, 1907	121	191–192	Oct. 16, 1913–Nov. 17, 1913
57	99	June 1, 1907–June 30, 1907	122	193–194	Nov. 18, 1913–Dec. 25, 1913
58	100	July 1, 1907–July 31, 1907	123	195–196	Dec. 26, 1913–Mar. 6, 1914
59	101–102	Aug. 1, 1907–Sept. 30, 1907	124	197	Mar. 7, 1914–Mar. 31, 1914
60	103	Oct. 1, 1907–Nov. 3, 1907	125	198–199	Apr. 1, 1914–Apr. 30, 1914
61	104–105	Nov. 11, 1907–Mar. 31, 1908	126	200–201	May 1, 1914–June 10, 1914
62	106–107	Apr. 1, 1908–Aug. 10, 1908	127	202–203	June 11, 1914–July 31, 1914
63	108	Aug. 11, 1908–Oct. 17, 1908	128	204–205	Aug. 1, 1914–Oct. 30, 1914
64	109	Oct. 17, 1908–Dec. 31, 1908	129	206–207	Nov. 1, 1914–Sept. 30, 1915
65	110–111	Jan. 10, 1909–Apr. 5, 1909	130	208–209	Oct. 1, 1915–Nov. 30, 1916
66	112	Apr. 7, 1909–May 16, 1909	131	210–211	Dec. 1, 1916–Aug. 3, 1917
67	113	May 17, 1909–June 20, 1909	132	212–213	Sept. 1, 1917–June 30, 1918
68	114	June 21, 1909–July 31, 1909	133	214–215	July 6, 1918–May 22, 1919
69	115–116	Aug. 8, 1909–Oct. 3, 1909	134	216–217	May 22, 1919–Oct. 31, 1919
70	117	Oct. 9, 1909–Nov. 21, 1909	135	218–219	Nov. 1, 1919–Apr. 28, 1920
71	118	Nov. 22, 1909–Dec. 15, 1909	136	220–221	May 1, 1920–Aug. 25, 1920
72	119–120	Dec. 27, 1909–Mar. 3, 1910	137	222–223	Aug. 26, 1920–Oct. 31, 1920
73	121	Mar. 4, 1910–Mar. 23, 1910	138	224–225	Nov. 1, 1920–Feb. 17, 1921
74	122	Mar. 23, 1910–Apr. 6, 1910	139	226–227–228	Feb. 18, 1921–Mar. 11, 1921
75	123	Apr. 7, 1910–Apr. 17, 1910	140	229–230	Mar. 3, 1921–Mar. 15, 1921
76	124	Apr. 20, 1910–May 3, 1910	141	231–232	Mar. 16, 1921–Apr. 20, 1921
77	125	May 4, 1910–May 9, 1910	142	233–234–235	Apr. 21, 1921–May 29, 1921
78	126	May 11, 1910–May 29, 1910	143	236–237–238	May 29, 1921–Oct. 26, 1921
79	127	June 1, 1910–June 15, 1910	144	239–240	Oct. 28, 1921–July 29, 1922
80	128	June 25, 1910–July 3, 1910	145	241–242	July 24, 1922–Dec. 28, 1922
81	129	July 14, 1910–July 21, 1910	146	243	Jan. 1, 1923–Apr. 26, 1923
82	130	Aug. 1, 1910–Aug. 24, 1910	147	244	Apr. 23, 1923–July 2, 1923
83	131	Sept. 1, 1910–Sept. 27, 1910	148	245	July 2, 1923–Aug. 6, 1923
84	132	Oct. 5, 1910–Oct. 15, 1910	149	246	Aug. 10, 1923–Sept. 7, 1923
85	133	Oct. 25, 1910–Nov. 17, 1910	150	246a	May 10, 1907–Oct. 23, 1921
86	134–135	Nov. 21, 1910–Dec. 31, 1910	151	247–248	Sept. 8, 1923–Dec. 1, 1923
87	136–137	Jan. 1, 1911–Mar. 5, 1911	152	249–250	Dec. 2, 1923–Aug. 11, 1924
88	138–139	Mar. 6, 1911–Apr. 11, 1911	153	251	Aug. 8, 1924–Dec. 26, 1924
89	140–141	Apr. 14, 1911–May 15, 1911	154	252–253	Jan. 1, 1924–Jan. 31, 1926
90	142	May 16, 1911–May 31, 1911	155	254	Feb. 8, 1926–Aug. 8, 1926
91	143	June 1, 1911–June 19, 1911	156	255	Aug. 9, 1926–Dec. 31, 1926
92	144	June 20, 1911–July 11, 1911	157	256–257	Jan. 3, 1927–Nov. 21, 1927
93	145	July 12, 1911–July 31, 1911	158	258–259	Dec. 11, 1927–Oct. 31, 1928
94	146	Aug. 1, 1911–Aug. 31, 1911	159	260–261	Nov. 1, 1928–Aug. 31, 1929
95	147	Sept. 1, 1911–Sept. 19, 1911	160	262–263	Sept. 1, 1929–June 30, 1930
96	148	Sept. 20, 1911–Oct. 15, 1911	161	264–265	July 1, 1930–Mar. 28, 1931
97	149	Oct. 16, 1911–Nov. 7, 1911	162	266–267	Apr. 2, 1931–Dec. 31, 1931
98	150–151	Nov. 8, 1911–Dec. 18, 1911	163	268–269	Jan. 1, 1932–Aug. 31, 1932
99	152–153	Dec. 19, 1911–Feb. 14, 1912	164	270–271	Sept. 1, 1932–July 30, 1933
100	154–155	Feb. 15, 1912–Mar. 31, 1912	165	272–273	Aug. 3, 1933–Apr. 28, 1934
101	156–157	Apr. 1, 1912–May 9, 1912	166	274–275	May 2, 1934–Feb. 24, 1935
102	158–159	May 11, 1912–June 4, 1912	167	276–277	Mar. 3, 1935–Sept. 30, 1935
103	160–161	June 6, 1912–July 9, 1912	168	278–279	Oct. 2, 1935–May 31, 1936
104	162–163	July 10, 1912–Aug. 16, 1912	169	280–281	June 3, 1936–Dec. 29, 1936
105	164–165	Aug. 17, 1912–Sept. 17, 1912	170	282–283	Jan. 3, 1937–Oct. 31, 1937
106	166–167	Sept. 18, 1912–Oct. 21, 1912	171	284–285	Nov. 4, 1937–Aug. 31, 1938
107	168	Oct. 22, 1912–Nov. 9, 1912	172	286–287	Sept. 1, 1938–June 25, 1939
108	169–170	Nov. 11, 1912–Dec. 11, 1912	173	288–289	July 2, 1939–June 20, 1940
109	171	Dec. 12, 1912–Dec. 30, 1912	174	290–291	July 2, 1940–June 29, 1941
110	172–173	Jan. 1, 1913–Mar. 8, 1913	175	292	July–Dec. 1941
111	174–175	Mar. 9, 1913–Apr. 9, 1913	176	293	Jan. 1, 1942–June 27, 1943
112	176	Apr. 10, 1913–Apr. 17, 1913	177	F–294	July 1, 1943–May 27, 1944
113	177	Apr. 18, 1913–May 4, 1913	178	F–295	May 30, 1944–Feb. 28, 1945
114	178	May 5, 1913–May 18, 1913	179	F–296	Mar. 2, 1945–Aug. 9, 1945
115	179–180	May 19, 1913–June 12, 1913	180	F–297	Aug. 10, 1945–Oct. 22, 1945

Roll	Volumes	Dates*
181	F–298	Oct. 23, 1945–Dec. 31, 1945

Lists were filmed as they appeared in volumes; date spans may overlap.

Portland, Maine

Index to Passengers Arriving at Portland, ME, January 29, 1893–November 22, 1954. T524. 1 roll. 16mm.

Book Indexes to Portland, ME, Passenger Lists, 1907–1930. T793. 12 rolls.

Roll	Dates
1	Apr. 1907–Mar. 12, 1910
2	Mar. 27, 1910–Apr. 24, 1911
3	Nov. 22, 1911–Mar. 18, 1912
4	Mar. 18, 1912–Apr. 22, 1912
5	Nov. 30, 1912–Mar. 8, 1913
6	Mar. 11, 1913–Apr. 9, 1913
7	Apr. 9, 1913–Nov. 7, 1913
8	Dec. 16, 1913–Apr. 1, 1914
9	Apr. 4, 1914–Apr. 12, 1915
10	Apr. 12, 1915–Feb. 25, 1919
11	Apr. 2, 1919–Oct. 1, 1923
12	Nov. 1, 1923–Apr. 6, 1930

Passenger Lists of Vessels Arriving at Portland, ME, November 29, 1893–March 1943. T1151. 35 rolls.

The Immigration and Naturalization Service filmed these records as they appeared in volumes. The date spans overlap and gaps appear as indicated in the listings below. The records are arranged by volume letter or number.

Roll	Volumes	Dates
1	A–B	Nov. 29, 1893–July 22, 1906
2	C	Nov. 24, 1895–Feb. 15, 1900
3	D	Feb. 13, 1900–May 1901
4	E	May 26, 1901–Jan. 19, 1904
5	F	Jan. 19, 1904–May 27, 1906
6	G	Nov. 29, 1907–May 10, 1908
7	H	Sept. 1908–Apr. 24, 1909
8	I	Nov. 22, 1909–Mar. 3, 1910
9	J	Mar. 11–May 25, 1910
10	K–L	July 1, 1906–Apr. 25, 1907
11	1	Nov. 24, 1910–Mar. 20, 1911
12	2	Mar. 23–Apr. 23, 1911
13	3	Nov. 22, 1911–Mar. 5, 1912
14	4	Mar. 9–Apr. 2, 1912
15	5	Apr. 4–Apr. 7, 1912
16	6	Apr. 18–Apr. 29, 1912
17	7	Nov. 30, 1912–Jan. 28, 1913
18	8	Feb. 1–Mar. 11, 1913
19	9	Mar. 11–Mar. 24, 1913
20	10	Mar. 27–Apr. 3, 1913
21	11	Apr. 3–Apr. 13, 1913
22	12	Apr. 13–Apr. 17, 1913
23	13	Apr. 19–May 17, 1913
24	14	May 29–June 18, 1913
25	15	Nov. 25, 1913–Feb. 26, 1914
26	16	Mar. 7–Apr. 5, 1914
27	17–18	Apr. 6, 1914–Apr. 22, 1915
28	19–20	Aug. 13, 1915–June 18, 1919
29	21	June 3, 1919–May 1, 1921
30	22	July 13, 1921–June 30, 1923

Roll	Volumes	Dates
31	23	Mar. 1–Nov. 1, 1923
32	24	Nov. 1–June 30, 1924
33	25	July 1, 1924–June 30, 1925
34	26	July 1, 1928–Dec. 31, 1932
35	27	Jan. 1933–Mar. 1943

Providence, Rhode Island

Index to Passengers Arriving at Providence, RI, June 18, 1911–October 5, 1954. T518. 2 rolls.

Roll	Contents
1	Aabed–Pitochelli
2	Pizza–Zveruy

Book Indexes to Providence Passenger Lists, 1911–1934. T792. 15 rolls.

Roll	Dates
1	Dec. 13, 1911–Mar. 21, 1913
2	Apr. 18, 1913–Apr. 25, 1914
3	May 4, 1914–Apr. 2, 1916
4	July 8, 1916–June 17, 1920
5	July 1, 1920–Apr. 29, 1921
6	May 26, 1921–Nov. 28, 1921
7	Jan. 7, 1922–Aug. 1, 1923
8	Sept. 1, 1923–June 29, 1924
9	June 30, 1924–Sept. 12, 1925
10	Oct. 1, 1925–Dec. 18, 1926
11	Dec. 31, 1926–Mar. 13, 1928
12	Apr. 8, 1928–July 7, 1929
13	Aug. 9, 1929–Feb. 20, 1931
14	Apr. 2, 1931–Nov. 25, 1931
15	Jan. 6, 1932–June 26, 1934

Passenger Lists of Vessels Arriving at Providence, RI, 1911–1943. T1188. 49 rolls.

Roll	Volumes	Dates
1	1	June 17–Dec. 23, 1911
	2	Jan. 8–Apr. 16, 1912
2	3	May 8–July 27, 1912
3	4	Aug. 1–Dec. 31, 1912
4	5	Jan. 1–Mar. 31, 1913
	6	Apr. 1–May 30, 1913
5	7	June 1–July 30, 1913
	8	Aug. 1–Oct. 15, 1913
6	9	Oct. 16–Dec. 31, 1913
	10	Jan. 1–Mar. 31, 1914
7	11	Apr. 1–May 31, 1914
8	12	June 1–Aug. 31, 1914
	13	Sept. 1–Dec. 31, 1914
9	14	Jan. 8–Sept. 30, 1915
	15	Oct. 15, 1915–Mar. 3, 1916
10	16	Apr. 1–Apr. 30, 1916
11	17	Oct. 6, 1916–Apr. 30, 1917
12	18	May 1–Dec. 31, 1917
	19	June 1918–Nov. 1919
13	20	Dec. 1919–Mar. 1920
14	21	Apr. 1–June 15, 1920
	22	June 16–July 15, 1920
15	23	July 16–Aug. 31, 1920
16	24	Sept. 1–Oct. 31, 1920
	25	Nov. 22–Dec. 31, 1920
17	26	Jan. 1–Mar. 31, 1921
	27	Apr. 2–Apr. 29, 1921

Roll	Volumes	Dates
18	28	May 30–June 30, 1921
	29	July 11–Aug. 27, 1921
19	30	Sept.–Dec. 1921
	31	Jan. 1–Jan. 31, 1922
20	32	Aug. 1–Oct. 31, 1922
21	33	Nov. 1, 1922–June 30, 1923
22	34	July 1–Aug. 31, 1923
23	35	Sept. 5–Oct. 19, 1923
24	36	Nov. 1, 1923–Feb. 11, 1924
25	37	Mar. 3–May 31, 1924
26	38	June–Oct. 1924
27	39	Nov. 1924–Jan. 1925
	40	Feb.–Mar. 1925
28	41	May 7–June 25, 1925
29	42	Aug. 17–Oct. 20, 1925
30	43	Nov. 4, 1925–Feb. 13, 1926
31	44	Mar. 4–Apr. 30, 1926
32	45	May 6–July 31, 1926
	46	Aug. 4–Oct. 22, 1926
33	47	Nov. 10, 1926–Feb. 27, 1927
34	48	Mar. 28–May 27, 1927
34	49	May 30–July 30, 1927
	50	Aug. 9–Sept. 9, 1927
35	51	Oct. 2–Dec. 6, 1927
36	52	Jan. 1–Mar. 15, 1928
37	53	Apr. 8–June 23, 1928
38	54	July 8–Aug. 31, 1928
39	55	Sept. 12–Nov. 26, 1928
40	56	Dec. 11, 1928–Feb. 8, 1929
	57	Mar. 1–Apr. 24, 1929
41	58	May 4–July 25, 1929
42	59	Aug. 9–Sept. 15, 1929
43	60	Oct. 2–Nov. 26, 1929
	61	Dec. 1929–Mar. 1930
44	62	Apr.–June 1930
	63	July–Aug. 1930
45	64	Sept.–Oct. 1930
	65	Nov.–Dec. 1930
46	66	Jan.–Mar. 1931
	67	Apr. 1931
	68	May–June 1931
47	69	July–Sept. 1931
	70	Oct.–Nov. 1931
	71	Jan.–Mar. 1932
48	72	Apr.–Nov. 1932
	73	Feb.–Oct. 1933
	74	Jan. 1934–Jan. 1943

St. Albans, Vermont, District

★ Soundex Index to Canadian Border Entries through the St. Albans, VT, District, 1895–1924. M1461. 400 rolls. (Roll 218 not used). 16mm.

Roll	Contents
1	A-000 Aarne–A-160 Ivy Mary
2	A-160 Herbert–A-220 Teiji
3	A-220 Teiji–A-246 Golde
4	A-246 Gregoire–A-300 Maurice
5	A-300 May–A-350 Margaret
6	A-350 Margaret–A-400 Joseph
7	A-400 Joseph Goodwin–A-425 Catherine
8	A-425 Alexander Caustine–A-450 Catherine
9	A-450 Catherine–A-453 Rebecca
10	A-453 Robert–A-524 Albert
11	A-524 Albert–A-535 Luigi
12	A-535 Luigi–A-536 Elizabeth
13	A-536 Elizabeth–A-536 Juzef
14	A-536 Julius Alfred–A-536 William
15	A-536 William–A-623 Consalato
16	A-623 Boyd–A-650 Annie
17	A-650 Annie–A-656 Jean
18	A-656 Jean–B-150 Phileman
19	B-150 Philias–B-200 George
20	B-200 George–B-200 Zulma
21	B-200 Zaida–B-224 Vlodimir
22	B-224 Pietro–B-236 Herbert
23	B-236 Henry–B-246 Ovila
24	B-246 Nellie–B-253 Bernadette
25	B-253 Bernice–B-260 Edwin
26	B-260 Edwin Lartnop–B-260 Yvonne
27	B-260 Yvonne–B-300 Francesco
28	B-300 Francis–B-320 Stephen
29	B-320 Stephen–B-346 Josephine
30	B-346 Josephine Jette–B-356 Audrej
31	B-356 Audrzeq–B-400 Alfred H.
32	B-400 Alfred H.–B-400 Katherine H.M.
33	B-400 Kathleen–B-415 Paul
34	B-415 Paul–B-420 Marie Louise
35	B-420 Marie Louise–B-424 Johann
36	B-424 John–B-430 Ozias
37	B-430 Pasquale–B-450 Dan Blaney
38	B-450 E.J.–B-452 Jaui
39	B-452 Jean–B-456 Azarre
40	B-456 B.J. Bloomers–B-500 Iwan
41	B-500 J.A. James–B-520 Hyman
42	B-520 Ida–B-526 Fritz
43	B-526 Gabriel–B-532 Evelyn
44	B-532 Fajos–B-552 Lucile
45	B-552 Magdalena–B-600 John
46	B-600 John A.–B-615 Lynia
47	B-615 Maggie–B-620 Edit
48	B-620 Edith–B-620 Joseph
49	B-620 Joseph–B-620 Thomas
50	B-620 Thomas–B-622 Szaja J.
51	B-622 Taube–B-624 John Alfred
52	B-624 John Black–B-625 Uzenio
53	B-625 Valentino–B-626 Willard
54	B-626 William–B-630 Myrtle
55	B-630 Nahma–B-632 Rutheda
56	B-632 "S"–B-635 Burach
57	B-635 Calogero–B-636 Lydia
58	B-636 Mabel–B-646 Zenaide
59	B-650 "One"–B-650 Ezra A.
60	B-650 Mrs. F.–B-650 Leona M.
61	B-650 Leonard–B-650 Volney, M.
62	B-650 "W"–B-652 Henriette
63	B-652 Henry–B-653 Charles W.
64	B-653 Charley–B-654 Prosper
65	B-654 Rachel–B-650 Krumann
66	B-656 L. Leon–C-000 Lyn
67	C-000 "M"–C-130 Ewilda
68	C-130 Fanny–C-150 Duncan
69	C-150 E. Barton–C-160 Lysander
70	C-160 Mabel–C-200 Elja
71	C-200 Ella–C-200 Sara Grace
72	C-200 Sarah–C-232 Ivan Joseph
73	C-232 Jacob–C-245 Martha

Roll	Contents	Roll	Contents
74	C-245 Mary–C-256 Zuzanna	139	E-525 Hans–E-625 Eyvind
75	C-260 Miss–C-300 Joseph	140	E-625 "F"–F-146 Pietra
76	C-300 Joseph A.–C-336 Guiseppe	141	F-150 Alex–F-220 Justyna
77	C-340 Ada–C-362 Yonica	142	F-220 "K"–F-250 Otto
78	C-363 Ada–C-410 Myrtle	143	F-250 Pacific–F-320 Fredrich
79	C-410 Nado–C-420 Martus	144	F-320 Gaton–F-400 Zacharia
80	C-420 Mary–C-435 Alice	145	F-410 Aaron–F-430 Ewa
81	C-435 Alice–C-451 Giovannina	146	F-430 Fannie–F-450 Martin
82	C-451 Giovannina–C-455 Sarah	147	F-450 Mary–F-463 Iva
83	C-455 Sarah–C-462 Joe Robert	148	F-463 Jack–F-524 Czarue
84	C-462 John–C-500 Chum	149	F-524 Daniel–F-560 Winifred
85	C-500 Chun–C-500 Mariano	150	F-361 Eugen–F-620 Branislaw
86	C-500 Marie–C-500 Zoel	151	F-620 Caesidio–F-623 Emilia
87	C-510 "Mrs."–C-514 Izy	152	F-626 Emile–F-626 Clara
88	C-514 "J"–C-516 Kiva	153	F-626 Clarence–F-630 Symeon
89	C-516 LaPelle–C-520 Son Yin	154	F-630 Takka–F-636 Croce
90	C-520 Song–C-534 Pramono	155	F-636 Daginar–F-651 Winnered
91	C-534 Dre–C-552 Alfred W.	156	F-652 "Miss"–F-652 Toiles
92	C-552 Alice–C-563 Brother	157	F-652 Tom–F-656 Martha
93	C-563 C.G.–C-600 Fililpo	158	F-656 Mary–G-120 Yan
94	C-600 Frances–C-612 Zofia	159	G-121 Aleksei–G-160 Bvail
95	C-613 "Mrs."–C-616 Jno Frances	160	G-160 C.F.–G-221 Stoian
96	C-616 Joseph–C-620 Rodney W.	161	G-222 Atonas–G-260 Cyril
97	C-620 Roland–C-623 Izzy	162	G-250 Daisy–G-260 Bruno
98	C-623 J.Barret–C-625 Ella Maud	163	G-260 C.A.–G-320 Josefa
99	C-625 Ellen–C-631 William	164	G-320 Joseph–G-350 Guy
100	C-632 "Miss"–C-636 Gwendoline	165	G-350 Hajke–G-360 Martha
101	C-636 H. Adams–C-642 Ann Mackey	166	G-360 Mary–G-410 Iza
102	C-642 Anna–C-650 Agathe-Addy	167	G-410 Jacob–G-420 Dolly
103	C-650 Antonio–C-652 Dmytro	168	G-420 Domenico–G-426 Bune
104	C-652 Domenico–C-656 Exilda	169	G-426 Caroline–G-431 Morrin
105	C-656 Fabian–D-100 Annibale	170	G-431 Morris–G-435 Violet
106	D-100 Annie–D-120 Catharine E.	171	G-435 Walter–G-453 Martha
107	D-120 Catherine–D-120 Ozora	172	G-453 Mary–G-514 Blanche C.
108	D-120 P.V.–D-132 Davitti	173	G-514 Camillo–G-534 Guisseppe
109	D-132 Dawson–D-143 Zulma	174	G-534 Gladys–G-600 Frya
110	D-144 Aline–D-161 Peter	175	G-600 Georg–G-612 Antonette B.
111	D-161 Peter–D-200 John	176	G-612 Anton–G-615 Andres
112	D-200 John–D-221 Zalmen	177	G-615 Andrew–G-620 Jane M.M.
113	D-222 Adriana–D-235 Oren	178	G-620 Janet–G-623 Kunez
114	D-235 Padre–D-246 Morris	179	G-623 Lars O.–G-630 Francziszek
115	D-246 Napolean–D-250 Luigi	180	G-630 Frank–G-635 James
116	D-251 M.Louis–D-260 Zotique	181	G-635 James A.–G-650 Annie
117	D-261 A. Margaretee–D-266 Victor	182	G-650 Annie C.–G-651 Sara
118	D-300 Ditta–D-352 Cila	183	G-651 Sara–G-655 Anne M.
119	D-352 Dalrymple–D-400 Qwenie	184	G-655 Annie–H-100 Cyrus M.
120	D-400 "R"–D-424 Kennith	185	H-100 Daniel–H-161 Jacob B.
121	D-424 Laura–D-455 Boruch	186	H-161 Johanna–H-200 Myrtle E.
122	D-455 Carl–D-500 James	187	H-200 Hayashi N.–H-235 Hyman
123	D-500 James–D-514 Zmis	188	H-235 Ida–H-252 Hy. G.
124	D-515 Ada M.–D-520 Dong Shi Kuing	189	H-252 I.J.–H-310 Hilda
125	D-520 Shirley–D-526 Frida	190	H-310 Josepha–H-350 Myrtle
126	D-526 Gabriel–D-541 Everett	191	H-350 Mary–H-400 Leroy D.
127	D-541 Federizo–D-522 Volpe	192	H-400 Leslie–H-425 Anna
128	D-552 Waleria–D-566 Leanordi	193	H-425 Anna–H-452 John
129	D-600 Thos.–D-616 Wladyslaw	194	H-452 John A.–H-513 Kristiana
130	D-620 Mrs. Samuel–D-625 Izzy	195	H-513 Latham Alex–H-525 Cyril S.
131	D-625 J.C.–D-650 Muriel	196	H-525 "D"–H-534 Evangeline A.
132	D-650 Napoleon–E-130 William	197	H-534 F.G.–H-543 Fredricka
133	E-131 Clara–E-210 Ivar	198	H-543 Gail–H-600 Cyril T.
134	E-210 Jacob–E-250 Johann	199	H-449 D. M.–H-620 Mary Getrude
135	E-250 John–E-350 Louise	200	H-620 Mary J.–H-630 Eloise
136	E-350 Mabel–E-420 Hyman	201	H-630 Elsie–H-636 Dorothy A.
137	E-450 I.W.–E-452 Bertran	202	H-636 Earl–I-125 William
138	E-452 Carl–E-525 Gustav	203	I-126 Hija–I-460 Winnie

Roll	Contents
204	I-461 Neno–J-100 Gustav
205	J-100 Hannah–J-212 Louie
206	J-212 Louis–J-255 Juho
207	J-255 Julio–J-520 David A.
208	J-520 David B.–J-520 William
209	J-520 William A.–J-525 Carl G.
210	J-525 Carl H.–J-525 Johan
211	J-525 Johan–J-525 Sarah G.
212	J-525 Sarah J.–J-635 Alice J.
213	J-635 Alma–K-142 Zuzanna
214	K-143 "A"–K-200 Stephen
215	K-200 Steve–K-245 Zalmen
216	K-246 Abel–K-320 Ben
217	K-320 Benjamin–K-400 Heinrich
218	roll no. 218 not used
219	K-400 Helen–K-421 Lars M.
220	K-421 Lojze–K-453 Pawla
221	K-453 Peter–K-510 Jakob J.
222	K-510 James–K-521 Gustav V.
223	K-521 Guy–K-532 Hilmar
224	K-532 Hilmar–K-600 Herbert
225	K-600 Herman–K-620 Willi D.
226	K-620 William–K-626 Philip
227	K-626 William–K-652 Shlome
228	K-652 Sidor–L-000 Kik
229	L-000 Kim–L-000 Patrizia T.
230	L-000 Patrick–L-000 Sara
231	L-000 Sarah–L-130 Emanuel
232	L-130 Emile–L-145 Marita
233	L-145 Mary–L-155 Pinkel
234	L-155 Philip–L-162 Joseph L.
235	L-162 Joseph A.–L-200 Fun Hon
236	L-200 Fred–L-220 Albany
237	L-220 Albert–L-240 Andrea
238	L-240 Andrew–L-252 Jaywood
239	L-252 Jean–L-263 Fredrick
240	L-263 Fredrico–L-325 Axel
241	L-325 Baltaser–L-363 Yvonne
242	L-364 Adelle–L-500 Into-N.
243	L-500 Irene–L-516 Nichola
244	L-516 Nicholas–L-520 Thloon
*245	L-523 Isabella–L-530 Franz-Alex (This roll is of very poor quality. Much of the information is illegible.)
246	L-530 Fred–L-535 Kalle
247	L-535 Kaol–L-562 Armas
248	L-562 Arthur–L-625 Carl
249	L-625 Carl–L-653 Fritz
250	L-653 Genevieve–M-200 Antonio
251	M-200 Antonio P.–M-200 Mose Pasqual
252	M-200 Moses–M-216 Ambrose
253	M-216 Amelia–M-222 Justin
254	M-222 "K"–M-234 Voicak
255	M-234 W.D.–M-235 Martina
256	M-235 Mary–M-240 Keith
257	M-240 Kenneth–M-242 Peter O.
258	M-242 Peter S.–M-245 Fortunato
259	M-245 Frances–M-250 Danechi
260	M-250 Daniel–M-252 Catherine
261	M-252 Catherine A.–M-253 Forbes J.
262	M-253 Frances–M-255 Allison
263	M-255 Alma–M-260 Joseph
264	M-260 Joseph A.–M-263 Margaret
265	M-263 Margaret A.–M-320 Chanaje
266	M-320 Charles–M-325 Alfons
267	M-325 Alfred–M-360 Jan
268	M-360 Jane–M-420 Pattie
269	M-420 Paul–M-450 Arsene
270	M-450 Arthur–M-460 Augoton
271	M-460 August–M-463 Slyvestro
272	M-463 Thelma D.–M-522 Anita
273	M-522 Anna–M-532 Wildred
274	M-532 William–M-563 Helen L.
275	M-563 Hermance–M-600 Joseph P.
276	M-600 Joseph R.–M-610 Theresa
277	M-610 Thos–M-620 Milroy
278	M-620 Milton–M-624 Betty R.
279	M-624 Beulah–M-625 Minerva
280	M-625 Minnie–M-634 Paul
281	M-634 Paul B.–M-635 Rosalie
282	M-635 Rosanna–M-650 Petra
283	M-650 Petro–N-143 William O.
284	N-144 Raefaelo–N-320 Josefa
285	N-220 Joseph–N-245 Hilda
286	N-245 Hrye–N-325 Josef
287	N-325 Koupel–N-425 Dorothea
288	N-425 Dorothy–N-500 Alice M.
289	N-500 Alma–N-630 Angus
290	N-630 Anna–O-165 Eva
291	O-165 Evelyn–O-242 Izaja
292	O-242 James–O-410 Walenty
293	O-412 Aasi–O-425 Ole
294	O-425 Ole A.–O-520 Lyle H.
295	O-520 "M"–O-625 Yeta
296	O-653 Anna–P-162 Zugniard
297	P-163 Abrane–P-320 Antoniette
298	P-230 Antonio–P-250 Viltorio
299	P-250 Walter–P-320 Rocco
300	P-320 Roger F.–P-360 Slyvia
301	P-360 Tahuo–P-362 John R.
302	P-362 John S.–P-400 Frank
303	P-400 Frank B.–P-420 Anezaras
304	P-420 Andrea–P-430 Emily
305	P-430 Emma–P-451 William J.
306	P-452 Paulhaus–P-500 Jakim
307	P-500 James–P-535 Josef
308	P-535 Joseph–P-612 Dan
309	P-612 Dan–P-620 Ruwen
310	P-620 Sadie–P-625 Gust M.
311	P-625 Gustaf–P-630 Paul Ernest
312	P-630 Pauline–P-643 Yvonne
313	P-644 Onhi–Q-142 Mile
314	Q-145 Albert–R-000 Lucienne
315	R-000 Lucy–R-134 Donat
316	R-134 Dorilda–R-152 Willard
317	R-152 William–R-163 Rial
318	R-163 Richard–R-200 Hugh
319	R-200 Hugh A.–R-214 Ben
320	R-214 Bernard–R-240 Jalmari
321	R-240 James–R-252 Franjo
322	R-252 Frank–R-263 Andree
323	R-263 Andrew–R-300 Jan
324	R-300 Jane–R-324 Douglas H.
325	R-324 Ehm–R-352 Gudrun
326	R-352 Hanna–R-430 Leonidas
327	R-430 Liborio–R-520 Eva
328	R-520 Eva–R-526 Kurt Horst
329	R-526 Lavis–R-536 Mike
330	R-536 Mildred–S-000 Alice M.
331	S-000 Alice W.–S-120 Isaek

Roll	Contents
332	S-120 Israel–S-140 Zayda
333	S-141 Abram –S-155 Yrjo
334	S-156 Schaffer–S-163 Henry
335	S-163 Herbert–S-212 Gunnar
336	S-212 Gunnar–S-240 Pierina
337	S-240 Pietro–S-300 Annie
338	S-300 Annie A.–S-314 John
339	S-314 John–S-320 Ihel
340	S-320 Itzek–S-344 Ann
341	S-340 Anna–S-350 Solomon
342	S-350 Solomon–S-356 Gotfrid
343	S-356 Gottlieb–S-362 Zygmind
344	S-363 Statford–S-364 Loretta J.
345	S-364 Louis–S-400 Sanni
346	S-400 Sarah–S-420 Ava
347	S-420 Averski–S-432 Mike
348	S-432 Mike–S-455 Jakob
349	S-455 James–S-500 Willem
350	S-500 William–S-520 Karol
351	S-520 Karolina–S-525 Shone
352	S-525 Sidney O.–S-530 Ethel
353	S-530 Ethel–S-530 Madelin
354	S-530 Madeline–S-531 Kirsteus
355	S-531 Knuit K.–S-535 Ermete
356	S-535 Ernest–S-540 Carl
357	S-540 Carl–S-552 Kasimir
358	S-552 Kasimir–S-600 Dimitre
359	S-600 Dine–S-620 Emil
360	S-620 Emile–S-632 Fannie
361	S-632 Fanny–S-653 Zigmonti
362	S-654 Albert E.–T-143 Ovide
363	T-143 Ovidi–T-225 Arsene
364	T-225 Arsene–T-263 Joe
365	T-263 Johan B.–T-400 Jalmar
366	T-400 James–T-460 Henry Wilson
367	T-460 Herbert–T-512 Edith L.
368	T-512 Edith M.–T-520 George E.
369	T-520 George–T-525 Lemen
370	T-525 Lena–T-600 Willard Henry
371	T-600 William–T-623 Emily
372	T-623 Emma–T-640 Matteo
373	T-640 Matthew–T-653 Deborah
374	T-653 Della–U-423 Joseph
375	U-423 Klard Heydig–V-240 Janko
376	V-240 J.D.A.–V-410 Sevine
377	V-500 Shebe–V-513 Williamina
378	V-514 "Mr"–V-536 Flvie
379	V-536 Frances–V-645 William
380	V-646 Charles–W-162 Carl
381	W-162 Catherine–W-234 Johan
382	W-234 Johan A.–W-255 Schmiel
383	W-255 Sebastian–W-300 Hyosuke
384	W-300 Ian Rene G.–W-320 Marvin
385	W-320 Mary–W-340 Klyde
386	W-340 Konstontin–W-365 Joseph
387	W-365 Justine A.–W-420 Froma
388	W-420 G.S.–W-425 Albert
389	W-425 Albert C.–W-425 Roxa
390	W-425 Roy–W-435 Ernest
391	W-435 Ernest–W-452 Ivan
392	W-452 Ivan E.–W-510 William George
393	W-512 Adeline–W-532 Zirle
394	W-524 Aarot–W-600 Winfield Scott
395	W-600 Winnie–W-630 Merle
396	W-630 Michael–Y-000 Myrtle

Roll	Contents
397	Y-000 Nahman–Y-520 Agnes D.
398	Y-520 Agnes H.–Y-621 Yerko
399	Y-622 Addie–Z-310 Victoria
400	Z-312 Anton–Z-565 Yankel

★ **Alphabetical Index to Canadian Border Entries through Small Ports in Vermont, 1895–1924. M1462. 6 rolls. 16mm.**

This microfilm publication reproduces alphabetical indexes to records of arrivals through various small ports in Vermont. The records include permanent and temporary admissions on Record of Registry, on card manifests, or Primary Inspection Memoranda. Some have photographs of the alien.

Roll	Contents
	Admissions at Norton and Island Pond, VT
1	Aangeenbrug, Cornelius–Godin, Alphonse
2	Godin, Antonio–Zewalicz, Agatia
	Admissions at Beecher Falls, VT
3	Abas, Philmine–Young, Joseph
	Admissions at Highgate Springs, Swanton, Alburg, and Richford, VT
4	Abarie, Fred–Young, Ruth
	Entries and Departures through St. Albans and Canaan, VT
5	Abare, John–Farley, Annunciata
6	Farley, Joseph–Zuger, Rose

★ **Soundex Index to Entries into the St. Albans, VT, District through Canadian Pacific and Atlantic Ports 1924–1952. M1463. 98 rolls. 16mm.**

Roll	Contents
1	A-000 Alexander–A-352 Erna May
2	A-352 Ernest–A-536 Dorothy
3	A-536 Dorothy M.T.–B-135 Mary Ann D.
4	B-140 Adolf–B-242 Walter Siegbert
5	B-243 Abram I–B-300 Marguerite
6	B-300 Maria–B-400 Elizabeth L.
7	B-400 Elizabeth Jane–B-430 Marie Gratia
8	B-430 Marie Gratia–B-514 Gerald Joseph
9	B-514 James–B-614 Wilfred Michael
10	B-615 Adelard–B-625 James Harold
11	B-625 James Herbert–B-636 Anthony
12	B-636 Antoine–B-652 Howard
13	B-652 Howard–C-145 Yetta nee Whitta
14	C-146 Adolphe–C-250 Fabiola M.
15	C-250 Fannie–C-413 Janet N.
16	C-413 Jean–C-462 Ivy Christiana
17	C-462 J.A.–C-516 Kenneth H.
18	C-516 Laura–C-600 J.
19	C-600 J.C. Henri–C-625 Sadie M.
20	C-625 Samuel–C-652 Duncan R.
21	C-652 Earl Daniel–D-120 Regina
22	D-120 Reginald–D-225 Philamene
23	D-225 R. Armand–D-262 Jeanne
24	D-262 Jeanne–D-460 Evan
25	D-460 Felix–D-541 Yvette M.
26	D-542 Donalson–D-650 Elsie
27	D-650 Elzabeth–E-423 Arthur
28	E-423 Arthur H.–F-255 Andress
29	F-255 Angelo–F-460 Ivyrose
30	F-460 J. Damase–F-626 Catherine
31	F-626 Catherine–F-655 Zulema
32	F-656 Ferner–G-255 David
33	G-255 Delcia–G-400 Yvonne
34	F-410 Ada Jane–G-453 Anicet
35	F-453 Anna–G-614 Maria S.

Roll	Contents
36	G-614 Marie T.–G-650 Henry
37	G-650 Henry–H-123 Wilfred
38	H-125 A.M.–H-246 Zoa
39	H-250 Adda E.–H-400 Ederie L.
40	H-400 Edward–H-510 William
41	H-512 Anna–H-550 Zerila
42	H-551 Ellen–H-634 Earl W.
43	H-634 Earle V.–J-212 Ann
44	J-212 Ann–J-523 Harry
45	J-523 Harry A.–K-156 Xavor
46	K-163 Abram S.–K-450 Ilko
47	K-450 Ilse–K-564 Willis R.
48	K-565 Ernestina–L-100 Richard C.
49	L-100 Robert–L-145 Omer
50	L-145 Omer–L-200 Jan
51	L-200 Jane–L-260 Anna
52	L-260 Anna–L-416 Gemma
53	L-416 Gerard–L-524 John W.
54	L-524 Joseph–L-600 Yvonne
55	L-610 Agnes Elizabeth–M-200 Lavina
56	M-200 Lawrence–M-226 Alfred
57	M-226 Allan–M-235 Marian
58	M-235 Marie–M-243 Janie
59	M-243 Jean–M-250 Mike
60	M-250 Mildred–M-254 Lyle Tilton
61	M-254 Lyman–M-263 James O.
62	M-263 James P.–M-362 Walter
63	M-363 Charles–M-460 Helen Edith
64	M-460 Helen Elizabeth–M-560 Robertin
65	M-560 Robert (20)–M-620 Henry
66	M-620 Henry–M-630 Matilda
67	M-630 Maurice–M-654 Zofja Serejska
68	M-655 Merriman–N-361 Sidney L.
69	N-362 Alexander–O-220 Wilson
70	O-221 Joseph–O-600 Phyllis
71	O-600 Phyllis–P-230 Zepherin
72	P-232 Alexandros–P-365 Wasyl
73	P-366 Adrien–P-456 Dorothy
74	P-456 Edith–P-620 Joseph J. Paul
75	P-620 Joseph L.–P-652 Frank
76	P-652 Frederick–R-125 Zata
77	R-126 Marie Lucie Zelia–R-200 Josef
78	R-200 Joseph–R-263 Alban
79	R-263 Albenie–R-362 Zepherine
80	R-363 Emil Walter–R-562 Victor
81	R-563 Achille–S-163 John W.
82	S-163 Joseph–S-253 William
83	S-254 Fryma–S-350 Antonio
84	S-350 Archie–S-365 Siri
85	S-365 Sivert–S-500 Ne
86	S-500 Nellie–S-530 Linda Mae
87	S-530 Lionel–S-550 Anne Marie
88	S-550 Annie–S-652 Joseph
89	S-652 Jozef–T-400 Zella
90	T-410 Alice–T-552 Yvonne
91	T-553 Agnes–T-651 Rosaria N.
92	T-651 Rose–V-451 Jacqueline
93	V-451 James–W-230 George I.
94	W-230 George Leo–W-330 Winnifred Irene
95	W-334 Anne Rosamond–W-425 John Duff
96	W-425 John E.–W-526 Lloyd J.
97	W-526 Lloyd R.–Y-621 Zelman
98	Y-622 Anthony (Anton)–Z-660 Oscar

★ **Manifests of Passengers Arriving in the St. Albans, VT, District through Canadian Pacific and Atlantic Ports, 1895–1954. M1464. 640 rolls.**

Roll	Contents	Volume
1	Jan. 11, 1895, VANCOUVER–Oct. 25, 1896, SARDINIAN	
2	Oct. 28, 1896, LAKE HURON–Oct. 28, 1896, LAKE ONTARIO	
3	Aug. 12, 1898, LAURENTIAN–Apr. 13, 1899, GALLIA	
4	May 14, 1899, VANCOUVER–Oct. 1, 1899, VANCOUVER	
5	Oct. 2, 1899, BAVARIAN–Mar. 26, 1900, NUMIDIAN	
6	Mar. 27, 1900, LAKE SUPERIOR–July 8, 1900, CORINTHIAN	
7	July 12, 1900, LAKE HURON–Nov. 2, 1900, LAKE ONTARIO	
8	Nov. 4, 1900, CAMBROMAN–Apr. 30, 1901, ELDER DEMPSTER	
9	May 7, 1901, BUENOS AYREAN–July 20, 1901, TUNISIAN	
10	July 27, 1901, LAKE ONTARIO–Nov. 29, 1901, LAKE SUPERIOR	
11	Dec. 1, 1901, LAKE SUPERIOR–Mar. 31, 1902, LAKE SUPERIOR	
12	Mar. 15, 1902, LAKE ONTARIO–May 1902, MONTREAL MANIFEST	
13	May 2, 1902, MANCHESTER SHIPPER–July 24, 1902, LAKE CHAMPLAIN	
14	July 27, 1902, NUMIDIAN–Sept. 30, 1902, SICILIAN	
15	Oct. 2, 1902, LAKE CHAMPLAIN–Nov. 29, 1902, LAKE ERIE	
16	Dec. 6, 1902, NUMIDIAN–Feb. 24, 1903, PRETORIAN	
17	Mar. 1, 1903, CANADA–Apr. 25, 1903, ASSYRIA	
18	May 1, 1903, SYBERIAN–June 30, 1903, SICILIAN	
19	July 1, 1903, ADRIA–Aug. 29, 1903, MONTROSE	
20	Sept. 1, 1903, SARDINAIAN–Nov. 29, 1903, BAVARIAN	
21	Dec. 1, 1903, CAMBROMAN–Feb. 29, 1904, LAKE ERIE	
22	Mar. 4, 1904, CANADA–June 27, 1904, PRETORIAN	
23	July 2, 1904, IONIAN–Sept. 30, 1904, BAVARIAN	
24	Oct. 1, 1904, LAKE ERIE–Nov. 28, 1904, LAKE CHAMPLAIN	
25	Dec. 2, 1904, CANADA–Mar. 28, 1905, LAURENTIAN	
26	Apr. 1, 1905, VICTORIAN–Apr. 25, 1905, MONGOLIAN	
27	May 2, 1905, IONIAN–May 31, 1905, MONGOLIAN	
28	June 3, 1905, SARDINIAN–June 30, 1905, LAKE MANITOBA	
29	July 1, 1905, POMERANIAN–July 29, 1905, SARMAJIAN	
30	Aug. 2, 1905, BUENOS AYREAN–Aug. 29, 1905, KASTALIA	
31	Sept. 1, 1905, CANADA–Sept. 30, 1905, KENSINGTON	

Roll	Contents	Volume
32	Oct. 3, 1905, VICTORIAN–Oct. 27, 1905, OTTAWA	
33	Nov. 1, 1905, MONTROSE–Dec. 28, 1905, MONTREAL	
34	Jan. 1, 1906, SICILIAN–Feb. 25, 1906, LAKE CHAMPLAIN	
35	Feb. 27, 1906, CORINTHIAN–Apr. 24, 1906, PRETORIAN	
36	Apr. 30, 1906, PARISIEN–May 25, 1906, LAKE ERIE	
37	May 26, 1906, MOUNT TEMPLE–June 24, 1906, KENSINGTON	
38	June 26, 1906, SIBERIAN–July 23, 1906, MOUNT TEMPLE	
39	July 27, 1906, VIRGINIAN–Aug. 25, 1906, LAKE MANITOBA	
40	Aug. 27, 1906, MONTEZUMA–Sept. 25, 1906, MONGOLIAN	
41	Sept. 26, 1906, MONMOUTH–Oct. 23, 1906, MOANA	
42	Sept. 26, 1906, MONMOUTH–Oct. 23, 1906, MOANA	
43	Oct. 26, 1906, MOUNT TEMPLE–Nov. 23, 1906, MIOWERA	
44	Oct. 26, 1906, MOUNT TEMPLE–Nov. 23, 1906, MIOWERA	
45	Nov. 25, 1906, PARISIAN–Dec. 22, 1906, ATHENIAN	
46	Dec. 26, 1906, LAKE MICHIGAN–Jan. 23, 1907, NUMIDIAN	
47	Jan. 25, 1907, MONTEZUMA–Feb. 22, 1907, CORINTHIAN	
48	Feb. 25, 1907, VICTORIAN–Mar. 23, 1907, VICTORIAN	
49	Mar. 26, 1907, VANCOUVER–Apr. 24, 1907, MONTEAGLE	
50	Mar. 1907, BLACK ROCK, NY–Apr. 1907, SUMAS, WA	
51	Apr. 25, 1907, LAURENTIAN–May 24, 1907, CARTHAGINIAN	
52	May 1907, BORDER PORTS–May 1907, SUMAS, WA	
53	May 25, 1907, POMERANIAN–June 30, 1907, LAKE CHAMPLAIN	
54	June 1907, BLACK ROCK, NY–June 1907, SUMAS, WA	
55	July 3, 1907, MONTROSE–July 22, 1907, OGDENSBURG, NY	1-2
56	July 1907, PORT HURON, MI–July 1907, SUMAS, WA	3
57	July 26, 1907, ATLANTIC SEAPORTS– Aug. 24, 1907, OGDENSBURG, NY	
58	Aug. 1907, PORT HURON, MI–Aug. 1907, RICHFORD, VT	6
59	Aug. 26, 1907, ATLANTIC SEAPORTS– Sept. 24, 1907, VANCOUVER	7
60	Sept. 1907, ALBURG, VT–Sept. 1907, OGDENSBURG, NY	8
61	Sept. 1907, ST. ALBANS, VT	9
62	Oct. 1907, ST. ALBANS, VT–Oct. 24, 1907, NEWPORT, VT	10
63	Oct. 1907, ST. ALBANS, VT–Oct. 1907, SUMAS, WA	11-12
64	Oct. 25, 1907 ST. ALBANS. VT–Nov. 22, 1907, VANCOUVER	13

Roll	Contents	Volume
65	Nov. 1907, MONTREAL–Nov. 1907, ALBURG, VT	14
66	Nov. 1907, ST. ALBANS, VT–Nov. 1907, SUMAS, WA	15-16
67	Nov. 1907, ST. ALBANS, VT–Dec. 1907, PORTAL, ND	17-18
68	Dec. 1907, ST. ALBANS, VT–Jan. 1908, NEWPORT, VT	19-20
69	Jan. 1908, ST. ALBANS, VT–Feb. 1908, NEWPORT, VT	21-22
70	Feb. 1908, ST. ALBANS, VT–Mar. 1908, MORRISTOWN, NY	23-24
71	Mar. 1908, ST. ALBANS, VT–Mar. 1908, RICHFORD, VT	25
72	Apr. 1908, ST. ALBANS, VT–Apr. 24, 1908, MORRISTOWN, NY	26
73	Apr. 1908, ST. ALBANS, VT–May 7, 1908, VANCOUVER	27-28
74	May 1908, ST. ALBANS, VT–May 1908, SUMAS, WA	29-30
75	May 1908, ST. ALBANS, VT–June 1908, OGDENSBURG, NY	31–32
76	June 1908, ST. ALBANS, VT–July 25, 1908, VANCOUVER	33-34
77	July 1908, ST. ALBANS, VT–July 1908, SUMAS, WA	35-36
78	July 22, 1908, ST. ALBANS, VT–Aug. 1908, NIAGARA FALLS, NY	37-38
79	July 1908, ST. ALBANS, VT–Sept. 22, 1908, VICTORIA, BC	39-40
80	Sept. 1908, ST. ALBANS, VT–Sept. 24, 1908, NIAGARA FALLS, NY	41
81	Sept. 25, 1908, ST. ALBANS, VT–Oct. 24, 1908, DETROIT, MI	42-43
82	Oct. 1908, DULUTH, MN–Oct. 1908, MANITOBA	44
83	Oct. 1908, QUEBEC–Oct. 1908, SUMAS, WA	45
84	Oct. 25, 1908, QUEBEC–Nov. 21, 1908, EASPORT, ID	46
85	Nov. 1908, FORT FAIRFIELD, ME–Nov. 1909, PLUM COULEE, MB 47	
86	Nov. 27, 1908, NORTH DAKOTA–Dec. 24, 1908, ISLAND POND, VT	48-49
87	Dec. 1908, OLD TOWN, ME–Dec. 1908, SUMAS, WA	50-51
88	Jan. 17, 1909, ST. JOHN, NB–Jan. 23, 1909, MARCUS, WA	52
89	Jan. 1909, NO. STRATFORD, NH–Jan. 1909, PORTAL, ND	53
90	Jan. 27, 1909, ST. JOHN, NB–Feb. 23, 1909, MORDEN, MB	54
91	Feb. 1909, MARCUS, WA–Feb. 1909, SUMAS, WA	55
92	Feb. 25, 1909, HALIFAX, NS–Mar. 24, 1909, PORT HURON, MI	56-57
93	Mar. 25, 1909, PORTAL, ND–April 23, 1909, DULUTH, MN	58-59
94	Apr. 1909, EASTPORT, ME–Apr. 1909, PEMBINA, ND	60
95	Apr. 1909, PORTAL, ND–Apr. 1909, SUMAS, WA	61
96	Apr. 25, 1909, ST. JOHN, NB–May 23, 1909, BLACK ROCK, NY	62

Roll	Contents	Volume
97	May 1909, BLAINE, WA–May 1909, NECHE, ND	63
98	May 1909, OGDENSBURG, NY–May 1909, RICHFORD, VT	64
99	May 25, 1909, QUEBEC–June 24, 1909, NIAGARA FALLS, NY	65-66
100	June 25, 1909, NECHE, ND–July 24, 1909, VANCOUVER	67-68
101	July 1909, QUEBEC–July 1909, RICHFORD, VT	69-70
102	July 25, 1909, QUEBEC–Aug. 24, 1909, QUEBEC	71
103	Aug. 1909, VICTORIA, BC–Aug. 1909, NEWPORT, VT	72
104	Aug. 26, 1909, NIAGARA FALLS, NY–Sept. 25, 1909, QUEBEC	73-74
105	Sept. 13, 1909, QUEBEC–Sept. 24, 1909, VICTORIA, BC	75
106	Sept. 1909, QUEBEC–Sept. 1909, NEWPORT, VT	76
107	Sept. 24, 1909, NIAGARA FALLS, NY–Sept. 30, 1909, PORTAL, ND	77
108	Sept. 25, 1909, QUEBEC–Oct. 24, 1909, QUEBEC	78-79
109	Oct. 1909, MONTREAL–Oct. 1909, RICHFORD, VT	80-81
110	Oct. 23, 1909, QUEBEC–Nov. 23, 1909, MONTREAL	82-83
111	Nov. 1909, MALONE, NY–Nov. 1909, RICHFORD, VT	84-85
112	Nov. 26, 1909, ST. JOHN, NB–Dec. 21, 1909, DETROIT, MI	86
113	Dec. 1909, DULUTH, MN–Dec. 1909, NIAGARA FALL, NY	87
114	Dec. 1909, ST. ALBANS, VT–Dec. 1909, RICHFORD, VT	88
115	Dec. 25, 1909, ST. ALBANS, VT–Jan. 23, 1910, MONTREAL	89
116	Jan. 1910, ST. ALBANS, VT–Jan. 11, 1910, PORTAL, ND	90
117	Jan. 26, 1910, ST. ALBANS, VT–Feb. 24, 1910, MEGANTIC, QUEBEC	91
118	Feb. 1910, ST. ALBANS, VT–Feb. 1910, RICHFORD, VT	92
119	Feb. 25, 1910, ST. ALBANS, VT–Mar. 23, 1910, PORT HURON, MI	93-94
120	Mar. 1910, ST. ALBANS, VT–Mar. 1910, RICHFORD, VT	95
121	Mar. 1910, ST. ALBANS, VT–Apr. 1910, MEGANTIC, QUEBEC	96-97
122	Apr. 1910, ST. ALBANS, VT–Apr. 1910, MALONE, NY	98-99
123	Apr. 1910, ST. ALBANS, VT–May 1910, MEGANTIC, QUEBEC	100-101
124	May 1910, ST. ALBANS, VT–May 1910, PORT HURON, MI	102
125	May 1910, ST. ALBANS, VT–June 1910, HALIFAX	103-104
126	June 1910, ST. ALBANS, VT–June 1910, PEMBINA, ND	105-106
127	June 1910, ST. ALBANS, VT–July 17, 1910, QUEBEC	107-108
128	July 1910, ST. ALBANS, VT–July 1910, PEMBINA, ND	109-110

Roll	Contents	Volume
129	July 1910, ST. ALBANS, VT–Aug. 1910, QUEBEC	111-112
130	Aug. 1910, ST. ALBANS, VT–Aug. 24, 1910, DETROIT, MI	113
131	Aug. 1910, ST. ALBANS, VT–Aug. 1910, PORT HURON, MI	114
132	Aug. 1910, ST. ALBANS, VT–Aug. 25, 1910, QUEBEC	115-116
133	Sept. 1910, ST. ALBANS, VT–Sept. 1910, QUEBEC	117
134	Sept. 1910, ST. ALBANS, VT–Sept. 1910, PORT HURON, MI	118-119
135	Sept. 1910, ST. ALBANS, VT–Sept. 1910, MALONE, NY	120
136	Sept. 1910, ST. ALBANS, VT–Oct. 23, 1910, EASTPORT, ID	121-122
137	Oct. 1910, ST. ALBANS, VT–Oct. 1910, PORT HURON, MI	123
138	Oct. 1910, ST. ALBANS, VT–Oct. 1910, MALONE, NY	124
139	Oct. 1910, ST. ALBANS, VT–Nov. 1910, MONTREAL	125-126
140	Nov. 1910, ST. ALBANS, VT–Nov. 1910, MALONE, NY	127-128
141	Nov. 1910, ST. ALBANS, VT–Dec. 24, 1910, DETROIT, MI	129
142	Dec. 1910, ST. ALBANS, VT–Dec. 1910, OGDENSBURG, NY	130
143	Dec. 1910, ST. ALBANS, VT–Dec. 1910, MALONE, NY	131
144	Dec. 1910, ST. ALBANS, VT–Dec. 27, 1910, MONTREAL	132
145	Jan. 1911, ST. ALBANS, VT–Jan. 1911, MALONE, NY	133
146	Jan. 25, 1911, ST. ALBANS, VT–Feb. 21, 1911, MONTREAL	134
147	Feb. 1911, ST. ALBANS, VT–Feb. 26, 1911, CHARLOTTE, NY	135-136
148	Mar. 1911, ST. ALBANS, VT–Mar. 1911, MALONE, NY	137-138
149	Mar. 1911, ST. ALBANS, VT–Apr. 24, 1911, VICTORIA, BC	139
150	Apr. 1911, ST. ALBANS, VT–Apr. 1911, NIAGARA FALLS, NY	140
151	Apr. 1911, ST. ALBANS, VT–Apr. 1911, MALONE, NY	141
152	Apr. 27, 1911, ST. ALBANS, VT–May 24, 1911, VICTORIA, BC	142
153	May 1911, ST. ALBANS, VT–May 1911, NIAGARA FALLS, NY	143
154	May 1911, ST. ALBANS, VT–May 1911, MALONE, NY	144
155	May 1911, ST. ALBANS, VT–June 15, 1911, VICTORIA, BC	145
156	June 1911, ST. ALBANS, VT–June 1911, NIAGARA FALLS, NY	146
157	June 1911, ST. ALBANS, VT–June 1911, MALONE, NY	147
158	June 25, 1911, ST. ALBANS, VT–July 24, 1911, VANCOUVER, BC	148
159	July 1911, ST. ALBANS, VT–July 1911, NYAUDO, NY	149
160	July 1911, ST. ALBANS, VT–July 1911, VANCOUVER, BC	150

Roll	Contents	Volume
161	July 26, 1911, ST. ALBANS, VT–Aug. 20, 1911, QUEBEC	151
162	Aug. 1911, ST. ALBANS, VT–Aug. 1911, HOULTON, ME	152
163	Aug. 1911, ST. ALBANS, VT–Aug. 1911, VANCOUVER, BC	153-154
164	Sept. 1911, ST. ALBANS, VT–Sept. 1911, DETROIT, MI	155-156
165	Sept. 1911, ST. ALBANS, VT–Sept. 1911, PEMBINA, ND	157
166	Sept. 1911, ST. ALBANS, VT–Oct. 1911, MONTREAL	158-159
167	Oct. 1911, ST. ALBANS, VT–Oct. 1911, PORTAL, ND	160-161
168	Oct. 1911, ST. ALBANS, VT–Oct. 25, 1911, VANCOUVER, BC	162-163
169	Nov. 1911, ST ALBANS, VT–Nov. 1911, MONTREAL	164
170	Nov. 1911, ST. ALBANS, VT–Nov. 1911, VANCOUVER, BC	165-166
171	Nov. 25, 1911, ST. ALBANS, VT–Dec. 1911, PORTAL, ND	167-168
172	Dec. 1911, ST. ALBANS, VT–Dec. 1911, EASTPORT, ID	169-170
173	Jan. 1912, ST. ALBANS, VT–Jan. 1912, VANCOUVER, BC	171-172
174	Jan. 1912, ST. ALBANS, VT–Feb. 1912, PORTAL, ND	173-174
175	Feb. 1912, ST. ALBANS, VT–Mar. 1912, CALAIS, ME	175-176
176	Mar. 1912, ST. ALBANS, VT–Apr. 1912, VANCOUVER, BC	177-178
177	Apr. 1912, ST. ALBANS, VT–Apr. 1912, LOWELLTOWN, ME	179-180
178	Apr. 1912, ST. ALBANS, VT–Apr. 1912, PORTAL, ND	181
179	Apr. 1912, ST. ALBANS, VT–Apr. 1912, VANCOUVER, BC	182
180	May 1912, ST. ALBANS, VT–Apr. 1912, EASTPORT, ID	183-184
181	May 1912, ST. ALBANS, VT–May 1912, PORT HURON, MI	185
182	May 1912, ST. ALBANS, VT–June 1912, HALIFAX, NS	186-187
183	June 1912, ST. ALBANS, VT–June 24, 1912, DETROIT, MI	188
184	June 1912, ST. ALBANS, VT–June 1912, VANCOUVER, BC	189-190
185	July 1912, ST. ALBANS, VT–July 1912, HANNAH, ND	191-192
186	July 1912, ST. ALBANS, VT–July 1912, PORT HURON, MI	193
187	July 1912, ST. ALBANS, VT–July 28, 1912, QUEBEC	194-195
188	Aug. 1912, ST. ALBANS, VT–Aug. 1912, PORT HURON, MI	196-197
189	Aug. 1912, ST. ALBANS, VT–Aug. 1912, VANCOUVER, BC	198
190	Aug. 9, 1912, ST. ALBANS, VT–Aug. 9, 1912, VICTORIA, BC	199-200
191	Sept. 1912, ST. ALBANS, VT–Sept. 1912, MALONE, NY	201
192	Sept. 1912, ST. ALBANS, VT–Sept. 1912, VANCOUVER, BC	202-203
193	Sept. 1912, ST. ALBANS, VT–Oct. 1912, QUEBEC	204
194	Oct. 1912, ST. ALBANS, VT–Oct. 1912, MADAWASKA, ME	205
195	Oct. 1912, ST. ALBANS, VT–Oct. 1912, ROUSES POINT, NY	206
196	Oct. 1912, ST. ALBANS, VT–Oct. 1912, VANCOUVER, BC	207
197	Oct. 1912, ST. ALBANS, VT–Nov. 1912, HALIFAX, NS	208
198	Nov. 1912, ST. ALBANS, VT–Nov. 1912, MALONE, NY	209
199	Nov. 1912, ST. ALBANS, VT–Nov. 1912, RAINIER, MN	210
200	Nov. 1912, ST. ALBANS, VT–Dec. 1912, BUFFALO, NY	211-212
201	Dec. 1912, ST. ALBANS, VT–Dec. 1912, ST. CLAIR, MI	213-214
202	Dec. 1912, ST. ALBANS, VT–Dec. 1912, VANCOUVER, BC	215
203	Dec. 1912, ST. ALBANS, VT–Jan. 1913, OGDENSBURG, NY	216-217
204	Jan. 1913, ST. ALBANS, VT–Feb. 1913, CALAIS, ME	218-219
205	Feb. 1913, ST. ALBANS, VT–Feb. 1913, NECHE, ND	220
206	Feb. 1913, ST. ALBANS, VT–Mar. 1913, VICTORIA, BC	221-222
207	Mar. 1913, ST. ALBANS, VT–Mar. 1913, RANIER, MN	223-224
208	Mar. 1913, ST. ALBANS, VT–Mar. 1913, HALIFAX	225-226
209	Mar. 1913, ST. ALBANS, VT–Apr. 1913, MONTREAL	227-228
210	Apr. 1913, ST. ALBANS, VT–Apr. 1913, ST. JOHN, NB	229
211	Apr. 1913, ST. ALBANS, VT–May 1913, HALIFAX	230-231
212	May 1913, ST. ALBANS, VT–May 1913, QUEBEC	232
213	May 1913, ST. ALBANS, VT–May 1913, MONTREAL	233-234
214	May 1913, ST. ALBANS, VT–May 1913, ST. JOHN, NB	235
215	May 1913, ST. ALBANS, VT–June 1913, QUEBEC and MONTREAL	236-237
216	June 1913, ST. ALBANS, VT–June 1913, HALIFAX	238-239
217	June 1913, ST. ALBANS, VT–June 1913, EASTPORT, ME	240
218	June 1913, ST. ALBANS, VT–June 1913, ST. JOHN, NB	241-242
219	June 1913, ST. ALBANS, VT–July 1913, HALIFAX	243-244
220	July 1913, ST. ALBANS, VT–July 1913, QUEBEC	245
221	July 1913, ST. ALBANS, VT–July 1913, INTERNATIONAL FALLS, MN	246-247
222	July 1913, ST. ALBANS, VT–July 1913, SUMAS, WA	248-249
223	July 1913, ST. ALBANS, VT–Aug. 1913, QUEBEC	250-251
224	Aug. 1913, ST. ALBANS, VT–Aug. 1913, MONTREAL	252

Roll	Contents	Volume
225	Aug. 1913, ST. ALBANS, VT–Aug. 1913, NYANDO, NY	253-254
226	Aug. 1913, ST. ALBANS, VT–Aug. 1913, ST. ALBANS, VT	255
227	Aug. 1913, ST. ALBANS, VT–Sept. 1913, QUEBEC and MONTREAL	256-257
228	Sept. 1913, ST. ALBANS, VT–Sept. 1913, EASTPORT, ME	258-259
229	Sept. 1913, ST. ALBANS, VT–Sept. 1913, NYANDO, NY	260
230	Sept. 1913, ST. ALBANS, VT–Sept. 1913, ST. ALBANS, VT	261
231	Sept. 1913, ST. ALBANS, VT–Oct. 1913, HALIFAX	262-263
232	Oct. 1913, ST. ALBANS, VT–Oct. 1913, FERRY, WA	264-265
233	Oct. 1913, ST. ALBANS, VT–Oct. 1913, NIAGARA FALLS, NY	266
234	Oct. 1913, ST. ALBANS, VT–Oct. 1913, VANCOUVER, BC	267-268
235	Oct. 1913, ST. ALBANS, VT–Nov. 1913, MONTREAL	269-270
236	Nov. 1913, ST. ALBANS, VT–Nov. 1913, GATEWAY, MT	271
237	Nov. 1913, ST. ALBANS, VT–Nov. 1913, HALIFAX	272
238	Nov. 1913, ST. ALBANS, VT–Nov. 1913, ST. MARY, MI	273
239	Nov. 1913, ST. ALBANS, VT–Dec. 1913, ST. JOHN, NB	274-275
240	Dec. 1913, ST. ALBANS, VT–Dec. 1913, NIAGARA FALLS, NY	276-277
241	Dec. 1913, ST. ALBANS, VT–Dec. 1913, VANCOUVER, BC	278-279
242	Dec. 1913, ST. ALBANS, VT–Jan. 1914, DETROIT, MI	280
243	Jan. 1914, ST. ALBANS, VT–Jan. 1914, OROIVILLE, WA	281
244	Jan. 1914, ST. ALBANS, VT–Jan. 1914, VANCOUVER, BC	282
245	Feb. 1914, ST. ALBANS, VT–Feb. 1914, OROVILLE, WA	283-284
246	Feb. 1914, ST. ALBANS, VT–Feb. 1914, VANCOUVER, BC	285
247	Feb. 1914, ST. ALBANS, VT–Mar. 1914, MONTREAL	286-287
248	Mar. 1914, ST. ALBANS, VT–Mar. 1914, VANCOUVER, BC	288-289
249	Mar. 1914, ST. ALBANS, VT–Apr. 1914, CALAIS, ME	290-291
250	Apr. 1914, ST. ALBANS, VT–Apr. 1914, ST. JOHN, NB	292-293
251	Apr. 1914, ST. ALBANS, VT–May 1914, QUEBEC	294-295
252	May 1914, ST. ALBANS, VT–May 1914, MADAWASKA, ME	296-297
253	May 1914, ST. ALBANS, VT–May 1914, PORTAL, ND	298
254	May 1914, ST. ALBANS, VT–June 1914, QUEBEC and MONTREAL	299-300
255	June 1914, ST. ALBANS, VT–June 1914, MADAWASKA, ME	301-302
256	June 1914, ST. ALBANS, VT–June 1914, PORTAL, ND	303
257	June 1914, ST. ALBANS, VT–June 1914, QUEBEC	304-305
258	July 1914, ST. ALBANS, VT–July 1914, NEWPORT, VT	306-307
259	July 1914, ST. ALBANS, VT–July 1914, VANCOUVER, BC	308-309
260	July 1914, ST. ALBANS, VT–Aug. 1914, QUEBEC	310-311
261	Aug. 1914, ST. ALBANS, VT–Aug. 1914, FORT FAIRFIELD, ME	311-312
262	Aug. 1914, ST. ALBANS, VT–Aug. 1914, NIAGARA FALLS, NY	313
263	Aug. 1914, ST. ALBANS, VT–Aug. 1914, ST. JOHN, NB	314
264	Aug. 1914, ST. ALBANS, VT–Aug. 1914, VANCOUVER, BC	315
265	Aug. 1914, ST. ALBANS, VT–Sept. 1914, QUEBEC	316
266	Sept. 1914, ST. ALBANS, VT–Sept. 1914, LEWISTON, NY	317-318
267	Sept. 1914, ST. ALBANS, VT–Sept. 1914, NECHE, ND	319
268	Sept. 1914, ST. ALBANS, VT–Sept. 1914, VANCOUVER, BC	320-321
269	Oct. 1914, ST. ALBANS, VT–Oct. 1914, CLEVELAND, OH	322
270	Oct. 1914, ST. ALBANS, VT–Oct. 1914, NORTHGATE, ND	323-324
271	Oct. 1914, ST. ALBANS, VT–Oct. 1914, SWEET GRASS, MT	325
272	Oct. 1914, ST. ALBANS, VT–Oct. 24, 1914, VANCOUVER, BC	326
273	Oct. 1914, ST. ALBANS, VT–Nov. 1914, MARCUS, WA	327-328
274	Nov. 1914, ST. ALBANS, VT–Nov. 1914, VANCOUVER, BC	329-330
275	Nov. 1914, ST. ALBANS, VT–Dec. 1914, PORT HURON, MI 331-332	
276	Dec. 1914, ST. ALBANS, VT–Jan. 1915, INTERNATIONAL FALLS, MN	333-334
277	Jan. 1915, ST. ALBANS, VT–Jan. 1915, VANCOUVER, BC	335-336
278	Feb. 1915, ST. ALBANS, VT–Feb. 24, 1915, PEMBINA, ND	337-338
279	Feb. 1915, ST. ALBANS, VT–Mar. 1915, ISLAND POND, VT	339-340
280	Mar. 1915, ST. ALBANS, VT–Mar. 1915, VANCOUVER, BC	341-342
281	Apr. 1915, ST. ALBANS, VT–Apr. 1915, PORTHILL, ID	343-344
282	Apr. 1915, ST. ALBANS, VT–May 15, 1915, INTERNATIONAL FALLS, MN	345-346
283	May 15, 1915, ST. ALBANS, VT–May 24, 1915, WINNIPEG, MN	347-348
284	May 25, 1915, ST. ALBANS, VT–June 1915, PORTAL, ND	349-350
285	June 1915, ST. ALBANS, VT–July 1915, ISLAND POND, VT	351-352
286	July 1915, ST. ALBANS, VT–July 1915, VANCOUVER, BC	353-354
287	Aug. 1915, ST. ALBANS, VT–Aug. 1915, PEMBINA, ND	355-356
288	Aug. 1915, ST. ALBANS, VT–Aug. 1915, VANCOUVER, BC	357

Roll	Contents	Volume
289	June 26, 1915, ST. ALBANS, VT–Sept. 1915, INTERNATIONAL FALLS, MN	358
290	Sept. 1915, ST. ALBANS, VT–Sept. 1915, PORT HURON, MI	359
291	Sept. 1915, ST. ALBANS, VT–Sept. 1915, VANCOUVER, BC	360
292	Aug. 11, 1915, ST. ALBANS, VT–Oct. 1915, INTERNATIONAL FALLS, MN	361
293	Oct. 1915, ST. ALBANS, VT–Oct. 1915, PEMBENA, ND	362
294	Oct. 1915, ST. ALBANS, VT–Oct. 25, 1915, EASTPORT, ID	363-364
295	Nov. 1915, ST. ALBANS, VT–Nov. 1915, ST. JOHN, NB	365-366
296	Nov. 1915, ST. ALBANS, VT–Dec. 22, 1915, HANNAH, ND	367-368
297	Dec. 1915, ST. ALBANS, VT–Dec. 1915, PORT HURON, MI	369
298	Dec. 1915, ST. ALBANS, VT–Dec. 1915, VANCOUVER, BC	370
299	Dec. 26, 1915, ST. ALBANS, VT–Jan. 1916, OROVILLE, WA	371-372
300	Jan. 1916, ST. ALBANS, VT–Feb. 1916, HOULTON, ME	373-374
301	Feb. 1916, ST. ALBANS, VT–Feb. 1916, VANCOUVER, BC	375-376
302	Mar. 6, 1916, ST. ALBANS, VT–Mar. 1916, ISLAND POND, VT 377	
303	Mar. 1916, ST. ALBANS, VT–Mar. 24, 1916, PORT HURON, MI 378	
304	Mar. 24, 1916, ST. ALBANS, VT–Mar. 29, 1916, DULUTH, MN	379-380
305	Apr. 1916, ST. ALBANS, VT–Apr. 1916, ST. CLAIR, MI	381-382
306	Apr. 1916, ST. ALBANS, VT–Apr. 1916, VANCOUVER, BC	383
307	May 1916, ST. ALBANS, VT–May 1916, MONTREAL	384-385
308	May 1916, ST. ALBANS, VT–May 1916, VANCOUVER, BC	386-387
309	June 1916, ST. ALBANS, VT–June 1916, MONTREAL	388-389
310	June 1916, ST. ALBANS, VT–June 1916, QUEBEC	390
311	June 1916, ST. ALBANS, VT–July 1916, CLEVELAND, OH	391-392
312	July 1916, ST. ALBANS, VT–July 1916, PORTAL, ND	393-394
313	July 1916, ST. ALBANS, VT–Aug. 1916, CLEVELAND, OH	395-396
314	Aug. 1916, ST. ALBANS, VT–Aug. 1916, MONTREAL	397
315	Aug. 1916, ST. ALBANS, VT–Aug. 1916, VANCOUVER, BC	398-399
316	Sept. 1916, ST. ALBANS, VT–Sept. 1916, MADAWASKA, ME	400-401
317	Sept. 1916, ST. ALBANS, VT–Sept. 1916, OROVILLE, WA	402
318	Sept. 1916, ST. ALBANS, VT–Sept. 1916, MONTREAL	403-404
319	Oct. 1916, ST. ALBANS, VT–Oct. 1916, DETROIT, MI	405
320	Oct. 1916, ST. ALBANS, VT–Oct. 1916, NYAUDO, NY	406

Roll	Contents	Volume
321	Oct. 1916, ST. ALBANS, VT–Oct. 24, 1916, ST. CLAIR, MI	407
322	Oct. 1916, ST. ALBANS, VT–Oct. 24, 1916, VANCOUVER, BC	408
323	Oct. 1916, ST. ALBANS, VT–Nov. 1916, MADAWASKA, ME	409-410
324	Nov. 1916, ST. ALBANS, VT–Nov. 1916, ST. JOHN, NB	411-412
325	Nov. 1916, ST. ALBANS, VT–Dec. 24, 1916, DETROIT, MI	413-414
326	Dec. 1916, ST. ALBANS, VT–Dec. 1916, ST. CLAIR, MI	415-416
327	Dec. 1916, ST. ALBANS, VT–Dec. 24, 1916, VANCOUVER, BC	417
328	Dec. 1916, ST. ALBANS, VT–Jan. 24, 1917, NIAGARA FALLS, NY	418-419
329	Jan. 1917, ST. ALBANS, VT–Jan. 1917, VANCOUVER, BC	420-421
330	Feb. 1917, ST. ALBANS, VT–Feb. 1917, MADAWASKA, ME	422
331	Feb. 1917, ST. ALBANS, VT–Feb. 1917, ROUSES POINT, NY	423
332	Feb. 1917, ST. ALBANS, VT–Mar. 1917, HANNAH, ND	424-425
333	Mar. 1917, ST. ALBANS, VT–Mar. 24, 1917, WINNIPEG, MN	426-427
334	Apr. 1917, ST. ALBANS, VT–Apr. 30, 1917, DETROIT, MI	428
335	Apr. 1917, ST. ALBANS, VT–Apr. 1917, ST. JOHN, NB	429-430
336	Apr. 1917, ST. ALBANS, VT–May 1917, NEWPORT, VT	431-432
337	May 1917, ST. ALBANS, VT–May 24, 1917, VANCOUVER, BC	433
338	June 1917, ST. ALBANS, VT–June 30, 1917, OROVILLE, WA	434-435
339	June 1917, ST. ALBANS, VT–June 1917, VANCOUVER, BC	436
340	July 1917, ST. ALBANS, VT–July 24, 1917, MONTREAL	437-438
341	Aug. 1917, ST. ALBANS, VT–Aug. 1917, MORRISTOWN, NY	439
342	Aug. 1917, ST. ALBANS, VT–Aug. 8, 1917, VANCOUVER, BC	440
343	Sept. 1917, ST. ALBANS, VT–Sept. 1917, YARMOUTH, NS	441-442
344	Nov. 1917, ST. ALBANS, VT–Nov. 1917, MONTREAL	433-444
345	Nov. 1917, ST. ALBANS, VT–Nov. 23, 1917, MONTREAL	445-446
346	Dec. 1917, ST. ALBANS, VT–Dec. 1917, YARMOUTH, NS	447-448
347	Jan. 1918, ST. ALBANS, VT–Jan. 24, 1918, MONTREAL	449-450
348	Jan. 1918, ST. ALBANS, VT–Feb. 1918, VANCOUVER, BC	451-452
349	Mar. 1918, ST. ALBANS, VT–Mar. 1918, WINNIPEG, MB	453-454
350	Apr. 1918, ST. ALBANS, VT–Apr. 1918, VANCOUVER, BC	455-456
351	May 1918, ST. ALBANS, VT–May 1918, VANCOUVER, BC	457-458
352	June 1918, ST. ALBANS, VT–June 1918, NYANDO, NY	459

Roll	Contents	Volume
353	June 1918, ST. ALBANS, VT–June 1918, MORRISTOWN, NY	460-461
354	July 1918, ST. ALBANS, VT–Aug. 1918, MORRISTOWN, NY	462-463
355	Aug. 1918, ST. ALBANS, VT–Sept. 1918, NEWPORT, VT	464-465
356	Sept. 1918, ST. ALBANS, VT–Oct. 1918, MORRISTOWN, NY	466-467
357	Oct. 1918, ST. ALBANS, VT–Nov. 1918, MORRISTOWN, NY	468-469
358	Nov. 1918, ST. ALBANS, VT–Dec. 1918, MORRISTOWN, NY	470-471
358a	Dec. 1918, ST. ALBANS, VT–Dec. 1918, NEWPORT, VT	472
359	Jan. 1919, ST. ALBANS, VT–Jan. 1919, MONTREAL	473
360	Jan. 1919, ST. ALBANS, VT–Jan. 1919, MONTREAL	474
361	Jan. 1919, ST. ALBANS, VT–Feb. 1919, MONTREAL	475
362	Feb. 1919, ST. ALBANS, VT–Mar. 1919, DETROIT, MI	476-477a
363	Mar. 1919, ST. ALBANS, VT–Mar. 1919, MONTREAL	477b
364	Mar. 1919, ST. ALBANS, VT–Mar. 1919, MONTREAL	478
365	Apr. 1919, ST. ALBANS, VT–Apr. 1919, HANNAH, ND	479
366	Apr. 1919, ST. ALBANS, VT–Apr. 1919, OGDENSBURG, NY	480
367	Apr. 1919, ST. ALBANS, VT–Apr. 1919, VANCOUVER, BC	481
368	May 1919, ST. ALBANS, VT–May 1919, OGDENSBURG, NY	482-483
369	May 1919, ST. ALBANS, VT–May 1919, MONTREAL	484
370	June 1919, ST. ALBANS, VT–June 1919, BUFFALO, NY	485
371	June 1919, ST. ALBANS, VT–June 1919, QUEBEC	486-487
372	June 1919, ST. ALBANS, VT–July 1919, DETROIT, MI	488-489
373	July 1919, ST. ALBANS, VT–July 1919, OGDENSBURG, NY	490
374	July 1919, ST. ALBANS, VT–July 1919, VANCOUVER, BC	491
375	Aug. 1919, ST. ALBANS, VT–Aug. 1919, MORRISTOWN, NY 492-493	
376	Aug. 1919, ST. ALBANS, VT–Aug. 1919, MONTREAL	494-495
377	Sept. 1919, ST. ALBANS, VT–Sept. 1919, CLEVELAND, OH	496
378	Sept. 1919, ST. ALBANS, VT–Sept. 1919, MONTREAL	497
379	Sept. 1919, ST. ALBANS, VT–Sept. 1919, RAINIER, MN	498
380	Sept. 1919, ST. ALBANS, VT–Oct. 1919, BUFFALO, NY	499-500
381	Oct. 1919, ST. ALBANS, VT–Oct. 1919, RAINIER, MN	501-502
382	Oct. 1919, ST. ALBANS, VT–Oct. 1919, VANCOUVER, BC	503
383	Nov. 1919, ST. ALBANS, VT–Nov. 1919, MADAWASKA, ME	504-505
384	Nov. 1919, ST. ALBANS, VT–Nov. 1919, PORT HURON, MI	506
385	Nov. 1919, ST. ALBANS, VT–Dec. 1919, CAPE VINCENT, NY	507-508
386	Dec. 1919, ST. ALBANS, VT–Dec. 1919, ST. JOHN, NB	509-510
387	Dec. 1919, ST. ALBANS, VT–Jan. 1920, HALIFAX, NS	511-512
388	Jan. 1920, ST. ALBANS, VT–Jan. 1920, MONTREAL	513-514
389	Feb. 1920, ST. ALBANS, VT–Feb. 1920, INTERNATIONAL FALLS, MN	514-515
390	Feb. 1920, ST. ALBANS, VT–Feb. 1920, MONTREAL	516-517
391	Mar. 1920, ST. ALBANS, VT–Mar. 1920, JACKMAN, ME	518
392	Mar. 1920, ST. ALBANS, VT–Mar. 1920, VANCOUVER, BC	519-520
393	Apr. 1920, ST. ALBANS, VT–Apr. 1920, MORRISTOWN, NY 521-522	
394	Apr. 1920, ST. ALBANS, VT–Apr. 1920, RAINIER, MN	523
395	Apr. 1920, ST. ALBANS, VT–May 1920, BUFFALO, NY	524-525
396	May 1920, ST. ALBANS, VT–May 1926, NIAGARA FALLS, NY	526-527
397	May 1920, ST. ALBANS, VT–May 1920, VANCOUVER, BC	528-529
398	June 1920, ST. ALBANS, VT–June 1920, MALONE, NY	530-531
399	June 1920, ST. ALBANS, VT–June 1920, SWANTON, VT	532-533
400	June 1920, ST. ALBANS, VT–July 1920, LOUISVILLE LANDING, NY	534-536
401	June 1920, ST. ALBANS, VT–July 19, 1920, VANCOUVER, BC	537-539
402	Aug. 1920, ST. ALBANS, VT–Aug. 1920, NYANDO, NY	540-542
403	Aug. 1920, ST. ALBANS, VT–Sept. 11, 1920, QUEBEC	543-545
404	Sept. 1920, ST. ALBANS, VT–Sept. 24, 1920, NIAGARA FALLS, NY	546-548
405	Sept. 1920, ST. ALBANS, VT–Sept. 24, 1920, MONTREAL	549-550
406	Sept. 1920, ST. ALBANS, VT–Sept. 24, 1920, MADAWASKA ME	551-552
407	Sept. 1920, ST. ALBANS, VT–Oct. 1920, MONTREAL	553-554
408	Oct. 25, 1920, ST. ALBANS, VT–Nov. 16, 1920, QUEBEC	555
409	Nov. 2, 1920, ST. ALBANS, VT–Nov. 1920, NEWPORT, VT	556-557
410	Nov. 1920, ST. ALBANS, VT–Nov. 1920, MONTREAL	558-559
411	Dec. 1920, ST. ALBANS, VT–Nov. 24, 1920, CAPE VINCENT, NY	560-561
412	Dec. 1920, ST. ALBANS, VT–Dec. 1920, ST. JOHN, NB	562-563
413	Dec. 1920, ST. ALBANS, VT–Jan. 24, 1921, ST. JOHN, NB	564-565
414	Jan. 1921, ST. ALBANS, VT–Jan. 1921, MONTREAL	566-567
415	Feb. 1921, ST. ALBANS, VT–Feb 24, 1921, NIAGARA FALLS, NY	568-569

Roll	Contents	Volume
416	Feb. 1921, ST. ALBANS, VT–Mar. 1921, FORT KENT, ME	570-571
417	Mar. 1921, ST. ALBANS, VT–Feb. 26, 1921, MONTREAL	572-573
418	Apr. 1921, ST. ALBANS, VT–Apr. 1921, MONTREAL	574-575
419	Apr. 1921, ST. ALBANS, VT–Apr. 1921, MONTREAL	576-577
420	May 1921, ST. ALBANS, VT–May 1921, MONTREAL	578-579
421	May 1921, ST. ALBANS, VT–May 1921, MONTREAL	580-581
422	June 1921, ST. ALBANS, VT–June 1921, PORT HURON, MI	582-583
423	June 1921, ST. ALBANS, VT–July 1921, BEECHER FALLS, VT	584-585
424	July 1921, ST. ALBANS, VT–July 1921, YARMOUTH, NS	586-587
425	July 1921, ST. ALBANS, VT–Aug. 1921, PORTAL, ND	588-589
426	Aug. 1921, ST. ALBANS, VT–Sept. 24, 1921, FORT COVINGTON, NY	591-593
427	Sept. 1921, ST. ALBANS, VT–Sept. 1921, MONTREAL	594-595
428	Oct. 1921, ST. ALBANS, VT–Oct. 24, 1921, NIAGARA FALLS, NY	596-597
429	Oct. 1921, ST. ALBANS, VT–Nov. 16, 1921, QUEBEC	598-599
430	Nov. 1921, ST. ALBANS, VT–Nov. 1921, PORTAL, ND	600-601
431	Nov. 1921, ST. ALBANS, VT–Dec. 1921, OGDENSBURG, NY	602-604
432	Dec. 1921, ST. ALBANS, VT–Jan. 24, 1922, ROUSES POINT, NY	605-607
433	Jan. 1922, ST. ALBANS, VT–Feb. 24, 1922, CAPE VINCENT, NY	608-609
434	Feb. 1922, ST. ALBANS, VT–Mar. 24, 1922, FT. COVINGTON, NY	610-612
435	Mar. 1922, ST. ALBANS, VT–Oct. 3, 1921, VANCOUVER, BC	613-614
436	Apr. 1922, ST. ALBANS, VT–Apr. 1922, PORT HURON, MI 615-616	
437	Apr. 1922, ST. ALBANS, VT–May 15, 1922, QUEBEC	617-618
438	May 1922, ST. ALBANS, VT–May 1922, PORTAL, ND	619-620
439	May 1922, ST. ALBANS, VT–May 18, 1922, QUEBEC	621-622
440	June 1922, ST. ALBANS, VT–June 1922, ROCHESTER, NY	623-624
441	June 1922, ST. ALBANS, VT–July 23, 1922, QUEBEC	625-626
442	July 1922, ST. ALBANS, VT–July 24, 1922, ROUSES POINT, NY	627-628
443	July 1922, ST. ALBANS, VT–July 24, 1922, FORT COVINGTON, NY	629-631
444	Aug. 1922, ST. ALBANS, VT–June 22, 1922, VANCOUVER, BC	632-633
445	Sept. 1922, ST. ALBANS, VT–Sept. 9, 1922, QUEBEC	634-635
446	Sept. 1922, ST. ALBANS, VT–Sept. 1922, OGDENSBURG, NY	636-637
447	Sept. 1922, ST. ALBANS, VT–Oct. 13, 1922, QUEBEC	638-639
448	Sept. 1922, ST. ALBANS, VT–Oct. 1922, MORRISTOWN, NY	640-641
449	Sept. 1922, ST. ALBANS, VT–Sept. 1922, VANCOUVER, BC	642-643
450	Nov. 1922, ST. ALBANS, VT–Nov. 1922, EASTPORT, ME	644-645
451	Nov. 1922, ST. ALBANS, VT–Nov. 1922, ST. CLAIR, MI	646-647
452	Nov. 1922, ST. ALBANS, VT–Nov. 1922, CAPE VINCENT, NY	648-649
453	Dec. 1922, ST. ALBANS, VT–Dec. 1922, ST. JOHN, NB	650-651
454	Dec. 1922, ST. ALBANS, VT–Jan. 1923, CAPE VINCENT, NY	652-653
455	Jan. 1923, ST. ALBANS, VT–Jan. 1923, ST. JOHN, NB	654-655
456	Jan. 1923, ST. ALBANS, VT–Feb. 1923, DETROIT, MI	656-657
457	Feb. 1923, ST. ALBANS, VT–Feb. 1923, ST. JOHN, NB	658-659
458	Mar. 1923, ST. ALBANS, VT–Mar. 1923, JACKMAN, ME	660-661
459	Mar. 1923, ST. ALBANS, VT–Mar. 12, 1923, VANCOUVER, BC	662-663
460	Apr. 1923, ST. ALBANS, VT–Apr. 23, 1923, HALIFAX, NS	664
461	Apr. 1923, ST. ALBANS, VT–Apr. 24, 1923, DETROIT, MI	665
462	Apr. 1923, ST. ALBANS, VT–Apr. 24, 1923, FORT KENT, ME	666
463	Apr. 1923, ST. ALBANS, VT–Apr. 1923, RANIER, MN	667
464	Apr. 1923, ST. ALBANS, VT–May 13, 1923, QUEBEC	668-669
465	May 1923, ST. ALBANS, VT–May 24, 1923, DETROIT, MI	670-671
466	May 1923, ST. ALBANS, VT–May 24, 1923, PORT HURON, MI	672-673
467	May 1923, ST. ALBANS, VT–May 17, 1923, VICTORIA, BC	674-675
468	June 1923, ST. ALBANS, VT–June 1923, HANNAH, ND	676-677
469	June 1923, ST. ALBANS, VT–June 24, 1923, PORTAL, ND	678-679
470	June 1923, ST. ALBANS, VT–June 1923, VANCOUVER, BC	680
471	June 1923, ST. ALBANS, VT–Aug. 8, 1923, QUEBEC and MONTREAL	681-682
472	July 1923, ST. ALBANS, VT–July 19, 1923, FT. COVINGTON, NY	683-684
473	July 1923, ST. ALBANS, VT–July 1923, ST. ALBANS, VT 685-686	
474	July 1923, ST. ALBANS, VT–July 28, 1923, QUEBEC and MONTREAL	687-688
475	Aug. 1923, ST. ALBANS, VT–Aug., 24, 1923, DETROIT, MI	689-690
476	Aug. 1923, ST. ALBANS, VT–Aug. 24, 1923, PORTAL, ND	691-692
477	Aug. 1923, ST. ALBANS, VT–Aug. 14, 1923, VICTORIA, BC	693-694
478	Sept. 1923, ST. ALBANS, VT–Sept. 16, 1923, QUEBEC	695-696
479	Sept. 1923, ST. ALBANS, VT–Sept. 1923, HALIFAX, NS	697-698

Roll	Contents	Volume
480	Sept. 1923, ST. ALBANS, VT–Sept. 24, 1923, ST. JOHN, NB	699-700
481	Sept. 1923, ST. ALBANS, VT–Oct. 7, 1923, QUEBEC	701-702
482	Sept. 1923, ST. ALBANS, VT–Oct. 1923, CLEVELAND, OH	703-704
483	Sept. 1923, ST. ALBANS, VT–Oct. 1923, OGDENSBURG, NY	705-706
484	Sept. 1923, ST. ALBANS, VT–Oct. 1923, VANCEBORO, ME	707
485	Oct. 1923, ST. ALBANS, VT–Nov. 11, 1923, QUEBEC	708-709
486	Nov. 1923, ST. ALBANS, VT–Nov. 24, 1923, FT. COVINGTON, NY	710-711
487	Nov. 1923, ST. ALBANS, VT–Nov. 1923, MONTREAL	712
488	Nov. 1923, ST. ALBANS, VT–Nov. 1923, VANCEBORO, ME	713-714
489	Nov. 1923, ST. ALBANS, VT–Dec. 24, 1923, CLEVELAND, OH	715-716
490	Dec. 1923, ST. ALBANS, VT–Dec. 24, 1923, PORT HURON, MI	717-718
491	Dec. 1923, ST. ALBANS, VT–Dec. 24, 1923, WARROAD, MN	719
492	Dec. 1923, ST. ALBANS, VT–Dec. 14, 1923, VICTORIA, BC	720
493	Jan. 1924, ST. ALBANS, VT–Jan. 1924, MORRISTOWN, NY	721-722
494	Jan. 1924, ST. ALBANS, VT–Jan. 24, 1924, ST. CLAIR, MI	723
495	Jan. 1924, ST. ALBANS, VT–Feb. 1924, CLEVELAND, OH	724-725
496	Feb. 1924, ST. ALBANS, VT–Feb. 1924, NYANDO, NY	726-727
497	Feb. 1924, ST. ALBANS, VT–Feb. 1924, NEW BRUNSWICK	728-729
498	Mar. 1924, ST. ALBANS, VT–Mar. 1924, MADAWASKA, ME	730-731
499	Mar. 1924, ST. ALBANS, VT–Mar. 1924, RICHFORD, VT	732
500	Mar. 1924, ST. ALBANS, VT–Apr. 1924, CLEVELAND, OH	733-734
501	Apr. 1924, ST. ALBANS, VT–Apr. 24, 1924, ISLAND POND, VT	735
502	Apr. 1924, ST. ALBANS, VT–Apr. 24, 1924, ST. JOHN, NB	736-737
503	Apr. 1924, ST. ALBANS, VT–Mar. 31, 1924, VANCOUVER, BC	738
504	Apr. 1924, ST. ALBANS, VT–May 24, 1924, DETROIT, MI	739-740
505	May 1924, ST. ALBANS, VT–May 1924, PORTAL, ND	741-742
506	May 1924, ST. ALBANS, VT–Apr. 21, 1924, VANCOUVER, BC	734-735
507	June 1924, ST. ALBANS, VT–June 24, 1924, DETROIT, MI	745-746
508	June 1924, ST. ALBANS, VT–June 24, 1924, RANIER, MN	747-748
509	June 1924, ST. ALBANS, VT–June 24, 1924, WINNIPEG, MB	749
510	June 1924, ST. ALBANS, VT–Aug. 1924, QUEBEC	750-752
511	Aug. 1924, ST. ALBANS, VT–Sept. 13, 1924, QUEBEC	753-755

Roll	Contents	Volume
512	Sept. 1924, ST. ALBANS, VT–Oct. 3, 1924, QUEBEC	756-757
513	Oct. 1924, ST. ALBANS, VT–Nov. 16, 1924, QUEBEC	758-760
514	Dec. 1924, ST. ALBANS, VT–Feb. 24, 1925, MONTREAL	761-763
515	Mar. 1925, ST. ALBANS, VT–Apr. 6, 1925, VANCOUVER, BC	764-765
516	Apr. 1925, ST. ALBANS, VT–May 1925, ST. JOHN, NB	766a-766b
517	May 1925, ST. ALBANS, VT–July 16, 1925, VANCOUVER, BC	767-768
518	July 1925, ST. ALBANS, VT–Sept. 4, 1925, QUEBEC	769-771
519	Sept. 6, 1925, ST. ALBANS, VT–Oct. 4, 1925, QUEBEC and MONTREAL	772-774
520	Oct. 5, 1925, ST. ALBANS, VT–Nov. 14, 1925, VANCOUVER, BC	775-776
521	Nov. 25, 1925, ST. ALBANS, VT–Mar. 24, 1926, MONTREAL	777-779
522	Apr. 1926, ST. ALBANS, VT–May 10, 1926, QUEBEC	780-781
523	May 1926, ST. ALBANS, VT–June 19, 1926, QUEBEC	782a-783
524	June 1926, ST. ALBANS, VT–July 15, 1926, HALIFAX, NS	784
525	July 1926, ST. ALBANS, VT–Aug. 12, 1926, HALIFAX, NS	785-786
526	Aug. 1926, ST. ALBANS, VT–Sept. 11, 1926, QUEBEC	787-788
527	Sept. 1926, ST. ALBANS, VT–Oct. 16, 1926, HALIFAX, NS	789-790
528	Oct. 1926, ST. ALBANS, VT–Oct. 1, 1926, QUEBEC	791-792
529	Oct. 1926, ST. ALBANS, VT–Nov. 1926, MONTREAL	793
530	Nov. 1926, ST. ALBANS, VT–Feb. 1927, ST. JOHN, NB	794
531	Feb. 1927, ST. ALBANS, VT–May 8, 1927, QUEBEC	795a-796
532	May 7, 1927–June 28, 1927	797-798
533	July 1, 1927–Aug. 6, 1927	799-800
534	Aug. 6, 1927–Aug. 21, 1927	801-802
535	Sept. 22, 1927–Sept. 23, 1927	803-804
536	Sept. 24, 1927–Oct. 23, 1927	805-806
537	Oct. 23, 1927–Dec. 30, 1927	807-808
538	Dec. 31, 1927–Feb. 29, 1928	809
539	Mar. 2, 1928–Apr. 29, 1928	810
540	Apr. 29, 1928–May 13, 1928	811
541	May 15, 1928–June 29, 1928	812-813
542	June 30, 1928–July 8, 1928	814
543	July 14, 1928–Aug. 10, 1928	815-816
544	Aug. 17, 1928–Aug. 25, 1928	817-818
545	Aug. 26, 1928–Sept. 9, 1928	819-820
546	Sept. 9, 1928–Sept. 22, 1928	821-822
547	Sept. 24, 1928–Oct. 20, 1928	823-824
548	Oct. 21, 1928–Nov. 5, 1928	825
549	Nov. 11, 1928–Dec. 8, 1928	826
550	Dec. 1928–Jan. 1929	827
551	Feb. 1929–Mar. 1929	828
552	Mar. 30, 1929–May 1929	829-830
553	May 21, 1929–June 29, 1929	831-832
554	June 29, 1929–July 28, 1929	833-834
555	July 1929–Aug. 1929	835-836
556	Aug. 11, 1929–Aug. 24, 1929	837-838

Roll	Contents	Volume
557	Aug. 24, 1929–Sept. 7, 1929	839-840
558	Sept. 7, 1929–Sept. 22, 1929	841-842
559	Sept. 22, 1929–Oct. 13, 1929	843-844
560	Oct. 13, 1929–Nov. 30, 1929	845-846
561	Dec. 11, 1929–Feb. 25, 1920	847-848
562	Mar. 1, 1930–Apr. 30, 1930	849-850
563	May 2, 1930–May 31, 1930	851
564	June 1, 1930–June 22, 1930	852
565	June 23, 1930–July 19, 1930	853
566	July 19, 1930–Aug. 2, 1930	854
567	Aug. 2, 1930–Aug. 26, 1930	855-856
568	Aug. 28, 1930–Sept. 12, 1930	857-858
569	Sept. 13, 1930–Sept. 29, 1930	859
570	Sept. 27, 1930–Oct. 12, 1930	860
571	Oct. 12, 1930–Nov. 21, 1930	861
572	Nov. 21, 1930–Mar. 28, 1931	862
573	Apr. 4, 1931–May 31, 1931	863
574	June 1, 1931–Aug. 9, 1931	864-865
575	Aug. 7, 1931–Aug. 31, 1931	866
576	Sept. 1, 1931–Oct. 23, 1931	867-868
577	Oct. 26, 1931–June 27, 1932	869-870
578	June 28, 1932–Sept. 6, 1932	871-872
579	Oct. 2, 1932–Nov. 24, 1932	873
580	Sept. 6, 1932–Sept. 30, 1932	874
581	Nov. 29, 1932–Oct. 6, 1933	875
582	Apr. 16, 1933–July 10, 1933	876
583	July 13, 1933–Aug. 31, 1933	877
584	Sept. 1, 1933–Oct. 29, 1933	878
585	Nov. 1, 1933–May 28, 1934	879
586	May 30, 1934–Sept. 1, 1934	880-881
587	Sept. 13, 1934–Apr. 29, 1935	882-883
588	May 1, 1935–Aug. 18, 1935	884-885
589	Aug. 22, 1935–Oct. 19, 1935	886-887
590	Oct. 20, 1935–June 30, 1936	888-889
591	July 2, 1936–Aug. 30, 1936	890-891
592	Sept. 2, 1936–Sept. 21, 1936	892
593	Sept. 24, 1936–May 18, 1937	893-894
594	May 20, 1937–July 18, 1937	895
595	July 18, 1937– Aug. 21, 1937	896
596	Aug.22, 1937–Sept. 9, 1937	897
597	Sept. 10, 1937–Sept. 29, 1937	898
598	Oct. 1, 1937–Nov. 19, 1937	899
599	Nov. 20, 1937–May 14, 1938	900
600	May 15, 1938–June 29, 1938	901
601	July 1, 1938–July 31, 1938	902
602	Aug. 3, 1938–Sept. 3, 1938	903
603	Sept. 4, 1938–Sept. 25, 1938	904
604	Sept. 26, 1938–Oct. 31, 1938	905
605	Nov. 1, 1938–Apr. 29, 1939	906
606	May 1, 1939–June 30, 1939	907
607	July 1, 1939–July 31, 1939	908
608	Aug. 1, 1939–Aug. 30, 1939	909
609	Sept. 2, 1939–Dec. 23, 1939	910
610	Jan. 6, 1940–Aug. 30, 1940	911
611	Sept. 6, 1940–Dec. 31, 1940	912
612	Jan. 2, 1941–June 27, 1941	913
613	July 2, 1941–Dec. 30, 1941	914
614	Jan. 1, 1942–Dec. 29, 1942	915-916
615	Jan. 10, 1943–Feb 16, 1944	917-918
616	Jan. 2, 1945–Sept. 29, 1945	919-920
617	Oct. 1, 1945–Dec. 31, 1945	921
618	Jan. 1, 1946–June 9, 1946 RMS MAURETANIA	
619	June 11, 1946–Jan. 2, 1947 RMS MANCHESTER PORTS	

Roll	Contents	Volume
620	Sept. 23, 1947–Sept. 23, 1946 RMS AQUITANIA*	
621	Jan. 10, 1947–May 3, 1947	
622	May 5, 1947–Oct. 6, 1947	
623	Oct. 6, 1947 SS CANADIAN CHALLENGER–June 13, 1948 MANCHESTER REGIMENT	
624	June 5, 1948 SS BEAVERBURN–Jan. 25, 1949 BEAVERFORD	
625	Jan. 26, 1949 SS EMPRESS OF FRANCE–Sept. 8, 1949 ASCANIA	
626	Sept. 8, 1949 SS IRISH PINE–Apr. 26, 1950 FLIGHT TEAL 2211/36	
627	Apr. 26, 1950 BOAC FLT BA601B/232–Sept. 4, 1950 SS EMPRESS OF FRANCE	
628	Sept. 4, 1950 BOAC FLT BA601/288–Feb. 13, 1951 SS THORSISLE	
629	Feb 13, 1951 AIR FRANCE FLT 015/12–Aug. 9, 1951 SS ASCANIA	
630	Aug. 9, 1951 LISMORIA–Nov. 20, 1951 CAIRNVALONIA	
631	Nov. 20, 1951 IRISH OAK–June 29, 1952 KLM FLT 654/154	
632	June 29, 1952 SS MANCHESTER SHIPPER–Sept. 15, 1952 EMPRESS OF FRANCE	
633	Sept. 15, 1952 AIR FRANCE FLT 005–Apr. 15, 1953 BOAC FLT 601/581	
634	Apr. 15, 1953 KLM FLT 649–Apr. 15, 1953 SS BASSANO	
635	Aug. 2, 1953 AIR FRANCE FLT 007–Sept. 2, 1953 SS BRITANNIC	
636	Oct. 2, 1953 SS AMN SALEN–Mar. 19, 1954 EMPRESS OF AUSTRALIA	
637	Mar. 18, 1954 KLM FLT 656–July 17, 1954 SS SAMARIA	
638	July 17, 1954 KLM FLT 656–Sept. 24, 1954 SS ATLANTIC	
639	Sept. 24, 1954 SS ZUIDERKRUIS–Nov. 30, 1954 TRANS ATLANTIC	

*dates are out of order

★ **Manifests of Passengers Arriving in the St. Albans, VT, District through Canadian Pacific Ports, 1929–49. M1465. 25 rolls.**

Roll	Contents
1	July 9, 1929, SS ARABIA MARU–Jan. 1, 1930 RMS NIAGARA
2	Jan. 3, 1930, RMS NIAGARA–July 17,1930, RMS AORANGI
3	July 17, 1930, RMS AORANGI–Feb. 26, 1931, RMS AORANGI
4	Feb. 26, 1931 RMS AORANGI–Aug. 5, 1931, EMPRESS OF JAPAN
5	Aug. 5, 1931, EMPRESS OF JAPAN–Feb. 22, 1932, EMPRESS OF ASIA
6	Feb. 22, 1932, EMPRESS OF ASIA–Aug. 12, 1932, RMS NIAGARA
7	Aug. 12, 1932 RMS NIAGARA–May 19, 1933, RMS NIAGARA
8	May 19, 1933, RMS NIAGARA–Dec. 19, 1933, EMPRESS OF JAPAN

Roll	Contents
9	Dec. 28, 1933, RMS NIAGARA–July 18, 1934, EMPRESS OF CANADA
10	July 18, 1934, EMPRESS OF CANADA–Mar. 25, 1935, EMPRESS OF RUSSIA
11	Mar. 25, 1935, EMPRESS OF RUSSIA–Aug. 12, 1935, EMPRESS OF ASIA
12	Aug. 12, 1935, HIYU MARU–Mar. 24, 1936, EMPRESS OF JAPAN
13	Apr. 6, 1935, EMPRESS OF ASIA–Aug. 7, 1936, RMS NIAGARA
14	Aug. 7, 1936, RMS NIAGARA–Sept. 12, 1936, EMPRESS OF RUSSIA
15	Dec. 12, 1936, EMPRESS OF RUSSIA–Apr. 9, 1937, RMS NIAGARA
16	Apr. 9, 1937, RMS NIAGARA–July 28, 1937, EMPRESS OF CANADA
17	July 28, 1937, EMPRESS OF CANADA–Nov. 17, 1937, EMPRESS OF CANADA
18	Nov. 17, 1937, EMPRESS OF CANADA–Apr. 20, 1938, EMPRESS OF JAPAN
19	Apr. 20, 1938, EMPRESS OF JAPAN–July 13, 1938, EMPRESS OF CANADA
20	July 13, 1938, EMPRESS OF CANADA–Oct. 21, 1938, RMS NIAGARA
21	Oct. 21, 1938, RMS NIAGARA–Apr. 4, 1939, EMPRESS OF JAPAN
22	Apr. 4, 1939, EMPRESS OF JAPAN–June 28, 1939, EMPRESS OF CANADA
23	June 28, 1939, EMPRESS OF CANADA–Sept. 23, 1939, RMS NIAGARA
24	Sept. 23, 1939, RMS NIAGARA–Aug. 1, 1940, RMS AORANGI
25	Aug. 4, 1940, RMS AORANGI–June 24, 1949, SS THOR I

San Francisco, California

★ **Indexes to Passenger Lists of Vessels Arriving at San Francisco, CA, 1893–1934. M1389. 28 rolls. 16mm.**

This microfilm publication reproduces three alphabetical card indexes to passenger arrival records for the port of San Francisco, May 1, 1893–May 9, 1934. The first 21 rolls reproduce the general index to passengers. The second alphabetical index on rolls 22–27, relates to individuals arriving from the Philippines, from Honolulu (September 30, 1902–June 12, 1907), and from Insular Possesions (May 28, 1907–October 28, 1911).

The records, which are arranged alphabetically by name of passenger, were extracted from the San Francisco passenger lists. Each entry provides the date of arrival and the vessel name. In the upper right hand corner of each index card there is a reference to the manifest number, the page number, and the line number on which the passenger's name appears. For example, 10383/15/23 refers to manifest number 10383, page 15, line 23.

These records were transferred to the National Archives on microfilm. Errors in arrangement and ommisions cannot be corrected. Defective images, which were identified when the records were filmed, were microfilmed again, and the corrections were spliced on the beginning of each roll as retakes.

Roll	Contents
1	Aaga, Kichiemon–Baribeau, Theodore
2	Barich, Christ.–Campbell, Charles
3	Campbell, Charles G.–Cross, William Joseph
4	Crossan, James–Fishel, C.J.
5	Fisher, Mr.–Gonzalez, Luz De
6	Gonzales, Micaela–Herbertz, Rudolph
7	Herbertz, Rudolph–Inouye, Sashichi
8	Inouye, Sawa–Kashiwaga, T.
9	Kashiwagi, Chiaki–Kozo, Osumi
10	Kozono, Hatsutaro–MacKenzie, Vera
11	MacKenzie, Vera–Melina, Carlos E.
12	Melin, Cecile–Muramato, Chiyochi
13	Maramatsu, Asaichi–Nomura, Kanbei
14	Nomura, Kane–Parkenson, Richard
15	Parker, Miss–Robins, Richard William
16	Robinson, Mrs. A.–Scott, Eliza
17	Scott, Elizabeth–Stephenson, Magnus L.
18	Stephenson, A.–Tatehara, Toki
19	Tatekhi, Juichi–Valkenburg, Samuel
20	Valla, Honorene–Wocke, Rudolph
21	Worker, Wilhelm–Zylva, Susan E.
22	Aalberg, Master J.–Cormick, C.H.
23	Corn, Dorothy–Huruta
24	Harvey, Dr.–Marh, Young Choon
25	Mari, Felipe–Resurrection, Eueseba
26	Reta, Epifanto–Wakimoto, S.
27	Wakino–Zwilling, W.P.
28	Singh–Singh, Yhakar

★ **Passenger Lists of Vessels Arriving at San Francisco, CA, 1893–1953. M1410. 429 rolls.**

Roll	Contents
1	May 1, 1893, CITY OF PUBLA–February 7, 1896, GAELIC
2	March 4, 1896, AUSTRALIA–October 2, 1898, SAN BLAS
3	October 26, 1898, ACAPULAN–October 1, 1899, INVERCAULA
4	November 1, 1899, CITY OF PUBLA–October 31, 1900, CURACAO
5	October 31, 1900, CURACAO–December 23, 1901, CITY OF PUEBLO
6	December 23, 1901, CITY OF PUEBLO–December 8, 1902, SIERRA
7	December 11, 1902, ACAPULCO–June 8, 1903, KOREA
8	June 8, 1903, KOREA–October 26, 1903, RAMSES
9	October 28, 1903, PERU–November 25, 1903, HONG KONG MARU
10	November 25, 1903, HONG KONG MARU–April 25, 1904, SONOMA
11	May 2, 1904, MELANOPE–August 31, 1904, ACAPULCO
12	August 3, 1904, LINDFIELD–December 17, 1904, MONGOLIA
13	December 17, 1904, MONGOLIA–May 24, 1905, MONGOLIA
14	May 25, 1905, CITY OF PANAMA–October 23, 1905, SIBERIA
15	October 23, 1905, SIBERIA–January 31, 1906, CHINA
16	January 31, 1906, CHINA–May 5, 1906, SAN JUAN
17	May 7, 1906, DORIC–September 2, 1906, ACAPULCO
18	September 2, 1906, ACAPULCO–November 8, 1906, KOREA

Roll	Contents
19	November 8, 1906, KOREA–Feburay 26, 1907, MONGOLIA
20	March 3, 1907, CURACAO–June 7, 1907, COPTIC
21	May 11, 1907, COPTIC–August 31, 1907, SONOMA
22	September 1, 1907, MELVILLE DOLLAR–October 30, 1907, CITY OF PUEBLO
23	November 1, 1907, CURACAO–December 12, 1907, SIBERIA
24	December 12, 1907, SIBERIA–February 19, 1908, AMERICA MARU
25	February 19, 1908, AMERICA MARU–April 17, 1908, HAZEL DOLLAR
26	April 17, 1908, ALESSIUIA–June 8, 1908, SAN JUAN
27	June 8, 1908, SAN JUAN–August 1, 1908, SIBERIA
28	August 1, 1908, SIBERIA–September 27, 1908, KOREA
29	September 27, 1908, KOREA–November 22, 1908, MONGOLIA
30	November 22, 1908, MONGOLIA–January 9, 1909, CHINA
31	January 9, 1909, CITY OF VICTORIA–March 15, 1909, SIBERIA
32	March 15, 1909, SIBERIA–May 3, 1909, TENYO MARU
33	May 3, 1909, TENYO MARU–June 14, 1909, MANCHURIA
34	June 14, 1909, MANCHURIA–July 27, 1909, KOREA
35	July 28, 1909, CURACAO–September 13, 1909, CITY OF PARA
36	September 13, 1909, ASIA–October 23, 1909, CITY OF PUEBLO
37	October 28, 1909, SIBERIA–November 24, 1909, CITY OF PARA
38	November 26, 1909, ASIA–January 6, 1910, NIPPON MARU
39	January 6, 1910, NIPPON MARU–February 4, 1910, CITY OF PARA
40	February 5, 1910, SENATOR–April 3,1910, AMASIS
41	April 7, 1910, MARIPOSA–May 14, 1910, MONGOLIA
42	May 14, 1910, MONGOLIA–June 25, 1910, CHINA
43	June 25, 1910, CHINA–August 6,1910, TENYO MARU
44	August 6, 1910, TENYO MARU–September 23, 1910, CHIYO MARU
45	September 23, 1910, CHIYO MARU– November 12, 1910, NIPPON MARU
46	November 12, 1910, NIPPON MARU–December 31, 1910, MONGOLIA
47	December 31, 1910, MONGOLIA–March 4, 1911, ASIA
48	March 4, 1911, ASIA–March 31, 1911, PERSIA
49	March 31, 1911, PERSIA–June 11, 1911, PERSIA
50	June 11, 1911, PERU–July 26, 1911, PERU
51	July 27, 1911, CHIYO MARU–September 14, 1911, MAITAI
52	September 14, 1911, MAITAI–November 9, 1911, MAITAI
53	November 9, 1911, MAITAI–December 28, 1911, CHIYO MARU
54	December 30, 1911, SENATOR–February 26, 1912, NEWPORT
55	February 26, 1912, NEWPORT–April 11, 1912, TENYO MARU

Roll	Contents
56	April 11, 1912, TENYO MARU–May 28, 1912, CITY OF SYDNEY
57	May 28, 1912, CITY OF SYDNEY–July 11, 1912, MANUKA
58	July 11, 1912, MANUKA–August 19, 1912, CHIYO MARU
59	August 19, 1912, CHIYO MARU–September 27, 1912, PERU
60	September 27, 1912, PERU–November 19, 1912, MONGOLIA
61	November 19, 1912, MONGOLIA–January 25, 1913, AORANGI
62	January 25, 1913, AORANGI–March 20, 1913, MOANA
63	March 17, 1913, BUFFALO–May 15, 1913, TAHITI
64	May 15, 1913, TAHITI–June 23, 1913, CHIYO MARU
65	June 23, 1913, CHIYO MARU–August 1, 1913, SIERRA
66	August 2, 1913, KOREA–August 30, 1913, THOMAS
67	September 1, 1913, MANCHURIA–September 14, 1913, LOGAN
68	September 14, 1913, NILE–October 22, 1913, SHINYO MARU
69	October 24, 1913, SIERRA–November 30, 1913, POLARIS
70	December 2, 1913, LURLINE–January 14, 1914, SIBERIA
71	January 14, 1914, SIBERIA–March 7, 1914, PERSIA
72	March 7, 1914, PERSIA–April 22, 1914, MANCHURIA
73	April 22, 1914, MANCHURIA–June 3, 1914, SAN JUAN
74	June 3, 1914, SAN JUAN– July 15, 1914, TENYO MARU
75	July 15, 1914, TENYO MARU–August 1, 1914, NEWPORT
76	August 1, 1914, NEWPORT–August 28, 1914, SIBERIA
77	August 31, 1914, CHIYO MARU–October 16, 1914, NEWPORT
78	October 15, 1914, TENYO MARU–November 27, 1914, PENNSYLVANIA
79	November 27, 1914, PENNSYLVANIA–January 18, 1915, KOREA
80	January 18, 1915, KOREA–March 1, 1915, NORTHERN
81	March 3, 1915, VENTURA–April 17, 1915, PERU
82	April 19, 1915, CHIYO MARU–June 1, 1915, MONGOLIA
83	June 1, 1915, MONGOLIA–July 13, 1915, CHINA
84	July 13, 1915, CHINA–August 23, 1915, SHINYO MARU
85	August 23, 1915, SHINYO MARU–October 6, 1915, MANCHURIA
86	October 6, 1915, MANCHURIA–November 8, 1915, SHINYO MARU
87	November 8, 1915, SHINYO MARU–January 25, 1916, SIERRA
88	January 25, 1916, SIERRA–April 2, 1916, NIPPON MARU
89	April 2, 1916, NIPPON MARU–May 22, 1916, CHEHALIS
90	May 23, 1916, WILHEMINA–July 24, 1916, NEWPORT

Roll	Contents
91	July 24, 1916, NEWPORT–September 14, 1916, SEIYO MARU
92	September 14, 1916, SEIYO MARU–November 10, 1916, SAN JOSE
93	November 10, 1916, SAN JOSE–December 24, 1916, KOREA MARU
94	December 24, 1916, KOREA MARU–February 18, 1917, KIYO–MARU
95	February 18, 1917, KIYO MARU–April 2, 1917, TENYO MARU
96	April 2, 1917, TENYO MARU–May 15, 1917, GOLDEN STATE
97	May 16, 1917, PERSIA MARU–June 22, 1917, TENYO MARU
98	June 22, 1917, TENYO MARU–July 19, 1917, PERU
99	July 19, 1917, PERU–Setember 10, 1917, CITY OF PARA
100	September 10, 1917, CITY OF PARA–September 29, 1917, GERLADINE WOLVIN
101	September 29, 1917, COLUSA–October 8, 1917, LOGAN
102	October 30, 1917, S.S. WILHELMINA–Dec. 12, 1917, S.S. CHINA
103	Dec. 12, 1917, S.S. CHINA–Jan. 1, 1918, S.S. BARK KOHALA
104	Dec. 29, 1917, S.S. KOHALA–Jan. 27, 1918, S.S. KAWI
105	Janaury 27, 1918, KAWI–February 19, 1918, KIYO MARU
106	February 17, 1918, TENYO MARU–April 22, 1918, ANYO MARU
107	April 22, 1918, ANYO MARU–May 4, 1918, SUPERIOR
108	May 4, 1918, SUPERIOR–May 13, 1918, KIYO MARU
109	May 13, 1918, KIYO MARU–July 23, 1918, TENYO MARU
110	July 23, 1918, TENYO MARU–August 10, 1918, PERU
111	August 10, 1918, PERU–October 7, 1918, WILLIS
112	October 7, 1918, WILLIS–November 1, 1918, ANYO MARU
113	November 1, 1918, ANYO MARU–December 5, 1918, EQUADOR
114	December 9, 1918, CENTRALIA–December 24, 1918, PERU
115	December 26, 1918, TENYO MARU–February 9, 1919, NANKING
116	February 9, 1919, NANKING–March 1, 1919, SIBERIA MARU
117	March 1, 1919, SIBERIA MARU–March 26, 1919, COLUMBIA
118	March 26, 1919, SAN JOSE–April 29, 1919, NANKING
119	April 27, 1919, ANYO MARU–May 14, 1919, KIYO MARU
120	May 14, 1919, KIYO MARU–June 3, 1919, TENYO MARU
121	June 3, 1919, TENYO MARU–June 25, 1919, SS SACHEM
122	June 30, 1919, TENYO MARU–July 27, 1919, SS CHINA
123	July 27, 1919, SS CHINA–August 20, 1919, KIYO MARU
124	August 20, 1919, SS KIYO MARU–September 15, 1919, SS COLUSA
125	September 15, 1919, SS COLUSA–October 11, 1919, SS SAN JUAN
126	October 10, 1919, SAN JUAN–October 15, 1919, ANYO MARU
127	October 16, 1919, J.B. STETSON–November 11, 1919, KIYU MARU
128	November 11, 1919, KIYU MARU–December 16, 1919, ALLIANCE
129	December 17, 1919, CHINA–January 14, 1920, TENYO MARU
130	January 14, 1920, TENYO MARU–February 18, 1920, SIBERIA MARU
131	February 18, 1920, SIBERIA MARU–March 21, 1920, KOREA MARU
132	March 21, 1920, KOREA MARU–April 18, 1920, SIBERIA MARU
133	April 18, 1920, LOGAN–May 1, 1920, SENATOR
134	May 2, 1920, MT. VERNON–June 12, 1920, CHINA
135	June 12, 1920, CHINA–June 23, 1920, TENYO MARU
136	June 23, 1920, NEWPORT–July 6, 1920, MATSONIA
137	July 6, 1920, ANYO MARU–July 31, 1920, SAN JOSE
138	July 31, 1920, SAN JOSE–August 27, 1920, SIBERIA MARU
139	August 27, 1920, SIBERIA MARU–September 26, 1920, NILE
140	September 26, 1920, NILE–October 16, 1920, ANYO MARU
141	October 16, 1920, ANYO MARU–November 8, 1920, CUBA
142	November 9, 1920, SONOMA–December 3, 1920, VENEZUELA
143	December 3, 1920, VENEZUELA–December 21, 1920, SHINYO MARU
144	December 21, 1920, SHINYO MARU–January 12, 1921, WILHEMINA
145	January 12, 1921, WILHEMINA–January 26, 1921, MAUI
146	February 2, 1921, COLUSA–February 25, 1921, TAHITI
147	February 25, 1921, KIYO MARU–March 22, 1921, CHINA
148	March 23, 1921, MANOA–April 25, 1921, TAHITI
149	April 28, 1921, NANKING–May 18, 1921, VENEZUELA
150	May 18, 1921, VENEZUELA–June 21, 1921, VENTURA
151	June 21, 1921, VENTURA–July 27, 1921, TENYO MARU
152	July 27, 1921, TENYO MARU–August 30, 1921, NILE
153	August 30, 1921, NILE–August 30, 1921, TAIYO MARU
154	September 13, 1921, MAUI–October 18, 1921, KOREA MARU
155	October 18, 1921, KOREA MARU–November 30, 1921, SAN JUAN
156	November 30, 1921, SS SAN JUAN–January 2, 1922, SS GOLDEN STATE
157	January 2, 1922, SS GOLDEN STATE–January 14, 1922, SS MATSONIA
158	January 16, 1922, MATSONIA–March 26, 1922, KOREA MARU

Roll	Contents
159	March 26, 1922, SANTA ANA–May 1, 1922, TAHITI
160	May 1, 1922, TAHITI–May 29, 1922, MARAMA
161	May 29, 1922, MARAMA–June 27, 1922, June 27, 1922, PRESIDENT HAYES
162	June 27, 1922, PRESIDENT HAYES–Jyly 27, 1922, PRESIDENT CLEVELAND
163	July 27, 1922, PRESIDENT CLEVELAND–September 9, 1922, GUERREO
164	September 4, 1922, TAHITI–October 8, 1922, TAIYO MARU
165	October 8, 1922, TAIYO MARU–November 7, 1922, VENTURA
166	November 7, 1922, VENTURA–December 11, 1922, CUBA
167	December 11, 1922, CUBA–January 1, 1923, NAYARI
168	January 17, 1923, NAYARIT–February 24, 1923, PRESIDENT PIERCE
169	February 23, 1923, PRESIDENT PIERCE–March 27, 1923, PRESIDENT LINCOLN
170	March 27, 1923, PRESIDENT LINCOLN–April 29, 1923, CHIAPAS
171	April 29, 1923, CHIAPAS– May 19, 1923, ECQUADOR
172	May 19, 1923, ECQUADOR–June 22, 1923, TENYO MARU
173	August 13, 1923, TENYO MARU–July 16, 1923, DINTELDYK
174	July 16, 1923, DINTELDYK–August 13, 1923, TAIYO MARU
175	August 13, 1923, TAIYO MARU–September 12, 1923, VENEZUELA
176	September 12, 1923, VENEZUELA–October 15, 1923, SIBERIA MARU
177	October 15, 1923, SIBERIA MARU–November 19, 1923, FINLAND
178	November 20, 1923, MATSONIA–December 17, 1923, NAYARIT
179	December 18, 1923, MATSONIA–January 14, 1924, PRESIDENT CLEVELAND
180	January 15, 1924, MATSONIA–February 19, 1924, SONOMA
181	February 19, 1924, KOREA MARU–March 20, 1924, MANOA
182	March 20, 1924, COLUMBIA–April 18, 1924, PRESIDENT WILSON
183	April 18, 1924, PRESIDENT WILSON–May 16, 1920, TAHITI
184	May 16, 1924, SAMARIA–June 11, 1924, TAIYO MARU
185	June 11, 1924, TAIYO MARU–June 27, 1924, PRESIDENT WILSON
186	June 27, 1924, LURLINE–August 6, 1924, MANOA
187	August 7, 1924, SIBERIA MARU–September 3, 1924, TENYO MARU
188	September 3, 1924, TENYO MARU–October 4, 1924, SHINYO MARU
189	October 4, 1924, SHINYO MARU–November 3, 1924, FINLAND
190	November 3, 1924, SIERRA–December 12, 1924, PRESIDENT LINCOLN
191	December 12, 1924, PRESIDENT LINCOLN–January 14, 1925, MATSONIA
192	January 15, 1925, RAKUYO MARU–March 2, 1925, RAKUYO MARU
193	March 2, 1925, RAKUYO MARU–March 30, 1925, SONOMA
194	April 1, 1925, COLUSA–April 30, 1925, KOREA MARU
195	April 30, 1925, KOREA MARU–May 21, 1925, COLUMBIA
196	May 23, 1925, WASHINGTON–June 22, 1925, VENTURA
197	June 22, 1925, SACHSEN–July 25, 1925, SINALOA
198	July 27, 1925, COLUMBIA–August 22, 1925, HESSEN
199	August 23, 1925, LONDON MERCHANT–September 24, 1925, PRESIDENT LINCOLN
200	September 24, 1925, PRESIDENT LINCOLN–November 2, 1925, CORINTO
201	November 2, 1925, CARINTO–December 7, 1925, FINLAND
202	December 7, 1925, FINLAND–January 13, 1926, PRESIDENT TAFT
203	January 13, 1926, PRESIDENT TAFT–February 13, 1926, WEST CAJCOT
204	February 14, 1926, CITY OF SAN FRANCISCO–March 18, 1926, SIBERIA MARU
205	March 19, 1926, COLUSA–April 15, 1926, SONOMA
206	April 15, 1926, ZENON–April 29, 1926, HECTRONZUMA
207	April 30, 1926, KOREA MARU–May 24, 1926, BUENOS AIRES
208	May 25, 1926, SIERRA–June 6, 1926, CITY OF PANAMA
209	June 9, 1926, MANOA–June 30, 1910, PRESIDENT LINCOLN
210	June 30, 1926, PRESIDENT LINCOLN–July 28, 1926, PRESIDENT PIERCE
211	July 28, 1926, PRESIDENT PIERCE–August 23, 1926, TAIYO MARU
212	August 23, 1926, TAIYO MARU–September 15, 1926, WILHEMINA
213	September 17, 1926, KOREA MARU–October 15, 1926, SIBERIA MARU
214	October 15, 1926, SIBERIA MARU–November 16, 1926, COLUSA
215	November 17, 1926, PRESIDENT LINCOLN–December 14, 1926, MATSONIA
216	December 15, 1926, LONDON SHIPPER–January 19, 1927, ANTON
217	January 21, 1927, MAKURA–February 23, 1927, PRESIDENT PIERCE
218	February 23, 1927, PRESIDENT PIERCE–March 23, 1927, PRESIDENT ADAMS
219	March 24, 1927, PRESIDENT JEFFERSON–April 18, 1927, TAIYO MARU
220	April 18, 1927, CORINTO–May 13, 1927, KOREA MARU
221	May 13, 1927, KOREA MARU–June 8, 1927, MANOA
222	June 8, 1927, NORFOLK MARU–June 30, 1927, PRESIDENT PIERCE
223	June 30, 1927, PRESIDENT PIERCE–July 24, 1927, WEST CAROB
224	July 26, 1927, CROSS KEYS–August 19, 1927, NORFOLK MARU
225	August 20, 1927, AXEL JOHNSON–September 16, 1927, TENYO MARU

Roll	Contents
226	September 10, 1927, DRECHTDYK–October 17, 1927, SHINYO MARU
227	October 17, 1927, SHINYO MARU–November 7, 1927, WEST NOTUS
228	November 6, 1927, PACIFIC TRADER–December 1, 1927, CITY OF PANAMA
229	December 1, 1927, CITY OF PANAMA–January 6, 1928, SIBERIA MARU
230	January 6, 1928, SIBERIA MARU–February 8, 1928, CONTENIAL
231	February 9, 1928, PRESIDENT GRANT–March 9, 1928, SONOMA
232	March 9, 1928, SONOMA–April 3, 1928, MATSONIA
233	April 4, 1928, MALOLO–April 30, 1928, RIALTO
234	May 1, 1928, MATSONIA–May 31, 1928, PRESIDENT McKINLEY
235	May 31, 1928, PRESIDENT McKINLEY–June 27, 1928, CLEVELAND
236	June 27, 1928, CLEVELAND–July 24, 1928, MATSONIA
237	July 24, 1928, PRESIDENT MONROE–August 21, 1928, MATSONIA
238	August 22, 1928, MALOLO–September 14, 1928, TENYO MARU
239	September 14, 1928, TENYO MARU–October 12, 1928, SHINYO MARU
240	October 12, 1928, SHINYO MARU–November 12, 1928, TAIYO MARU
241	November 12, 1928, TAIYO MARU–December 6, 1928, VENTURA
242	December 7, 1928, KOREA MARU–January 5, 1929, SIBERIA MARU
243	January 5, 1929, SIBERIA MARU–January 23, 1929, PRESIDENT JACKSON
244	Januaay 23, 1929, ECUADOR–February 20, 1929, PRESIDENT GRANT
245	February 20, 1929, MALOLO–March 29, 1929, MALOLO
246	March 21, 1929, SONOMA–April 15, 1929, TAIYO MARU
247	April 15, 1929, TAIYO MARU–April 15, 1929, LA PERLA
248	April 21, 1929, GOLDEN TIDE–May 14, 1929, MAUI
249	May 14, 1929, CONRITO–June 7, 1929, TAHITI
250	June 7, 1929, TAHITI–June 25, 1929, ESPARTA
251	June 26, 1929, PRESIDENT GRANT–July 17, 1929, GRANT
252	July 22, 1929, CUBA MARU–August 15, 1929, VENTURA
253	August 15, 1929, VENTURA–September 9, 1929, VENEZUELA
254	September 9, 1929, VENEZUELA–October 7, 1929, ESPARTA
255	October 8, 1929, TAIYO–November 7, 1929, FELTRE
256	November 7, 1929, SIERRA–November 19, 1929, DELFTDYK
257	November 30, 1929, CAMBRAI–December 25, 1929, COLUMBIA
258	December 26, 1929, SEATTLE–January 1, 1930, TAIYO MARU
259	January 1, 1930, TAIYO MARU–February 28, 1930, KOREA MARU

Roll	Contents
260	February 28, 1930, KOREA MARU–March 21, 1930, ASAMA MARU
261	March 21, 1930, ASAMA MARU–April 13, 1930, GUATAMALA
262	April 13, 1930, SURINAME–May 7, 1930, MALOLO
263	May 7, 1930, MANOA–May 24, 1930, CORINTO
264	May 24, 1930, EQUADOR–June 15, 1930, SARAMACCA
265	June 16, 1930, CALIFORNIA–July 8, 1930, BORDEAUX MARU
266	July 8, 1930, PRESIDENT GARFIELD–August 5, 1930, OREGON MARU
267	August 6, 1930, PRESIDENT PIERCE–September 1, 1930, VENTURA
268	September 1, 1930, VENTURA–September 29, 1930, GINYO MARU
269	September 29, 1930, GINYO MARU–October 29, 1930, CHICHIBU MARU
270	October 29, 1930, CHICHIBU MARU–December 10, 1930, PRESIDENT PIERCE
271	December 10, 1930, PRESIDENT PIERCE– January 1, 1931, CITY OF PANAMA
272	January 9, 1931, CALIFORNIA–February 16, 1931, PARRAKOOLA
273	February 16, 1931, COLUMBIA–March 25, 1931, CHICHIBU MARU
274	March 25, 1931, CHICHIBU MARU–April 22, 1931, ASAMA MARU
275	April 4, 1931, ASAMA MARU–May 20, 1931, CHICHIBU MARU
276	May 20, 1931, MANOA–June 19, 1931, EL SALVADOR
277	June 20, 1931, EUROPA–July 28, 1931, HABUBASAN MARU
278	July 29, 1931, TATASUTA MARU–August 26, 1931, SONOMA
279	August 27, 1931, VANCOUVER–October 4, 1931, PRESIDENT GRANT
280	October 5, 1931, CALIFORNIA–November 17, 1931, MAUNAWILI
281	November 17, 1931, PRESIDENT McKINLEY–December 29, 1931, PRESIDENT COOLIDGE
282	December 29, 1931, PRESIDENT COOLIDGE–February 8, 1931, PRESIDENT COOLIDGE
283	February 9, 1932, PRESIDENT JACKSON–March 20, 1932, EMPRESS OF BRITAIN
284	March 29, 1932, EMPRESS OF BRITAIN–April 30, 1932, SILVER RAY
285	May 2, 1932, PRESIDENT HOOVER–June 2, 1932, ANNIE JOHNSON
286	June 3, 1932, MAUNGANUL–July 8, 1932, EUROPA
287	July 11, 1932, SS PRES. COOLIDGE–August 9, 1932, SS PRES. HOOVER
288	August 9, 1932, SS BOKUYO MARU–September 21, 1932, SS MANULANI
289	September 23, 1932, SS MAKURA–November 9, 1932, SS TATSUTA MARU
290	November 9, 1932, SS TATSUTA MARU–November 21, 1932, SS CHICHIBU MARU
291	December 23, 1932, SS SANTA ELISA–February 7, 1933, SS SANTA ROSA
292	February 7, 1933, SS SANTA ROSA–March 20, 1933, SS PRES. COOLIDGE
293	March 20, 1933, SS PRES. COOLIDGE–May 3, 1933, SS PRES. MCKINLEY

Roll	Contents
294	May 3, 1933, SS PRES. MCKINLEY–June 5, 1933, SS GENERAL LEE
295	June 8, 1933, SS MALOLO–July 10, 1933, SS PRES. LINCOLN
296	July 10, 1933, SS PRES. LINCOLN–August 14, 1933, SS SAN FRANCISCO
297	August 15, 1933, SELANDIA–September 16, 1933, SANTA ANA
298	September 16, 1933, SANTA ANA–October 18, 1933, SANTA LUCIA
299	October 16, 1933, SANTA LUCIA–November 24, 1933, NELSON TRAVELER
300	November 25, 1933, SANATA ELISA–January 3, 1934, TATSUTA MARU
301	January 3, 1934, TATSUTA MARU–February 15, 1934, MALOLO
302	February 16, 1934, TAIYO MARU–March 28, 1934, ASAMA MARU
303	March 28, 1934, ASAMA MARU–April 23, 1934, GENERAL LEE
304	May 5, 1934, LISBON MARU–May 21, 1934, TACOMA
305	May 21, 1934, TACOMA–July 6, 1934, PRESIDENT HOOVER
306	July 9, 1934, BUENOS AIRES–August 15, 1934, PORTLAND
307	August 15, 1934, PORTLAND–September 16, 1934, PRESIDENT WILSON
308	September 17, 1934, DRECHTKYK–October 16, 1934, PRESIDENT PIERCE
309	October 16, 1934, PACIFIC PIONEER–November 14, 1934, SILVER BEECH
310	November 16, 1934, MAKURA–December 21, 1934, TACOMA
311	December 21, 1934, TACOMA–January 26, 1935, CALIFORNIA EXPRESS
312	February 3, 1935, PRESIDENT WILSON–March 8, 1935, PACIFIC TRADER
313	March 9, 1935, CHARCAS–April 10, 1935, PRESIDENT HOOVER
314	April 10, 1935, PRESIDENT HOOVER–May 8, 1935, PRESIDENT COOLIDGE
315	May 8, 1935, PRESIDENT COOLIDGE–June 6, 1935, MALOLO
316	June 9, 1935, PRESIDENT LINCOLN–July 9, 1935, TUTUSTA MARU
317	July 9, 1935, TATUSTA–August 14, 1935, AORANGI
318	August 14, 1935, AORANGI–September 9, 1935, MARIPOSA
319	September 9, 1935, MARIPOSA–October 11, 1935, TAIYO MARU
320	October 11, 1935, TAIYO MARU–November 14, 1935, TRICOLOR
321	November 12, 1935, SANTA ELONA–December 18, 1935, PRESIDENT COOLIDGE
322	December 18, 1935, PRESIDENT COOLIDGE–January 30, 1936, LURLINE
323	January 30, 1936, LURLINE–March 11, 1936, PRESIDENT HOOVER
324	March 11, 1936, PRESIDENT HOOVER–April 11, 1936, PRESIDENT COOLIDGE
325	April 11, 1936, PRESIDENT COOLIDGE–May 14, 1936, TATSUTA MARU
326	May 14, 1936, TATSUTA MARU–June 9, 1936, SANTA ELENA

Roll	Contents
327	June 9, 1936, SANTA ELENA–July 30, 1936, ESTE
328	July 13, 1936, MARIPOSA–August 17, 1936 BUENOS AIRES
329	August 17, 1936, U.S. GRANT–September 15, 1936, PRESIDENT CLEVELAND
330	September 15, 1936, PRESIDENT CLEVELAND–October 16, 1936, MAUNGANUI
331	October 16, 1936, OAKLAND–November 28, 1936, MONTEREY
332	December 1, 1936, ST. MIHIEL–February 18, 1937, MAUNALEI
333	February 21, 1937, WEST MAHWAH–March 29, 1937, U.S. GRANT
334	March 29, 1937, TOSARI–May 1, 1937, GRETE MARERSK
335	May 3, 1937, CALIFORNIA–May 25, 1937, SANTA PAULA
336	May 26, 1937, CHINA CLIPPER–June 24, 1937, CHICHIBU MARU
337	June 26, 1937, CHICHIBU MARU–July 30, 1937, ASAMA MARU
338	July 10, 1937, ASAMA MARU–August 23, 1937, REPUBLIC
339	August 23, 1937, VIRGINIA–September 27, 1937, OREGON
340	September 3, 1937, CANADA–October 28, 1937, LURLINE
341	October 29, 1937, SS AMER. AIRWAYS–December 9, 1937, SS LURLINE
342	December 9, 1937, SS LURLINE–January 27, 1938, SS PRES. COOLIDGE
343	January 27, 1938, SS PRES. COOLIDGE–March 9, 1938, SS TITIBU MARU
344	March 9, 1938, SS TITIBU MARU–April 9, 1938, SS PHILIPPINE CLIPPER
345	April 11, 1938, SS CHAUMONT–May 17, 1938, SS PRES. TAFT
346	May 17, 1938, SS MARIPOSA–June 24, 1938, SS DAMSTERDYK
347	June 24, 1938, SS HENDERSON–August 9, 1938, SS MONTEREY
348	August 9, 1938, SS MONTEREY–September 23, 1938, NANKAI MARU
349	September 25, 1938, UNIVERSITY OF LEON–November 16, 1938, ASAMA MARU
350	November 17, 1938, HAURAKI–January 12, 1939, TATUTA MARU
351	Janaury 12, 1939, TATUTA MARU–February 26, 1939, WASHINGTON
352	February 26, 1939, WASHINGTON–March 31, 1939, PACIFIC RANGER
353	March 29, 1939, CHINA CLIPPER–May 8, 1939, ASAMA MARU
354	May 8, 1939, ASAMA MARU–June 14, 1939, MARIPOSA
355	June 13, 1939, AZUMASAN MARU–July 19, 1939, LURLINE
356	July 19, 1938, LURLINE– August 18, 1939, PRESIDENT COOLDIGE
357	August 18, 1939, PRESIDENT COOLIDGE–September 20, 1939, TATUTA MARU
358	September 20, 1939, TATUTA MARU–November 9, 1939, MODJOKERTO
359	November 9, 1939, MODJOKERTO–January 18, 1940, PRESIDENT PIERCE

Roll	Contents
360	January 18, 1940, PESIDENT PIERCE–March 21, 1940, TATUTA MARU
361	March 21, 1940, TATUTA MARU–May 14, 1940, MARIPOSA
362	May 14, 1940, MARIPOSA–June 24, 1940, TATANO MARU
363	June 25, 1940, HONOLULU CLIPPER–August 13, 1940, NITTA MARU
364	August 13, 1940, NITTA MARU–September 23, 1940, AMERICAN CLIPPER
365	September 22, 1940, CITY OF SAN FRANCISCO–November 13, 1940, TATSUTA MARU
366	November 13, 1940, TATUTA MARU–December 29, 1940, PRESIDENT CLEVELAND
367	December 29, 1940, PRESIDENT CLEVELAND–February 20, 1941, YAWATA MARU
368	February 20, 1941, YAWATA MARU–April 1, 1941, NITTA MARU
369	April 2, 1941, MAYA–May 20, 1941, PHILIPPINE CLIPPER
370	May 23, 1941, MATSONIA–July 3, 1941, PRESIDENT COOLIDGE
371	July 3, 1941, PRESIDENT COOLIDGE–August 28, 1941, PRESIDENT COOLIDGE
372	August 28, 1941, PRESIDENT COOLIDGE–Novembe 4, 1941, MARIPOSA
373	November 4, 1941, MARIPOSA–March 22, 1942, PACIFIC EXPORTER
374	March 24, 1942, AQUITANIA–August 15, 1942, ETOTIN
375	August 15, 1942, PRESIDENT JOHNSON–January 22, 1943, FELIX DZERJINSKY
376	January 21, 1943, Army Airplane–July 9, 1943, HENDERSON
377	July 9, 1943, REPUBLIC–January 11, 1944, GENERAL JOHN POPE
378	January 11, 1944, KIT CARSON–August 2, 1944, Aircraft NC 18604
379	August 2, 1944, Aircraft NC 18604–February 24, 1945, TAWALI
380	February 24, 1945, TAWALI–July 30, 1945, KILPFONTEIN
381	July 30, 1945, KILPFONTEIN–December 18, 1945, TORRIALRA
382	December 21, 1945, S.S. MONTEREY–April 2, 1946, COUNCIL BLUFFS
383	April 18, 1946, ARTHUR MIDDLETON– June 24, 1946, GENERAL H.W. BUTNER
384	June 25, 1946, MARGUERITE LE HAND–August 27, 1946, DAVID C. SHANKS
385	August 27, 1946, DAVID C. SHANKS–October 19, 1946, MOORING KNOT
386	October 21, 1946, SEA HARE–January 8, 1947, MATSONIA
387	January 8, 1947, MATSONIA–February 24, 1947, GENERAL WILLIAM WEIGEL
388	Februay 24, 1947, ALSHAIN–April 7, 1947, MARINE LYNX
389	April 7, 1947, MARINE LYNX–May 31, 1947, LOCHMONAR
390	May 31, 1947, LOCHMONAR–July 14, 1947, GENERAL W.H. GORDON
391	July 14, 1947, GENERAL W.H. GORDON–August 25, 1947, GENERAL Mc. MEIGS

Roll	Contents
392	August 25, 1947, GENERAL Mc. MEIGS–October 1, 1947, MARINE SWALLOW
393	October 1 1947, MARINE SWALLOW–November 11, 1947, PRESIDENT TAFT
394	November 11, 1947, ALAMO VICTORY–December 31, 1947, GENERAL E.T. COLLINS
395	December 31, 1947, GENERAL E.T. COLLINS–February 9, 1948, PRES. CLEVELAND
396	February 9, 1948, PRESIDENT CLEVELAND–March 23, 1948, LOCH GARTH
397	March 24, 1948, PARRAKOOLA–May 7, 1948, USAT HOPE
398	May 8, 1948, CONTEST–June 14, 1948, PRESIDENT WILSON
399	June 14, 1948, PRESIDENT WILSON–September 10, 1948, GENERAL WILLIAM MITCHELL
400	September 10, 1948, GENERAL WILLIAM MITCHELL–September 8, 1948, GENERAL Mc. MEIGS
401	September 8, 1948, GENERAL Mc. MEIGS–December 13, 1948, GENERAL A.W. GREELY
402	December 13, 1948, GENERAL A.W. GREELY–February 19, 1949, MV DURANGO
403	February 19, 1949, MV DURANGO–April 7, 1949, GENERAL W.H. GORDON
404	April 7, 1949, GENERAL W.H. GORDON–May 24, 1949, GENERAL J.C. BRECKINRIDGE
405	May 24, 1949, J.C. BRECKINRIDGE–June 30, 1949, PRESIDENT MADISON
406	July 1, 1949, PRESIDENT WILSON–July 24, 1949, GREAT REPUBLIC
407	July 24, 1949, OROHENA–September 17, 1949, IVAN VICTORY
408	August 20, 1949, LOS ANGELES–November 24, 1949, GENERAL W.H. GORDON
409	November 24, GENERAL W.H. GORDON–January 30, 1950, PRESIDENT CLEVELAND
410	January 30, 1950, PRESIDENT CLEVELAND–March 31, 1950, CHINA BEAR
411	April 1, 1950, GENERAL G.M. RANDALL–May 23, 1950, PRESIDENT WILSON
412	May 23, 1950, PRESIDENT WILSON–July 7, 1950, VENTURA
413	July 10, 1950, LIMON–August 16, 1950, GENERAL R.L. HOWZE
414	August 16, 1950, GENERAL R.L. HOWZE–November 27, 1950, IVARAI
415	November 27, 1950, PRESIDENT McKINLEY–February 22, 1951, GUAYANA
416	February 22, 1951, GUAYANA–May 12, 1951, DONA ALICIA
417	May 12, 1951, SANTA ADELA–July 22, 1951, PRESIDENT WILSON
418	July 12, 1951, PRESIDENT WILSON–September 12, 1951, SLAMAT
419	September 3, 1951, PARAGUAY–October 5, 1951, TUDOR
420	November 1, 1951, DAVID SHANKS–November 30, 1951, GENERAL MANN
421	December 1, 1951, GENERAL MANN–January 31, 1952, COTTON STATE
422	February 1, 1952, FLYING ARROW–April 6, 1952, PRESIDENT WILSON
423	April 6, 1952, PRESIDENT WILSON–June 5, 1952, GENERAL AULTMAN

Roll	Contents
424	June 5, 1952, GENERAL AULTMAN–August 13, 1952, GENERAL C.C. MORTON
425	August 13, 1952, GENERAL C.C. MORTON–October 13, 1952, PRESIDENT CLEVELAND
426	October 14, 1952, LOCH AVON–December 22, 1952, CARNIA
427	December 22, 1952, PRESIDENT WILSON–February 26, 1953, PRSIDENT WILSON
428	February 26, 1953, PRESIDENT WILSON–April 28, 1953, HAWAIIAN WHOLESALER
429	April 28,1953, PHILIPPINE BEAR–May 31, 1953, RYUZAN MARU

★ **Passenger and Crew Lists of Vessels Arriving at San Francisco, CA, December 1, 1954–February 1, 1957. M1411. 19 rolls.**

Inbound passenger manifests, crew lists, and related form I-489 (statement of changes in crew). Arranged in chronological order by date of arrival. Passenger lists are form I-415 (manifest of inbound passengers, alien) and I-416 (manifest of inbound passengers, US citizens or nationals). These records were transferred to the National Archives on microfilm. Errors in arrangement and omissions cannot be corrected. Defective images, which were identified when the records were filmed, were microfilmed again, and the corrections were spliced on the beginning of each roll as "retakes." There is a gap between September 18, 1955 and November 8, 1955.

Roll	Contents
1	December 1, 1954, CARAIBE–December 31, 1954, SALLY MAERSK
2	December 31, 1954, SALLY MAERSK–February 3, 1955, CALLAO
3	February 3, 1955, HAWAIIAN PACKER–March 3, 1955, LURLINE
4	March 3, 1955, LURINE–April 5, 1955, GOLDEN BEAR
5	April 6,1955, GEN. D.E. AULTMAN–May 15, 1955, PRESIDENT HARRISON
6	May 15, 1955, PRESIDENT HARRISON–June 30, 1955, HAWAIIAN FARMER
7	June 30, 1955, HEREDIA–August 12, 1955, WONOGIRI
8	August 13, 1955, ALAMO VICTORY–September 18, 1955, SOUTHERN BREEZE
9	This roll is missing
10	November 8, 1955, DRINA–December 17, 1955, HUGH J. GAFFEY
11	December 17, 1955, HUGH J. GAFFEY–January 31, 1956, PETER MAERSK
12	February 1, 1956, HAWAIIAN LUMBERMAN–March 20, 1956, W.H. BERG
13	March 20, 1956, C.G. MORTON–April 27, 1956, ORION
14	April 27, 1956, ORION–June 7, 1956, PARDALINA
15	June 8, 1956, ANDROS SEA–July 17, 1956, BAWEAN
16	July 16, 1956, CONSTITUTION STATE–August 28, 1956, TALLEYRAND
17	August 26, 1956, ANTE TOPIC–October 19, 1956, ESPARTA
18	October 19, 1956, FAIRPORT–December 2, 1956, STEEL DESIGNER
19	December 1, 1956, H.D. COLLIER–January 17, 1957, KYUSHU MARU

Roll	Contents
20	January 18, 1957, ASOHARU MARU–February 28, 1957, STEEL FABRICATOR

★ **Customs Passenger Lists of Vessels Arriving at San Francisco, CA, January 2, 1903–April 1, 1918. M1412. 13 rolls.**

This microfilm publication reproduces copies of U.S. Customs Service passenger lists filed by masters of vessels entering the port of San Francisco between January 2, 1903 and April 1, 1918. The records were used by the Immigration and Naturalization Service to supplement the lists filed with immigration officials in the same port.

The records are arranged chronologically by date of arrival. The lists were originally bound in volumes and are microfilmed as they appeared in the volumes. At the beginning of each of the volumes is a typed list of vessels.

Roll	Contents
1	Jan. 2, 1903, CITY OF PUEBLA–Apr. 21, 1904, SS SENATOR
2	Apr. 22, 1904, SS HERMONTHIS–Aug. 21, 1905, SS VENTURA
3	Aug. 26, 1905, SS CHINA–Nov. 19, 1906, SS AMERICA MARU
4	Nov. 19, 1906, SS AMERICA MARU–Jan. 21, 1908, MS DOLLAR
5	Jan. 25, 1908, CITY OF SYDNEY–July 27, 1909, SS KOREA
6	July 27, 1909, SS KOREA–Dec. 17, 1910, SS ASIA
7	Dec. 17, 1910, SS ASIA–July 1, 1912, TENYO MARU
8	July 1, 1912, PENNSYLVANIA–Aug. 25, 1913, SS CHINA
9	Aug. 15, 1913, SIBERIA–May 20, 1914, SS NEWPORT
10	May 23, 1914, HONG KONG MARU–June 1, 1915, SS MONGOLIA
11	June 1, 1915, SS MONGOLIA–Jan. 30, 1916, SS PERU
12	July 5, 1916, SS MATSONIA–Feb. 4, 1917, SS GOVERNOR
13	Mar. 24, 1917, SIBERIA MARU–Apr. 18, 1918, SS GOVERNOR

★ **Registers of Chinese Laborers Arriving at San Francisco, CA, 1882–88. M1413. 12 rolls.**

Roll	Contents
1	June 6, 1882, SS OCEANIC–Dec. 18, 1882, SS SYDNEY
2	Dec. 16, 1882, SS GAELIC–Sept. 27, 1883, SS OCEANIC
3	September 27, 1883, SS OCEANIC–Jan. 15, 1884, SS RIO DE JANERIO
4	Jan. 15, 1884, SS OCEANIC–Sept. 25, 1884, SS SAN PABLO
5	Sept. 25, 1884, SS SAN PABLO–Dec. 6, 1884, SS TOKIO
6	Dec. 6, 1884, SS TOKIO–Aug. 1, 1885, SS ARABIC
7	Aug. 1, 1885, SS ARABIC–Dec. 19, 1885, SS SAN PABLO
8	Dec. 19, 1885, SS SAN PABLO–Sept. 21,. 1886, SS RIO
9	Sept. 21, 1886, SS RIO–Apr. 28, 1887, SS BELGIC
10	Apr. 28, 1887, SS SAN PABLO–Nov. 29, 1887, SS BELGIC

Roll	Contents
11	Nov. 29, 1887, SS BELGIC–Aug. 21, 1888, SS ARABIC
12	Aug. 21, 1888, SS ABYSSINIA–Oct. 9, 1888, SS NEW YORK

★ Lists of Chinese Passengers Arriving at San Francisco, CA, 1888–1914. M1414. 32 rolls.

Roll	Contents
1	Aug. 9, 1882, GRENADA–MAY 22, 1885, SAN PABLO
2	May 23, 1885, TEALANDIA–Mar, 16, 1887, SS G.W. ELDER
3	Mar. 15, 1887, CITY OF NEW YORK–Dec. 23, 1888, TROPIC BIRD
4	Dec. 22, 1888, SS BELGIC–Apr. 13, 1892, SS CHINA
5	Apr. 5, 1892, SAN JUAN–Nov. 17, 1894, SS UMATILLA
6	Nov. 14, 1894, SS PERU–Sept. 19, 1899, SS COLON
7	Sept, 16, 1899, SAN JUAN–Nov. 19, 1903, SS KOREA
8	Nov. 9, 1903, SS SONOMA–Sept. 23, 1904, SS GAELIC
9	Sept. 23, 1904, SS GAELIC–Aug. 15, 1905, SS MAGNOLIA
10	Aug. 15, 1905, SS MAGNOLIA–Apr. 16, 1906, SS ACAPULCO
11	Apr. 19, 1906, SS CHINA–Nov. 26, 1906, SS SIBERIA
12	Nov. 26, 1906, SS SIBERIA–June 14, 1907, SS HONG KONG MARU
13	June 14, 1907, SS HONG KONG MARU–Nov. 28, 1907, SS KOREA
14	Nov. 28, 1907, SS KOREA–May 14, 1908, SS SIBERIA
15	May 14, 1908, SS SIBERIA–Sept. 15, 1908, SS TENYO MARU
16	Sept. 15, 1908, CITY OF PARA–Jan. 1, 1909, SS SIBERIA
17	Jan. 1, 1909, SS SIBERIA–May 21, 1909, SS SAN JOSE
18	May 21, 1909, SS NIPPON MARU–Sept. 13, 1909, CITY OF PARA
19	Sept. 14, 1909, SS ASIA–Dec. 26, 1909, SS KOREA
20	Dec. 28, 1909, SS CURACAO–May 27, 1910, SS KOREA
21	June 3, 1910, CITY OF SYDNEY–Oct. 15, 1910, SS MONGOLIA
22	Oct. 15, 1910, SS MONGOLIA–Feb. 17, 1911, SS MANCHURIA
23	Feb. 18, 1911, SS ACAPULCO–Aug. 11, 1911, SS MONGOLIA
24	Aug. 11, 1911, SS MONGOLIA–Dec. 14, 1911, SS CHINA
25	Dec. 15, 1911, SS NEWPORT–June 3, 1912, SS CHIYO MARU
26	June 11, 1912, SS NILE–Sept. 30, 1912, SS KOREA
27	Sept. 30, 1912, SS KOREA–Mar. 24, 1913, SS CHINA
28	Mar. 31, 1913, SS MANCHURIA–Sept. 30, 1913, SS SIBERIA
29	Sept. 1, 1913, SS SIBERIA–Nov. 10, 1913, SS CHINA
30	Nov. 17, 1913, SS MANCHURIA–Apr. 22, 1914, SS MANCHURIA
31	Apr. 23, 1914, SS SONOMA–Sept. 1, 1914, SS MATSONIA

Roll	Contents
32	Sept. 4, 1914, SS SIERRA–Dec. 25, 1914, SS SIERRA

★ Crew Lists of Vessels Arriving at San Francisco, CA, December 28, 1905–October 30, 1954. M1416. 174 rolls.

Roll	Contents
1	Dec. 28, 1905, INVERMARK–Sept. 14, 1906, STRATHFILLAN
2	Sept. 3, 1906, GANTOCK ROCK–Aug. 5, 1907, YEDDO
3	Aug. 4, 1907, WATERLOO–Apr. 30, 1908, AZTEX
4	Apr. 30, 1908, PRINCE GEORGE–July 17, 1909, DAKOTAH
5	July 17, 1909, KANSAS CITY–Oct. 1, 1909, BALASARE
6	Dec. 30, 1910, BOVERIZ–June 8, 1911, GEORGE BILLINGS
7	June 12, 1911, HORNBY CASTLE–Feb. 15, 1912, SHINYO MARU
8	Feb 15, 1912, SHINYO MARU–Aug. 9, 1912, AORANGI
9	Aug. 9, 1912, AORANGI–Dec. 13, 1912, CLAN MACIVER
10	Dec. 10, 1912, PERU–Apr. 26, 1913, THOR
11	Apr. 26, 1913, LISAK–Sept. 1, 1913, MANCHURIA
12	Sept. 1, 1913, MANCHURIA–Mar. 31, 1914, MASCANOMO
13	Dec. 13, 1913, SANTA MARIA–Apr. 8, 1914, CANADA CAPE
14	Apr. 7, 1914, MANOA–July 31, 1914, MARY E. FOSTER
15	May 5, 1914, NEPTUNE–Nov. 13, 1914, CAPE FINISTERRE
16	Nov. 14, 1914, MALAKKA–Mar. 28, 1915, CACIQUE
17	Mar. 28, 1915, CUZCO–July 20, 1915, MANCHURIA
18	July 20, 1915, WILHELMINA–Dec. 12, 1915, EDGAR H. VANCE
19	Dec. 12, 1915, CARLOS–May 13, 1916, NEWPORT
20	May 9, 1916, BARGE SIMLA–Oct. 6, 1916, NEWPORT
21	Oct. 7, 1916, RMS MAITAI–Feb. 22, 1917, SS SHINYO MARU
22	Jan. 28, 1917, SS TOKAI MARU–June 30, 1917, SS TENYO MARU
23	June 20, 1917, GEORGE W. ELDER–Oct. 9, 1917, W.H. TALBOT
24	Oct. 10, 1917, WACHUSETT–Jan. 8, 1918, TJIKEMBANG
25	Jan. 27, 1918, VEINDYK–Apr. 17, 1918, GEORGE WASHINGTON
26	May 5, 1918, SUPERIOR–Aug. 11, 1918, PRESIDENT
27	Aug. 14, 1918, SS CORONA–Dec. 12, 1918, SS SIBERIA MARU
28	Dec. 12, 1918, SS OTTILLIE–Mar. 17, 1919, SS KOREA MARU
29	Mar. 21, 1919, SS KOREA MARU–June 26, 1919, SS RAJAH
30	June 27, 1919, JOHN ENA–Oct. 7, 1919, LURLINE
31	Oct. 8, 1919, SS CHINA–Jan. 10, 1920, SAN JOSE
32	Jan. 11, 1920, SS PRIMERA–Apr. 18, 1920, SIBERIA
33	Apr. 17, 1920, TECUMSEH–July 12, 1920, LIMA MARU

Roll	Contents
34	July 13, 1920, WEST HIMROD–Oct. 9, 1920, EL LOBO
35	Oct. 10, 1920, EASTERN GALE–Jan. 12, 1921, MONTROLITE
36	Jan. 12, 1921, GRIFFSON–Mar. 29, 1921, MAUI
37	Mar. 30, 1921, PERSIA–May 27, 1921, FAIRHAVEN
38	June 30, 1921, IRONITE–Aug. 20, 1921, MARAMA
39	Sept. 22, 1921, BAJA, CALIF.–Dec. 31, 1921, CANADIAN WINNER
40	Jan. 1, 1922, TJISALAK–May 2, 1922, GENEA MARU
41	Apr. 18, 1922, ARAKAN–July 21, 1922, TAIYO MARU
42	July 1, 1922, ASTRAL–Nov. 6, 1922, TAHITI
43	DATE NOT SHOWN, GYMERIC–Jan. 26, 1923, EMPRESS OF FRANCE
44	Feb. 8, 1923, EMPRESS OF FRANCE–May 14, 1923, AMARIA
45	May 14, 1923, SAMARIA–Aug. 9, 1923, PRES. LINCOLN
46	Aug. 9, 1923, PRES. LINCOLN–Nov. 14, 1923, PRES. CLEVELAND
47	Nov. 14, 1923, DAUNTLESS–Feb. 7, 1923, USAT THOMAS
48	Feb. 8, 1924, TASCALUSA–May 11, 1924, SHINYO MARU
49	May 17, 1924, YACHT MARINER–Sept. 2, 1924, TENYO MARU
50	Aug. 20, 1924, CARGOYLE–Dec. 11, 1924, SHINYO MARU
51	Dec. 12, 1924, PRES. LINCLON–Mar. 23, 1925, CITY OF SAN FRANCISCO
52	Mar. 23, 1925, MITRA–June 16, 1925, PRES. TAFT
53	June 16, 1925, LIEBRE–Sept. 10, 1925, ROMULUS
54	Sept. 11, 1925, MAUNA ALA–Dec. 25, 1925, WEST NIGER
55	Dec. 24, 1925, HOYEISAN MARU–May 11, 1926, ARGUN MARU
56	May 11, 1926, DUCHESSA D'AOSTA–Aug. 29, 1926, PORT ANGELO
57	Sept. 9, 1926, SS POINT LOBOS–Feb. 27, 1927, SS STANLEY DOLLAR
58	Feb. 4, 1927, MOTORSHIP LIO–June 24, 1927, SS MANULANI
59	June 26, 1927, SS WEST ISLIP–Oct. 31, 1927, SS CATHWOOD
60	Nov. 1, 1927, W.H. LIBBY–Mar. 5, 1928, WAIHEMO
61	Mar. 8, 1928, SS ROCHELIE–July 27, 1928, AMALTHUS
62	July 28, 1928, WEST CACTUS–Nov. 21, 1928, YARRAVILLE
63	Nov. 21, 1928, ARGUN MARU–Mar. 14, 1929, FLORIDA MARU
64	Mar. 16, 1929, HOYEISAN MARU–July 10, 1929, VINE MOOR
65	July 11, 1929, IBUKISAN MARU–Nov. 16, 1929, LINCOLN ELLSWORTH
66	Nov. 16, 1929, GOLDEN CLOUD–Mar. 14, 1930, SS IOWA
67	Mar. 16, 1930, LA PERLA–July 22, 1930, SS WISCONSIN
68	July 20, 1930, SARACACCA–Nov. 20, 1930, MARECHAL FOCH
69	Nov. 21, 1930, MAKURA–Apr. 11, 1931, MORDANGER
70	Apr. 13, 1931, DUCHESSA D'AOSTA–Sept. 10, 1931, WIRUNA
71	Sept. 11, 1931, SURINAME–Jan. 17, 1932, SACRAMENTO VALLEY
72	Jan. 19, 1932, YAHIKO MARU–July 10, 1932, IOWA
73	July 11, 1932, SAXICAVA–Jan. 13, 1933, VARDAAS
74	Jan. 13, 1933, TOKAI MARU–May 5, 1933, RMS MAKURA
75	May 6, 1933, RUTH ALEXANDER–Aug. 6, 1933, MS HAURAHI
76	Aug. 7, 1933, SHOHEI MARU–Nov. 8, 1933, SANTA PAULA
77	Nov. 8, 1933, HOLLAND MARU–Feb. 24, 1934, EMMA ALEXANDER
78	Feb. 25, 1934, GOLDEN WALL–June 6, 1934, HEIAN MARU
79	June 9, 1934, WARWICK–Oct. 2, 1934, SANTA LUCIA
80	Oct. 2, 1934, ROCHELIE–Feb. 23, 1935, HAURAKI
81	Feb. 24, 1935, INDIA MARU–June 19, 1935, SAN LUIS MARU
82	June 20, 1935, H.F. ALEXANDER–Sept. 25, 1935, EMMA ALEXANDER
83	Sept. 27, 1935, LACKLAN–Mar. 25, 1936, VARANGER
84	Mar. 27, 1936, ROCHELIE–July 19, 1936, NORE
85	July 21, 1936, KINGSLEY–Nov. 11, 1936, BAHREIN
86	Nov. 13, 1936, RMS MAKURA–May 25, 1937, WAIOTAPU
87	May 25, 1937, DORNOCH–Oct. 18, 1937, ST. MIHIEL
88	Oct. 16, 1937, SAMOAN–Apr. 29, 1938, DISTRICT OF COLUMBIA
89	Apr. 30, 1938, NORDEN–Sept. 22, 1938, O.A. KNUDSEN
90	Sept. 22, 1938, MOSTUN–Mar. 6, 1939, SAN CIPRIANO
91	Mar. 7, 1939, SAN CLEMENTE–Aug. 28, 1939, MARUSCEBEL
92	Aug. 28, 1939, SS KINGSLEY–Jan. 10, 1940, OMUROSAN MARU
93	Jan. 12, 1940, SS ROSE BANK–Aug. 15, 1940, DAISAN OGURA MARU
94	Aug. 19, 1940, FRESNO STAR–Jan. 20, 1941, KIM
95	Jan. 20, 1941, USAT LEONARD WOOD–July 10, 1941, MOVERIA
96	July 11, 1941, BOYACA–Mar. 28, 1942, PRES. JOHNSON
97	Mar. 23, 1942, THOR-I–Oct. 12, 1942, PARRAKOOLA
98	Oct. 14, 1942, FORT FORK–Feb. 28, 1943, ULUA
99	Feb. 28, 1943, CALAMARES–June 16, 1943, MORMACLARK
100	June 17, 1943, USAT RORRENS–Sept. 21, 1943, SMMELSOIJK
101	Sept. 21, 1943, KANANGOORA–Nov. 29, 1943, CAPE MAY
102	Nov. 30, 1943, JOSIAH SNELLING–Feb. 7, 1944, TRADE WIND
103	Feb. 9, 1944, DONBASS–Apr. 1, 1944, MORMACTERN
104	Apr. 1, 1944, CAPE ALEXANDER–June 1, 1944, WILLARD A. HOLBROOK

Roll	Contents
105	June 1, 1944, AMERICAN PACKER–July 16, 1944, THOR-I
106	July 16, 1944, DAVID DIDLEY FIELD–Aug. 26, 1944, CELESTIAL
107	Aug. 26, 1944, SEA PIKE–Aug. 30, 1944, SARAH J. HALE
108	Oct. 1, 1944, JAPARA–Nov. 23, 1944, CAPE CANSO
109	Nov. 23, 1944, FRANCISCO CORONADO–Jan. 3, 1945, KLIPFONTEIN
110	Jan. 3, 1945, JEREMIAH M. DAILY–Feb. 6, 1945, JOSE J. ACOSTA
111	Feb. 6, 1945, CAPE COD–Mar. 17, 1945, FAIRLAND
112	Mar. 16, 1945, PINE RIDGE–Apr. 19, 1945, EDGAR W. NYE
113	Apr. 19, 1945, H. WEIR COOK–May 19, 1945, DASTHING WADE
114	May 19, 1945, MERIDIAN VICTORY–June 18, 1945, LURLINE
115	June 18, 1945, LURLINE–July 18, 1945, LUCY STONE
116	July 17, 1945, FRANCIS E. WILLARD–Aug. 12, 1945, SS WM. J. RIDDLE
117	Aug. 13, 1945, GUATEMALA VICTORY–Sept. 9, 1945, HOKE SMITH
118	Sept. 8, 1945, WS RHEEMS–Oct. 7, 1945, SANTA LEONOR
119	Oct. 8, 1945, EDMUND RANDOFF–Nov. 22, 1945, ATCHISON VICTORY
120	Nov. 21, 1945, ALCOA PORITAN–Jan. 8, 1946, CHAS. KEFFER
121	Jan. 8, 1946, LAKE FRANCIS–Mar. 19, 1946, CAPE NEWENHAM
122	Mar. 19, 1946, GREAT REPUBLIC–June 3, 1946, MARINE PANTHER
123	June 3, 1946, LIGHTNING–Aug. 24, 1946, SHEEPSHANK
124	Aug. 23, 1946, PANAMA VICTORY–Oct. 16, 1946, H.T. HODGES
125	Oct. 16, 1946, PERCY FOXWORTH–Dec. 26, 1946, GEN. H.F. HODGES
126	Dec. 26, 1946, MOSES BROWN–Feb. 18, 1947, W.G. HAAN
127	Feb. 19, 1947, PRES. JEFFERSON–Apr. 21, 1947, ADM. W.S. SIMS
128	Apr. 21, 1947, SAN MATEO VICTORY–July 12, 1947, JOSEPH A. BROWN
129	July 12, 1947, APPLETON VICTORY–Sept. 28, 1947, PACIFIC TRANSPORT
130	Sept. 29, 1947, W.G. HAAN–Dec. 11, 1947, W.F. HASE
131	Nov. 29, 1947, SURPRISE–Mar. 1, 1948, MASON PATRICK
132	Mar. 1, 1948, FERDINAND WESTDAL–May 15, 1948, GOV. COMER
133	May 16, 1948, WM. KENT–July 20, 1948, IMPERIAL EDMONTON
134	July 20, 1948, HAWAIIAN CRAFTSMAN–Oct. 11, 1948, PRES. TAFT
135	July 11, 1948, WM. PEPPERELL–Jan 29, 1949, NELSON M. WALKER
136	Jan. 3, 1949, SS MUMEWORI–Apr. 19, 1949, PACHITEA
137	Apr. 19, 1949, PACIFIC BEAR–July 9, 1949, JOPLIN VICTORY

Roll	Contents
138	July 10, 1949, MISSION SAN DIEGO–Sept. 20, 1949, NUENA GLORIA
139	Sept. 20, 1949, ANCHOR HITCH–Dec. 10, 1949, FLYING CLOUD
140	Dec. 11, 1949, THOR-I–Dec. 30, 1949, LAKELAND VICTORY
141	Jan. 1, 1950, CONTEST–Jan. 31, 1950, BRAZILIAN PRINCE
142	Feb. 2, 1950, SONOMA–Apr. 17, 1950, TRADE WIND
143	Apr. 18, 1950, C.G. MORTON–June 30, 1950, SS HEREDIA
144	July 1, 1950, D.E. AULTMAN–Aug. 31, 1950, P&T EXPLORER
145	Sept. 1, 1950, ESPARTA–Oct. 31, 1950, LOVELAND
146	Nov. 1, 1950, WESTPORT–Apr. 30, 1950, GEO. LUCKENBACK
147	Dec. 2, 1950, GRETE MAERSK–Jan. 31, 1951, PADUCAH VICTORY
148	Feb. 1, 1951, GREEN VALLEY–Mar. 31, 1951, SONOMA
149	Apr. 1, 1951, JIHI TURTLE–May 31, 1951, BELGIUM VICTORY
150	June 1, 1951, SS LIMON–July 31, 1951, TARANGER
151	Aug. 1, 1951, VESTAN–Aug. 31, 1951, GOLDEN OCEAN
152	Sept. 1, 1951, COASTAL ADVENTURER–Oct. 14, 1951, JOSEPH F. MERRELL
153	Oct. 14, 1951, ALTNES–Oct. 30, 1951, KONGSGAARD
154	Dec. 1, 1951, NICOLINE MAERSK–Jan. 31, 1952, NORTHLEIGH
155	Feb. 1, 1952, FLYING ARROW–Mar. 1, 1952, TONEGAWA MARU
156	Apr. 1, 1952, SHOOTING STAR–Apr. 30, 1952, J.H. TUTTLE
157	May 1, 1952, PETER MAERSK–May 31, 1952, SALLY MAERSK
158	June 1, 1952, LOCH AVON–July 16, 1952, DVISBURG
159	July 17, 1952, PHILIPPINE TRANSPORT–Aug. 31, 1952, CARDINAL O'CONNELL
160	Sept 1, 1952, CLOVIS VICTORY–Oct. 14, 1952, LOCH AVON
161	Oct. 14, 1952, TAMESIS–Dec. 7, 1952, WAGON BOX
162	Dec. 8, 1952, NAVAJO VICTORY–Jan. 24, 1953, HAWAIIAN PACKER
163	Jan. 24, 1953, THORSISLE–Feb. 28, 1953, WESTERN OCEAN
164	Mar. 1, 1953, HOEGH CLAIR–Apr. 21, 1953, FLYING SCUD
165	Apr. 21, 1953, ALASKA BEAR–May 31, 1953, RYUZAN MARU
166	June 2, 1953, EURYCLEIA–July 18, 1953, OLYMPIA MARU
167	July 18, 1953, EMPIRE STATE–Aug. 31, 1953, MV AJAX
168	Sept. 1, 1953, CHARLES E. MOWER–Oct. 14, 1953, KEYSTONE MARINER
169	Oct. 23, 1953, AWOBASAN MARU–Dec. 28, 1953, FERNDALE
170	Dec. 28, 1953, DONA NATI–Mar. 11, 1954, SERAMPORE

Roll	Contents
171	Mar. 11, 1954, SERAMPORE–May 24, 1954, SUVA
172	May 11, 1954, TUNGAHA–Aug. 2, 1954, SHOOTING STAR
173	Aug. 2, 1954, SIMON B. BUCKNER–Oct. 13, 1954, AKITA MARU
174	Oct. 13, 1954, PRESIDENT GRANT–Oct. 30, 1954, MV MANISA

★ **Alien Crew Manifests of Vessels Arriving at San Francisco, CA, Sept. 1, 1896–Sept. 24, 1921. M1436. 8 rolls.**

Arranged chronologically by date of arrival, these passenger manifest forms list alien seamen admitted to the United States. There are very few lists dated before 1902.

Roll	Contents
1	Sept. 1, 1896, DIMSDALE–May 19, 1917, RENDAJANI
2	May 1, 1917, SS MONTANA–Mar. 31, 1918, SS EQUADOR
3	March 31, 1918, SS OMEGA–July 20, 1918, SS ALEXA
4	July 20, 1918, SS MAKAWELI–Feb. 26, 1919, SS NORWOOD
5	Jan. 6, 1919, SS RAUPO–Aug. 15, 1919, LA MERCED
6	Aug. 16, 1919, WM. E. BURNHAM–March 6, 1920, CITY OF PARA
7	Mar. 7, 1920, SCOTIA MAIDEN–Jan. 26, 1921, SS WEST BORA
8	Jan. 31, 1921, LAS VEGAS–Sept. 24, 1921, MERIDEN

★ **Indexes to Vessels Arriving at San Francisco, CA, 1882–1957. M1437. 2 rolls. 16mm.**

Roll	Contents
1	AAGOT–WHITTIER, M.H.
2	SS WICHITA–SS ZVIR

★ **Passenger Lists of Vessels Arriving at San Francisco, CA, from Insular Possessions, 1907–1911. M1438. 2 rolls.**

Roll	Contents
1	Vol I: May 28, 1907, SS ALAMEDA–Mar. 1, 1910, SS ALAMEDA
2	Vol II: Mar. 2, 1910, SS WILHELMENIA–Oct. 28, 1911, SS MONGOLIA

★ **Passenger Lists of Vessels Arriving at San Francisco, CA, from Honolulu, HI, Sept. 30, 1902–May 17, 1907. M1440. 1 roll.**

Roll	Contents
1	Sept. 30, 1902, SIERRA–May 17, 1907, SIERRA

★ **Lists of Chinese Applying for Admission to the United States through the Port of San Francisco, 1903–1947. M1476. 27 rolls.**

Roll	Contents
1	July 7, 1903, SS PEKING–Oct. 23, 1905, SS SIBERIA
2	Oct. 24, 1905, SS VENTURA–Oct. 28, 1907, SS ASIA
3	Oct. 28, 1907, SS ASIA–Nov. 22, 1908, SS MONGOLIA
4	Nov. 22, 1908, SS MONGOLIA–Sept. 25, 1909, SS MONGOLIA
5	Sept. 25, 1909, SS MONGOLIA–Sept. 10, 1910, SS CHINA
6	Sept. 10, 1910, SS CHINA–Oct. 24, 1911, SS COLUMBIAN

Roll	Contents
7	Oct. 28, 1911, SS MONGOLIA–Dec. 2 1912, SS TENYO MARU
8	Dec. 11, 1912, SS PERSIA–June 13, 1914, SS SIBERIA
9	June 15, 1914, SS CHIO MARU–June 21, 1915, SS KOREA
10	June 22, 1915, SS WILHELMINA–Sept. 30, 1916, SS CHINA
11	Sept. 16, 1916, SS CHINA–Mar. 8, 1918, SS SHINYO MARU
12	Mar. 23, 1918, SS PERSIA MARU–Jan. 22, 1920, SS NILE
13	Jan. 22, 1920, SS NILE–Mar. 21, 1921, SS TAIYO MARU
14	Mar. 21, 1921, SS CHINA–Jan. 4, 1922, SS KOREA MARU
15	Jan. 5, 1922, NANKING–Nov. 18, 1922, NANKING
16	Nov. 18, 1922, NANKING–Dec. 2, 1923, PRES. PIERCE
17	Dec. 2, 1923, PRES. PIERCE–Mar. 5, 1925, SHINO MARU
18	Mar. 5, 1925, SHINO MARU–Apr. 1, 1926, PRES. WILSON
19	Apr. 7, 1926, PRES. WILSON–Dec. 29, 1926, PRES. TAFT
20	Dec. 29, 1926, PRES. TAFT–Sept. 29, 1927, KOREA MARU
21	Sept. 29, 1927, KOREA MARU–June 22, 1928, TAIYO MARU
22	June 22, 1928, TAIYO MARU–Nov. 11, 1929, TAIYO MARU
23	Nov. 13, 1929, PRES. CLEVELAND–Nov. 3, 1931, PRES. JACKSON
24	Nov. 3, 1931, PRES. JACKSON–Nov. 21, 1934, PRES. COOLIDGE
25	Dec. 11, 1934, PRES. LINCOLN–Mar. 1, 1938, PRES. TAFT
26	Mar. 22, 1938, PRES. COOLIDGE–Nov. 22, 1940, PRES. COOLIDGE
27	Nov. 22, 1940, PRES. COOLIDGE–Jan. 7, 1947, ADM. C.E. HUGHES

Savannah, Georgia

Passenger Lists of Vessels Arriving at Savannah, GA, 1906–1945. T943. 4 rolls.

Roll	Volumes	Dates
1	1	June 5, 1906–June 19, 1917
2	2	July 5, 1917–May 22, 1923
3	3–4	June 18, 1923–May 14, 1942
4	5	Apr. 16, 1944–Dec. 6, 1945

Seattle, Washington, and Other Washington Ports

★ **Lists of Chinese Passengers Arriving at Seattle [Port Townsend], WA, 1882–1916. M1364. 10 rolls.**

This microfilm publication reproduces lists of Chinese passengers arriving at Seattle and Port Townsend, WA, from 1882–1916. The lists are arranged chronologically by date of arrival beginning in June 1882.

Roll	Contents
1	June 23, 1882–Feb. 28, 1890
2	Mar. 3, 1890–Oct. 30, 1900
3	Nov. 2, 1900–Aug. 11, 1907
4	Sept. 6, 1907–July 4, 1909
5	July 6, 1909–June 14, 1910
6	July 11, 1910–Mar. 20, 1912
7	Apr. 4, 1912–Apr. 12, 1913
8	Apr. 16, 1913–July 8, 1914
9	July 8, 1914–Dec. 24, 1915
10	Dec. 28, 1915–Nov. 16, 1916

★ **Certificates of Head Tax Paid by Aliens Arriving at Seattle, WA, from Foreign Contiguous Territory, 1917–1924. M1365. 10 rolls. 16mm.**

Roll	Certificate Numbers	Dates
1	1–5628	1917–1918
2	5629–12965	1918–1919
3	12966–20519	1919–1920
4	20520–26296	1920–1921
5	26297–38729	1921–1922
6	38730–45686	1921–1922
7	45687–51050	1921–1923
8	51051–57728	1921–1923
9	57729–76416	1923–1924
10	76417–79500	1923–1924
	113901–113950	March–April 1929
	227659–227800	1917
	231201–249950	1917

★ **Passenger and Crew Lists of Vessels Arriving at Seattle, WA, 1890–1957. M1383. 357 rolls.**

Roll	Contents
1	Aug. 29, 1890, VESTA–Apr. 17, 1900, SS GOODWIN
2	Apr. 17, 1900, SS GOODWIN–Jan. 17, 1904, SS TOSA MARU
3	Jan. 18, 1904, SS TREMONT–Mar. 22, 1905, IVYDENE
4	Apr. 11, 1905, SS THODE FAGELUND–May 24, 1906, SS SHAWMUT
5	May 24, 1906, SS SHAWMUT–Nov. 17, 1906, SS AL-KI
6	Sept. 27, 1906, SS KOHALA–June 26, 1907, SS SHINANO MARU
7	June 26, 1907, SS SHINANO MARU–Dec. 27, 1907, SS TANGO MARU
8	Dec. 30, 1907, SS CYCLOPS–June 25, 1908, SS AKI MARU
9	June 25, 1908, SS AKI MARU–Feb. 19, 1909, SS TANGO MARU
10	Feb. 19, 1909, SS TANGO MARU–Oct. 31, 1910, SS SHIMANO MARU
11	Oct. 15, 1909, SS HUMBOLT–May 25, 1910, SS INABA MARU
12	May 25, 1910, SS INABA MARU–Oct. 31, 1910, SS EMPRESS OF JAPAN
13	Oct. 31, 1910, SS EMPRESS OF JAPAN–May 17, 1911, SS CHICAGO MARU
14	May 17, 1911, SS CHICAGO MARU–Oct. 30, 1911, SS SADO MARU
15	Oct. 30, 1911, SS SADO MARU–May 11, 1912, SS SANUKI MARU
16	May 11, 1912, SS SANUKI MARU–Oct. 3, 1912, SS CITY OF SEATTLE
17	Oct. 4, 1912, SS IROQUIS–Apr. 5, 1913, SS CANADA MARU

Roll	Contents
18	Apr. 5, 1913, SS CANADA MARU–Aug. 16, 1913, SS RICHARD DE SOLER
19	Aug. 17, 1913, SS ALEX T. BROWN–Jan. 16, 1914, SS SADO MARU
20	Jan. 16, 1914, SS SADO MARU–June 11, 1914, SS SPOKANE
21	June 11, 1914, SS SPOKANE–Nov. 6, 1914, SS MATSON A. WEST
22	Nov. 7, 1914, Schr. M. TURNER–May 7, 1915, SS TAMBA MARU
23	May 7, 1915, SS TAMBA MARU–Oct. 7, 1915, SS AKI MARU
24	Oct. 7, 1915, SS AKI MARU–Mar. 17, 1916, ARIEL
25	Mar. 23, 1916, SS SPOKANE–July 20, 1916, SS MANILA MARU
26	July 20, 1916, SS MANILA MARU–Dec. 7, 1916, SS PRINCESS ADELAIDE
27	Dec. 8, 1916, SS PRINCESS ADELAIDE–Apr. 27, 1917, SS SHIDZUCKA MARU
28	Apr. 27, 1917, SS SHIDZUCKA MARU–July 24, 1917, (Canadian Entries)
29	July 24, 1917, (Canadian Entries)–Oct. 12, 1917, SS CHICAGO MARU
30	Sept. 29,1917, SS MEITEN MARU–Dec. 26, 1917, SS CHICAGO MARU
31	Dec. 26, 1917, SS CHICAGO MARU–Mar. 24, 1918, (Canadian Entries)
32	Mar. 24, 1918, (Canadian Entries)–Apr. 30, 1918, SS MAKURA
33	Apr. 30, 1918, SS MAKURA–June 22, 1918, SS MEIGEN MARU
34	June 26, 1918, SS GAIFUKU MARU–Aug. 17, 1918, SS SENATOR
35	Aug. 17, 1918, SS SENATOR–Oct. 9, 1918, SS FUSHINI
36	Oct. 11, 1918, SS ATSUTA MARU–Dec. 16, 1918, SS RUSH
37	Dec. 21, 1918, SS BARGE BORADA–Feb. 13, 1919, ROBERT LEWERS
38	Feb. 14, 1919, SS WESTHAM–Apr. 7, 1919, SS KASHIMA MARU
39	Apr. 7, 1919, SS KASHIMA MARU–June 24, 1919 SS CANADIAN PACIFIC
40	June 24, 1919, SS CANADIAN PACIFIC–July 23, 1919, SS FUSHIMI MARU
41	July 23, 1919, SS FUSHIMI MARU–Aug. 25, 1919, SS EMPRESS OF ASIA
42	Aug. 25, 1919, (Canadian Entries)–Oct. 1, 1919, SS QUNADRA
43	Oct. 1, 1919, SS PRINCESS ADELAIDE–Nov. 14, 1919, SS STEVESTON
44	Nov. 19, 1919, SS MANILA MARU–Jan. 15, 1920, SS EMPRESS OF RUSSIA
45	Jan. 15, 1920, SS EMPRESS OF RUSSIA–Feb. 1, 1920, SS WESTHAM
46	Feb. 4, 1920, SS WESTHAM–Mar. 26, 1920, SS KASHIMA MARU
47	Mar. 26, 1920, SS KASHIMA MARU–Apr. 17, 1920, SS FUSHIMI MARU
48	Apr. 17, 1920, SS FUSHIMI MARU–May 15, 1920, SS SOL DUC
49	May 9, 1920, SS INDO MARU–June 23, 1920, SS KASHIMA MARU
50	June 23, 1920, SS KASHIMA MARU–July 10, 1920, SS CASCADE

Roll	Contents
51	July 13, 1920, SS QUADRA–Aug. 14, 1920, SS ARIZONA MARU
52	Aug. 29, 1920, SS EURYDAMAS–Sept. 21, 1920, SS KASHIMA MARU
53	Sept. 21, 1920, SS KASHIMA MARU–Nov. 12, 1920, SS NIAGARA
54	Nov. 12, 1920, SS NIAGARA–Dec. 19, 1920, SS TAHITI
55	Dec. 19, 1920, SS TAHITI–Jan. 24, 1921, (Canadian Entries)
56	Jan 24, 1921, (Canadian Entries)–Feb. 16, 1921, SS ARIZONA MARU
57	Feb. 16, 1921, SS ARIZONA MARU–Mar. 31, 1921, SS PRINCESS VICTORIA
58	Mar. 29, 1921, SS BELFAST–May 5, 1921, SS NIAGARA
59	May 5, 1921, SS NIAGARA–June 24, 1921, (Canadian Entries)
60	June 24, 1921, (Canadian Entries)–July 24, 1921, (Canadian Entries)
61	July 24, 1921, (Canadian Entries)–Aug. 24, 1921, (Canadian Entries)
62	Aug. 24, 1921, (Canadian Entries)–Sept. 1, 1921, SS AMER. WESTERN KNIGHT
63	Aug. 30, 1921, SS SHAMROCK–Oct. 7, 1921, SS HAWAII MARU
64	Oct. 7, 1921, SS HAWAII MARU–Nov. 7, 1921, SS OSAGE
65	Nov. 18, 1921, SS HAKATA MARU–Jan. 7, 1922, SS NIAGARA
66	Jan. 7, 1922, SS NIAGARA–Feb. 5, 1922, SS ARABIA MARU
67	Feb. 5, 1922, SS ARABIA MARU–Mar. 27, 1922, SS SILVER STATE
68	Mar. 27, 1922, SS SILVER STATE–May 8, 1922, SS EMPRESS OF RUSSIA
69	May 8, 1922, SS EMPRESS OF RUSSIA–June 22, 1922, SS EMPRESS OF CANADA
70	June 22, 1922, SS EMPRESS OF CANADA–July 18, 1922, SS EMPRESS OF JAPAN
71	July 18, 1922, SS EMPRESS OF JAPAN–Aug. 24, 1922, (Canadian Entries)
72	Aug. 24, 1922, (Canadian Entries)–Sept. 16, 1922, SS NIAGARA
73	Sept. 16, 1922, SS NIAGARA–Oct. 23, 1922, SS EMPRESS OF RUSSIA
74	Oct. 23, 1922, SS EMPRESS OF RUSSIA–Nov. 24, 1922, (no vessel)
75	Nov. 24, 1922, (Canadian Entries)–Dec. 24, 1922, (Canadian Entries)
76	Dec 24, 1922, (Canadian Entries)–Jan. 2, 1923, SS PRES. JACKSON
77	Jan. 2, 1923, SS PRES. JACKSON–Feb. 27, 1923, SS GRIFCO
78	Feb. 7, 1923, SS COMANCHE–Mar. 21, 1923, SS SWELL
79	Mar. 10, 1923, SS PRINCESS VICTORIA–Apr. 3, 1923, SS FUKU MARU
80	Apr. 11, 1923, SS GRADAC–May 18, 1923, SS HOWE SOUND III
81	May 18, 1923, SS HOWE SOUND III–June 24, 1923, (Canadian Entries)
82	June 24, 1923, (Canadian Entries)–June 28, 1923, SS BRITISH EASTHOLM
83	June 30, 1923, SS PRINCESS MARY–July 16, 1923, SS TOKIWA MARU
84	July 15, 1923, SS BR.JWP–Aug. 5, 1923, SS WESTHAM
85	Aug. 6, 1923, SS PRINCESS VICTORIA–Sept. 24, 1923, (Canadian Entries)
86	Sept. 24, 1923, (Canadian Entries)–Sept. 23, 1923, SS EMPRESS OF ASIA
87	Sept. 23, 1923, SS EMPRESS OF ASIA–Oct. 5, 1923, TUG TYREE
88	Oct. 1, 1923, SS WAIHEMO–Nov. 26, 1923, (Canadian Entries)
89	Nov. 26, 1923, (Canadian Entries)–Dec. 24, 1923, SS FRENCH CATINAT
90	Oct. 17, 1923, SS ANNE COMYN–Dec. 19, 1923, SS PRES. MCKINLEY
91	Dec. 19, 1923, SS PRES MCKINLEY–Jan. 18, 1924, SS SEIRSTAD
92	Jan. 14, 1924, SS RUTH KAYSER–Feb. 14, 1924, SS HAWAII MARU
93	Feb. 14, 1924, SS HAWAII MARU–Mar. 10, 1924, SS GLENIFFER
94	Mar. 13, 1924, SS PRINCESS VICTORIA–Apr. 21, 1924, SS EMPRESS OF RUSSIA
95	Apr. 21, 1924, SS EMPRESS OF RUSSIA–May 24, 1924, (Canadian Entries)
96	May 24, 1924, (Canadian Entries)–May 18, 1924, SS YONEYAMA MARU
97	May 19, 1924, SS MILAN–June 11,1924, SS SHIDZUOKA MARU
98	June 11, 1924, SS SHIDZUOKA MARU–June 28, 1924, SS MISHIMA MARU
99	June 28, 1924, SS MISHIMA MARU–Aug. 4, 1924, SS EMPRESS OF CANADA
100	Aug. 4, 1924, SS EMPRESS OF CANADA–Sept. 7, 1924, SS PRES. JEFFERSON
101	Sept. 7, 1924, SS PRES. JEFFERSON–Oct. 19, 1924, SS HAKUSHIKA
102	Oct. 22, 1924, SS ARABIA MARU–Nov. 26, 1924, SS SOMEDONO
103	Nov. 28, 1924, SS TOHGU MARU–Jan. 15, 1925, SS CLYDE MARU
104	Jan. 16, 1925, SS KOSHIN MARU–Mar. 7, 1924, SS RESPOND
105	Mar. 14, 1925, SS RESPOND–Apr. 10, 1925, SS PRES. GRANT
106	Apr. 10, 1925, SS PRES GRANT–May 18, 1925, SS PROJECTIVE
107	May 21, 1925, SS SHIDZUOKA MARU–June 26, 1925, SS NIAGARA
108	June 26, 1925, SS NIAGARA–July 27, 1925, SS EMPRESS OF CANADA
109	July 27, 1925, SS EMPRESS OF CANADA–Sept 9, 1925, SS EMPRESS OF ASIA
110	Sept. 9, 1925, SS EMPRESS OF ASIA–Nov. 16, 1925, SS EMPRESS OF CANADA
111	Nov. 16, 1925, SS EMPRESS OF CANADA–Aug. 7, 1925, SS OLYMPIA #2
112	June 15, 1925, SS G.S. ORIENT–Jan. 17, 1926, SS ASIA
113	Jan. 6, 1926, SS GRIFFCO–Mar. 4, 1926, SS AORANGI
114	Mar. 4, 1926, SS AORANGI–Mar. 27, 1926, SS KAGA MARU

Roll	Contents	Roll	Contents
115	Mar. 31, 1926, SS SWELL–May 5, 1926, SS EMPRESS OF AUSTRALIA	147	Mar. 25, 1929, SS STANLEY DOLLAR–Apr. 26, 1926, SS ALKE FRANCIS
116	May 3, 1926, SS RUTH JANET–June 8, 1926, SS ARABIA MARU	148	Jan. 24, 1929, SS PRINCESS CHARLOTTE–May 22, 1929, SS BUCHANNESS
117	June 8, 1926, SS ARABIA MARU–July 12, 1926, SS DEWEY	149	May 31, 1929, SS MISHIMA MARU–June 20, 1929, SS SEATTLE
118	July 7, 1926, SS ENSLEY CITY–August 14, 1926, SS TUG CLAYBURN	150	June 20, 1929, SS OLYMPIA–July 31, 1929, SS CACIQUE
119	Aug. 19, 1926, 13th Tug RFM–Sept. 9, 1926, SS PARANA	151	July 29, 1929, SS PRES. JACKSON–Sept. 6, 1929, SS PRINCESS KATHLEEN
120	Sept. 13, 1926, SS EASTERN KNIGHT–Sept. 28, 1926, SS BORDER KING	152	Sept. 3, 1929, SS LORNET–Oct. 21, 1929, SS ARIZONA MARU
121	Oct. 4, 1926, SS EMPRESS OF RUSSIA–Nov. 22, 1926, SAMEDONO MARU	153	Oct. 13, 1929, SS GLAMORGANSHIRE–Nov. 14, 1929, SS SOUTHHOLM
122	Dec. 2, 1926, SS FUKUYO MARU–Jan. 11, 1927, SS ASAKA MARU	154	Nov. 17, 1929, SS TAMAHOKO MARU–Dec. 16, 1929, SS PRES. MCKINLEY
123	Jan. 11, 1927, SS ASAKA MARU–Mar. 4, 1927, SS NIAGARA	155	Dec. 16, 1929, SS PRES. MCKINLEY–Jan. 31, 1930, SS COLUMBIA
124	Mar. 4, 1927, SS NIAGARA–Apr. 25, 1927, SS YONEYAMA MARU	156	Feb. 2, 1930, SS PRINCESS CHARLOTTE–Mar. 10, 1930, SS SEISHO MARU
125	Mar. 29, 1927, SS YONEYAMA MARU–May 8, 1927, SS AFRICA MARU	157	Mar. 11, 1930, SS SPRAY–Apr. 19, 1930, SS PRES. MCKINLEY
126	May 17, 1927, SS AFRICA MARU–May 27, 1927, SS BOSTON MARU	158	Apr. 19, 1930, SS PRES. MCKINLEY–May 21, 1930, PRINCETON
127	May 26, 1927, SS GRIFFCO–July 1, 1927, SS ORIDONO	159	May 24, 1930, SS PRES MCKINLEY–July 22, 1930, SS TOPILA
128	July 1, 1927, SS ORIDONO–Aug. 6, 1927, SS HARRIET E.	160	July 2, 1930, SS MANILA MARU–Aug. 15, 1930, SS PIKES PEAK
129	Aug. 27, 1927, SS HARRIET E.–Sept. 10, 1927, SS PROTESILAUS	161	Aug. 5, 1930, SS WALES MARU–Sept. 7, 1930, SS COLUMBIA MARU
130	Sept. 10, 1927, SS PROTESILAUS–Oct. 16, 1927, SS LURLINE	162	Sept. 5, 1930, Tanker WARWICK–Oct. 25, 1930, SS HIKAWA MARU
131	Oct. 16. 1927, SS ARABIA MARU–Nov. 21, 1927, SS GEIFFUKU MARU	163	Oct. 14, 1930, SS LOCHKATRINE–Nov. 29, 1930, SS MISHIMA MARU
132	Nov. 22, 1927, SS TOYAMA–Oct. 17, 1927, SS G. MITKOFF	164	Nov. 29, 1930, SS MISHIMA MARU–Jan. 4, 1931, SS PRINCESS KATHLEEN
133	Feb. 26, 1927, SS L. MILDRED–Feb. 17, 1928, SS WEST HIMROD	165	Jan. 3, 1931, SS BORDER KING–Feb. 11, 1931, SS M.V. COASTER
134	Feb. 1, 1928, SS BORDER KING–Mar. 4, 1928, SS EMPRESS OF CANADA	166	Feb. 12, 1931, SS GYOKOH MARU–Apr. 3, 1931, SS PRES. MADISON
135	Mar. 5, 1928, SS STRATH–Apr. 8, 1928, SS SUBLAY	167	Apr. 3, 1931, SS PRES. MADISON–May 14, 1931, SS WATCO
136	Apr. 8, 1928, SS SUBLAY–May 7, 1928, SS PRES. PIERCE	168	May 13, 1931, SS HARDANGER–June 22, 1931, SS PRINCESS MARGUERITE
137	May 7, 1928, SS PRES. PIERCE–June 7, 1928, SS SUNDOWN	169	June 20, 1931, SS MALOLO–Aug. 2, 1931, SS CROWN CITY
138	June 5, 1928, SS ROBERT H. MERRICK–July 2, 1928, SS GRIFFCO	170	Aug. 1, 1931, SS EVERETT–Sept. 24, 1931, SS DAUNTLESS
139	July 2, 1928, SS GRIFFCO–Aug. 6, 1928, SS SHELTON	171	Sept. 9, 1931, SS MALOLO–Oct. 25, 1931, SS PRINCESS MARGUERITE
140	Aug. 14, 1928, SS FELTRE–Sept. 21, 1928, SS YOKAHAMA MARU	172	Oct. 25, 1931, SS PRINCESS MARGUERITE–Nov. 29, 1931, SS PACIFIC EXPORTER
141	Sept. 10, 1928, SS PRINCESS KATHLEEN–Oct. 8, 1928, SS PRES. JEFFERSON	173	Nov. 25, 1931, SS FRENCH–Jan. 28, 1932, SS NORTHHOLM
142	Oct. 8, 1928, SS PRES. JEFFERSON–Nov. 10, 1928, SS EMPRESS OF RUSSIA	174	Jan. 10, 1932, SS PACIFIC GROVE–Mar. 31, 1932, SS NORTHLAND
143	Nov. 10, 1928, SS EMPRESS OF RUSSIA–Dec. 17, 1928, SS PRES. GRANT	175	Mar. 2, 1932, SS COLUMBIA MARU–Apr. 27, 1932, Barge DRUMWELL
144	Dec. 17, 1928, SS PRES. GRANT–Jan. 8, 1929, SS TYDAREUS	176	Apr. 13, 1932, SS TEIHEIMAUR–May 24, 1932, SS PRINCESS ADELAIDE
145	Jan. 9, 1929, SS PRINCESS CHARLOTTE–Feb. 25, 1929, SS TALTHYBIUS	177	May 24, 1932, SS PRINCESS ADELAIDE–June 30, 1932, SS PRINCESS MARGARITA
146	Feb. 25, 1929, SS SCHWAREN–Mar. 25, 1929, SS PACIFIC RELIANCE	178	June 30, 1932, SS PRINCESS MARGARITA–Aug. 9, 1932, SS SHIDZUOKA MARU

Roll	Contents	Roll	Contents
179	Aug. 9, 1932, SS SHIDZUOKA MARU–Sept. 13, 1932, SS PROTESILAUS	211	Dec. 2, 1935, SS PRINCESS CHARLOTTE–Jan. 9, 1936, SS HIYE MARU
180	Sept. 13, 1932, SS PROTESILAUS–Oct. 14, 1932, SS VICTORY BAY	212	Jan. 17, 1936, SS HIYE MARU–Mar. 14, 1936, SS COOSTER
181	Oct. 14, 1932, SS GREGALIA–Dec. 2, 1932, SS EASTHOLM	213	Mar. 2, 1936, SS BORDER PRINCE–Apr. 6, 1936, SS STORM KING
182	Dec. 8, 1932, SS EASTHOLM–Jan. 17, 1933, SS STORM KING	214	Apr. 16, 1936, SS BERWIN–May 15, 1936, SS RACE ROCK
183	Jan. 12, 1933, SS ISLAND PLANET–Mar.3, 1933, SS LA REINE	215	May 13, 1936, SS PRES. GRANT–June 27, 1936, SS WESTERN PILOT
184	Mar. 11, 1933, SS LA REINE–Apr. 18, 1933, SS PRES. TAFT	216	June 9, 1936, SS PRINCESS CHARLOTTE–July 24, 1936, SS PACIFIC SHIPPER
185	Apr. 18, 1933, SS PRES. TAFT–May 31, 1933, SS DERBLAY	217	July 13, 1936, SS LIVELY–Aug. 11, 1936, SS PRINCESS MARGUERITE
186	Apr. 2, 1933, SS PRINCESS CHARLOTTE–July 28, 1933, SS LA PALOMA	218	Aug. 12, 1936, SS PRINCESS MARGUERITE–Sept. 7, 1936, SS PRINCESS MARGUERITE
187	July 5, 1933, SS NIELSON–Aug. 8, 1933, SS NORFOLK MARU	219	Sept. 8, 1936, SS SOUTHHOLM–Oct. 14, 1936, SS ALEUTIAN NATIVE
188	Aug. 14, 1933, SS NORFOLK MARU–Sept. 16, 1933, SS ADMIRAL GOVE	220	Oct. 17, 1936, SS ALEUTIAN NATIVE–Nov. 26, 1936, SS CARLODA "N"
189	Sept. 18, 1933, SS VICTORY BAY–Oct. 31, 1933, SS PRES. JACKSON	221	Nov. 24, 1936, SS MARTHA FOSS–Feb. 9, 1937, SS CANADIAN TUG
190	Oct. 31, 1933, SS PRES. JACKSON–Dec. 31, 1933, SS SALVAGE QUEEN	222	Feb. 11, 1937, SS BRITISH TUG–Mar. 26, 1937, SS SANTA CLARA VALLEY
191	Dec. 1, 1933, SS VIGILANT–Jan. 9, 1934, SS PACIFIC COMMERCE	223	Mar. 29, 1937, SS CORRIENTES–May 1, 1937, SS IROQUIS
192	Jan. 10, 1934, SS GRACIA–Feb. 26, 1934, SS MARY D.	224	May 1, 1937, SS PRINCESS KATHLEEN–June 2, 1937, SS PRINCESS MARGUERITE
193	Feb. 28, 1934, SS LOYAL–Apr. 3, 1934, SS PRES. MCKINLEY	225	June 2, 1937, SS PRINCESS MARGUERITE–July 2, 1937, SS SULAWATI
194	Apr. 3, 1934, SS PRES. MCKINLEY–May 10, 1934, SS WEST NILUS	226	July 1, 1937, SS QUILOENE–Aug. 19, 1937, (Canadian Entries)
195	May 10, 1934, SS WILMURDELL–June 27, 1934, SS PRES. JEFFERSON	227	Aug. 27, 1937, SS BURRARD CHIEF–Aug. 1937, (Canadian Entries)
196	June 27, 1934, SS PRES. JEFFERSON–Aug. 6, 1934, SS IXION	228	Sept. 1, 1937, SS MODAVIA–Sept. 30, 1937, SS EEIAN MARU
197	Aug. 5, 1934, SS EVERETT–Sept. 20, 1934, SS SHELLCO	229	Sept. 30, 1937, SS PRES. GRANT–Oct. 19, 1937, SS EEIAN MARU
198	Sept. 7, 1934, SS ADMIRAL CHASE–Oct. 4, 1934, SS MOLDANGER	230	Oct. 28, 1937, SS EEIAN MARU–Nov. 22, 1937, SS GRACIA
199	Oct. 3, 1934, SS ALEUTIAN–Nov. 6, 1934, SS HIKAWA MARU	231	Nov. 30, 1937, SS GRACIA–Dec. 21, 1937, SS TYNDAREUS
200	Nov. 6, 1934, SS HAKAWA MARU–Dec. 10, 1934, SS SHELTON	232	Dec. 21, 1937, SS TYNDAREUS–Feb. 21, 1938, SS SOUTHHOLM
201	Dec. 13, 1934, SS TALTHYBIUS–Feb. 28, 1935, SS IROQUOIS	233	Feb. 2, 1938, SS ROSARIO–Mar. 6, 1938, SS BERNARD CHIEF
202	Feb. 1, 1935, SS ISLAND COMET–Mar. 12, 1935 SS MOLDANGER	234	Mar. 6, 1938, SS SALVAGE PRINCESS–Apr. 8, 1938, SS S.B.&Y.
203	Mar. 12, 1935, SS MOLDANGER–Apr. 21, 1935, SS ADMIRAL MULTON	235	Apr. 8, 1938, SS B.C. CLIPPER–May 28, 1938, SS ALEUTIAN NATIVE
204	Apr. 22, 1935, BEATRICE–June 1, 1935, SS TANTALUS	236	May 4, 1938, SS SEAROCK–June 4, 1938, SS SOUTHHOLM
205	May 23, 1935, SS CELLIAN–June 21, 1935, SS LANE	237	June 5, 1938, SS WESTERN CHIEF–July 25, 1938, SS STORM KING
206	June 21, 1935, SS PRINCESS MARGUERITE–July 30, 1935, SS HARRIET	238	July 5, 1938, SS SPRAY–Aug. 31, 1938, SS NORTH SEA
207	July 18, 1935, SS NEPTUNE–Aug. 30, 1935, SS GRAINIER	239	Aug. 31, 1938, SS NORTH SEA–Sept. 1, 1938, SS OLYMPIC
208	Aug. 17, 1935, SS ZAPORA–Sept. 20, 1935, SS TANESSE	240	Sept. 1, 1938, SS OLYMPIC–Oct. 1, 1938, SS PRINCESS KATHLEEN
209	Sept. 13, 1935, SS STORM KING–Oct. 21, 1935, SS ALMARA	241	Oct. 1, 1938, SS PRINCESS KATHLEEN–Nov. 8, 1938, SS DENALI
210	Oct. 17, 1935, SS DEVON CITY–Dec. 30, 1935, SS GRAINIER	242	Nov. 3, 1938, SS DENALI–Dec. 12, 1938, SS LORNA FOSS

Roll	Contents
243	Dec. 13, 1938, SS STRATH–Jan. 21, 1939, SS MARTHA FOSS
244	Jan. 17, 1939, SS WASHINGTON EXPRESS–Mar. 8, 1939, SS HIE MARU
245	Mar. 8, 1939, SS HIE MARU–Apr. 25, 1939, SS HIE MARU
246	Apr. 27, 1939, SS NORTHLAND–June 21, 1939, SS OL. S. FREYA
247	June 3, 1939, SS PIONEER III–July 10, 1939, SS BERVIU
248	July 21, 1939, SS BERVIU–Aug. 22, 1939, SS CORDILLERA
249	Aug. 23, 1939, SS BALBOA–Oct. 6, 1939, SS CHARLOTTE
250	Oct. 6, 1939, SS CHARLOTTE–Nov. 23, 1939, SS HIE MARU
251	Nov. 23, 1939, SS HIE MARU–Jan. 11, 1940, SS HIE MARU
252	Jan. 11, 1940, SS HIE MARU–Mar. 21, 1940, SS ISLAND ROVER
253	Mar. 7, 1940, SS TATIBANA MARU–May 6, 1940, SS CHILLIMACK
254	May 4, 1940, SS SMOHOMISH–June 23, 1940, SS YACHT HAIDA
255	June 22, 1940, SS MARGUERITE–Aug. 8, 1940, SS NORTH SEA
256	Aug. 24, 1940, SS NORTH SEA–Sept. 25, 1940, SS MARTHA #2
257	Sept. 26, 1940, SS SHELLCO–Nov. 7, 1940, SS SHELLCO
258	Nov. 26, 1940, SS SHELLCO–Jan. 30, 1941, SS BORDER KING
259	Jan. 2, 1941, SS BONILLAN–Mar. 26, 1941, SS NORCO
260	Mar. 1, 1941, SS TYEE–Apr. 22, 1941, SS UTOCARBON
261	Apr. 28, 1941, SS HIKAWA MARU–June 27, 1941, SS EMPIRE CANNERY
262	June 2, 1941, SS PRINCESS MARGUERITE–July 7, 1941, SS HIE MARU
263	July 7, 1941, SS HIE MARU–Aug. 15, 1941, SS OLD KINGFISHER
264	Aug. 17, 1941, SS MAIDALENE–Oct. 25, 1941, SS OL. S. ALRITA
265	Oct. 25, 1941, SS OL. S. FAITH II–Jan. 30, 1942, SS AMUR
266	Jan. 7, 1942, SS R.F.M.–Mar. 11, 1942, SS OLD FAITH
267	Mar. 11, 1942, SS CONSTITUTION–May 27, 1942, SS ARGO
268	May 13, 1942, SS ANTLER–July 26, 1942, SS PIERCE
269	July 5, 1942, SS DOLA–Sept. 22, 1942, U.S. 3OC510
270	Sept. 22, 1942, SS ARNE–Dec. 29, 1942, SS GEORGE A. CUSTER
271	Dec. 28, 1942, SS ISLAND WARRIOR–Apr. 3, 1943, SS JOSEPH McKENNA
272	Apr. 9, 1943, SS MINSK–June 14, 1943, SS WESTFORD
273	June 10, 1943, SS DNEPROSTROY–Sept. 10, 1943, SS ZENITH
274	Sept. 11, 1943, SS CHERNISHINSKI–Dec. 2, 1943, SS SOUTHHOLM

Roll	Contents
275	Dec. 5, 1943, SS BURRARD CHIEF–Feb. 24, 1944, SS LORD TEMPLETON
276	Feb 25, 1944, SS TONGASS–May 27, 1944, SS MIMROD
277	May 20, 1944, SS VITEBSK–July 11, 1944, SS ELEONARA
278	July 11, 1944, SS LANE–Sept. 30, 1944, SS STALIN
279	Sept. 30, 1944, SS STALIN–Dec.19, 1944, SS BERWIN
280	Dec. 19, 1944, SS CHELAN–Feb. 27, 1945, SS NORTHLAND
281	Feb. 26, 1945, SS ROSARAH–May 19, 1945, SS ISLAND WARRIOR
282	May 1, 1945, MV INDIAN–June 18, 1945, SS CALIFORNIA
283	June 18, 1945, SS DOLPHIN–Aug. 8, 1945, SS CAPE PALMAS
284	Aug. 8, 1945, SS CAPE PALMAS–Oct. 10, 1945, SS NORTH SEA
285	Oct. 10, 1945, SS NORTH SEA–Dec. 10, 1945, SS GEORGE ROSS
286	Dec. 10, 1945, SS ISLAND STAR–Feb. 6, 1946, SS WAIMEA
287	Feb. 8, 1946, SS BRANDON VICTORY–Apr. 25, 1946, SS LA REINE
288	Apr. 1, 1946, SS LE MARS–May 20, 1946, SS EMPRESS
289	May 20, 1946, SS IDEAL–July 17, 1946, SS BELLINGHAM VICTORY
290	July 17, 1946, SS BELLINGHAM VICTORY–Sept. 30, 1946, SS SMOHOMISH
291	Sept. 9, 1946, SS BELLINGHAM–Sept. 30, 1946, SS SMOHOMISH
292	Nov. 8, 1946, SS FAITH II–Jan. 26, 1947, SS CAPE IGVAK
293	Jan. 24, 1947, SS CORAL–Mar. 31, 1947, SS CORNELIUS
294	Mar. 28, 1947, SS THISTLEDALE–May 24, 1947, SS TAWALI
295	Mar. 23, 1947, SWS ATHENIA–July 26, 1947, SS RUFUS W. PECKHAM
296	July 27, 1947, SS TRONDANGER–Sept. 27, 1947, SS CHEERFUL
297	Sept. 18, 1947, SS CELTIC–Nov. 28, 1947, SS ISLAND CHAMPION
298	Nov. 4, 1947, SS PROVO VICTORY–Jan. 6, 1948, SS BURRARD CHIEF
299	Jan. 6, 1948, SS BURRARD CHIEF–Mar. 10, 1948, SS GRANT
300	Mar. 11, 1948, SS ISLAND RANGER–May 6, 1948, SS MANX FISHER
301	May 8, 1948, SS GENERAL W.C. LANGFITT–June 20, 1948, SS KENYON VICTORY
302	June 21, 1948, SS ALEUTIAN CHIEF–Aug. 13, 1948, SS J.H. TUTTLE
303	Aug. 13, 1948, SS PARAGUAY–Oct. 2, 1948, SS CANADA MAIL
304	Oct. 5, 1948, SS SOUTHHOLM–Dec. 15, 1948, SS ISLAND RANGER
305	Dec. 3, 1948, SS MASTER–Feb. 7, 1949, SS SPRAY
306	Feb. 4, 1949, SS SWELL–Apr. 21, 1949, SS STANDFAST
307	Apr. 22, 1949, SS MUSKETEER–June 26, 1949, SS SEATAC

Roll	Contents
308	June 19, 1949, SS ARGO–Aug. 17, 1949, SS FORREST FRIEND
309	Aug. 12, 1949, SS JANE–Oct. 28, 1949, SS R.F.M.
310	Oct. 12, 1949, SS TACONITE–Dec. 22, 1949, SS ARCHER GAMMON
311	Dec. 21, 1949, SS ETHEL–Mar. 27, 1950, SS MARPOLE
312	Mar. 5, 1950, SS R.F.M.–May 31, 1950, SS FAITH II
313	May 12, 1950, SS IDEAL–July 10, 1950, SS REGINA
314	July 8, 1950, SS SWIFT II–Sept. 4, 1950, SS SIRMAC
315	Sept. 4, 1950, SS TAHSIS KING–Oct. 28, 1950, SS W.I. JOAN
316	Oct. 27, 1950, SS MORANG–Dec. 15, 1950, SS MERLAMAC II
317	Dec. 11, 1950, SS PATRICIA FOSS–Feb. 16, 1951, SS ARTHUR FOSS
318	Feb 16, 1951, SS IRENE–Apr. 24, 1951, SS GEN. M.C. MEIGS
319	Apr. 24, 1951, SS GEN. M.C. MEIGS–June 9, 1951, SS ARGUS
320	June 9, 1951, SS BARNEY JR.–Aug. 6, 1951, SS NOVA
321	Aug. 6, 1951, SS OCIANUS–Oct. 4, 1951, SS ISLAND WARRIOR
322	Oct. 4, 1951, SS EVER FOSS–Dec. 3, 1951, SS FLEETWOOD
323	Dec. 3, 1951, SS FLEETWOOD–Feb. 4, 1952, SS R.F.M.
324	Feb. 3, 1952, SS SELMA VICTORY–Mar. 31, 1952, SS BRAZILIAN PRINCE
325	Mar. 29, 1952, SS F.E. LOVEJOY–May 16, 1952, SS LA FORCE
326	May 17, 1952, SS LA SALLE–June 27, 1952, SS F.E. LOVEJOY
327	June 28, 1952, SS GLENEVON–Aug. 21, 1952, SS ISLAND DESPATCHER
328	Aug. 21, 1952, SS ISLAND ROVER–Oct. 8, 1952, SS PACIFIC DRAGON
329	Oct. 7, 1952, SS PULASKI–Nov. 23, 1952, SS MASTER
330	Nov. 22, 1952, SS MOHAWK–Jan. 16, 1953, SS MARPOLE
331	Jan. 15, 1953, SS PRODUCER–Mar. 1, 1953, SS INDIA MAIL
332	Mar. 3, 1953, SS HAWAIAN LOGGER–Apr. 23, 1953, USNS MARINE LYNX
333	Apr. 23, 1953, SS SANTA FLAVIA–June 14, 1953, SS LA BONNE
334	June 14, 1953, SS LA FILLE–Aug. 5, 1953, SS ISLAND WARRIOR
335	Aug. 5, 1953, SS JAMES LICK–Oct. 19, 1953, SS PATRICK TAP
336	Oct. 15, 1953, SS ARIMASON MARU–Dec. 15, 1953, SS WASHINGTON
337	Dec. 15, 1953, SS WASHINGTON–Mar. 4, 1954, SS ISLAND BOOSTER
338	Mar. 4, 1954, SS ISLAND KING–May 24, 1954, SS B.C. STANDARD
339	May 24, 1954, SS TULCREST–Aug. 14, 1954, SS MARINE ADDER
340	Aug. 14, 1954, SS MARINE ADDER–Nov. 6, 1954, SS SEAMAID
341	Nov. 6, 1954, SS TAIKYU MARU–Nov. 30, 1954, SS STANDFAST
342	Dec. 1, 1954, SS OCEAN MAIL–Oct. 22, 1955, USS GEN. WA. MANN
343	Feb. 25, 1955, SS MASTER–May 19, 1955, SS LEVIATHAN
344	May 20, 1955, SS CALIFORNIA–July 30, 1955, SS EDGAR F. LUCKENBACK
345	July 30, 1955, SS EDGAR F. LUCKENBACK–Oct. 10, 1955, SS STANDARD SERVICE
346	Oct. 11, 1955, SS GEN. H.B. FREEDMAN–Dec. 11, 1955, (Airline manifest)
347	Dec. 12, 1955, SS LA REINE–Feb. 12, 1956, SS JULIA LUCKENBACH
348	Feb. 12, 1956, SS JULIA LUCKENBACH–Apr. 10, 1956, USNS FREDERICK FUNSTON
349	Apr. 10, 1956, USNS FREDRICK FUNSTON–June 1, 1956, MV THEA FOSS
350	June 2, 1956, USNS JAMES O'HARA–July 7, 1956, SS WENDELL FOSS
351	July 7, 1956, SS SANTA LEONOR–Aug. 7, 1956, SS CANADIAN MV MOGUE
352	Aug. 7, 1956, SS STANDARD SERVICE–Aug. 31, 1956, SS SIRANGER
353	Aug. 8, 1956, SS CANADIAN MAIL–Aug. 18, 1956, US 30S1019
354	Aug. 31, 1956, SS SIRANGER–Oct. 1, 1956, USNS GEN. HUGH J. GAFFEY
355	Oct. 1, 1956, USNS GEN. HUGH J. GAFFEY–Nov. 24, 1956, SS WESTERN TRADER
356	Nov. 25, 1956, SS CHINA MAIL–Jan. 18, 1957, SS PRINCESS JOAN
357	Jan. 18, 1957, SS TAIKYU MARU–Mar. 6, 1957, M/S YAMATERU MARU

★ **Passenger Lists of Vessels Arriving at Seattle, WA, 1949–54. M1398. 5 rolls.**

Roll	Contents
1	Jan. 4, 1949, MS MANOERAN–May 24, 1950, GEN. MASON M. PATRICK
2	May 24, 1950, GEN. MASON M. PATRICK–Dec. 21, 1951, FREDERICK FUNSTON
3	Dec. 20, 1951, GEN. H.B. FREEMAN–Dec. 21, 1952, GEN. SIMON B. BUCKNER
4	Dec. 21, 1952, GEN. SIMON B. BUCKNER–Dec. 16, 1953, GEN. SIMON B. BUCKNER
5	Dec. 16, 1953, GEN. SIMON B. BUCKNER–Nov. 29, 1954, SS TRADEWIND

★ **Crew Lists of Vessels Arriving at Seattle, WA, 1903–1917. M1399. 15 rolls.**

Roll	Contents
1	Sept. 16, 1903, LEICESTER CASTLE–July 21, 1905, IYO MARU
2	June 17, 1905, NIXE–June 6, 1906, HELENE BLUM
3	May 14, 1906, B.K. KILLERAN–Aug. 22, 1907, KAGA MARU
4	Aug. 22, 1907, KAGA MARU–June 16, 1908, ADMIRAL DUPERRE
5	June 16, 1908, ADMIRAL DUPERRE–Sept. 1, 1909, MINNESOTA
6	Sept. 1, 1909, MINNESOTA–Aug. 17, 1910, HAZEL DOLLAR
7	Aug. 20, 1910, CAPE FINISTERRE–July 3, 1911, ARIZONAN

Roll	Contents
8	July 8, 1911, ADMIRAL–Mar. 10, 1912, HENRIETTE
9	Mar. 12, 1912, OTTER–Oct. 2, 1912, VERCUIGETARIX
10	Nov. 16, 1912, PANAMA MARU–June 5, 1913, SANUKI MARU
11	June 17, 1913, BENICIA–Feb. 16, 1914, QUEEN MARGARET
12	Mar. 9, 1914, ECHO–Dec. 4, 1914, AKI MARU
13	Dec. 4, 1914, AKI MARU–Oct. 21, 1915, ALUMNA
14	Oct. 22, 1915, RESOLUTE–Aug. 11, 1916, HENRIK IBSEN
15	Aug. 31, 1916, DAUNTLESS–Mar. 8, 1917, PUERTO MONTT

★ **Customs Passenger Lists of Vessels Arriving at Port Townsend and Tacoma, WA, 1894–1909. M1484. 1 roll.**

★ **Passenger Lists of Vessels Arriving at Seattle, WA, from Insular Possessions, 1908–1917. M1485. 1 roll.**

Guide to the Soundex System

The Soundex filing system, alphabetic for the first letter of surname and numeric thereunder as indicated by divider cards, keeps together names of the same and similar sounds but of variant spellings.

To search for a particular name, you must first work out the code number for the surname of the individual. No number is assigned to the first letter of the surname. If the name is Kuhne, for example, the index card will be in the "K" segment of the index. The code number for Kuhne, worked out according to the system below, is 500.

Soundex Coding Guide

Code	Key Letters and Equivalents
1	b,p,f,v
2	c,s,k,g,j,q,x,z
3	d,t
4	l
5	m,n
6	r

The letters a, e, i, o, u, y, w, and h are *not* coded. The first letter of the surname is *not* coded.

Every Soundex number must be a 3-digit number. A name yielding no code numbers, as Lee, would thus be L-000; one yielding only one code number would have two zeros added, as Kuhne, coded as K-500; and one yielding two code numbers would have one zero added, as Ebell, coded as E-140. Not more than three digits are used, so Ebelson would be coded as E-142, *not* E-1425.

When two key letters or equivalents appear together, or one key letter immediately follows or precedes an equivalent, the two are coded as one letter, by a single number, as follows: *Kelly*, coded as K-400; *Buerck*, coded as B-620, *Lloyd*, coded as L-300; and *Schaefer*, coded as S-160.

If several surnames have the same code, the cards for them are arranged alphabetically by given name. There are divider cards showing most code numbers, but not all. For instance, one divider may be numbered 350 and the next one 400. Between the two divider cards there may be names coded 353, 350, 360, 365, and 355, but instead of being in numerical order they are interfiled alphabetically by given name.

Such prefixes to surnames as "van," "Von," "Di," "de," "le," "Di," "D'," "dela," or "du" are sometimes disregarded in alphabetizing and in coding.

The following names are examples of Soundex coding and are given only as illustrations.

Name	Letters Coded	Code No.
Allricht	l,r,c,	A-462
Eberhard	b,r,r	E-166
Engebrethson	n,g,b	E-521
Heimbach	m,b,c	H-512
Hanselmann	n,s,l	H-524
Henzelmann	n,z,l	H-524
Hildebrand	l,d,b	H-431
Kavanagh	v,n,g	K-152
Lind, Van	n,d	L-530
Lukaschowsky	k,s,s	L-222
McDonnell	c,d,n	M-235
McGee	c	M-200
O'Brien	b,r,n	O-165
Opnian	p,n,n	O-155
Oppenheimer	p,n,m	O-155
Riedemanas	d,m,n	R-355
Zita	t	Z-300
Zitzmeinn	t,z,m	Z-325

Native Americans, Orientals, and Religious Nuns

Researchers using the Soundex system to locate religious nuns or persons with American Indian or oriental names should be aware of the way such names were coded. Variations in coding differed from the normal coding system.

Phonetically spelled oriental and Indian names were sometimes coded as if one continuous name, or, if a distinguishable surname was given, the names were coded in the normal manner. For example, the American Indian name Shinka-Wa-Sa may have been coded as "Shinka" (S-520) or "Sa" (S-000). Researchers should investigate the various possibilities of coding such names.

Religious nun names were coded as if "Sister" were the surname, and they appear in the Soundex indexes under the code "S-236." Within the code S-236, the names may not be in alphabetical order.

Index to Publication Numbers

M 237	13	M 1465	143
M 255	6	M 1476	155
M 259	11	M 1477	24
M 261	12	M 1478	32
M 265	7	M 1479	33
M 272	12	M 1484	162
M 277	9	M 1485	162
M 326	6	T 517	23
M 327	5	T 518	129
M 334	3	T 519	39
M 360	20	T 520	23
M 425	22	T 521	25
M 575	4	T 522	35
M 596	7	T 523	34
M 1066	18	T 524	129
M 1357	33	T 526	126
M 1358	33	T 527	10
M 1359	33	T 612	46
M 1364	155	T 617	25
M 1365	156	T 618	35
M 1383	156	T 621	40
M 1389	144	T 715	55
M 1398	161	T 790	25
M 1399	161	T 791	127
M 1410	144	T 792	129
M 1411	151	T 793	129
M 1412	151	T 840	127
M 1413	151	T 843	26
M 1414	152	T 844	23
M 1416	152	T 905	35
M 1417	126	T 938	30
M 1436	155	T 939	37
M 1437	155	T 940	34
M 1438	155	T 941	34
M 1440	155	T 942	35
M 1461	130	T 943	155
M 1462	133	T 944	35
M 1463	133	T 1151	129
M 1464	134	T 1188	129

Index to Publications by Port

Alabama, Florida, Georgia, and South Carolina
  Index to passenger lists, 1890–1924 23
Atlantic, Gulf, and Great Lakes Ports
  Index to passenger lists, 1820–1874 3
  Passenger lists, 1820–1873 4
Baltimore, Maryland
  Indexes to passenger lists
    1820–1897 (federal lists) 5
    1833–1866 (city lists) 6
    1897–1952 23
  Passenger lists
    1820–1891 6
    1891–1909 23
    1954–1957 24
  Quarterly abstracts of passenger lists,
    1820–1869 7
Boston, Massachusetts
  Crew lists, 1917–1943 .30
  Indexes to passenger lists
    1848–1891 7
    1899–1940 25
    1902–1906 25
    1906–1920 25
  Passenger lists
    1820–1891 9
    1891–1943 26
Brownsville, Texas
  See Galveston, Texas
Canada
  See St. Albans, Vermont, District
Detroit, Michigan
  Card manifests of entries, 1906–1954 32
  Passenger and alien crew lists, 1946–1957 33
Galveston, Texas and Other Texas Ports
  Index to passenger lists, 1896–1906 33
  Index to passenger lists, 1906–1951 33
  Passenger lists, 1896–1951 33
Gloucester, Massachusetts
  Crew lists, 1918–1943 .34
Gulfport, Mississippi
  Index to passenger arrivals, 1904–1954 34
Houston, Texas
  See Galveston, Texas
Key West, Florida
  Passenger lists, 1898–1945 34
New Bedford, Massachusetts
  Crew lists, 1917–1943 .35
  Index to passenger arrivals, 1902–1954 35
  Passenger lists, 1902–1942 35

New Orleans, Louisiana
  Crew lists,
    1903–1945 35
    1910–1945 37
  Indexes to passenger lists
    Before 1900 10
    1900–1952 35
  Passenger lists
    1820–1902 11
    1903–1945 35
  Quarterly abstracts of passenger lists,
    1820–1875 12
New York, New York
  Indexes to passenger lists
    1820–1846 12
    1897–1902 39
    1902–1943 40
    1906–1942 46
    1944–1948 126
  Passenger lists
    1820–1897 13
    1897–1957 (includes crew lists) 55
  Registers of vessels, 1789–1919 18
Pascagoula, Mississippi
  Index to passenger arrivals, 1903–1935 34
Philadelphia, Pennsylvania
  Indexes to passenger lists
    1800–1906 20
    1883–1948 126
    1906–1926 127
  Passenger lists
    1800–1882 22
    1883–1945 127
Port Townsend, Washington
  See Seattle, Washington
Portland, Maine
  Indexes to passenger lists
    1893–1954 129
    1907–1930 129
  Passenger lists, 1893–1943 129
Providence, Rhode Island
  Indexes to passenger lists
    1911–1934 129
    1911–1954 129
  Passenger lists, 1911–1943 129

St. Albans, Vermont, District
  Indexes to Canadian border entries
    Alphabetical, miscellaneous small ports,
        1895–1924 133
      Soundex, 1895–1924 130
      Soundex, 1924–1952 133
  Manifests of passenger arrivals
    From Canadian Atlantic ports, 1895–1954 . 134
    From Canadian Pacific ports, 1895–1954 . . 134
    From Canadian Pacific ports, 1929–1949 . . 143
San Francisco, California
  Crew lists
    (Alien) 1896–1921 155
    1905–1954 152
    1954–1957 151
  Index to vessels, 1882–1957 155
  Index to passenger lists, 1893–1934 144
  Passenger lists
    1893–1953 144
    1954–1957 151
    1902–1907 (from Honolulu) 155
    1903–1918 151
    1907–1911 (from insular possessions) 155
    Chinese passengers only
      1882–1888 151
      1888–1914 152
      1903–1947 155
Savannah, Georgia
  Passenger lists, 1906–1945 155
Seattle, Washington and Other Washington Ports
  Certificates of head tax paid by alien passengers,
      1917–1924 156
  Crew lists
    1890–1957 156
    1903–1917 161
  Passenger lists
    1882–1916 (Chinese passengers only) 155
    1890–1957 156
    1894–1909 162
    1908–1917 (from insular possessions) 162
    1949–1954 161
Tacoma, Washington
  See Seattle, Washington

Index to Publication Numbers by Port

Alabama, Florida, Georgia, and South Carolina
  T517. 23
Atlantic, Gulf, and Great Lakes Ports
  M334 3
  M575 4
Baltimore, Maryland
  M255 6
  M326 6
  M327 5
  M596 7
  M1477 24
  T520 23
  T844 23
Boston, Massachusetts
  M265 7
  M277 9
  T521 25
  T617 25
  T790 25
  T843 26
  T938 30
Brownsville, Texas
  M1358 33
Detroit, Michigan
  M1478 32
  M1479 33
Galveston, Texas
  M1357 33
  M1358 33
  M1359 33
Gloucester, Massachusetts
  T941 34
Gulfport, Mississippi
  T523 34
Houston, Texas
  M1358 33
Key West, Florida
  T940 34
New Bedford, Massachusetts
  T522 35
  T942 35
  T944 35
New Orleans, Louisiana
  M259 11
  M272 12
  T527 10
  T618 35
  T905 35
  T939 37

New York, New York
  M237 13
  M261 12
  M1066 18
  M1417 126
  T519 39
  T612 46
  T621 40
  T715 55
Pascagoula, Mississippi
  T523 34
Philadelphia, Pennsylvania
  M360 20
  M425 22
  T526 126
  T791 127
  T840 127
Port Townsend, Washington
  M1484 162
Portland, Maine
  T524 129
  T793 129
  T1151 129
Providence, Rhode Island
  T518 129
  T792 129
  T1188 129
St. Albans, Vermont, District
  M1461 130
  M1462 133
  M1463 133
  M1464 134
  M1465 143
San Francisco, California
  M1389 144
  M1410 144
  M1411 151
  M1412 151
  M1413 151
  M1414 152
  M1416 152
  M1436 155
  M1437 155
  M1438 155
  M1440 155
  M1476 155
Savannah, Georgia
  T943 155

Seattle, Washington
    M1364 155
    M1365 156
    M1383 156
    M1398 161
    M1399 161
    M1484 162
    M1485 162
Tacoma, Washington
    M1484 162

Index to Microfilm Holdings in the Regional Archives

New England Region
  Record Group 36
    M277 9
    M575 4
  Record Group 85
    M1357 33
    M1358 33
    M1359 33
    M1461 130
    M1462 133
    M1463 133
    M1464 134
    M1465 143
    T790 25
    T843 26
    T938 30
    T944 35

Northeast Region
  Record Group 36
    M237 13
    M261 12
  Record Group 85
    M1357 33
    M1358 33
    M1359 33
    M1417 126
    M1462 133
    M1463 133
    M1465 143
    T519 39
    T715 55

Mid Atlantic Region
  Record Group 36
    M326 6
    M327 5
    M334 3
    M360 20
    M425 22
  Record Group 85
    M1357 33
    M1358 33
    M1359 33
    T520 23
    T526 126
    T791 127
    T840 127
    T844 23

Southeast Region
  Record Group 36
    M575 4
    T527 10
  Record Group 86
    M1357 33
    M1358 33
    M1359 33
    T517 23
    T523 34
    T940 34
    T943 155

Great Lakes Region
  Record Group 36
    M237 13
    M261 12
    M575 4
  Record Group 85
    M1357 33
    M1358 33
    M1359 33
    T519 39

Central Plains Region
  Record Group 85
    M1357 33
    M1358 33
    M1359 33

Southwest Region
  Record Group 36
    M261 12
    M326 6
    M327 5
    M334 3
    M360 20
    M425 22
    M575 4
    M1066 18
    T527 10
  Record Group 85
    M1357 33
    M1358 33
    M1359 33
    T521 25
    T790 25
    T840 127
    T843 26
    T944 35

Rocky Mountain Region
  Record Group 36
    M237 13
    M255 6
    M261 12
    M360 20
    M575 4
    M1066 18
  Record Group 85
    M1357 33
    M1358 33
    M1359 33
    T519 39
    T844 23
Pacific Southwest Region
  Record Group 36
    M261 12
  Record Group 85
    M1357 33
    M1358 33
    M1359 33
    M1410 144
    M1437 155
    M1438 155
    M1440 155
Pacific Sierra Region
  Record Group 85
    M1357 33
    M1358 33
    M1359 33

M1364 155
M1389 144
M1410 144
M1411 151
M1412 151
M1413 151
M1414 152
M1416 152
M1436 155
M1438 155
M1440 155
M1462 133
M1465 143
M1476 155
Pacific Northwest Region
  Record Group 36
    M237 13
    M327 5
  Record Group 85
    M1357 33
    M1358 33
    M1359 33
    M1364 155
    M1365 156
    M1383 156
    M1398 161
    M1399 161
    M1484 162
    M1485 162

Instructions for Ordering Microfilm Publications

Positive copies of microfilm may be purchased from the National Archives. Single rolls may be purchased separately. Effective August 1, 1990, the price per roll was $23 for orders shipped to domestic U.S. addresses and $30 for rolls shipped to foreign addresses. Shipping is included. These prices are subject to change without separate notice to you. For current prices, write to the Publications Services Staff (NEPS), National Archives and Records Administration, Washington, DC 20408, or call 202-501-5240.

Submit your order on NATF Form 36, Microfilm Order. Copies of this form appear at the end of this catalog. Photocopies of the form are acceptable. Additional order forms will be sent on request. Include the microfilm publication number(s), roll number(s), and prices in your order. Titles and dates of publications are not required.

Prepayment is required. You may charge your order to your VISA or MasterCard credit card, or attach a check or money order payable in U.S. dollars and drawn on a U.S. bank. U.S. Treasury regulations require a minimum amount of $25.00 for foreign checks. Make your check or money order payable to National Archives Trust Fund (NEPS). Do NOT send cash.

Purchase orders are accepted only from Federal, State or quasi-government agencies or from domestic U.S. colleges, universities, or libraries.

Check your order immediately upon receipt for errors, completeness, or damage in shipping. You must notify the Publications Services Staff of any problems within 60 days. Do not return microfilm orders without written permission from the Publications Services Staff.

MICROFILM ORDER
(Prices subject to change.)

Microfilm publication numbers (preceded by an "M" or "T") are assigned to each microfilm publication. Please enter the microfilm publication number and roll number(s) in the proper columns. Because we accept orders for individual rolls, as well as for complete microfilm publications, we must know which rolls you wish to purchase.

Effective August 1, 1990, the price for each roll of microfilm is $23 for U.S. orders. The price is $30 per roll for foreign orders. Shipping is included. These prices are subject to change without notice. For current price information, write to the Publications Services Staff (NEPS), National Archives and Records Administration, Washington, DC 20408, or call 202-501-5240.

Sample of correctly completed form.

MICRO. PUB. NUMBER	ROLL NUMBER(S)	PRICE
T624	1138	$23.
T1270	88 - 89	$46.

Additional order forms are available upon request.

ORDERED BY *(Include organization if shipping to a business address.)*	Name	
	Organization *(if applicable)*	
	Address *(Number and Street)*	
	City, State & ZIP Code	
	Daytime Telephone Number *(Include area code)*	

PAYMENT TYPE

Send your order to:

CREDIT CARD

Check one and enter card number below. ☐ VISA ☐ MasterCard

Exp. Date

Signature

*National Archives Trust Fund
Cashier (NAJC)
Washington, DC 20408*

OTHER ☐ Check ☐ Money Order

Make payable to: National Archives Trust Fund.

Amount Enclosed $

*National Archives Trust Fund
P.O. Box 100793
Atlanta, GA 30384-0793*

IDENTIFY THE ROLLS YOU WISH TO ORDER

MICRO. PUB. NUMBER	ROLL NUMBER(S)	PRICE		MICRO. PUB. NUMBER	ROLL NUMBER(S)	PRICE
					Subtotal (this column)	
					Subtotal from first column	
	Subtotal (this column)				**TOTAL PRICE**	

NATIONAL ARCHIVES TRUST FUND BOARD   NATF Form 36 (rev. 4-91)

MICROFILM ORDER
(Prices subject to change.)

Microfilm publication numbers (preceded by an "M" or "T") are assigned to each microfilm publication. Please enter the microfilm publication number and roll number(s) in the proper columns. Because we accept orders for individual rolls, as well as for complete microfilm publications, we must know which rolls you wish to purchase.

Effective August 1, 1990, the price for each roll of microfilm is $23 for U.S. orders. The price is $30 per roll for foreign orders. Shipping is included. These prices are subject to change without notice. For current price information, write to the Publications Services Staff (NEPS), National Archives and Records Administration, Washington, DC 20408, or call 202-501-5240.

Sample of correctly completed form.

MICRO. PUB. NUMBER	ROLL NUMBER(S)	PRICE
T624	1138	$23.
T1270	88 - 89	$46.

Additional order forms are available upon request.

ORDERED BY *(Include organization if shipping to a business address.)*	Name	
	Organization *(if applicable)*	
	Address *(Number and Street)*	
	City, State & ZIP Code	
	Daytime Telephone Number *(Include area code)*	

PAYMENT TYPE

Send your order to:

CREDIT CARD	Check one and enter card number below. ☐ VISA ☐ MasterCard
	Exp. Date
	Signature

National Archives Trust Fund Cashier (NAJC) Washington, DC 20408

| OTHER | ☐ Check ☐ Money Order *Make payable to: National Archives Trust Fund.* | Amount Enclosed $ |

National Archives Trust Fund P.O. Box 100793 Atlanta, GA 30384-0793

IDENTIFY THE ROLLS YOU WISH TO ORDER

MICRO. PUB. NUMBER	ROLL NUMBER(S)	PRICE	MICRO. PUB. NUMBER	ROLL NUMBER(S)	PRICE
				Subtotal (this column)	
				Subtotal from first column	
	Subtotal (this column)			**TOTAL PRICE**	

NATIONAL ARCHIVES TRUST FUND BOARD   NATF Form 36 (rev. 4-91)

MICROFILM ORDER
(Prices subject to change.)

Microfilm publication numbers (preceded by an "M" or "T") are assigned to each microfilm publication. Please enter the microfilm publication number and roll number(s) in the proper columns. Because we accept orders for individual rolls, as well as for complete microfilm publications, we must know which rolls you wish to purchase.

Effective August 1, 1990, the price for each roll of microfilm is $23 for U.S. orders. The price is $30 per roll for foreign orders. Shipping is included. These prices are subject to change without notice. For current price information, write to the Publications Services Staff (NEPS), National Archives and Records Administration, Washington, DC 20408, or call 202-501-5240.

Sample of correctly completed form.

MICRO. PUB. NUMBER	ROLL NUMBER(S)	PRICE
T624	1138	$23.
T1270	88 - 89	$46.

Additional order forms are available upon request.

ORDERED BY *(Include organization if shipping to a business address.)*	Name	
	Organization *(if applicable)*	
	Address *(Number and Street)*	
	City, State & ZIP Code	
	Daytime Telephone Number *(Include area code)*	

PAYMENT TYPE

		Send your order to:
CREDIT CARD	Check one and enter card number below. ☐ VISA ☐ MasterCard [ ][ ][ ][█][ ][ ][ ][█][ ][ ][ ][█][ ][ ][ ][ ] Exp. Date Signature	*National Archives Trust Fund Cashier (NAJC) Washington, DC 20408*
OTHER	☐ Check ☐ Money Order *Make payable to: National Archives Trust Fund.* Amount Enclosed $	*National Archives Trust Fund P.O. Box 100793 Atlanta, GA 30384-0793*

IDENTIFY THE ROLLS YOU WISH TO ORDER

MICRO. PUB. NUMBER	ROLL NUMBER(S)	PRICE	MICRO. PUB. NUMBER	ROLL NUMBER(S)	PRICE
				Subtotal (this column)	
				Subtotal from first column	
	Subtotal (this column)			**TOTAL PRICE**	

MICROFILM ORDER
(Prices subject to change.)

Microfilm publication numbers (preceded by an "M" or "T") are assigned to each microfilm publication. Please enter the microfilm publication number and roll number(s) in the proper columns. Because we accept orders for individual rolls, as well as for complete microfilm publications, we must know which rolls you wish to purchase.

Effective August 1, 1990, the price for each roll of microfilm is $23 for U.S. orders. The price is $30 per roll for foreign orders. Shipping is included. These prices are subject to change without notice. For current price information, write to the Publications Services Staff (NEPS), National Archives and Records Administration, Washington, DC 20408, or call 202-501-5240.

Sample of correctly completed form.

MICRO. PUB. NUMBER	ROLL NUMBER(S)	PRICE
T624	1138	$23.
T1270	88 - 89	$46.

Additional order forms are available upon request.

ORDERED BY *(Include organization if shipping to a business address.)*

Name	
Organization *(if applicable)*	
Address *(Number and Street)*	
City, State & ZIP Code	
Daytime Telephone Number *(Include area code)*	

PAYMENT TYPE

CREDIT CARD

Check one and enter card number below. ☐ VISA ☐ MasterCard

| | | | | | | | | | | | | Exp. Date |

Signature

Send your order to:

National Archives Trust Fund Cashier (NAJC) Washington, DC 20408

OTHER ☐ Check ☐ Money Order

Make payable to: National Archives Trust Fund.

Amount Enclosed $

National Archives Trust Fund P.O. Box 100793 Atlanta, GA 30384-0793

IDENTIFY THE ROLLS YOU WISH TO ORDER

MICRO. PUB. NUMBER	ROLL NUMBER(S)	PRICE	MICRO. PUB. NUMBER	ROLL NUMBER(S)	PRICE
				Subtotal (this column)	
				Subtotal from first column	
	Subtotal (this column)			**TOTAL PRICE**	